SOCIAL PSYCHOLOGY
OF HEALTH

Key Readings in Social Psychology

General Editor: ARIE W. KRUGLANSKI, University of Maryland at College Park

The aim of this series is to make available to advanced undergraduate and graduate students key articles in each area of social psychology in an attractive, user-friendly format. Many professors want to encourage their students to engage directly with research in their fields, yet this can often be daunting for students coming to detailed study of a topic for the first time. Moreover, declining library budgets mean that articles are not always readily available, and course packs can be expensive and time-consuming to produce. *Key Readings in Social Psychology* aims to address this need by providing comprehensive volumes, each one of which will be edited by a senior and active researcher in the field. Articles will be carefully chosen to illustrate the way the field has developed historically as well as current issues and research directions. Each volume will have a similar structure, which will include:

- an overview chapter, as well as introductions to sections and articles
- questions for class discussion
- annotated bibliographies
- full author and subject indexes

Published Titles

The Self in Social Psychology	Roy F. Baumeister
Stereotypes and Prejudice	Charles Stangor
Motivational Science	E. Tory Higgins and Arie W. Kruglanski
Social Psychology and Human Sexuality	Roy F. Baumeister
Emotions in Social Psychology	W. Gerrod Parrott
Intergroup Relations	Michael A. Hogg and Dominic Abrams
The Social Psychology of Organizational Behavior	Leigh L. Thompson
Social Psychology: A General Reader	Arie W. Kruglanski and E. Tory Higgins
Social Psychology of Health	Peter Salovey and Alexander J. Rothman

Titles in Preparation

Attitudes	Richard E. Petty and Russell Fazio
Persuasion	Richard E. Petty and Russell Fazio
Close Relationships	Harry Reis and Caryl Rusbult
Group Processes	John Levine and Richard Moreland
Interface of Social and Clinical Psychlogy	Robin M. Kowalski and Mark R. Leary
Language and Communication	Gün R. Semin
Political Psychology	John Jost and Jim Sidanius
Social Cognition	David Hamilton
Social Comparison	Diederik Stapel and Hart Blanton
Social Neuroscience	John T. Cacioppo and Gary Berntson

For contiualy updated information about published and forthcoming titles in the Key Readings in Social Psychology series, please visit: www.keyreadings.com

SOCIAL PSYCHOLOGY OF HEALTH
Key Readings

Edited by

Peter Salovey
Yale University

Alexander J. Rothman
University of Minnesota

CRC Press
Taylor & Francis Group
Boca Raton London New York

CRC Press is an imprint of the
Taylor & Francis Group, an informa business

Reprinted 2010 by CRC Press

CRC Press
6000 Broken Sound Parkway, NW
Suite 300, Boca Raton, FL 33487

270 Madison Avenue
New York, NY 10016

2 Park Square, Milton Park
Abingdon, Oxon OX14 4RN, UK

Published in 2003 by
Psychology Press
29 West 35th Street
New York, NY 10001
www.psypress.com

Published in Great Britain by
Psychology Press
27 Church Road
Hove, East Sussex
BN3 2FA
www.psypress.co.uk

Library of Congress Cataloging-in-Publication Data

Social psychology of health : key readings / edited by Peter Salovey, Alexander J. Rothman.
    p. cm. — (Key readings in social psychology)
    Includes bibliographical references and index.
    ISBN 1-84169-016-3 — ISBN 1-84169-017-1 (pbk.)
    1. Social medicine. 2. Health attitudes. 3. Medicine and psychology. 4. Social psycholgoy.
  I. Salovey, Peter. II. Rothman, Alexander J. III. Series.

RA418.S6428 2003
613'.0'9—dc21

2003043109

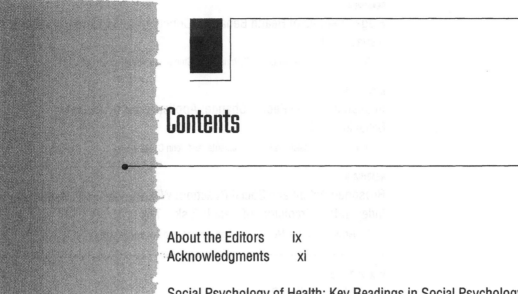

Contents

About the Editors   ix
Acknowledgments   xi

Social Psychology of Health: Key Readings in Social Psychology
An Overview   1
    Peter Salovey and Alexander J. Rothman

PART 1
Mental Models of Health and Illness   5

READING 1
Common-Sense Models of Illness: The Example of Hypertension   9
    Daniel Meyer, Howard Leventhal, and Mary Gutmann

READING 2
A Longitudinal Study of the Reciprocal Nature of Risk Behaviors
and Cognitions in Adolescents: What You Do Shapes
What You Think, and Vice Versa   21
    Meg Gerrard, Frederick X. Gibbons, Alida C. Benthin, and Robert M. Hessling

READING 3
Testing Four Competing Theories of Health-Protective Behavior   33
    Neil D. Weinstein

PART 2
Health Beliefs and Health Behavior   47

READING 4

Stage Theories of Health Behavior: Conceptual and Methodological Issues 50

Neil D. Weinstein, Alexander J. Rothman, and Stephen R. Sutton

READING 5

In Search of How People Change: Applications to Addictive Behaviors 63

James O. Prochaska, Carlo C. DiClemente, and John C. Norcross

READING 6

Reasoned Action and Social Reaction: Willingness and Intention as Independent Predictors of Health Risk 78

Frederick X. Gibbons, Meg Gerrard, Hart Blanton, and Daniel W. Russell

PART 3

Health Information Processing 95

READING 7

Understanding the Impact of Risk Factor Test Results: Insights From a Basic Research Program 98

Peter H. Ditto and Robert T. Croyle

READING 8

Defensive Processing of Personally Relevant Health Messages 118

Akiva Liberman and Shelly Chaiken

READING 9

Alcohol Myopia and Condom Use: Can Alcohol Intoxication Be Associated With More Prudent Behavior? 130

Tara K. MacDonald, Geoffrey T. Fong, Mark P. Zanna, and Alanna M. Martineau

PART 4

Social Influence and Health and Illness:
Social Comparison and Social Norms 147

READING 10

Social Comparison in Adjustment to Breast Cancer 151

Joanne V. Wood, Shelley E. Taylor, and Rosemary R. Lichtman

READING 11

Predicting Young Adults' Health Risk Behavior 166

Frederick X. Gibbons and Meg Gerrard

READING 12

Pluralistic Ignorance and Alcohol Use on Campus: Some
Consequences of Misperceiving the Social Norm 183

Deborah A. Prentice and Dale T. Miller

READING 13

Social Comparison and Affiliation Under Threat: Effects on Recovery
From Major Surgery 199

James A. Kulik, Heike I. M. Mahler, and Philip J. Moore

PART 5

Social Support and Health and Illness 215

READING 14

Social Relationships and Health 218

James S. House, Karl R. Landis, and Debra Umberson

READING 15

Psychosocial Models of the Role of Social Support in the Etiology
of Physical Disease 227

Sheldon Cohen

PART 6

Changing Behavior 245

READING 16

Experimental Evidence for Stages of Health Behavior Change:
The Precaution Adoption Process Model Applied to Home Radon
Testing 249

Neil D. Weinstein, Judith E. Lyon, Peter M. Sandman, and Cara L. Cuite

READING 17

Attributions of Responsibility and Persuasion: Increasing
Mammography Utilization Among Women Over 40 With
an Internally Oriented Message 261

Alexander J. Rothman, Peter Salovey, Carolyn Turvey, and Stephanie A. Fishkin

READING 18

Inducing Hypocrisy as a Means of Encouraging Young Adults
to Use Condoms 272

Jeff Stone, Elliot Aronson, A. Lauren Crain, Matthew P. Winslow, and Carrie B. Fried

READING 19

The Systematic Influence of Gain- and Loss-Framed Messages on
Interest in and Use of Different Types of Health Behavior 286

Alexander J. Rothman, Steven C. Martino, Brian T. Bedell, Jerusha B. Detweiler,
and Peter Salovey

P A R T   7

Personality and Health 301

READING 20

The "Disease-Prone Personality": A Meta-Analytic View
of the Construct 305

Howard S. Friedman and Stephanie Booth-Kewley

READING 21

Hostility and Health: Current Status of a Psychosomatic
Hypothesis 325

Timothy W. Smith

READING 22

Dispositonal Optimism and Recovery From Coronary Artery
Bypass Surgery: The Beneficial Effect on Physical and
Psychological Well-Being 342

Michael F. Scheier, Karen A. Matthews, Jane F. Owens, George J. Magovern, Sr.,

R. Craig Lefebvre, R. Anne Abbott, and Charles S. Carver

READING 23

Writing About Emotional Experiences as a Therapeutic Process 362

James W. Pennebaker

Appendix: How to Read a Journal Article in Social Psychology 369

Christian H. Jordan and Mark P. Zanna

Author Index 379

Subject Index 389

About the Editors

Peter Salovey is the Chris Argyris Professor of Psychology at Yale University, where he completed his graduate work and now serves as Dean of the Graduate School of Arts and Sciences. His work concerns the psychological functions of moods and emotions; emotional intelligence; and the use of social psychological theory to guide interventions designed to change health behaviors, especially health messages motivating cancer and HIV/AIDS-relevant behaviors. Professor Salovey is also the Deputy Director of Yale's Center for Interdisciplinary Research on AIDS (CIRA). At Yale University, Professor Salovey has received the William Clyde DeVane Medal for Distinguished Scholarship and Teaching in Yale College in 2000 and the Lex Hixon '63 Prize for Teaching Excellence in the Social Sciences in 2002.

Alexander J. Rothman is an associate professor of psychology at the University of Minnesota. His research program involves a synthesis of basic research on how people process and evaluate health information with the development and evaluation of theory-based interventions to promote healthy behavior. In recognition of his work, Professor Rothman was awarded the 2002 Distinguished Scientific Award for Early Career Contributions to Psychology in the area of Health Psychology by the American Psychological Association.

Acknowledgments

The authors and publishers are grateful to the following for permission to reproduce the articles in this book:

Reading 1: D. Meyer, H. Leventhal, and M. Gutmann, Common-sense models of illness: The example of hypertension. *Health Psychology, 4,* 115–135. Copyright © 1985 by Lawrence Erlbaum Associates. Reprinted with permission.

Reading 2: M. Gerrard, F. X. Gibbons, A. C. Benthin, and R. M. Hessling, A longitudinal study of the reciprocal nature of risk behaviors and risk cognitions in adolescents: What you do shapes what you think and vice versa. *Health Psychology, 15,* 344–354. Copyright © 1996 by the American Psychological Association. Reprinted/adapted with permission.

Reading 3: N. D. Weinstein, Testing four competing theories of health-protective behavior. *Health Psychology, 12,* 324–333. Copyright © 1993 by the American Psychological Association. Reprinted/adapted with permission.

Reading 4: N. D. Weinstein, A. J. Rothman, and S. R. Sutton, Stage theories of health behavior: Conceptual and methodological issues. *Health Psychology, 17,* 290–299. Copyright © 1998 by the American Psychological Association. Reprinted/adapted with permission.

Reading 5: J. O. Prochaska, C. C. DiClemente, and J. C. Norcross, In search of how people change: Applications to addictive behaviors. *American Psychologist, 47,* 1102–1114. Copyright © 1992 by the American Psychological Association. Reprinted/adapted with permission.

Reading 6: F. X. Gibbons, M. Gerrard, H. Blanton, and D. W. Russell, Reasoned action and social reaction: Willingness and intention as independent predictors of health risk. *Journal of Personality and Social Psychology, 74,* 1164–1180. Copyright © 1998 by the American Psychological Association. Reprinted/adapted with permission.

Reading 7: P. H. Ditto and R. T. Croyle, Understanding the impact of risk factor test results: Insights from a basic research program. From *Psychosocial effects of screening for disease prevention and detection,* edited by Robert T. Croyle. Copyright © 1995 by Oxford University Press, Inc. Used by permission of Oxford University Press, Inc.

Reading 8: A. Liberman and S. Chaiken, Defensive processing of personally relevant health messages. *Personality and Social Psychology Bulletin, 18,* 669–679. Copyright © 1992 by the Society for Personality and Social Psychology, Inc. Reprinted by permission of Sage Publications, Inc.

Reading 9: T. K. MacDonald, G. T. Fong, M. P. Zanna, and A. M. Martineau, Alcohol myopia and condom use: Can alcohol intoxication be associated with more prudent behavior? *Personality and Social Psychology Bulletin, 22,* 763–775. Copyright © 2000 by the Society for Personality and Social Psychology, Inc. Reprinted by permission of Sage Publications, Inc.

Reading 10: J. V. Wood, S. E. Taylor, and R. R. Lichtman, Social comparison in adjustment to breast cancer. *Journal of Personality and Social Psychology, 49,* 1169–1183. Copyright © 1985 by the American Psychological Association. Reprinted/adapted with permission.

Reading 11: F. X. Gibbons and M. Gerrard, Predicting young adults' health risk behavior. *Journal of Personality and Social Psychology, 69,* 505–517. Copyright © 1995 by the American Psychological Association. Reprinted/adapted with permission.

Reading 12: D. A. Prentice and D. T. Miller, Pluralistic ignorance and alcohol use on campus: Some consequences of misperceiving the social norm. *Journal of Personality and Social Psychology, 64,* 243–256. Copyright © 1993 by the American Psychological Association. Reprinted/adapted with permission.

Reading 13: J. A. Kulik, H. I. M. Mahler, and P. J. Moore, Social comparison and affiliation under threat: Effects on recovery from major surgery. *Journal of Personality and Social Psychology, 71,* 967–979. Copyright © 1996 by the American Psychological Association. Reprinted/adapted with permission.

Reading 14: J. S. House, K. R. Landis, and D. Umberson, Social relationships and health. *Science, 241,* 540–545. Reprinted with permission from *Science.* Copyright © 1988 American Association for the Advancement of Science.

Reading 15: S. Cohen, Psychosocial models of the role of social support in the etiology of physical disease. *Health Psychology, 7,* 269-297. Copyright © 1988 by Lawrence Erlbaum Associates. Reprinted with permission.

Reading 16: N. D. Weinstein, J. E. Lyon, P. M. Sandman, and C. L. Cuite, Experimental evidence for stages of health behavior change: The precaution adoption process model applied to home radon testing. *Health Psychology, 17,* 445–453. Copyright © 1998 by the American Psychological Association. Reprinted/adapted with permission.

Reading 17: A. J. Rothman, P. Salovey, C. Turvey, and S. A. Fishkin, Attributions of responsibility and persuasion: Increasing mammography utilization among women over 40 with an internally oriented message. *Health Psychology, 12,* 39–47. Copyright © 1993 by the American Psychological Association. Reprinted/adapted with permission.

Reading 18: J. Stone, E. Aronson, A. L. Crain, M. P. Winslow, and C. B. Fried, Inducing hypocrisy as a means of encouraging young adults to use condoms. *Personality and Social Psychology Bulletin, 20,* 116–128. Copyright © 1994 by the Society for Personality and Social Psychology, Inc. Reprinted by permission of Sage Publications, Inc.

Reading 19: A. J. Rothman, S. C. Martino, B. T. Bedell, J. B. Detweiler, and P. Salovey, The systemic influence of gain- and loss-framed messages on interest in and use of different types of health behavior. *Personality and Social Psychology Bulletin, 25,* 1355–1369. Copyright © by the Society for Personality and Social Psychology, Inc. Reprinted by permission of Sage Publications, Inc.

Reading 20: H. S. Friedman and S. Booth-Kewley, The "disease-prone personality: A meta-analytic view of the construct." *American Psychologist, 42,* 539–555. Copyright © 1987 by the American Psychological Association. Reprinted/adapted with permission.

Reading 21: T. W. Smith, Hostility and health: Current status of a psychosomatic hypothesis. *Health Psychology, 11,* 139–150. Copyright © 1992 by Lawrence Erlbaum Associates. Reprinted with permission.

Reading 22: M. F. Scheier, K. A. Matthews, J. F. Owens, G. J. Magovern, Sr., R. C. Lefebvre, R. A. Abbott, and C. S. Carver, Dispositional optimism and recovery from coronary artery bypass surgery: The beneficial effect on physical and psychological well-being. *Journal of Personality and Social Psychology, 57,* 1024–1040. Copyright © 1992 by the American Psychological Association. Reprinted/adapted with permission.

Reading 23: J. W. Pennebaker, Writing about emotional experiences as a therapeutic process. *Psychological Science, 8,* 162–166. Copyright © 1997 by Blackwell Publishing. Reprinted with permission.

Social Psychology of Health: Key Readings in Social Psychology An Overview

Peter Salovey • Yale University
Alexander J. Rothman • University of Minnesota

People want to live long, healthy lives. This universal motive should make the promotion of healthy behaviors easy, or so one might think. Such is not the case, however. Consider the following examples:

- Most college students know that, if one is sexually active, the only effective way to stop the spread of sexually transmitted diseases, such as HIV or HPV, is to use a condom. Yet, the majority of college students did not use a condom the last time they had sex.
- The early detection of breast cancer allows women to have many more alternatives for treatment and may even save lives (although this is still controversial). Nonetheless, in a typical year, only about half of the women who should obtain a screening mammogram actually do so.
- Most folks know it is healthy to stay trim and fit—and believe they look better when they do so. Yet, most of the people who lose weight by dieting will gain it all back. And more.
- People purchase cellular car telephones in order to be able to call for help in the unlikely event of an emergency; however, merely talking on a cellular phone while driving increases the risk of traffic accidents to the same extent as driving while intoxicated.
- Despite the fact that people increasingly appreciate the risk of melanoma associated with tanning at the beach or salon, tanned skin is considered a sign of health and vitality.
- Cancer patients undergoing chemotherapy who have few side effects sometimes terminate treatment because they believe it is ineffective; individuals taking a placebo medication with dramatic side effects—for example, it turns their urine brown—actually report feeling better.
- Adolescents and young adults are well aware of the health risks associated with cigarette smoking and even recognize how changes in their own behavior affect their chance of developing a life-threatening disease. Yet, they continue to choose to smoke.

We think you get the idea. Perhaps designing strategies that can motivate people to make healthy behavioral choices is not so easy. What directs people's decisions to adopt a particular

1

pattern of behavior? Traditionally, psychologists as well as other social scientists have assumed that people's behavior is guided by a rational analysis of the costs and benefits associated with the behavior—that is, people act to maximize benefits and minimize costs. However, the specific costs and benefits that come to mind can change depending upon the circumstances in which people find themselves. In a doctor's office, the health benefits associated with using a condom are clear and compelling, but in a romantic setting these same beliefs may not readily come to mind. Under those circumstances, the social costs associated with talking about or using condoms may be most salient. At any given point in time, people may feel like they are making a reasoned choice—that is, they are selecting the behavior that they believe affords the most beneficial outcomes. What they may not recognize is that their beliefs about the behavior do not represent an unbiased assessment of the issue at hand.

What are the principles that people rely on to motivate the choices they make? Yale University professor emeritus William McGuire has proposed that there are at least 16 different goals that may shape people's behavioral choices (McGuire, 1991). Although people may often act based on a desire to maximize their "expected utility," there are times when they will act in the service of goals such as to maximize immediate pleasure, minimize effort, distinguish themselves from others, conform to others' expectations, or increase their acceptance by other people. And people's assessments of the relative costs and benefits associated with a behavior at a given moment may be filtered through these motives. Thus, the value associated with a particular outcome lies in the mind of the person considering that outcome. Because different goals are associated with a unique set of ideas and concerns, the specific goal that underlies a person's behavior can influence the likelihood that someone would consider a particular outcome regardless of its value. Consequently, what appears to be a cost or a benefit may change from moment to moment and from situation to situation, and one of the major purposes of this volume is to explore the social psychological factors that influence these intuitive cost-benefit ratios regarding health-relevant behavior.

Understanding and modifying health behavior is likely to be complicated. Moreover, some public health officials believe that the next big improvement in our nation's health will be attributable to advances in the biomedical science—the isolation of new antigens and antibodies, the formulation of new vaccines. So, is the effort to change behavior worth it? A government blueprint containing health goals for the next millennium, *Healthy People 2010,* asserts that health promotion and disease prevention objectives depend heavily on modifying human behavior. It is change in behavior that is likely to be the most efficient way of reducing disease morbidity and premature mortality. If the entire population quit smoking, there would be a 25% reduction in cancer deaths and 350,000 fewer fatal heart attacks each year. A 10% weight loss through dietary modification and physical exercise would produce a 20% decrease in coronary artery disease as well as lower incidences of stroke, some cancers, diabetes, and other kinds of heart disease in the population (from Taylor, 1990; see also Matarazzo, 1984). Dramatic reductions in disease morbidity would be possible if individuals engaged reliably in prevention behaviors such as regular physical exercise and screening behaviors such as mammography and Pap testing. Moreover, the health benefits that are to come from the overwhelming majority of advances in biomedical sciences critically depend upon people's behavioral decision making. For example, as evidenced by innovations in medical treatments for persons living with AIDS, people must adhere to their prescription if they are to experience the benefits of the drugs. In fact, poor rates of adherence may produce adverse health consequences, as not taking medications as prescribed allows the virus to become drug-resistant.

Nonetheless, encouraging people to modify their behavior has proven to be an especially intractable problem. Many efforts to change behavior have failed. The "war on drugs" has likely been lost, violence in our schools has escalated despite the proliferation of conflict resolution programs, and the weight of the average American increases annually, despite changes in the definition of obesity and concerted media campaigns that make salient the health risks of carrying extra poundage. In the face of these difficulties, why spend energy trying to under-stand and change people's health behavior? Why not adopt a live-and-let-live attitude in which each person is welcome to choose his or her own poison? Although individuals may be will-ing to assume the personal risk of engaging in unhealthy practices, when aggregated in the population, the burden to society can be unacceptable. Even a small reduction in medical costs attributable to changes in individual behavior would free up countless dollars that could be spent on other priorities—depending on your political views, education, mass transporta-tion, or foreign aid. Small changes in individual health behavior ramify and produce large benefits for a society. Moreover, there are domains in which efforts to change behaviors have been successful.

The phenomena with which we opened this chapter are paradoxes. The question is not whether to label them as rational or irrational, but to understand them. The purpose of the collection of articles selected for this volume is to examine the social psychological basis of health behavior and attempts to modify it. Instead of complaining about the shortcomings of the human psyche and how they appear to motivate self-destruction, we bring to you articles that focus on identifying and explaining the complex social psychological determinants of health behavior with the goal of demonstrating how one can capitalize on them to motivate desired behavior.

In this volume, the articles in the first section focus on how people organize and store memory information about health and illness. The second section grapples with the links between attitudes about health and subsequent health behavior, with a particular eye toward whether there are stages in how individuals approach an opportunity to engage in or modify a healthy or unhealthy practice. Why are interventions that effectively help people initiate a change in behavior for the first time not useful in preventing relapse?

The third section of the book contains articles that explore the factors that influence how people understand incoming health information—factors such as whether the information itself is threatening or whether the receiver of the information is under the influence of alcohol.

The fourth and fifth sections of the book examine how perceived and objective features of the social context affect people's health. In section four, the series of articles examines how our perceptions of social norms and our reliance on social comparison processes affect how we think and reason about our health.

In the fifth section of the book, the contributors look at how social relationships can have health consequences of various sorts. Relationships with friends and family members can both inspire us to engage in salubrious behavior and motivate us to take unnecessary risks. Social support may be health-enhancing (and sometimes health-damaging) in direct and indi-rect ways, and the contributors address why individuals who are able to protect themselves with the warm fabric of social relationships live longer than those who cannot.

By the time we get to the sixth section of the book, we present articles that address the modification of health behavior head-on. These contributors present work in which decidedly social psychological approaches to health behavior change were tested. For instance, how can motives to appear consistent (and not hypocritical) be capitalized upon to motivate people to behave in healthy ways? How can health messages be tailored and framed so as to make them especially effective? These approaches illustrate how the design of interventions can be influ-enced by our understanding of how people think and reason about their health.

Finally, the last section of the book looks at variables of concern to personality psycholo-gists, such as negative affectivity, hostility, optimism, and the willingness to confront trau-matic experiences, and whether these affective aspects of personality can be linked reliably to particular illnesses or health habits. Does the positive worldview of cockeyed optimists, for example, make them more likely to take care of themselves or ignore obvious risks?

Throughout this volume, we have selected articles from investigators who adopt a uniquely social psychological perspective. What this means is that they are phenomenologists—they consider the person as an active constructor of his or her reality. Health behavior can only be understood in the context of an individual's perceptions, construals, and resulting belief system, and these behaviors are motivated by the interaction of individual dispositions and situational affordances. Moreover, a social psychological approach places health behavior in the context of other social behaviors of the individual and considers the diverse set of human needs that may underlie people's health practices.

In adopting this mode of analysis, many of the authors focus on the social psychological processes that underlie people's behavioral practices rather than the specific behavioral practices themselves—the person who smokes rather than smoking behavior per se. Although we are committed to the goal of developing interventions and technologies that maximize people's chances of changing their behavior, we believe that the likelihood of significant advances in health behavior change are contingent on the identification of the psychological processes that facilitate or inhibit healthy behavior. Moreover, we believe that understanding why a particular intervention technique is effective—for example, why does setting a group quit date in a smoking cessation program increase the likelihood of cessation?—raises the probability that this procedure can be integrated into interventions across health domains.

This focus on processes that generalize beyond the health domain in which they were first studied accounts for our decision not to organize this book around diseases or particular health behaviors, or even around specific theoretical models. Rather, we feel the most useful level of analysis is one focused on social cognitive processes—how do people think about their health, how do they regulate their exposure to health information?—and social influence processes— how do people compare their own health to others, what social norms guide behavioral decision-making? From this vantage point, our contributors tend to look "down" at individual behaviors and diseases and look "up" toward theoretical models, all with an eye toward offering a general set of determinants of healthy and risky behavior that can be shaped to the advantage of the individual and the improvement of society. We believe that the information in these readings has important implications for efforts that can and need to be taken at both the basic and applied level of analysis. The basic principles discussed in this volume have clear implications for the design of interventions. Although the value of these interventions rests considerably on their ability to address important practical problems effectively, they will also provide crucial opportunities to test and, when necessary, refine our basic principles.

We hope that this introductory essay creates in you the same excitement about the social psychology of health and illness that we feel about our work every day. We have not tried to review this enormous field systematically, of course. If you would like a thorough background to all of the issues raised by the contributors, we recommend that you take a look at our chapter in the *Handbook of Social Psychology* (Salovey, Rothman, & Rodin, 1998). However, we encourage you simply to plunge right in to the articles that follow here. They were selected for the importance of their content as well as for their readability. We think you will find them incredibly stimulating.

REFERENCES

Matarazzo, J. D. (1984). Behavioral health. In J. D. Matarazzo, S. M. Weiss, J. A. Herd, N. E. Miller, & S. M. Weiss (Eds.), *Behavioral health: A handbook of health enhancement and disease prevention* (pp. 3-40). New York: Wiley.

McGuire, W. J. (1991). Using guiding-idea theories of the person to develop educational campaigns against drug abuse and other health-threatening behavior. *Health Education Research, 6,* 173–184.

Salovey, P., Rothman, A. J., & Rodin, J. (1998). Health behavior. In D. Gilbert, S. Fiske, & G. Lindzey (Eds.), *Handbook of social psychology* (4th ed., Vol. 2, pp. 633–683). New York: McGraw-Hill.

Taylor, S. E. (1990). Health psychology: The science and the field. *American Psychologist, 45,* 40–50.

Mental Models of Health and Illness

It's been 3 days and you can't take it any longer. You've been running a fever, sneezing, and coughing incessantly. Worst of all, the pain in your face and head is intolerable. You drag yourself out of bed and go to the doctor, who diagnoses a sinus infection. Four days later, you're feeling great; the antibiotics the doctor prescribed did the trick. Although 6 days of pills remain in the bottle, since you feel better and were never particularly fond of the stomach cramps, you decide to save the medication for the next time you're sick. A week later you're back in the doctor's office, coughing, sneezing, and feeling as bad as ever. You thought you had acted wisely and taken care of yourself. What happened?

Mental models of health and illness are sets of beliefs that people hold that guide their decisions and actions. Because these models specify the attributes that people ascribe to a specific health problem, in order to understand people's health behaviors it is essential that investigators attend to them. Failing to take all of the antibiotics that have been prescribed might appear to be irrational, as it, not surprisingly, can result in relapse. However, such behavior may be understandable if one examines the links between it and a person's underlying belief system. If your mental model of an illness such as a sinus infection includes the belief that the absence of symptoms indicates that the disease has been cured, we should not be surprised when medication is discontinued prematurely. Although this belief about illness is incorrect, the behavior based on it—terminating antibiotic use—follows logically from it. Behavior that appears irrational to an outside observer might actually be consistent with an actor's underlying beliefs.

The three articles in this section explore the contents of the belief systems that guide people's health practices. Meyer, Leventhal, and Gutmann (1985) assert that people's mental models of illness are organized around four themes: (1) symptoms, (2) causes, (3) consequences, and (4) duration. In a creative study, in which they interviewed 230 patients with high blood pressure, they demonstrate that the features patients ascribe to hypertension determines the extent to which they adhere to their treatment regimen. For example, despite the fact that hypertension is asymptomatic, those patients who believe they can tell whether or not their blood pressure is elevated use this information to decide whether to continue the treatment. Thus, people may think they are acting appropriately, consistent with their understanding of the health problem, but still not make the right decision.

The path between mental models and behavior is not a one-way street. Just as people's beliefs guide their actions, these behaviors, in turn, feed back to and change these beliefs. For example, people who feel at risk for a sexually transmitted disease (STD) may be motivated to use condoms when sexually active. However, over time, the regular use of condoms should decrease how vulnerable they feel to being infected by an STD. Gerrard and colleagues (1997) provide a rich description of the relation between adolescents' beliefs and behavior over a 3-year period across three behaviors (reckless driving, drinking alcohol, and smoking cigarettes). These investigators not only delineate the reciprocal relation between beliefs and behavior, but also reveal why investigators need to assess a broad set

of beliefs that underlie people's behavior. Consistent with the perspective put forth by Meyer et al. (1985), the risky behaviors only make sense after considering the constellation of beliefs on which they are based.

The dominant theories of the psychological antecedents of health behavior all point to certain beliefs as critical. What appears important in motivating intentions to take healthy actions includes one's evaluations of these action as pleasant or unpleasant, one's beliefs about what other people are or are not doing, and one's appreciation that the required actions are under one's control. Because different theorists use different terminology, students of the social psychology of health behavior often are confused regarding the similarities and differences among the dominant models of health behavior. Weinstein (1993) asserts that meaningful progress in understanding the relative value of these models can only come if we accurately describe where these models converge and diverge with respect to each other. To this end, Weinstein translates the factors specified by four leading models of precautionary behavior into a common framework.

The complex relationship between belief and behavior is a fundamental question in the field of social psychology. Because of their importance in day-to-day social interaction, indeed to life itself, health and illness provide an excellent testing ground for exploring when belief systems motivate behavior, when behavior guides belief, and when both of these processes are operating at the same time. As such, the explication of people's mental models of illness represents the quintessential starting point in the study of social psychology and health.

REFERENCES

Gerrard, M., Gibbons, F. X., Benthin, A. C., & Hessling, R. M. (1997). A longitudinal study of the reciprocal nature of risk behaviors and risk cognitions in adolescents: What you do shapes what you think and vice versa. *Health Psychology, 15,* 344–354.

Meyer, D., Leventhal, H., & Gutmann, M. (1985). Common-sense models of illness: The example of hypertension. *Health Psychology, 4,* 115–135.

Weinstein, N. D. (1993). Testing four competing theories of health-protective behavior. *Health Psychology, 12,* 324–333.

Discussion Questions

1. Consider the last time you had the flu. How would you describe your "mental model" of the flu? To what extent do the features you associate with the flu affect how you did or did not take care of your illness? Can you think of ways in which people's mental models of common health problems might be different from their models of severe health problems such as hypertension or cancer?

2. According to Gerrard and her colleagues, the more adolescents believe that their peers are drinking alcohol, the more likely they are to drink themselves. What are the different ways that your peers might influence your behavior? Do you think peers exert a similar influence on the behavior of college students? How about the behavior of older adults?

3. Researchers often gather information about people's beliefs and behavior at a single point in time (i.e., a cross-sectional survey). Why might it be important for researchers to examine the relation between beliefs and behavior over time (i.e., a longitudinal survey)?

4. Recall the last time you did not follow a treatment regimen specified by your doctor (e.g., failed to complete your antibiotic prescription). Why do you think you made this decision?

5. Joe is 21 years old, smokes a pack of Marlboros each day, and says he enjoys smoking. Would you say his behavior is "rational" or "irrational"? Why?

Suggested Readings

Lau, R. R., & Hartman, K. A. (1983). Common sense representations of common illnesses. *Health Psychology, 2,* 167–185.
> Another perspective on mental models of illness but one that reveals somewhat different dimensions than Meyer, Leventhal, and Gutmann (1985).

Petrie, K. J., & Weinman, J. A. (1997). *Perceptions of health and illness: Current research and applications.* London: Harwood Academic Press.
> A helpful collection of work on mental models of illness by the leading researchers in this area.

Salovey, P., Rothman, A. J., & Rodin, J. (1998). Health behavior. In D. T. Gilbert, S. T. Fiske, & G. Lindzey (Eds.), *The handbook of social psychology* (Vol. 2, pp. 633–683). Boston, MA: McGraw-Hill.
A comprehensive review of the social psychology and health behavior literature organized around competing theoretical perspectives and general issues.

Common-Sense Models of Illness: The Example of Hypertension

Daniel Meyer, Howard Leventhal, and Mary Gutmann

University of Wisconsin, Madison, and Mount Sinai Hospital, Milwaukee

Our premise was that actions taken to reduce health risks are guided by the actor's subjective or common-sense constructions of the health threat. We hypothesized that illness threats are represented by their labels and symptoms (their identity), their causes, consequences, and duration. These attributes are represented at two levels: as concrete, immediately perceptible events and as abstract ideas. Both levels guide coping behavior. We interviewed 230 patients about hypertension, presumably an asymptomatic condition. When asked if they could monitor blood pressure changes, 46% of 50 nonhypertensive, *clinic control* cases said yes, as did 71% of 65 patients *new to treatment*, 92% of 50 patients in *continuing treatment*, and 94% of 65 *re-entry patients*, who had previously quit and returned to treatment. Patients in the *continuing treatment* group, who believed the treatment had beneficial effects upon their symptoms, reported complying with medication and were more likely to have their blood pressure controlled. Patients new to treatment were likely to drop out of treatment if: (1) they had reported symptoms to the practitioner at the first treatment session, or (2) they construed the disease and treatment to be acute. The data suggest that patients develop implicit models or beliefs about disease threats, which guide their treatment behavior, and that the initially most common model of high blood pressure is based on prior acute, symptomatic conditions.

O ur study was designed to achieve both practical and theoretical goals. Its practical purpose was to uncover some of the variables that affect failure to adhere to treatment regimens for high blood pressure. Its theoretical goal was to determine how common-sense representations of high blood pressure—that is, lay cognitive models of this disease—affect compliance behaviors. Hypertension, or high blood pressure, seemed a particularly suitable focus for the study of the way illness representations affect behavior for several reasons. First, since high blood pressure is considered a silent or asymptomatic condition, how people come to identify it in themselves is of special interest (Galton, 1973). Second, hypertension requires the long-term adoption of a variety of prescribed behaviors, such as medication taking, weight loss, and diet change. Thus, it is possible to see how the perception or representation of hypertension affects these behaviors. Third, the

Possible explanation of w-adherence

treatment of high blood pressure is a significant public health problem. Early estimates suggest that blood pressure is uncontrolled in 70% to 80% of hypertensives (Schoenberger, Stamler, Shekelle, & Shekelle, 1972). One third to one half of those initially identified with high readings fail to seek treatment, and an additional one third to one half of those who seek treatment drop out. An equally high proportion of those who remain in treatment are inconsistent in taking medication and are poorly controlled. Thus, even though regular use of medication can control blood pressure and reduce its associated risks of morbidity and mortality, the majority of hypertensives remain unprotected (National High Blood Pressure Education Program, 1979a, 1979b; Schoenberger et al., 1972). In summary, both the asymptomatic quality and the long duration of hypertension suggest that the patient's understanding of the disease may be important in achieving long-term adherence to a potentially costly treatment.

Conclusion

It is also clear that the low levels of treatment adherence are likely to reflect a succession of failures to communicate to the patient the nature of the disease at each of the steps from discovery to continuation of treatment. Thus, when a high reading is first discovered, the individual is asked to return for another checkup. If that second reading also is elevated, it is suggested that he or she enter treatment with a personal physician or at a clinic. When the diagnosis is confirmed, the patient is asked to take medications designed to control the condition. After some experimentation with drug type and dosage, the patient is told to continue treatment on a daily basis for an unlimited period. Each step requires that the patient receive and understand information about this disease: that it is a potential threat, that the threat is a personal one, that a regimen of treatment must be accepted, and, finally, that the treatment requires continued adherence. Failure to achieve compliance, therefore, suggests a failure to produce changes in attitude and behavior at one or more of these steps.

How can we account for communication failures such as the above? Our examination of the literature on both compliance and attitude change suggests that investigators have accounted for compliance failures in three different ways (Leventhal, Meyer, & Gutmann, 1980): (1) as a consequence of relatively fixed patient characteristics such as social class or personality (Haynes, 1976); (2) as a result of situational barriers such as the high cost or poor access to treatment (Finnerty, Shawl, & Himmelsback, 1973), or inadequate social support for medication taking (Caplan, Robinson, French, Caldwell, & Shinn, 1976); and (3) as a consequence of inadequate motivation or the absence of a desire to seek information and treatment for self-protection. Although each of these approaches has added to our understanding of noncompliance, none of the other three approaches has provided a fully satisfying account of the compliance problem. Studies comparing compliant to noncompliant patients have reported few if any consistent differences between them in either personality (Finnerty et al., 1973) or demographic characteristics (Sackett et al., 1975). Thus, defining compliance failures in a dispositional framework, which may be encouraged by the practitioner's role as an expert observer (Jones & Nisbett, 1971), appears to have done little more than cast blame on the patient (Leventhal, Zimmerman, & Gutmann, 1984; Stimson, 1974).

The situational approach, which has been adopted by some medical investigators, has proven more fruitful. For example, the removal of situational barriers (e.g., setting individualized appointment times) has substantially reduced noncompliance in some settings (Finnerty et al., 1973). Physician monitoring of patient behavior has also been shown to be of value (Svarstad, 1976). Unfortunately, compliance has not always been improved by situational manipulations. Individualized appointments have failed to reduce noncompliance in some studies (Levine et al., 1979), as have efforts to remove situational barriers by the introduction of prepaid (hence, free) services (e.g., Kegeles, Lotzkar, & Andrews, 1959). It is clear, therefore, that situational variables must be viewed in a theoretical framework if we are to understand how and when they work. This has been done in very few of the studies reviewed.

Finally, studies designed to test the impact of altered motivation have used educational programs that have increased knowledge and developed more favorable attitudes toward treatment (Levine et al., 1979), but have not always led to improved behavior (Sackett et al., 1975). The literature on attitude and behavior suggests two possible reasons for this failure. First, patients may believe treatments are ineffective and, therefore, will fail to adopt and use them (Becker & Maiman, 1975; Chu, 1966; Dabbs & Leventhal, 1966; Rosenstock & Kirscht, 1979). Second, patients are less likely to comply if they lack specific instructions on when and how to act (Leventhal, Singer, & Jones, 1965), or if they feel incompetent or unable to act (Bandura, 1977; Leventhal, 1970; Rosen, Terry, & Leventhal, 1982). Given the known efficacy of antihypertensive medication, the relative simplicity of the behaviors—for example, taking a diuretic pill twice daily—and the efforts to instruct patients on the proper utilization of medication, neither of the above mentioned factors appear to provide a sufficient explanation for the problem of noncompliance. This review led us to the conclusion that the patient's understanding of the disorder, that is, how he or she experienced high blood pressure and its treatment, may be critical for understanding his or her failure to continue treatment and control his or her blood pressure level (Leventhal, Meyer, & Gutmann, 1980).

We began with three assumptions. The first was that patients are motivated to protect themselves from health dangers. The second was that patients will identify the danger (e.g., hypertension) by concrete, perceptual signs as well as by its abstract label. Third, we assumed that concrete signs would exert an important influence on behavior as they define the perceptual field that directs behavior. If these assumptions are correct, how will a patient represent or construe his or her problem when told that he or she has high blood pressure, that it is asymptomatic, and that it requires a lifelong regimen of medication? Our assumptions make clear that such information does not fall on a blank mind. From a patient's earliest childhood, a diagnosed illness has been accompanied by symptoms—stomachaches, a runny nose, pain, and so on. In many cases, the symptomatic stage is followed by treatment and by the alleviation of symptoms—that is, by cure. This history may lead patients to expect and perceive hypertension as following this same pattern. Symptoms that are felt at or near the time blood pressure is taken and/or hypertension is diagnosed are likely to be seen as indicators of the disorder. Moreover, the environmental events that precede these symptoms, for example, stress leading to headaches, are likely to be seen as causes of hypertension. The disappearance of symptoms after treatment may be perceived as a cure, while the intensification of symptoms may make treatment seem counterproductive. If the motivated patient adheres to treatment on the basis of hypotheses such as these, the control of blood pressure will depend on the overlap between the hypothesis and the mechanism causing the disorder.

Our study was designed to investigate whether people develop such common-sense models and to evaluate their impact on patients' adherence to treatment. Our specific hypotheses were as follows: (1) Patients will develop representations of hypertension that include both abstract information and concrete attributes, that is, symptoms; (2) the representation of the disorder will be similar to that for prior acute illness episodes and have an acute (short-lived) time frame; (3) the representation will serve as a guide to the patients' behavior: patients who have been in treatment continually over a long period of time will likely use symptoms as a guide to medication taking, and patients who have just entered treatment are likely to drop out of treatment if they identify and monitor symptoms of this disorder and if they believe that hypertension is an acute (short-lived) disorder.

Method

Design and Subjects

Clinical groups. Four groups of patients were interviewed at different stages in the diagnosis and treatment of hypertension: (1) *normotensive clinic controls* ($n = 50$), patients with normal blood pressure visiting the clinic for reasons other than blood pressure treatment; (2) *newly treated* ($n = 65$), patients in treatment for hypertension for the first time; (3) *continuing treatment* ($n = 50$), patients who had been in continuous treatment for 3 months to 15 years ($\overline{X} = 7.75$ years); and (4) *re-entry* ($n = 65$), patients who had dropped out of and then returned to treatment. An audit of medical records at a 6-month follow-up provided data on treatment outcome and dropout rates for both newly treated and re-entry patients. Longitudinal data were also obtained from a 6-month follow-up interview with the newly treated patients.

Subjects were randomly selected from among those presenting themselves for screening and/or treatment at the primary care and renal clinics of Mount Sinai Medical Center in Milwaukee and at the downtown hypertension clinic of the Milwaukee Blood Pressure Program; these clinics serve a predominantly inner-city population. Mean initial blood pressure for the hypertensive groups was 150/103, with 75% of the patients classified as mild-to-moderate (i.e., with diastolic pressures between 90 and 110 mm/Hg). A diuretic was the sole treatment for 65% of the patients. The mean age was 47 years. Sixty percent of the subjects were black and 55% of the subjects were female. Differences in age and sex between the groups were negligible.

The Interview and Representation of High Blood Pressure

A 45-minute structured interview was used to elicit the patient's view of high blood pressure. Open-ended questions obtained spontaneous reactions and were followed by structured probes to explore in depth the patient's perceptions of the causes, mechanisms, and consequences of high blood pressure. For example, the open-ended question, "In your own words, what do you think high blood pressure means?" was followed by systematic probes: "Do you think something in the heart causes high blood pressure? In the brain . . . ? In the blood vessels . . . ? The blood . . . ? The kidneys . . . ? Other parts of the body?" Answers that were stereotyped or that repeated generally accepted ideas were followed by questions such as, "Well, what do you think?" or "What about for yourself?"

These probes allowed us to distinguish clearly between the patient's report of what she or he had been told and believed about high blood pressure and its treatment, and between what she or he believed to be true in general and thought was true about his or her own blood pressure. Patients had no difficulty with these distinctions. To determine how patients could tell that changes in their blood pressure had occurred, open-ended questions were followed by explicit ones about bodily sensations and the interpretations of changes in these symptoms with treatment.

Coping and adherence. A later section of the interview assessed adherence to the medication regimens. To make it acceptable to report deviations from prescribed regimens, the first of the four questions opened by saying that there were many reasons why people missed their medications. The

patients were then asked why they had missed taking medication on specific occasions. The second question probed more specific reasons for missing medication; the third asked for an estimate of the number of pills missed per week. The fourth question was designed to tap experimentation with the medication regimen. It opened with the statement that many people experiment with the amount of medication and asked respondents if they had ever attempted to reduce their medication. Responses to the four questions were coded to form a three-level index of adherence: taking as prescribed, missing randomly and infrequently, and systematically departing from the regimen. Data on adherence are reported only for *continuing treatment* patients.

Protecting against interviewing biases. Because the interviewers (the senior author and three medical students) knew whether the respondent was *newly treated, re-entry,* and so on, the following precautions were taken to avoid bias. First, the interview protocol, including predetermined probes, was strictly adhered to. Second, the questions used to assess symptom monitoring and medication taking were in separate sections of the interview. Third, coding was done by three students who were not interviewers. Neither the student interviewers nor the coders were informed of the hypotheses. Reliabilities on the items reported were 88% agreement or better. Fourth, we expected symptoms to be related to medication taking, but we did not try to anticipate the rich array of symptom models and behavioral determinants that the patients reported. Finally, we saw our task to be recording and making explicit the patients' views of their disorders. This was consistent with our basic premise that patient behavior is logical within the context of the patient's view of hypertension, regardless of the medical validity of that viewpoint.

Blood pressure control. All patients in the actively treated group were classified as being in good, borderline, or poor control of their blood pressure on the basis of age, sex, and blood pressure readings on the last three clinic visits. Criteria for classification were taken from published national guidelines (Report of the Joint National Committee on Detection, Evaluation, and Treatment of High Blood Pressure: A cooperative study, 1977). The classifications were made by two nephrologists and one general internist. Clinical judgment also entered into the categorizations.

Disagreement occurred for only 4 of the 50 cases, and these were just one step apart. We also looked for correlations between these blood pressure readings and symptom reports.

Results

We present data to address our two major hypotheses: first, that patients construct representations of high blood pressure using both concrete symptoms and conceptual notions (time-line, causes, and physiology of the disease); second, that this representation exerts an important influence on coping behaviors, that is, taking medications and staying in treatment.

The Representation of Hypertension

A series of questions assessed the patients' perceptions of high blood pressure with respect to the following attributes: (1) its *identity*, or the signs or symptoms used to tell when blood pressure is elevated ("Do you think you can tell when your blood pressure is up?" "How do you tell?"); (2) its *time-line* ("How long do you think it will take for the treatment to control your high blood pressure?" and "How long do you think you'll need to be on treatment?"); (3) its *causes* ("How do you think high blood pressure started in your case?"); and (4) notions about the underlying physiological factors causing high blood pressure.

The symptomatic identification of high blood pressure. Medical authorities assert that hypertension is asymptomatic, but our respondents thought otherwise. When asked, "Do you think you can tell when your blood pressure is up?" 46% of the *normotensive* clinic control group, 71% of the *newly treated* group, 92% of the *continuing treatment* group, and 94% of the *re-entry* group identified symptoms for detecting elevated pressure. The group differences, which are highly significant ($\chi^2 = 44.65, df\, 3, p < .01$), suggest a developmental progression, with more patients identifying symptoms with blood pressure the longer they have been diagnosed as having the disease. Although the progression could also be due to a selective dropping out of treatment, the developmental hypothesis is supported by data from the *newly treated* patients:

71% reported symptoms of high blood pressure on the initial interview, as compared to 92% by the 6-month follow-up ($\chi^2 = 9.72, df\, 1, p < .01$). Although patients perceived their hypertension as symptomatic, 80% of the patients in the *continuing treatment* group agreed with the statement, "People can't tell when their blood pressure is up." They had understood what is advertised on TV and printed in pamphlets, and accepted this information as their abstract view of the disorder. But their concrete, personal view of illness led them to separate themselves from these more abstract, medically accepted generalizations with statements like: "My doctor tells me that people can't tell, but *I* can." They were clearly aware of the inconsistency, as 64% of these same *continuing treatment* patients spontaneously requested that their ideas not be communicated to the treating physician.

Time-line. Overall, 43% of the patients made clear that they had a chronic model of high blood pressure. When asked, "How long do you think you'll need to be on treatment?" they said, "For a lifetime." About one quarter of the patients expected to be cured (acute model); one third expected the disease to come and go (cyclic model). *Newly treated* patients were much more likely to anticipate an acute time-line (40%) than either *re-entry* (18%) or *continuing treatment* patients (12%), and *continuing treatment* patients were by far the most likely to hold a chronic model of the disorder (64% vs. 43% for *re-entry* and 28% for *newly treated*; $\chi^2 = 20.99, df\, 4, p < .01$)

The causes of high blood pressure. Seventy-five to 80% of the patients had ideas about the cause of their condition. The causes of high blood pressure most likely to be mentioned by *re-entry* and *newly treated* patients were eating and drinking (31%) or home and job situation (26%); these patients were also most likely to give "Don't know" (19% and 26%, respectively) responses. (The questions were: "How do you think high blood pressure started in your case?" and its probes "Things you eat or drink?" "Things in your life—like your home or job situation?" "Your weight?" "Anything else?") *Continuing treatment* patients were most likely to cite heredity (40%) and least likely to say they didn't know (12%). (Due to the small number of subjects in many cells of the table, no statistical analysis will be presented.)

Physiological mechanisms. When asked, "Do you think something in the heart . . . brain . . .

blood . . . blood vessels . . . other parts of the body . . . causes your high blood pressure?" 60% of the *continuing treatment*, 65% of the *re-entry*, and 56% of the *newly treated* patients agreed to brain and/or blood. *Newly treated* patients were least likely to give two or more responses and most likely to say that they didn't know. None of the differences, however, were significant.

Linkages Between Attributes

We tabulated whether patients linked their physiological hypotheses to their perceptions of the cause, symptoms, or treatment of high blood pressure. When we compared those who made all three linkages to those who made fewer or none, the percentage making three was highest for *continuing treatment* (36%), next highest for *re-entry* (12%), and lowest for *newly treated* (11%) patients. The comparison of the proportions across conditions was statistically significant ($\chi^2 = 14.48$, $df\, 2$; $p < .001$). Identifying all three links suggests a more organized representation of the disease, but the number of patients making three links was relatively small. The most common link was between physiology and treatment.

The Representation and Behavior

We examined the impact of two attributes of the representation on two types of behavior: adherence to medication and dropping out or remaining in treatment. Adherence to medication was the most appropriate measure to use with the *continuing treatment* group, as these subjects have remained in treatment—some for a very long time— and they are less likely to drop out. On the other hand, dropping out of treatment is the appropriate measure to use with the *newly treated* patient group, as these patients have yet to decide whether treatment is necessary. It was also the most appro-

priate measure for the *re-entry* group, as these patients have a history of regulating their treatment by entering and then leaving the medical care system.

Adherence to medication. As stated before, 92% (46 of 50) of the patients in the *continuing treatment* group identified symptoms of high blood pressure. If these patients expected treatment to reduce their blood pressure and modify their symptoms, their symptoms should have influenced how they adhered to their medication regimens. When asked if treatment affected their symptoms, 17 of the 46 said yes; 12 of the 17 (70%) were taking medications as prescribed. Blood pressure was in good control in 9 of the 17 (53%) patients. Five of the 17 patients who believed treatment affected their symptoms and did not take medication as prescribed treated their blood pressure as though it were an acute illness, that is, they took medication when symptoms were present and did not when symptoms were absent.

In contrast, medication was taken as prescribed by only 9 of the 29 (31%) patients who believed treatment did *not* affect their symptoms; 7 of 29 (24%) were in good control of their blood pressure. A comparison of the data on compliance (70% vs. 31%) yielded a chi-square of 5.25 (1 *df* and *p* <.05). For blood pressure control (scored as good, fair, or poor), the chi-square of 5.93 was significant at the .06 level, with superior control for the 17 patients reporting that treatment affected their symptoms. There was also a clear relationship between reports of compliance and blood pressure control. For example, of the patients who believed that medication had a beneficial effect on their symptoms and took medication as prescribed, 7 of the 9 in good control reported excellent compliance. For all 50 *continuing treatment* patients, adherence was significantly related to blood pressure control ($\chi^2 = 12.81$, 2 *df*, *p* < .005). (See Table 1.1).

TABLE 1.1. Relationship of Reported Adherence to Blood Pressure Control for Continuing Treatment Group

Adherence as prescribed	Blood pressure control			
	Good	Borderline	Poor	Total
Yes	13	6	2	21
No	4	16	9	29
Total	17	22	11	50

Because of the small number of patients per group, we could not find an association between the patients' temporal expectations (chronic, cyclic, acute) and the three levels of adherence (as prescribed, with random misses, and with systematic misses). But patients with a chronic view of their problem did seem less likely to report systematic misses of medication (3.1%, 1 of 32) than did patients holding either cyclic and/or acute views (27.8%, 5 of 18; $\chi^2 = 4.50$, df 1, $p < .05$).

We also failed to detect any association between compliance and the perceived cause of high blood pressure, the perceived underlying physiological process, and the linkages between cause, physiology, and so on. The absence of a relationship between perceived cause and compliance was not surprising since the two most common causes, stress (home situation) and ingestion (salt intake), can be stable (life can always be stressful) or episodic. Finally, not all actively treated patients adhered to treatment for symptomatic reasons. For example, ten patients justified close adherence to the regimen by stating that they felt better about themselves for doing something about their health. Three others reported strict adherence "because the doctor told me to."

Dropping out. For the *newly treated* patients, both symptoms and time-line were related to decisions to enter and remain in treatment. When the initial interview was used to divide the *newly treated* patients into those who did and those who did not identify symptoms with their high blood pressure, a greater percentage of those who reported symptoms had dropped out of treatment by the 6-month follow-up (43.4%, 20 of 46 vs. 21.1%, 4 of 19; $\chi^2 = 2.90$, df 1, $p < .10$). Further examination of these data revealed the following unexpected effect: 23 of the 46 patients who identified a symptom with blood pressure indicated they had specifically mentioned that symptom on the first visit to their practitioner. When this subgroup of 23 patients was compared with the 42 (23 symptomatic, 19 asymptomatic) who did not say they reported symptoms to their doctor, we found that 61% (14 of 23) of the former had dropped treatment, compared with 24% (10 of 42) of the latter ($\chi^2 = 8.56$, df 1, $p < .01$). Thus, *newly treated* patients who said they told their doctor about their high blood pressure symptoms were more likely to drop out. Follow-up interviews with dropout patients indicated that they interpreted the disappearance of symptoms as a cure of the disease and the continued presence of symptoms as a failure in the treatment.

The time-line, the expected duration of hypertension and its treatment, also influenced decisions to remain in or drop out of treatment. *Newly treated* patients who saw their problem as chronic (28%, 18 of 65) had a low proportion of dropouts over the next 6 months, 17% (3 of 18). Those *newly treated* patients who saw their problem as cyclic or episodic (32%, 21 of 65) had a higher dropout rate (29%, 6 of 21), while those who saw the problem as acute (40%, 26 of 65) had the highest dropout rate (58%, 15 of 26; $\chi^2 = 8.62$, df 2, $p < .05$). The perceived time factor appears to be a good predictor of patients' remaining in treatment.

Given that both reports of symptoms and time-line related to decisions to remain in treatment, we examined the relationship between the two and then used both to see how well they would predict behavior. More symptoms were reported by patients with acute representations (80%; 21 of 26) than were reported by patients with either cyclic (71%; 15 of 21) or chronic representations (66%; 10 of 18), but the differences were not significant ($\chi^2 = 3.27$, df 2). A logistical regression analysis using temporal expectations (3 levels) and presence of symptoms (2 levels) showed that both were related to remaining in treatment ($\chi^2 = 8.47$, $p < .05$); together, they accounted for 21% of the variance in dropping out of treatment.

Finally, we examined the relationship of symptom monitoring to the decision to return to treatment among the *re-entry* patients. Fully 94% of the *re-entry* patients thought they could tell when their blood pressure was up. But only 32% (21 of 65) returned to treatment because of their symptoms: The remaining 44 patients returned for reasons such as discovering that their blood pressure was elevated although they were asymptomatic ($n = 20$) or finding that it was elevated when they were seeking care for some other symptomatic problem ($n = 24$). Six months later, only 29% (6 of 21) of the *re-entry* patients who had returned to treatment because of symptoms they related to high blood pressure had dropped out, compared to 39% (17 of 44) who dropped out for those who had returned to treatment without identifying a blood pressure symptom. While the difference is not statistically reliable, it is opposite to that for the *newly treated* patients. One possible explanation for the apparent reversal is that almost three quarters (71%, 15 of 21) of those who returned because of symptoms of high blood pressure had a symptom different from the one that had brought them into treatment on the first occasion; 93% (14 of 15) of these patients were in treatment at the time of the 6-month follow-up. The appearance of a new symptom may have decreased their confidence in the validity of symptoms as indicators of high blood pressure and increased their likelihood of remaining in treatment.

Validity of Sensations as Indicators of Blood Pressure

To see if symptoms are related to blood pressure, point biserial correlations were calculated between the presence or absence of each symptom and blood pressures measured at the initial interview. The highest correlation for systolic pressure was to dizziness (+.106), and the lowest was to warmth (−.076). The highest correlation for diastolic blood pressures was to headaches (+.076), and the lowest to nervousness (−.035). Thus, while adherence to treatment and blood pressure outcomes are affected by the perception of symptoms, there is no evidence in this clinic population of a relationship between symptoms and blood pressure. These data are consistent with previous reports (Berglund, Ander, Lindstrom, & Tibblin, 1975; Bulpitt, Dollery, & Carne, 1976). A better test of the relationship, however, would be to take blood pressure readings in both the presence and absence of symptoms using a within-subject design (Pennebaker, 1982). One study using such a design in the work setting is reported by Baumann and Leventhal (1985).

Discussion

Our data suggest that people construct common-sense models of hypertension. These models appear to have strong similarities to prior illness experiences. Thus, our subjects, both normotensive and hypertensive, believed that symptoms were associated with and could be used to monitor elevations in blood pressure, that the problem would be of limited duration, and that it was caused by a variety of environmental conditions such as work,

family, stress, and diet. These findings are comparable to those we have found for patients undergoing chemotherapy treatment for cancer (Nerenz, 1979; Ringler, 1981) and are similar to those reported by Lau and Hartman (1983) in their study of illness cognition in college undergraduates.

The data also show that common-sense models evolve over time. A higher percentage of patients in those groups in treatment for a long period of time reported monitoring their symptoms, and a greater proportion of the *newly treated* subjects reported symptom monitoring at 6 months after their initial treatment than on the initial interview. Moreover, temporal expectations clearly change from an acute, or time-limited, to a *chronic* frame of reference. The increase in symptom monitoring suggests that individuals feel a need to define abstract concepts such as hypertension in concrete terms. The result is a symmetry between labels and symptoms: (1) given an undefined state of body arousal, subjects will seek labels (Schachter & Singer, 1962); (2) given a label, subjects will seek and find symptoms (Leventhal, Meyer, & Nerenz, 1980; Pennebaker, 1982). The symmetry appears to hold for emotions as well as for illness (Pennebaker, 1982). We do not know what type of experiences are responsible for these changes and how these experiences are processed. Leventhal and Nerenz (1983) have speculated that labeling leads to a search for supportive, concrete evidence and have suggested that the subject will formulate hypotheses on the basis of cues present at or near the time of diagnosis. If these cues stimulate imagery of prior episodes with similar cues and if the events recalled along with them fit common-sense notions of the causes of hypertension, they will be accepted as signs of the disorder; for example, the subject notices headaches when diagnosed, and the headache cues recall prior headaches when the patient is under stress. Pennebaker (1982) has reported evidence relevant to this process. Coping reactions that are associated with the disappearance of symptoms may also reinforce the notion that symptoms are linked to hypertension and may develop the belief that the disorder is curable (Lau & Hartman, 1983).

Our data also suggest that people's common-sense representations of hypertension are not coherent and well-organized: Only 36% of the *continuing treatment*, 12% of the *re-entry*, and 11% of the *newly treated* patients recognized clear connections between cause, symptoms, and the physiological mechanisms of their disorder. Moreover, people with linked models were no more likely to take medication as prescribed. There are many reasons why only a few patients will form better-integrated models of their illness over time. First, when a person is ill there is a very strong tendency to focus upon the specific aspect of the illness at that moment: for example, the symptoms and their meaning, the treatment and its effects on symptoms. Concerns about cause are likely to remain in the background until the symptoms resolve and the individual can, if he or she is so inclined, turn to issues of prevention. Consequences may be more generally salient if the disease intrudes itself on daily functioning, something hypertension tends not to do. Finally, few patients are curious enough or believe it their responsibility to understand the mechanisms underlying their illness—that is the doctor's job! There may indeed be little incentive for them to engage in such thought, as doing so may have little positive consequence. This issue, however, merits further exploration.

The third and most important set of findings concerned the relationship between the common-sense attributes of hypertension and behavior. The belief that variations in blood pressure were manifested in symptoms was related to compliance with the therapeutic regimen, that is, to the absence of systematic misses and to the adequacy of blood pressure control. Prior studies failed to show relationships between compliance with treatment regimens and symptomatology, either related to the disease or produced as "side effects" of treatment (see Haynes, 1979). In the present study, symptoms were related to treatment compliance for patients who had entered and remained in treatment (the *continuing treatment* group) when one took account of the patients' interpretations of the relationship between symptoms and treatment. The perception that treatment had beneficial effects on symptoms was critical in the prediction of compliance. Such effects were not controlled for in prior studies.

Symptoms also related to dropping out of treatment for patients in the *newly treated* sample, and this relationship was strongest when we took into account the subjects' reports that the practitioner had been told of the symptom. We suspect that patients who reported the symptom as a sign of blood pressure were either more convinced of its validity or believed that the practitioner agreed with their interpretation unless he or she stated otherwise. Analysis of tape recordings of practitioner–patient encounters for hypertension treatment from a recent study strongly suggests that practitioners rarely attempt to correct patients' symptom models; indeed, they reinforce these models when they ask about symptoms to explore drug side effects and to review systems (Steele, Gutmann, & Leventhal, 1983). It should come as no surprise, therefore, that when patients infer that the practitioner accepts their diagnostic indicators, patients are more likely to use these indicators in making decisions to discontinue treatment.

The patients' views of the duration of the illness and treatment were also good predictors of their staying in or dropping from treatment. Compliance with medication and remaining in treatment were not predicted by any of the other attributes—for example, the perceived cause of the high blood pressure, the perceived consequences, the perceived physiological basis of the problem, or the perceived connection between cause, symptom, physiological basis, and treatment. None of these factors, however, should have a simple relationship to our compliance criteria. For example, a patient may believe that life stress, at home or at work, causes high blood pressure, and because life stress may be constant or periodic, the patient's compliance may be either stable or episodic. These factors may predict compliance only when investigators measure other variables that connect these attributes to the compliance behavior. It is possible, though, that perceived causes relate to other types of self-generated treatments, such as efforts to alter diet, reduce stress, and so on. But we did not measure attempts to control disease by such additions or subtractions from life patterns (Hayes-Bautista, 1976, 1978; Kleinman, 1980).

One important question that can be raised about our findings concerns their specificity to a relatively poor inner-city population with limited education. Because there was virtually no variance in income or education within our sample, it was not possible to relate the findings to socioeconomic status (SES). We did, however, obtain similar data on two samples of respondents at the Wisconsin State Fair, an exposition held on the west side of Milwaukee, where the attendance is largely white and suburban (85% of our sample). Of 51 respondents found to have high readings for the first time,

52% thought they could monitor their blood pressure, whereas 48% of the 37 normotensive respondents interviewed believed they could monitor their pressure. These figures are similar to the 46% reported by our inner-city nonhypertensive visitors to the medical clinics.

These findings also raise a number of questions about the more general issue of the weak or nonexistent relationships between attitudes and behavior (Wicker, 1969). Our earlier studies on threat messages and preventive health actions showed that action followed attitude change if the threat message, either strong or weak, was accompanied by specific instructions for implementing the action in the subject's daily life (Leventhal, 1970). Specific instructions did not, however, lead to action in the absence of a threat message. As the level of threat aroused by the message was not critical in the combination of threat message and specific action instructions, it was apparent that some undefined cognitive component was the key. We believe that component is what we have identified as the illness representation. Indeed, one purpose of the present study was to discover the cognition component that combines with specific action instructions so as to sustain long-term behavior.

Ajzen and Fishbein (1973, 1977) recommend a quite different solution to this attitude/action problem. They suggest that attitudes will predict action when the action is perceived as normative and when the measure of attitude is specific to the action. We have no problem with their first suggestion—there is clear evidence of the importance of normative factors for health actions—and we suspect these effects operate because the norms reflect specific attributes of the health problem. (See, e.g., the study of the use of rooming-in service and breast-feeding for new mothers by Mazen & Leventhal, 1972.) We also agree with their second suggestion, that measures of attitude toward behavior will be better predictors than attitudes toward the goals of action. But in this instance, we do not believe that improved prediction is equivalent to improved explanation. Increasing the specificity of the attitude measure—for example, "Are you favorable toward taking your antihypertensive medication?" "Are you favorable to taking your antihpertensive medication right now?" ("right now" being the time it is supposed to be taken)—would undoubtedly improve prediction, but the most specific way of assessing attitude comes increasingly close to duplicating the measurement of the reaction and does less and less to explain why the action occurs. Unlike the assessment of attitudes toward the action or the assessment of intentions, assessment of common-sense representations of illness yields, in our judgment, information about the substantive knowledge and the mechanisms that underlie, or are the reasons for and the mediators of, the action.

A final point concerns whether or not the measures of the representation of high blood pressure are related to factors making up the subjects' perceived effectance (Bandura, 1977) or ability to generate self-instructions for action (Kanfer, 1977; Karoly & Kanfer, 1982; Leventhal, 1970). A very crude measure of effectance or action planning was included in the interview: The subject received 1 to 3 points if he or she responded with specific actions to each of four questions, which asked what he or she would do with respect to each of the steps from discovery to taking medications for a problem such as elevated cholesterol or a symptomatic chest X ray. Scores on this factor (ranging from 4 to 9) were unrelated to adherence for the *continuing treatment* sample. The *newly treated* sample showed an interesting relationship to dropping out: The two groups with the highest scores on the effectance-action-planning factor were the patients with an acute or short-term view of high blood pressure who dropped out of treatment and the patients with chronic time-lines who remained in treatment. The data suggest, therefore, that self-effectance or skill is predictive of taking the action that fits the patient's view of the problem and it is not predictive of taking the action recommended by the authorities. While the relationship was not significant statistically, it is clearly inconsistent with any suggestion that the attributes of the representation are equivalent to self-effectance; thus, commonsense representations are definitions of problems or statements of conditions for goals that guide performance and are among the factors important for understanding health and illness behaviors.

ACKNOWLEDGMENTS

This research was supported by research funds from the Department of Medicine of the University of Wisconsin at Mount Sinai Hospital, Milwaukee, and by grant HL 24543 from the National Heart, Lung, and Blood Institute. Our thanks to Dr. Thomas Jackson of Mount Sinai Hospital for his many helpful suggestions.

REFERENCES

Ajzen, I., & Fishbein, M. (1973). Attitudinal and normative variables as predictors of specific behaviors. *Journal of Personality and Social Psychology, 27,* 41–57.

Ajzen, I., & Fishbein, M. (1977). Attitude-behavior relations: A theoretical analysis and review of empirical research. *Psychological Bulletin, 84,* 888–918.

Bandura, A. (1977). Self-efficacy: Toward a unifying theory of behavioral change. *Psychological Review, 84,* 191–215.

Baumann, L., & Leventhal, H. (1985). "I can tell when my blood pressure is up: Can't I?" *Health Psychology, 4,* 203–218.

Becker, M. H., & Maiman, L. A. (1975). Sociobehavioral determinants of compliance with health and medical care recommendations. *Medical Care, 13,* 10–24.

Berglund, G., Ander. S., Lindstrom, B., & Tibblin, G. (1975). Personality and reporting of symptoms in normo- and hypertensive 50-year-old males. *Journal of Personality and Social Behavior, 19,* 139–145.

Bulpitt, C. J., Dollery, C. T., & Carne. S. (1976). Change in symptoms of hypertensive patients after referral to hospital clinic. *British Heart Journal, 38,* 121–128.

Caplan, R. D., Robinson, E., French, J., Caldwell, J., & Shinn, M. (1976). *Adhering to medical regimens: Pilot experiments in patient education and social support.* Ann Arbor: Institute for Social Research, University of Michigan.

Chu, G. C. (1966). Fear arousal, efficacy, and imminency. *Journal of Personality and Social Psychology, 4,* 517–524.

Dabbs, J. M., & Leventhal. H. (1966). Effects of varying the recommendations in a fear-arousing communication. *Journal of Personality and Social Psychology, 4,* 525–531.

Finnerty, F., Shawl, L., & Himmelsback, F. (1973). Hypertension in the inner city. II: Detection and follow-up. *Circulation, 47,* 76–78.

Galton, L. (1973). *The silent disease: Hypertension.* New York: Crown.

Hayes-Bautista, D. E. (1976). Modifying the treatment: Patient compliance, patient control and medical care. *Social Science and Medicine, 10,* 233–238.

Hayes-Bautista, D. E. (1978). Chicano patients and medical practitioners: A sociology of knowledge paradigm of lay-professional interaction. *Social Science and Medicine, 12,* 83–90.

Haynes, R. B. (1976). A critical review of the "determinants" of patient compliance with therapeutic regimens. In D. L. Sackett & R. B. Haynes (Eds.), *Compliance with therapeutic regimens* (pp. 26–39). Baltimore: Johns Hopkins University Press.

Haynes, R. B. (1979). Determinants of compliance: The disease and the mechanics of treatment. In R. B. Haynes, D. W. Taylor, & D. L. Sackett (Eds.), *Compliance in health care* (pp. 49–62). Baltimore: Johns Hopkins University Press.

Jones, E. E., & Nisbett, R. E. (1971). *The actor and the observer: Divergent perceptions of the causes of behavior.* New York: General Learning Press.

Kanfer, F. H. (1977). The many faces of self-control, or behavior modification changes its focus. In R. B. Stuart (Ed.), *Behavioral self-management: Strategies, techniques, and outcomes* (pp. 1–48). New York: Brunner-Mazel.

Karoly, F., & Kanfer, P. (Eds.). (1982). *Self-management and behavior change.* New York: Pergamon Press.

Kegeles, S. S., Lotzkar, S., & Andrews, L. W. (1959). *Dental care for the chronically ill and aged. II. Some factors relevant for predicting the acceptance of dental care by nursing home residents.* Unpublished manuscript. Washington, DC: U.S. Department of Health, Education, and Welfare, Public Health Service.

Kleinman, A. (1980). *Healers and patients in the context of culture: The interface of anthropology, medicine, and psychiatry.* Berkeley, CA: University of California Press.

Lau. R. R., & Hartman, K. A. (1983). Common sense representations of common illnesses. *Health Psychology, 2,* 167–185.

Leventhal, H. (1970). Findings and theory in the study of fear communications. In L. Berkowitz (Ed.), *Advances in experimental social psychology* (pp. 119–186). New York: Academic Press.

Leventhal. H., Meyer. D., & Gutmann, M. (1980). The role of theory in the study of compliance to high blood pressure regimes. In R. B. Haynes, M. E. Mattson, & T. O. Engbetson (Eds.), *Patient compliance to prescribed antihypertensive medication regimens: A report to the National Heart, Lung, and Blood Institute* (N.I.H. Publication No. 1–2102). Washington, DC: U.S. Department of Health and Human Services.

Leventhal. H., Meyer, D., & Nerenz, D. (1980). The common-sense representation of illness danger. In S. Rachman (Ed.), *Medical psychology* (Vol. 2, pp. 7–30). New York: Pergamon Press.

Leventhal. H., & Nerenz, D. (1983). Implications of stress research for the treatment of stress disorders. In D. Meichenbaum & M. Jaremko (Eds.), *Stress reduction and prevention* (pp. 5–38). New York: Plenum Press.

Leventhal, H., Singer, R. P., & Jones, S. (1965). Effects of fear and specificity of recommendations upon attitudes and behavior. *Journal of Personality and Social Psychology, 2,* 20–29.

Leventhal, H., Zimmerman, R., & Gutmann, M. (1984). Compliance: A self-regulation perspective. In D. Gentry (Ed.), *Handbook of behavioral medicine* (pp. 369–436). New York: Guilford Press.

Levine, D. M., Green, L. W., Deeds, S. G., Chwalow, J., Russell, P., & Finlay, J. (1979). Health education for hypertensive patients. *Journal of the American Medical Association, 241,* 1700–1703.

Mazen, R., & Leventhal, H. (1972). The influence of communicator-recipient similarity upon the beliefs and behavior of pregnant women. *Journal of Experimental Social Psychology, 8,* 289–302.

National High Blood Pressure Education Program. (1979a). Hypertension detection and follow-up program of the cooperative group. Five-year findings of the hypertension detection and follow-up program: 1. Reduction in mortality of persons with high blood pressure, including mild hypertension. *Journal of the American Medical Association, 242,* 2562–2571.

National High Blood Pressure Education Program. (1979b). Hypertension detection and follow-up program of the cooperative group. Five-year findings of the hypertension detection and follow-up program: II. Mortality by race, sex, and age. *Journal of the American Medical Association, 242,* 2572–2577.

Nerenz, D. R. (1979). *Control of emotional distress in cancer chemotherapy.* Unpublished doctoral dissertation, University of Wisconsin at Madison.

Pennebaker, J. (1982). *The psychology of physical symptoms.* New York: Springer-Verlag.

Report of the Joint National Committee on Detection, Evaluation, and Treatment of High Blood Pressure: A cooperative study. (1977). *Journal of the American Medical Association, 237,* 255–262.

Ringler, K. (1981). *Process of coping with cancer chemotherapy.* Unpublished doctoral dissertation. University of Wisconsin at Madison.

Rosen, T. J., Terry, N. S., & Leventhal, H. (1982). The role of esteem and coping in response to a threat communication. *Journal of Research in Personality, 16,* 90–107.

Rosenstock, I. M., & Kirscht, J. P. (1979). Why people seek health care. In G. C. Stone, F. Cohen, & N. E. Adler (Eds.), *Health psychology: A handbook* (pp. 161–188). San Francisco: Jossey-Bass.

Sackett, D. L., Haynes, R. B., Gibson, E. S., Hackett, B. C., Taylor, D. W., Roberts, R. S., & Johnson, A. L. (1975). Randomized clinical trial of strategies for improving medi-

cation compliance in primary hypertension. *The Lancet, 1,* 1205–1207.

Schachter, S., & Singer, J. E. (1962). Cognitive, social, and physiological determinants of emotional state. *Psychological Review, 69,* 377–399.

Schoenberger, J., Stamler, J., Shekelle, R., & Shekelle, S. (1972). Current status of hypertension control in an industrial population. *Journal of the American Medical Association, 222,* 559–562.

Steele, D., Gutmann, M., & Leventhal, H. (1983, May). *Symposium on coping and models of hyptertension.* Paper presented at the meeting of the Midwest Psychological Association, Chicago.

Stimson, G. V. (1974). Obeying doctor's orders: A view from the other side. *Social Sciences and Medicine, 8,* 97–104.

Svarstad, B. (1976). Physician–patient communication and patient conformity with medical advice. In D. Mechanic (Ed.), *The growth of bureaucratic medicine* (pp. 220–238). New York: Wiley.

Wicker, A. W. (1969). Attitudes versus actions: The relationship of verbal and overt behavioral responses to attitude objects. *Journal of Social Issues, 25,* 41–78.

A Longitudinal Study of the Reciprocal Nature of Risk Behaviors and Cognitions in Adolescents: What You Do Shapes What You Think, and Vice Versa

Meg Gerrard, Frederick X. Gibbons, Alida C. Benthin, and Robert M. Hessling • Iowa State University

Adolescents' reckless driving, drinking, and smoking, along with their cognitions about these behaviors, were assessed in a 3-year longitudinal design. Consistent with most models of health behavior, the results indicated that health cognitions predict risk behavior. In addition, the current data demonstrate that increases in risk behavior are accompanied by increases in perceptions of vulnerability and prevalence and by decreases in the influence of concerns about health and safety. Furthermore, the changes in prevalence estimates and concern about health and safety predicted subsequent risk behavior. These results demonstrate reciprocity between risk behaviors and related cognitions and suggest that adolescents are aware of the risks associated with their behavior but modify their thinking about these risks in ways that facilitate continued participation in the behaviors.

Key words: adolescent, risk behavior, health cognitions

Most health behavior models suggest that cognitions, such as perceptions of vulnerability to harm and perceptions of the costs and benefits of adopting precautions, guide decisions to engage in both risk and preventive behaviors. In fact, there is a wealth of research documenting the influence of such cognitions on health risk behaviors (cf. Harrison, Mullen, & Green, 1992; Janz & Becker, 1984). What is surprising, however, is that there has been little research on the reciprocal nature of the relation between health cognitions and health behavior. The primary purpose of the current study was to examine the hypothesis that, in addition to health cognitions influencing participation in risk behavior, engaging in risk behaviors influences health cognitions.

21

Impact of Health-Related Cognitions on Risk Behavior

Implementation of a wide variety of health educational programs over the last 2 decades is responsible for increases in awareness of the risks associated with smoking, drinking, driving, and unprotected sex (Eiser, Eiser, & Lang, 1989; Finn & Bragg, 1986; Finn & Brown, 1981; Gerrard, Gibbons, & Warner, 1991; Gerrard & Luus, 1995; Leventhal, Glynn, & Fleming, 1987). Unfortunately, however, these increases in awareness about health risks and personal vulnerability have not been accompanied by corresponding declines in risk behaviors (Janus & Janus, 1993; Public Health Service, 1993; Roscoe & Kruger, 1990; Rotheram-Borres & Koopman, 1991). In fact, the prevalence of many risk behaviors among adolescents may actually be increasing (Centers for Disease Control, 1992, 1993). Thus, it appears that adolescents are aware of the risks, but this awareness does not inhibit them from engaging in the behaviors. A secondary purpose of the current study, then, was to address the question of how adolescents can continue to engage in behaviors that they apparently know are putting them at risk.

The Reciprocal Relation Between Risk Behaviors and Cognitions

The idea that health behaviors affect health-relevant cognitions is not new. In fact, almost 40 years ago Festinger (1957) discussed the predicament of a hypothetical smoker who had recently learned that smoking was harmful. He proposed that individuals who continued smoking could choose between two alternative ways of dealing with this information: They could deny the relation between their behavior and potential negative consequences, or they could engage in various cognitive strategies that would enable them to continue smoking (e.g., deciding that the benefits of smoking outweigh the dangers or that the risk is negligible in comparison with that of other activities; cf. Lawton & Goldman, 1961; Pervin & Yatko, 1965). Since this early work, however, little attention has been paid to the impact that engaging in risk behavior has on health-related cognitions. Given the prominence of perceptions of vulner-

ability in models of health behavior, it is particularly surprising that there is a paucity of research on the impact of risk behavior on this specific cognition.

Until recently, thinking about the effects of risk taking on perceptions of vulnerability has been dominated by a long tradition in clinical research suggesting that people deny or minimize their vulnerability to alleviate anxiety over the potential negative consequences of their behavior. In an early statement of this principle, Janis (1958) hypothesized that as individuals approach a risk, the proximity of the threat elicits denial. This premise suggests, then, that one reason that people continue to engage in behaviors that they know are risky is that they deny the possibility of negative consequences.

We suggest that educational programs implemented over the last 2 decades have made it exceedingly difficult for people to engage in what Weisman (1972) refers to as "first-order" denial of health risks (e.g., refusing to believe that smoking increases the likelihood of cancer). In spite of evidence that people tend to minimize the seriousness of potential health risks (Croyle, 1990; Croyle & Sande, 1988; Ditto, Jemmott, & Darley, 1988), a number of recent studies have suggested that perceptions of vulnerability reflect awareness of risk rather than denial (cf. Weinstein & Nicolich, 1993). For example, a cross-sectional examination of 14 different risk behaviors indicated that adolescents who participated most in a risk behavior reported feeling the most vulnerability to the negative consequences associated with that behavior (Cohn, Macfarlane, Yanez, & Imai, 1995). Similarly, college students' perceptions of vulnerability have been shown to correlate with their actual probability of experiencing a variety of health hazards (Rothman, Klein, & Weinstein, 1996). In addition, a meta-analysis of studies of the relation between sexual risk behavior and perceptions of vulnerability to HIV indicated that people who engage in more sexual risk behaviors have higher estimates of their likelihood of contracting HIV than do people who engage in fewer risk behaviors (Gerrard, Gibbons, & Bushman, 1996). Thus, it appears that people typically do not cope with the apparent contradiction between their behavior and their awareness of its potential negative consequences by engaging in first-order denial. We propose that, instead, adolescents who engage in risk behaviors deal with this contradiction by altering or manipulating their cognitions about the behaviors in two specific ways. First, they convince themselves that many others are also taking the same risks, and, second, they avoid thinking about the dangers associated with their behavior.

Cognitive Shifts Associated With Increased Risk Behavior

Prevalence Estimates

Snyder and Wicklund (1981) theorized that when people do something they think is undesirable, they normalize their actions by engaging in a process of "claiming consensus," thus making the behavior seem more benign. A number of studies have demonstrated this type of "false consensus" effect (Ross, Greene, & House, 1977) in relation to health risk behaviors: The frequency of individuals' participation in specific risk behaviors has been shown to be associated with their estimates of the prevalence of smoking, drug use, and drinking (Gibbons, Helweg-Larsen, & Gerrard, 1995; Kandel, 1980; Leventhal et al., 1987; Sherman, Presson, Chassin, Corty, & Olshansky, 1983; Sussman et al., 1988). Using a longitudinal design, Collins et al. (1987) demonstrated that adolescents' prevalence estimates predicted onset of and increases in smoking at a 16-month follow-up. In addition, a study by Marks, Graham, and Hansen (1992) demonstrated that adolescents' alcohol consumption is positively associated with their concurrent estimates of the number of their peers who drink. These prevalence estimates, in turn, are positively associated with subsequent alcohol consumption. These studies did not, however, examine adjustments in prevalence estimates associated with increased drinking.

Disregarding Consequences

Another (and perhaps less intuitive) cognitive adjustment that people can make when dealing with the knowledge that their behavior has increased their vulnerability to negative consequences has to do with the extent to which they consider this information when making decisions. Specifically, one option is to disregard the potential negative consequences by decreasing the influence such

thoughts have on one's behavior. Although first-order denial of risk is uncommon, people can engage in a "denial-like process" (Lazarus, 1983) of avoiding thinking about the danger; in other words, the fear associated with awareness of the danger inherent in risk behavior can be brought under control by avoiding thinking about it. According to Lazarus, "A terminal patient may know full well that he or she is dying, but prefer not to think or talk about it. This is not denial, but avoidance" (p. 10).

Impact on Subsequent Risk Behavior

Some people who initiate or increase risk behavior undoubtedly respond to their awareness of increased risk by decreasing or even ceasing the risk behavior. Others, however—and we suspect that many adolescents fall into this category—recognize their vulnerability but continue to engage in the behavior. We suggest that these two cognitive shifts, normalizing the behavior and decreasing the influence of concerns about negative consequences, result in continuation of, or even an increase in, the behavior.

Current Study

The current study examined the reciprocal relation between health cognitions and adolescents' participation in three health risk behaviors: reckless driving, drinking, and smoking. On the basis of previous research, four hypotheses were generated. First, we hypothesized that adolescents' estimates of the prevalence of specific risk behaviors and their concerns about health and safety are predictive of their subsequent risk behavior. Second, when adolescents initiate or increase specific risk behaviors, they increase their perceptions of vulnerability to the negative consequences associated with those behaviors (cf. Gerrard, Gibbons, Warner, & Smith, 1993; Weinstein & Nicolich, 1993). Third, as adolescents initiate or increase a specific risk behavior, they will increase their estimates of the prevalence of that behavior among their friends and report a decline in the extent to which the potential negative consequences of that behavior are likely to influence their thinking. (The opposite of each of these effects would be expected for adolescents who decrease their risk behavior; however, the relatively small number of adolescents decreasing risk behaviors makes it difficult to test these effects.) Fourth, we hypothesized that these increases in prevalence estimates and decreases in consideration of negative consequences are associated with subsequent increases in risk behavior

Method

Participants

Participants in this study were 231 male and 246 female adolescents who completed the first two waves of data collection (Time 1 [T1] and Time 2 [T2]) in an ongoing longitudinal study of health risk behaviors conducted in rural areas of Iowa (T1 to T2 retention rate = 95%; Gibbons & Gerrard, 1995; Gibbons, Gerrard, & Boney-McCoy, 1995; Gibbons, Helweg-Larsen, & Gerrard, 1995). The 220 boys and 233 girls who participated in a third wave of data collection (Time 3 [T3]) were included in follow-up analyses of subsequent risk behavior (T2 to T3 retention rate = 93%). Half of the adolescents were in the 8th grade, and half were in the 10th grade, at T1; their mean age at that time was 14. (It is legal for 14-year-olds to drive in rural Iowa.)

Procedure

The adolescents' families' participation in the study was solicited via mailings to the parents of all 8th and 10th graders in chosen rural public schools throughout the state. To be included, target adolescents had to have a sibling within 2 years of their age, and the sibling and custodial parent(s) had to be willing to participate in the study. Of the families that met these criteria, 73% agreed to participate.

Questionnaires were administered in the families' homes by a trained interviewer at each time period, approximately 1 year apart. After presenting instructions and obtaining informed consent, the interviewer asked the adolescents (and other family members) to complete the questionnaire in private. Anonymity was stressed, and all family members were reminded several times that they were not to discuss each other's responses at any time. Each family was paid $50 for their participation at T1 and T2 and $55 at T3. The data collected from family members other than the target adolescent were intended for another study.

Measures

Risk behaviors. Reckless driving was assessed through the following item: "Sometimes both adults and teenagers drive carelessly or recklessly (too fast or in a dangerous way). How many times in the last 3 months have you driven recklessly?" The options were *never* (1), *once or twice* (2), *a few times* (3), *more than a few times* (4), and *regularly* (5). The drinking question was "How many times in the last 3 months have you had a whole drink of alcohol (for example, a bottle of beer, a glass of wine, or a whole mixed drink)?" The response options for this question were *never* (1), *once or twice* (2), *a few times* (3), *more than a few times (up to once a week)* (4), and *regularly (at least two times a week)* (5). Smoking was assessed with the question "How often do you smoke now?" Response options were *not at all* (1), *a few times every month* (2), *several times a week* (3), and *every day* (4).

In an effort to check the validity of the adolescents' self-reports of their behavior, we also asked parents to estimate their child's participation in these behaviors (cf. Stacy, Widaman, Hays, & DiMatteo, 1985). Although the parents consistently underestimated relative to their son's or daughter's self-report, the correlations between both parents' estimates and the adolescents' self-reports of all three risk behaviors were significant and ranged from .24 to .68 (*p*s < .01). These correlations, together with the emphasis placed on accuracy and anonymity in the instructions given to all participants, suggest that the adolescents' reports were reasonably valid indicators of their behaviors. Previous research has also suggested that these types of self-reports among adolescents have reasonable validity (see Brown, Clasen, & Eicher, 1986).

Perceived vulnerability. Perceptions of vulnerability were assessed via two questions for each risk behavior. The questions for accident risk were "How likely is it that your driving will cause a car or motorcycle accident that injures someone at some time in the future?" (1 = *no chance*, 7 = *definitely will happen*) and "Compared to others your age, how likely is it that your driving will cause a car (or motorcycle) accident that injures someone at some time in the future?" (1 = *much less likely than others*, 7 = *much more likely than others*). The drinking risk questions were "How likely is it that you will have a drinking problem at some time in the future?" and "Compared to others your age, how likely is it that you will have a drinking problem at some time in the future?" For smoking risk, the questions were "How likely is it that you will have a smoking-related illness (e.g., lung cancer) at some time in the future?" and "Compared to others your age, how likely is it that you will have a smoking-related illness (e.g., lung cancer) at some time in the future?" (Responses to the drinking and smoking risk questions were made on the scales just described.) T1 alphas on the perceptions of vulnerability questions for specific risks ranged from .68 to .76; T2 alphas ranged from .65 to .81.

Avoidance of thoughts about health and safety. Avoidance of thoughts about health and safety were assessed via one question for each risk behavior (e.g., "How likely is concern for your health and safety to influence your drinking behavior?"). Participants responded to these questions on a scale ranging from *not at all* (1) to *very much* (7).

Estimated prevalence. The adolescents' estimates of the prevalence of reckless driving, drinking, and smoking were each assessed with two questions about their friends' and peers' behaviors (e.g., "How many of your friends smoke?" and "How many people your age do you think smoke?"). Responses to these questions were recorded as percentages. Alphas for these measures ranged from .63 to .81.

Results

Overview

The results are organized into four sections. The first describes the adolescents' risk behaviors, changes in those behaviors over time, and the correlations between the three risk behaviors. The second reports the effect of health and safety concerns and perceived prevalence (T1) on changes in risk behavior (from T1 to T2). The third includes analyses related to the hypothesis that these cognitions change as a function of change in risk behavior (from T1 to T2). The fourth set of analyses tested the hypothesis that subsequent increases in risk behaviors (from T2 to T3) are associated with adolescents' altered cognitions

about their health and safety and the prevalence of the risk behaviors.

Behavior and Behavior Change

Participants were divided into the following four behavior change categories based on their reports of participation in each of the four risk behaviors: no risk, increasing risk, decreasing risk, and same risk. Adolescents in the no risk category reported minimal risk behaviors at both T1 and T2 (i.e., they drove recklessly or drank alcohol no more than once or twice, or they did not smoke). Adolescents in the increasing risk category reported at least a 1-point increase between T1 and T2 on the scales measuring the frequency of the specific behavior. For example, adolescents who reported drinking once or twice at T1 and reported drinking a few times at T2 were classified as increasers. Similarly, those in the decreasing risk category reported at least a 1-point decrease in their frequency between T1 and T2. Those in the same risk category reported engaging in the behavior at least "a few times" at T1 and the same amount at T2. Table 2.1 presents the percentage of adolescents who reported engaging in the behaviors at T1, T2, and T3, as well as the percentage in each T1–T2 behavior change category.

The smoking and drinking behavior reported by this sample was similar to national norms for this age group (U.S. Department of Health and Human Services, 1990). Although we are not aware of national data on self-reported reckless driving, we assumed that the prevalence of this risk behavior was higher in this sample than elsewhere because of the lower than average legal driving age in rural Iowa. Eighty percent of the adolescents reported driving at T1, 95% reported driving at T2, and 98% reported driving at T3.

As expected, there were significant increases in the proportion of adolescents engaging in all three risk behaviors from T1 to T2 and from T2 to T3 (all $ps < .01$). The risk behaviors were moderately correlated with each other and had moderate to high stability over time.

Changes in Risk Behavior as a Function of Health Cognitions

To assess the effect of T1 cognitions on changes in behavior between T1 and T2, we conducted two

TABLE 2.1. Percentage of Participants Reporting Risk Behavior and Behavior Change

Time	Reckless driving[a] %		Drinking[a] %		Smoking[b] %	
T1	32		28		6	
T2	51		43		9	
T3	59		48		14	

T1–T2 change category	%	M	%	M	%	M
No risk	34		54		90	
T1		1.0		1.0		1.0
T2		1.0		1.0		1.0
Decrease	11		8		2	
T1		3.0		3.0		2.6
T2		1.7		1.9		1.1
Increase	43		27		6	
T1		1.5		1.5		1.3
T2		3.0		3.0		3.0
Same risk	11		11		2	
T1		2.4		2.8		2.5
T2		2.4		2.8		2.5

Note. The scales for drinking and reckless driving were as follows: 1 = *never*, 2 = *once or twice*, 3 = *a few times*, 4 = *more than a few times*, and 5 = *regularly*. The scale for smoking was as follows: 1 = *not at all*, 2 = *a few times a month*, 3 = *several times a week*, and 4 = *every day*. Sample sizes were 476 at Time 1 (T1), 476 at Time 2 (T2), and 453 at Time 3 (T3). See text for details on behavior change categories.
[a]Percentage who reported engaging in the behavior more than once or twice during the last 3 months.
[b]Percentage reporting currently smoking at least a few times a month.

hierarchical regression analyses predicting T2 behavior from T1 risk behavior and T1 cognitions (prevalence of risk behaviors among peers, and ratings of the influence of concerns about health and safety) for each of the three risk behaviors (reckless driving, drinking, and smoking). In each of these six analyses, T1 behavior was entered in Step 1 (thereby controlling for T1 behavior), followed by T1 cognition in Step 2. For example, in the first analysis, we predicted T2 reckless driving from the adolescents' estimates of the prevalence of reckless driving, controlling for T1 reckless driving. Thus, these analyses, in effect, predicted T1 to T2 changes in behavior from T1 cognitions about the behavior.

The adolescents' reckless driving, drinking, and smoking at T1 were significant predictors of these behaviors at T2 (βs = .49, .64, and .49, respectively, all ps < .001). In addition, estimates of the prevalence of these behaviors, and the influence of concerns about health and safety, predicted all three risk behaviors at T2 after the influence of T1 behavior had been controlled. Thus, as expected,

these cognitions at T1 predicted changes in behavior between T1 and T2.

Changes in Cognitions as a Function of Behavior Change

To assess the effect of T1–T2 behavior change on T1–T2 changes in risk-relevant cognitions, we conducted a set of three hierarchical regression analyses predicting T2 cognitions (perceptions of vulnerability, prevalence of risk behaviors among peers, and ratings of the influence of concerns about health and safety) for each of the three risk behaviors. In each of these nine analyses, T1 behavior and T1 cognition were entered in Step 1, followed by T2 behavior in Step 2 (therefore, both T1 behavior and T1 cognitions were controlled). Thus, these analyses predicted changes in cognitions from changes in behavior.

Reckless driving. T1 to T2 changes in reckless driving behavior predicted changes in perceptions of vulnerability to the negative consequences of reckless driving ($\beta = .28$, $p < .01$), in estimates of the prevalence of reckless driving ($\beta = .27$, $p < .01$), and in the influence of health and safety concerns ($\beta = -.23$, $p < .01$). The pattern of these regressions indicated that increases in reckless driving between T1 and T2 were accompanied by increased perceptions of risk, increased prevalence estimates, and decreases in reported influence of concerns about health and safety.

In an effort to examine potentially differential patterns of cognitive changes in adolescents whose risk behavior increased, decreased, and remained stable, we also conducted a series of 2×4 (Time × Behavior Change Category) repeated measures analyses of variance (ANOVAs) on the adolescents' cognitions. These analyses included a separate ANOVA for each cognition. The Time × Behavior Change Category interactions were significant for all three driving-related cognitions: influence of health and safety concerns, $F(3, 369) = 4.45$, $p < .01$; perceptions of vulnerability, $F(3, 371) = 5.34$, $p < .001$; and prevalence estimates, $F(3, 328) = 8.16$, $p < .001$. The pattern of these interactions was as expected in that simple effects analyses (paired t-test repeated measures analyses of the differences in cognitions from T1 to T2) indicated that the group of primary interest, the increasers, increased their perceptions of their personal risk as well as their estimates of the prevalence of reckless driving among their peers but reported reduced influence of concerns about health and safety (all $ps < .01$). In contrast, the decreasers showed a significant increase in reported influence of health and safety concerns ($p < .01$) and a marginally significant decrease in perceptions of risk ($p < .10$), and they were the only group that showed a tendency to decrease (although not significantly) their estimates of the prevalence of reckless driving, in spite of the significant increase in actual reckless driving among their peers (see Table 2.1). All other groups recognized the increase in prevalence of this risk behavior ($ps < .05$). It should also be noted that, with the exception of the no risk group, all adolescents clearly overestimated the prevalence of reckless driving among their peers (cf. Gibbons, Helweg-Larsen, & Gerrard, 1995; Goethals, Messick, & Allison, 1991; Ross et al., 1977; Suls, Wan, & Sanders, 1988).

Drinking. The regression analyses revealed that T1 to T2 changes in drinking were accompanied by changes in cognitions relevant to drinking. Spe-

cifically, increases in drinking were also associated with increases in risk perception ($\beta = .41$, $p < .01$), increases in prevalence estimates ($\beta = .23$, $p < .01$), and decreases in the influence of health and safety concerns ($\beta = -.29$, $p < .01$)

As was the case with the change category analyses for reckless driving, the Time × Behavior Change Category interactions were significant for all three drinking cognitions: perceptions of vulnerability, $F(3, 468) = 12.52$, $p < .001$; estimated prevalence, $F(3, 467) = 11.84$, $p < .001$; and influence of health and safety concerns, $F(3, 464) = 4.57$, $p < .01$. The pattern of changes among increasers followed predictions; members of this group increased their perceived personal risk and prevalence estimates and reported reduced influence of concerns about health and safety (all $ps < .01$). In contrast, decreasers significantly lowered their perceptions of vulnerability ($p < .01$) and reported no change in influence of health and safety concerns.

All groups showed an awareness that the level of drinking among their peers and friends had risen from T1 to T2, $F(1, 467) = 98.56$, $p < .001$. This main effect was qualified by a significant Time × Behavior Change Category interaction, such that the largest increase in prevalence estimates occurred among the increasers and the smallest occurred among the decreasers ($Ms = 21.2$ and 6.8, respectively). The no risk group was the only group that did not dramatically overestimate the prevalence of drinking among peers at both T1 and T2.

Smoking. Finally, in spite of the small number of participants who changed their frequency of smoking from T1 to T2, the pattern of changes in smoking-related cognitions was similar to that for drinking and reckless driving: Increases in smoking were associated with increases in risk perception ($\beta = .35$, $p < .01$), increases in prevalence estimates ($\beta = .11$, $p < .05$), and decreases in influence of health and safety concerns ($\beta = -.20$, $p < .01$).

The ANOVAs revealed that the anticipated Time × Behavior Change Category interactions for perceptions of vulnerability and prevalence estimates were significant, $F(3, 466) = 10.02$, $p < .01$, and $F(3, 467) = 5.46$, $p < .01$, respectively, and the interaction for health and safety concerns was marginal, $F(3, 471) = 2.45$, $p = .06$. Again, simple effects analyses across time revealed that those adolescents who increased their smoking behavior increased their perceived personal risk and prevalence estimates and reported reduced influence of concerns about health and safety ($ps < .01$). As with the other two behaviors, the decreasers were the only group to report a decrease in their estimates of prevalence and an increase in influence of concerns about health and safety (although neither change was significant). All groups significantly overestimated the prevalence of smoking at both T1 and T2.

Associations Between Changes in Cognitions

Next, to determine whether the observed changes in risk perceptions, influence of concern about health and safety, and estimated prevalence were redundant with each other, we examined the correlations among these changes. The pattern of correlations between risk perceptions and influence of concern about health and safety was consistent across all three behaviors: Increases in risk perceptions were associated with decreases in the reported influence of health and safety concerns (rs ranged from $-.15$ [$p < .01$] for drinking to $-.10$ [$p < .05$] for reckless driving); prevalence estimates were not correlated with influence of health and safety concerns; and two of the three correlations between estimated prevalence and perceptions of vulnerability were not significant (the exception was reckless driving; $r = .11$, $p < .05$). Thus, it appears that although all three cognitions changed in the predicted directions, these changes were not redundant with each other.

Changes in Subsequent Behavior as a Function of Changes in Cognitions

To test our hypothesis that the newly adjusted thinking about health and safety and prevalence of the behavior would predict subsequent behavior changes, we conducted a series of three hierarchical regression analyses predicting T3 reports of each risk behavior from T2 concern about health and safety and estimated prevalence, controlling for T2 behavior. In these analyses, T2 behavior was entered first, followed by T2 health and safety concern and, finally, T2 prevalence estimates. Self-

reported influence of health and safety at T2 was a significant predictor of all three risk behaviors at T3 ($ps < .01$), such that low levels of health and safety influence were associated with subsequent increases in risk behavior. Estimated prevalence (at T2) significantly predicted changes in both drinking and smoking above and beyond the influence of health and safety ($ps < .01$), such that high prevalence estimates predicted increases in drinking and smoking. T2 prevalence estimates for reckless driving, however, did not predict changes in reckless driving after the influence of health and safety concerns had been removed.

Discussion

Impact of Increased Risk Behavior on Perceptions of Vulnerability

The current study demonstrates that adolescents perceptions of vulnerability to the negative consequences of specific risk behaviors increase as their participation in these behaviors increases. Thus, these young adolescents apparently understand the relation between risk behaviors and vulnerability to negative outcomes and apply this knowledge to themselves. It appears, then, that the reason that adolescents engage in risk behavior in spite of their awareness of the potential consequences is not first-order denial of risk. Instead, these adolescents apparently engage in cognitive manipulations that allow them to deal with the inherent contradiction between their behavior and their knowledge of the danger. Two of these manipulations were identified in this study. First, those adolescents who increased their risk normalized their actions by overestimating their peers' risk behaviors to a greater extent than did other adolescents. Second, they decreased the influence health and safety concerns had on their risk behavior. Thus, they apparently avoided thinking about health and safety issues by putting such concerns out of their mind. In doing so, they engaged in what appears to be a "Scarlett O'Hara strategy" in which they say to themselves, "I won't think about this now." Furthermore, the data indicate that these cognitive manipulations were associated with subsequent increases in all three risk behaviors.

The Reciprocal Relation Between Health Behavior and Health Cognitions

The findings of this study are consistent with the traditional hypothesis that health cognitions predict subsequent health behaviors. That is, T1 concern about health and safety and prevalence estimates predicted T2 risk behavior after the influence of T1 risk behavior had been controlled, and changes in these cognitions between T1 and T2 predicted T3 risk behavior. More important, these data also provide evidence that increases in risk behavior are associated with adjustments in health cognitions. Thus, the current data suggest a more complex picture of the evolving nature of the relation between these cognitions and behaviors over time than most health behavior models do. They suggest that health cognitions affect participation in health risk behaviors and that engaging in health risk behaviors is associated with subsequent changes in health cognitions.

Whereas data collection at 12-month intervals makes it impossible to determine whether changes in cognition occur before changes in behavior, or vice versa, our conclusions regarding the impact of risk behavior on cognitions are consistent with two previous studies of the association between changes in risk behavior and a different kind of risk cognition: images of the "typical smoker." First, Gibbons, Gerrard, Lando, and McGovern (1991) demonstrated that smokers' perceptions or images of the typical smoker became significantly more negative over time as they tried to quit smoking. Another, more recent study demonstrated that young adults' risk prototypes (i.e., images of the typical smoker, drinker, unwed parent, and reckless driver) also changed as a function of changes in these risk behaviors (Gibbons & Gerrard, 1995). That is, the images became more negative among those whose risk behavior declined (as was the case in the smoker study), whereas those who increased each risk behavior reported an increase in the favorability of the prototypes associated with these behaviors. The favorability of these prototypes, in turn, predicted future involvement in the behavior.

Together, the current study and the prototype studies indicate that a variety of influential cognitions shift as a result of involvement in various kinds of risk behaviors. This suggests that much of the previous research, which has relied almost exclusively on nonreciprocal models in examining the relation between cognitions and risk behavior, has perhaps addressed a set of limited questions. Specifically, previous research has demonstrated the importance of cognitions in influencing behavior by focusing on whether cognitions about risk behaviors predict who begins to smoke, drink, and so forth and who does not. Because most adolescents experiment with risk behaviors at an early age, however, it is also important to determine what pattern of reciprocal shifts in cognitions and behaviors predicts further increases in these behaviors. The current study demonstrates the relation between behaviors and cognitions over time and, in so doing, draws attention to the need to develop more complex methodologies for examining these linkages (cf. Fiske & Taylor, 1991).

Motivated Shifts?

It is likely that adolescents whose initial experimentation leads them to the conclusion that they enjoy a specific risk behavior will begin to associate with others who engage in that behavior (Sheppard, Wright, & Goodstadt, 1985), and this exposure will lead to increased prevalence estimates. Similarly, the decision to engage in a risk behavior in spite of its dangerousness is, ipso facto, evidence that one has decided to ignore or defer thoughts about the health and safety of the behavior. The correlational nature of the current study did not allow us to address the question of whether the shifts in prevalence estimates and influence of health and safety concerns we observed reflected cognitive strategies for dealing with one's increased vulnerability or were the result of unmotivated cognitive adjustments accompanying increased experience with the behaviors and increased exposure to peers who participate in the behaviors.

A recent series of studies, however, has provided evidence that these cognitive shifts may be self-serving in that they are more pronounced among people with high self-esteem. First, Smith, Gerrard, and Gibbons (1997) reported two studies designed to test the hypothesis that individuals with high self-esteem are more likely than those with low self-esteem to interpret their health behavior in a self-serving manner. In the first study, we employed an experimental paradigm to demonstrate that self-esteem moderates the effect of reviewing sexual and contraceptive risk behavior on women's perceptions of vulnerability to unplanned pregnancy. In this study, reviewing risk behavior increased vulnerability estimates among women with low self-esteem, but not among women with high self-esteem. In the second study, we employed a longitudinal design to demonstrate a similar moderation of the relation between naturally occurring changes in sexual behavior and changes in risk perception: Women with low self-esteem show greater increases in their vulnerability estimates after increasing their risk behavior than do those with low self-esteem. Together, these two studies demonstrated that self-esteem can mitigate the acknowledgment of the relation between behavior and vulnerability to the consequences of that behavior.

Limits of Increases in Perceived Vulnerability

The narrow range in age and experience in the current sample demands caution in extrapolating from these results to older, more experienced adolescents or adults. More specifically, the pattern in these data suggests a linear relation between risk behavior and perceptions of vulnerability that is unlikely to persist as these adolescents mature. In fact, there is reason to believe that when people continue risk behaviors without experiencing negative consequences, they develop what Weinstein (1989) has labeled an "absent/exempt" perspective. Although the relation is linear in the early stages of the development of risk behaviors, it is likely that instead of resulting in ever-increasing perceptions of vulnerability, these perceptions will eventually at least stabilize and perhaps decrease, leading the individual to believe that "if it hasn't happened to me so far, it isn't likely to happen to me at all." This decline in the association between perceptions of vulnerability and risk behavior may, once again, eventually "allow" or facilitate future increases in risk.

Implications for Intervention

The current data point to a need for further research on the combination of cognitive shifts promoting increases in risk behaviors. More specifi-

cally, given that most adolescents at least experiment with a variety of risk behaviors at a very early age, it is important that future research examine specific patterns of cognitive shifts that promote the progression from initiation of and experimentation with such behaviors to increased involvement. Two groups of researchers have recently proposed interventions compatible with the current findings. Graham, Marks, and Hansen (1991) have argued that alcohol and drug educational programs should be designed to include efforts to correct misperceptions about the prevalence—specifically overestimations—of use among peers (cf. Graham, Collins, Wugalter, Chung, & Hansen, 1991). Similarly, Prentice and Miller (1993) have demonstrated that college students who mistakenly believe that their negative attitudes about excessive drinking are not shared by others are motivated to conform to their (mis)perception that overindulgence is both normative and expected. Thus, these authors suggest that encouraging college students to share private attitudes about drinking, thereby exposing this pluralistic ignorance, will promote social changes by demonstrating that negative attitudes about excessive drinking are not deviant. Although the current data are consistent with both of these proposals, the finding that both misperceptions of prevalence and influence of health and safety concerns are altered by engaging in the risk behavior suggests that interventions designed to reduce pluralistic ignorance and overestimation of prevalence will be most effective if directed at young people before they begin to experiment with the risk behaviors, that is, before the process of engaging in the behavior has affected their cognitions about the prevalence and riskiness of the behavior.

ACKNOWLEDGMENTS

This research was supported by National Institute of Mental Health Grant 1 P50 MH48165-01, National Institute on Drug Abuse Grant DA07534A, and National Institute on Alcohol Abuse and Alcoholism Grant AA10208. We would like to thank Hart Blanton and Susan Cross for their comments on an earlier version of this article.

REFERENCES

Brown, B. B., Clasen, D. N., & Eicher, S. A. (1986). Perceptions of peer pressure, peer conformity dispositions, and self-reported behavior among adolescents. *Developmental Psychology, 22,* 521–530.

Centers for Disease Control (1992). Recent trends in adolescent smoking, smoking-uptake correlates, and expectations about the future. *Advance Data, 221.*

Centers for Disease Control. (1993). Teenage pregnancy and birth rates—United States 1990. *Morbidity and Mortality Weekly Report, 42,* 39.

Cohn, L. D., Macfarlane, S., Yanez, C., & Imai, W. K. (1995). Risk-perceptions: Differences between adolescents and adults. *Health Psychology, 14,* 217–222.

Collins, L. M., Sussman, S., Rauch, J. M., Dent, C. W., Johnson, C. A., Hansen, W. B., & Flay, B. R. (1987). Psychosocial predictors of young adolescent cigarette smoking: A sixteen-month, three-wave longitudinal study. *Journal of Applied Social Psychology, 17,* 554–573.

Croyle, R. T. (1990). Biased appraisal of high blood pressure. *Preventive Medicine, 19,* 40–44.

Croyle, R. T., & Sande, G. N. (1988). Denial and confirmatory search: Paradoxical consequences of medical diagnosis. *Journal of Applied Social Psychology, 18,* 473–490.

Ditto, P. H., Jemmott, J. B., & Darley, J. M. (1988). Appraising the threat of illness: A mental representational approach. *Health Psychology, 7,* 183–201.

Eiser, C., Eiser, J. R., & Lang, J. (1989). Adolescent beliefs about AIDS prevention. *Psychology and Health, 3,* 287–296.

Festinger, L. A. (1957). *A theory of cognitive dissonance.* Evanston, IL: Row, Peterson.

Finn, P., & Bragg, B. W. (1986). Perception of the risk of an accident by young and older drivers. *Accident Analysis and Prevention, 18,* 289–298.

Finn, P., & Brown, J. (1981). Risks entailed in teenage intoxication as perceived by junior and senior high school students. *Journal of Youth and Adolescence, 10,* 298.

Fiske, S. T., & Taylor, S. E. (1991). *Social cognition.* New York: Random House.

Gerrard, M., Gibbons, F. X., & Bushman, B. J. (1996). The relation between perceived vulnerability to HIV and precautionary sexual behavior. *Psychological Bulletin, 119,* 390–409.

Gerrard, M., Gibbons, F. X., & Warner, T. D. (1991). Effects of reviewing risk-relevant behaviors on perceived vulnerability of women marines. *Health Psychology, 10,* 173–179.

Gerrard, M., Gibbons, F. X., Warner, T. D., & Smith, G. E. (1993). Perceived vulnerability to AIDS and AIDS preventive behavior: A critical review of the evidence. In J. Pryor & G. Reeder (Eds.), *The social psychology of HIV infection* (pp. 59–84). Hillsdale, NJ: Erlbaum.

Gerrard, M., & Luus, C. E. (1995). Judgments of vulnerability to pregnancy: The role of risk factors and individual differences. *Personality and Social Psychology Bulletin, 21,* 158–169.

Gibbons, F. X., Eggleston, T., & Benthin, A. C. (1997). Cognitive reactions to smoking relapse: The reciprocal relation between dissonance and self-esteem. *Journal of Personality and Social Psychology, 72,* 184–195.

Gibbons, F. X., & Gerrard, M. (1995). Predicting young adults' health risk behavior. *Journal of Personality and Social Psychology, 69,* 505–517.

Gibbons, F. X., Gerrard, M., & Boney-McCoy, S. (1995). Prototype perception predicts (lack of) pregnancy prevention. *Personality and Social Psychology Bulletin, 21,* 85–93.

Gibbons, F. X., Gerrard, M., Lando, H. A., & McGovern, P. G. (1991). Social comparison and smoking cessation: The role of the "typical smoker." *Journal of Experimental Social Psychology, 27,* 239–258.

Gibbons, F. X., Helweg-Larsen, M., & Gerrard, M. (1995). Prevalence estimates and adolescent risk behavior: Cross-cultural differences in social influence. *Journal of Applied Psychology, 80,* 107–121.

Gibbons, F. X., McGovern, P. G., & Lando, H. A. (1991). Relapse and risk perception among members of a smoking cessation clinic. *Health Psychology, 10,* 42–45.

Goethals, G. R., Messick, D. M., & Allison, S. T. (1991). The uniqueness bias: Studies of constructive social comparison. In J. Suls & T. A. Wills (Eds.), *Social comparison: Contemporary theory and research* (pp. 149–176). Hillsdale, NJ: Erlbaum.

Graham, J. W., Collins, L. M., Wugalter, S. E., Chung, N. K., & Hansen, W. B. (1991). Modeling transitions in latent stage-sequential processes: A substance use prevention example. *Journal of Consulting and Clinical Psychology, 59,* 48–57.

Graham, J. W., Marks, G., & Hansen, W. B. (1991). Social influence processes affecting adolescent substance use. *Journal of Applied Psychology, 76,* 291–298.

Harrison, J. A., Mullen, P. D., & Green, L. W. (1992). A meta-analysis of studies of the health belief model with adults. *Health Education Research, 7,* 107–116.

Janis, I. L. (1958). *Psychological stress.* New York: Wiley.

Janus, S., & Janus, C. (1993). *Janus report on sexual behavior.* New York: Wiley.

Janz, N. K., & Becker, M. H. (1984). The health belief model: A decade later. *Health Education Quarterly, 11,* 1–47.

Kandel, D. (1980). Drug and drinking behavior among youth. *Annual Review of Sociology, 6,* 235–285.

Lawton, M. P., & Goldman, A. E. (1961). Cigarette smoking and attitude toward the etiology of lung cancer. *Journal of Social Psychology, 54,* 235–248.

Lazarus, R. S. (1983). The costs and benefits of denial. In S. Breznitz (Ed.), *The denial of stress* (pp. 1–30). New York: International Universities Press.

Leventhal, H., Glynn, K., & Fleming, R. (1987). Is the smoking decision an "informed choice"?: The effect of smoking risk factors on smoking beliefs. *Journal of the American Medical Association, 257,* 3373–3376.

Marks, G., Graham, J. W., & Hansen, W. B. (1992). Social projection and social conformity in adolescent alcohol use: A longitudinal analysis. *Personality and Social Psychology Bulletin, 18,* 96–101.

Pervin, L. A., & Yatko, R. J. (1965). Cigarette smoking and alternative methods of reducing dissonance. *Journal of Personality and Social Psychology, 2,* 30–36.

Prentice, D. A., & Miller, D. T. (1993). Pluralistic ignorance and alcohol use on campus: Some consequences of misperceiving the social norm. *Journal of Personality and Social Psychology, 64,* 243–256.

Public Health Service. (1993). *Prevention: Federal programs and progress.* '91/'92. Washington, DC: Office of Disease Prevention.

Roscoe, B., & Kruger, T. L. (1990). Late adolescents' knowledge and its influence on sexual behavior. *Adolescence, 25,* 38–48.

Ross, L., Greene, D., & House, P. (1977). The false consensus phenomenon: An attributional bias in self-perception and social-perception processes. *Journal of Experimental Social Psychology, 13,* 279–301.

Rotheram-Borres, M. L., & Koopman, C. (1991). Sexual risk behaviors, AIDS knowledge, and beliefs about AIDS among runaways. *American Journal of Public Health, 81,* 206–208.

Rothman, A. J., Klein, W. M., & Weinstein, N. D. (1996). Absolute and relative biases in estimation of personal risk. *Journal of Applied Social Psychology, 26,* 1213–1236.

Sheppard, M. A., Wright, D., & Goodstadt, M. S. (1985). Peer pressure and drug use—Exploding the myth. *Adolescence, 20,* 949–958.

Sherman, S. J., Presson, C. C., Chassin, L., Corty, E., & Olshansky, R. (1983). Mechanisms underlying the false consensus effect: The special role of threats to the self. *Personality and Social Psychology Bulletin, 10,* 127–138.

Smith, G. E., Gerrard, M., & Gibbons, F. X. (1997). Self-esteem and the relation between risk behavior and perceived vulnerability to unplanned pregnancy in college women. *Health Psychology, 16,* 137–146.

Snyder, M. L., & Wicklund, R. A. (1981). Attribute ambiguity. In J. H. Harvey, W. Ickes, & R. F. Kidd (Eds.), *New directions in attribution research* (Vol. 3, pp. 197–221). Hillsdale, NJ: Erlbaum.

Stacy, A. W., Widaman, K. F., Hays, R., & DiMatteo, M. R. (1985). Validity of self-reports of alcohol and other drug use: A multitrait-multimethod assessment. *Journal of Personality and Social Psychology, 49,* 219–232.

Suls, J., Wan, C. K., & Sanders, G. S. (1988). False consensus and false uniqueness in estimating the prevalence of health-protective behaviors. *Journal of Applied Social Psychology, 18,* 66–79.

Sussman, S., Dent, C. W., Mestel-Rauch, J., Johnson, C. A., Hansen, W. B., & Flay, B. R. (1988). Adolescent nonsmokers, triers, and regular smokers' estimates of cigarette smoking prevalence: When overestimations occur and by whom? *Journal of Applied Social Psychology, 18,* 537–551.

U.S. Department of Health and Human Services. (1990). *Healthy people 2000: National health promotion and disease prevention objectives* (DHHS Publication No. PHS 91-50212). Washington, DC: Author.

Weinstein, N. D. (1989). Effects of personal experience on self-protective behavior. *Psychological Bulletin, 105,* 31–50.

Weinstein, N. D., & Nicolich, M. M. (1993). Correct and incorrect interpretations of correlations between risk perceptions and risk behaviors. *Health Psychology, 12,* 235–245.

Weinstein, N. D., Rothman, A. J., & Nicolich, M. M. (1995). *Use of correlational data to examine the effects of risk perceptions on precautionary behavior.* Manuscript submitted for publication.

Weisman, A. D. (1972). *On dying and denying.* New York: Behavioral Publications.

Testing Four Competing Theories of Health-Protective Behavior

Neil D. Weinstein • Rutgers University

Four competing theories of health-protective behavior are reviewed: the health belief model, the theory of reasoned action, protection motivation theory, and subjective expected utility theory. In spite of their commonalities, these models are seldom tested against one another. The review points out the similarities and differences among these theories and the data and analyses needed to compare them. In addition to describing the content of the models, their conceptualization of key variables, and the combinatorial rules used to make predictions, some general problems in theory development and testing for health behaviors are examined. The article's goal is to help investigators design studies that will clarify the strengths and weaknesses of these models, leading toward a better understanding of health behavior.

Key words: health behavior, health belief model, theory of reasoned action, protection motivation theory, subjective expected utility theory

Many theories have been proposed to explain the adoption of health-protective behavior. Because these theories contain at least a grain of truth, empirical tests typically yield some degree of confirmation, enough to keep the theory under scrutiny from being rejected. Rarely, though, is one theory pitted against another. Thus, despite a large empirical literature, there is still no consensus that certain models of health behavior are more accurate than others, that certain variables are more influential than others, or that certain behaviors or situations are understood better than others. In general, researchers have failed to carry out the winnowing process that is necessary for scientific progress.

This article reviews four theories of health pro-

tective behavior—the health belief model (Becker, 1974; Janz & Becker, 1984; Kirscht, 1988), subjective expected utility theory (Edwards, 1954; Ronis, 1992; Sutton, 1982), protection motivation theory (Maddux & Rogers, 1983; Prentice-Dunn & Rogers, 1986; Rogers, 1983), and the theory of reasoned action (Ajzen & Fishbein, 1980; Fishbein & Ajzen, 1975)—with special emphasis on the differences among these theories and the kinds of data and analyses needed to compare them. These theories were chosen for two reasons. First, the theories emphasize beliefs about health hazards and health-protective behaviors and have many features in common, although the similarities are seldom recognized. Second, as a group, the theories under discussion are probably used more frequently than any other type of model in research on health behavior.

Because of the similarities among the four theories, little effort would be needed in an investigation to compare their relative success. Nevertheless, such comparisons are rare; researchers typically select one theory to test or to guide their choice of explanatory variables as if the other theories did not exist. A recent search of the PsychLit database (Silver Platter, Inc., 1992) revealed 205 articles between 1974 and 1991 which mentioned one of these four theories in the title, abstract, or index terms. Nevertheless, there were only 10 articles that listed more than one theory, and only 4 of these articles were empirical comparisons.

Many reviews of these and other theories of health-protective behavior exist (e.g., Becker, 1991; Cummings, Becker, & Maile, 1980; Glanz, Lewis, & Rimer, 1990; Hays, 1985; Mullen, Hersey, & Iverson, 1987; Nelson & Moffit, 1988; Wallston & Wallston, 1984), but they overlook many of the similarities (an exception is Sutton, 1987) and do not offer the detailed, point-by-point comparison that will be provided here. This article will also discuss several areas of theory development and testing that need further attention. The intent is not to review the available empirical research or to conclude that one theory is better than another. Rather, the goal is to help investigators design studies that will clarify the strengths and weaknesses of these models. Such studies should eventually lead to models of greater accuracy, either by suggesting refinements in the present models or, if the results of rigorous testing so indicate, by leading researchers to reject this type of model and develop different theoretical approaches.

Mental Content and Motivation to Take Action

Each of the four theories assumes that anticipation of a negative health outcome and the desire to avoid this outcome or reduce its impact creates motivation for self-protection. The expected aversiveness of the outcome is discussed in terms of the *perceived severity* of health consequences in the health belief model and in protection motivation theory, negative *utility* in subjective ex-

pected utility theory, and negative *evaluation* in the theory of reasoned action. These various terms have the same underlying meaning, and the questions used to assess these terms are essentially indistinguishable from one theory to another.

The models agree that the impact of a negative outcome on the motivation to act also depends on beliefs about the likelihood that this outcome will occur. Likelihood is usually referred to as *perceived vulnerability* or *perceived susceptibility* in the health belief model and in protection motivation theory, *subjective probability* in subjective expected utility theory, and *expectancy* in the theory of reasoned action. Again, these differing terms have the same underlying meaning and are assessed with questions that are essentially interchangeable. (Sometimes susceptibility is misinterpreted as general susceptibility to illness rather than as referring to the likelihood of specific consequences. This interpretation would only be appropriate if the precaution in question, such as exercise or good diet, were intended to improve overall health.) I will use SEV (severity) to refer to the individual's evaluation of the health outcome that might occur assuming no change in behavior and PROB (probability) to refer to the perceived likelihood that this outcome will occur.

According to these theories, the motivation to act arises from the expectation that action can reduce the likelihood or severity of harm. In subjective expected utility theory and in the theory of reasoned action, the expected benefit can be determined from the difference between (a) beliefs about the magnitude and likelihood of harm assuming no change in behavior and (b) beliefs about these same issues assuming the adoption of a protective measure. In practice, though, research that is based on the theory of reasoned action frequently omits questions about present behavior (Sutton, 1987). Sometimes this omission can be justified because outcomes are phrased in terms of changes that would occur from adopting the recommended action (e.g., Brubaker & Wickersham, 1990). For example, an outcome may be described as an earlier detection of cancer, and this outcome can be rated for likelihood (i.e., will detection actually be earlier) and desirability (i.e., how beneficial is early detection). However, researchers often forget to consider current behavior and ask questions that have no logical implications for action. For example, subjects can rate the likelihood that if they perform a testicular self-examination, it will be possible to "treat cancer when curable" (Steffen, 1990, p. 690), but this rating does not tell us whether subjects think cancer is more likely to be curable if they perform a self-examination than if they do not. Thus, a careful application of the theory of reasoned action requires rating expectations from current behavior and from the alternative behavior under consideration (or, alternately, phrasing all outcomes in terms of changes). The health belief model and protection motivation theory, in contrast, are typically presented in terms of the likelihood and severity of health consequences if current behavior does not change and a separate variable is used to indicate the perceived effectiveness or efficacy (EFFECT) of the precaution.

Nonrisk Variables

All four theories assume that the expected benefits in risk reduction must be weighed against the expected costs of acting (COST) to predict changes in behavior. The costs considered by these theories include time, effort, money, inconvenience, and the loss of satisfactions obtained from current behavior. In the health belief model these various costs or barriers are represented by a single variable, though multiple questions may be asked to evaluate the costs. Protection motivation theory explicitly separates the perceived cost of performing a new protective behavior from the perceived self-efficacy (SE) for performing this response and the loss of current internal rewards (IR) and external rewards (ER) that will result from this behavioral change.

The theory of reasoned action differs from the health belief model and protection motivation theory by considering a much wider range of consequences of continuing the current behavior (not just the possibility of health problems) and by considering a wider range of consequences of the alternative behavior under consideration (not just the explicit cost and the reduced health risk). The list of consequences that need to be considered is not stated a priori but is developed during pilot research in which subjects are asked about the consequences that they foresee. The impact of each possible consequences on the motivation to act is determined by its expected value (VALUE) and

by the expectation (i.e., PROB) that the consequence will occur. Thus, in the theory of reasoned action some consequences can be seen as costs, some as health outcomes, and others as nonhealth outcomes (such as the amount of worry about an illness). Investigators often seem to think that perceptions of the likelihood and severity of health outcomes are not part of the theory of reasoned action (e.g., Henning & Knowles, 1990; Hoogstraten, de Haan, & ter Horst, 1985; Ried & Christensen, 1988; Steffen, 1990). This is incorrect.

The theory of reasoned action also differs from the preceding models by explicitly incorporating social influence. It does this in terms of how much other relevant people want the individual to perform a given behavior (i.e., normative beliefs; NB), and how much the individual is motivated to comply (MC) with each of their preferences.

Research based on subjective expected utility theory may use COST as a single variable to be estimated by subjects or list various costs as possible outcomes and ask subjects to rate the likelihood and undesirability of each cost. A wide range of positive outcomes can also be accommodated by subjective expected utility theory, but often applications focus on the perceived reduction of risk likelihood, severity, or both (Ronis, 1992; Sutton, 1982).

Combinatorial Rules

Aside from variations in the range of nonrisk issues that are considered, the greatest differences among these four models concern the rules they use to combine the independent variables when predicting action.

It is important, though, to recognize that none of these models actually predict the amount of precautionary behavior that will occur. Instead, what is predicted is the relative likelihood of action by different individuals or by individuals in different treatment groups. It is a telling sign of the incompleteness of existing theories that they do not even attempt to predict the amount of action that will occur. Finding that the correlation between predicted behavior and observed behavior is .6 may seem reassuring, but it does not allow us to predict whether 20%, 50%, or 80% of the population will act.

The prediction rule associated with each theory

Table 3.1. Four Cognitive Theories of Health-Protective Behavior

Theory	Principal variables	Prediction of health-protective behavior[a]
Health belief model (HBM)	$PROB_c$, SEV_c, EFFECT, COST	$w_1PROB_c + w_2SEV_c + w_3EFFECT - w_4COST$[b]
Protection motivation theory (PMT)	$PROB_c$, SEV_c, EFFECT, COST[c], IR, ER, SE	$w_1PROB_c + w_3SEV_c + w_3EFFECT - w_4COST_{PMT}$ (where $COST_{PMT}$ = COST + $w_5IR + w_6ER - w_7SE$)
Subjective expected utility theory (SEU)	$PROB_c$, SEV_c, $PROB_a$, SEV_a, COST, $PROB_{c'}$, $VALUE_{c'}$, $PROB_{a'}$, $VALUE_{a'}$	$PROB_cSEV_c - PROB_aSEV_a - COST_{SEU}$ or $PROB_cSEV_cEFFECT - COST_{SEU}$[d] (where $COST_{SEU} = \Sigma_{a'}PROB_{a'}VALUE_{a'} - \Sigma_{c'}PROB_{c'}VALUE_{c'}$)
Theory of reasoned action (TRA)	$PROB_c$, SEV_c, $PROB_a$, SEV_a, $PROB_{c'}$, $VALUE_{c'}$, $PROB_{a'}$, $VALUE_{a'}$, $NB_{c,k}$, $NB_{a,k}$, MC_k	$PROB_cSEV_c - PROB_aSEV_a - COST_{TRA}$ (where $COST_{TRA} = \Sigma_{a'}PROB_{a'}VALUE_{a'} - \Sigma_{c'}PROB_{c'}VALUE_{c'} - \alpha\Sigma_k[(NB_{a,k} - NB_{c,k}) MC_k]$)

Note. PROB = Perceived probability that a particular outcome will occur; SEV = Perceived severity of a health outcome; EFFECT = Perceived effectiveness of the precaution; IR = Perceived internal rewards from current behavior; ER = Perceived external rewards from current behavior; SE = Self-efficacy; NB = Normative beliefs (strength of the desire of another person that the individual perform a particular behavior); MC = Motivation to comply with the other person's desire; COST = Perceived costs and barriers to action; VALUE = Perceived value of a nonhealth outcome; a = Health consequences under alternate behavior (the precaution); a' = Consequences of alternate behavior other than health effects; c = Health consequences under current behavior; c' = Consequences of current behavior other than health effects; k = Various individuals whose desires might influence behavior; $w_1, w_2, \ldots, \alpha$ = Parameters (>0) to be determined empirically.
[a] The relative likelihood of action is assumed to be proportional to the value of the expression in the table.
[b] The HBM is not explicit about the functional relationship between the independent variables and behavior. It is presented here in the simplest possible form, the form examined in most research.
[c] In PMT, COST refers to all anticipated barriers to action other than IR, ER, and SE.

is presented in Table 3.1. A subscript c on variables in Table 3.1 indicates beliefs about what might happen assuming no change in current behavior, and subscript a refers to beliefs about what might happen if an alternative behavior (i.e., the precaution) were adopted. The expressions in Table 3.1 have been deliberately arranged to reveal the strong similarities among the models. The rule presented for the theory of reasoned action assumes that both the current behavior and the alternative behavior are examined in reaching a prediction. The rule listed for subjective expected utility theory assumes a detailed calculation of costs in terms of the perceived likelihood and utility of nonhealth consequences.

One major difference in these four combinatorial rules is that protection motivation theory assumes severity and probability are additive in influencing behavior, whereas subjective expected utility theory and the theory of reasoned action assume a multiplicative relationship.[1] The multiplicative relationship reflects the assumption (compatible with both expectancy–value theory and

probability theory) that threats will be ignored if either their severity or their likelihood is zero. This assumption certainly seems reasonable, but many studies, both experimental and nonexperimental (Beck & Lund, 1981; Rogers & Mewborn, 1976; Ronis & Harel, 1989; Steffen, 1990; Sutton & Eiser, 1990), have not found such an interaction.

A common misinterpretation of the theory of reasoned action is to add together the likelihood ratings of the various consequences, add the de-

_____

[1] The similarity of the theory of reasoned action to other models has been emphasized in Table 3.1 by separating out the perceived likelihood and severity of expected health consequences from the perceived likelihood and desirability of the other possible consequences of each behavior. When the issue is the adoption of a recommended health-protective behavior, health consequences are likely to be among the various consequences salient to people, but proponents of the theory of reasoned action would not separate these health consequences from other consequences. The rule presented in Table 3.1 thus highlights one type of consequence, but this highlighting is only an algebraic rearrangement of the standard expression and does not affect the predictions that would be made from the theory.

sirability ratings, and then multiply these sums together (e.g., Henning & Knowles, 1990; Ried & Christensen, 1988). According to the theory, the likelihood and desirability of each outcome should be multiplied together, and then these products should be added (Ajzen & Fishbein, 1980; Fishbein & Ajzen, 1975).

The health belief model as originally proposed (Hochbaum, 1958; Leventhal, Hochbaum, & Rosenstock, 1960) involved the product of severity, likelihood, and effectiveness, but more recent uses of the theory (e.g., Cummings, Jette, Brock, & Haefner, 1979; Peterson, Farmer, & Kashani, 1990; Sheppard, Solomon, Atkins, Foster, & Frankowski, 1990) have not assumed any particular relationship among the four central variables. Without any combinatorial rule, the health belief model is more accurately described as a short list of variables than as a theoretical model.

A second difference concerns the number of parameters in the prediction rule that are not specified by the theory and must be determined from the data. With probability measured on a 0–1 scale and with severity and cost measured on a common scale of utility, subjective expected utility theory has no adjustable parameters. For this reason, no unspecified coefficients are shown in front of the terms in the subjective expected utility theory prediction rule in Table 3.1. With probabilities and expectancies measured on the same 0–1 scale and with severity, cost, and value all measured on a common scale, the theory of reasoned action has only one adjustable parameter, α, indicating the relative importance of perceived social pressure versus perceived direct consequences.[2] In contrast, the addition of variables in protection motivation theory and the health belief model that have different units (e.g., probability, severity, self-efficacy) means that there are unspecified coefficients that need to be determined after measurement scales are selected. These theories seem to suggest, though, that once these coefficients are

determined, the coefficients should remain constant from one study to the next so long as the scales are not changed.

There is a problem in protection motivation theory concerning the interaction effects that are assumed to occur. Regarding these interactions, Prentice-Dunn and Rogers (1986, p. 156) state that

> if response efficacy and/or self-efficacy are high, then increases in severity and/or vulnerability will produce a positive main effect [on the motivation to act]. On the other hand, if response efficacy and/or self-efficacy are low, then increases in severity and/or vulnerability will either have no effect or a boomerang effect, actually reducing intentions to comply with the health recommendation.

This statement is internally inconsistent. If, for example, response efficacy is high and self-efficacy is low, the first part of the statement says that action increases with severity and/or vulnerability, whereas the second part of the statement says that increases in severity and/or vulnerability will either have no effect or will boomerang. It does not seem possible to combine the two components of protection motivation theory, perceptions of the *adaptive response*—which is said to be dependent on the sum of self-efficacy and response effectiveness—and perceptions of the *maladaptive response*—which is said to be dependent on the sum of severity and likelihood—and produce an interaction like that quoted.

Other Points of Comparison

Costs

The theories under discussion differ in the extent to which they specify various kinds of costs. The health belief model implies that general questions about the costs or barriers to action might be sufficient, or at least that different types of costs can all be added together. Protection motivation theory adds distinct variables concerning the internal and external rewards lost by giving up the current behavior. Empirical research can determine whether various kinds of costs have differential effects, and need to be kept separate, or whether they can simply be added together to form a single variable. For example, the loss of internal rewards, which

---

[2]Since interpersonal influences are also consequences of taking a behavior, it is not clear why interpersonal influences need to be differentiated from the remaining consequences. If all other consequences can be assessed on a common metric, it seems that interpersonal consequences could be assessed in the same way (on the basis of the expected likelihood of different reactions from each significant person and the value placed on each reaction). This formulation would eliminate the arbitrary constant α.

is often experienced multiple times, might have more impact on behavior than an external, monetary cost that is experienced only once.

Self-Efficacy

Protection motivation theory differs from the health belief model, subjective expected utility theory, and the theory of reasoned action in explicitly referring to self-efficacy (Bandura, 1977). Self-efficacy is assessed with questions that refer to the problems individuals expect to encounter in adopting the precaution or to doubts about their ability to change current patterns of behavior. Although theorists (e.g., Beck & Lund, 1981; Rogers, 1983) point out the difference between self-efficacy and response efficacy, they overlook the similarity between self-efficacy and barriers to action. Many of the problems people expect to encounter in carrying out protective measures (e.g., "Taking calcium supplements on a daily basis would be hard for me to do"; Wurtele, 1988, p. 631) would simply be labeled costs or barriers to action by other theories, not self-efficacy. Health belief model researchers, for example, might see the difficulty of acting as part of the expected cost of acting. Thus, the distinction between self-efficacy (as typically measured) and costs is not clear.

People are sometimes unsure about their ability to carry out health precautions (such as losing weight or stopping smoking). Doubts about one's ability to carry out an action are not the same as beliefs about the cost or trouble involved. It is one thing to ask whether the benefits of some precaution will outweigh the costs; it is something else to ask whether an attempt to carry out this precaution, because it may fail, will provide any benefits at all. In discussing applications of subjective expected utility theory to smoking, for example, Sutton (1987) suggests that the perceived likelihood that stopping smoking will lead to desired outcomes, such as lowered risk of heart disease (i.e., action efficacy) should be multiplied by the perceived likelihood that a quit attempt will lead to stopping smoking (i.e., self-efficacy) to correctly describe the expected benefits of attempting to stop. However, the effects of self-efficacy and action efficacy on quit attempts were additive in the data reported by Sutton.

The theory of planned behavior (Ajzen, 1985; Ajzen & Madden, 1986) modifies the theory of reasoned action to recognize that doubts about one's ability to carry out an action (i.e., perceived behavioral control) can affect the motivation to act. Perceived behavioral control is described as the perceived probability of succeeding in enacting the behavior and is equated in discussions of the theory of planned behavior with self-efficacy. Like Sutton (1987), the theory of planned behavior introduces the likelihood of succeeding as a multiplicative factor (i.e., multiplying the attitude toward taking the action).

Although self-efficacy, when defined as the likelihood of successfully carrying out a preventive action, can be differentiated from the perceived barriers that must be overcome, these two variables are likely to be strongly correlated. It may be that the nature of their influence on behavior is similar. To test this idea one must determine whether predictions of behavior are significantly better when self-efficacy is kept separate (and allowed to have an independent effect on action) or when it is combined with variables (either added to other measures of the costs to be borne or, as suggested by Sutton and the theory of planned behavior, multiplying the benefits expected from the precaution).

The Range of Nonhealth Considerations

The theory of reasoned action differs from the other models in trying to identify all of the main consequences of action or inaction, including consequences from obeying or disobeying the preferences of important others. (Some applications of subjective expected utility theory also take this approach.) The fundamental question raised by this difference is the extent to which hazard reduction is the reason for action and can explain and predict such action. Although there are some actions for which hazard reduction appears to be the dominant motive (e.g., taking blood pressure medication or avoiding foods with additives), the performance of many health-related actions (e.g., losing weight or using a condom during sexual intercourse) appears to be governed by a much wider array of motives. The importance of motives other than hazard reduction in any particular instance is indicated by the accuracy of action predictions based only on risk considerations and by the improvement in accuracy that can be achieved by adding nonrisk variables to these predictions.

Effectiveness

Another difference concerns the perceived effectiveness of the precaution. The health belief model and protection motivation theory usually ask respondents directly about the effectiveness of the precaution in reducing risk (e.g., Seydel, Taal, & Wiegman, 1990; Wurtele, 1988). Subjective expected utility theory and some theory of reasoned action studies ask respondents about the likelihood and severity of harmful outcomes under the current behavior and under the alternative behavior and infer perceptions of effectiveness from the answers (e.g., Ronis, 1992; Ronis & Harel, 1989; Sutton & Eiser, 1990). Other theory of reasoned action studies have used *changes* in health—such as a reduction in risk or an improved chance of successful treatment—as the consequences considered by subjects, asking subjects about the likelihood of these changes and the value they place on this change. Logically, these different strategies should yield the same results. For example, effectiveness in the health belief model assessed through direct questioning should be the same as effectiveness in subjective expected utility theory inferred from beliefs about the risk present with and without preventive action. After all, the effectiveness *is* the reduction in risk. Nevertheless, the way that people naturally think about these issues may be closer to one conceptualization than another. A person, for example, may have a definite opinion about the effectiveness of automobile seat belts but be unable to answer questions about the probability and severity of injuries for drivers who buckle up and those who don't. Which approach produces the best predictions has never been tested.

These alternative ways of looking at effectiveness raise a general issue. Theories framed in terms of concepts that people actually use in thinking about hazards will undoubtedly lead to better predictions and interventions than theories framed in terms of concepts that might appear to be logically equivalent but do not match the actual mental representations of these issues.

The Process That Leads to Health-Protective Behavior

These four theories specify variables that are supposed to determine whether someone will view a health-protective action as more attractive than current behavior. The health belief model and subjective expected utility theory say nothing about factors that might intervene between the perceived attractiveness of a precaution and precaution adoption. Although subjective expected utility theory, with its decision-theory origin, might be interpreted as specifying which of two actions will be selected, it is only used to predict the relative likelihood of action (i.e., it is used to predict that Person A is more likely to act than Person B but not to predict whether Person A will or will not act). This usage reflects the implicit assumption that knowing which action is most attractive is not sufficient to predict what people will do. Nevertheless, neither the health belief model nor subjective expected utility theory make any additional testable predictions about the process that leads to behavior change.

The theory of reasoned action, however, is formulated in terms of behavioral intentions, not behavior, and the prediction rule in Table 3.1 actually concerns the prediction of these intentions. The theory of reasoned action is explicit in assuming that intentions are sufficient for predicting behavior when they are stable and measured at the same level of specificity as behavior and when the behavior is under volitional control.[3] Although intentions are said to be sufficient for accurate predictions, the fact that the intentions (like Equation 1 in subjective expected utility theory) are only used to predict the relative likelihood of action implies that other issues must intervene. Whether these intervening factors are essentially random, as implied by the theory of reasoned action, or identifiable, is a testable question. Studies can examine whether variables within or outside the theory of reasoned action have a direct effect on behavior beyond their contributions to behavioral intentions. This issue is one that has received a considerable amount of empirical attention (e.g., Brubaker & Wickersham, 1990; Sutton & Eiser, 1990; Sutton & Hallett, 1988; for a thorough review, see Liska, 1984).

Protection motivation theory, like the theory of reasoned action, was formulated in terms of an

---

[3]The theory of planned behavior (Ajzen, 1985; Ajzen & Madden, 1986) holds that many problems may intervene between intentions and successful action. It uses perceived behavioral control as an indirect measure of the actual control an individual has over his or her behavior.

intervening variable, protection motivation, rather than in terms of health behavior. It asserts that protection motivation is most appropriately assessed by behavioral intentions (Prentice-Dunn & Rogers, 1986). As just discussed, the adequacy of describing the process that leads to the adoption of precautions solely in terms of the formation of intentions is open to question. However, Prentice-Dunn and Rogers also discuss the role of self-efficacy in determining an individual's persistence in the face of obstacles. Thus, they are implicitly suggesting a temporal process in which people form intentions to act, attempt to carry out these intentions, encounter difficulties, and eventually either succeed or fail. If this is the process of precaution adoption, intentions and action are certainly not interchangeable.

Implications for Model Testing and Development

The preceding review suggests a number of critical issues that must be addressed to advance our understanding of health-promotive action. These issues can be classified under three broad headings: model testing, concept differentiation, and static versus dynamic models. *Model testing* refers to the specific strategies to be followed and problems to be overcome in establishing the accuracy of existing theories. *Concept differentiation* emphasizes the need for a better understanding of key variables and their origins. Tension will exist between those who advocate more carefully controlled tests of current models and variables (e.g., "Are the effects of susceptibility and severity on behavior additive or multiplicative?") and those who advocate a reexamination of the underlying concepts and phenomena themselves ("What does the term *susceptibility* really mean? Is it a single concept or does it refer to a set of concepts?"). The research designed to answer these questions will look quite different.

The *static versus dynamic* distinction separates those researchers who search for a single prediction rule to explain health-protective behavior from researchers who see the adoption of health behaviors as the end of a sequence of stages, with different issues—and hence different prediction rules—involved at different stages. A researcher interested in stages would be particularly interested in people who have only vague opinions about the health hazard and who give "don't know" answers on survey questions. Investigators searching for the single best prediction rule, however, may not even allow respondents to give "don't know" answers.

Model Tests Matched to Model Content

Two fundamental questions are encountered in model testing: (a) "Which variables need to be included in the model?" and (b) "How do these variables combine to influence behavior?" An example of the first question concerns the necessity of including variables pertaining to social influence on health behavior, as suggested by the theory of reasoned action.

Testing integration rules, more difficult statistically, requires multivariate research designs. In nonexperimental research, one would normally test the accuracy of a prediction rule—and the superiority of one rule over another—in terms of the correlation between the behavior predicted by the theory and the behavior actually observed. Note, however, that all these theories predict the relative likelihood of *changes* in behavior (i.e., certain factors in the model are assumed to lead people to take new actions), and generally require prospective designs to test them. For example, the correlation between perceived risk and current risk behavior indicates the accuracy of these perceptions (i.e., a strong positive correlation implies accuracy), whereas the correlation between perceived risk and future risk behavior indicates the effects of perceptions on behavior (i.e., a strong negative correlation implies that perception of risk leads people to adopt safer behavior). It is usually not appropriate to test the theories by examining the correlation between predicted behavior and current behavior (Weinstein & Nicolich, 1993).

In addition to examining the overall prediction of behavior change, hierarchical regression, path analysis (i.e., sequential, hierarchical regression), or structural modeling should be used to determine whether the specific relationships between the independent variables and behavior claimed by the theory match the relationships actually observed. Furthermore, the more completely specified theories, such as the theory of reasoned action and subjective expected utility theory, prescribe not only the presence of particular terms, but the coefficients of these terms in the prediction rule. In subjective expected utility theory, for example, the coefficients of the three terms in Table 3.1, $PROB_c SEV_c$, $PROB_a SEV_a$, and COST, are all supposed to be the same. Similarly, the theory of reasoned action assumes that all outcomes have equal influence on behavior once perceptions of likelihood and value are taken into account (hence all terms have equal coefficients within the summations in Table 3.1). One should investigate these theories with statistical models that include all of the variables in the theory and their interactions, and test whether the coefficients that are predicted to be the same (or to be zero) really are.

Testing details like these is essential. There is considerable evidence, for example, that people do not act like the optimal problem solvers assumed by subjective expected utility theory (Fischhoff, Goitein, & Shapira, 1982; Schoemaker, 1982). Their behavior, for example, may be influenced more by a concrete short-term cost than by a hypothetical reduction in future vulnerability. Such an effect would appear in the statistical analysis as a difference in the size of the coefficients for these terms. The difference would be missed, however, if only the overall agreement between predicted and observed behavior were examined.

In an experimental paradigm, one would test the predicted main and interaction effects. However, because a single experiment is unlikely to manipulate more than a few variables, it will not test the overall prediction rule. There is no reason, however, why experimental designs cannot assess variables that are not manipulated and perform nonexperimental tests of prediction rules using a combination of manipulated and nonmanipulated variables. Because some of the theories differ only slightly from one another, researchers should always test the various integration rules that differentiate among these theories and take care to include the variables that are present in one theory but not in another.

Problems in Model Testing

When predicted effects fail to appear, why don't researchers trust their own results and reject the theory they have been testing? Among the more familiar problems are questions of reliability and validity. Researchers may doubt, for example, that a survey has adequately measured abstract concepts like susceptibility or self-efficacy or may be skeptical that self-reports of health behavior are an adequate substitute for independent observation.

Adequacy of experimental manipulations. Expected effects may also fail to appear because an intervention does not sufficiently alter independent variables. Not only are most experimental treatments quite brief, but ethical considerations further limit the potential differences between experimental and control conditions. No one wants to leave study participants with the impression that a serious health problem presents no danger. The further one moves from the laboratory, where debriefing is possible (and behavioral intentions rather than actual behavior are the outcome measured), toward realistic, community-based investigations, the narrower the range of experimental treatments that is ethically defensible.

The apparent success of the intervention, however, may be exaggerated because of the demand characteristics of the experimental setting. Subjects who have just been told that they are susceptible to an illness may be reluctant to indicate on manipulation checks that they remain unconvinced. (Demand characteristics may also exaggerate the apparent effects of the experimental intervention on behavioral intentions.) The persistence of the changes produced is also open to question. Manipulation checks are almost always conducted immediately after the intervention; changes in behavior, in contrast, are usually assessed much later when the effects of the treatments may have worn off.

Finally, even when the intervention produces a highly significant change in an independent variable and the relationship between the independent variable and the behavioral outcome is relatively strong, the impact of the treatment on the behavioral outcome may not be statistically significant. Experiments are actually tests of simple, two-step models in which an intervention is presumed to affect the independent variable, which is then supposed to affect the behavior under study (Weinstein, Sandman, & Roberts, 1990). In such a model, the proportion of the variance in behavior explained by the intervention is the product of the variances explained in each separate step. For instance, assume that the intervention affects the independent variable, such that 20% of the postintervention variance in the independent variable is accounted for by experimental condition. Furthermore, assume that the independent variable accounts for 20% of the variance in behavior (in correlational terms, $r = .45$). The intervention will then account for only 4% of the variance in behavior (20% of 20%). Unless the sample is large, the effects of the intervention may not be statistically significant, even though the premise of the experiment, that the independent variable has a substantial, causal influence on behavior, is perfectly correct.

Effects dependent on the levels of other variables. Particularly in studying health behaviors, the effects of one variable may depend on the values of other relevant variables; that is, there may be interactions. Fear appeals, for example, may lead people to adopt a precaution only if this precaution is believed to be effective in reducing the risk. If investigators believe that the failure of the experimental manipulation to have an effect is a consequence of the levels of the other variables, they should feel an obligation to specify these proposed interactions and should acknowledge that a theory without such interactions is inadequate to explain their data.

It is difficult to determine whether the level of a secondary variable might explain the absence of treatment effects unless the value of this variable is known. Consequently, experimenters should assess and report, in addition to the levels and variance of the variable they have set out to manipulate, the mean levels and variances of other potentially important variables. Given a series of such research reports, it might be discovered, for example, that variations in perceptions of illness likelihood are important when perceived severity is high but not when it is low.

The absence of predicted interaction effects cannot be evaluated without knowing whether both of the independent variables involved are distributed over a suitably wide range. Frequently this requirement is not met. Variances may be small because there is little variation in a sample (e.g., the range of perceived severity in any study dealing with cancer is likely to be small), because the variation that is observed is due to errors of measurement, or because the intervention failed to affect the variables involved. Only if both the variables in a two-way interaction term are successfully manipulated in an experiment is it possible for interaction effects to appear.

Problems in testing multiplicative models. Improper statistical analysis of models containing multiplicative terms is common (Evans, 1991). Except under unusual circumstances, the effects of multiplicative terms should be tested after the variables are first added individually to the statistical model, even if the theory does not assume the presence of such main effects.

It is also important to recognize that statistical tests of multiplicative terms in survey data are strongly affected by the reliability of measurement of their components (Busemeyer & Jones, 1983). The poorer the measurement, the less significant the interaction will be. Furthermore, as declining reliability causes a decrease in the variance explained by the interaction term, significant main effects of the separate variables (i.e., simple additive terms) will appear (Dunlap & Kemery, 1988; Evans, 1985). These phantom main effects are due solely to the imperfect measurement. This reliability-related phenomenon may explain why tests of the probability by severity interaction using survey data often do not prove significant.

Concept Differentiation

We have already noted a number of instances in which the conceptualization of similar variables differs across theories. These instances include various ways of specifying costs (raising the issue of which types of costs need to be considered and whether they need to be treated separately), whether self-efficacy needs to be distinguished from other barriers to action, and whether people think of effectiveness as a distinct concept or as the difference between the risk one faces with and without precautionary action.

Similarly, we need to ask whether the threat to health that is presumed to form the motivation to act is always built from separate perceptions of likelihood and severity—as the theories suggest—or whether people can have a conception of threat without having any ideas about these separate perceptions (Weinstein, 1988). In other words, is threat an essential, intervening construct, and what variables other than perceptions of likelihood and severity (the only hazard attributes explicitly considered by these theories) might influence perceived threat?

Even concepts shared by many of these theories, like susceptibility, fear arousal, or efficacy, need critical examination. How many different dimensions are concealed beneath these individual labels? Research on the perceived risk of various technologies and activities suggests that risk is a multidimensional concept (Slovic, Fischhoff, & Lichtenstein, 1985). It cannot be summarized by a single probability statistic; in fact, laypeople have great difficulty understanding such statistics. Moreover, we know that concrete case histories have more impact on decisions than abstract statistics (Borgida & Nisbett, 1977). The health hazard attributes that may influence the perceived need for action include not only beliefs about likelihood and severity, but also the vividness of images of harm, the frequency of reminders, the availability of the issue in memory, the sensory experiences associated with the hazard, the time till onset and expectations of warnings prior to onset, the social meaning attached to victimization, and even the part of the body affected. Meyer, Leventhal, and Gutmann (1985), for example, hypothesize that responses to illness threats reflect their labels and symptoms, their causes, their consequences, and their duration. We need to discover which dimensions of health hazards need to be kept separate because of their differential effects on behavior and which can be combined because of their simple additive effects.

Similarly, none of these theories provide a conceptual model of protective behaviors. In addition to difficulty and effectiveness, there may be other issues (such as familiarity vs. novelty or initiating new behaviors vs. stopping old behaviors) that influence decisions to act. What attributes of these issues other than beliefs about likelihood and value are important?

Static Versus Dynamic Models

The four theories examined here try to specify the combination of variables that determines whether people take action. They differ in the particular variables considered, but all aim toward a single prediction rule. Recently, however, there has been growing interest in the idea that the adoption of health behaviors is too complex to be summarized by one decision rule (Baranowski, 1989–1990;

Prochaska & DiClemente, 1983, 1984; Safer, Tharps, Jackson, & Leventhal, 1979; Weinstein 1988; Weinstein & Sandman, 1992). According to this perspective, an adequate view of precautionary behavior has to explain several distinct steps along the route to action. Not only must we explain why people decide that they should act, but we must also explain how people first come to consider a problem as requiring their attention and describe the issues that intervene between decisions and action. Furthermore, the factors that lead people to initiate actions are not sufficient to explain whether they are successful in maintaining these actions (Leventhal, Diefenbach, & Leventhal, 1992; McCaul, Glasgow, & O'Neill, 1992).

The identification of more than two distinct stages suggests that progress toward taking health-protective action cannot be adequately explained by the change in the value of a single prediction rule. Since different issues may be important at different stages, a series of prediction rules may be required. Stage theories thus require specification of the different stages (how they are defined; how they can be assessed; how people at one stage differ from those at another) and specification of the rules that govern transitions from one stage to the next. This is clearly more complicated than generating a single prediction rule, but may better reflect the reality of the precaution adoption process.

Conclusion

Although each of the theories discussed here is presented in various forms in the literature, some readers may argue that the version presented in this article is not the right one. The real goal, however, should not be to decide which theory is best, but to decide which variables and processes in these theories improve our understanding of health-protective behavior. Finding that one theory correlates .4 with observed behavior and that another theory correlates .5 is not nearly as helpful as discovering what features of the theories account for the difference. The substantive issues that have been identified in the preceding pages are summarized in Table 3.2. These are the questions that really need to be addressed, and these are the questions whose answers will lead to better theories of health-protective behavior.

TABLE 3.2. Key Questions Suggested by Model Comparisons

1. To what extent do beliefs about the likelihood and severity of health outcomes combine to influence behavior? Are their effects additive, multiplicative, or some other function?
2. How important are perceptions of risk compared to beliefs about other nonrisk issues in influencing behavior? Are there categories of nonrisk issues (such as emotional experience, self-esteem, social approval, etc.) that are useful to distinguish? Are there certain nonrisk issues that are always relevant, or is each health threat unique?
3. Do doubts about one's ability to carry out a precaution have a different impact on behavior than do other obstacles (such as perceived cost and inconvenience)? Does the expected cost of carrying out a precaution need to be considered separately from the expected loss of internal and external rewards resulting from abandoning current behavior, or can they be combined?
4. Do people derive notions of risk reduction effectiveness from separate beliefs about the risk presented from current behavior and from the recommended alternative, or do they have notions of effectiveness that arise separately?
5. What variables intervene between intentions and actions? Is reaching a decision to take action a discrete event that can be defined by a dichotomy, or should decisions to act be described along a continuum? Are there other distinct stages to the precaution adoption process that can be identified?
6. Do dimensions of risk other than likelihood and severity (e.g., familiar vs. novel, visible vs. invisible, imminent vs. delayed) need to be considered? How do they affect behavior?
7. What attributes of precautions other than the beliefs about costs and effectiveness considered in these models (e.g., past patterns of behavior, complexity of action, need for repetition, elimination of risk vs. reduction in risk, etc.) influence behavior?

ACKNOWLEDGMENT

The many valuable suggestions offered by Howard Leventhal during the preparation of this article are gratefully acknowledged.

REFERENCES

Ajzen, I. (1985). From intentions to actions: A theory of planned behavior. In J. Kuhl & J. Beckmann (Eds.), *Action control: From cognition to behavior* (pp. 11–40). Berlin: Springer-Verlag.

Ajzen, I., & Fishbein, M. (1980). *Understanding attitudes and predicting behavior.* Englewood Cliffs, NJ: Prentice-Hall.

Ajzen, I., & Madden, T. J. (1986). Prediction of goal-directed behavior: Attitudes, intentions, and perceived behavioral control. *Journal of Experimental Social Psychology, 22,* 453–474.

Bandura, A. (1977). Self-efficacy: Toward a unifying theory of behavioral change. *Psychological Review, 84,* 191–215.

Baranowski, T. (1989–1990). Reciprocal determinism at the stages of behavior change: An integration of community, personal, and behavioral perspectives. *International Quarterly of Community Health Education, 10,* 297–327.

Beck, K. H., & Lund, A. K. (1981). The effects of health threat seriousness and personal efficacy upon intentions and behavior. *Journal of Applied Social Psychology, 11,* 401–415.

Becker, M. H. (Ed.). (1974). The health belief model and personal health behavior. *Health Education Monographs, 2*(4).

Becker, M. H. (1991). Theoretical models of adherence and strategies for improving adherence. In S. A. Shumaker, E. B. Schron, & J. K. Ockene (Eds.), *The handbook of health behavior change* (pp. 5–43). New York: Springer.

Becker, M. H., & Maiman, L. A. (1975). Sociobehavioral determinants of compliance with health and medical care recommendations. *Medical Care, 13,* 10–24.

Borgida, E., & Nisbett, R. E. (1977). The differential impact of abstract vs. concrete information on decisions. *Journal of Applied Social Psychology, 7,* 258–271.

Brubaker, R. G., & Wickersham, D. (1990). Encouraging the practice of testicular self-examination: A field application of the theory of reasoned action. *Health Psychology, 9,* 154–163.

Busemeyer, J. R., & Jones, L. E. (1983). Analysis of multiplicative combination rules when the causal variables are measured with error. *Psychological Bulletin, 93,* 549–562.

Cummings, K. M., Becker, M. H., & Maile, M. C. (1980). Bringing the models together: An empirical approach to combining variables used to explain health actions. *Journal of Behavioral Medicine, 3,* 123–145.

Cummings, K. M., Jette, A. M., Brock, B. M., & Haefner, D. P. (1979). Psychosocial determinants of immunization behavior in a swine influenza campaign. *Medical Care, 17,* 639–649.

Davidson, A. R., & Beach, L. R. (1981). Error patterns in the prediction of fertility behavior. *Journal of Applied Social Psychology, 11,* 475–488.

Dunlap, W. P., & Kemery, E. R. (1988). Effects of predictor intercorrelations and reliabilities on moderated multiple regression. *Organizational Behavior and Human Decision Processes, 41,* 248–258.

Edwards, W. (1954). The theory of decision making. *Psychological Bulletin, 51,* 380–417.

Evans, M. G. (1985). A Monte Carlo study of the effects of correlated method variance in moderated multiple regression analysis. *Organizational Behavior and Human Decision Processes, 36,* 305–323.

Evans, M. G. (1991). The problem of analyzing multiplicative composites. *American Psychologist, 46,* 6–15.

Fischhoff, B., Goitein, B., & Shapira, Z. (1982). The experienced utility of expected utility approaches. In N. T. Feather (Ed.), *Expectations and actions: Expectancy-value models in psychology* (pp. 315–339). Hillsdale, NJ: Erlbaum.

Fishbein, M., & Ajzen, I. (1975). *Belief, attitude, intention and behavior: An introduction to theory and research.* Reading, MA: Addison-Wesley.

Glanz, K., Lewis, F. M., & Rimer, B. K. (Eds.). (1990). *Health behavior and health education.* San Francisco: Jossey-Bass.

Hays, R. (1985). An integrated value-expectancy theory of alcohol and other drug use. *British Journal of Addictions, 80,* 379–384.

Henning, P., & Knowles, A. (1990). Factors influencing women over 40 years to take precautions against cervical cancer. *Journal of Applied Social Psychology, 20,* 1612–1621.

Hochbaum, G. (1958). *Public participation in medical screening programs: A sociopsychological study.* (U.S. Public Health Service Publication No. 572). Washington, DC: U.S. Government Printing Office.

Hoogstraten, J., de Haan, W., & ter Horst, G. (1985). Stimulating the demand for dental care: An application of Ajzen and Fishbein's theory of reasoned action. *European Journal of Social Psychology, 15,* 401–415.

Janz, N. K., & Becker, M. H. (1984). The health belief model: A decade later. *Health Education Quarterly, 11,* 1–47.

Kirscht, J. P. (1988). The health belief model and predictions of health actions. In D. Gochman (Ed.), *Health Behavior* (pp. 27–41). New York: Plenum Press.

Leventhal, H., Diefenbach, M., & Leventhal, E. A. (1992). Illness cognition: Using common sense to understand treatment adherence and affect cognition interaction. *Cognitive Therapy and Research, 16,* 143–163.

Leventhal, H., Hochbaum, G. M., & Rosenstock, I. (1960). *The impact of Asian influenza on community life: A study in five cities.* (U.S. Public Health Service Publication No. 766). Washington, DC: U.S. Government Printing Office.

Liska, A. E. (1984). A critical examination of the causal structure of the Fishbein/Ajzen attitude-behavior model. *Social Psychology Quarterly, 47,* 61–74.

Luce, R. D., & Raiffa, H. (1957). *Games and decisions.* New York: Wiley.

Maddux, J. E., & Rogers, R. W. (1983). Protection motivation and self-efficacy: A revised theory of fear appeals and attitude change. *Journal of Experimental Social Psychology, 19,* 469–479.

McCaul, K. D., Glasgow, R. E., & O'Neill, H. K. (1992). The problem of creating habits: Establishing health-protective dental behaviors. *Health Psychology, 11,* 101–110.

Meyer, D., Leventhal, H., & Gutmann, M. (1985). Commonsense models of illness: The example of hypertension. *Health Psychology, 4,* 115–135.

Mullen, P. D., Hersey, J. C., & Iverson, D. C. (1987). Health behavior models compared. *Social Science & Medicine, 11,* 973–981.

Nelson, G. D., & Moffit, P. B. (1988). Safety belt promotion: Theory and practice. *Accident Analysis and Prevention, 20,* 27–38.

Peterson, L., Farmer, J., & Kashani, J. H. (1990). Parental injury prevention endeavors: A function of health beliefs? *Health Psychology, 9,* 177–191.

Prentice-Dunn, S., & Rogers, R. W. (1986). Protection motivation theory and preventive health: Beyond the health belief model. *Health Education Research, 1,* 153–161.

Prochaska, J. O., & DiClemente, C. C. (1983). Stages and processes of self-change in smoking: Toward an integrative model. *Journal of Consulting and Clinical Psychology, 51,* 390–395.

Prochaska, J. O., & DiClemente, C. C. (1984). *The transtheoretical approach: Crossing traditional boundaries of change.* Homewood, IL: J. Irwin.

Prothero, J., & Beach, L. R. (1984). Retirement decisions: Expectation, intention, and action. *Applied Social Psychology, 14,* 162–174.

Ried, L. D., & Christensen, D. B. (1988). A psychosocial perspective in the explanation of patients' drug-taking behavior. *Social Science and Medicine, 27,* 277–285.

Rogers, R. W. (1983). Cognitive and psychological processes in fear appeals and attitude change: A revised theory of protection motivation. In J. T. Cacioppo & R. E. Petty (Eds.), *Social psychophysiology* (pp. 153–176). New York: Guilford Press.

Rogers, R. W., & Mewborn, C. R. (1976). Fear appeals and attitude change: Effects of a threat's noxiousness, probability of occurrence, and the efficacy of coping responses. *Journal of Personality and Social Psychology, 34,* 54–61.

Ronis, D. L. (1992). Conditional health threats: Health beliefs, decisions, and behaviors among adults. *Health Psychology, 11,* 127–134.

Ronis, D. L., & Harel, Y. (1989). Health beliefs and breast examination behaviors: Analysis of linear structural equations. *Psychology and Health, 3,* 259–285.

Rosenstock, I. M. (1974). The health belief model: Origins and correlates. *Health Education Monographs, 2,* 336–353.

Safer, M. A., Tharps, Q., Jackson, T., & Leventhal, H. (1979). Determinants of three stages of delay in seeking care at a medical clinic. *Medical Care, 17,* 11–29.

Schoemaker, P. J. H. (1982). The expected utility model: Its variants, purposes, evidence and limitations. *Journal of Economic Literature, 20,* 529–563.

Seydel, E., Taal, E., & Wiegman, O. (1990). Risk-appraisal, outcome and self-efficacy expectancies: Cognitive factors in preventive behavior related to cancer. *Psychology and Health, 4,* 99–109.

Sheppard, S. L., Solomon, L. J., Atkins, E., Foster, R. S. J., & Frankowski, B. (1990). Determinants of breast self-examination among women of lower income and lower education. *Journal of Behavioral Medicine, 13,* 359–371.

Silver Platter, Inc. (1992). *PsychLit (1974–1983, 1983–1991).* CD-ROM disc. Norwood, MA: Author.

Slovic, P., Fischhoff, B., & Lichtenstein, S. (1985). Characterizing perceived risk. In C. Hohenemser & J. Kasperson (Eds.), *Perilous progress: Managing the hazards of technology* (pp. 91–125). Boulder, CO: Westview Press.

Steffen, V. (1990). Men's motivation to perform the testicle self-exam: Effects of prior knowledge and an educational brochure. *Journal of Applied Social Psychology, 20,* 681–702.

Sutton, S. R. (1982). Fear arousing communications: A critical examination of theory and research. In J. R. Eiser (Ed.), *Social psychology and behavioral medicine* (pp. 303–338). New York: Wiley.

Sutton, S. (1987). Social-psychological approaches to understanding addictive behaviors: Attitude-behaviour and decision-making models. *British Journal of Addiction, 82*, 355–370.

Sutton, S. R., & Eiser. J. R. (1990). The decision to wear a seat belt: The role of cognitive factors, fear, and prior behavior. *Psychology and Health, 4*, 111–123.

Sutton, S., & Hallett, R. (1988). Understanding the effects of fear-arousing communications: The role of cognitive factors and amount of fear arousal. *Journal of Behavioral Medicine, 11*, 353–360.

Wallston, B. S., & Wallston, K. A. (1984). Social psychological models of health behavior: An examination and integration. In A. Baum, S. E. Taylor, & J. E. Singer (Eds.), *Handbook of psychology and health*. (Vol. 4, pp. 23–54). Hillsdale, NJ: Erlbaum.

Weinstein, N. D. (1988). The precaution adoption process. *Health Psychology, 7*, 355–386.

Weinstein, N. D., & Nicolich, M. M. (1993). Correct and incorrect interpretations of correlations between risk perceptions and risk behaviors. *Health Psychology, 12*, 235–245.

Weinstein. N. D., & Sandman, P. M. (1992). A model of the precaution adoption process: Evidence from home radon testing. *Health Psychology, 11*, 170–180.

Weinstein, N. D., Sandman, P. M., & Roberts, N. E. (1990). Determinants of self-protective behavior: Home radon testing. *Journal of Applied Social Psychology, 20*, 783–801.

Wurtele, S. K. (1988). Increasing women's calcium intake: The role of health beliefs, intentions, and health value. *Journal of Applied Social Psychology, 18*, 627–639.

Wurtele, S. K., & Maddux, J. E. (1987). Relative contributions of protection motivation theory components in predicting exercise intentions and behavior. *Health Psychology, 6*, 453–466.

Health Beliefs and Health Behavior

Consider two cigarette smokers. Angela has given a lot of thought to quitting, renewed her commitment to giving up her habit, and scans newspapers and magazines for information about new approaches to cessation. Another smoker, Noah, rarely thinks about the need to quit and has a difficult time coming up with arguments for quitting. How might one best characterize the difference between these two individuals? Research on health behavior change provides two contrasting approaches to this question. One approach suggests that a specific and consistent set of variables (e.g., attitudes, perceived norms, intentions) can be used to predict the likelihood of health behavior change among everyone, and that the difference observed between people such as the two smokers is best characterized by differences on these dimensions (e.g., Angela holds more negative beliefs about smoking than does Noah). One implication of this "continuum-based" approach is that health promotion efforts that address these core factors can be effective across all individuals.

The second approach suggests that the behavior change process is best conceptualized as a series of stages through which people must pass. From this vantage point, the observed differences between Angela and Noah indicate that they are at different stages in the behavior change process. According to a "stage-based" approach, different factors need to be addressed in order to facilitate transitions between different stages. Thus, the factors predicted to help Angela implement her desire to quit are different from those predicted to help Noah first recognize the need to quit smoking.

The articles in this section provide a good overview of these two approaches to health behavior change. One challenge to understanding the relative promise of these two approaches is to recognize their similarities and differences. Weinstein, Rothman, and Sutton (1998) provide a guide to differentiating between "continuum-based" and "stage-based" models of behavior change and suggest the experimental evidence that is needed to determine which of these two approaches is more appropriate.

The dominant stage-based model in health psychology is the transtheoretical model of behavior change. Prochaska, DiClemente, and Norcross (1992) provide a broad overview of this theory and suggest its applicability to various health behaviors. In contrast, Gibbons and his colleagues (1998) reveal how the same factors can be used to predict people's behavior, regardless of their readiness to change. Although their work is grounded in health beliefs emanating from the theory of reasoned action—attitudes about the health behavior and beliefs about what other people are doing in the formation of an intention to change—these investigators argue that certain health behaviors, in particular those that put us at risk, are not necessarily predicated on our intentions to take action. Although people don't intend to have unprotected sex or to drive while intoxicated, Gibbons and his colleagues have shown that they do differ in their willingness, under certain circumstances, to engage in these risky behaviors.

REFERENCES

Gibbons, F. X., Gerrard, M., Blanton, H., & Russell, D. W. (1998). Reasoned action and social reaction: Willingness and intention as independent predictors of health risk. *Journal of Personality and Social Psychology, 74,* 1164–1180.

Prochaska, J.O., DiClemente, C. C., & Norcross, J. C. (1992). In search of how people change: Applications to addictive behaviors. *American Psychologist, 47,* 1102–1114.

Weinstein, N. D., Rothman, A. J., & Sutton, S. R. (1998). Stage theories of health behavior: Conceptual and methodological issues. *Health Psychology, 17,* 290–299.

Discussion Questions

1. Are there certain health behaviors for which a stage-based model seems more or less appropriate?
2. Stage-based approaches to behavior change such as the transtheoretical model primarily focus on differences in people's readiness to enact a change in behavior. Yet the benefits afforded by most health behaviors only accrue if they are maintained over time. What differentiates the incentives that are needed to get someone to an initiate a new behavior for the first time as opposed to maintain a behavior in which they already engage?

3. Consider the array of healthy and risky behaviors that you are currently faced with. Are there behaviors that you have no intention of doing, but could imagine a circumstance in which you would be willing to engage in them? Are there behaviors that you intend to do, but could imagine circumstances in which you would be unwilling to initiate them?

4. In what ways are stage-based models of health behavior similar to or different from other stage models you may have studied in psychology (e.g., stage models of moral behavior; stage models of cognitive development in childhood)?

5. In designing interventions to promote healthy patterns of behavior, why might investigators be more likely to ground the intervention on a continuum-based rather than a stage-based framework?

Suggested Readings

Albarracin, D., Johnson, B. T., Fishbein, M., & Muellerleile, P. A. (2001). Theories of Reasoned Action and Planned Behavior as models of condom use: A meta-analysis. *Psychological Bulletin, 127,* 142–161.
The authors examine evidence from more than 22,000 individuals concerning the strength of several theoretically based predictors of condom use: attitudes, norms, behavioral control, and intentions.

Bandura, A. (1997). *Self-efficacy: The exercise of control.* New York: W. H. Freeman.
The role of beliefs concerning one's confidence in carrying out required behaviors is discussed in many different domains. An especially useful chapter on health behavior is included.

Herzog, T. A., Abrams, D. B., Emmons, K. M., Linnan, L. A., & Shadel, W. G. (1999). Do processes of change predict smoking stage movements? A prospective analysis of the transtheoretical model. *Health Psychology, 18,* 369–375.
An investigation of the underlying stage-linked change processes predicted by the transtheoretical model of change.

Janz, N. K., & Becker, M. H. (1984). The health belief model: A decade later. *Health Education Monographs, 2,* 387–402.
Although other theories of health behavior have superseded the health belief model, it still represents the classic starting point for many psychological theories in this domain.

Weinstein, N. D. (1988). The precaution adoption process. *Health Psychology, 7,* 355–386.
The leading alternative stage theory to the transtheoretical model.

Stage Theories of Health Behavior: Conceptual and Methodological Issues

Neil D. Weinstein • Rutgers University
Alexander J. Rothman • University of Minnesota
Stephen R. Sutton • University College, London

Despite growing interest in stage theories of health behavior, there is considerable confusion in the literature concerning the essential characteristics of stage theories and the manner in which such theories should be tested. In this article, the four key characteristics of a stage theory—a category system, an ordering of categories, similar barriers to change within categories, and different barriers to change between categories—are discussed in detail. Examples of stage models of health behavior also are described. Four major types of research designs that might be used for testing stage theories are examined, including examples from the empirical literature. The most commonly used design, which involves cross-sectional comparisons of people believed to be in different stages, is shown to have only limited value for testing whether behavior change follows a stage process.

Key words: stage theories, health behavior, methodology, research design

Stage theories are being used increasingly to investigate health-protective behaviors. They have been applied to the adoption of preventive behaviors (Blalock et al., 1996; Weinstein & Sandman, 1992); to attempts to stop unhealthy behaviors (DiClemente et al., 1991; Prochaska, Redding, & Velicer, 1994); and to the use of medical services (Rakowski et al., 1992). An example may help to illustrate why stage models are so attractive.

Consider AIDS prevention. A great many variables (e.g., social norms, knowledge, efficacy beliefs, and risk perceptions) are likely to influence the performance of unsafe sexual behavior. However, given a list of such variables, how do we de-sign a program to encourage safer behavior? Do different categories of people need different kinds of help? Do certain topics (such as information about vulnerability) need to be addressed before others (such as skills for negotiating condom use)? A stage theory of safer sex behavior would specify an ordered set of categories into which people could be classified and would identify the factors that can induce movement from one category to the next. Given such a theory, a health educator approaching a new population could identify the dominant stage or stages and focus resources on those issues that would move people to the next stage. Thus, if health behavior change proceeds through a series of stages, a theory that correctly describes these stages makes possible the matching of treatments to individuals (because people in different stages have different needs) and the sequencing of treatments (because the stages have a temporal order).

Despite their popularity, there is a great deal of confusion about stage theories. In this article, we discuss the essential characteristics of stage theories. We briefly describe two current stage theories of health behavior and then review the types of tests that should be used to distinguish between stage and continuum processes. Finally, we consider challenges facing the implementation of stage-based behavior change programs. Our aim is to provide guidance in the development and testing of stage theories. Given the limitations in the present empirical literature, it is not possible to determine whether one current stage theory of health behavior is better than another.

What Is a Stage Theory of Health Behavior?

Many of the most familiar theories of health behavior (e.g., theory of reasoned action [Fishbein & Ajzen, 1975]; theory of planned behavior [Ajzen & Madden, 1986]; health belief model [Janz & Becker, 1984]; protection motivation theory [Maddux & Rogers, 1983]; and subjective expected utility theory [Ronis, 1992]) can be called *continuum theories*. Their approach is to identify variables that influence action (such as perceptions of risk and precaution effectiveness) and to combine them in a prediction equation. When applied to a particular individual, the value generated by the equation indicates the probability that this person will act. Thus, each person is placed along a continuum of action likelihood. Because each theory has only a single prediction equation, the way in which variables combine to influence action is expected to be the same for everyone.

Is it reasonable to assume that behavior change can be described by a single prediction equation? Many natural phenomena pass through qualitatively different stages. Water, for example, changes from solid to liquid to gas. Insects of the order Lepidoptera develop from egg to caterpillar to chrysalis to butterfly. To test whether behavior

change also occurs through stages, we first need to understand the four defining properties of a stage theory of health behavior.

1. A Classification System to Define the Stages

Every stage theory needs a set of rules that assign each individual to one of a limited number of categories. As a consequence of this assignment, members of a given stage automatically share the attributes that define the stage. This is not to say, however, that members of a stage are identical, even on the attributes used to assign them to stages, or that there is complete discontinuity between one stage and the next. Stages are theoretical constructs. We can define a prototype for each stage, but few people will match this ideal perfectly. Thus, health behavior stages are categories with relatively small differences among people in the same stage and relatively large differences between people in different stages.

2. An Ordering of the Stages

At atmospheric pressure, liquid water always intervenes between water vapor and solid ice. The pupal stage always intervenes between the caterpillar and the winged butterfly. It is this sequential nature that distinguishes a stage theory from a theory that merely identifies different categories of individuals (such as one that might suggest different interventions for men and women). Specifying the sequence of stages is a start toward identifying the interventions needed to help people change.

The requirement of a sequence of stages does not imply that progression is either inevitable or irreversible, as Bandura (1995) has asserted. In this respect, behavior change is different from biological development. Furthermore, because of the flexibility of human behavior, people do not need to spend a fixed or minimum length of time in any stage. If all the factors needed to convince people to act and to carry out an action are present simultaneously, people may pass through all of the stages in a few moments. Yet, if an essential component is missing, people may never get beyond their current stage.

Rather than resembling stages of biological

development, stages of health behavior are more like the stages of buying a house. First, people decide that they need a new home. Then, they search for a house that matches their needs. Once such a house is found, they enter into negotiations with the owner over the final price and the terms of sale. Next, they apply for a mortgage. Finally, the sale is completed and they own a new home. Acquiring a new house is not a steady, incremental process. Quite different issues are important at different times, and at any point the process can be halted, reversed, or even abandoned. Like buying a house, people may pass through some stages of health behavior several times before they succeed in reaching the final end point. Attempting to use a single equation to model the process of purchasing a house would inevitably distort the complex and changing issues involved.

Stages of health behavior resemble the stages of buying a house in another respect. Although there may be a single, most prevalent path through the stages, other paths to action are possible. Just as one can inherit a new home, bypassing all the stages just described, there may be a number of routes to the adoption of a health behavior. A woman's attempt to stop smoking may be sparked by the prohibition of smoking at work and have nothing to do with health considerations. A homeowner might decide to test for radon because a friend offers him a test kit, bypassing any period of information acquisition. If there are many paths to action and few people follow the sequence of stages laid out in a particular theory, the theory will not be very useful. If a substantial majority follow the specified sequence, a theory can be considered accurate and useful even if other paths to action are possible.

3. Common Barriers to Change Facing People in the Same Stage

The principal goals of research on health-protective behavior are to understand and to influence behavior. Stage ideas will be helpful in reaching these goals if people at one stage have to address similar issues before they can progress to the next stage. Thus, the third feature of a stage theory of health behavior is the requirement that people at a given stage face similar barriers and, consequently,

that they can be helped by similar interventions. For example, people who have only heard about a precaution on television may share a need for information about its relevance to their own personal situation before they can be convinced to act.

4. Different Barriers to Change Facing People in Different Stages

If the factors producing movement toward action were the same regardless of a person's stage, a single intervention could be used for everyone. The concept of stages would be superfluous; a continuum model would be adequate.

To justify calling health behavior a stage process, some barriers must be more important at certain stages than others. Acknowledgment of personal risk, for instance, might be required before people will decide to act, whereas training might be needed before people will carry out that decision. Other factors, however, might facilitate progress regardless of stage. For example, knowing people who have adopted a precaution may encourage movement toward action, irrespective of a person's stage.

It is easier to point out the differences between caterpillars and butterflies than to understand how the transformation occurs. Similarly, it may be easier to describe stages of health behavior than to identify the factors that produce transitions between these stages. Defining the stages and specifying their sequence (Criteria 1 and 2) are initial steps toward demonstrating that health behavior change follows a stage process. However, discovering the barriers between stages and showing the benefits of using different interventions as people move through the stages (Criteria 3 and 4) constitute the ultimate tests.

Although the stages described by a theory may apply to a wide range of behaviors, the specific factors responsible for transitions between adjacent stages probably vary from one health behavior to another. The factors that help people decide to lose weight, for example, may be quite different from the factors that help people decide to use condoms. A model that describes a specific sequence of stages in the change process could be correct even if it does not identify the barriers between stages. Nevertheless, there is no way to find out if the model is correct without testing its predictions for a concrete behavior; to do so, one must describe the barriers between the stages of this behavior.

Differences in Structure Between Continuum and Stage Theories

Given the prevalence of linear methods in the analysis of behavioral data, it is not surprising that linear models also dominate continuum theories of health behavior. Yet, it is questionable whether linear models are capable of capturing the complex processes that underlie decisions to engage in health behaviors (McGuire, 1973).

An example is the implicit assumption in linear prediction equations that there are no limits to the values that the independent and dependent variables can take on. Many health-relevant variables do have limits. Self-efficacy, for instance, can vary only between complete certainty that one cannot carry out the action and complete certainty that one can. Once people are convinced that they can act successfully, this variable cannot be affected further. Obviously, if a variable has reached its limit and people have still not acted, interventions need to shift their focus to other variable. Although the assessment scales used in research recognize variables' limits, the theoretical implications of these limits are not discussed. Variables are simply combined, usually in linear equations. These equations imply that matching of treatments to individuals because of limits on variables is unnecessary.

Intention to act and likelihood of action are often represented in continuum models as a sum of variables without interaction terms. In such an equation, each variable's contribution is independent of all others' contributions. If perceived risk has a large positive coefficient in a linear regression equation, for example, an increase in perceived risk should produce the same increase in action from people who think the precaution is worthless as from people who think the precaution is highly effective. Thus, in a second respect, linear prediction equations assume implicitly that matching interventions to individuals is unnecessary.

If prediction equations include interaction terms,

and are no longer strictly linear, the consequence of increasing one variable depends on the values of the variables with which it interacts. For example, protection motivation theory (Maddux & Rogers, 1983) predicts an interaction between perceived threat and perceived efficacy. The effect of a high-threat message is said to increase with the perceived effectiveness of the preventive action. Interactions like this imply that matching interventions to audiences will be beneficial. However, even with such an equation, it makes no difference whether an intervention changes perceived threat first or perceived efficacy first, or whether both are altered simultaneously. *Sequencing of treatments is unnecessary if behaviors can be predicted by a single equation.*

Pseudostage Models

Stage-like categories, or "pseudostages," can be created out of any continuum. For example, pseudostages can be created by dividing a continuous scale that measures intentions to act into a small number of categories. The cutpoints and the number of categories would be essentially arbitrary. De Vries and Backbier (1994), for example, created categories of "precontemplators" and "contemplators" by dichotomizing a 5-point intentions scale.

Pseudostages created from a continuum provide a category system, so they satisfy Criterion 1. They also seem to satisfy Criterion 2 because the categories can be arranged in a sequence, with some appearing closer to action than others. However, if the underlying continuum model is correct, people can move to action from any category; they do not need to pass through all the intervening stages first. Furthermore, neither the third nor the fourth stage criteria are met. There is no reason to expect that people in the same region of the continuum are held back by the same barriers or that the nature of the barriers changes from one region of the continuum to another.

In general, an investigator needs to determine whether a proposed set of categories satisfies the requirements of a stage theory or is simply a set of pseudostages masking a continuous process. To answer this question, it is necessary to know how results would differ if behavior change were a stage process rather than a continuous process. The results expected from stages and pseudostages in different types of studies are examined in a later section.

Current Stage Models of Health Behavior

To test the validity of stage models, it helps to understand how such models are formulated. A number of stage-based theories have appeared in the health literature. Some emphasize a particular issue or behavior (e.g., AIDS risk reduction [Catania, Kegeles, & Coates, 1990] or delay in seeking medical care [Andersen, Cacioppo, & Roberts, 1995; Safer, Tharps, Jackson, & Leventhal, 1979]), whereas others offer a theoretical framework that can be applied to a broad range of health behaviors (e.g., the transtheoretical model [Prochaska, DiClemente, & Norcross, 1992], the health action process approach [Schwarzer, 1992], and the precaution adoption process model [Weinstein & Sandman, 1992]). The category systems of the Prochaska et al. (1992) and the Weinstein and Sandman (1992) models are briefly summarized here. Although they have important differences, they both distinguish among three classes of people: those who have not yet decided to change their behavior, those who have decided to change, and those who are already changing.

Transtheoretical Model of Behavior Change (TTM)

The TTM (DiClemente & Prochaska, 1982; Prochaska & DiClemente, 1983; Prochaska et al., 1992) is currently the most widely used stage model in health psychology. Although initially developed to examine smoking cessation and recovery in psychotherapy, its theoretical framework has been applied to a broad array of behaviors (e.g., safer sex behavior, exercise adoption, mammography utilization; for a recent summary, see Prochaska, Velicer, et al., 1994; for a detailed critique, see Sutton, 1996, 1997).

The TTM separates behavior change into five discrete stages that are defined in terms of a person's past behavior and his or her plans for fu-

ture action (Prochaska et al., 1992). To understand these stages, consider the issue of smoking cessation. At the initial stage, *precontemplation*, a smoker expresses no intention of stopping in the near future, typically operationalized as the next 6 months. A smoker who is thinking about quitting sometime in the next 6 months (but is not planning to quit in the next month) is said to have reached the *contemplation* stage. *Preparation* indicates that the smoker intends to take action within the next month and, furthermore, that she or he reports at least one unsuccessful 24-hour quit attempt in the past year. (It is not apparent how it is possible for someone to reach the preparation stage the very first time.) *Action* involves successfully altering a behavior for any period of time between 1 day and 6 months. After 6 months, someone is said to have reached *maintenance*. Although progression is primarily forward and sequential, relapse to an earlier stage can occur. Multiple attempts and relapses can result in a spiral-like progression through the behavior-change process (Prochaska, DiClemente, & Norcross, 1992).

Investigators usually assign people to stages on the basis of their responses to questions concerning their prior behavior and current behavioral intentions (e.g., DiClemente et al., 1991; but see McConnaughy, Prochaska, & Velicer, 1983). Although the five stages are designed to be mutually exclusive, the specific time points used to distinguish between stages are somewhat arbitrary. Any shift in these points would alter the distribution of people across stages.

In addition to specifying a classification scheme, stage theories attempt to identify the factors that determine whether people move between stages. The TTM includes a large array of factors that are thought to facilitate movement through the five stages (e.g., Prochaska et al., 1992). For example, 10 processes of change have been identified to represent the cognitive and behavioral strategies people use when attempting to change their behavior (Prochaska, Velicer, DiClemente, & Fava, 1988). Although research has indicated that people at different stages use different techniques and hold different beliefs about the behavior (e.g., Prochaska, DiClemente, Velicer, Ginpil, & Norcross, 1985), the specific strategies and beliefs that cause them to move from one stage to the next are currently not well identified.

Precaution Adoption Process Model (PAPM)

The PAPM (Weinstein, 1988; Weinstein & Sandman, 1992) identifies seven stages in the process by which people come to adopt a precaution. At some initial point, people are unaware of the health issue (Stage 1). When people first learn something about the issue, they are no longer unaware, but they are not necessarily engaged by it either (Stage 2). People who reach the decision-making stage (Stage 3) have become engaged by the issue and are considering their response. This decision-making process can result in one of two outcomes. If the decision is made not to take any action, the precaution adoption process ends (Stage 4), at least for the time being. But once people have decided to adopt the precaution (Stage 5), the next step is to initiate the behavior (Stage 6). A seventh stage, if relevant, indicates that the behavior has been maintained over time.

Although the PAPM stages resemble those specified by the TTM, the PAPM identifies people at two new stages. First, it distinguishes between people who are unaware of an issue (Stage 1) and those who know something about an issue but have never actively thought about it (Stage 2). Second, people who have decided not to adopt the precaution (Stage 4) are differentiated from people who are not taking action because they have yet to give the issue serious consideration (Stages 1 and 2).

This conceptual framework has been applied to home radon testing (Weinstein & Sandman, 1992), osteoporosis prevention (Blalock et al., 1996), and hepatitis B vaccination (Hammer, 1997). To assign people to stages, respondents are first asked whether they have ever heard about the action (a "no" answer places a person in Stage 1). People who have heard about it are then asked whether they have never thought about taking the action (Stage 2); are thinking about the behavior, but are undecided (Stage 3); have decided not to act (Stage 4); have decided to adopt the precaution (Stage 5); or have already adopted the precaution (Stage 6). Unlike the TTM, the classification does not involve past behavior or any particular time frame.

The PAPM identifies some of the variables that influence whether people proceed through each of the seven stages. For example, perceptions of per-sonal vulnerability are thought to be crucial in determining whether someone decides to take precautionary action (moving from Stage 3 to Stage 5), whereas going from an intention to act (Stage 5) to actually adopting the behavior (Stage 6) is believed to be strongly influenced by situational obstacles.

Testing the Validity of Stage Theories

Research designs differ greatly in their ability to distinguish between stage and continuum processes. After briefly discussing the assessment of stages, this section examines four kinds of empirical evidence that have been or could be interpreted as supporting a stage model. When possible, examples from the published literature are provided. The examples are all based on the transtheoretical model or the precaution adoption process model, the two models that have received the most empirical attention to date. Because our primary aim is to identify the types of data needed to confirm or disconfirm claims that behavior change follows a stage process, predictions derived from a stage model are compared with those from two pseudostage models: a simple linear continuum model and a more general continuum model that includes interactions. Table 4.1 summarizes the predictions made by these various models.

Assessing Stages

Not only must one identify the characteristics that distinguish one stage from another, one must measure these characteristics. Because the attributes that define stages of health behavior are usually internal to the individual (e.g., beliefs, plans, attributions), measurement can be imperfect. Small changes in the assessment procedure might make a large difference. For example, of 400 participants in a study of radon testing, 23.7% said that they "planned" to test, but only 13.7% said they had "decided" to test (Weinstein, Lyon, & Sandman, 1996).

Furthermore, people participating in a study of a specific precaution may exaggerate their inclination to take that precaution. A tendency to ex-

TABLE 4.1. Effects Predicted by Stage and Pseudostage Models in Different Types of Studies

Type of study/effect	Stage model	Pseudostages created from linear equation without interactions or limits	Pseudostages created from a general algebraic equation, including interactions and limits on variables
1. Cross-sectional comparisons			
a. Attributes of people differ across stages	+	+	+
b. The patterns of differences across stages vary from one attribute to another	+	−[a]	+
2. Observed sequences of stages			
Successive stages follow the hypothesized sequence	+[b]	+[b]	+[b]
3. Longitudinal prediction of stage transitions			
Predictors of stage transitions vary from stage to stage	+	−	+
4. Experimental studies of matched and mismatched interventions			
a. Interventions matched to stage produce more progress toward action than unmatched or mismatched interventions	+	−	−
b. Sequencing of interventions according to the sequence of stages maximizes progress toward action	+	−	−

Note. "+" or "−" indicates whether an effect is or is not predicted by a model.
[a]Although the amount by which a variable differs between adjacent stages can change from stage to stage if these pseudostages are unequally spaced, a linear model does not permit a variable to differ between some adjacent stages and not between others, nor can a variable increase between one pair of adjacent stages and decrease between another pair.
[b]Expected but cannot be reliably tested because of the likelihood of missed transitions.

aggerate interest in action would weaken predictions from stage models because people who appear to be in a particular stage would be a mixture of those who actually belong in that stage and those who belong in earlier stages.

Research Design 1: Cross-Sectional Comparisons of People in Different Stages

The approach used most often to study stage theories is to compare people in different stages on variables that the theories say should differ across stages (e.g., Blalock et al., 1996; De Vries & Backbier, 1994; Prochaska, 1994; Rakowski et al., 1992; Weinstein & Sandman, 1992). In a study of smoking cessation during pregnancy, for example, De Vries and Backbier (1994) compared pregnant women classified as precontemplators, contemplators, or actors. Contemplators and actors held stronger beliefs about the negative consequences

of smoking than did precontemplators, whereas actors had significantly higher scores on self-efficacy for quitting than did precontemplators and contemplators. A third variable, social influences, showed an approximately linear increase across the three groups.

Although important variables should differ across the stages of a stage process, such differences can also be created by pseudostages (see Table 4.1). To see this, assume that two people are in different pseudostages. Because the pseudostages conceal an underlying continuum, the individuals are at different places along this continuum. Thus, they must have different standing on the variables that go into the equation that creates this continuum.

Rakowski et al. (1992), for example, measured the perceived pros and cons of mammography and found that these two variables differed among people in different stages of the transtheoretical model. However, the pros and cons changed smoothly and linearly from one stage to the next, as if the stages represented an underlying continuum that was a linear function of the pros and cons. Such data are more suggestive of a pseudostage model than of a genuine stage process.

What if there is a small difference on some variable between Stages A and B but a large difference between Stages B and C? If the magnitudes of the differences vary across stages and the patterns differ from one variable to the next, the data are suggestive of a stage model. Still, these results also could be produced by a pseudostage model in which the underlying continuum dimension is a nonlinear function of the independent variables.

Overall, cross-sectional comparisons provide a weak test of stage ideas. If there are no differences across stages, if the differences change linearly from one stage to the next, or if the pattern of differences is the same for all variables, it argues against a stage theory. Changes that differ by variable could indicate a stage process or a nonlinear continuum process. The particular stage or nonlinear theory able to predict which variables will change most between which stages is the one that would be supported by such results; merely observing that different variables have different patterns is not conclusive support for either type of theory.

Research Design 2: Examination of Stage Sequences

Longitudinal data can be used to test the assumption that people pass through stages in the sequence hypothesized. Although all stage transitions are of interest, most studies to date have emphasized transitions from pre-action stages to action (DiClemente et al., 1991; Weinstein & Sandman, 1992). For example, Weinstein and Sandman (1992) found that homeowners who ordered radon test kits came predominantly from those who had said earlier that they planned to test; the rates of testing from all other stages were much lower and were about the same. Such evidence can be interpreted as supporting two assumptions of the PAPM: (a) that its stages represent qualitative distinctions rather than incremental differences and (b) that the stages are temporally ordered, with the planning-to-test stage being "closest" to action. Furthermore, the results suggest that planning to test approximates a necessary but not a sufficient condition for action because testing from the decided-to-act stage was still only about 25%.

Given suitable data, longer sequences can be examined. For example, Prochaska, Velicer, DiClemente, Guadagnoli, and Rossi (1991) reported data on smokers and ex-smokers who completed questionnaires every 6 months over a 2-year period and were classified on each occasion as being in the precontemplation (PC), contemplation (C), action (A), or maintenance (M) stage. Over the 2 years, 16% of participants progressed from one stage to the next in the sequence without experiencing any reverses (e.g., PC-PC-PC-C-C), whereas 36% stayed in the same stage (e.g., C-C-C-C-C). The number who skipped stages was not reported.

Although movement that occurs mainly to adjacent stages in the expected sequence suggests a stage process, such movement is also consistent with a pseudostage model (see Table 4.1). One would expect small, naturally occurring shifts along a continuum to be more common than large shifts, so movement to nearby pseudostages would be more likely than movement to distant pseudostages.

Any test based on the observed sequence of stages implicitly assumes that the measurement schedule gives a complete picture of the stage transitions that occur. If the measurement interval is too long or individuals can move rapidly through several stages, transitions will be missed. Because of this, it is difficult to argue that signs of skipped stages disprove the idea of a stage process; the intermediate steps might have been overlooked.[1]

If the probability of transitions between pairs of stages is found to decline gradually the farther apart the stages are, this tends to suggest a continuum process. A pattern in which transitions occur almost exclusively from adjacent stages tends to suggest a stage process. But labeling a changing pattern of transition probabilities as "gradual" or "abrupt" is somewhat subjective, so sequence data may not be very conclusive.

Research Design 3: Longitudinal Prediction of Stage Transitions

Prospective studies can be used to test the assumption that different causal factors are important at

[1]The assumption that stage transitions are not overlooked is also relevant to the next two types of evidence to be discussed but is less problematic because the time intervals involved are likely to be shorter.

different stages. If perceived risk proves to be a better predictor of movement between Stages 1 and 2 than between Stages 2 and 3, whereas self-efficacy is a better predictor of the latter transition, it would support a three-stage model of change. The focus of the analysis would be on predicting movement from a given stage to the next stage in the sequence, though prediction of movement to the preceding stage could also be of interest.

We are unaware of any studies that have examined predictors of stage transitions in this way. In a sample of smokers and ex-smokers, Prochaska et al. (1985) used stepwise discriminant analysis to study movement among the stages of the transtheoretical model, but their analysis focused on transitions *out* of a stage (to all other stages), not transitions to the next predicted stage in the sequence.

In a linear prediction equation, the variables that predict movement along a continuum are independent of one another. Thus, predictors of progress are independent of where an individual stands on the continuum. A longitudinal study of a pseudostage model derived from a linear equation would not find different predictors at different stages. If the model of action contained interactions or limits on variables, however, predictors of progress could depend on a person's initial standing. Thus, the observation that predictors vary with stage could indicate either a stage process or a nonlinear continuum model. Again, the ability of a theory to predict the observed results would determine whether the data should be seen as supporting that theory.

Research Design 4: Experimental Studies of Matched and Mismatched Interventions

Experiments provide better tests of stage ideas than do correlational research designs. Two specific types of experiments can provide converging evidence of a stage-based process.

Matching treatments to stage. If different variables influence movement at different stages in the postulated sequence, treatments designed to influence these variables will be most effective when applied to people in the appropriate stage. Thus, individuals in a given stage should respond better to an intervention that is matched to their stage than to one that is mismatched (i.e., matched to a different stage). Table 4.2 presents the expected results of an idealized experiment in a situation containing three stages. As Part I illustrates, the model assumes that Intervention A is necessary to get people in Stage 1 to advance to Stage 2 and that Intervention B is necessary to get people in Stage 2 to move to Stage 3. It follows from these assumptions that combining the matched and mismatched treatments into a single treatment (A + B) will be no better in moving people forward from Stage 2 than the matched treatment alone.

Part II of Table 4.2 reveals the predictions from this same model when the dependent variable is movement all the way to the final stage (action) rather than simply movement toward action. The key prediction is that neither A nor B alone is sufficient to shift people from Stage 1 to Stage 3. Both treatments are necessary.

TABLE 4.2. Predictions From a Stage Model Under Different Interventions

Pretreatment stage	Treatment			
	Control	A	B	A + B
I. Predicted progress to one or more stages toward action (fraction progressing)				
Stage 1	0	a	0	a
Stage 2	0	0	b	b
II. Predicted progress to the action stage (i.e., Stage 3; fraction acting)				
Stage 1	0	0	0	ab
Stage 2	0	0	b	b

Note. The model specifies a sequence of three stages. It is assumed that each intervention has an effect on one stage and no other and that the no-intervention control condition has zero effect.
a = success of Treatment A in moving Stage 1 people to Stage 2 (i.e., fraction who advance to next stage).
b = success of Treatment B in moving Stage 2 people to Stage 3.

Of course, the assumptions in Table 4.2 are rather unrealistic. For instance, it is assumed that no change occurs in the control condition even though events external to the experiment may well lead to some change. It is also assumed that the "mismatched" treatment has no effect, even though a perfectly mismatched treatment may be as difficult to find as a perfectly matched treatment. Furthermore, some of the people stopped at Stage 1 may already possess the resources needed to go from Stage 2 to Stage 3, so Intervention A delivered to people in Stage 1 may be sufficient to move some of them all the way to Stage 3. In a real experiment, a stage process would be indicated if the matched treatment was more effective than the mismatched treatment in moving people to the next stage (i.e., one would look for an interaction between treatment and stage).

In a study of home radon testing, Weinstein, Lyon, Sandman, and Cuite (1998) created a "high-risk" treatment intended to convince people in the undecided stage of the PAPM to decide to test and a "low-effort" treatment intended to make it easier for people who had decided to test to carry out this intention. The treatments were combined factorially into four conditions, exactly as in Table 4.2, and were assigned at random to people in the undecided and decided-to-test stages. As predicted, the data revealed a significant interaction between stage and condition. The high-risk treatment was good at getting undecided people to decide to test but not at getting people to order tests. The low-effort treatment, in contrast, proved quite helpful in getting decided-to-test people to act but produced few test orders from people who were undecided. In addition, as predicted by the last row in Part II of Table 4.2, the condition in which decided-to-test people received both treatments generated no more testing than the condition in which they received only the low-effort treatment.

Several studies based on the transtheoretical model have compared tailored interventions with standardized interventions (e.g., Campbell et al., 1994; Prochaska, DiClemente, Velicer, & Rossi, 1993; Skinner, Strecher, & Hospers, 1994). Although standardized interventions are not mismatched in the sense in which we have been using the term, according to a stage theory perspective they should be less effective than stage-matched interventions. These studies have kept track of overall changes in behavior but they have not assessed transitions to the next stage in the model.

Table 4.3 presents the results expected from the experiment in Table 4.2 under the assumption of a linear continuum process rather than a true stage process. Here, Stages 1 and 2 represent pseudostages created from the variable "commitment to act." The likelihood of acting (i.e., reaching Stage 3) is assumed to be proportional to commitment to act, and commitment to act is itself assumed to be a linear function of underlying variables. For a linear equation, the effects of any intervention will be independent of the person's position on the continuum (hence independent of the person's pseudostage), and the effect of the combination treatment in Table 4.3 will equal the sum of the effects of the separate treatments. In clear contrast to Table 4.2, action is expected from all conditions and stages. Main effects of stage and treatment, but no Stage × Treatment interaction, are predicted. Thus, an experiment using matched and mismatched treatments can readily distinguish between a stage model and an additive continuum model.

Nonadditive continuum models, in contrast, can produce Stage × Treatment interactions. For ex-

TABLE 4.3. Predictions From a Continuum (Pseudostage) Model Under Different Interventions

Pretreatment "stage"	Treatment			
	Control	A	B	A + B
Stage 1	αc_1	$\alpha(c_1 + a)$	$\alpha(c_1 + b)$	$\alpha(c_1 + a + b)$
Stage 2	αc_2	$\alpha(c_2 + a)$	$\alpha(c_2 + b)$	$\alpha(c_2 + a + b)$

Note. Commitment to act (C) is assumed to be an additive function of its underlying causes, and action is assumed to be proportional to commitment (i.e., action = αC). The continuum of commitment to act is divided into pseudostages (1, 2) and action represents the final stage (3). Stage 1 has mean commitment of c_1, and Stage 2 has mean commitment of c_2 ($c_1 < c_2$). Treatment A produces a positive shift of a along the continuum, and Treatment B produces a positive shift of size b. The no-intervention control condition is assumed to produce no movement along the continuum.

ample, the theory of planned behavior (Ajzen & Madden, 1986) proposes an interaction between an individual's intentions to act and his or her actual control over that action: An intervention to increase control should produce more action when applied to people in a high-intention pseudostage than in a low-intention pseudostage.

There is no intervention, however, that, according to the theory of planned behavior, would be more effective in a low-intention pseudostage than in a high-intention pseudostage. To produce a stage-like, matching prediction (i.e., one variable particularly effective at an early stage, another at a later stage) would require a more complex theory containing at least two separate interaction terms. Furthermore, if, as stage models often suggest, some variables are effective at particular stages and ineffective (rather than less effective) at others, this would require a prediction equation that has not only several interaction terms but also nonlinearity. Thus, although a continuum model could be created to mimic stage predictions, it would have to be much more complicated than any continuum model of health behavior yet proposed.

Because a Treatment × Intervention interaction can be observed with both stage and nonadditive continuum theories, an observed interaction supports one theory over another only if that theory actually predicts which interventions will produce an interaction and predicts the nature of the interaction. Finding an unanticipated interaction does not provide strong support for either type of theory.

Sequencing of treatments. Only stage models predict that the sequencing of treatments is important. For maximum effectiveness, the sequence of interventions should follow the hypothesized sequence of stages (see Table 4.1). Thus, for people in Stage 1, Intervention A followed later in time by Intervention B should be more effective in producing movement to Stage 3 than Intervention B followed by Intervention A. In fact, according to Table 4.2, the former sequence should lead the fraction a × b to act (i.e., the proportion in Stage 1 that moves to Stage 2 under Intervention A times the proportion in Stage 2 that moves to Stage 3 under the influence of Intervention B), whereas the latter sequence should lead no one (i.e., 0 × 0) to act.

In contrast, according to continuum or pseudostage models, whether based on linear or nonlinear equations, the sequence of treatments

should be unimportant.[2] Thus, sequence effects are the most convincing evidence of a stage process. Unfortunately, they are also the most difficult to study.

It would be naive to expect differences due to sequencing if the interventions were to be presented in the same session but in different orders. Experimental tests of sequencing effects need to allow a suitable time interval between treatments. There is a further practical difficulty in that participants who know they are in an experiment are likely to pay attention to all treatments, even treatments that they might ignore under more naturalistic conditions. Thus, effects due to variations in treatment sequence may be diluted as compared with those in situations where the participants are not aware that they are part of a research study. No investigations comparing different sequences of treatments have been published to date.

Summary. As Table 4.1 indicates, various types of data differ greatly in their ability to distinguish between different models. Unfortunately, the great majority of existing studies use cross-sectional comparisons, one of the least diagnostic approaches. With cross-sectional designs, both stage and pseudostage models predict differences among groups. Investigators using cross-sectional designs should focus on whether the patterns of between-stage differences vary from one predictor variable to the next, a pattern that would rule out linear continuum models.

Sequenced interventions that are matched or mismatched are the only unequivocal way to distinguish between stages and pseudostages based on a nonadditive continuum model. Yet, although the effects listed in Table 4.1 under Categories 1b, 2, 3, and 4a are consistent with both types of models, the models may differ greatly in their ability to predict these effects.

---

[2]The ability of an intervention to alter a variable may sometimes depend on preceding events regardless of whether change follows a continuum or stage process. For example, *intervention A* may have a bigger effect on *variable A* if it is presented after *intervention B* than before *B*. This is not the sequencing issue under consideration here. Rather, we are concerned with a situation in which the effects of the treatments on behavior change or on change in stage depend on the treatment order, even if the change in *variable A* produced by *intervention A* and the change in *variable B* produced by *intervention B* are independent of treatment order.

Designing and Evaluating Interventions to Change Behavior

Conclusions about the advantages and disadvantages of stage-based theories must be drawn with caution. First, stage theories are no less diverse than continuum theories. Attempts to demonstrate that change in health behavior is a stage process may fail because the stages have not been correctly identified or assessed, because the barriers between stages have not been correctly identified, or because the behavior change does not proceed by stages. Consequently, if a test of a particular stage model fails to produce the expected results, it does not prove that a stage theory is inapplicable.

A stage model is useful in creating interventions only if it is possible to identify and alter the particular factors that help people move from one stage to the next. In evaluating the advantages of a stage-matched approach, attention should be paid to the possibility that merely describing an intervention as tailored or personalized might increase its effectiveness. Both tailoring and personalizing an intervention may lead participants to feel they are receiving special attention, and this in turn may lead them to process the information provided more thoroughly. Although this factor may enhance the effectiveness of a tailored intervention relative to a standardized intervention, it has no direct bearing on the validity of a stage model.

Tailored interventions are not the exclusive province of stage models. Interventions are frequently designed so that particular versions are targeted to particular subpopulations (e.g., Kalichman, Kelly, Hunter, Murphy, & Tyler, 1993). The same message is delivered to more than one person only if their beliefs match perfectly (e.g., Strecher et al., 1994). This type of approach uses a classification scheme with some similarities to a stage model, but the sequence in which information should be communicated is not considered.

The advantage of a stage-based intervention depends on one's ability to identify stages accurately and efficiently. If a complex assessment process is required, it may be difficult to apply in a large-scale campaign. Finally, the value of a particular stage-matched intervention must be measured against that of the best available standardized treatment (e.g., Prochaska et al., 1993). The added complexity of implementing a stage-based intervention can be justified only if it significantly outperforms an effective standardized treatment.

There are other challenges facing investigators who choose to implement and evaluate stage-based interventions. The speed with which stage transitions occur must be considered. For some behaviors, transitions between stages could occur quickly, and one might choose to present all of the theoretically necessary information in a single intervention. In general, a public health campaign would need to monitor the stage distribution in the population, changing the amount of information pertaining to each stage as people progress toward action.

Despite these potential problems, stage models offer the possibility of creating programs and treatments that will be more effective and efficient than one-size-fits-all interventions. Most of the evidence produced so far in support of stage models, however, is weak and is consistent with continuum models. It is our hope that this article will help researchers focus on the designs and analyses that are most appropriate for determining the existence of stages of health behavior and the as-yet-untested potential of stage-based programs.

ACKNOWLEDGMENTS

This research was supported by National Cancer Institute Grant 1 R01 CA60890. We are grateful to Charles Abraham, Mark Conner, Nick Heather, Robert Jeffery, Paul Norman, Peter Salovey, and Paschal Sheeran for their thoughtful suggestions during the preparation of this article.

REFERENCES

Ajzen, I., & Madden, T. J. (1986). Prediction of goal-directed behavior: Attitudes, intentions, and perceived behavioral control. *Journal of Experimental Social Psychology, 22,* 453–474.

Andersen, B. L., Cacioppo, J. T., & Roberts, D. C. (1995). Delay in seeking a cancer diagnosis: Delay stages and psychophysiological comparison processes. *British Journal of Social Psychology, 34,* 33–52.

Bandura, A. (1995, March). *Moving into forward gear in health promotion and disease prevention.* Address presented at the annual meeting of the Society of Behavioral Medicine, San Diego.

Blalock, S. J., DeVellis, R. F., Giorgino, K. B., DeVellis, B. M., Gold, D., Dooley, M. A., Anderson, J. B., & Smith, S. L. (1996). Osteoporosis prevention in premenopausal women: Using a stage model approach to examine the predictors of behavior. *Health Psychology, 15,* 84–93.

Campbell, M. K., DeVellis, B. M., Strecher, V. J., Ammerman,

A. S., DeVellis, R. F., & Sandler, R. S. (1994). Improving dietary behavior: The effectiveness of tailored messages in primary care settings. *American Journal of Public Health, 84,* 783–787.

Catania, J. A., Kegeles, S. M., & Coates, T. J. (1990). Towards an understanding of risk behavior: An AIDS risk reduction model (ARRM). *Health Education Quarterly, 17,* 53–72.

De Vries, H., & Backbier, E. (1994). Self-efficacy as an important determinant of quitting among pregnant women who smoke: The Ø-pattern. *Preventive Medicine, 23,* 167–174.

DiClemente, C. C., & Prochaska, J. O. (1982). Self-change and therapy change of smoking behavior: A comparison of processes of change in cessation and maintenance. *Addictive Behaviors, 7,* 133–142.

DiClemente, C. C., Prochaska, J. O., Fairhurst, S. K., Velicer, W. F., Velasquez, M. M., & Rossi, J. S. (1991). The process of smoking cessation: An analysis of precontemplation, contemplation, and preparation stages of change. *Journal of Consulting and Clinical Psychology, 59,* 295–304.

Fishbein, M., & Ajzen, I. (1975). *Belief, attitude, intention and behavior: An introduction to theory and research.* Reading, MA: Addison-Wesley.

Hammer, G. P. (1997). *Hepatitis B vaccine acceptance among nursing home workers.* Unpublished dissertation, Department of Health Policy and Management, Johns Hopkins University.

Janz, N. K., & Becker, M. H. (1984). The health belief model: A decade later. *Health Education Quarterly, 11,* 1–47.

Kalichman, S. C., Kelly, J., Hunter, T., Murphy, D., & Tyler, R. (1993). Culturally tailored HIV-AIDS risk-reduction messages targeted to African-American urban women: Impact on risk sensitization and risk reduction. *Journal of Consulting and Clinical Psychology, 61,* 291–295.

Maddux, J. E., & Rogers, R. W. (1983). Protection motivation and self-efficacy: A revised theory of fear appeals and attitude change. *Journal of Experimental Social Psychology, 19,* 469–479.

McConnaughy, E. A., Prochaska, J. O., & Velicer, W. F. (1983). Stages of change in psychotherapy: Measurement and sample profiles. *Psychotherapy: Theory, Research, and Practice, 20,* 368–373.

McGuire, W. J. (1973). The yin and yang of progress in social psychology. *Journal of Personality and Social Psychology, 26,* 446–456.

Prochaska, J. O. (1994). Strong and weak principles for progressing from precontemplation to action on the basis of twelve problem behaviors. *Health Psychology, 13,* 47–51.

Prochaska, J. O., & DiClemente, C. C. (1983). Stages and processes of self-change in smoking: Toward an integrative model of change. *Journal of Consulting and Clinical Psychology, 51,* 390–395.

Prochaska, J. O., DiClemente, C. C., & Norcross, J. C. (1992). In search of how people change: Applications to addictive behaviors. *American Psychologist, 47,* 1102–1114.

Prochaska, J. O., DiClemente, C. C., Velicer, W., Ginpil, S., & Norcross, J. C. (1985). Predicting change in smoking status for self-changers. *Addictive Behaviors, 10,* 395–406.

Prochaska, J. O., DiClemente, C. C., Velicer, W., & Rossi, J. S. (1993). Standardized, individualized, interactive, and personalized self-help programs for smoking cessation. *Health Psychology, 12,* 399–405.

Prochaska, J. O., Redding, C. A., & Velicer, W. F. (1994). The transtheoretical model of change and HIV prevention: A review. *Health Education Quarterly, 21,* 471–521.

Prochaska, J. O., Velicer, W. F., DiClemente, C. C., & Fava, J. S. (1988). Measuring processes of change: Applications to the cessation of smoking. *Journal of Consulting and Clinical Psychology, 56,* 520–528.

Prochaska, J. O., Velicer, W. F., DiClemente, C. C., Guadagnoli, E., & Rossi, J. S. (1991). Patterns of change: Dynamic typology applied to smoking cessation. *Multivariate Behavioral Research, 26,* 83–107.

Prochaska, J. O., Velicer, W. F., Rossi, J. S., Goldstein, M. G., Marcus, B. H., Rakowski, W., Fiore, C., Harlow, L. L., Redding, C. A., Rosenbloom, D., & Rossi, S. R. (1994). Stages of change and decisional balance for 12 problem behaviors. *Health Psychology, 13,* 39–46.

Rakowski, W., Dube, C. E., Marcus, B. H., Prochaska, J. O., Velicer, W. F., & Abrams, D. B. (1992). Assessing elements of women's decisions about mammography. *Health Psychology, 11,* 111–118.

Ronis, D. L. (1992). Conditional health threats: Health beliefs, decisions, and behaviors among adults. *Health Psychology, 11,* 127–134.

Safer, M. A., Tharps, Q., Jackson, T., & Leventhal, H. (1979). Determinants of three stages of delay in seeking care at a medical clinic. *Medical Care, 17,* 11–29.

Schwarzer, R. (1992). Self-efficacy in the adoption and maintenance of health behaviors: Theoretical approaches and a new model. In R. Schwarzer (Ed.), *Self-efficacy: Thought control of action* (pp. 217–243). Washington, DC: Hemisphere.

Skinner, C. S., Strecher, V. J., & Hospers, H. (1994). Physicians' recommendations for mammography: Do tailored messages make a difference? *American Journal of Public Health, 84,* 43–49.

Strecher, V. J., Kreuter, M., Den-Boer, D-J., Kobrin, S., Hospers, H. J., & Skinner, C. (1994). The effects of computer-tailored smoking cessation messages in family practice settings. *The Journal of Family Practice, 39,* 262–268.

Sutton, S. R. (1996). Can "stages of change" provide guidance in the treatment of addictions? A critical examination of Prochaska and DiClemente's model. In G. Edwards & C. Dare (Eds.), *Psychotherapy, psychological treatments and the addictions* (pp. 189–205). Cambridge, England: Cambridge University Press.

Sutton, S. R. (1997). Transtheoretical model of behavior change. In A. Baum, C. McManus, S. Newman, J. Weinman, & R. West (Eds.), *Cambridge handbook of psychology, health and medicine* (pp. 180–183). Cambridge, England: Cambridge University Press.

Weinstein, N. D. (1988). The precaution adoption process. *Health Psychology, 7,* 355–386.

Weinstein, N. D., Lyon, J. E., & Sandman, P. M. (1996). *Pilot study of radon testing interventions.* Unpublished manuscript, Department of Human Ecology, Rutgers University.

Weinstein, N. D., Lyon, J. E., Sandman, P. M., & Cuite, C. L. (1998). Experimental evidence for stages of health behavior change: The precaution adoption process model applied to home radon testing. *Health Psychology, 17,* 445–453.

Weinstein, N. D., & Sandman, P. M. (1992). A model of the precaution adoption process: Evidence from home radon testing. *Health Psychology, 11,* 170–180.

In Search of How People Change: Applications to Addictive Behaviors

James O. Prochaska • Cancer Prevention Research Consortium.
University of Rhode Island
Carlo C. DiClemente • University of Houston
John C. Norcross • University of Scranton

How people intentionally change addictive behaviors with and without treatment is not well understood by behavioral scientists. This article summarizes research on self-initiated and professionally facilitated change of addictive behaviors using the key transtheoretical constructs of stages and processes of change. Modification of addictive behaviors involves progression through five stages—precontemplation, contemplation, preparation, action, and maintenance—and individuals typically recycle through these stages several times before termination of the addiction. Multiple studies provide strong support for these stages as well as for a finite and common set of change processes used to progress through the stages. Research to date supports a transtheoretical model of change that systematically integrates the stages with processes of change from diverse theories of psychotherapy.

Hundreds of psychotherapy outcome studies have demonstrated that people successfully change with the help of professional treatment (Lambert, Shapiro, & Bergin, 1986; Smith, Glass, & Miller, 1980). These outcome studies have taught us relatively little, however, about *how* people change with psychotherapy (Rice & Greenberg, 1984). Numerous studies also have demonstrated that many people can modify problem behaviors without the benefit of formal psychotherapy (Marlatt, Baer, Donovan, & Divlahan, 1988; Schachter, 1982; Shapiro et al., 1984; Veroff, Douvan, & Kulka, 1981a, 1981b). These studies have taught us relatively little, however, about *how* people change on their own.

Similar results are found in the literature on addictive behaviors. Certain treatment methods consistently demonstrate successful outcomes for alcoholism and other addictive behaviors (Miller & Hester, 1980, 1986). Self-change has been documented to occur with alcohol abuse, smoking, obesity, and opiate use (Cohen et al., 1989; Orford, 1985; Roizen, Cahaland, & Shanks, 1978; Schachter, 1982; Tuchfeld, 1981). Self-change of addictive behaviors is often misnamed "spontaneous remission," but such change involves external influence and individual commitment (Orford, 1985; Tuchfeld, 1981). These studies demonstrate that intentional modification of addictive behaviors occurs both with and without expert assistance.

Moreover, these changes involve a process that is not well understood.

Over the past 12 years, our research program has been dedicated to solving the puzzle of how people intentionally change their behavior with and without psychotherapy. We have been searching for the structure of change that underlies both self-mediated and treatment-facilitated modification of addictive and other problem behaviors. We have concentrated on the phenomenon of intentional change as opposed to societal, developmental, or imposed change. Our basic question can be framed as follows: Because successful change of complex addictions can be demonstrated in both psychotherapy and self-change, are there basic, common principles that can reveal the structure of change occurring with and without psychotherapy?

This article provides a comprehensive summary of the research on the basic constructs of a model that helps us understand self-initiated and professionally assisted changes of addictive behaviors. The key transtheoretical concepts of the stages and processes of change are examined, and their applications to a variety of addictive behaviors and populations are reviewed. This transtheoretical model offers an integrative perspective on the structure of intentional change.

Stages of Change

One objective of treatment outcome research in the addictions is to establish the efficacy of interventions. However, study after study demonstrates that not all clients suffering from an addictive disorder improve: Some drop out of treatment, and others relapse following brief improvement (Kanfer, 1986; Marlatt & Gordon, 1985). Inadequate motivation, resistance to therapy, defensiveness, and inability to relate are client variables frequently invoked to account for the imperfect outcomes of the change enterprise. Inadequate techniques, theory, and relationship skills on the part of the therapist are intervention variables frequently blamed for lack of therapeutic success.

In our earliest research we found it necessary to ask *when* changes occur, in order to explain the relative contributions of client and intervention variables and to understand the underlying structure of behavior change (DiClemente & Prochaska, 1982; Prochaska & DiClemente, 1983). Individu-

als modifying addictive behaviors move through a series of stages from precontemplation to maintenance. A linear schema of the stages was discovered in research with smokers attempting to quit on their own and with smokers in professional treatment programs (DiClemente & Prochaska, 1982). People were perceived as progressing linearly from precontemplation to contemplation, then from preparation to action, and finally into maintenance. Precursors of this stage model can be found in the writings of Horn and Waingrow (1966), Cashdan (1973), and Egan (1975). Variations of and alternatives to our stage model can be found in more recent writings of Beitman (1986); Brownell, Marlatt, Lichtenstein, and Wilson (1986); Dryden (1986); and Marlatt and Gordon (1985).

Several lines of research support the stages of change construct (Prochaska & DiClemente, 1992). Stages of change have been assessed in outpatient therapy clients as well as self-changers (DiClemente & Hughes, 1990; DiClemente & Prochaska, 1985; DiClemente, Prochaska, & Gilbertini, 1985; Lam, McMahon, Priddy, & Gehred-Schultz, 1988; McConnaughy, DiClemente, Prochaska, & Velicer, 1989). Clusters of individuals have been found in each of the stages of change, whether the individuals were presenting for psychotherapy or attempting to change on their own. Stages of change have been ascertained by two different self-report methods: a discrete categorical measure, which assesses the stage from a series of mutually exclusive questions (DiClemente et al., 1991), and a continuous measure, which yields separate scales for precontemplation, contemplation, action, and maintenance (McConnaughy et al., 1989; McConnaughy, Prochaska, & Velicer, 1983).

In our original research we had identified five stages (Prochaska & DiClemente, 1982). But in principal component analyses of the continuous measure of stages, we consistently found only four scales (McConnaughy et al., 1983, 1989). We misinterpreted these data to mean that there were only four stages. For 7 years we worked with a four-stage model, omitting the stage between contemplation and action (Prochaska & DiClemente, 1983, 1985, 1986). We now realize that in the same studies on the continuous measures, cluster analyses had identified groups of individuals who were in the preparation stage (McConnaughy et al.,

1983, 1989). They scored high on both the contemplation and action scales. Unfortunately we paid more attention to principal component analyses rather than the cluster analyses and ignored the preparation stage. Recent research has supported the importance of assessing preparation as a fifth stage of change (DiClemente et al., 1991; Prochaska & DiClemente, 1992). Following are brief descriptions of each of the five stages.

Precontemplation is the stage at which there is no intention to change behavior in the foreseeable future. Many individuals in this stage are unaware or underaware of their problems. As G. K. Chesterton once said, "It isn't that they can't see the solution. It is that they can't see the problem." Families, friends, neighbors, or employees, however, are often well aware that the precontemplators have problems. When precontemplators present for psychotherapy, they often do so because of pressure from others. Usually they feel coerced into changing the addictive behavior by a spouse who threatens to leave, an employer who threatens to dismiss them, parents who threaten to disown them, or courts who threaten to punish them. They may even demonstrate change as long as the pressure is on. Once the pressure is off, however, they often quickly return to their old ways.

In our studies using the discrete categorization measurement of stages of change, we ask whether the individual is seriously intending to change the problem behavior in the near future, typically within the next 6 months. If not, he or she is classified as a precontemplator. Even precontemplators can *wish* to change, but this seems to be quite different from intending or seriously considering change in the next 6 months. Items that are used to identify precontemplation on the continuous stage of change measure include "As far as I'm concerned, I don't have any problems that need changing" and "I guess I have faults, but there's nothing that I really need to change." Resistance to recognizing or modifying a problem is the hallmark of precontemplation.

Contemplation is the stage in which people are aware that a problem exists and are seriously thinking about overcoming it but have not yet made a commitment to take action. People can remain stuck in the contemplation stage for long periods. In one study of self-changers, we followed a group of 200 smokers in the contemplation stage for 2 years. The modal response of this group was to remain in the contemplation stage for the entire 2 years of the project without ever moving to significant action (DiClemente & Prochaska, 1985; Prochaska & DiClemente, 1984).

The essence of the contemplation stage is communicated in an incident related by Benjamin (1987). He was walking home one evening when a stranger approached him and inquired about the whereabouts of a certain street. Benjamin pointed it out to the stranger and provided specific instructions. After readily understanding and accepting the instructions, the strange began to walk in the opposite direction. Benjamin said, "You are headed in the wrong direction." The stranger replied, "Yes, I know. I am not quite ready yet." This is contemplation: knowing where you want to go but not quite ready yet.

Another important aspect of the contemplation stage is the weighing of the pros and cons of the problem and the solution to the problem. Contemplators appear to struggle with their positive evaluations of the addictive behavior and the amount of effort, energy, and loss it will cost to overcome the problem (DiClemente, 1991; Prochaska & DiClemente, 1992; Velicer, DiClemente, Prochaska, & Brandenburg, 1985). On discrete measures, individuals who state that they are seriously considering changing the addictive behavior in the next 6 months are classified as contemplators. On the continuous measure these individuals would be endorsing such items as "I have a problem and I really think I should work on it" and "I've been thinking that I might want to change something about myself." Serious consideration of problem resolution is the central element of contemplation.

Preparation is a stage that combines intention and behavioral criteria. Individuals in this stage are intending to take action in the next month and have unsuccessfully taken action in the past year. As a group, individuals who are prepared for action report some small behavioral changes, such as smoking five cigarettes less or delaying their first cigarette of the day for 30 minutes longer than precontemplators or contemplators (DiClemente et al., 1991). Although they have made some reductions in their problem behaviors, individuals in the preparation stage have not yet reached a criterion for effective action, such as abstinence from smoking, alcohol abuse, or heroin use. They are intending, however, to take such action in the very near future. On the continuous measure they score high on both the contemplation and action scales. Some investigators prefer to conceptualize the preparation stage as the early stirrings of the action stage. We originally called it *decision making*.

Action is the stage in which individuals modify their behavior, experiences, or environment in order to overcome their problems. Action involves the most overt behavioral changes and requires considerable commitment of time and energy. Modifications of the addictive behavior made in the action stage tend to be most visible and receive the greatest external recognition. People, including professionals, often erroneously equate action with change. As a consequence, they overlook the requisite work that prepares changers for action and the important efforts necessary to maintain the changes following action.

Individuals are classified in the action stage if they have successfully altered the addictive behavior for a period of from 1 day to 6 months. Successfully altering the addictive behavior means reaching a particular criterion, such as abstinence. With smoking, for example, cutting down by 50% and changing to lower-tar and -nicotine cigarettes are behavior changes that can better prepare people for action but do not satisfy the field's criteria for successful action. On the continuous measure, individuals in the action stage endorse statements such as "I am really working hard to change" and "Anyone can talk about changing; I am actually doing something about it." They score high on the action scale and lower on the other scales. Modification of the target behavior to an acceptable criterion and significant overt efforts to change are the hallmarks of action.

Maintenance is the stage in which people work to prevent relapse and consolidate the gains attained during action. Traditionally, maintenance was viewed as a static stage. However, maintenance is a continuation, not an absence, of change. For addictive behaviors this stage extends from 6 months to an indeterminate period past the initial action. For some behaviors maintenance can be considered to last a lifetime. Being able to remain free of the addictive behavior and being able to consistently engage in a new incompatible behavior for more than 6 months are the criteria for considering someone to be in the maintenance stage. On the continuous measure, representative maintenance items are "I may need a boost right now

to help me maintain the changes I've already made" and "I'm here to prevent myself from having a relapse of my problem." Stabilizing behavior change and avoiding relapse are the hallmarks of maintenance.

Spiral Pattern of Change

As is now well-known, most people taking action to modify addictions do not successfully maintain their gains on their first attempt. With smoking, for example, successful self-changers make an average of from three to four action attempts before they become long-term maintainers (Schachter, 1982). Many New Year's resolvers report 5 or more years of consecutive pledges before maintaining the behavioral goal for at least 6 months (Norcross & Vangarelli, 1989). Relapse and recycling through the stages occur quite frequently as individuals attempt to modify or cease addictive behaviors. Variations of the stage model are being used increasingly by behavior change specialists to investigate the dynamics of relapse (e.g., Brownell et al., 1986; Donovan & Marlatt, 1988).

Because relapse is the rule rather than the exception with addictions, we found that we needed to modify our original stage model. Initially we conceptualized change as a linear progression through the stages; people were supposed to progress simply and discretely through each step. Linear progression is a possible but relatively rare phenomenon with addictive behaviors.

A spiral pattern can be used to illustrate how most people actually move through the stages of change. In this spiral pattern, people can progress from contemplation to preparation to action to maintenance, but most individuals will relapse. During relapse, individuals regress to an earlier stage. Some relapsers feel like failures—embarrassed, ashamed, and guilty. These individuals become demoralized and resist thinking about behavior change. As a result, they return to the precontemplation stage and can remain there for various periods of time. Approximately 15% of smokers who relapsed in our self-change research regressed back to the precontemplation stage (Prochaska & DiClemente, 1986).

Fortunately, this research indicates that the vast majority of relapsers—85% of smokers, for example—recycle back to the contemplation or preparation stages (Prochaska & DiClemente, 1984). They begin to consider plans for their next action attempt while trying to learn from their recent efforts. To take another example, fully 60% of unsuccessful New Year's resolvers make the same pledge the next year (Norcross, Ratzin, & Payne, 1989; Norcross & Vangarelli, 1989). The spiral model suggests that most relapsers do not revolve endlessly in circles and that they do not regress all the way back to where they began. Instead, each time relapsers recycle through the stages, they potentially learn from their mistakes and can try something different the next time around (DiClemente et al., 1991).

On any one trial, successful behavior change is limited in the absolute numbers of individuals who are able to achieve maintenance (Cohen et al., 1989; Schachter, 1982). Nevertheless, in a cohort of individuals, the number of successes continues to increase gradually over time. However, a large number of individuals remain in contemplation and precontemplation stages. Ordinarily, the more action taken, the better the prognosis. Much more research is needed to better distinguish those who benefit from recycling from those who end up spinning their wheels.

Additional investigations will also be required to explain the idiosyncratic patterns of movement through the stages of change. Although some transitions, such as from contemplation to preparation, are much more likely than others, some people may move from one stage to any other stage at any time. Each stage represents a period of time as well as a set of tasks needed for movement to the next stage. Although the time an individual spends in each stage may vary, the tasks to be accomplished are assumed to be invariant.

Treatment Implications

Professionals frequently design excellent action-oriented treatment and self-help programs but then are disappointed when only a small percentage of addicted people register, or when large numbers drop out of the program after registering. To illustrate, in a major health maintenance organization (HMO) on the West Coast, over 70% of the eligible smokers said they would take advantage of a professionally developed self-help program if one was offered (Orleans et al., 1988). A sophisticated action-oriented program was developed and of-

fered with great publicity. A total of 4% of the smokers signed up. As another illustration, Schmid, Jeffrey, and Hellerstedt (1989) compared four different recruitment strategies for home-based intervention programs for smoking cessation and weight control. The recruitment rates ranged from 1% to 5% of those eligible for smoking cessation programs and from 3% to 12% for those eligible for weight control programs.

The vast majority of addicted people are *not* in the action stage. Aggregating across studies and populations (Abrams, Follick, & Biener, 1988; Gottlieb, Galavotti, McCuan, & McAlister, 1990; Pallonen, Fava, Salonen, & Prochaska, 1992), 10–15% of smokers are prepared for action, approximately 30–40% are in the contemplation stage, and 50–60% are in the precontemplation stage. If these data hold for other populations and problems, then professionals approaching communities and worksites with only action-oriented programs are likely to underserve, misserve, or not serve the majority of their target population.

Moving from recruitment rates to treatment outcomes, we have found that the amount of progress clients make following intervention tends to be a function of their pretreatment stage of change (e. g., Prochaska & DiClemente, 1992; Prochaska, Norcross, Fowler, Follick, & Abrams, 1992). Figure 5.1 presents the percentage of 570 smokers who were not smoking at four follow-ups over an 18-month period as a function of the stage of change before random assignment to four home-based self-help programs. Figure 5.1 indicates that the amount of success smokers reported after treatment was directly related to the stage they were in before treatment (Prochaska & DiClemente, 1992). To treat all of these smokers as if they were the same would be naive. And yet that is what we traditionally have done in many of our treatment programs.

If clients progress from one stage to the next during the first month of treatment, they can double their chances of taking action during the initial 6 months of the program. Of the precontemplators who were still in precontemplation at 1-month follow-up, only 3% took action by 6 months. For the precontemplators who progressed to contemplation at 1 month, 7% took action by 6 months. Similarly, of the contemplators who remained in contemplation at 1 month, only 20% took action by 6 months. At 1 month, 41% of the

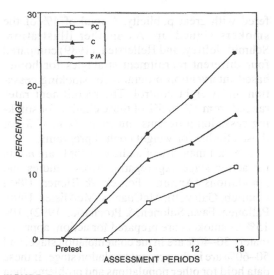

FIGURE 5.1 ■ Percentage abstinent over 18 months for smokers in precontemplation (PC), contemplation (C), and preparation (P/A) stages before treatment ($N = 570$).

contemplators who progressed to the preparation stage attempted to quit by 6 months. These data demonstrate that treatment programs designed to help people progress just one stage in a month can double the chances of participants taking action on their own in the near future (Prochaska & DiClemente, 1992).

Mismatching Stage and Treatment

A person's stage of change provides proscriptive as well as prescriptive information on treatments of choice. Action-oriented therapies may be quite effective with individuals who are in the preparation or action stages. These same programs may be ineffective or detrimental, however, with individuals in precontemplation or contemplation stages.

An intensive action- and maintenance-oriented smoking cessation program for cardiac patients was highly successful for those patients in action and ready for action. This same program failed, however, with smokers in the precontemplation and contemplation stages (Ockene, Ockene, & Kristellar, 1988). Patients in this special care program received personal counseling in the hospital and monthly telephone counseling calls for 6 months following hospitalization. Of the patients

who began the program in action or preparation stages, an impressive 94% were not smoking at 6-month follow-up. This percentage is significantly higher than the 66% nonsmoking rate of the patients in similar stages who received regular care for their smoking problem. The special care program had no significant effects, however, with patients in the precontemplation and contemplation stages. For patients in these stages, regular care did as well or better.

Independent of the treatment received, there were clear relationships between pretreatment stage and outcome. Twenty-two percent of all precontemplators, 43% of the contemplators, and 76% of those in action or prepared for action at the start of the study were not smoking 6 months later.

A mismatched stage effect occurred with another smoking program. An HMO-based self-help smoking cessation program for pregnant women was successful with patients prepared for action but had negligible impact on those in the precontemplation stage. Of the women in the preparation stage who received a series of seven self-help booklets through the mail, 38% were not smoking at the end of pregnancy (which was approximately 6 months posttreatment). This was triple the 12% success rate obtained for those who received regular care of advice and fact sheets. For precontemplators, however, 6% of those receiving special care and 6% receiving regular care were not smoking at the end of pregnancy (Ershoff, Mullen, & Quinn, 1987). These two illustrative studies portend the potential importance of matching treatments to the client's stage of change (DiClemente, 1991; Prochaska, 1991).

Stage Movements During Treatment

What progress do patients in formal treatment evidence on the stages of change? In a cross-sectional study we compared the stages of change scores of 365 individuals presenting for psychotherapy with 166 clients currently engaged in therapy (Prochaska & Costa, 1989). Patients entering therapy could usually be characterized as prepared for action because their highest score was on the contemplation scale and second highest was on the action scale. The contemplation and action scores crossed over for patients in the midst of treatment.

Patients in the middle of therapy could be characterized as being in the action stage because their highest score was on the action scale. Compared with patients beginning treatment, those in the middle of therapy were significantly higher on the action scale and significantly lower on the contemplation and precontemplation scales.

We interpreted these cross-sectional data as indicating that, over time, patients who remained in treatment progressed from being prepared for action into taking action. That is, they shifted from thinking about their problems to doing things to overcome them. Lowered precontemplation scores also indicated that, as engagement in therapy increased, patients reduced their defensiveness and resistance. The vast majority of the 166 patients who were in the action stage were participating in more traditional insight-oriented psychotherapies. The progression from contemplation to action is postulated to be essential for beneficial outcome, regardless of whether the treatment is action oriented or insight oriented (also see Wachtel, 1977, 1987).

This crossover pattern from contemplation to action was also found in a longitudinal study of a behavior therapy program for weight control (Prochaska, Norcross, et al., 1992). Figure 5.2 presents the stages of change scores at pre- and midtreatment. As a group, these subjects entering treatment could be characterized as prepared for action. During the first half of treatment, members of this contingent progressed into the action stage, with their contemplation scores decreasing significantly and their action scores increasing significantly.

The more clients progressed into action early in therapy, the more successful they were in losing weight by the end of treatment. The stages of change scores were the second-best predictors of outcome; they were better predictors than age, socioeconomic status, problem severity and duration, goals and expectations, self-efficacy, and social support. The only variables that outperformed the stages of change as outcome predictors were the processes of change the clients used early in therapy.

Processes of Change

The stages of change represent a temporal dimension that allows us to understand *when* particular

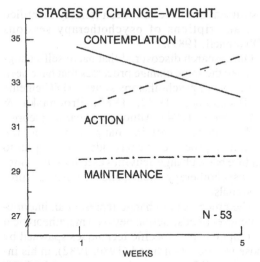

FIGURE 5.2 ■ A longitudinal comparison of stages of change scores for clients before (Week 1) and midway through (Week 5) a behavioral program for weight reduction.

shifts in attitudes, intentions, and behaviors occur. The processes of change are a second major dimension of the transtheoretical model that enable us to understand *how* these shifts occur. Change processes are covert and overt activities and experiences that individuals engage in when they attempt to modify problem behaviors. Each process is a broad category encompassing multiple techniques, methods, and interventions traditionally associated with disparate theoretical orientations. These change processes can be used within therapy sessions, between therapy sessions, or without therapy sessions.

The change processes were first identified theoretically in a comparative analysis of the leading systems of psychotherapy (Prochaska, 1979). The processes were selected by examining recommended change techniques across different theories, which explains the term *transtheoretical*. At least 10 subsequent principal component analyses on the processes of change items, conducted on various response formats and diverse samples, have yielded similar patterns (Norcross & Prochaska, 1986; Prochaska & DiClemente, 1983; Prochaska & Norcross, 1983; Prochaska, Velicer, DiClemente, & Fava, 1988). Extensive validity and reliability data on the processes have been reported elsewhere (Prochaska et al., 1988). The processes are typically assessed by means of a self-report instrument but have also been reliably identified in transcriptions of psychotherapy sessions (O'Connell, 1989).

Our research discovered that naive self-changers used the same change processes that have been at the core of psychotherapy systems (DiClemente & Prochaska, 1982, 1985; Prochaska & DiClemente, 1984). Although disparate theories will emphasize certain change processes, the breadth of processes we have identified appear to capture basic change activities used by self-changers, psychotherapy clients, and mental health professionals.

The processes of change represent an intermediate level of abstraction between metatheoretical assumptions and specific techniques spawned by those theories. Goldfried (1980, 1982), in his influential call for a rapprochement among the therapies, independently recommended change principles or processes as the most fruitful level for psychotherapy integration. Subsequent research on proposed therapeutic commonalities (Grencavage & Norcross, 1990) and agreement on treatment recommendations (Giunta, Saltzman, & Norcross, 1991) has supported Goldfried's view of change processes as the content area or level of abstraction most amenable to theoretical convergence.

Although there are 250–400 different psychological therapies (Herink, 1980; Karasu, 1986) based on divergent theoretical assumptions, we have been able to identify only 12 different processes of change based on principal components analysis. Similarly, although self-changers use over 130 techniques to quit smoking, these techniques can be summarized by a much smaller set of change processes (Prochaska et al., 1988).

Table 5.1 presents the 10 processes receiving the most theoretical and empirical support in our work, along with their definitions and representative examples of specific interventions. A common and finite set of change processes has been repeatedly identified across such diverse problem areas as smoking, psychological distress, and obesity (Prochaska & DiClemente, 1985). There are striking similarities in the frequency with which the change processes were used across these problems. When processes were ranked in terms of how frequently they were used for each of these three problem behaviors, the rankings were nearly identical. Helping relationships, consciousness raising, and self-liberation, for example, were the top three ranked processes across problems, whereas contingency management and stimulus control were the lowest-ranked processes.

TABLE 5.1. Titles, Definitions, and Representative Interventions of the Processes of Change

Process	Definitions: Interventions
Consciousness raising	Increasing information about self and problem: observations, confrontations, interpretations, bibliotherapy
Self-reevaluation	Assessing how one feels and thinks about oneself with respect to a problem: value clarification, imagery, corrective emotional experience
Self-liberation	Choosing and commitment to act or belief in ability to change: decision-making therapy, New Year's resolutions, logotherapy techniques, commitment enhancing techniques
Counterconditioning	Substituting alternatives for problem behaviors: relaxation, desensitization, assertion, positive self-statements
Stimulus control	Avoiding or countering stimuli that elicit problem behaviors: restructuring one's environment (e.g., removing alcohol or fattening foods), avoiding high-risk cues, fading techniques
Reinforcement management	Rewarding oneself or being rewarded by others for making changes: contingency contracts, overt and covert reinforcement, self-reward
Helping relationships	Being open and trusting about problems with someone who cares: therapeutic alliance, social support, self-help groups
Dramatic relief	Experiencing and expressing feelings about one's problems and solutions: psychodrama, grieving losses, role playing
Environmental reevaluation	Assessing how one's problem affects physical environment: empathy training, documentaries
Social liberation	Increasing alternatives for nonproblem behaviors available in society: advocating for rights of repressed, empowering, policy interventions

Significant differences occurred, however, in the absolute frequency of the use of change processes across problems. Individuals relied more on helping relationships and consciousness raising for overcoming psychological distress than they did for weight control and smoking cessation. Overweight individuals relied more on self-liberation and stimulus control than did distressed individuals (Prochaska & DiClemente, 1985).

Processes as Predictors of Change

The processes have been potent predictors of change for both therapy changers and self-changers. As indicated earlier, in a behavioral weight control program, the processes used early in treatment were the single best predictors of outcome (Prochaska, Norcross, et al., 1992). For self-changers with smoking, the change processes were better predictors of progress across the stages of change than were a set of 17 predictor variables, including demographics, problem history and severity, health history, withdrawal symptoms, and reasons for smoking (Prochaska, DiClemente, Velicer, Ginpil, & Norcross, 1985; Wilcox, Prochaska, Velicer, & DiClemente, 1985).

The stages and processes of change combined with a decisional balance measure were able to predict with 93% accuracy which patients would drop out prematurely from psychotherapy. At the beginning of therapy, premature terminators were much more likely to be in the precontemplation stage. They rated the cons of therapy as higher than the pros, and they relied more on willpower and stimulus control than did clients who continued in therapy or terminated appropriately (Medieros & Prochaska, 1992).

Integrating the Processes and Stages of Change

The prevailing zeitgeist in psychotherapy is the integration of leading systems of psychotherapy (Norcross, Alford, & DeMichele, 1992; Norcross & Goldfried, 1992). Psychotherapy could be enhanced by the integration of the profound insights of psychoanalysis, the powerful techniques of behaviorism, the experiential methods of cognitive

therapies, and the liberating philosophy of existentialism. Although some psychotherapists insist that such theoretical integration is philosophically impossible, ordinary people in the natural environment can be remarkably effective in finding practical means of synthesizing powerful change processes.

The same is true in addiction treatment and research. There are multiple interventions but little integration across theories (Miller & Hester, 1980). One promising approach to integration is to begin to match particular interventions to key client characteristics. The Institute of Medicine's (1989) report on prevention and treatment of alcohol problems identifies the stages of change as a key matching variable. A National Cancer Institute report of self-help interventions for smokers also used the stages as a framework for integrating a variety of interventions (Glynn, Boyd, & Gruman, 1990). The transtheoretical model offers a promising approach to integration by combining the stages and processes of change.

A Cross-Sectional Perspective

One of the most important findings to emerge from our self-change research is an integration between the processes and stages of change (DiClemente et al., 1991; Norcross, Prochaska, & DiClemente, 1991; Prochaska & DiClemente, 1983, 1984). Table 5.2 demonstrates this integration from cross-sectional research involving thousands of self-changers representing each of the stages of change for smoking cessation and weight loss. Using the data as a point of departure, we have interpreted how particular processes can be applied or avoided at each stage of change. During the precontemplation stage, individuals used eight of the change processes significantly less than people in any of the other stages. Precontemplators processed less information about their problems, devoted less time and energy to reevaluating themselves, and experienced fewer emotional reactions to the negative aspects of their problems. Furthermore, they were less open with significant others about their problems, and they did little to shift their attention or their environment in the direction of overcoming problems. In therapy, these would be the most resistant or the least active clients.

Individuals in the contemplation stage were

Table 5.2. Stages of Change in Which Particular Processes of Change Are Emphasized

Precontemplation	Contemplation	Preparation	Action	Maintenance
Consciousness raising				
Dramatic relief				
Environmental reevaluation				
	Self-reevaluation			
		Self-liberation		
			Reinforcement management	
			Helping relationships	
			Counterconditioning	
			Stimulus control	

most open to consciousness-raising techniques, such as observations, confrontations, and interpretations, and they were much more likely to use bibliotherapy and other educational techniques (Prochaska & DiClemente, 1984). Contemplators were also open to dramatic relief experiences, which raise emotions and lead to a lowering of negative affect if the person changes. As individuals became more conscious of themselves and the nature of their problems, they were more likely to reevaluate their values, problems, and themselves both affectively and cognitively. The more central their problems were to their self-identity, the more their reevaluation involved altering their sense of self. Contemplators also reevaluated the effects their addictive behaviors had on their environments, especially the people with whom they were closest. They struggled with questions such as "How do I think and feel about living in a deteriorating environment that places my family or friends at increasing risk for disease, poverty, or imprisonment?"

Movement from precontemplation to contemplation and movement through the contemplation stage entailed increased use of cognitive, affective, and evaluative processes of change. Some of these changes continued during the preparation stage. In addition, individuals in preparation began to take small steps toward action. They used counterconditioning and stimulus control to begin reducing their use of addictive substances or to control the situations in which they relied on such substances (DiClemente et al., 1991).

During the action stage, people endorsed higher levels of self-liberation or willpower. They increasingly believed that they had the autonomy to change their lives in key ways. Successful action also entailed effective use of behavioral processes, such as counterconditioning and stimulus control, in order to modify the conditional stimuli that frequently prompt relapse. Insofar as action was a particularly stressful stage, individuals relied increasingly on support and understanding from helping relationships.

Just as preparation for action was essential for success, so too was preparation for maintenance. Successful maintenance builds on each of the processes that came before. Specific preparation for maintenance entailed an assessment of the conditions under which a person was likely to relapse and development of alternative responses for coping with such conditions without resorting to self-defeating defenses and pathological responses. Perhaps most important was the sense that one was becoming the kind of person one wanted to be. Continuing to apply counterconditioning and stimulus control was most effective when it was based on the conviction that maintaining change supports a sense of self that was highly valued by oneself and at least one significant other.

A Longitudinal Perspective

Cross-sectional studies have inherent limitations for assessing behavior change, and we, therefore, undertook research on longitudinal patterns of change. Four major patterns of behavior change were identified in a 2-year longitudinal study of smokers (Prochaska, DiClemente, Velicer, Rossi, & Guadagnoli, 1992): (a) *Stable* patterns involved subjects who remained in the same stage for the entire 2 years; (b) *progressive* patterns involved linear movement from one stage to the next; (c) *regressive* patterns involved movement to an earlier stage of change; and (d) *recycling* patterns involved two or more revolutions through the stages of change over the 2-year period.

The stable pattern can be illustrated by the 27 smokers who remained in the precontemplation stage at all five rounds of data collection. Figure 5.3 presents these precontemplators' standardized scores ($M = 50$, $SD = 10$) for the 10 change processes being used at 6-month intervals over the 2-year period. All 10 processes remained remarkably stable over the 2-year period, demonstrating little increase or decrease over time.

This figure graphically illustrates what individuals resistant to change were likely to be experiencing and doing. Eight of 10 change processes, like self-reevaluation and self-liberation, were between 0.4 and 1.4 standard deviations below the mean (i.e., 50). In brief, these subjects were doing very little to control or modify themselves or their problem behavior.

This static pattern was in marked contrast to the pattern representing people who progressed from contemplation to maintenance over the 2-year study. Significantly, many of the change processes did not simply increase linearly as individuals progressed from contemplation to maintenance. Self-reevaluation, consciousness raising, and dramatic relief—processes most associated with the contemplation stage—demonstrated significant decreases as self-changers moved through the action stage into maintenance. Conversely, self-liberation, stimulus control, contingency control, and counterconditioning—processes most associated with the action stage—evidenced dramatic increases as self-changers moved from contemplation to action. These change processes then leveled off or decreased when maintenance was reached (Prochaska, DiClemente, et al., 1992).

Progressive self-changers demonstrated an almost ideal pattern of how change processes can be used most effectively over time. They seemed to increase the particular cognitive processes most important for the contemplation stage and then to increase more behavioral processes in the action and maintenance stages. Before overidealizing the

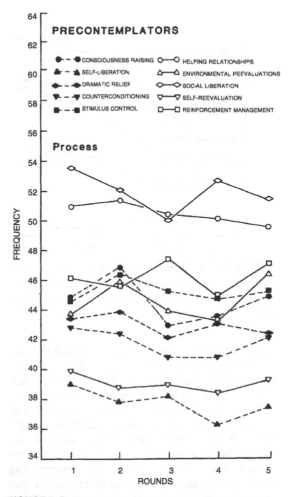

FIGURE 5.3 ■ Use of change processes (T scores) for 23 smokers who remained in the precontemplation stage at each of five assessment points over 2 years.

wisdom of self-changers, note that only 9 of 180 contemplators found their way through this progressive pattern without relapsing at least once.

The longitudinal results of the 53 clients completing a behavior therapy program for weight control provide additional support for an integration of the processes and stages of change (Prochaska, Norcross, et al., 1992). As mentioned earlier, this group progressed from contemplation to action during the 10-week therapy program. Figure 5.4 presents the six change processes that evidenced significant differences over the course of treatment. As predicted by the transtheoretical

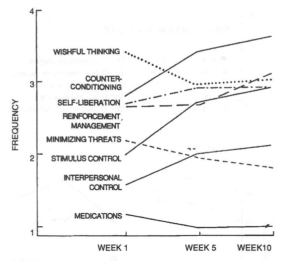

FIGURE 5.4 ■ Change processes that significantly increased or decreased during a 10-week behavioral program for weight reduction on a Likert scale ranging From 1 (*Never Use*) to 5 (*Almost Always Use*) (*N* = 53).

model, clients reported significantly greater use of four action-related change processes: counter-conditioning, stimulus control, interpersonal control, and contingency management. They also increased their reliance on social liberation and decreased their reliance on medications, wishful thinking, and minimizing threats. In other words, these clients were substituting alternative responses for overeating; they were restructuring their environments to include more stimuli that evoked moderate eating; they reduced stimuli that prompted overeating; they modified relationships to encourage healthful eating; and they paid more attention to social alternatives that allow greater freedom to keep from overeating.

Integrative Conclusions

Our search for how people intentionally modify addictive behaviors encompassed thousands of research participants attempting to alter, with and without psychotherapy, a myriad of addictive behaviors, including cigarette smoking, alcohol abuse, and obesity. From this and related research, we have discovered robust commonalities in how people modify their behavior. From our perspective the underlying structure of change is neither technique-oriented nor problem specific. The evidence supports a transtheoretical model entailing (a) a cyclical pattern of movement through specific stages of change, (b) a common set of processes of change, and (c) a systematic integration of the stages and processes of change.

Probably the most obvious and direct implication of our research is the need to assess the stage of a client's readiness for change and to tailor interventions accordingly. Although this step may be intuitively taken by many experienced clinicians, we have found few references to such tailoring before our research (Beutler & Clarkin, 1990; Norcross, 1991). A more explicit model would enhance efficient, integrative, and prescriptive treatment plans. Furthermore, this step of assessing stage and tailoring processes is rarely taken in a conscious and meaningful manner by self-changers in the natural environment. Vague notions of willpower, mysticism, and biotechnological revolutions dominate their perspectives on self-change (Mahoney & Thoreson, 1972).

We have determined that efficient self-change depends on doing the right things (processes) at the right time (stages). We have observed two frequent mismatches. First, some self-changers appear to rely primarily on change processes most indicated for the contemplation stage—consciousness raising, self-reevaluation—while they are moving into the action stage. They try to modify behaviors by becoming more aware, a common criticism of classical psychoanalysis: Insight alone does not necessarily bring about behavior change. Second, other self-changers rely primarily on change processes most indicated for the action stage—reinforcement management, stimulus control, counter-conditioning—without the requisite awareness, decision making, and readiness provided in the contemplation and preparation stages. They try to modify behavior without awareness, a common criticism of radical behaviorism: Overt action without insight is likely to lead to temporary change.

We have generated a number of tentative conclusions from our research that require empirical confirmation. Successful change of the addictions involves a progression through a series of stages. Most self-changers and psychotherapy patients will recycle several times through the stages before achieving long-term maintenance. Accordingly, intervention programs and personnel expecting people to progress linearly through the stages are likely to gather disappointing and discouraging results.

With regard to the processes of change, we have tentatively concluded that they are distinct and measurable both for self- and therapy changers. Similar processes appear to be used to modify diverse problems, and similar processes are used within, between, and without psychotherapy sessions. Dynamic measures of the processes and stages of change outperform static variables, like demographics and problem history, in predicting outcome.

Competing systems of psychotherapy have promulgated apparently rival processes of change. However, ostensibly contradictory processes can become complementary when embedded in the stages of change. Specifically, change processes traditionally associated with the experiential, cognitive, and psychoanalytic persuasions are most useful during the precontemplation and contemplation stages. Change processes traditionally associated with the existential and behavioral traditions, by contrast, are most useful during action and maintenance. People changing addictive behaviors with and without therapy can be remarkably resourceful in finding practical means of integrating the change processes, even if psychotherapy theorists have been historically unwilling or unable to do so. Attending effective self-changers in the natural environment and integrating effective change processes in the consulting room may be two keys to unlocking the elusive structure of how people change.

ACKNOWLEDGMENTS

This research was supported in part by Grants CA27821 and CA50087 from the National Cancer Institute.

REFERENCES

Abrams, D. B., Follick, M. J., & Biener, L. (1988, November). Individual versus group self-help smoking cessation at the workplace: Initial impact and 12-month outcomes. In T. Glynn (Chair), *Four National Cancer Institute–funded self-help smoking cessation trials: Interim results and emerging patterns*. Symposium conducted at the annual meeting of the Association for the Advancement of Behavior Therapy, New York.

Beitman, B. D. (1986). *The structure of individual psychotherapy*. New York: Guilford Press.

Benjamin, A. (1987). *The helping interview*. Boston: Houghton Mifflin.

Beutler, L. E., & Clarkin, J. F. (1990). *Systematic treatment selection*. New York: Brunner/Mazel.

Brownell, K. D., Marlatt, G. A., Lichtenstein, E., & Wilson G. T. (1986). Understanding and preventing relapse. *American Psychologist, 41*, 765–782.

Cashdan, S. (1973). *Interactional psychotherapy: Stages and strategies in behavioral change*. New York: Grune & Stratton.

Cohen, S., Lichtenstein, E., Prochaska, J. O., Rossi, J. S., Gritz, E. R., Carr, C. R., Orleans, C. T., Schoenbach, V. J., Biener, L., Abrams, D., DiClemente, C. C., Curry, S., Marlatt, G. A., Cummings, K. M., Emont, S. L., Giovino, G., & Ossip-Klein, D. (1989). Debunking myths about self-quitting: Evidence from 10 prospective studies of persons quitting smoking by themselves. *American Psychologist, 44*, 1355–1365.

DiClemente, C. C. (1991). Motivational interviewing and the stages of change. In W. R. Miller & S. Rollnick (Eds.), *Motivational interviewing: Preparing people for change* (pp. 191–202). New York: Guilford Press.

DiClemente, C. C., & Hughes, S. L. (1990). Stages of change profiles in alcoholism treatment. *Journal of Substance Abuse, 2*, 217–235.

DiClemente, C. C., & Prochaska, J. O. (1982). Self-change and therapy change of smoking behavior: A comparison of processes of change in cessation and maintenance. *Addictive Behaviors, 7*, 133–142.

DiClemente, C. C., & Prochaska, J. O. (1985). Processes and stages of change: Coping and competence in smoking behavior change. In S. Shiffman & T. A. Wills (Eds.), *Coping and substance abuse* (pp. 319–343). San Diego, CA: Academic Press.

DiClemente, C. C., Prochaska, J. O., Fairhurst, S. K., Velicer, W. F., Velasquez, M. M., & Rossi, J. S. (1991). The process of smoking cessation: An analysis of precontemplation, contemplation, and preparation stages of change. *Journal of Consulting and Clinical Psychology, 59*, 295–304.

DiClemente, C. C., Prochaska, J. O., & Gilbertini, M. (1985). Self-efficacy and the stages of self-change of smoking. *Cognitive Therapy and Research, 9*, 181–200.

Donovan, D. M., & Marlatt, G. A. (Eds.). (1988). *Assessment of addictive behaviors: Behavioral, cognitive, and physiological procedures*. New York: Guilford Press.

Dryden, W. (1986). Eclectic psychotherapies: A critique of leading approaches. In J. C. Norcross (Ed.), *Handbook of eclectic psychotherapy*. New York: Brunner/Mazel.

Egan, G. (1975). *The skilled helper: A model for systematic helping and interpersonal relating*. Monterey, CA: Brooks/Cole.

Ershoff, D. H., Mullen, P. D., & Quinn, V. (1987, December). *Self-help interventions for smoking cessation with pregnant women*. Paper presented at the Self-Help Intervention Workshop of the National Cancer Institute, Rockville, MD.

Giunta, L. C., Saltzman, N., & Norcross, J. C. (1991). Whither integration? An exploratory study of contention and convergence in the Clinical Exchange. *Journal of Integrative and Eclectic Psychotherapy, 10*, 117–129.

Glynn, T. J., Boyd, G. M., & Gruman, J. C. (1990). Essential elements of self-help/minimal intervention strategies for smoking cessation. *Health Education Quarterly, 17*, 329–345.

Goldfried, M. R. (1980). Toward the delineation of therapeutic change principles. *American Psychologist, 35*, 991–999.

Goldfried, M. R. (1982). *Converging themes in psychotherapy*. New York: Springer.

Gottlieb, N. H., Galavotti, C., McCuan, R. S., & McAlister, A. L. (1990). Specification of a social cognitive model predicting smoking cessation in a Mexican-American population: A prospective study. *Cognitive Therapy and Research, 14*, 529–542.

Grencavage, L. M., & Norcross, J. C. (1990). Where are the commonalities among the therapeutic common factors? *Professional Psychology: Research and Practice, 21*, 372–378.

Herink, R. (Ed.). (1980). *The psychotherapy handbook*. New York: Meridian.

Horn, D., & Waingrow, S. (1966). Some dimensions of a model for smoking behavior change. *American Journal of Public Health, 56*, 21–26.

Institute of Medicine. (1989). *Prevention and treatment of alcohol problems: Research opportunities*. Washington, DC: National Academy Press.

Kanfer, F. H. (1986). Implications of a self-regulation model of therapy for treatment of addictive behaviors. In W. R. Miller & N. Heather (Eds.), *Treating addictive behaviors: Processes of change* (pp. 29–50). New York: Plenum Press.

Karasu, T. B. (1986). The specificity versus nonspecificity dilemma: Toward identifying therapeutic change agents. *American Journal of Psychiatry, 143*, 687–695.

Lam, C. S., McMahon, B. T., Priddy, D. A., & Gehred-Schultz, A. (1988). Deficit awareness and treatment performance among traumatic head injury adults. *Brain Injury, 2*, 235–242.

Lambert, M. J., Shapiro, D. A., & Bergin, A. E. (1986). The effectiveness of psychotherapy. In S. L. Garfield & A. E. Bergin (Eds.), *Handbook of psychotherapy and behavior change* (3rd ed.). New York: Wiley.

Mahoney, M. J., & Thoreson, C. E. (1972). Behavioral self-control: Power to the person. *Educational Researcher, 1*, 5–7.

Marlatt, G. A., Baer, J. S., Donovan, D. M., & Divlahan, D. R. (1988). Addictive behavior: Etiology and treatment. *Annual Review of Psychology, 39*, 223–252.

Marlatt, G. A., & Gordon, J. R. (1985). *Relapse prevention: A self-control strategy for the maintenance of behavior change*. New York: Guilford Press.

McConnaughy, E. A., DiClemente, C. C., Prochaska, J. O., & Velicer, W. F. (1989). Stages of change in psychotherapy: A follow-up report. *Psychotherapy, 26*, 494–503.

McConnaughy, E. A., Prochaska, J. O., & Velicer, W. F. (1983). Stages of change in psychotherapy: Measurement and sample profiles. *Psychotherapy, 20*, 368–375.

Medieros, M., & Prochaska, J. O. (1992). *Predicting premature termination from psychotherapy*. Unpublished manuscript.

Miller, W. R., & Hester, R. R. (1980). Treating the problem drinker: Modern approaches. In W. R. Miller (Ed.), *The addictive behaviors: Treatment of alcoholism, drug abuse, smoking and obesity* (pp. 11–141). Oxford, England: Pergamon Press.

Miller, W. R., & Hester, R. R. (1986). The effectiveness of alcoholism treatment. In W. R. Miller & N. Heather (Eds.), *Treating addictive behaviors: Processes of change* (pp. 121–174). New York: Plenum Press.

Norcross, J. C. (1991). Prescriptive matching in psycho-therapy: Psychoanalysis for simple phobias? *Psychotherapy, 28*, 439–443.

Norcross, J. C., Alford, B. A., & DeMichele, J. T. (1992). The future of psychotherapy: Delphi data and concluding observations. *Psychotherapy, 29*, 150–158.

Norcross, J. C., & Goldfried, M. R. (Eds.). (1992). *Handbook of psychotherapy integration*. New York: Basic Books.

Norcross, J. C., & Prochaska, J. O. (1986). Psychotherapist heal thyself: 1. The psychological distress and self-change of psychologists, counselors, and laypersons. *Psychotherapy, 23*, 102–114.

Norcross, J. C., Prochaska, J. O., & DiClemente, C. C. (1991). *The stages and processes of behavior change: Two replications with weight control*. Unpublished manuscript.

Norcross, J. C., Ratzin, A. C., & Payne, D. (1989). Ringing in the New Year: The change processes and reported outcomes of resolutions. *Addictive Behaviors, 14*, 205–212.

Norcross, J. C., & Vangarelli, D. J. (1989). The resolution solution: Longitudinal examination of New Year's change attempts. *Journal of Substance Abuse, 1*, 127–134.

Ockene, J., Ockene, I., & Kristellar, J. (1988). *The coronary artery smoking intervention study*. Worcester, MA: National Heart, Lung, and Blood Institute.

O'Connell, D. (1989). *An observational coding scheme for therapists' processes of change*. Unpublished doctoral dissertation, University of Rhode Island, Kingston.

Orford, J. (1985). *Excessive appetites: A psychological view of addictions*. New York: Wiley.

Orleans, C. T., Schoenback, V. J., Salmon, M. A., Wagner, E. A., Pearson, D. C., Fiedler, J., Quade, D., Porter, C. Q., & Kaplan, B. A. (1988, November). Effectiveness of self-help quit smoking strategies. In T. Glynn (Chair), *Four National Cancer Institute–funded self-help smoking cessation trials: Interim results and emerging patterns*. Symposium presented at the annual meeting of the Association for the Advancement of Behavior Therapy, New York.

Pallonen, U. E., Fava, J. L., Salonen, J. T., & Prochaska, J. O. (1992). Readiness for smoking change among middle-aged Finnish men. *Addictive Behaviors, 17*, 415–423.

Prochaska, J. O. (1979). *Systems of psychotherapy: A transtheoretical analysis*. Homewood, IL: Dorsey Press.

Prochaska, J. O. (1991). Prescribing to the stages and levels of change. *Psychotherapy, 28*, 463–468.

Prochaska, J. O., & Costa, A. (1989). *A cross-sectional comparision of stages of change for pre-therapy and within-therapy clients*. Unpublished manuscript, University of Rhode Island, Kingston.

Prochaska, J. O., & DiClemente, C. C. (1982). Transtheoretical therapy: Toward a more integrative model of change. *Psychotherapy: Theory, Research and Practice, 20*, 161–173.

Prochaska, J. O., & DiClemente, C. C. (1983). Stages and processes of self-change in smoking: Toward an integrative model of change. *Journal of Consulting and Clinical Psychology, 5*, 390–395.

Prochaska, J. O., & DiClemente, C. C. (1984). *The transtheoretical approach: Crossing traditional boundaries of change*. Homewood, IL: Dorsey Press.

Prochaska, J. O., & DiClemente, C. C. (1985). Common processes of change in smoking, weight control, and psychological distress. In S. Shiffman & T. Wills (Eds.), *Coping and substance abuse* (pp. 345–363). San Diego, CA: Academic Press.

Prochaska, J. O., & DiClemente, C. C. (1986). Toward a comprehensive model of change. In W. R. Miller & N. Heather (Eds.), *Treating addictive behaviors: Processes of change* (pp. 3–27). New York: Plenum Press.

Prochaska, J. O., & DiClemente, C. C. (1992). Stages of change in the modification of problem behaviors. In M. Hersen, R. M. Eisler, & P. M. Miller (Eds.), *Progress in behavior modification* (pp. 184–214). Sycamore, IL: Sycamore Press.

Prochaska, J. O., DiClemente, C. C., Velicer, W. F., Ginpil, S., & Norcross, J. C. (1985). Predicting change in smoking status for self-changers. *Addictive Behaviors, 10,* 395–406.

Prochaska, J. O., & Norcross, J. C. (1983). Psychotherapists' perspectives on treating themselves and their clients for psychic distress. *Professional Psychology: Research and Practice, 14,* 642–655.

Prochaska, J. O., Norcross, J. C., Fowler, J. L., Follick, M. J., & Abrams, D. B. (1992). Attendance and outcome in a worksite weight control program: Processes and stages of change as process and predictor variables. *Addictive Behaviors, 17,* 35–45.

Prochaska, J. O., Velicer, W. F., DiClemente, C. C., & Fava, J. S. (1988). Measuring processes of change: Applications to the cessation of smoking. *Journal of Consulting and Clinical Psychology, 56,* 520–528.

Prochaska, J. O., Velicer, W. F., Guadagnoli, E., Rossi, J. S., & DiClemente, C. C. (1991). Patterns of change: Dynamic typology applied to smoking cessation. *Multivariate Behavioral Research, 26,* 83–107.

Rice, L. N., & Greenberg, L. (Eds.). (1984). *Patterns of change.* New York: Guilford Press.

Roizen, R., Cahaland, D., & Shanks, R. (1978). Spontaneous remission among untreated problem drinkers. In D. Randell (Ed.), *Longitudinal research on drug use: Empirical findings and methodological issues.* Washington, DC: Hemisphere.

Schachter, S. (1982). Recidivism and self-cure of smoking and obesity. *American Psychologist, 37,* 436–444.

Schmid, T. L., Jeffrey, R. W., & Hellerstedt, W. L. (1989). Direct mail recruitment to home-based smoking and weight control programs: A comparison of strengths. *Preventive Medicine, 18,* 503–517.

Shapiro, S., Skinner, E., Kessler, L., Van Korff, M., German, P., Tischler, G., Leon, P., Bendham, L., Cottler, L., & Regier, D. (1984). Utilization of health and mental health services. *Archives of General Psychiatry, 41,* 971–978.

Smith, M. L., Glass, G. V., & Miller, T. I. (1980). *The benefits of psychotherapy.* Baltimore: John Hopkins University Press.

Tuchfeld, B. (1981). Spontaneous remission in alcoholics: Empirical observations and theoretical implications. *Journal of Studies on Alcohol, 42,* 626–641.

Velicer, W. F., DiClemente, C. C., Prochaska, J. O., & Brandenburg, N. (1985). A decisional balance measure for assessing and predicting smoking status. *Journal of Personality and Social Psychology, 48,* 1279–1289.

Veroff, J., Douvan, E., & Kulka, R. A. (1981a). *The inner America.* New York: Basic Books.

Veroff, J., Douvan, E., & Kulka, R. A. (1981b). *Mental health in America.* New York: Basic Books.

Wachtel, P. L. (1977). *Psychoanalysis and behavior therapy: Toward an integration.* New York: Basic Books.

Wachtel, P. L. (1987). *Action and insight.* New York: Guilford Press.

Wilcox, N., Prochaska, J. O., Velicer, W. F., & DiClemente, C. C. (1985). Client characteristics as predictors of self-change in smoking cessation. *Addictive Behaviors, 40,* 407–412.

READING 6

Reasoned Action and Social Reaction: Willingness and Intention as Independent Predictors of Health Risk

Frederick X. Gibbons, Meg Gerrard, Hart Blanton, and
Daniel W. Russell • Iowa State University

Three* studies are described that assess elements of a new model of adolescent health-risk behavior, the prototype/willingness (P/W) model (F. X. Gibbons & M. Gerrard, 1995, 1997). The 1st analysis examined whether a central element of the prototype model, behavioral willingness, adds significantly to behavioral expectation in predicting adolescents' smoking behavior. The 2nd set of analyses used structural-equation-modeling procedures to provide the 1st test of the complete model in predicting college students' pregnancy-risk behavior. Finally, the 3rd study used confirmatory factor analysis to assess the independence of elements of the model from similar elements in other health behavior models. Results of the 3 studies provided support for the prototype model and, in particular, for 2 of its primary contentions: (a) that much adolescent health-risk behavior is not planned and (b) that willingness and intention are related but independent constructs, each of which can be an antecedent to risk behavior.

Most models of attitude–behavior consistency are based on an assumption that the decision to engage in a particular behavior is the result of a rational process that is goal-oriented and that follows a logical sequence. That is, behavioral options are considered, consequences or outcomes of each are evaluated, and a decision to act or not act is made. That decision is generally referred to as *behavioral intention* (BI). This approach is perhaps best exemplified by Fishbein and Ajzen's (1980) theory of reasoned action and its update, Ajzen's theory of planned behavior (Ajzen, 1985, 1988, 1991), but it is typical of a number of social

psychological theories (e.g., subjective expected utility theory, Ronis, 1992; protection motivation theory, Rogers, 1983). A central tenet of these rational approaches is that because all behaviors involve premeditation or planning, the only proximal antecedent of a particular action is the individual's intention to engage in that action.

These approaches have fared very well in predicting behavior. In the domain of health, for example, rational-based theories have been very

*The original article contained three studies, only studies 1 and 2 are included here.

effective at predicting a variety of health-promoting actions, such as dieting (Schifter & Ajzen, 1985), exercise (Godin, Valois, & Lepage, 1993), reducing dietary fat (Sparks & Shepherd, 1992), condom use (Fisher, Fisher, & Rye, 1995), and health screening (McCaul, Sandgren, O'Neill, & Hinsz, 1993; see Conner & Sparks, 1996; Sheppard, Hartwick, & Warshaw, 1988, for reviews). This success is not surprising given that these are intentional behaviors that are premeditated and logical. They are also goal-oriented and therefore fit well within a rational framework. As Ajzen (1985) has suggested, "strictly speaking, every intended behavior is a goal whose attainment is subject to some degree of uncertainty" (p. 24).

Not all behaviors are logical or rational, however. Again using health as an example, it would be hard to argue that behaviors that impair one's health or well-being, such as having sex without contraception when pregnancy is not desired, or drunk driving, are either goal-oriented or rational; the question of whether they are premeditated or intended remains open. Nonetheless, these behaviors are common, especially among young persons. In fact, the prevalence of some of them seems to be increasing of late (University of Michigan Survey Research Center, 1995). In general, predicting this type of behavior is more difficult for models that rely on an assumption of rational forethought (Boldero, Moore, & Rosenthal, 1992; L. K. Brown, DiClemente, & Reynolds, 1991; Johnson, 1988; Kilty, 1978; Stacy, Bentler, & Flay, 1994; cf. Conner & Sparks, 1996). In particular, whereas rational or deliberative theories, such as the theories of reasoned action and planned behavior, have been successful at predicting intentions to engage in some health-impairing behaviors, such as reckless driving (Parker, Manstead, Stradling, Reason, & Baxter, 1992), excess drinking (Schlegel, D'Avernas, Zanna, DeCourville, & Manske, 1992), and smoking (Godin, Valois, Lepage, & Desharnais, 1992), they have been less effective at predicting other health-impairing behaviors, such as substance use (Morojele & Stephenson, 1994; see Van den Putte, 1993, for a review), drunk driving, and smoking (Stacy et al., 1994). It should be kept in mind, however, that most of the studies generated by or testing these theories have not included intention and behavior (separated temporally) in the same design, and very few have focused on health risk as opposed to health promotion. The latter is consistent with these studies' emphasis on rational behavior.

Adolescent Health Risk

Elsewhere we have presented a model, called the prototype/willingness (P/W) model (Gibbons & Gerrard, 1995, 1997; Gibbons, Gerrard, Ouelette, & Burzette, 1998), that was intended to explain and predict these relatively complex behaviors within a population that has proven somewhat problematic for rational behavior theories, namely, adolescents and young adults (van den Putte, 1993; cf. L. K. Brown et al., 1991). The model is based on three related assumptions, which reflect its relative emphasis (compared with most health models) on social reactivity rather than rational planning. The first assumption is that for young persons, more so than adults, behaviors related to health risk are volitional, but they are often neither rational nor intentional. Rather, they are reactions to risk-conducive circumstances that most adolescents are likely to encounter from time to time. Second, health-risk behaviors are social events for adolescents; they seldom engage in these behaviors alone (cf. Nadler & Fisher, 1992). Third, because of their social nature, these behaviors have clear social images associated with them that are widely recognized. When adolescents consider engaging in the behaviors, the images have a significant impact on their decisions.

Support for these assumptions has come mostly from our own research (Gerrard, 1987; Gerrard, Gibbons, & Boney McCoy, 1993; Gibbons, Gerrard, & Boney-McCoy, 1995), although similar opinions have been expressed by several researchers. Others have suggested, for example, that adolescent sexual activity is often spontaneous rather than planned (Brooks-Gunn & Furstenberg, 1989; L. K. Brown et al., 1991; Chilman, 1983). Consistent with this notion, surveys conducted with sexually active teens have suggested that much of their sexual activity is reactive and not premeditated (Ingham, Woodcock, & Stenner, 1991; Winter, 1988), which may be one reason why more than 80% of adolescent pregnancies are unintended (S. Brown & Eisenberg, 1995). Moreover, it does not appear to be the case that this behavior is a result of ignorance of the risks involved (Gerrard & Luus, 1995; Terry, Galligan, &

Conway, 1993). On the contrary, adolescents do know, for example, which kinds of sexual behaviors are safe (or rational) and which are not. When asked, they will typically say they do not intend to engage in behaviors in the latter category. Often, however, they end up doing so anyway (Kegeles, Adler, & Irwin, 1988; Turtle et al., 1989; cf. Blanton, Gibbons, Gerrard, Conger, & Smith, 1997; Zabin, 1994). This lack of correspondence between attitude and behavior suggests two things: (a) Attitudes—especially those toward risky behaviors—change and (b) there is an additional, nonintentional component involved in the decision to engage in risky behavior. That component, called *behavioral willingness* (BW), is the focus of the P/W model. The model shares a number of constructs and assumptions with the theory of reasoned action. It also adds two new constructs, one of which is BW. The two constructs and the model itself are described below.

The P/W Model

Willingness

Although many adolescents do not intend to engage in risky behaviors, they do frequently find themselves in situations in which the opportunity to perform these actions is presented to them (e.g., a party where cigarettes are available, an enthusiastic boyfriend or girlfriend who wants to have sex). In these settings, the issue is more appropriately framed as "What are you willing to do?", which is not the same as "What do you plan to do?" BW is distinguished from BI in several ways, including a relative lack of planning or premeditation and self-focus associated with BW compared with BI. The primary distinction, however, involves the reactive rather than deliberative nature of BW (see Gibbons et al., 1998). According to the model, this reactive component is a function of four factors. Three of these factors are also related to BI, as outlined in the theory of reasoned action. First, subjective norms are operationalized in the P/W model in a manner quite similar to that in the theory of reasoned action. In particular, perceptions that important others (e.g., peers) engage in the behavior, and would not disapprove of one's own participation, are associated with greater BW to engage (Gibbons, Helweg-Larsen, & Gerrard,

1995), just as it is with greater BI. Second, positive attitudes toward the behavior are generally associated with more BI and more BW to engage. Measurement of attitudes, however, is somewhat more outcome-focused in the P/W model than in the theory of reasoned action, because of the model's focus on risk behavior. In particular, the less danger or the less likelihood of negative outcome an individual associates with a particular risk behavior, the more willing he or she is to engage in that behavior (Gibbons et al., 1998). Third, having engaged in the behavior in the past should be associated with a more favorable attitude toward the behavior (Bentler & Speckart, 1981), more positive subjective norms (Gerrard, Gibbons, Benthin, & Hessling, 1996), and greater BI (Bagozzi, 1981) and BW to engage again. The fourth antecedent to BW, which is unique to the P/W model, is the social image or prototype that the adolescent associates with the behavior, in other words, his or her perception of the type of person who does it.

Prototypes

In general, adolescents are preoccupied with social images and identities—their own and others' (Erikson, 1963; Manning & Allen, 1987; Youniss & Haynie, 1992)—and that may be even more true for the images associated with risk behaviors (cf. Chassin, Tetzloff, & Hershey, 1985). In fact, previous research has indicated that adolescents are quite familiar with risk images (Chassin, Presson, Sherman, McCoughlin, & Gioia, 1985; Leventhal & Cleary, 1980) and that these images are positively associated with attitudes and subjective norms, as well as intention to engage in the associated behavior. The more favorable an adolescent's image of smokers, for example, the more likely he or she is to intend to smoke (Chassin, Presson, Sherman, Corty, & Olshavsky, 1981). According to the P/W model, the influence that images or prototypes have on behavior is mediated by BW. Briefly, the reasoning is as follows. Adolescents have a clear image of the type of person who engages in different risk behaviors (e.g., the typical smoker). They also realize that if they engage in risky behaviors within a social context, which is where these behaviors are most likely to occur (Assumption 2 of the model; Gibbons & Gerrard, 1995), they will acquire the image themselves. If they smoke in public, for example, they will become a typical smoker in the eyes of their peers. In some sense, then, the images are social consequences as well as antecedents of the behavior. These images tend not to be very favorable, however, even among those who do engage in the behavior. Thus, the images themselves (or their acquisition), although influential, are usually not goals for young people. Instead, the question is how acceptable the image is to them—the more acceptable it is, the more willing they are to do the behavior. Thus, social images or prototypes relate directly to BW in the model but not directly to BI.

Empirical Support

Previous research has supported this aspect of the P/W model by demonstrating a relation between risk prototypes and willingness to engage in a related risk behavior. Specifically, maintaining a favorable image of the typical unwed teenage parent has been shown to be positively associated with adolescents' willingness to engage in unprotected sex (Gibbons, Gerrard, et al., 1995, Study 1; Gibbons, Helweg-Larsen, et al., 1995). In addition, alcohol prototypes (i.e., images of the typical drinker) have been shown to predict changes in drinking behavior among adolescents (Blanton et al., 1997) and college students (Gibbons & Gerrard, 1995). To date, however, no studies have examined the extent to which the impact of prototypes on behavior is mediated by BW and not BI, as is hypothesized in the model. That question was explored in the current research.

Measuring Intentions and Willingness

Intentions Versus Expectations

In a revision of the theory of reasoned action, Sheppard et al. (1988) recommended that a distinction be made between BI, which they defined as the extent to which plans (i.e., commitment) have been formulated to perform a behavior, and what they call *behavioral expectation* (BE), which they suggested is the individual's perceived likelihood that she or he will actually perform the behavior. The latter construct takes into account a number of additional factors besides BI that could affect performance of the behavior, such as opportunity, previous behavior or habits, and alternative behaviors available to the individual. Thus, BE appears to be more appropriate for certain types of behaviors, such as substance use (Morojele & Stephenson, 1994). Reports of BE are also less constrained by social desirability than is BI (Beck & Ajzen, 1991). Because most adolescent health-risk behaviors are not socially desirable and are largely context-dependent, we assumed that a BE measure would be a more effective predictor than would a typical BI measure (e.g., "How likely is it that you will drive drunk?" vs. "Do you intend to drive drunk?"; cf. Stacy et al., 1994; Stacy, Newcomb, & Bentler, 1991). Consequently, we used BE measures in this study.

Willingness

In assessing BW, risk-conducive circumstances are first described to respondents and then respondents are asked how willing they would be to react in several different ways if they were in such a situation. These reactions vary in terms of level of risk (e.g., say no, do something less risky). Respondents are told that no assumption is being made that they would ever be in such a situation. In this manner, the construct emphasizes social as well as situational influences on behavior, and it shifts some of the focus of responsibility for the behavior from the adolescent, which is where it rests for most BI measures, and places it on the context (Gibbons et al., 1998). Because it involves some estimation of the likelihood of a particular behavior (given an opportunity), BW does include an element of expectation. Like BE, it is also less affected by social desirability constraints. In short, willingness measures are more similar to expectation measures than they are to "traditional" intention measures. Using BE rather than BI items, then, provides a more conservative test of the difference between reasoned and reactive behavior.

Summary

Previous studies have examined various aspects of the P/W model; as of yet, however, no study has examined the entire model. In particular, the most basic assumption of the P/W model, which is that much adolescent risk behavior is not intended or planned, has not yet been assessed. Moreover, the hypothesis that BW relates to behavior independent of BI has been examined in only one study (Gibbons et al., 1998). Hence, the purpose of the first study was to test the second half of the P/W model, which links BW to risk behavior. Specifically, the study examined the relations among BW, BE, and change in adolescents' cigarette smoking over time. The following hypotheses were examined: (a) Adolescent risk behaviors have an extraintentional component, which is captured in the BW construct and (b) accordingly, this construct will add significantly to the predictive power of BE. Study 2 then presents the first test of all elements of the model in a single prospective study, using structural-equation-modeling procedures.

Study 1

Method

PARTICIPANTS AND PROCEDURE

The Time 1 (T1) sample consisted of 245 boys and 255 girls from small towns in Iowa who had been recruited along with their families to participate in a study of social psychological factors related to health behavior. Half of the sample was age 13 at T1 and half was age 15. From that group, 470 completed all of the measures at T1, 464 at Time 2 (T2), and 447 at Time 3 (T3); 430 completed all measures at all three time periods. Data collection occurred in the families' homes at intervals of approximately 1 year. Families were paid $50 at T1 and T2 and $55 at T3 (for additional description of the sample and measures, see Gerrard et al., 1996; Gibbons et al., 1995). Behavior was assessed at T1 (i.e., prior behavior), at T2, and then, as the criterion, at T3. BW and BE were both assessed at T2.

MEASURES

Two measures of smoking behavior were used: (a) lifetime, "What is the most you have ever smoked cigarettes?" followed by a 6-point scale with anchors *never* (1) to *I have smoked every day* (6) and (b) current, "How often do you smoke

now?" followed by a 4-point scale from *not at all* (1) to *every day* (4). For analysis, the two items were standardized and then averaged together (alphas at T1 and T3 = .83 and .89, respectively).

BE was assessed with a single global item, "Do you think that you will smoke cigarettes in the future?", followed by a 7-point scale with anchors *I definitely will not* (1) to *I definitely will* (7). We chose to keep the time frame open, assuming that a specific time period (e.g., 1 year) would produce a more conservative (lower) BE value. BW was assessed by asking participants to imagine themselves in different situations and then think about how they might respond if they were in the situation. For smoking, the situation was "Suppose you were with some friends and one of them offered you a cigarette. How likely is it that you would do *each* of the following?" This was followed by three responses: "Take it and try it," "Tell them 'no thanks,'" and "Leave the situation," each with a 7-point scale with anchors *not at all likely* (1) to *very likely* (7). The second two items were reversed, and then the three were averaged together to form a BW index ($\alpha = .80$).

Results

DESCRIPTIVE STATISTICS

The means, standard deviations, and correlations for the primary measures are presented in Table 6.1. As indicated in the table, BW was greater than BE, but the correlation between the two was very high ($r = .69$). Nonetheless, responses on the BE measure suggested that much of these adolescents' smoking behavior was not intended. For example, among those who reported smoking during the

TABLE 6.1. Correlations, Means, and Standard Deviations for Adolescent Smoking (Study 1)

Variable	1	2	3	4
1. T1 behavior	—			
2. T2 BE	.44	—	.69	.56
3. T2 BW	.41		—	.62
4. T3 behavior	.52			—
M	2.64	1.86	2.93	3.40
SD	1.40	1.41	1.69	2.16

Note. N = 430. Scales BE and BW = 1–7; behavior = 2–10 (i.e., sum of the behavior items). BE = behavioral expectation; BW = behavioral willingness; T = time.

period from T2 to T3, 55% had responded with either a 1 or 2 on the prior (T2) BE question. Among those who initiated the behavior during this time period, 64% had responded with a 1 and 25% a 2 on the BE question.

REGRESSION ANALYSES

A hierarchical regression analysis was conducted in which T1 behavior, then T2 BE, and finally T2 BW were entered as predictors of T3 behavior. In addition, a commonality analysis was also conducted to determine the increment in R^2 accounted for by each of the three predictors individually and then BE and BW together (i.e., their unique and also their shared explanatory ability). Results of this analysis, presented in Table 6.2 and Figure 6.1, indicated that the three variables together explained 45% of the variance in T3 smoking behavior, with previous smoking explaining the greatest amount. In addition, in spite of their high correlation, BE and BW each explained a significant percentage of the variance in behavior independently, after accounting for previous behavior. Moreover, BW was a significantly stronger predictor than was BE (R^2 increment for BE = 1.4%, for BW = 7.3%; both $ps < .001$; the difference between the BE and BW betas was significant, $p < .001$). The two constructs together, however, accounted for a larger proportion of the variance in behavior (12.9%) than did either by itself. These results remained essentially unchanged when the adolescents who were regular smokers were excluded from the analyses, when nonsmokers were excluded, and when the criterion was switched to current smoking only. Also, there were no sex differences on any measures or in the regression analyses.

Discussion

As expected, BW and BE were highly correlated. The two constructs are clearly related, and the overlap between the two, as indicated by the commonality analysis, predicted changes in smoking quite well. Consistent with the P/W model, however, there was a significant element of this adolescent risk behavior that apparently was not intended. That element, which we have called BW, related more strongly to smoking behavior than did BE. One likely reason for this is the fact that smoking is not yet habitual for most adolescents, which is probably why the BE measure was not as effective at predicting this behavior as it usually is for adults. In fact, for many adolescents, smoking is neither planned nor premeditated. Rather, it is a response to opportunity—situations that they are likely to encounter that are risk-conducive. Being at a party where cigarettes or alcohol are available would be a prime example. This combination of availability and willingness can lead to risk, even when there was little or no intention in the first place.

Regarding the distinction between BW and BE and their relation to behavior, several factors are worth noting. First, the long period of time between the measurement of BE and behavior most likely attenuated their relation somewhat (Ajzen, 1988; of course, the same was true for the relation between BW and behavior). Similarly, the fact that previous behavior was included in the regression means that this was a conservative test of the predictive ability of both BE and BW (Grube & Morgan, 1990; Huba, Wingard, & Bentler, 1981; Sutton, 1994); some expectation and some willingness are most likely subsumed by previous behavior. Third, because BE is conceptually more

TABLE 6.2. Hierarchical Regression and Commonality Analysis Predicting Adolescent Smoking (Study 1)

Variable	Regression[a]			Commonality[b]	
	β	Z	R^2	R^2 (unique)	R^2 (shared)
Step 1: T1 behavior	.26	6.53	.24		
Step 2: T2 BE	.17	3.33	.38	.01	
Step 3: T2 BW	.39	7.76	.45	.07	.13

Note. N = 430. BE = behavioral expectation; BW = behavioral willingness; T = time. For all values, p ≤ .001.
[a] For regression, β and *t* are at final step; R^2 reflects increment in R^2 at time of entry.
[b] For commonality analysis, R^2 = increment associated with the predictor.

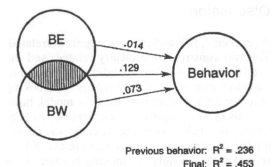

Previous behavior: R^2 = .236
Final: R^2 = .453

FIGURE 6.1 ■ Shared and unique variance of behavioral expectation (BE) and behavioral willingness (BW) predicting adolescent smoking (Study 1). N = 430.

similar to BW than to BI, it seems likely that the statistical distinction between BW and BI would be more pronounced and that the BW index would have explained even more of the variance in behavior, if BW had been used in conjunction with a BI measure instead of the more encompassing BE measure. Finally, the fact that BE was assessed with a single item and BW with an index does raise the possibility that the reliability for BE was lower, which could have affected its predictive power. (The alpha across the three waves of data collection for this measure was .76, which suggests its reliability was reasonable, however.) This issue was addressed in Study 2.

Study 2

Although most individual components of the P/W model have been examined empirically, to date, no study has provided an assessment of the overall model. The second study provided this initial test. All components of the P/W model (see Figure 6.2), including those it shares with the theory of reasoned action (subjective norms, attitudes, and BE) as well as its two unique elements (BW and risk prototypes), and previous behavior were incorporated into a single analysis.

According to the model, BW is expected to relate to behavior in two ways: directly, independent of BE, and indirectly, through BE. This latter path reflects the shared variance of the two constructs identified in the commonality analysis in Study 1. It is also consistent with another tenet of the model, which is that being willing to perform

a behavior will lead to an increase in the perceived likelihood or expectation of performing that behavior. This sequence is thought to be more likely than the reverse (i.e., intending to engage leads to a willingness to engage; see Gibbons & Gerrard, 1997, for further discussion). Thus, a path from BW to BE was freed in the model. In addition, one pathway depicted in the figure that has not yet been examined is the relation between previous behavior and BW. Having engaged in the behavior previously should result in greater BW and greater expectation of engaging again (cf. Gerrard et al., 1996; Gordon, 1989).

Method

OVERVIEW

This study included an older sample, college students, and a different risk behavior, sexual intercourse without contraception. Consistent with previous studies, the image that we hypothesized would be related to lack of contraception was that of the young unwed parent (Gibbons & Gerrard, 1995; Gibbons, Gerrard, et al., 1995). We used the LISREL VIII program to assess the fit of the model.

PARTICIPANTS AND PROCEDURE

Participants were college students who had responded to three waves of data collection in an ongoing longitudinal study of health-risk behaviors (see Gibbons & Gerrard, 1995, for further description of the sample). There were 628 students at the first wave, which was collected during spring semester of the students' freshman year. From that group, 84 dropped out of school and 18 others dropped out of the study (i.e., declined or could not be scheduled for the subsequent sessions).[1] In addition, 57 individuals had enough

[1] Those participants who dropped out of the study (most of whom dropped out of school) reported engaging in more pregnancy-risk behavior than did those who stayed in the study through all three waves and answered all of the items. We do not believe this alters the conclusions of the study, however, for two reasons: (a) As a result of this attrition, there was less variance in the behavior to predict, which most likely attenuated the power of our model; and (b) there were no differences between attriters and participants in terms of the relations between prototypes and BW, as measured at the initial wave (prior to T1), and between these central constructs and

missing data to be excluded from the analysis, leaving a total across the three waves of 469 cases. This sample had a mean age of 18 at T1 and 19 at T3 and was 44% male. Each wave of data collection was separated by 6 months. Participants' pregnancy-risk behavior was assessed at T1 and T3. At T2, all elements of the P/W model, plus BE, were assessed.

MEASURES

Behavior. Two measures of pregnancy-risk behavior were used to operationalize the behavior latent construct. The first was a direct question ("In the past 6 months, have you ever had sexual intercourse without using any kind of birth control?", followed by a scale from 1 = *never* to 5 = *all the time*). The second question asked participants what type of birth control they had used the last time they had intercourse. Their responses were then coded in the following manner: 3 = *none*, 2 = *less effective (withdrawal or rhythm)*, 1 = *effective (pill or condom)*, 0 = virgin (28% of the sample were virgins at T3).

Subjective norms. There were four measures of subjective norms. Two items assessed perceptions of prevalence of the behavior, one among friends and the other among peers: "How many of your friends [people your age] have had sexual intercourse without using birth control?" each followed by a scale from 1 = *none* to 7 = *almost all*. The other two questions assessed perceptions of friends' and parents' reactions to the behavior: "How do you think your friends [parents] would respond if they thought you had had sexual intercourse *without using birth control?*" each followed by a scale from 1 = *have a strong negative reaction and tell you to stop* to 5 = *encourage you to continue*. The two friend questions (reaction and prevalence) were added together, as were the peer prevalence and parent reaction questions, to form two indicators of a subjective-norms latent construct. Finally, consistent with the theory of reasoned action, we did include two measures of motivation to comply, each of which was multi-

plied by the corresponding perceived norm items (i.e., parents' and friends' reactions). These product scores did not load as highly on the subjective-norm latent construct as did the individual items, however, so we used the latter. Problems with this product term (see also Footnote 2) are not unprecedented in studies of the theory (Ajzen, 1991; Ajzen & Fishbein, 1970).

Attitude. There were five measures of attitudes and beliefs (referred to here simply as attitude measures). The first three pertained to the theory of reasoned action concept of behavioral belief (i.e., perceived pregnancy risk), one for the self, the second for a couple: "If you [a couple] were to have sexual intercourse *regularly* (say once a week for a year) *without using birth control*, what do you think the chances are that you [the woman] would get pregnant?" The third item replaced "regularly" in the self question with "once or twice." Each of the three items was followed by a scale ranging from 1 = *no chance* to 7 = *definitely would happen*. The last two items pertained to the reasoned action concept of outcome evaluation: "In general, how dangerous do you think unprotected sex is?", followed by a scale ranging from 1 = *not at all dangerous* to 7 = *very dangerous*, and "How would you feel if you had [caused] an unplanned pregnancy sometime in the future?", followed by a 7-point scale with anchors *very happy* (1) to *very unhappy* (7). This last item did not correlate well with the others, however, and so it was not included in the latent construct. The couple pregnancy risk over a year and the perceived danger items were combined as were the other two (self) pregnancy-risk items to form two separate indicators of a latent attitude construct.

Prototype. A definition of a prototype was provided (see Gibbons, Gerrard, et al., 1995, for the description) and then participants were asked to indicate their opinion of the "type of person (your age) who gets [a woman] pregnant" using 12 adjectives (smart, confused, popular, immature, "cool" [sophisticated], self-confident, independent, careless, unattractive, dull [boring], considerate, and self-centered); items were reversed where necessary, so that a high score reflected a positive perception. Exploratory (oblique) factor analysis of these 12 items in previous studies (e.g., Blanton et al., 1997) consistently produced evidence of three correlated factors, labeled mature, self-assured, and attractive. A mean was calculated for

---

T1 behavior. Moreover, the model shown in Figure 6.2 was reestimated using various methods of missing data estimation (i.e., sensitivity analyses) for participants who dropped out of the sample. Use of these estimated measures did not substantively alter the results.

each of the four-item subscales defined by the three factors; these three scores constituted the prototype latent construct.

Expectation. There were two BE items: "Do you think you will have sex in the next year without using birth control?" (from 1 = *I definitely will not* to 7 = *I definitely will*) and "If you were to have sexual intercourse in the next year, how likely is it that you would use the following kinds of birth control?" This second item was followed by a list of six types of birth control, each accompanied by a 7-point scale ranging from *not at all likely* (1) to *very likely* (7). The list included "no birth control," which was the second measure used in the BE construct.

Willingness. BW was assessed beginning with a description of a scenario in which participants were asked to imagine being with their boyfriend or girlfriend who wanted to have sex, but with no birth control available. They were then asked how likely it was that they would do each of the following: have sex, but use withdrawal (which was defined); not have sex; have sex without any birth control. Each statement was accompanied by a scale ranging from 1 = *not at all likely* to 7 = *very likely*. The second item was reversed, and then the three were included as indicators of the latent BW construct.

Results

DESCRIPTIVE STATISTICS

Twenty-two percent of respondents at T1 and 17% at T3 indicated they had had sex without any birth control during the previous 6 months. In addition, 5% at each time period reported using relatively ineffective birth control (rhythm or withdrawal) during their last intercourse. Correlations among the BW and BE measures were more modest than in Study 1 (mean $r = .38$). Once again, many of the participants who indicated at T3 that they had engaged in the risk behavior in the previous 6 months had reported little or no expectation of doing so at the previous wave: 47% of this group responded with either a 1 or 2 on the BE question at T2. Of those who had risky sex for the first time during this period, 60% responded with a 1 and 27% with a 2 on the BE question at T2.

STRUCTURAL EQUATION ANALYSES

Structural equation analysis with latent variables was used to test the causal model shown in Figure 6.2, as operationalized by the maximum likelihood methods of LISREL VIII (Jöreskog & Sörbom, 1993). Evaluation of model fit was based on the

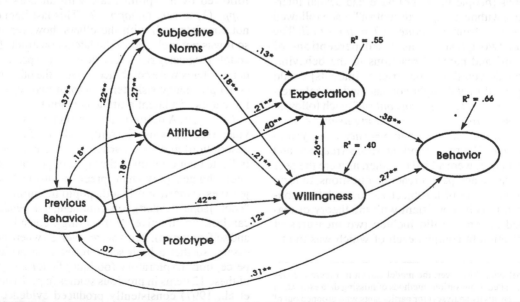

FIGURE 6.2 ■ Structural model for pregnancy risk (Study 2). $N = 469$. Goodness-of-fit index = .95.
*$p < .05$. **$p < .001$.

goodness-of-fit (GFI) statistic, which represents the proportion of the variation and covariation of the measured variables that is explained by the model (Tanaka & Huba, 1985), and the Comparative Fit Index (CFI; Bentler, 1990), which is based on the noncentral chi-square value for two models, the one being tested and a null model which specifies that the variables are uncorrelated.

Correlated measurement error. Because behavior was assessed using identical items at two points in time (i.e., T1 and T3), systematic response biases due to the wording or nature of the questions may have affected self-reports. Systematic or correlated measurement error serves to increase the apparent stability of the latent variables, thereby lessening the potential causal effects of other variables (cf. Ulrich-Jakubowski, Russell, & O'Hara, 1988). In addition, the overall goodness of model fit is negatively affected by correlated error (see, e.g., Krause, Liang, & Yatomi, 1989). We therefore included the possibility of correlated measurement error between the parallel measures of behavior at T1 and T3 that were included in the model. We also constrained the factor loadings of the two indicators of behavior to be constant over time.

Testing the measurement model. To evaluate the adequacy of the measurement model, a confirmatory factor analysis was conducted using the maximum likelihood estimation algorithm from the LISREL VIII program. A seven-factor oblique model was tested, with the factors hypothesized to underlie the measured variables as described above (i.e., Behavior at T1; Prototype, Attitude, Subjective Norms, BE, and BW at T2; and behavior at T3). This model was found to provide a very good fit to the data, χ^2 (82, $N = 469$) = 192.4, $p < .001$, GFI = .95, CFI = .96. All of the hypoth-

esized factor loadings of the measured variables on the latent variables were highly significant. Table 6.3 presents the correlations among the latent variables derived from the confirmatory factor analysis. Several relations are worth noting. First, T1 behavior was correlated with all of the T2 cognitive variables (all $rs \geq .19$), except prototype; T1 behavior was also highly correlated with T3 behavior ($r = .66$). Second, as expected, subjective norms and attitude were related to BE (all $rs \geq .43$), and BW was related to the prototype construct ($r = .23$). Finally, BW and BE were once again related to each other ($r = .60$), and both were related to T3 behavior ($rs \geq .65$).

Testing the full structural model. Given that the specification of the latent variables through the measurement model appeared adequate, we then tested the overall structural equation model. The model was found to fit the data well, χ^2 (86, $N = 469$) = 196.5, $p < .001$, GFI = .95, CFI = .96. The standardized path coefficients from this model are presented in Figure 6.2. As expected, BW at T2 was significantly (and positively) predicted by T1 behavior, as well as the T2 predictors of attitude toward the behavior, subjective norms, and a (positive) prototype regarding individuals who engage in the behavior. In combination, these variables accounted for 40% of the variation in the latent BW variable. Also consistent with predictions, BE at T2 was significantly and positively predicted by T1 behavior, as well as T2 attitudes, subjective norms, and BW. In combination, these variables accounted for 55% of the variation in scores on the latent BE variable.

Predicting behavior. As in Study 1, the T2 measures of BE and BW were again significant and independent predictors of T3 behavior. As indi-

TABLE 6.3. Correlations Among the Latent Constructs (Study 2)

Construct	1	2	3	4	5	6	7
1. Subjective norms	—	.27	.44	.42	.22	.37	.41
2. Attitude		—	.43	.38	.19	.19	.22
3. BE			—	.60	.13	.63	.73
4. BW				—	.23	.54	.65
5. Prototype					—	.08†	.18
6. T1 behavior						—	.66
7. T3 behavior							—

Note. BE = behavioral expectation; BW = behavioral willingness; T = time.
†*ns*; for all other values, $p < .001$.

cated by the standardized path coefficients (see Figure 6.2), both BE and BW uniquely explained variation in T3 behavior net T1 behavior. In this sample, however, BE was a stronger predictor than was BW.

Indirect effects. The results presented in Figure 6.2 suggest that the three exogenous variables assessed at T2, plus T1 behavior, have an indirect influence on behavior at T3, through their effects on BE and BW at T2. To evaluate this, we tested the statistical significance of the indirect effects of these four predictor variables on T3 behavior, using a procedure developed by Sobel (1987). All four variables were found to have statistically significant indirect effects on behavior 6 or 12 months later, through the intervening cognitive variables assessed at T2 (all $Zs > 2.18$, $p < .05$). Also, as expected, BW significantly influenced subsequent behavior indirectly, through BE ($Z = 2.82$, $p < .005$). The total amount of variance accounted for in T3 behavior was 66%, which compares favorably with applications of rational models to health behavior (van den Putte, 1993; cf. Conner & Sparks, 1996).

Removing BW–T3 behavior path. To evaluate the importance of the direct effect of BW on T3 behavior, the modeling analysis was repeated with the path from BW to T3 behavior fixed at zero. This resulted in a significant reduction in the fit of the model, χ^2 (1, $N = 469$) = 12.1, $p < .001$, even though the explained variation in behavior declined only slightly, from 66% to 65%. Examination of the results for this latter version of the model indicated that, with the path from BW to T3 behavior fixed at zero, the path from BE to T3 behavior increased substantially, from .38 to .50. However, the indirect effect of BW on T3 behavior through BE also increased substantially, from .10 to .15. These results indicate that the fit of the model is improved by including the path from BW to T3 behavior and, when that direct path is removed, BW has a substantial indirect effect on T3 behavior through BE. Finally, a different model that did not include either BW or prototypes produced an R^2 of .61 for T3 behavior, as opposed to .66 for the entire BW model. That figure dropped to .52 when previous behavior was excluded. In short, the new elements from the model did add significantly to behavioral prediction.

Sex differences. Analyses were also conducted testing for sex differences in the structural param-

eters of the model, using the multiple-group procedure in the LISREL VIII program. It should be noted that in conducting these analyses, the measurement model (i.e., the factor loadings) was held constant across the two groups. A comparison of a model in which the causal paths were also forced to be equivalent for the two sexes with a model where the causal paths were allowed to vary was nonsignificant, χ^2 (11, $N = 469$) = 12.2, $p > .30$. Therefore, it appears that the causal paths were essentially equivalent for male and female participants. Finally, a separate analysis conducted on just those participants who indicated at T3 that they were not virgins ($n = 343$) produced a model that was almost identical to the full model described here. All paths remained significant and the overall fit was good (CFI = .97).[2]

Discussion

The data conformed to the pattern outlined by the P/W model, as the relations among all of the variables were as predicted and were statistically significant. Thus, the results indicate the full P/W model can predict changes in pregnancy-risk behavior reasonably well, just as elements of the model (e.g., prototypes) have been shown in previous studies to predict adolescent drinking and willingness to engage in risky sex (Blanton et al., 1997; Gibbons & Gerrard, 1995). Moreover, these results indicated, once again, that BW is strongly related to BE, that the two predict risk behavior jointly, and that they predict behavior independent of one another.

The primary purpose of Study 2 was to assess the entire P/W model, rather than to compare it

---

[2]Also, we assessed refusal efficacy (Ellickson & Hays, 1991) by presenting an additional, altered version of the BW scenario in which participants were asked to assume that they did not want to have sex but that their boyfriend or girlfriend did. This single item did correlate with the three BW items ($rs = .35, .47,$ and $.52$). Of more importance, when refusal efficacy replaced BW in the model, it was related to contraception BE ($p = .03$), but it was not related to any of the other constructs, including T3 behavior ($p = .09$). Moreover, when the refusal efficacy item was included as a fourth indicator of BW, it did load moderately well on the construct (.58); however, the BW to behavior path coefficient declined slightly, and the overall model did not fit as well as it did with the three-item BW construct. Thus, refusal efficacy does not appear to be as effective in this sample at predicting pregnancy risk as does BW.

directly with the theory of planned behavior or other rational models. Consequently, we operationalized constructs, some of which are shared with reasoned action and planned behavior theories, in a manner that was consistent with the P/W model. In particular, whereas the subjective norm and BE constructs were essentially as defined by those theories, the attitude construct placed more emphasis on outcome. Also, because we assumed that most college students believe they have control over their sexual behavior, we did not include a perceived behavioral control measure as planned behavior theory would suggest. Finally, we used only a BE measure and did not include a "traditional" BI measure.

Although these decisions were consistent with the goals of the study, they do raise an important question for the P/W model that could only be partly addressed in the first two studies. That is, how distinct are the two central constructs of the P/W model—prototypes and especially BW—from what appear to be similar constructs in rational behavior theories, at least one of which is highly correlated with BW, namely, BE and perceived behavioral control? If these constructs are redundant with one another, the need for these new elements would be harder to justify. Consequently, a third study was conducted in which a confirmatory factor analysis was performed on all of the elements of reasoned action and planned behavior theories, plus those of the P/W model. Again, the maximum likelihood estimation algorithm from LISREL VIII was used.

General Discussion

Although others have suggested that adolescents' risky sexual behavior is often reactive rather than planned (Brooks-Gunn & Furstenberg, 1989; see S. Brown & Eisenberg, 1995), to date no studies have directly assessed the first of the three basic assumptions of the P/W model, which is that this behavior, like other health-risk behaviors among young people, does have a significant nonintentional component. The current studies tested that assumption, and in so doing, provided prospective and retrospective evidence that pregnancy-risk and STD-risk behavior among college students, as well as adolescent smoking, are not always intended. Adding this to another recent study indicating that the same is true of drunk driv-

ing among college students (Gerrard, Gibbons, Smith, & Ouelette, 1998) suggests that this basic postulate of the P/W model is accurate.

Another tenet of the P/W model is that much of this nonintentional component of adolescent risk behavior can be captured by the BW construct, which is thought to be distinct from related constructs in rational models of behavior, namely, BI or BE. In previous studies, we have shown that BW and BE relate differently to perceptions of vulnerability to the negative outcomes associated with health-risk behaviors (e.g., drunk-driving expectation is related to perceived vulnerability to alcohol-related accidents, whereas willingness to drive drunk is not; in contrast, drunk-driving willingness is strongly related to defensiveness or denial of accident risk, whereas BE is not; Gibbons et al., 1998). The current studies add to this previous research by demonstrating, once again, that BE and BW are related to one another but show discriminable patterns in their relations with other variables, including behavior.

Discriminating Between Willingness and Intention

Study 1 indicated that BE and BW were highly correlated but still predicted change in adolescent smoking behavior independent of one another. They also predicted smoking behavior jointly, indicating that the overlap between the two constructs relates to future behavior, as do their unique components. Consistent with this latter finding, the structural equation modeling analyses in Study 2 indicated that both variables had a unique effect on pregnancy-risk behavior and that there was a significant indirect path from BW through BE to pregnancy risk as well. Thus, once again, BW and BE explained significant percentages of the behavioral variance by themselves and jointly. Finally, the confirmatory factor analysis in Study 3 provided direct evidence that BW and BE, this time for unprotected sex, are related to one another but are not redundant. In summary, converging evidence suggests that BE and BW have much in common—those who are intending to perform a behavior, for example, are also likely to be willing to do it. On the other hand, the direct relation between BW and behavior independent of intention, which was detected in the regression and the modeling analyses, indicates that BE is not a necessary antecedent to health behaviors of this nature; BW alone may sometimes be sufficient.

THE IMPACT OF PREVIOUS BEHAVIOR

One relation in the three studies worth noting is that between previous behavior and BE versus BW. In Study 1, behavior was assessed 1 year after both BE and BW, and the latter was a stronger predictor than the former. In Study 2, the time lag was 6 months, and this time behavior correlated somewhat more highly with BE than with BW (albeit in an older sample). Finally, in Study 3, when all of the constructs were assessed simultaneously, recent behavior was much more highly related to BE than to BW. Keeping in mind that the three studies involved three different behaviors, one interpretation of this result is that expectations relate more strongly to recent behavior because they are a reflection of the individual's current situation (cf. Liska, 1984). Using unprotected sex as an example, some of these college students may have been in a fairly committed relationship at the time in which they were using the pill but not condoms. They may have felt, or wanted to believe, that this relationship would last and, therefore, assumed that their current protection strategies (including lack of condom use) would continue. Thus, the relation between BE and their recent behavior would be high, and it would remain so unless, or until, their circumstances changed.

SPECIFICITY

The correlations of BE and BW with behavior, both previous and expected, also address another related issue that is relevant to the conceptualization and measurement of the two constructs. This concerns their respective degrees of specificity relative to one another and vis-à-vis behavior (Fishbein & Ajzen, 1975). On the one hand, the BE measure we used was of a global nature, whereas the BW measure was more specific to the scenario we described. On the other hand, the behavioral measure itself also was global and, in fact, matched the BE items on this dimension (including time frame) more closely than did the BW items. This match (what Ajzen, 1988, has termed *compatibility*) should bolster the relation between BE and both retrospective and pro-

spective reports of recent and imminent behavior (Fazio, 1990), and that appeared to be the case. What this suggests, more generally, is that BE measures, because they are a reflection of one's recent behavior and current situation, will predict behavior quite well—better than BW items—in the near future. Over time, however, circumstances change, which means the relation between BE and behavior will decline (cf. Liska, 1984). Also, as circumstances change, individuals will likely experience more types of risk situations in which their BW will have an opportunity to be expressed. In short, although the BW items are worded in a more specific manner, they may actually be less closely linked to specific (i.e., current or recent) circumstances than are the BE items. The result is that BE predicts much better than BW in the short run, but loses that predictive superiority over time.

SOCIAL DESIRABILITY

As indicated earlier, BE measures are less subject to social desirability constraints than are intention measures (Beck & Ajzen, 1991). By the same token, it may also be true that saying one is willing to do a risky behavior under conducive circumstances is more socially acceptable than stating that one intends or expects to do it. Although this might add to the (relative) predictive power of BW measures, we do not believe it is an important reason why BW measures supplement BE measures. Instead, we would argue that, in most cases, when people state they do not intend or expect to engage in a particular behavior they are being truthful. That does not mean, however, that they would not be willing to do the behavior if the opportunity presented itself, and they will acknowledge this. In fact, our data indicate that a significant percentage of young people report some level of BW for a number of risky behaviors while also stating no intention or expectation at all. Future studies should focus on this interesting (presumably at-risk) group, in order to determine why they maintain these seemingly inconsistent cognitions.

A TEMPORAL SEQUENCE

BW and BE were measured concurrently in the current studies, which means it is not possible to draw any definitive conclusions about the temporal sequencing of their respective influences. Results of Study 2 were consistent with the assumption of the P/W model that the "flow" of shared influence proceeds from BW through BE, however. Thus, if we were to conceptually partial out the effects of BW on behavior, some of it would be direct: If one is willing, one is simply more likely to do the behavior should the opportunity occur. Some of the effect is indirect, however: Being willing is likely to lead to an increase in perceived likelihood or expectation of performance. One reason for this is that risk opportunities are ubiquitous, and the willing individual is not likely to avoid the circumstances that provide these opportunities. Eventually that person will acknowledge that his or her BW is resulting in performance of the behavior; such an admission is tantamount to expectation. Similarly, BW may also develop into intention with age and experience (see below). Future analyses that look at the two constructs assessed at different time periods should allow for a more complete test of this hypothesis.

Relating BW to Other Variables

MODERATION

One factor that is likely to moderate the strength of the BW–behavior relation is age or experience. The adolescents in Study 1 who smoked reported higher BW than BE, and in fact BW was a better predictor of behavior for them. Although relatively few adolescents intend to smoke or have unprotected sex, a number are interested enough that they might consider it should the opportunity afford itself. Thus, BW may be more of a factor for younger people. As the individual gains experience with the behavior, BE should become a better predictor of future behavior. Experience is likely to evoke more consideration of the behavior and its consequences, and consideration is associated with BE (Gibbons et al., 1998). Also, should the behavior become habitual, as with smoking or heavy drinking, then BW will become much less of a factor. In either case, the BW–BE ratio should decline with both age and experience. Some evidence of this can be seen in Study 2, in which BE within this older sample was a stronger predictor of behavior than was BW, the opposite of what was found with the younger sample in Study 1. Notable exceptions to this age trajec-

tory would be situations in which an adult finds him- or herself presented with opportunities to engage in risky behaviors with which he or she has little experience. An example might be drunk driving. Perhaps a better example would be adultery, much of which is neither planned nor rational (Buunk & Gibbons, 1997). In such circumstances, the adult is not much more advantaged, in terms of predicting behavior, than is an adolescent, and so BW measures should prove to be better predictors of the behavior. Generally speaking, BW is likely to be less important for high-incidence risk behaviors.

MODEL PARAMETERS

The P/W model was originally intended to predict and explain a particular kind of behavior within a specific population: health risk among young people. Generally speaking, we believe it is most effectively applied to this context—*effective* being defined as the extent to which it adds explanatory power to existing (rational) models. More specifically, BW is not likely to add much predictive power vis-à-vis behaviors that are rational and involve premeditation, such as those that promote health or socially desirable behaviors, such as volunteerism. There are, however, a number of other behaviors that are reactive in nature, and therefore have a willingness component, that are not health-relevant. These would include other prosocial behaviors, such as bystander or emergency intervention, and other risky behaviors, such as income tax cheating or scientific dishonesty. Once again, these are actions that are often not intended or planned but instead are reactions to fortuitous opportunities. Moreover, another aspect of the P/W model, prototypes, is likely to be influential for any behaviors—positive or negative, health-relevant or not—that have an identifiable social image associated with them (cf. Gibbons & Gerrard, 1997). Future research on these issues should serve to further clarify the domain of the model.

Conclusion

Rational models, which emphasize intention as the only proximal antecedent, have been quite successful at predicting certain types of behaviors, especially when used with adult samples. For example, BI has been shown to relate strongly to protective actions that involve some planning, such as breast cancer screening (Hill, Gardner, & Rassaby, 1985), flossing (McCaul, O'Neill, & Glasgow, 1988), and childbearing among older, married women (Davidson & Jaccard, 1979). This is quite consistent with the rational approach, given that these are clearly reasoned actions that may be viewed, essentially, as goal states or behavioral achievements (Ajzen, 1985, 1991). For risky behaviors, however, especially among younger people, there is an additional element that is related to performance, and that is the individual's willingness to engage in the behavior when circumstances facilitate it. The current studies demonstrate the utility of this and related constructs in predicting, and thereby furthering understanding of, these important but enigmatic behaviors.

ACKNOWLEDGMENTS

This research was supported by National Institute on Mental Health Grant MH48165-01 and National Institute on Alcohol Abuse and Alcoholism Grant AA10208.

REFERENCES

Aberg, L. (1994). Relations among variables influencing drivers' intentions to drive after drinking. In D. R. Rutter & L. Quine (Eds.), *Social psychology and health: European perspectives* (pp. 89–100). Aldershot, England: Avebury.

Ajzen, I. (1985). From intentions to actions: A theory of planned behavior. In J. Kuhl & J. Beckman (Eds.), *Action control: From cognition to behavior* (pp. 11–39). Berlin, Germany: Springer-Verlag.

Ajzen, I. (1988). *Attitudes, personality, and behavior.* Chicago: Dorsey Press.

Ajzen, I. (1991). The theory of planned behavior: Special issue. Theories of cognitive self-regulation. *Organizational Behavior and Human Decision Processes, 50,* 179–211.

Ajzen, I., & Fishbein, M. (1970). The prediction of behavior from attitudinal and normative variables. *Journal of Experimental Social Psychology, 6,* 466–487.

Bagozzi, R. P. (1981). Attitudes, intentions, and behavior: A test of some key hypotheses. *Journal of Personality and Social Psychology, 41,* 607–627.

Beck, L., & Ajzen, I. (1991). Predicting dishonest actions using the theory of planned behavior. *Journal of Research in Personality, 25,* 285–301.

Bentler, P. M. (1990). Comparative fit indexes in structural models. *Psychological Bulletin, 107,* 238–246.

Bentler, P. M., & Speckart, G. (1981). Attitudes "cause" behaviors: A structural equation analysis. *Journal of Personality and Social Psychology, 40,* 226–238.

Blanton, H., Gibbons, F. X., Gerrard, M., Conger, K. J., & Smith, G. E. (1997). The role of family and peers in the development of prototypes associated with health risks. *Journal of Family Psychology, 11,* 271–288.

Boldero, J., Moore, S., & Rosenthal, D. (1992). Intention, context, and safe sex: Australian adolescents' responses to AIDS. *Journal of Applied Social Psychology, 22,* 1374–1396.

Brooks-Gunn, J., & Furstenberg, F. F., Jr. (1989). Adolescent sexual behavior. *American Psychologist, 44,* 249–257.

Brown, L. K., DiClemente, R. J., & Reynolds, L. A. (1991). HIV prevention for adolescents: Utility of the health belief model. *AIDS Education and Prevention, 3,* 50–59.

Brown, S., & Eisenberg, L. (1995). *The best intentions: Unintended pregnancy and the well-being of children and families.* Washington, DC: National Academy Press.

Buunk, B. P., & Gibbons, F. X. (1997). [Temptations: Can prototypes predict adultery?]. Unpublished raw data.

Chassin, L. A., Presson, C., Sherman, S. J., Corty, E., & Olshavsky, R. W. (1981). Self-images and cigarette smoking in adolescence. *Personality and Social Psychology Bulletin, 7,* 670–676.

Chassin, L. A., Presson, C., Sherman, S. J., McCoughlin, L., & Gioia, D. (1985). Psychosocial correlates of adolescent smokeless tobacco use. *Addictive Behaviors, 10,* 431–435.

Chassin, L. A., Tetzloff, C., & Hershey, M. (1985). Self-image and social-image factors in adolescent alcohol use. *Journal of Studies on Alcohol, 46,* 39–47.

Chilman, C. S. (1983). The development of adolescent sexuality. *Journal of Research and Development in Education, 16*(2), 16–26.

Conner, M., & Sparks, P. (1996). The theory of planned behavior and health behaviours. In M. Conner & P. Norman (Eds.), *Predicting health behaviour: Research and practice with social cognition models* (pp. 121–162). Buckingham, England: Open University Press.

Davidson, A. R., & Jaccard, J. J. (1979). Variables that moderate the attitude–behavior relation: Results of a longitudinal survey. *Journal of Personality and Social Psychology, 37,* 1364–1376.

Ellickson, P. L., & Hays, R. D. (1991). Antecedents of drinking among young adolescents with different alcohol use histories. *Journal of Studies on Alcohol, 52,* 398–408.

Erikson, E. H. (1963). *Childhood and society.* New York: Norton.

Fazio, R. H. (1990). Multiple processes by which attitudes guide behavior: The mode model as an integrative framework. In M. P. Zanna (Ed.), *Advances in experimental social psychology* (pp. 75–109). San Diego, CA: Academic Press.

Fishbein, M., & Ajzen, I. (1975). *Belief, attitude, intention and behavior: An introduction to theory and research.* Reading, MA: Addison-Wesley.

Fishbein, M., & Ajzen, I. (1980). Predicting and understanding consumer behavior: Attitude–behavior correspondence. In I. Ajzen & M. Fishbein (Eds.), *Understanding attitudes and predicting social behavior* (pp. 148–172). Englewood Cliffs, NJ: Prentice-Hall.

Fisher, W. A., Fisher, J. D., & Rye, B. J. (1995). Understanding and promoting AIDS-preventive behavior: Insights from the theory of reasoned action. *Health Psychology, 14,* 255–264.

Gerrard, M. (1987). Sex, sex guilt, and contraceptive use revisited: Trends in the 1980s. *Journal of Personality and Social Psychology, 42,* 153–158.

Gerrard, M., Gibbons, F. X., Benthin, A., & Hessling, R. (1996). The reciprocal nature of risk behaviors and cognitions: What you think shapes what you do and vice versa. *Health Psychology, 15*, 344–354.

Gerrard, M., Gibbons, F. X., & Boney-McCoy, S. (1993). Emotional inhibition of effective contraception. *Anxiety, Stress, and Coping, 6*, 73–88.

Gerrard, M., Gibbons, F. X., Smith, G. E., & Ouelette, J. (1998). [The impact of alcohol consumption on risk taking]. Unpublished raw data.

Gerrard, M., & Luus, C. E. (1995). Judgments of vulnerability to pregnancy: The role of risk factors and individual differences. *Personality and Social Psychology Bulletin, 21*, 158–169.

Gibbons, F. X., & Gerrard, M. (1995). Predicting young adults' health-risk behavior. *Journal of Personality and Social Psychology, 69*, 505–517.

Gibbons, F. X., & Gerrard, M. (1997). Health images and their effects on health behavior. In B. P. Buunk & F. X. Gibbons (Eds.), *Health, coping, and well-being: Perspectives from social comparison theory* (pp. 63–94). Mahwah, NJ: Erlbaum.

Gibbons, F. X., Gerrard, M., & Boney McCoy, S. (1995). Prototype perception predicts (lack of) pregnancy prevention. *Personality and Social Psychology Bulletin, 21*, 85–93.

Gibbons, F. X., Gerrard, M., Ouelette, J., & Burzette, B. (1998). Cognitive antecedents to adolescent health risk: Discriminating between behavioral intention and behavioral willingness. *Psychology and Health, 13*, 319–340.

Gibbons, F. X., Helweg-Larsen, M., & Gerrard, M. (1995). Prevalence estimates and adolescent risk behavior: Cross-cultural differences in social influence. *Journal of Applied Psychology, 80*, 107–121.

Godin, G., Valois, P., & Lepage, L. (1993). The pattern of influence of perceived behavioral control upon exercising behavior: An application of Ajzen's theory of planned behavior. *Journal of Behavioral Medicine, 16*, 81–102.

Godin, G., Valois, P., Lepage, L., Desharnais, R. (1992). Predictors of smoking behaviour: An application of Ajzen's theory of planned behaviour. *British Journal of Addiction, 87*, 1335–1343.

Gordon, R. A. (1989). Intention and expectation measures as predictors of academic performance. *Journal of Applied Social Psychology, 19*, 405–415.

Grube, J. W., & Morgan, M. (1990). Attitude–social support interactions: Contingent consistency effects in the prediction of adolescent smoking, drinking, and drug use. *Social Psychology Quarterly, 53*, 329–339.

Hill, D., Gardner, G., & Rassaby, J. (1985). Factors predisposing women to take precautions against breast and cervix cancer. *Journal of Applied Social Psychology, 15*, 59–79.

Huba, C. J., Wingard, J. A., & Bentler, P. M. (1981). Intentions to use drugs among adolescents: A longitudinal analysis. *International Journal of the Addictions, 16*, 331–339.

Ingham, R., Woodcock, A., & Stenner, K. (1991). Getting to know you . . . Young people's knowledge of their partners at first intercourse: Special issue. Social dimensions of AIDS. *Journal of Community and Applied Social Psychology, 1*(2), 117–132.

Johnson, V. (1988). Adolescent alcohol and marijuana use: A longitudinal assessment of a social learning perspective. *American Journal of Drug and Alcohol Abuse, 14*, 419–439.

Jöreskog, K. G., & Sörbom, D. (1993). *LISREL VIII: User's reference guide* (1st ed.). Chicago: Scientific Software International.

Kegeles, S. M., Adler, N. E., & Irwin, C. E. (1988). Sexually-active adolescents and condoms: Changes over one year in knowledge, attitudes and use. *American Journal of Public Health, 78*, 460–461.

Kilty, K. M. (1978). Attitudinal and normative variables as predictors of drinking behavior. *Journal of Studies on Alcohol, 39*, 1178–1194.

Krause, N., Liang, J., & Yatomi, N. (1989). Satisfaction with social support and depressive symptoms: A panel analysis. *Psychology and Aging, 4*, 88–97.

Leventhal, H., & Cleary, P. D. (1980). The smoking problem: A review of the research and theory in behavioral risk modification. *Psychological Bulletin, 88*, 370–405.

Liska, A. E. (1984). A critical examination of the causal structure of the Fishbein/Ajzen attitude–behavior model. *Social Psychology Quarterly, 47*, 61–74.

Manning, M. L., & Allen, M. G. (1987). Social development in early adolescence: Implications for middle school educators. *Childhood Education, 63*, 172–176.

McCaul, K. D., O'Neill, H. K., & Glasgow, R. E. (1988). Predicting the performance of dental hygiene behaviors: An examination of the Fishbein and Ajzen model and self-efficacy expectations. *Journal of Applied Social Psychology, 18*, 114–128.

McCaul, K. D., Sandgren, A. K., O'Neill, H. K., & Hinsz, V. B. (1993). The value of the theory of planned behavior, perceived control, and self-efficacy for predicting health-protective behaviors. *Basic and Applied Social Psychology, 14*, 231–252.

Morojele, N. K., & Stephenson, G. M. (1994). Addictive behaviours: Predictors of abstinence intentions and expectations in the theory of planned behavior. In D. R. Rutter & L. Quine (Eds.), *Social psychology and health: European perspectives* (pp. 47–70). Aldershot, England: Avebury.

Nadler, A., & Fisher, J. D. (1992). Volitional personal change and interpersonal environment. In Y. Klar, J. Fisher, J. Chinsky, & A. Nadler (Eds.), *Initiating self changes: Social psychological and clinical perspectives* (pp. 213–230). New York: Springer-Verlag.

Parker, D., Manstead, A. S., Stradling, S. G., Reason, J. T., & Baxter, J. S. (1992). Intention to commit driving violations: An application of the theory of planned behavior. *Journal of Applied Psychology, 77*, 94–101.

Rogers, R. W. (1983). Cognitive and psychological processes in fear appeals and attitude change: A revised theory of protection motivation. In J. T. Cacioppo & R. E. Petty (Eds.), *Social psychophysiology* (pp. 153–176). New York: Guilford Press.

Ronis, D. L. (1992). Conditional health threats: Health beliefs, decisions, and behaviors among adults. *Health Psychology, 11*, 127–134.

Schifter, D. E., & Ajzen, I. (1985). Intention, perceived control, and weight loss: An application of the theory of planned behavior. *Journal of Personality and Social Psychology, 49*, 843–851.

Schlegel, R. P., D'Avernas, J. R., Zanna, M. P., DeCourville, N. H., & Manske, S. R. (1992). Problem drinking: A problem for the theory of reasoned action? *Journal of Applied Social Psychology, 22*, 358–385.

Sheppard, B. H., Hartwick, J., & Warshaw, P. R. (1988). The

theory of reasoned action: A meta-analysis of past research with recommendations for modifications and future research. *Journal of Consumer Research, 15*, 325–343.

Sobel, M. E. (1987). Direct and indirect effects in linear structural equation models. *Sociological Methods and Research, 16*, 155–176.

Sparks, P., & Shepherd, R. (1992). Self-identity and the theory of planned behavior: Assessing the role of identification with "green consumerism." *Social Psychology Quarterly, 55*, 388–399.

Stacy, A. W., Bentler, P. M., & Flay, B. R. (1994). Attitudes and health behavior in diverse populations: Drunk driving, alcohol use, binge eating, marijuana use, and cigarette use. *Health Psychology, 13*, 73–85.

Stacy, A. W., Newcomb, M. D., & Bentler, P. M. (1991). Cognitive motivation and drug use: A 9-year longitudinal study. *Journal of Abnormal Psychology, 100*, 502–515.

Sutton, S. (1994). The past predicts the future: Interpreting behaviour-behaviour relationships in social psychological models of health behaviour. In D. R. Rutter & L. Quine (Eds.), *Social psychology and health: European perspectives* (pp. 71–88). Aldershot, England: Avebury.

Tanaka, J. S., & Huba, G. J. (1985). A fit index for covariance structure models under arbitrary GLS estimation. *British Journal of Mathematical and Statistical Psychology, 38*, 197–201.

Terry, D. J., Galligan, R. F., & Conway, V. J. (1993). The prediction of safe sex behavior: The role of intentions, attitudes, norms and control beliefs. *Psychology and Health, 8*, 355–368.

Triandis, H. C. (1980). Values, attitudes and interpersonal behavior. In H. E. Howe, Jr. & M. M. Page (Eds.), *Nebraska Symposium on Motivation* (Vol. 28, pp. 195–259). Lincoln: University of Nebraska Press.

Turtle, A. M., Ford, B., Habgood, R., Grant, M., Bekiaris, J., Constantinou, C., Maack, M., & Polyzoidis, H. (1989). AIDS-related beliefs and behaviors of Australian university students. *The Medical Journal of Australia, 150*, 371–376.

Ulrich-Jakubowski, D., Russell, D. W., & O'Hara, M. W. (1988). Marital adjustment difficulties: Cause or consequence of depressive symptomatology? *Journal of Social and Clinical Psychology, 7*, 312–318.

University of Michigan Survey Research Center. (1995). *Monitoring the future.* Ann Arbor, MI: Author.

van den Putte, B. (1993). *On the theory of reasoned action.* Unpublished doctoral dissertation, University of Amsterdam, Amsterdam, the Netherlands.

Winter, L. (1988). The role of sexual self-concept in the use of contraceptives. *Family Planning Perspective, 20*, 123–127.

Youniss, J., & Haynie, D. L. (1992). Friendship in adolescence. *Developmental and Behavioral Pediatrics, 13*, 59–66.

Zabin, L. S. (1994). Addressing adolescent sexual behavior and childbearing: Self-esteem or social change. *Women's Health Issues, 4*, 93–97.

INTRODUCTION TO PART 3

Health Information Processing

Throughout their lives, people receive a tremendous amount of information that is relevant to their health and well-being. Although health professionals are an important source of information, health information can also be gleaned from newspapers, magazines, and websites as well as on radio and television. What happens to all of this information? Given that people's health practices are a function of their health beliefs, how people process health information is of great importance. Do people attend to and evaluate all information similarly or are they selective in what they focus on and in how they determine what information is valuable?

The articles in this section examine how people process and use health information from three different perspectives. Imagine that scientists had discovered that drinking coffee posed a substantial health threat. It would be important to communicate this information widely, especially to those people who drink a lot of coffee. In a creative study, Liberman and Chaiken (1992) demonstrate that communicating information to the very people who need to hear it is fraught with challenges. In particular, people who are actively engaging in a risk behavior—in this case, drinking coffee—may approach information about the risks posed by the behavior with a preconceived bias that causes them to assess it with a more critical eye.

The premise that people may not approach adverse health information with an open mind has also been the focus of a innovative line of research by Robert Croyle and Peter Ditto. These investigators have focused on how people react to information about their health status, such as the results of a diagnostic test. Across a series of studies (described in Ditto and Croyle [1995]), these authors have observed that people are quicker to accept favorable health information (e.g., learning one does not have a health problem) than unfavorable health information (e.g., learning one does have a health problem). In addition to delineating how people process information about their health status, these authors demonstrate how a laboratory-based experimental paradigm can be used to provide crucial insights into important aspects of the health system (i.e., the communication of diagnostic test results).

People have to make inferences about a broad range of issues that could potentially affect their health. One of the more complex judgments people have to make are those concerning sexual behavior and the need to take precautions to prevent the transmission of disease and/or pregnancy. This judgment process can become even more complicated after people have a few drinks. Tara MacDonald and her colleagues (2000) have examined how alcohol consumption affects the judgment process and provide a fascinating analysis of how intoxication can at times make people take greater risks and at times make them take fewer risks.

REFERENCES

Ditto, P. H., & Croyle, R. T. (1995). Understanding the impact of risk factor test results: Insights from a basic research program. In R. T. Croyle (Ed.), *Psychosocial effects of screening for disease prevention and detection*. Oxford, England: Oxford University Press.

Liberman, A., & Chaiken, S. (1992). Defensive processing of

personally relevant health messages. *Personality and Social Psychology Bulletin, 18*, 669–679.

MacDonald, T. K., Fong, G. T., Zanna, M. P., & Martineau, A. M. (2000). Alcohol myopia and condom use: Can alcohol intoxication be associated with more prudent behavior? *Personality and Social Psychology Bulletin, 22*, 763–775.

Discussion Questions

1. It would appear from the articles in this section that the more involved people are in a health issue, the more likely they are to process information in a critical manner. Why might this not always be true? What conditions might lead people who are highly involved in an issue to process information in a more accepting manner?

2. To what extent are people aware that aspects of their current behavior or their current health status affect how they evaluate health information?

3. When people are informed that they have a serious health condition, they frequently seek out a second opinion. Should the decision to get a second opinion be interpreted as a sign of biased processing? Why or why not?

4. In light of the findings reported in this section, what strategies might you recommend to health professionals so that they communicate health information more effectively?

Suggested Readings

Aspinwall, L. G., & Brunhart, S. M. (1996). Distinguishing optimism from denial: Optimistic beliefs predict attention to health threats. *Personality and Social Psychology Bulletin, 22*, 993–1003.

An illustration of factors that increase people's attention to health risk information.

Ditto, P. H., & Lopez, D. F. (1992). Motivated skepticism: Use of differential decision criteria for preferred and nonpreferred conclusions. *Journal of Personality and Social Psychology, 63*, 568–584.

A compelling demonstration of the lengths people will go to question unwanted health information.

Leary, M. R., Tchividjian, L. R., & Kraxberger, B. E. (1994). Self-presentation can be hazardous to your health: Impression management and health risk. *Health Psychology, 13*, 461–470.

The authors discuss how a range of motivational concerns can affect how people respond to health risk information.

Martin, R., Gordon, E. I., & Lounsbury, P. (1998). Gender disparities in the attribution of cardiac-related symptoms: Contributions of common sense models of illness. *Health Psychology, 17*, 346–357.

A demonstration of how people's stereotypes regarding health problems can affect their response to health information.

McCaul, K. D., Thiesse-Duffy, E., & Wilson, P. (1992). Coping with medical diagnosis: The effects of at-risk versus disease labels over time. *Journal of Applied Social Psychology, 22*, 1340–1355.

An example of how people respond to actual treatment information about oral health.

Understanding the Impact of Risk Factor Test Results: Insights From a Basic Research Program

Peter H. Ditto and Robert T. Croyle

As part of an optional "wellness" program offered by his company, John makes an appointment to take a battery of medical screening tests. John feels well and has no obvious physical complaints. John arrives for his appointment at a medical building, completes a brief health history questionnaire, and has his blood pressure taken. John is then told about a condition called hypercholesterolemia, a high level of cholesterol in the blood, which is a risk factor for cardiovascular disease. John is administered a blood cholesterol test—his finger is pricked and he waits the few minutes to get his total cholesterol count. John is surprised when he is told that his cholesterol level is high (245 mg/dl).

As part of an extra-credit option in her introductory psychology course at college, Jane makes an appointment to serve as a subject in a research project on the health characteristics of college students. Jane feels well and has no obvious physical complaints. Jane arrives for her appointment at the research wing of the psychology department, completes a brief health history questionnaire, and has her blood pressure taken. Jane is then told about a condition called thioamine acetylase (TAA) enzyme deficiency, a risk factor for a complex of mild but irritating pancreatic disorders. Jane is told

how to self-administer a test for the presence of TAA—she dips a chemically coated test strip in a sample of her saliva and is told that if the test strip changes color it indicates that she has TAA deficiency. Jane is surprised when her test strip changes from its original yellow color to a dark green.

There are several salient differences between the two scenarios described above. The scenarios differ in the physical context within which the medical test is given, the specifics of how the test is administered, the age and gender of the individuals receiving the diagnostic information, and the familiarity and seriousness of the diagnosed risk factor and its ultimate medical consequences. And yet, it is easy to imagine that John and Jane might have quite similar reactions to the risk factor information each received in their respective scenarios. In fact, it will be our contention in this chapter that these two scenarios are, at least at the level of the psychological reactions expected from the two individuals, very similar. This is important because the central way that the two scenarios differ is that the first describes an actual risk factor screening situation, whereas the second describes one of our laboratory experiments. To the extent that the latter situation is a reasonable psychological analogue of the former, the cognitive, motivational, and social determinants of reactions to actual risk factor information become subject to careful examination in a highly controlled laboratory environment.

In this chapter, we begin by discussing limitations of research on the impact of risk factor testing in public health settings. We then provide a detailed description of our procedure for studying cognitive appraisals of risk factor information in the laboratory and describe the major findings generated by a series of studies using this procedure. In these studies, participants are randomized to different test result conditions. We will focus in particular on the two most commonly observed phenomena in our experimental studies: the denial of the threat represented by an unfavorable test result and the use of social comparison information to evaluate the seriousness and behavioral implications of the health threat. Next, we will examine the generalizability of the experimental findings. The data will show that the results from our basic experimental paradigm are readily replicated when tests are conducted in more realistic contexts, when tests for actual risk factors are used, and when the effects of several well-known individual difference variables are controlled.

Finally, the last part of this chapter will discuss another issue related to generalization: the relationship between cognitive appraisals (the dependent variable in most of our experiments) and health-related behavior (usually the focus of risk factor screening programs). We will discuss a consistent finding in our research that has both theoretical and practical importance: defensive cognitive appraisals and problem-focused coping behavior are functionally independent. If defensively optimistic assessments of the threat represented by a risk factor do not necessarily interfere with adaptive coping behavior, then attempts to "correct" these assessments may be misguided and, ultimately, counterproductive.

Limitations of Previous Risk Factor Labeling Research

The other chapters in this volume review the public health research literature concerning labeling effects. As noted by the other contributors, interpreting this scattered body of work is a difficult task. Not only is the amount of research limited, it

is also characterized by a number of methodological limitations. One of the most critical limitations is that most of the studies utilize designs that do not test cause-and-effect relationships. The vast majority of studies rely on observational designs that greatly limit the ability of investigators to identify causal links between risk notification and psychosocial responses. Most of the prospective studies do not include control groups. Because risk status is often correlated with many other variables, the effect of communicating different test results is heavily confounded. The only way to eliminate confounds is to randomly assign study participants to different types of test feedback. Therefore, only an experiment that utilizes some form of deception can provide a pure examination of the effects of risk factor test results and the psychological processes underlying these effects.

Although the use of temporary deception in basic psychological research is unfamiliar to many public health researchers, deception has long been used by social psychologists to investigate issues such as conformity, impression formation, persuasion, group conflict, prejudice, and aggression (Aronson, Ellsworth, Carlsmith, & Gonzales, 1990). One reason why deception is used so often in this research is that social behavior is highly reactive. It is also subject to social desirability motives. For example, research subjects are often unwilling to admit to possessing racist attitudes and beliefs. Therefore, it is not surprising that when Silverman (1974) asked college students to pick a hypothetical roommate, the race of the potential roommate had no influence on selections. On the other hand, when subjects were told that their decision would determine their actual roommate (a deception), race became a significant determinant of selections. This illustrates another reason why deception is used: judgments and behaviors are often substantially different when individuals are highly involved in a situation that has direct personal relevance.

The Feasibility of an Experimental Approach to Studying Risk Factor Testing

The psychological dynamics of risk factor screening differ in some important ways from diagnosis in traditional primary care. Primary care patients are often motivated to seek care because of their physical symptoms. They expect and desire a diagnosis, prognosis, and treatment. In these settings, diagnoses are often communicated to individuals who already perceive themselves as ill.

In the case of risk factor screening, many of the individuals who are confronted with risk information are asymptomatic. The central goal in studying labeling effects, therefore, is to achieve an understanding of the psychological effects of *subjective health status*—for example, the belief that one has an elevated risk for a life-threatening disease. By randomizing study participants to different risk information conditions, perceived risk status can be studied in a highly controlled manner. Because risk factor information is typically communicated to individuals who are asymptomatic, healthy populations can be used as subjects.

The TAA Enzyme Paradigm

Spurred on by the belief that risk factor labeling could be studied experimentally in the laboratory, our first step was to develop a viable laboratory analogue of the risk factor testing situation. In collaboration with John Jemmott, we developed a procedure that was intended to recreate the psychological experience of an actual risk factor screening situation while remaining sensitive to the ethical constraints required by an experimental approach. In addition, the procedure was intended to be flexible. Flexibility was important because we hoped to model many different real-world settings, manipulate a wide range of independent variables, and measure many different dependent variables, all while using a standard set of procedures.

The core of the procedure involves bringing study participants into the laboratory and "testing" them for the presence of a fictitious risk factor. Two aspects of the procedure rely on deception. Participants are told that the risk factor is real. In addition, participants are randomly assigned to receive either a positive or a negative test result. Why use a fictitious risk factor? We had four primary reasons. First, the use of a fictitious risk factor controls for individual differences in knowledge and experience. This source of variance has been one of the primary barriers to progress in research on labeling effects. Second, the use of a

fictitious risk factor allows for more effective debriefing in that subjects can be told not only that they do not have the risk factor but that the risk factor itself does not exist. Third, the perceived seriousness of a fictitious risk factor can be controlled and consequently set at a level that is minimally sufficient to produce the desired impact. Finally, the use of a fictitious risk factor provides a great deal of experimental flexibility; the investigator is free to control and test the impact of a wide variety of independent variables without contradicting prior knowledge.

So far, all of the studies that have used the enzyme test procedure have employed college students as subjects. Participants are recruited for a study of college students' health characteristics. When students arrive for their appointment, they are met by an experimenter in a white laboratory coat and seated in a room filled with medical paraphernalia (e.g., posters, pamphlets, charts). Participants generally begin the session by completing a health history and having their blood pressure taken. With this context created, subjects are told about a diagnostic test for a condition called "Thioamine Acetylase (TAA) Deficiency." TAA deficiency is said to be a recently discovered enzyme condition that is a risk factor for a complex of "mild but irritating pancreatic disorders."

Participants are told that there is a simple diagnostic test for TAA deficiency that involves dipping a chemically coated test strip in a saliva sample and looking for a color reaction. Participants then self-administer the test. They begin by rinsing their mouths with mouth-wash (ostensibly to cleanse their mouths for the test). The student then places a saliva sample in a cup and "tests" this saliva by immersing a "TAA test strip." This test strip is actually a common urinary glucose test strip. Because a small amount of dextrose has been dissolved in the mouthwash, the test strip turns from yellow to green when placed in contact with the saliva. All participants see this color reaction but are led to interpret it in different ways. The meaning of the test result is manipulated by telling some subjects that the color reaction indicates a positive test result (i.e., TAA deficiency) and telling others that it indicates a negative test result (i.e., normal TAA presence).

After receiving their test result, subjects complete a series of questionnaires in which questions about the fictitious condition and diagnostic test are embedded in similar questions about actual health disorders and diagnostic tests. Medical conditions that are likely to be as unfamiliar as TAA deficiency are included to mask our particular interest in judgments about TAA deficiency. Completion of these questionnaires typically takes less than 10 minutes, after which subjects are thoroughly debriefed.

Reports of subjects after participation suggest that the procedure is quite convincing without causing emotional upset. Although the paradigm relies on deception, suspicion rates are typically very low (5% or less). Subjects perceive TAA deficiency to be about as serious as laryngitis (Ditto, Jemmott, & Darley, 1988). The time between the diagnostic feedback and debriefing is kept at a minimum. Subjects high in hypochondriacal tendencies are often excluded from participation, as are diabetics and hypoglycemics (because of the use of dextrose in the procedure). For further discussion of the paradigm and its limitations, see Croyle and Ditto (1990).

Motivational and Social Determinants of Risk Factor Appraisal: An Initial Investigation

In the first experiment to utilize this procedure, Jemmott, Ditto, and Croyle (1986) provided initial evidence for two phenomena that have become the focus of much of our subsequent research. The first issue addressed by this experiment was whether this procedure could be used to uncover evidence of denial reactions in response to unfavorable medical information. Although denial and other forms of defensiveness in response to illness are well accepted clinically (Hackett & Cassem, 1969; Janis, 1958; Kubler-Ross, 1969; Lipowski, 1970), our review of the literature turned up only scattered and indirect empirical evidence of these phenomena. In fact, the very existence of such motivated biases in judgment have been a controversial issue in experimental psychology for over 40 years (Erdelyi, 1974; Miller & Ross, 1975; Tetlock & Levi, 1982). The TAA enzyme procedure is quite useful in exploring evidence of denial in that it isolates the independent variable of interest (level of threat) and allows a direct analysis of causal relationships.

The second issue of interest in the Jemmott et al. study was the role of prevalence information in reactions to risk factor information. Zola (1966) observed that ailments are less likely to stimulate a treatment-seeking response in populations where those ailments are relatively widespread. One interpretation of this finding is that people perceive health disorders as less serious to the extent that they appear to be common. Again, the TAA enzyme procedure seemed perfectly suited to examine this question. By providing participants with different information about the prevalence of TAA deficiency, we could examine the effects of this variable on seriousness judgments.

Jemmott et al. designed an experiment to examine these two issues. Half of the subjects were led to believe they tested positive for TAA deficiency, and half that they tested negative. In addition, half of the subjects were led to believe TAA deficiency was relatively common, and half that it was relatively rare. One obvious way we might have manipulated perceived prevalence was with statistical information. However, we wanted to manipulate prevalence information in a way that more closely resembled how such information is obtained in everyday life. Subjects participated in groups of two or three with each individual in a separate room, but all subjects were led to believe that five subjects were participating in the session. Each subject self-administered the enzyme test and reported the results to the experimenter. In the high-prevalence conditions, the experimenter then told the subject that four of the five students had tested positive for the deficiency. In the low-prevalence conditions, the subject was told that just one of the five students had the deficiency. In this way, the perceived prevalence of TAA deficiency was manipulated by altering its prevalence in the subject's immediate social comparison group.

The results of the study provided strong evidence for both of the predicted effects. Two common forms of denial described in medical patients are minimization of the seriousness of the health threat (Janis, 1958; Lazarus, 1983; Lipowski, 1970) and heightened skepticism regarding the validity of the diagnosis (Visotsky, Hamburg, Goss, & Lebovitz, 1961). After the diagnostic feedback, subjects rated the seriousness of TAA deficiency on a 100-point scale (where 0 = not serious, can be ignored, and 100 = very serious, life-threatening), and the accuracy of the diagnostic test for TAA on a 9-point scale (where 9 = very accurate).

Subjects who tested positive for TAA deficiency rated it as a significantly less serious threat to health than did subjects who tested negative. Similarly, positive-result subjects rated the saliva reaction test as a significantly less accurate indicator of TAA deficiency than did negative-result subjects. That this effect is due to denial is further supported by the finding that the tendency to denigrate the accuracy of the test was particularly pronounced when subjects believed that they alone had received the positive test result.

The effects of the prevalence manipulation also confirmed our expectations. When subjects believed that only one of the five students had tested positive for TAA deficiency, they perceived the deficiency as significantly more serious than when they believed four of the five students had tested positive. Thus, even though the medically significant information about the deficiency was exactly the same in both conditions, subjects rated the enzyme condition as more serious when it appeared to be rare than when it appeared to be common.

The Jemmott et al. experiment provided support for the viability of an experimental approach to studying risk factor appraisals as well as evidence of two important determinants of such appraisals. Subsequent research has expanded on both of the major findings of this study, and each of these lines of research will be discussed in turn.

Denial of Risk Factor Information

Are the relatively optimistic threat appraisals of positive-result subjects the project of a defensive motivational process like denial or of some more rational aspect of information processing? Given our desire to understand the labeling process, one focus of our subsequent research with the TAA paradigm has been to rule out competing, nonmotivational explanations for the effect of favorability of test results on threat-related appraisals. Not only has this work confirmed the motivational nature of this phenomenon, but, along the way, many interesting findings have emerged regarding the conditions under which denial reactions are most likely to be observed and the wide variety of forms such denial reactions are likely to take.

Denial and Confirmatory Symptom Reporting

One alternative explanation for the denial effects observed in the Jemmott et al. study hinges on the differential symptom information that was potentially available to positive and negative test result subjects. Healthy college students who are told that they have an abnormal health condition may have special knowledge about it—that people (like themselves) who have the disorder do not feel ill. In other words, if we assume that positive-result subjects feel well and are not experiencing symptoms, they might conclude that TAA deficiency is not serious or that the test is inaccurate. Because negative-result subjects are not privy to this information, they may be more likely to conclude that the condition is serious. If minimization occurs primarily when a tested person cannot uncover relevant symptoms, this would suggest that asymptomatic persons should be the least likely to acknowledge the validity of information concerning their heightened susceptibility.

This explanation, of course, presumes that when given the positive test result, subjects in the Jemmott et al. study did not perceive themselves as having symptoms consistent with the diagnosis. A study by Croyle and Sande (1988), however, suggests that this presumption is incorrect. Like the Jemmott et al. study, Croyle and Sande presented subjects with positive and negative test results for TAA deficiency. In addition to measures of perceived seriousness and test accuracy, subjects in this study also completed a symptom checklist after receiving their diagnosis. Subjects were told that symptoms on the list were suspected of being related to TAA deficiency.

The denial effect observed in the Jemmott et al. study was replicated in the Croyle and Sande study: Subjects who tested positive for TAA deficiency rated it as less serious and the diagnostic test as less accurate than subjects who tested negative for the condition. In addition, subjects' responses to the symptom checklist indicated that positive test result subjects were able to uncover substantial evidence from memory to confirm the presence of TAA deficiency. Positive-result subjects tended to recall more diagnosis-consistent symptoms than did other subjects. Furthermore, subjects receiving the positive result also recalled more behav-

TABLE 7.1. Mean Scores on Diagnosis-Consistent Symptom and Risk Behavior Recall Indices as a Function of Test Result

Recall measure	Test result	
	Positive	Negative
Symptoms	30.62	20.54
Risk behaviors	101.52	86.79

Source: Croyle & Sande (1988).
Note. Recall indices were calculated by summing (across 11 diagnosis-consistent symptoms and 9 risk-enhancing behaviors) the number of days during the previous month the subject reported experiencing the symptom or engaging in the behavior.

iors that were labeled as increasing the risk of TAA deficiency (see Table 7.1).

The Croyle and Sande experiment provided important experimental evidence that risk factor labeling has a direct impact on self-reports of symptoms and health behaviors. These data are also consistent with Leventhal's self-regulation model of illness behavior (Leventhal, Nerenz, & Steele, 1984), which states that individuals assume and seek symmetry between illness labels and symptoms (Leventhal, Meyer, & Nerenz, 1980). The study also provides evidence that is directly inconsistent with one alternative explanation of our findings. Participants do not minimize the seriousness of the risk factor simply because they are unaware of any relevant symptoms.

Denial and Perceived Treatability

Ditto et al. (1988) took a different approach to examine the motivated nature of reactions to unfavorable test results. Research and theory from the stress and coping literature suggest that denial and other forms of defensiveness are most likely to occur when an individual has no means of immediately reducing the threat (Cohen & Lazarus, 1973; Janis, 1984; Leventhal, 1970). Consequently, two quite different predictions can be made regarding how threat appraisals are likely to be affected by the perception that an unfavorable diagnosis is amenable to treatment. If we adopt the viewpoint of a rational actor, it is reasonable to assume that a treatable disease should be perceived as less threatening than an untreatable one (unless the treatment itself is aversive). From the viewpoint of a person motivated to deny threat, on the other hand, knowledge that the threat can be reduced in the future may allow the individual to more fully acknowledge its immediate seriousness. Following this reasoning, if motivated denial is operating, information that a given disorder is treatable should lead to a paradoxical *increase* in perceived threat among those labeled at risk.

In order to test these competing predictions, Ditto et al. again led some subjects to believe that they had TAA deficiency and some to believe that they did not. Before the risk factor test was conducted, however, half of the subjects were given additional information concerning the treatability of TAA deficiency. Subjects in the treatment-informed condition were told that "treatment for TAA deficiency is relatively simple and painless. A short-term medication program has been found to correct the deficiency in most people by stimulating TAA production."

The results of the study again provide evidence of motivated denial. Subjects who believed they had the deficiency and were not provided with treatment information made a series of judgments that downplayed the threat represented by their test result. In contrast, positive-result, treatment-informed subjects gave responses that did not differ significantly from the negative-result conditions (see Table 7.2).

TABLE 7.2. Mean Scores on Threat-Related Perceptions as a Function of Test Result and Treatment Information

Dependent measure	Positive test result		Negative test result	
	Uninformed	Informed	Uninformed	Informed
TAA test's false-positive rate (%)	24.62	13.95	13.73	12.33
Seriousness of TAA deficiency	22.14	31.43	44.67	39.33
Probability of pancreatic disease given TAA deficiency (%)	21.10	21.67	29.73	43.47
Seriousness of pancreatic disease	55.71	71.90	69.33	60.00
Color of TAA test strip	5.86	6.38	6.73	7.40

Source: Ditto et al. (1988).
Note. The estimated greenness of the TAA strip is on a scale from 1 to 10, where higher numbers indicate darker green. Higher numbers indicate greater perceived seriousness of TAA deficiency and pancreatic disease.

In addition to providing additional support for the existence of denial reactions, the Ditto et al. study illustrates the variety of forms such denial reactions can take. As can be seen in Table 7.2, positive-result, treatment-uninformed subjects showed evidence of denial on ratings of the seriousness of both TAA deficiency and pancreatic disease, on estimates of the false-positive rate of the TAA diagnostic test, and on estimates of the probability that TAA deficiency leads to pancreatic disease. Moreover, these subjects' desire not to have the diagnosed condition also manifested itself in perceptual distortion: when shown a color scale and asked to estimate how green their "TAA test strip" had turned, positive-result, treatment-uninformed subjects remembered a less pronounced color reaction than did other subjects.

Denial and Expectations

One last alternative explanation for the motivational account of our denial findings concerns the role of expectations in reactions to medical diagnosis. According to this account, subjects confronted with an unfavorable test result may rate it as less accurate, not because they don't *want* to be sick but rather because they don't *expect* to be sick. Sickness is statistically less common than health, particularly within a college student population. Positive-result subjects may thus discount the accuracy of the test compared with negative-result subjects because the positive result is less expected than the negative result and, consequently, less plausible.

A study by Ditto and Lopez (1992, Study 3) addresses this issue. In this study, all subjects were told that they had a relatively rare enzyme condition (present in only 5% of the general population); however, the desirability of this condition was manipulated. Half of the subjects were told, as in previous studies, that the enzyme condition was detrimental to health (increasing one's susceptibility to pancreatic disease). The other half, however, were told that the enzyme condition was actually *beneficial* to health (decreasing one's susceptibility to future pancreatic disease). In addition, half of the subjects completed denial-related dependent measures *after* receiving their diagnostic feedback, whereas the other half answered questions about their diagnosis after hearing the description of the condition but *before* taking the diagnostic test.

The results provided strong support for motivated denial. Subjects asked before receiving their diagnostic feedback rated the test as equally accurate whether the enzyme condition was described as beneficial or detrimental to health. Subjects asked after the diagnostic test, in contrast, rated the test as significantly less accurate when they believed it to indicate a detrimental condition than when they believed it to indicate a beneficial one (see Table 7.3). A similar pattern was shown when subjects were asked to list any recent irregularities in their diet, stress level, and so on that they believed might have affected the accuracy of their test. As can be seen in Table 7.3, like the perceived accuracy ratings, the number of irregularities cited by beneficial-to-health and detrimental-to-health subjects did not differ before receiving their diagnosis. When asked after receiving their diagnosis, however, subjects who believed they had the detrimental condition cited significantly more irregularities that might have affected the accuracy of their test than did subjects diagnosed with the beneficial condition. That these differences are due to the motivational implications of the feedback rather than its consistency with expectations is confirmed by an additional question asked of the

TABLE 7.3. Mean Perceived Accuracy of Diagnostic Test and Number of Life Irregularities Cited as a Function of Timing of Dependent Measure (Before vs. After Diagnosis) and Desirability of Enzyme Condition (Healthy vs. Unhealthy)

Dependent measure	Before diagnosis		After diagnosis	
	Healthy	Unhealthy	Healthy	Unhealthy
Perceived accuracy of TAA test	6.95	6.68	7.31	5.68
Number of life irregularities cited	1.30	1.21	.55	1.75

Source: Ditto & Lopez (1992).
Note. Higher numbers indicate greater perceived accuracy of TAA test.

pre-diagnosis subjects. When asked before receiving their diagnostic feedback, subjects believing the enzyme condition to be beneficial to health and those believing it to be detrimental to health did not differ in their perceived likelihood of testing positive for the condition.

The Nature of Denial

In addition to providing additional support for the existence of motivational biases in illness appraisals, Ditto and Lopez (1992) offer some specific insights into the nature of these biases. These authors argue that denial and other forms of motivated judgment are a product of the simple fact that more thought is given to information with undesirable implications than to information with desirable implications. That is, a variety of evidence suggests that information that is consistent with a preferred judgment conclusion (e.g., that one is smart, likable, or healthy) receives relatively little cognitive analysis. Because of this uncritical analysis, the validity of information we want to believe is often accepted "at face value." Information that is *inconsistent* with a preferred judgment conclusion, on the other hand (e.g., information suggesting that one is not so smart, difficult to like, or ill), seems to trigger relatively extensive, detail-oriented cognitive analysis. Several authors (e.g., Pratto & John, 1991; Schwarz, 1990) have suggested that from an adaptive perspective it makes sense that individuals should be relatively attentive to negative information because it, more often than positive information, requires an immediate behavioral response. However, because the relatively careful analysis given to unwanted information is likely to uncover alternative (and more palatable) explanations for it, a more skeptical view of its validity (i.e., denial) often results.

This view of denial as a kind of "motivated skepticism" has two important implications. First, denial is not an all-or-nothing phenomenon. Individuals confronted with an unfavorable medical diagnosis do not deny its validity and seriousness in toto, but rather are simply more likely to view that information as potentially explainable in other, less threatening ways. This is quite consistent with the results of our studies. Positive-result subjects do not view the diagnostic test as completely inaccurate or the diagnosed disorder as completely benign, but only as relatively inaccurate and rela-

tively benign in comparison with negative-result subjects. In fact, the best characterization of our positive-result subjects is that their responses indicate uncertainty about the validity and seriousness of the diagnosis.

The second and related implication is that individuals are quite responsive to negative information—eventually. Most people hold a variety of negative beliefs about themselves (Markus & Wurf, 1987), and even among individuals confronted with diagnoses of cancer, profound denial reactions are clearly the exception rather than the rule (Aitken-Swan & Easson, 1959; Gilbertson & Wangersteen, 1962). Ditto and Lopez suggest that rather than leading individuals to believe whatever they prefer to believe, motivational factors bias judgments more subtly by affecting *the amount of information* required to reach conclusions. People are responsive to incoming information and will generally follow the implications of that information to both preferred and nonpreferred conclusions. However, the greater processing given to undesirable information ought to lead individuals, all else being equal, to reach the point of acceptance somewhat more reluctantly (i.e., after a greater amount or quality of information is received) for nonpreferred conclusions than preferred ones.

To examine the idea that more information is required to reach a nonpreferred conclusion than a preferred one, Ditto and Lopez (1992, Study 2) again confronted subjects with either a positive or negative test result for TAA deficiency. In this study, however, this was accomplished by having the TAA test strip remain yellow after contact with saliva rather than turn green. The urinary glucose strips previously used as TAA test strips were replaced with yellow construction paper. When no color reaction was observed after dipping the construction paper in their saliva, half of the subjects perceived this to indicate that they had TAA deficiency (those who would have been negative-result subjects in past studies), and half perceived this to indicate that they did not have TAA deficiency (positive-result subjects in past studies). Subjects were then surreptitiously videotaped while they self-administered the TAA test. All subjects were told that if a color reaction was to take place, it was generally complete within 20 seconds. Subjects were also told that it was important that as soon as they thought their test result was clear, they were to seal their test strip in a provided envelope. The key dependent measure in this study was the amount of time subjects took to decide their test result was complete (i.e., to accept that their test strip was not going to turn green). This was operationalized as the number of seconds between when subjects dipped their test strip in their saliva and when they sealed their test strip in the provided envelope.

All subjects interpreted the test result consistent with instructions. As predicted, however, subjects took almost 30 seconds longer to decide that their test result was complete when they believed that the lack of a color reaction indicated that they had TAA deficiency than when they believed no color reaction to be a negative test result. Stated another way, subjects required more information (i.e., more time) to reach a nonpreferred conclusion (i.e., that they had the risk factor) than to reach a preferred conclusion (i.e., that they did not have the risk factor).

The extra time positive-result subjects required to make their decision was not spent idly. Judges also coded the videotapes for whether subjects "retested" the validity of their diagnosis after observing the initial lack of color reaction. It was found that negative-result subjects typically dipped their test strip once, observed it for a few seconds, and sealed it in the envelope. Positive-result subjects, in contrast, were significantly more likely to engage in retesting behaviors such as repeatedly dipping their test strip in their saliva, testing more than one test strip, testing more than one saliva sample, and so on.

One way to view this retesting behavior is as an experimental analogue of the well-known tendency of medical patients to "seek a second opinion." Both the results of this experiment and common sense suggest that individuals are more likely to seek a second opinion when the first opinion is not to their liking. The results may also have implications for home diagnostic testing. Individuals may violate proper testing procedures in order to increase their chance of achieving a favorable result.

Summary

Our studies on college students' reactions to experimentally manipulated diagnoses provide clear support for denial reactions to unfavorable medical test results. Several studies provide converging evidence that the relatively optimistic threat appraisals of positive-result subjects are a function of their desire not to receive this information rather than a rational conclusion based on available symptom or expectancy information. Our studies also suggest that denial is most pronounced when individuals perceive no possibility of a behavioral response to reduce the threat. This suggests that individuals are likely to respond more defensively to a risk factor perceived to be uncontrollable (e.g., one with a genetic basis) than one perceived to be more amenable to change (e.g., one with a behavioral basis). Finally, although the desire to downplay the threat of an unfavorable diagnosis is strong and shows up in many different forms, our data suggest that individuals are ultimately responsive to negative risk factor information. The evidential requirements for accepting an unfavorable diagnosis, however, are stricter than those for accepting a favorable diagnosis and, consequently, clear proof of risk factor status may be necessary before individuals fully acquiesce to its unwanted implications.

The Social Nature of Risk Factor Appraisal

Social comparison theory (Festinger, 1954) states that when clear evaluative standards are absent, people evaluate themselves by comparing themselves with others. The effects of prevalence information on risk factor appraisal is a clear example of just this sort of social comparison process. Confronted with an unfamiliar health condition of undetermined seriousness, subjects in the Jemmott et al. (1986) study turned to their immediate social environment for evaluative information. But why should an identically described health disorder be perceived as less serious when it appears to be common than when it appears to be rare?

One answer is that people use perceived prevalence to evaluate the seriousness of health disorders because in many judgmental domains prevalence information is quite predictive of evaluative extremity. Ditto and Jemmott (1989) argue that a basic principle of social comparison is that characteristics are evaluated extremely only to the extent that they differentiate one from others. This is true with both positive and negative characteristics. The ability to run a certain speed or jump a certain distance, for example, is evaluated more positively the fewer the number of other people who are able to match or surpass one's performance. Similarly, a poor performance on some task (e.g., the failure of a math test) is evaluated more negatively the more unusual it is perceived to be. The use of prevalence information to infer evaluation in these domains is quite reasonable. In fact, in these domains the evaluation of performance is almost solely determined by its prevalence.

Ditto and Jemmott argued that based on our experience with domains in which evaluation is socially determined, we come to rely on a *scarcity heuristic* when making all sorts of evaluative judgments. According to this decision-making shortcut, positive stimuli are evaluated more positively and negative stimuli are evaluated more negatively when they are perceived to be rare. When making evaluative judgments in a domain such as health in which evaluation is not socially determined (i.e., the commonness of a health disorder does not determine its seriousness), prevalence information is still used quite automatically to determine evaluative extremity. Ditto and Jemmott (1989) provided evidence for this account in two studies. In both studies, subjects were told about an enzyme condition that either increases or decreases susceptibility to pancreatic disease and is either relatively common or relatively rare. In one study, subjects were told that they had the condition and that either one or four of five fellow subjects had it. In the second study, subjects merely read about the condition. The perceived prevalence of the condition was varied by providing different subjects with different statistical information. Identical results were obtained in both studies: the enzyme condition was evaluated more extremely—more positively when it was said to be beneficial, more negatively when it was said to be detrimental—when it was perceived to be rare.

From these and other data, Ditto and Jemmott argue that the effect of prevalence information on risk factor evaluations is simply one example of our reliance on a quite general evaluation shortcut or heuristic. As is the case with other judgmental heuristics (e.g., Tversky & Kahneman, 1974), the scarcity heuristic is not an altogether unreasonable decision strategy. However, because it relies on a "shortcut" inference process, it may lead to erroneous conclusions in some circumstances (see

Ditto & Jemmott, 1989, for a fuller discussion of this point).

Illness Appraisals and Direct Social Influence

Prevalence information is not the only social influence on risk factor appraisals. Appraisals may also be affected more directly by the appraisals stated by others. This is important because prior to seeking formal medical attention, individuals often utilize "lay conferral" networks (e.g., Friedson, 1961) in which the appraisals of family and friends are actively sought in an attempt to interpret uncertain medical situations (Francis, Korsch, & Morris, 1969; Kleinman, Eisenberg, & Good, 1978).

In an initial attempt to capture this more direct form of social influence in the laboratory, Croyle and Hunt (1991) tested subjects for TAA deficiency in the presence of a same-sex confederate who played the role of a second subject. Subjects always tested positive for the deficiency; the test result of the confederate was varied. In addition, for half of the subjects, after receiving the diagnostic information the confederate made a comment that minimized the seriousness of the deficiency ("It doesn't seem like a big deal to me").

Croyle and Hunt found a complex pattern of social influence consistent with the Leventhal et al. (1984) model (see Table 7.4). Leventhal et al. argue that responses to health threats are characterized by two coping processes that occur in parallel. One process involves coping with the threat itself and often is manifested by efforts to reduce risk. A second process involves coping with the fear and other emotional responses to the threatening information. Croyle and Hunt's findings illustrate how these two processes can be affected by different factors. Subjects exposed to the confederate's minimizing comment expressed less *concern* about their diagnosis than did subjects not exposed to the comment. Subjects' *behavioral intentions* (plans to reduce risk), however, were not affected by the confederate's comments. Rather, intentions to engage in preventive behavior were significantly affected only by the confederate's *diagnosis*. When the confederate also tested positive for the deficiency, subjects reported fewer behavioral intentions than when he or she tested negative. Interestingly, these behavioral intentions

TABLE 7.4. Mean Concern and Behavioral Intention Scores as a Function of Confederate's Comment and Test Result

Dependent measure	No comment		Minimizing comment	
	Positive	Negative	Positive	Negative
Concern about TAA deficiency	36.77	45.16	29.23	29.29
Behavioral intention	20.26	23.26	19.69	24.70

Source: Croyle & Hunt (1991).
Note. Higher numbers indicate greater concern about TAA deficiency. The health behavior intention score was calculated by summing the ratings of seven behavior intention items. Higher numbers of the behavioral intention index indicate greater intention to engage in behaviors that decrease the risk of developing TAA deficiency.

were mediated by subjects' perceptions of the prevalence of the deficiency. Mediational analyses revealed that the confederate's positive test result led to perceptions of greater prevalence, which in turn resulted in weaker behavioral intentions. Thus, although this study reveals the importance of more direct forms of social influence on risk factor appraisals, prevalence perceptions again appear to be a key contributing factor.

Illness Appraisals and the False Consensus Bias

Prevalence perceptions not only affect risk factor appraisals but are also affected by them. A commonly observed bias in social psychological research is people's tendency to overestimate the commonness of their behaviors and characteristics. This *false consensus bias* (Ross, Greene, & House, 1977) is also a common finding in our research. Subjects told that they have TAA deficiency estimate its prevalence in the general population to be higher than do subjects told that they do not have TAA deficiency (e.g., Croyle & Sande, 1988; Ditto & Lopez, 1992).

Both motivational and information-processing interpretations of the false consensus bias have been posited (Goethals, 1986; Ross et al., 1977), and which is a better interpretation of the finding in the TAA paradigm is unclear. Given that a common disorder is perceived as less serious than a rare disorder, it is tempting to interpret this bias as another manifestation of defensiveness. Convincing oneself that one's affliction is common should also help convince oneself that it may not be serious. An equally plausible explanation, however, hinges on the differential information available to positive- and negative-result subjects. Positive-result subjects know one person who has the condition (themselves), whereas negative-result subjects

do not. Thus, positive-result subjects might reasonably infer from their own ostensible affliction that other people must also be unknowingly afflicted, whereas the basis for this inference is not available to negative-result subjects.

Whatever the genesis of these differential prevalence perceptions, once established they are likely to have some important implications. For example, unlike some of the other biases we have documented in college students' judgments, the false consensus bias is also manifested by physicians. Jemmott, Ditto, and Croyle (1988) sent questionnaires to 65 practicing physicians asking them about their experience with and beliefs about 13 well-known health disorders (e.g., migraine headaches, viral pneumonia). Physicians' estimates of the prevalence of the health disorders in the general population revealed a false consensus bias. Physicians who had experienced a given health problem gave higher estimates of its prevalence than did physicians who had never experienced the problem. For example, physicians who had herpes simplex virus infection of the lips estimated its population prevalence at 52%. Physicians who had never experienced the same problem estimated its prevalence to be only 15%.

These findings have implications for diagnostic reasoning. Medical textbooks suggest that physicians consider the prevalence of a particular disorder both in general and within a specific subpopulation when developing diagnostic hypotheses (Cutler, 1979; Petersdorf et al., 1983). Several studies have also shown that diagnostic reasoning is biased toward hypothesis confirmation (Elstein, Shulman, & Sprafka, 1978; Snyder, 1984). Putting these two facts together, it seems possible that physicians who believe that a particular disorder is prevalent because they have had it themselves may be more likely to entertain that disorder as a diagnostic hypothesis and, consequently, more likely to decide on it as the ultimate diagnosis. In the case of risk factor labeling, this suggests that physicians' beliefs concerning their own risk factor status may have a direct or indirect influence on their identification of important risk factors in their patients. The extent to which physicians' personal experience with health disorders influences their diagnostic strategies and ultimate diagnoses is an important topic for future research.

Summary

Our research suggests that risk factor appraisal has important social psychological aspects. Appraisals of the seriousness of a risk factor are affected by the appraisals offered by others. That this effect was demonstrated in a laboratory context with the appraisal of a stranger suggests that this effect is likely to be considerably more pronounced when such appraisals are offered by a good friend or family member. Seriousness judgments are also affected by the perceived prevalence of the risk factor. Although this may not at first glance seem unreasonable, the heuristic nature of this judgment strategy creates the possibility of misperceptions. One simple example of this in our studies is the fact that subjects readily base their prevalence estimates (and consequently their seriousness appraisals) on data gathered from very small samples. Even if the prevalence of a condition was perfectly predictive of its severity, a prevalence estimate based on a sample of one (Croyle & Hunt, 1991) or even five (Ditto & Jemmott, 1989; Jemmott et al., 1986) may be highly unrepresentative of the actual prevalence rate in the general population. Finally, our studies reveal a false census bias in risk factor appraisals. Although the specific causes of this bias are unclear, it is revealed by both physicians and laypersons and may have important consequences for both populations' subsequent decision making.

The Generalizability Issue

The preceding sections have reviewed some of the insights gained about risk factor appraisals from a series of laboratory experiments. The strengths of laboratory experimentation are clear. The ability of our experimental procedure to isolate the causal

contribution of specific factors to specific aspects of risk factor appraisals cannot be matched with more naturalistic methodologies. And yet, the weaknesses of laboratory experimentation are equally clear. The purchase price of internal validity is the greater assumptions that must be made about external validity. In the case of our TAA experiments, the question concerns the degree to which the phenomena we observe in our laboratory simulation generalize to people's appraisals of actual risk factors in actual risk factor screening situations.

In the sections that follow we discuss several of the most commonly mentioned generalization issues that arise concerning the results of our TAA studies. Where possible, we then describe data to address each issue. To foreshadow our conclusions, considerable data supports the generalizability of the basic findings obtained with the TAA enzyme paradigm.

Psychological Reactions to Well-Known Risk Factors

Perhaps the most often expressed concern about the TAA enzyme paradigm is its use of a fictitious and therefore completely unfamiliar risk factor. The assumption is that individuals might respond quite differently when confronted with evidence of some more familiar health condition.

Two different lines of research, however, suggest that the basic phenomena that are observed in reaction to TAA deficiency can be observed in reactions to actual risk factors as well. The first examines judgments about actual health conditions within a survey format. The second is a series of studies in which individuals are given experimentally engineered feedback about their status on some actual risk factor.

Jemmott et al. (1988, Study 1) asked college students to make a series of judgments about 12 well-known health disorders. Three major findings emerged. First, consistent with the minimization effect found in laboratory TAA studies, individuals who had experienced a given disorder rated that disorder as significantly less serious than did individuals who had not experienced that disorder. Second, consistent with the finding that prevalence information affects seriousness judgments, the average correlation between students' estimates of the prevalence of a given disorder in the general population and their rating of its seriousness was significant and negative. That is, the more common a given disorder was perceived to be, the less serious it was perceived to be and vice versa (see also Jemmott et al., 1986). Finally, a false consensus effect was also observed. Individuals who had experienced a given disorder gave higher estimates of its prevalence in the general population than did individuals with no experience with the disorder. Although the causal interpretation of the observed relationships is less clear in this correlational data than in the experimental data, the converging findings from the two approaches provide strong evidence for generalizability.

The results from experimental studies tell a similar tale. Croyle, Sun, and Louie (1993) gave subjects a standard blood cholesterol screening test and randomly assigned them to receive a total cholesterol reading that was either in the clearly low-risk range (174 mg/dl) or one that was borderline high (224 mg/dl). (Subjects were given their actual cholesterol readings during debriefing.) Appraisals of the cholesterol feedback were remarkably similar to appraisals of randomized TAA feedback. Subjects receiving the borderline-high feedback rated high cholesterol as a less serious threat to health, gave higher estimates of its population prevalence, and viewed the cholesterol test as less accurate than did subjects receiving the more desirable reading.

McCaul, Thiesse-Duffy, and Wilson (1991) found very similar results in appraisals of bogus gum disease feedback. Subjects volunteered to have a standard gum health exam at a campus dental office. After completing the examination, subjects were randomly assigned to receive one of three diagnoses from the dental hygienist. One third were told that they had gum disease, one third that they were at risk for gum disease, and the final third that they did not have gum disease. Subjects' postdiagnosis appraisals were consistent with previous research. Subjects told they had gum disease rated it as a more common condition than did subjects receiving at-risk feedback, who in turn perceived it as more common than did subjects receiving no-disease feedback. Disease and at-risk subjects also rated gum disease as a less serious threat to health than did no-disease subjects. Finally, the "paradoxical" relationship between denial and confirmatory symptom reporting (Croyle & Sande, 1988) was also replicated. Subjects re-

turned to the dental office to answer additional questions 2 days after receiving the diagnostic feedback. Subjects assigned the disease and at-risk feedback reported experiencing more bleeding from the gums (which they were told was a symptom of gum disease) than did no-disease subjects.*

Appraisals of experimentally manipulated blood pressure feedback also confirm findings from the TAA enzyme paradigm. In two experiments, Croyle (1990) measured subjects' blood pressure and then randomly assigned them to receive either high blood pressure feedback (140/97) or normal blood pressure feedback (110/80). The results of the studies mirror those of studies using the TAA paradigm: Subjects receiving the high blood pressure feedback rated high blood pressure as a less serious threat to health than did subjects receiving normal blood pressure feedback.

Confirmatory symptom reporting has also been demonstrated within the context of blood pressure testing. Baumann, Cameron, Zimmerman, and Leventhal (1989) randomly assigned subjects normal and high blood pressure feedback and found that high blood pressure subjects were more likely than normal blood pressure subjects to report symptoms laypersons commonly associate with hypertension. This effect was especially pronounced when high blood pressure subjects attributed their elevated reading to stress.

This latter finding illustrates that important insights can be gained from research on actual risk factors like hypertension that are unlikely to emerge from TAA research alone. A person's mental representations of the causes, consequences, and time course of health disorders have been shown to play an important role in appraisal processes (Ditto et al., 1988; Skelton & Croyle, 1991). Much of this research has concerned mental representations of hypertension (e.g., Meyer, Leventhal, & Gutmann, 1985). Building on this nonexperimental work, research on experimentally manipulated blood pressure feedback has confirmed that mental representations can both affect appraisals and be affected by them.

---

*Interestingly, the three groups of subjects did not differ in their perceptions of the accuracy of the diagnostic test. McCaul et al. argue that this is likely due to the fact that the professionally administered gum exam was perceived to be a highly valid indicator of gum disease. Consequently, it may have been difficult for disease and at-risk subjects to plausibly entertain the notion that the test result might be inaccurate.

Meyer et al. (1985), for example, have shown that mental representations of hypertension are characterized by one of three types of beliefs concerning the time course of the disorder. Some people view it as an acute condition, others as a cyclical condition that comes and goes, and still others adhere to the medically accepted chronic view of the disorder. Croyle (1990) found that which one of these views an individual ascribes to can be affected by diagnostic feedback. After they received their blood pressure results, subjects in Croyle's second experiment were asked whether they believed hypertension was an acute, cyclical, or chronic condition. Subjects told their blood pressure was high were less likely than low blood pressure subjects to endorse a chronic model of hypertension (see also Baumann et al., 1989). The findings also showed that minimization among subjects receiving the high blood pressure feedback was related to mental representations. Minimization occurred only among subjects who believed that hypertension was an acute or cyclical problem.

A study by Croyle and Williams (1991) makes a similar point regarding the interplay between mental representations and illness appraisals. The study examined the role of what Croyle and Williams call "illness stereotypes" in reactions to medical diagnoses. First, a small survey was conducted; it found that individuals who rated high blood pressure as a less serious threat to health also tended to associate the disorder with positive personal characteristics (e.g., professional employment, high intelligence). This relationship was then confirmed in a laboratory experiment. Subjects read information about high blood pressure that stated that it was associated either with undesirable personality characteristics, such as the tendency to panic under pressure, or with desirable personality characteristics leading to academic and professional success. When subjects were subsequently given false feedback indicating that their blood pressure was high, those given the positive stereotype information rated high blood pressure as a less serious threat to health and reported more hypertension-related symptoms than did subjects given the negative stereotype information.

In summary, both correlational and experimental research on appraisals of actual risk factors confirm the results found in the TAA enzyme paradigm. Minimization of risk factor seriousness and diagnostic test accuracy, the relationship between perceived prevalence and perceived seriousness, the false consensus bias, and confirmatory symptom reporting have all been demonstrated with appraisals of actual risk factors.

Research examining the impact of randomized feedback concerning actual risk factors, however, has not been limited to replications of phenomena discovered in the laboratory. Experimental studies using actual risk factors can also lead to novel insights regarding the determinants of risk factor appraisals. Although many of the important psychological processes underlying threat appraisal operate similarly across disease domains, each risk factor or disease also has unique features that raise some unique psychological issues. This is illustrated by the study of hypertension screening described earlier (Croyle, 1990). Another example is provided by the many tests now under development in the field of human genetics. Clearly, feedback on genetic tests have family and family-planning implications that nongenetic tests do not have. As field studies of new screening technologies begin to yield findings regarding psychosocial effects, the need to isolate and clarify these effects will influence the course of basic laboratory research on appraisal.

Diagnostic Context

Another obvious concern about the generalizability of results from the TAA enzyme paradigm is the artificial context within which subjects receive their diagnostic feedback. Is self-administering a saliva test in a psychological research lab the same as receiving diagnostic feedback from a medical professional?

We have two answers to that question. The first is that several studies have shown that similar patterns of risk factor appraisals are observed when the diagnostic test is professionally administered as when the test is self-administered. All of the studies cited above examining reactions to blood pressure and cholesterol feedback were administered by someone other than the subject. In addition, two studies have been done in which the test was conducted at a university healthy facility. Croyle and Sande (1988) tested students for TAA deficiency at a student infirmary. An experimenter in a nurse's uniform conducted the test. McCaul et al. (1991) tested subjects at the campus dental office. Testing was done by a professional dental hygienist. All of these studies produced results virtually identical to those found when subjects self-administer the TAA saliva test.

The second answer to the question is that reactions to self-administered and professionally administered tests might indeed show important differences. This does not, however, make reactions to self-diagnosis uninteresting. Quite the contrary, the recent proliferation of over-the-counter diagnostic tests makes reactions to self-administered tests an increasingly important topic of study. At-home assays can now be conducted for a variety of conditions, from pregnancy and ovulation to the examination of plasma or urinary glucose levels. More such tests are likely to be available in the near future. The TAA paradigm would seem a particularly good analogue of these types of self-administered diagnostic tests.

One potential difference between reactions to professionally administered and self-administered diagnostic tests concerns the level of ambiguity surrounding the meaning of the test result. Without a medical professional present, the individual self-administering a diagnostic test may be left with considerable uncertainty regarding interpretation of the test result. The more uncertainty, the more room for biased processing of the diagnostic information to operate. Croyle and Sande (1988), for example, found that when subjects were led to be relatively uncertain regarding the meaning of an unfavorable test result (i.e., that it was 75% accurate), they were *less* rather than more likely to request a second, more definite diagnostic test than subjects who were led to be more certain of the test's diagnostic value (i.e., that it was 95% accurate).

Another negative consequence of uncertainty is that it may be unsettling even when the test result is seemingly favorable. Cioffi (1991), in fact, has suggested that individuals may find a diagnosis of "uncertain wellness" uniquely troubling. Utilizing the TAA enzyme paradigm, Cioffi used instructions to manipulate both the favorability of the test result (deficiency or no deficiency) as well as its clarity (the color reaction in the test strip either clearly matched the color expected for the diagnosis or was a color that was at the perceptual midpoint between the diagnosis and an "invalid" reading). Her results indicated that, compared with subjects receiving the other diagnoses, subjects

receiving the unclear-well diagnosis reported more concern about their health, heightened perceived vulnerability to pancreatic disease, and a strong desire for treatment. Cioffi suggests that the unclear-well diagnosis may be emotionally unsettling because, while indicating some possibility of illness, it does not initiate the type of self-protective mechanisms typically observed in reaction to more unambiguous negative diagnoses. Consequently, the subjects are left with fear and uncertainty regarding their health status without the emotional buffer provided by threat-minimizing beliefs such as perceiving the looming disease as benign and/or the diagnostic test as potentially invalid.

In summary, experimental studies have shown that people respond similarly to risk factor information whether it is professionally administered or self-administered and whether or not the test is conducted in a formal medical context. Future studies might more specifically pursue differences in reactions to professionally administered and self-administered tests as well as examining the unique properties of the increasingly more common phenomenon of self-diagnosis.

Immediate Versus Delayed Reactions

Ethical concerns generally restrict the use of the TAA enzyme paradigm to the examination of immediate reactions to risk factor information. Immediate reactions to unfavorable risk factor information are theoretically interesting because the conflicting emotional and problem-focused coping demands placed on the individual are most intense at this time. Many important decisions, however, may not be made until some time after the risk factor information is initially received and "digested." Risk factor appraisals may change over time (Lazarus & Folkman, 1984; Lehman, Wortman, & Williams, 1987; Suls & Fletcher, 1985) as the individual gathers and integrates new information about the condition.

One study, however, suggests that the minimization response observed immediately after the receipt of diagnostic information may persist for at least a matter of days. McCaul et al. (1991) measured subjects' appraisals of gum disease immediately after receiving diagnostic feedback and again 2 days later. Appraisals measured after 2 days were virtually identical to those measured immediately. Subjects who were told they had gum disease still rated it as significantly less serious and more prevalent than did subjects in the at-risk and no-disease conditions 2 days after initially receiving the diagnosis. Two days is a relatively brief period of time, particularly in comparison to the time frames experienced in real-life coping situations. However, these data do show that the minimization effect observed immediately after receiving diagnostic information is not merely a transitory effect induced within a brief psychology experiment.

Reactions to Serious Medical Conditions

Ethical concerns also preclude experimental studies from examining reactions to extremely serious medical conditions. Although the TAA enzyme paradigm is likely to be a relatively close analogue to cholesterol and hypertension screening, its generalizability to appraisals of more immediately life-threatening medical conditions is more tenuous.

At one level, the TAA paradigm seems most likely to *underestimate* the effects observed in response to serious medical conditions. This would seem especially likely in terms of defensive reactions like minimization. Indeed, one fascinating aspect of the TAA enzyme paradigm is that defensive appraisals like those more typically expected in response to life-threatening conditions such as cancer or myocardial infarction can be reliably observed in subjects' reactions to a relatively benign and unfamiliar risk factor.

Other determinants of risk factor appraisals, however, may be less likely to operate when an individual is confronted with a clearly serious medical condition. The operation of judgmental biases and heuristics is most apparent under conditions of uncertainty (Kahneman, Slovic, & Tversky, 1982). To the extent that clear information is available about any judgmental dimension, therefore, judgments along this dimension are less likely to be affected by such extraneous factors. As just one example, the perceived prevalence of a condition is unlikely to affect seriousness judgments to the extent that other, more compelling evidence of the condition's seriousness is also available (Ditto & Jemmott, 1989).

Generalizing from Appraisal to Behavior

Experimental work on psychological reactions to risk factor information has been predominantly concerned with cognitive appraisals. Much less attention has been paid to obtaining measures of subjects' behavioral responses. For the most part, this emphasis on appraisal processes reflects our belief that the cognitive underpinnings of illness behavior are a crucial and understudied topic. Still, the individual's behavioral response to risk factor information—whether the individual seeks treatment or information, whether he or she enacts prescribed changes in behavior—remains of paramount practical importance. And while cognitive appraisals may provide important insights into an individual's likely behavioral response, research in social and personality psychology has clearly demonstrated that the cognition–behavior relationship is anything but simple (Quattrone, 1985; Schuman & Johnson, 1976; Wicker, 1969). Thus, a final issue that must be discussed is the nature of the relationship between cognitive appraisals of risk factor information and subsequent behavior.

Behavioral measures are not the strong suit of experimental research in social and personality psychology. However, our experiments have typically included "behavioroid" measures of some type. Behavioroid measures are those that assess behavioral intention or choice. The simplest (and consequently, least compelling) measure has been simply asking subjects to indicate on a scale their interest in obtaining additional information about TAA deficiency and pancreatic disease (Ditto et al., 1988). Several other studies have asked subjects to indicate their *intentions* (Ajzen & Fishbein, 1980) of engaging in a variety of preventive or reactive behaviors (Croyle & Hunt, 1991; Croyle et al., 1993). Finally, several studies have used a method in which subjects are offered the opportunity to review any or all of a series of informational services about TAA deficiency (a free pamphlet, a booklet costing 50 cents, a free physical examination) (Ditto & Jemmott, 1989; Jemmott et al., 1986). Subjects indicate which (if any) of these services they wish to receive and the number of services requested is used as the dependent measure.

Studies utilizing these types of behavioral measures have shown that in some instances the appraisal–behavior relationship is relatively straight-forward. Ditto and Jemmott (1989) found that the effect of prevalence information on perceptions of seriousness translated quite directly into behav-ior. Subjects led to believe that they had a rare enzyme condition not only perceived it to be more serious than subjects led to believe the condition was common, but were also significantly more likely to sign up to receive additional information about their condition. Behavioral intention data from Croyle and Hunt (1991) also confirm that conditions perceived to be rare provoke a relatively vigorous behavioral response.

Studies examining denial reactions to unfavor-able diagnostic information, however, suggest a more complex appraisal–behavior relationship. The simple assumption when considering denial reactions is that the lowered appraisals of threat offered by positive-result subjects should mani-fest themselves in similarly lower levels of behav-ioral responding. Denial, in other words, is often viewed as a maladaptive response (e.g., Haan, 1977) and one that is likely to interfere with adap-tive behavioral responses to threatening risk fac-tor information.

The results of several of our experimental stud-ies, however, have shown this not to be the case. Jemmott et al. (1986), for example, found that al-though positive-result subjects rated TAA defi-ciency as less serious and the TAA diagnostic test as less accurate than did negative-result subjects, they also requested significantly more additional information about TAA deficiency than did nega-tive-result subjects. Croyle et al. (1993) show a similar pattern in reactions to cholesterol feedback using a measure of behavioral intentions. Finally, the pattern of data found by Ditto et al. (1988) is particularly telling. These investigators found a more pronounced denial reaction when positive-result subjects believed TAA deficiency to be untreatable than when they perceived it to be treat-able. Still, positive-result, untreatable subjects showed interest in additional information about TAA deficiency and pancreatic disease that was just as high as positive-result, treatable subjects and significantly higher than that expressed by negative-result subjects. In other words, the more pronounced denial reactions observed by subjects perceiving their affliction as untreatable showed no evidence of dampening interest in additional information. This is particularly impressive in light of the fact that additional information is probably perceived as less likely to be useful if one's condi-tion is not thought to be amenable to treatment.

This seemingly paradoxical relationship be-tween denial and ameliorative behavior is remi-niscent of the relationship between denial and symptom reporting (Croyle & Sande, 1988; McCaul et al., 1991). Both findings are consistent with Lazarus and Folkman's (1984) distinction between emotion-focused and problem-focused coping and Leventhal et al.'s (1984) self-regula-tion theory of illness behavior. Both of these mod-els conceive of the coping process stimulated by a health threat as simultaneously proceeding along two parallel pathways. Lazarus and Folkman (1984) make a distinction between attempts to cope with the emotional upset resulting from the per-ception of threat (emotion-focused coping) and attempts to cope with the threatening agent itself (problem-focused coping). These two processes are thought to operate independently. Leventhal's self-regulation model similarly postulates a two-pathway coping process. One pathway corresponds to emotion-focused coping and involves "the cre-ation of an emotional response to the problem and the development of a coping plan for the manage-ment of emotion." The second pathway corre-sponds to problem-focused coping and involves "the creation of an objective view or representa-tion of an illness threat and the development of a coping plan to manage that threat" (1984, p. 220). In Leventhal et al.'s view, as in Lazarus and Folkman's, these processes are thought to operate semi-independently.

The denial processes observed in our studies are best conceived of as attempts to attenuate emo-tional upset. The search for relevant symptoma-tology and the construction of an adaptive behav-ioral response, on the other hand, represent the problem-focused pathway. Consistent with both theoretical models, our data suggest that these two processes operate independently. At the same time that the individual is minimizing the threat repre-sented by the risk factor information in an attempt to control emotional upset, she or he is attempting to construct an accurate representation of the ill-ness threat (sympton search) and taking active behavioral measures to cope with it. Additional evidence of independence comes from the fact that the two coping pathways appear to be affected by different variables (Croyle & Hunt, 1991).

An important implication of this separate pathways view of illnes behavior is that the defensive processes that are initiated by unfavorable test results may not deserve the negative connotations that are often placed on them. Rather than disrupting adaptive problem-focused coping attempts, casting a threatening situation in a relatively benign light may actually facilitate such attempts by keeping potentially disruptive emotional responses in check (Cohen & Lazarus, 1979; Lazarus, 1983; Taylor, 1983). This view of denial is consistent not only with data from the TAA paradigm, but also with other data suggesting an association between coping attempts characterized by denial and positive postsurgical outcomes (e.g., Cohen & Lazarus, 1973).

This more charitable view of denial is also consistent with Ditto and Lopez's (1992) characterization of motivational biases in judgment. According to this view, denial is rarely a total rejection of threatening information, but rather a kind of "motivated skepticism" fueled by heightened sensitivity to alternative explanations for unwanted information. Thus, the individual confronted with an unfavorable test result does not walk away convinced of its invalidity, but rather with a sense that the test result is potentially "confounded," and with some hope intact that a more agreeable interpretation is possible. This view of denial also removes the paradoxical nature from the appraisal–behavior relationship. Seeking treatment or information about a condition is paradoxical only if the individual is convinced that he or she is healthy.

In summary, more research is needed on the relationship between cognitive appraisals of risk factor information and subsequent behavioral responses. Our data suggest that this relationship is not necessarily a simple one. This is in large part due to the multiple coping demands faced by individuals confronted with an unfavorable diagnosis. Emotional and practical concerns must be dealt with simultaneously, resulting in a complex pattern of affective, cognitive, and behavioral responses. One implication from our data that is consistent with prominent theoretical models of illness behavior is that defensive biases in appraisal are not necessarily maladaptive. Denial processes may serve the important function of controlling potentially disruptive emotions. If this is the case, then disrupting this natural coping mechanism may have undesirable consequences.

Conclusions

This chapter reviewed experimental evidence on reactions to risk factor information. The majority of the studies reported utilized a research paradigm that was developed to investigate the psychological processes underlying the appraisal of risk factor test results by randomizing subjects to different test result conditions. Almost all of the studies have used college students as subjects and have focused on short-term reactions to risk information.

As a whole, the research provides strong and consistent evidence that initial appraisals are characterized by threat minimization. Subjects who receive test results indicative of a risk factor appraise it as less serious and the risk factor test as less accurate than do those who receive favorable test results. Subjects who are told they have a risk factor later perceive it as relatively common, but they also seek relevant information and express behavioral intentions that suggest the development of a plan for actively coping with the threat.

The research also provides consistent evidence that risk factor appraisals are affected by social factors. Both perceptions of the commonness of the risk factor and appraisals of the risk factor offered by others affect perceptions of its seriousness. Seriousness appraisals subsequently determine individuals' behavioral response to the risk factor information.

Substantial convergent evidence shows that findings regarding appraisal phenomena observed in the laboratory can be generalized to nonlaboratory settings. The findings from studies examining college students' reactions to fictitious risk factors have been replicated in studies utilizing real screening tests (e.g., cholesterol and blood pressure) and more diverse adult populations.

Laboratory experiments on risk factor testing cannot provide answers to all of the important questions concerning labeling effects. We do believe, however, that controlled studies of randomized feedback provide a critical and unique contribution to the body of work on the psychosocial impact of risk factor testing.

ACKNOWLEDGMENTS

Preparation of this manuscript was supported by grants from the National Institute of Mental Health (MH43097) and the Agency for Health Care Policy Research (HS 06660) awarded to the second author.

REFERENCES

Aitken-Swan, J., & Easson, E. C. (1959). Reactions of cancer patients on being told their diagnosis. *British Medical Journal, 1*, 779–783.

Ajzen, I., & Fishbein, M. (1980). *Understanding attitudes and predicting social behavior.* Englewood Cliffs, NJ: Prentice-Hall.

Aronson, E., Ellsworth, P. C., Carlsmith, J. M., & Gonzales, M. H. (1990). *Methods of research in social psychology* (2nd ed.). New York: McGraw-Hill.

Baumann, L. J., Cameron, L. D., Zimmerman, R. S., & Leventhal, H. (1989). Illness representations and matching labels with symptoms. *Health Psychology, 8*, 449–469.

Cioffi, D. (1991). Asymmetry of doubt in medical self-diagnosis: The ambiguity of "uncertain wellness." *Journal of Personality and Social Psychology, 61*, 969–980.

Cohen, F., & Lazarus, R. S. (1973). Active coping processes, coping dispositions, and recovery from surgery. *Psychosomatic Medicine, 35*, 357–389.

Cohen, F., & Lazarus, R. S. (1979). Coping with the stresses of illness. In G. Stone, F. Cohen, & N. Adler (Eds.), *Health psychology: A handbook* (pp. 217–254). San Francisco: Jossey-Bass.

Crowne, D. P., & Marlowe, D. (1964). *The approval motive: Studies in evaluative dependence.* New York: Wiley.

Croyle, R. T. (1990). Biased appraisal of high blood pressure. *Preventive Medicine, 19*, 40–44.

Croyle, R. T., Barger, S. D., & Sun, Y. (1992). Repressive coping style and appraisal of health threat. Unpublished data, University of Utah.

Croyle, R. T., & Ditto, P. H. (1990). Illness cognition and behavior: An experimental approach. *Journal of Behavioral Medicine, 13*, 31–52.

Croyle, R. T., & Hunt, J. R. (1991). Coping with health threat: Social influence processes in reactions to medical test results. *Journal of Personality and Social Psychology, 60*, 382–389.

Croyle, R. T., & Sande, G. N. (1988). Denial and confirmatory search: Paradoxical consequences of medical diagnoses. *Journal of Applied Social Psychology, 18*, 473–490.

Croyle, R. T., Sun, Y., & Louie, D. H. (1993). Psychological minimization of cholesterol test results: Moderators of appraisal in college students and community residents. *Health Psychology, 12*, 503–507.

Croyle, R. T., & Williams, K. D. (1991). Reactions to medical diagnosis: The role of illness stereotypes. *Basic and Applied Social Psychology, 12*, 227–241.

Cutler, P. (1979). *Problem solving in clinical medicine: From data to diagnosis.* Baltimore: Williams & Wilkins.

Ditto, P. H., & Jemmott, J. B., III (1989). From rarity to evaluative extremity: Effects of prevalence information on evaluations of positive and negative characteristics. *Journal of Personality and Social Psychology, 57*, 16–26.

Ditto, P. H., Jemmott, J. B., III, & Darley, J. M. (1988). Appraising the threat of illness: A mental representational approach. *Health Psychology, 7*, 183–200.

Ditto, P. H., & Lopez, D. F. (1992). Motivated skepticisim: The use of differential decision criteria for preferred and nonpreferred conclusions. *Journal of Personality and Social Psychology, 63*, 568–584.

Elstein, A. S., Shulman, L. S., & Sprafka, S. A. (1978). *Medi-cal problem solving: An analysis of clinical reasoning.* Cambridge, MA: Harvard University Press.

Erdelyi, M. H. (1974). A new look at the new look: Perceptual defense and vigilance. *Psychological Review, 81*, 1–25.

Festinger, L. (1954). A theory of social comparison processes. *Human Relations, 7*, 117–140.

Francis, V., Korsch, B. M., & Morris, M. J. (1969). Gaps in doctor-patient communications: Patients' response to medical advice. *New England Journal of Medicine, 280*, 535–540.

Friedson, E. (1961). *Patients' view of medical practice.* New York: Russell Sage Foundation.

Gilbertson, V. A., & Wangersteen, O. H. (1962). Should the doctor tell the patient that the disease is cancer? In *The Physician and the total care of the cancer patient* (pp. 80–85). New York: American Cancer Society.

Goethals, G. R. (1986). Fabricating and ignoring social reality. Self-serving estimates of consensus. In J. Olson, C. P. Herman, & M. P. Zanna (Eds.), *Relative deprivation and social comparison: The Ontario symposium* (Vol. 4, pp. 135–158). Hillsdale, NJ: Erlbaum.

Haan, N. (1977). *Coping and defending.* New York: Academic Press.

Hackett, T. P., & Cassem, N. H. (1969). Factors contributing to delay in responding to the signs and symptoms of acute myocardial infarction. *American Journal of Cardiology, 24*, 651–658.

Janis, I. L. (1958). *Psychological stress.* New York: Wiley.

Janis, I. L. (1984). Improving adherence to medical recommendations: Prescriptive hypotheses derived from recent research in social psychology. In A. Baum, S. Taylor, & J. Singer (Eds.), *Handbook of psychology and health: Vol. 4. Social psychological aspects of health* (pp. 113–148). Hillsdale, NJ: Erlbaum.

Jemmott, J. B., III, Ditto, P. H., & Croyle, R. T. (1986). Judging health status: Effects of preceived prevalence and personal relevance. *Journal of Personality and Social Psychology, 50*, 899–905.

Jemmott, J. B., III, Ditto, P. H., & Croyle, R. T. (1988). Commonsense epidemiology: Self-based judgments from laypersons and physicians. *Health Psychology, 7*, 55–73.

Kahneman, D., Slovic, P., & Tversky, A. (1982). *Judgment under uncertainty: Heuristics and biases.* New York: Cambridge University Press.

Kenrick, D. T., McCreath, H. E., Govern, J., King, R., & Bordin, J. (1990). Person-environment intersections: Everyday settings and common trait dimensions. *Journal of Personality and Social Psychology, 58*, 685–698.

Kleinman, A., Eisenberg, L., & Good, B. (1978). Culture, illness, and care. *Annals of Internal Medicine, 88*, 251–258.

Kubler-Ross, E. (1969). *On death and dying.* New York: Macmillan.

Lazarus, R. S. (1983). The costs and benefits of denial. In S. Breznitz (Ed.), *The denial of stress* (pp. 1–30). New York: International Universities Press.

Lazarus, R. S., & Folkman, S. (1984). *Stress, appraisal, and coping.* New York: Springer-Verlag.

Lehman, D. R., Wortman, C. B., & Williams, A. F. (1987). Long-term effects of losing a spouse or child in a motor vehicle crash. *Journal of Personality and Social Psychology, 52*, 218–231.

Leventhal, E. A., & Prohaska, T. R. (1986). Age, symptom interpretation, and health behavior. *Journal of the American Geriatric Society, 34*, 185–191.

Leventhal, H. (1970). Findings and theory in the study of fear communications. In L. Berkowitz (Ed.), *Advances in experimental social psychology* (Vol. 5, pp. 119–186). New York. Academic Press.

Leventhal, H., Meyer, D., & Nerenz, D. (1980). The commonsense representation of illness danger. In S. Rachman (Ed.), *Contributions to medical psychology* (Vol. 2, pp. 7–30). New York: Pergamon Press.

Leventhal, H., Nerenz, D. R., & Steele, D. J. (1984). Illness representations and coping with health threats. In A. Baum, S. Taylor, & J. Singer (Eds.), *Handbook of psychology and health, Vol. 4. Social psychological aspects of health* (pp. 219–252). Hillsdale, NJ: Erlbaum.

Lipowski, Z. J. (1970). Physical illness, the individual and the coping process. *International Journal of Psychiatry in Medicine, 1*, 91–102.

Markus, H., & Wurf, E. (1987). The dynamic self-concept: A social psychological perspective. In M. R. Rosenzweig & L. W. Porter (Eds.), *Annual review of psychology* (Vol. 38, pp. 299–337). Palo Alto, CA: Annual Reviews.

McCaul, K. D., Thiesse-Duffy, E., & Wilson, P. (1991). Coping with medical diagnosis: The effects of at-risk versus disease labels over time. *Journal of Applied Social Psychology, 22*, 1340–1355.

Meyer, D. L., Leventhal, H., & Gutmann, M. (1985). Common-sense models of illness: The example of hypertension. *Health Psychology, 4*, 115–135.

Miller, D. T., & Ross, M. (1975). Self-serving biases in attribution of causality: Fact or fiction? *Psychological Bulletin, 82*, 213–225.

Miller, S. M. (1987). Monitoring and blunting: Validation of a questionnaire to assess styles of information seeking under threat. *Journal of Personality and Social Psychology, 52*, 345–353.

Miller, S. M., Brody, D. S., & Summerton, J. (1988). Styles of coping with threat: Implications for health. *Journal of Personality and Social Psychology, 54*, 142–148.

Moore, K. A., & Ditto. P. H. (1991). *Hypochondriacal beliefs and reactions to unfavorable medical diagnoses*. Paper presented at the annual meeting of the American Psychological Association, San Francisco, CA.

Petersdorf, R. G., Adams, R. D., Brauwald, E., Isselbacher, K. J., Martin, J. B., & Wilson, J. D. (1983). *Harrison's principles of internal medicine* (10th ed.). New York: McGraw-Hill.

Pilowsky, I. (1967). Dimensions of hypochondriasis. *British Journal of Psychiatry, 113*, 89–93.

Pratto, F., & John, O. P. (1991). Automatic vigilance: The attention-grabbing power of negative social information. *Journal of Personality and Social Psychology, 61*, 380–391.

Prohaska. T. R., Keller. M. L., Leventhal. E. A., & Leventhal. H. (1987). Impact of symptoms and aging attribution on emotions and coping. *Health Psychology, 6*, 495–514.

Quattrone. G. A. (1985). On the congruity between internal states and action. *Psychological Bulletin, 98*, 3–40.

Rosenberg. M. (1965). *Society and the adolescent self-image*. Princeton, NJ: Princeton University Press.

Ross. L., Greene, D., & House, P. (1977). The false consensus phenomenon: An attributional bias in self-perception and social perception processes. *Journal of Experimental Social Psychology, 13*, 279–301.

Scheier, M. F., & Carver, C. S. (1985). Optimism, coping, and health: Assessment and implications of generalized outcome expectancies. *Health Psychology, 4*, 219–247.

Schuman, H., & Johnson, M. P. (1976). Attitudes and behavior. *Annual Review of Sociology, 2*, 161–207.

Schwarz, N. (1990). Feelings as information: Informational and motivational functions of affective states. In E. T. Higgins & R. M. Sorrentino (Eds.), *The handbook of motivation and cognition: Foundations of social behavior* (Vol. 2, pp. 527–561). New York: Guilford Press.

Silverman, I. (1974). Consequences, racial discrimination, and the principle of belief congruence. *Journal of Personality and Social Psychology, 29*, 497–508.

Skelton, J. A., & Croyle, R. T. (Eds.). (1991). *Mental representation in health and illness*. New York: Springer-Verlag.

Snyder, M. (1984). When belief creates reality. In L. Berkowitz (Ed.), *Advances in experimental social psychology* (Vol. 18, pp. 248–305). New York: Academic Press.

Suls, J., & Fletcher, B. (1985). The relative efficacy of avoidant and nonavoidant coping strategies: A meta-analysis. *Health Psychology, 4*, 249–288.

Taylor, S. E. (1983). Adjustment to threatening events: A theory of cognitive adaptation. *American Psychologist, 38*, 1161–1173.

Tetlock, P. E., & Levi, A. (1982). Attribution bias: On the inconclusiveness of the cognition-motivation debate. *Journal of Experimental Social Psychology, 18*, 68–88.

Tversky, A., & Kahneman, D. (1974). Judgment under uncertainty: Heuristics and biases. *Sciences, 185*, 1124–1131.

Ullman, L. P. (1962). An empirically derived MMPI scale which measures facilitation-inhibition of recognition of threatening stimuli. *Journal of Clinical Psychology, 18*, 127–132.

Visotsky, H. M., Hamburg, D. A., Goss, M. E., & Lebovitz, B. A. (1961). Coping under extreme stress: Observations of patients with severe poliomyelitis. *Archives of General Psychiatry, 5*, 423–448.

Weinstein, N. D. (1982). Unrealistic optimism about susceptibility to health problems. *Journal of Behavioral Medicine, 5*, 441–460.

Weinstein, N. D. (1987). Unrealistic optimism about susceptibility to health problems: Conclusions from a community-wide sample. *Journal of Behavioral Medicine, 10*, 481–500.

Wicker, A. W., (1969). Attitudes vs. actions: The relationship of verbal and overt behavioral responses to attitude objects. *Journal of Social Issues, 41*, 41–78.

Zola, I. K. (1966). Culture and symptoms—An analysis of patients' presenting complaints. *American Sociological Review, 31*, 615–630.

Defensive Processing of Personally Relevant Health Messages

Akiva Liberman and Shelly Chaiken • New York University

Subjects for whom a health threat was relevant or irrelevant were recruited and matched on prior beliefs in the health threat. Following exposure to either a low- or a high-threat message, high-relevance subjects were less likely to believe in the threat. Consistent with earlier work, no evidence was found to suggest that defensive inattention to the messages mediated subjects' final beliefs. Instead, processing measures suggested that high-relevance subjects processed threatening parts of both messages in a biased fashion. The relationship between biased judgment and biased processing is discussed, as are the difficulties in documenting the latter.

As you flip through the newspaper, you notice an article about radon contamination of homes. You have heard in the past that radon is a particularly serious problem in New Jersey. Usually, of course, this is just another amusing fact about New Jersey. Who would live there anyway? But now imagine that by some quirk of fate you actually live in New Jersey. Will you read this article differently than your friends in Arizona? Will you read it carefully to see whether you are at risk, will you quickly turn the page to avoid reading the article, or will you perhaps read it bent on finding reasons not to worry? As a psychologist, you make a unique defensive maneuver. Rather than thinking about radon, you turn your attention to the psychological question: How does personal relevance affect the processing of messages? You go to the library.

You are likely to leave the library with different conclusions depending on how you research the question. If you turn to recent research on persua-sion, you may conclude that people process a message more extensively or systematically when its topic is personally relevant (see Chaiken, 1987; Petty & Cacioppo, 1986). This tendency has been documented with messages concerning academic policies (e.g., Chaiken, 1980; Petty & Cacioppo, 1979b, 1984), consumer products (e.g., Maheswaran & Chaiken, 1991; Petty, Cacioppo, & Schumann, 1983), and public policy issues (e.g., Axsom, Yates, & Chaiken, 1987). In light of your radon problem, you may be even more interested to discover that the systematic processing motivated by personal relevance often appears to be objective (see Petty & Cacioppo, 1986).

Or you might read the literature on health messages and fear appeals. Here you may discover that some early research suggested that people defensively reject highly relevant messages (e.g., Berkowitz & Cottingham, 1960; Janis & Feshbach, 1953). How can you reconcile these apparently different conclusions?

The heuristic-systematic model (Chaiken, 1980, 1987; Chaiken, Liberman, & Eagly, 1989) suggests that these findings can be integrated by differentiating several types of motivation that may be induced by exposure to personally relevant messages and by differentiating biased from unbiased systematic processing. With nonthreatening messages, increased personal relevance will often increase motivation to arrive at an accurate conclusion, thereby prompting unbiased systematic processing. But with a threatening message, increased personal relevance may instead increase motivation to arrive at or defend a preferred conclusion or to reject an undesirable one. One active process that would serve this goal is biased systematic processing, in which threatening information is processed more critically than reassuring information. Other useful processes might include defensive inattention, motivated forgetting, and selective heuristic processing (Chaiken et al., 1989).

Early research on fear appeals and health messages investigated some of these defensive processes, with particular focus on defensive inattention to threatening messages. Some studies did find that threatening messages reduced persuasion, but little evidence was uncovered regarding mediating defensive processes. Instead, the main processing finding was that defensive inattention did *not* seem to account for defensive conclusions. Perhaps as a result, subsequent research on fear appeals has largely neglected defensive processing mechanisms (for a review, see Eagly & Chaiken, 1993).

We begin our review of studies investigating defensive processing with Janis and Feshbach's (1953) classic investigation of the effects of differentially fear-inducing messages. Their messages concerned dental hygiene. To induce fear, Janis and Feshbach made the message's language more personal, mentioned more threatening consequences of improper dental care, and accompanied the message with gruesome photographs. The messages were long and complex, mentioning from 18 to 71 negative consequences of improper dental care, depending on fear condition. Inattention to the message was assessed indirectly by a 23-item test about the message.

One week later, self-reports of behavior indicated that the high-fear message was less persuasive than the low-fear message. Moreover, when presented with counter-propaganda, high-fear sub-jects proved less resistant than low-fear subjects, and their open-ended comments referred less to the contents of the earlier message. However, high-fear subjects remembered the message as well as the low-fear subjects and had reported less "mind-wandering" (Janis & Feshbach, 1953, p. 88). Janis and Feshbach tentatively concluded that the high-fear message led to "subsequent defensive avoidance" (p. 89)—that is, avoidance of thought about the message after the initial experimental session.

Janis and Terwilliger (1962) had subjects think aloud while listening to a message that argued that heavy smoking causes cancer. Subjects stopped the message and thought aloud, into a microphone, after each of the message's 15 or 22 points (depending on condition) and at any other time they had a thought. The high-fear message changed attitudes somewhat less than the low-fear message, and it evoked significantly more major criticisms and less praise. This study thus provided an early demonstration of biased, critical processing of a threatening health message.

Although this early research primarily concerned the hypothesis that more *fearful* health messages might include defensive message processing, it also investigated the related hypothesis that more *personally relevant* health messages would induce defensive processing. It is this latter hypothesis that is the main focus of the present article. Janis and Feshbach (1953) conflated these two hypotheses because part of their fear manipulation was to make threatening consequences more personally relevant by means of more personal language (e.g., "This can happen to you," p. 79).

However, Janis and Terwilliger (1962, Note 4) investigated personal relevance independently of message-induced fear by comparing subjects who had earlier reported smoking more than five cigarettes a day ("smokers") or fewer than five cigarettes a day ("non-smokers"). Content analysis of subjects' thoughts revealed that smokers explicitly rejected the message more often and explicitly accepted it less often, but these trends did not prove reliable.

Berkowitz and Cottingham (1960) also investigated the hypothesis that personal relevance increases defensive processing of threatening messages. Subjects listened to a message about seat belts after being classified into low-relevance and high-relevance groups on the basis of their driving habits and whether they owned cars. In the high-fear message, gruesome photographs of automobile accidents were added, and the language was made more dramatic and personal. Study 2 used an 11-item memory test to explore inattention as a possible defensive process.

Berkowitz and Cottingham's low-relevance subjects were more persuaded by the high-fear than the low-fear message, but high-relevance subjects were not. Thus, high-relevance subjects' responses to the high-fear message seem to have been defensive, compared with low-relevance subjects' responses. However, no memory differences were found. Thus, inattention was apparently not responsible for high-relevance subjects' defensiveness. Subsequent studies have also compared the responses of high- and low-relevance subjects to health messages (see Sutton, 1982, for a brief review), but to our knowledge none have attempted to document the cognitive processes that might underlie any relevance effects.

A major problem with investigating the potential biasing effect of personal relevance by comparing the responses of people for whom an issue is more versus less personally relevant is that preexperimental differences in relevance are likely to be confounded with preexperimental beliefs and attitudes. Moreover, preexperimental attitudes can bias judgments of messages (e.g., Hovland, Harvey, & Sherif, 1957; Lord, Ross, & Lepper, 1979). Unfortunately, most studies have neglected to control preexperimental belief differences between high- and low-relevance subjects. One approach to rectifying this problem, used by Janis and Terwilliger (1962) and Berkowitz and Cottingham (1960), is to obtain both pre- and postmessage attitudes and analyze attitude change rather than postmessage attitudes alone.

More recently, Kunda (1987, Experiment 3) used a different strategy. To minimize preexperimental attitude differences between high- and low-relevance subjects, Kunda presented subjects with a message about an unfamiliar topic. To further guard against differing preexperimental beliefs, Kunda eliminated any subjects who indicated prior familiarity with the topic on a postexperimental questionnaire. Subjects read a short message asserting that caffeine consumption is related to fibrocystic disease. They then estimated their own likelihood of developing fibrocystic disease within the next 15 years and indicated how convinced they were of the connection between

caffeine and fibrocystic disease. Finally, subjects rated their own caffeine consumption, from *heavy* to *no consumption*. This final rating was used to divide subjects into high- and low-relevance groups.

High-relevance females were significantly less convinced of the link between caffeine and fibrocystic disease than low-relevance females. In a second study, using a weaker and presumably less threatening version of the message, Kunda (1987, Experiment 4) found no difference between high- and low-relevance subjects' postmessage beliefs. Thus, it was apparently the threatening message, rather than the topic itself, that motivated high-relevance subjects to be defensive. Neither study, however, included measures designed to assess mediating processes.

In summary, existing research has sometimes found that subjects defensively reject personally relevant and threatening health messages, but it has failed to document the mediating defensive mechanisms. However, studies exploring mediating processes have focused primarily on perhaps the most passive of defense mechanisms, inattention to the message. Only Janis and Terwilliger (1962) seriously attempted to find evidence for more active defensive processing mechanisms, and indeed their results suggest that such processes may be motivated by threatening, relevant messages. Thus, although some evidence of biased *judgment* has been obtained, very little evidence has been found of biased *processing*.

Experimental Overview

The present study was designed to investigate the processing mechanisms that mediate defensive conclusions regarding health messages. To minimize any confounding of prior beliefs with personal relevance, we used Kunda's (1987) unfamiliar topic. However, even with this topic, premessage beliefs might vary with personal relevance. That is, coffee drinkers may hold different beliefs about the general health effects of caffeine—including its relationship to cancer—than nondrinkers. Such beliefs may generalize even to unfamiliar cancer-related diseases, such as fibrocystic disease. In fact, initial pretesting among female introductory psychology students at New York University revealed a small negative correlation between self-reported coffee drinking and belief that caffeine was related to fibrocystic disease, $r(107) = -.21$, $p < .05$. Therefore, both personal relevance and prior belief in the relationship of caffeine to fibrocystic disease were assessed prior to the laboratory session, and coffee drinkers and nondrinkers were matched on this prior belief.

To facilitate detection of processing differences between high- and low-relevance subjects, we constructed two rather long and complex messages. The high-threat message concluded that this alleged health threat had been confirmed, whereas the low-threat message concluded that it had been refuted. In each message, an early medical report linking caffeine consumption and fibrocystic disease was reviewed and then followed by four subsequent reports. Methodological flaws were embedded in each medical report to allow vigilant subjects to criticize them. In both messages, at least one medical report supported belief in this health threat and one report failed to support it, so that all subjects responded both to threatening and to reassuring information. Recall and judgments were obtained separately for each medical report.

As in past research, a memory measure was included. However, in light of past research, we did not expect to find much evidence of inattention as a mediating defensive mechanism. Therefore, additional measures were included to facilitate detection of more active biased processing.

Method

Subjects

The subjects were 175 female New York University undergraduates enrolled in introductory psychology who had earlier completed our premeasures (see below) and were recruited for a study concerning health issues. For each coffee drinker recruited, a student who did not drink coffee was recruited with a very close, preferably equal, prior belief score (see Premeasures). Subjects participated in small groups and either received partial credit for a course requirement or were paid $5 for their participation.

Procedure

When subjects arrived at the laboratory, the experimenter explained that, as part of a study con-

cerning nonscientists' understanding of scientific and technical information, they would read one or—time permitting—two medical articles. Subjects were then given two articles to read at their own pace; they were instructed to proceed to the second article when they had finished the first. The first article concerned fibrocystic disease. The second article, which concerned Parkinson's disease, was included only to prevent faster readers from rereading the first article while slower readers finished it. When all subjects had finished reading the fibrocystic disease article, the experimenter interrupted and asked them to fill out questionnaires concerning that first article. Subjects were then debriefed and excused.

Premeasures

Premeasures were administered during mass testing of introductory psychology students at the beginning of the semester. To assess the personal relevance of this topic, subjects were asked whether they drank coffee and, if so, how many cups per day. Prior beliefs were assessed by asking: "To what extent do you agree or disagree that there is a strong association between caffeine consumption and fibrocystic disease (a disease associated with breast cancer)?" followed by a 10-point agreement scale.

Only women who reported drinking either no coffee at all (low relevance) or who reported drinking at least two cups of coffee per day (high relevance) were recruited. Coffee drinkers reported drinking two to seven cups per day ($M = 2.8$). For each coffee drinker recruited, a woman who did not drink coffee was recruited with a very close, and preferably equal, prior belief score. As a result, prior beliefs did not differ between relevance conditions (Ms = 5.74 and 5.52 for low- and high-relevance subjects, respectively; SDs = 2.02 and 2.03).

Message Threat

The message was described as an article from the *Health Today Newsletter* entitled "Coffee and Women, a New Health Risk?" It was three pages long, single-spaced, and contained approximately 1,600 words. Two versions were constructed. After describing fibrocystic disease, the *high-threat* version claimed that medical research had documented a link between caffeine and fibrocystic disease. In contrast, the *low-threat* version claimed that medical research had disconfirmed this purported health threat.

Both versions began by describing fibrocystic disease as a serious breast disease that, when advanced, is associated with breast cancer. The article then described the (fictitious) initial report in the *New England Journal of Medicine (NEJM)* linking caffeine and fibrocystic disease. According to this report, caffeine inhibits an enzyme, esteroziamine. Esteroziamine, in turn, controls levels in the breast of a toxic chemical called cAMP, which is associated with fibrocystic disease (see Kunda, 1987).

The high-threat message then continued:

Despite those who challenged the conclusion of the original *NEJM* article, the balance of newer research findings strongly supports the caffeine–fibrocystic disease link. Women who consume moderate to high amounts of caffeine are at a much higher risk for developing fibrocystic disease than women who are not caffeine users.

Four newer research reports were then described, three confirming the link (prolink) and one failing to confirm it (antilink). The article concluded by reiterating the existence of this threat and recommending that women eliminate caffeine from their diet.

The low-threat message, in contrast, followed the identical introductory report with the following statement:

Despite early research findings, the balance of newer research findings strongly argues against the caffeine–fibrocystic disease link. Women who consume moderate to high amounts of caffeine appear to be at no higher risk for developing fibrocystic disease than women who are not caffeine users.

Here, too, the message described four additional reports. These reports were very similar to those in the high-threat version, but with different results, so that three reports failed to find a link (antilink) and only one report suggested a link (prolink). The article then reiterated that a link probably does not exist and concluded that the recommendation for women to eliminate caffeine from their diet seems unwarranted.

To allow vigilant subjects the opportunity to be critical, methodological flaws or weaknesses were embedded in each research report, such as poorly matched control groups (e.g., women with fibrocystic disease compared against pregnant women), a high subject dropout rate in a longitudinal study, and potential confounds (e.g., fibrocystic disease patients ate more red meat). Thus, no report was irreproachable.

Checks on Experimental Design

To check the message's personal relevance, subjects were asked to indicate how personally important the topic was to them, on a 9-point scale.

To check our message threat manipulation, subjects were asked to indicate the message's conclusion concerning the relationship between caffeine intake and fibrocystic disease, on a scale from 1 (*concluded that there was no connection*) to 9 (*concluded that there was a very strong connection*).

Also included were additional 9-point measures that might be affected by the message threat manipulation, by personal relevance, or by both. Subjects were asked to indicate how interested they were in seeking out additional information about the topic and the extent to which they had felt fearful, tense, and anxious while reading the article. Responses to the latter three items were averaged to create one fear index (alpha = .81).

Dependent Measures

BELIEFS AND INTENTIONS

Subjects indicated their agreement with the statement that caffeine consumption is strongly associated with fibrocystic disease and their belief in the importance of women's reducing their caffeine intake to avoid developing fibrocystic disease, on 9-point scales. These two items correlated highly ($r = .62$) and were averaged to form one belief index.

Subjects were also asked to what extent they believed that they themselves should, and that they actually would, reduce their own caffeine consumption, on 9-point scales. These two measures were then averaged to form an index of behavioral intention ($r = .62$).

EFFORT

Subjects were asked to indicate on a 9-point scale how much effort they had put into "trying to understand and think about the content of the message."

RESPONSES TO INDIVIDUAL REPORTS

Subjects were also asked several open-ended questions concerning each medical report, in order to explore message processing. Because each message contained at least one report supporting belief in a link and one report arguing against it, we were able to examine whether prolink and antilink reports elicited differential processing.

Recall. Several specific questions tested recall of each report, such as "Describe the characteristics of the women who comprised the experimental (i.e., test-group) and the comparison groups." Recall scores ranged from 0 to 18. Two independent raters coded these protocols with 86% absolute agreement.

Support, strengths, and weaknesses. Subjects were also asked, in an open-ended format, how strongly or weakly each report supported or refuted the link between caffeine consumption and fibrocystic disease. Two independent raters, blind to relevance condition, coded three different scores from subjects' responses. First, responses were scored for how strongly they indicated that the report supported its own conclusion, along a scale from 1 (*strongly refutes the link*) to 7 (*strongly supports the link*). (Interrater correlations for the four reports ranged from .78 to .86; $M = .83$). For antilink reports, this perceived support measure was reversed, so that higher scores always indicated that the report more strongly supported its own pro- or antilink conclusion.

The other two scores coded were the number of strengths and the number of weaknesses listed for each report, with 91% absolute interrater agreement. (Weaknesses listed by subjects were scored without consideration of whether they corresponded to the flaws intentionally embedded in the reports.) The number of strengths listed for a report ranged from 0 to 2; the number of weaknesses ranged from 0 to 3.

For purposes of analysis, one prolink and one antilink score were created for each report measure (i.e., recall, perceived support, number of strengths, and number of weaknesses) by averaging across responses to the prolink and antilink reports, respectively.

Results

All measures were analyzed via 2×2 (Message Threat × Relevance) analyses of variance (ANOVAs).

Checks on Experimental Design

As expected, high-relevance subjects rated the topic as more personally important than low-relevance subjects ($Ms = 7.02$ vs. 5.99), $F(1, 171) = 9.51, p < .005$.

Also as expected, subjects perceived that the high-threat message more strongly advocated a caffeine–fibrocystic disease link than the low-threat message ($Ms = 6.79$ vs. 4.00), $F(1, 171), = 106, p < .001$. The high-threat message also spurred greater interest in seeking out additional information ($Ms = 5.88$ vs. 5.36), $F(1, 171) = 4.0, p < .05$. Message threat and relevance did not interact on these measures ($Fs < 1$).

The high-threat message induced more fear than the low-threat message ($Ms = 4.44$ vs. 3.85), $F(1, 171) = 3.9, p < .05$. High-relevance subjects also reported more fear than low-relevance subjects ($Ms = 4.45$ vs. 3.78), $F(1, 171) = 6.6, p < .05$. In neither case, however, was the mean above the scale midpoint. No Message Threat × Relevance interaction was found, $F < 1$.

Dependent Measures

BELIEFS AND INTENTIONS

As expected, subjects believed more strongly in the link between caffeine and fibrocystic disease after reading the high-threat rather than the low-threat message ($Ms = 6.81$ vs. 5.48), $F(1, 171) = 39.6, p < .001$. The high-threat message also motivated greater intention to reduce one's caffeine intake ($Ms = 5.19$ vs. 4.37), $F(1, 170) = 5.35, p < .05$.

More interesting, however, is the finding that relevance significantly reduced belief, so that high-relevance subjects believed in this link less than low-relevance subjects ($Ms = 5.60$ vs. 6.72), $F(1,$

TABLE 8.1. Postmessage Belief Among Low-Relevance and High-Relevance Subjects Reading Low-Threat or High-Threat Messages

Message threat	Relevance	
	Low	High
Low	6.18	4.77
High	7.21	6.39

Note. Higher numbers indicate greater belief in link between caffeine and fibrocystic disease.

171) = 27.8, $p < .001$. This apparent defensiveness on the part of high-relevance subjects was evident in response to both the low- and the high-threat message, with no significant Message Threat × Relevance interaction, $F(1, 171) = 1.9, p = .17$. Thus, even the low-threat message was apparently threatening enough to induce defensiveness. Means are shown in Table 8.1. In essence, then, high-relevance subjects agreed *less* with the high-threat message than low-relevance subjects but agreed *more* with the low-threat message.

EFFORT

In contrast to the defensive inattention hypothesis, high-relevance subjects reported expending somewhat more effort reading the articles than low-relevance subjects ($Ms = 7.16$ vs. 6.72), $F(1, 171) = 2.76, p = .098$. No other effects were found on this measure.

RESPONSES TO INDIVIDUAL REPORTS

Each message contained at least one report supporting belief in the link between caffeine and fibrocystic disease and one report disconfirming this belief. To examine whether pro- and antilink

reports elicited differential processing, pro- and antilink responses were analyzed as repeated measures (one score for each direction; see Method), with personal relevance and message threat as between-subjects factors. No between-subjects main effects were significant in these analyses ($Fs < 2.1$, $ps > .15$). All effects found thus reflect the within-subjects factor of report direction—that is, the *difference* between responses to the prolink and antilink reports.

Our main interest concerns how this difference is affected by personal relevance—that is, Personal Relevance × Report Direction interactions. This interaction emerged on two variables: (a) subjects' perceptions of how strongly each report supported its conclusion, and (b) the number of weaknesses subjects saw in each report. We begin with the former. Overall, subjects considered that the prolink reports supported their conclusions more strongly than the antilink reports ($Ms = 4.70$ vs. 3.80), $F(1, 131) = 23.69, p < .001$. More important, this tendency was qualified by personal relevance, $F(1, 131) = 5.08, p < .05$. As shown in the first two rows of Table 8.2, the tendency to regard prolink reports as superior to antilink reports was significantly less pronounced among high-relevance subjects (mean difference = .040; $F[1, 65] = 3.73, p = .06$) than among low-relevance subjects (mean difference = 1.40; $F[1, 66] = 23.49$, $p < .001$). Thus, compared with low-relevance subjects, high-relevance subjects were more partial to the antilink relative to prolink reports.

The Personal Relevance × Report Direction interaction also emerged on the number of weaknesses perceived in the reports. Overall, subjects listed somewhat more weaknesses for the prolink reports than the antilink reports ($Ms = 0.38$ vs. 0.30), $F(1, 171) = 3.08, p = .08$. However, this

TABLE 8.2. Personal Relevance × Report Direction Interactions on Processing Measures

Measure	Personal relevance	Report direction		
		Pro	Anti	Difference
Reports' support for	Low	4.86	3.46	+1.40
their own conclusions	High	4.54	4.14	+0.40
Weaknesses found in	Low	0.34	0.34	0.00
the reports	High	0.42	0.25	+0.17

Note. Higher numbers indicate that the reports were perceived to support their conclusions more strongly or to have more weaknesses.

tendency was restricted to high-relevance subjects, resulting in a marginally significant interaction, $F(1, 171) = 3.0$, $p = .08$. In fact, as shown in the last two rows of Table 8.2, low-relevance subjects listed the same number of weaknesses for pro- and antilink reports. High-relevance subjects, however, saw significantly more weaknesses in the prolink than in the antilink reports (mean difference = 0.17), $F(1, 84) = 4.30$, $p < .05$.

Little of theoretical interest was found on the remaining two process measures. Subjects listed very few strengths of any reports and were even less likely to list a strength of an antilink report ($M = 0.03$) than a prolink report ($M = 0.08$), $F(1, 171) = 6.71$, $p = .01$. On recall, the only effect to approach significance was the Message Threat × Report Direction interaction, $F(1, 171) = 2.8$, $p = .096$. For the low-threat message, the prolink report was recalled slightly better (mean difference = +.02), whereas for the high-threat message, the antilink report was recalled slightly better (mean difference = −.06). Apparently the dissenting report for either message was more salient than the other reports and was therefore slightly better recalled.

To summarize, high-relevance subjects processed the threatening versus nonthreatening parts of the message more defensively than low-relevance subjects. This was indicated on two measures: how strongly the prolink versus antilink reports were seen as supporting their conclusions, and how many weaknesses were seen in prolink versus antilink reports. This difference between high-relevance subjects' processing of the pro- and antilink reports could result from greater scrutiny of the threatening parts of the message or from less scrutiny of the reassuring part of the message. Our results are consistent with both possibilities. Means on both measures show high-relevance subjects being more critical of the prolink reports than low-relevance subjects *and* less critical of the antilink reports. However, on the perceived support measure, the latter difference is larger.

CORRELATIONS

To examine the relationship between message processing and postmessage beliefs, prolink minus antilink difference scores on each report measure were computed and then correlated with subjects' postmessage beliefs in the link between caffeine and fibrocystic disease.

These correlations indicate that recall did not significantly predict postmessage belief, $p = .29$, but that the other three measures did. Thus, the greater the difference between the perceived support the prolink reports and antilink reports provided for their respective conclusions, the more strongly subjects believed in the caffeine–fibrocystic disease link after reading the message, $r(135) = .48$, $p < .001$. In addition, the more subjects saw the prolink reports as flawed in comparison with the antilink reports (as indicated by weaknesses listed), the less subjects believed in the caffeine–fibrocystic disease link, $r(175) = −.17$, $p < .05$. And the more strengths subjects saw in the prolink reports compared with the antilink reports, the more they believed in the caffeine–fibrocystic disease link, $r(171) = .16$, $p < .05$

We also inspected the possibility that fear may have mediated the personal relevance effects obtained on processing but found that fear did not significantly correlate with any processing measure. Nor did entering fear as a covariate affect the Personal Relevance × Report Direction interactions obtained on these processing measures. Thus, fear per se did not appear to play any causal role in high-relevance subjects' defensive processing. This apparent absence of a mediating role of induced fear is consistent with current literature on fear appeals (for reviews, see Boster & Mongeau, 1984; Sutton, 1982).

These correlations supplement our ANOVA results and reinforce the conclusion that subjects' defensive conclusions were mediated by biased systematic processing, rather than by defensive inattention. Although this systematic processing became more biased as a result of high personal relevance, systematic processing predicted beliefs equally well for low- and high-relevance subjects. That is, the magnitude of these correlations did not differ appreciably for the two groups of subjects. This finding stands in interesting contrast to several other studies in which low-relevance subjects' final attitudes have apparently depended less on message content than high-relevance subjects.' We suggest two possible reasons. First, the current study's message may have been more involving—under low relevance—than the messages of many of these other studies. That is, low-relevance females may be more interested in risk factors for breast disease than college students are interested in academic policy proposals that will not affect them. Second, these other studies have provided clear, salient heuristic cues such as source likability (Chaiken, 1980), source expertise (Petty, Cacioppo, & Goldman, 1981), or consensus information (Axsom et al., 1987), which low-relevance subjects apparently used as alternative bases for judgment. In the absence of such obvious heuristic cues for judgment—as in the present study—even lower levels of motivation may be sufficient to motivate systematic message processing (see Chaiken et al., 1989).

Discussion

The current study demonstrates that high personal relevance can defensively bias systematic processing. Consistent with prior research on fear appeals, high-relevance subjects' defensive conclusions were apparently not mediated by inattention to the message. In fact, high-relevance subjects reported expending marginally more effort in reading the message. In addition, the present study goes beyond past research and finds evidence of an alternative mechanism, defensive systematic processing of the message. Compared with low-relevance subjects, high-relevance subjects were less critical of those parts of the message that were reassuring and more critical of those parts that were threatening.

Somewhat surprisingly, perhaps, this defensive processing did not differ noticeably across two message replications of differential threat. We can only speculate on why the high-threat message did not induce even more defensive processing. As both messages began by describing the purported health threat, perhaps the mixed evidence presented in the low-threat message was insufficiently reassuring—in the absence of defensive processing—despite its reassuring conclusion.

Defensive Mechanisms

Defensive judgment of the message was apparently mediated by defensive systematic processing. Although biased cognitive processing has long been hypothesized as a possible outcome of personal relevance (e.g., Festinger, 1957; Janis, 1967), little has been uncovered about mediating processes, as noted earlier in this article. A recent review by Kunda (1990) found numerous studies showing

self-serving judgment but surprisingly little direct evidence of mediating cognitive processes.

Why has so little evidence been found of the cognitive processes mediating defensive judgment? One reason may be that the process receiving the most attention in early laboratory research was defensive inattention. However, as Janis noted long ago, inattention to the message is least likely to be found with captive audiences, as in most laboratory situations (Hovland, Janis, & Kelley, 1953; Janis & Feshbach, 1953; see also Chaiken & Stangor, 1987). Hence, failures to find defensive inattention in the laboratory do not eliminate the very real possibility that people turn away from threatening information in less structured situations, such as while watching television, browsing through the newspaper, or waiting in supermarket checkout lanes.

Second, the defensive mechanisms found here are quite subtle. Defensiveness was found in more critical evaluations of more versus less threatening *parts* of the messages, rather than in processing of the message as a whole. These mechanisms would presumably not appear in the majority of studies that use one-sided, rather than mixed, messages.

We note, therefore, that several studies outside the health domain using mixed messages have indeed found biased judgment. Although these studies provide little direct evidence of the underlying message processing, their results seem to implicate biased processing. Lord et al. (1979) presented subjects with two research reports, one finding evidence for the deterrent effects of capital punishment and one refuting it. Subjects with strong prior attitudes rated the research report congenial to their own attitudes as better conducted and more convincing than the counterattitudinal report. Lord et al. suggested that these biased judgments may have been mediated by the type of biased processing found in the present study. Although these mediating processes were not explored systematically, several subjects' comments were presented to illustrate this possibility.

Similar results were reported by Pyszczynski, Greenberg, and Holt (1985). Subjects read two reports concerning the accuracy of a social sensitivity test, one supporting and one discrediting it, after themselves receiving positive or negative scores on the test. Subjects rated the report that was more congenial with their own test score as stronger than the other.

Wyer and Frey (1983) also obtained results that indirectly implicate biased message processing. Subjects received bogus feedback on an intelligence test and read a 24-argument mixed message concerning intelligence tests. Surprisingly, subjects' recall showed a counterattitudinal inclination; the arguments *supporting* the test were recalled better by negative- than positive-feedback subjects. Wyer and Frey speculated that this finding occurred because subjects had been trying to counterargue those arguments (see also Hastie, 1981; Pomerantz, Hazlewood, & Chaiken, 1991).

In sum, some evidence of biased judgment has accumulated, particularly in response to mixed messages. Several recent theoretical proposals have also been offered concerning possible processes (e.g., Chaiken et al., 1989; Frey, 1986; Kunda, 1990; Pyszczynski & Greenberg, 1987). Nonetheless, little direct evidence has been obtained of actual biased processing. Documenting these mechanisms has proved difficult, perhaps because defensive processing that is easily detectable is not very functional. After all, defensive processing must be subtle enough to allow people to maintain at least an "illusion of objectivity" about their own judgments if they are to have faith in their own conclusions (Pyszczynski & Greenberg, 1987).

Personal Relevance and Defensive Processing

The present study provides one demonstration of personal relevance heightening defensive processing. Defensiveness was induced by the content of the message, which threatened subjects' beliefs concerning their health. Some previous studies have provided similar illustrations of personal relevance amplifying defensive goals.

Howard-Pitney, Borgida, and Omoto (1986) reported personal relevance biasing message processing, although they did not assess subjects' postcommunication attitudes. As in the current study, defensiveness was induced by the content of the message. But rather than threatening subjects' health, the message threatened college student subjects' right to drink by way of a debate about raising the legal drinking age from 19 to 21. Subjects who had earlier indicated that the topic was of great personal relevance reported more thoughts about the arguments than subjects indicating little personal relevance. Moreover, high-relevance subjects listed somewhat more *negative* thoughts about those arguments that supported raising the drinking age. Apparently, high relevance motivated subjects to refute the threatening arguments.

Petty and Cacioppo (1979a) have also shown that personal relevance can heighten defensive processing. Here, however, defensiveness was not induced by the message's contents or conclusions, but rather by a warning that the message was intended to change subjects' attitudes. This warning apparently evoked reactance, a goal of avoiding influence (Brehm, 1966). The message advocated making comprehensive exams a prerequisite to college graduation. In contrast to unwarned subjects, subjects warned of persuasive intent were less influenced by the message and reported more negative thoughts about it. More important, this defensive effect of warning was heightened when subjects believed that the academic proposal was personally relevant, in that it might soon be imposed at their own school, than when they believed it was not personally relevant.

Personal Relevance and Objective Processing

Despite these demonstrations of the potential biasing effect of personal relevance, recent reviews seem to reach a different conclusion concerning personal relevance. The most identifiable cluster of recent persuasion studies seems to find quite the opposite, that personal relevance increases unbiased, objective message processing (see Petty & Cacioppo, 1986; cf. Johnson & Eagly, 1989). Why do these results differ from our own?

We suggest that the effect of personal relevance on message processing is contingent on people's processing *goals* (Chaiken et al., 1989). In the absence of any strongly preferred conclusion, accurate evaluation of a message will often be the predominant goal, and heightened relevance will simply motivate more, relatively unbiased processing toward this end. But people do sometimes strongly prefer a particular conclusion, whether because of a health threat, a threat to self-interest, or simply reactance against an influence attempt. Personal relevance can then motivate increased processing to support that conclusion, through either selective application of heuristic cues or biased systematic processing.

Many recent personal relevance studies, however, have been designed to isolate the goal of assessing the validity of a message and to minimize the intrusion of other goals. For example, as noted above, Petty and Cacioppo (1979a) found that forewarning of persuasive intent can induce defensiveness. These investigators have, therefore, carefully disguised the persuasive intent of the messages in studies finding more objective processing, precluding reactance goals (e.g., Petty & Cacioppo, 1979b, 1984).

Recent personal relevance research has also not sampled the range of possible messages very widely (for a review of message topics, see Johnson & Eagly, 1989). In particular, the messages are generally not very threatening. For example, one popular topic—requiring college seniors to pass comprehensive exams—often elicits quite neutral attitudes from college students (Johnson & Eagly, 1989; Liberman, Hazlewood, & Chaiken, 1991).

Moreover, these messages are often constructed with a pretesting criterion that may preclude testing the defensive processing hypothesis. One indication of objective—versus biased—processing is when high relevance increases acceptance of strong messages and increases rejection of weak messages (Petty & Cacioppo, 1986). Demonstrating this requires carefully differentiating strong and weak arguments. Therefore, Petty and Cacioppo (1979b, 1986, 1990) have advocated categorizing as strong only arguments eliciting primarily favorable thoughts in pretesting and categorizing as weak only arguments eliciting primarily unfavorable thoughts. However, one likely side effect of this pretesting criterion is to preclude categorizing as strong any threatening messages that elicit unfavorable, defensive thoughts. Were such messages used, they would instead be categorized as weak; increased rejection of these messages under high relevance would then be interpreted as objective, rather than biased.

Therefore, recent findings suggesting that personal relevance motivated unbiased processing cannot be taken as indicating the *general* effect of personal relevance. General conclusions must await continued research using a broader range of messages and varying message recipients' goals.

In conclusion, the present study demonstrates that threatening messages can evoke defensive

goals and that personal relevance can heighten this defensiveness. This demonstration supports the argument that whether personal relevance motivates objective or defensive processing depends on the goals activated by a message and the situation in which it is encountered. When defensive goals are activated, personal relevance can amplify biased message processing.

ACKNOWLEDGMENTS

This research was supported in part by National Institute of Mental Health Grant R01-MH43299 to Shelly Chaiken. We would like to thank Lily Chu, Victoria de la Hoz, Shirley Nadler, David Shechter, and Doug Hazlewood for research assistance and Ziva Kunda, Richard Petty, and an anonymous reviewer for comments on earlier drafts.

REFERENCES

Axsom, D., Yates, S. M., & Chaiken, S. (1987). Audience response as heuristic cue in persuasion. *Journal of Personality and Social Psychology, 53,* 30–40.

Berkowitz, L., & Cottingham, D. R. (1960). The interest value and relevance of fear arousing communications. *Journal of Abnormal and Social Psychology, 60,* 37–43.

Boster, F. J., & Mongeau, P. (1984). Fear arousing persuasive messages. In R. N. Bostrom (Ed.), *Communication yearbook 8* (pp. 330–375). Beverly Hills, CA: Sage.

Brehm, J. W. (1966). *A theory of psychological reactance.* New York: Academic Press.

Chaiken, S. (1980). Heuristic versus systematic information processing and the use of source versus message cues in persuasion. *Journal of Personality and Social Psychology, 39,* 752–766.

Chaiken, S. (1987). The heuristic model of persuasion. In M. P. Zanna, J. M. Olson, & C. P. Herman (Eds.), *Social influence: The Ontario Symposium* (Vol. 5, pp. 3–39). Hillsdale, NJ: Lawrence Erlbaum.

Chaiken, S., Liberman, A., & Eagly, A. H. (1989). Heuristic and systematic processing within and beyond the persuasion context. In J. S. Uleman & J. A. Bargh (Eds.), *Unintended thought* (pp. 212–252). New York: Guilford.

Chaiken, S., & Stangor, C. (1987). Attitudes and attitude change. *Annual Review of Psychology, 38,* 575–630.

Eagly, A. H., & Chaiken, S. (1993). *The psychology of attitudes.* San Diego, CA: Harcourt Brace Jovanovich.

Festinger, L. (1957). *A theory of cognitive dissonance.* New York: Harper & Row.

Frey, D. (1986). Recent research on selective exposure to information. In L. Berkowitz (Ed.), *Advances in experimental social psychology* (Vol. 19, pp. 41–80). New York: Academic Press.

Hastie, R. (1981). Schematic principles in human memory. In E. T. Higgins, C. P. Herman, & M. P. Zanna (Eds.), *Social cognition: The Ontario Symposium.* Hillsdale, NJ: Lawrence Erlbaum.

Hovland, C. I., Harvey, O. J., & Sherif, M. (1957). Assimilation and contrast effects in reactions to communication and attitude change. *Journal of Abnormal and Social Psychology, 55,* 244–252.

Hovland, C. I., Janis, I. L., & Kelley, H. H. (1953). *Communication and persuasion: Psychological studies of opinion change.* New Haven, CT: Yale University Press.

Howard-Pitney, B., Borgida, E., & Omoto, A. M. (1986). Personal involvement: An examination of processing differences. *Social Cognition, 4,* 39–57.

Janis, I. L. (1967). Effects of fear arousal on attitude change: Recent developments in theory and experimental research. In L. Berkowitz (Ed.), *Advances in experimental social psychology* (Vol. 3, pp. 166–224). New York: Academic Press.

Janis, I. L., & Feshbach, S. (1953). Effects of fear-arousing communications. *Journal of Abnormal and Social Psychology, 48,* 78–92.

Janis, I. L., & Terwilliger, R. (1962). An experimental study of psychological resistances to fear-arousing communications. *Journal of Abnormal and Social Psychology, 65,* 403–410.

Johnson, B. T., & Eagly, A. H. (1989). The effects of involvement on persuasion: A meta-analysis. *Psychological Bulletin, 106,* 290–314.

Kunda, Z. (1987). Motivated inference: Self-serving generation and evaluation of causal theories. *Journal of Personality and Social Psychology, 53,* 636–647.

Kunda, Z. (1990). The case for motivated reasoning. *Psychological Bulletin, 108,* 480–498.

Liberman, A., Hazlewood, D., & Chaiken, S. (1991). *The direct effect of personal relevance on attitudes.* Unpublished manuscript, New York University.

Lord, C. G., Ross, L., & Lepper, M. R. (1979). Biased assimilation and attitude polarization: The effects of prior theories on subsequently considered evidence. *Journal of Personality and Social Psychology, 37,* 2098–2109.

Maheswaran, D., & Chaiken, S. (1991). Promoting systematic processing in low motivation settings: The effect of incongruent information on processing and judgment. *Journal of Personality and Social Psychology, 61,* 13–25.

Petty, R. E., & Cacioppo, J. T. (1979a). Effects of forewarning of persuasive intent and involvement on cognitive responses and persuasion. *Personality and Social Psychology Bulletin, 5,* 173–176.

Petty, R. E., & Cacioppo, J. T. (1979b). Issue involvement can increase or decrease persuasion by enhancing message-relevant cognitive responses. *Journal of Personality and Social Psychology, 37,* 1915–1926.

Petty, R. E., & Cacioppo, J. T. (1984). The effects of involvement on responses to argument quantity and quality. Central and peripheral routes to persuasion. *Journal of Personality and Social Psychology, 46,* 69–81.

Petty, R. E., & Cacioppo, J. T. (1986). The elaboration likelihood model of persuasion. In L. Berkowitz (Ed.), *Advances in experimental social psychology* (Vol. 19, pp. 123–205). Orlando, FL: Academic Press.

Petty, R. E., & Cacioppo, J. T. (1990). Involvement and persuasion: Tradition versus integration. *Psychological Bulletin, 107,* 367–374.

Petty, R. E., Cacioppo, J. T., & Goldman, R. (1981). Personal involvement as a determinant of argument-based persuasion. *Journal of Personality and Social Psychology, 41,* 847–855.

Petty, R. E., Cacioppo, J. T., & Schumann, D. (1983). Central and peripheral routes to advertising effectiveness: The moderating role of involvement. *Journal of Consumer Research, 10,* 135–146.

Pomerantz, E. M., Hazlewood, D., & Chaiken, S. (1991, August). *Structural consistency, processing goals, and the attitude-memory relation.* Paper presented at the annual meeting of the American Psychological Association, San Francisco.

Pyszczynski, T. A., & Greenberg, J. (1987). Toward an integration of cognitive and motivational perspectives on social inference: A biased hypothesis-testing model. In L. Berkowitz (Ed.), *Advances in experimental social psychology* (Vol. 20, pp. 297–340). New York: Academic Press.

Pyszczynski, T. A., Greenberg, J., & Holt, K. (1985). Maintaining consistency between self-serving beliefs and available data: A bias in information evaluation. *Personality and Social Psychology Bulletin, 11,* 179–190.

Sutton, S. R. (1982). Fear-arousing communications: A critical examination of theory and research. In J. R. Eiser (Ed.), *Social psychology and behavioral medicine* (pp. 303–337). Chichester, England: Wiley.

Wyer, R. S., & Frey, D. (1983). The effects of feedback about self and others on the recall and judgments of feedback-relevant information. *Journal of Experimental Social Psychology, 19,* 540–559.

Alcohol Myopia and Condom Use: Can Alcohol Intoxication Be Associated With More Prudent Behavior?

Tara K. MacDonald • Queen's University
Geoffrey T. Fong and Mark P. Zanna • University of Waterloo
Alanna M. Martineau • San Diego State University

We tested two competing theories about the effects of alcohol on intentions to engage in risky behavior. Disinhibition predicts that intoxicated people will exhibit risky behavior regardless of environmental cues, whereas alcohol myopia (Steele & Josephs, 1990) predicts that intoxicated people will be more *or* less likely to exhibit risky behavior, depending on the cues provided. In four studies,* we found an interaction between intoxication and cue type. When impelling cues were present, intoxicated people reported greater intentions to have unprotected sex than did sober people. When subtle inhibiting cues were present, intoxicated and sober people reported equally cautious intentions (Studies 1–3). When strong inhibiting cues were present, intoxicated people reported *more prudent* intentions than did sober people (Study 4). We suggest that alcohol myopia provides a more comprehensive account of the effects of alcohol than does disinhibition.

There is a common assumption that alcohol causes people to engage in foolish and risky behaviors (Critchlow, 1986; MacAndrew & Edgarton, 1969). This belief is consistent with the notion that alcohol acts as a general disinhibitor, causing people to "let go" of the inhibitions that would normally constrain their behavior. Indeed, alcohol is commonly associated with many dan-

gerous, harmful, and risky acts that are costly to society, such as drinking and driving, unprotected sex, date rape, spousal or child abuse, and other forms of aggression. If the disinhibition theory of alcohol is correct, this has important implications for interventions designed to decrease the deleterious consequences of these behaviors that are associated with alcohol. If alcohol always leads to more risky behaviors, then the message is simple: People simply should not make decisions about health-relevant behaviors when they are intoxicated.

---

*The original article contained four studies, only Studies 1–3 are included here.

In their alcohol myopia theory, however, Steele and his associates (Steele, Critchlow, & Liu, 1985; Steele & Josephs, 1990; Steele & Southwick, 1985) provide a different perspective about how alcohol affects behavior. They have speculated that alcohol causes a restriction in cognitive capacity, and therefore intoxicated people no longer have the requisite processing skills to attend to all of the information in their environment. Instead, they are likely to focus on the aspects of their environment that are most salient. Alcohol myopia theory differs from disinhibition theory in both its explanation of the effects of alcohol and in its implications for designing effective change programs. Alcohol myopia theory predicts that alcohol intoxication may make a person more or less likely to engage in risky behaviors, depending on the types of cues that are salient in the environment: If powerful cues promoting safe behavior are made salient, alcohol myopia theory makes the counterintuitive prediction that alcohol could actually lead to more cautious or prudent behavior.

This research focuses on the social, or situational, determinants of the effects of alcohol on health-risk behavior. Many important health-relevant behaviors result from conscious, voluntary decisions (e.g., whether to wear a condom when having casual sex, whether to drink and drive, whether to wear a seat belt). It is widely recognized that engaging in behaviors such as drinking and driving or having unprotected casual sex can lead to extremely negative consequences. In too many instances, however, people do make the decision to drink and drive or have sex without a condom. The ultimate tragedy of outcomes resulting from these detrimental behaviors often lies in the fact that these events may have easily been avoided had people made better health-relevant decisions. Thus, it is critical to examine aspects of the situation that affect whether intoxicated people make decisions leading to risky behaviors that may endanger their own health and potentially the health of others.

In our previous research, we have demonstrated that in the presence of impelling cues, alcohol intoxication causes people to be more likely to report intentions to engage in risky behaviors. For example, in research assessing the effects of alcohol on the decision to drink and drive (MacDonald, Zanna, & Fong, 1995, 1998), we asked sober and intoxicated participants two types of questions

pertaining to their attitudes and intentions toward drinking and driving. In some of the questions, we simply asked participants about their intentions to drink and drive (e.g., "I would drive while intoxicated"). In contrast, some of the questions were impelling in nature; that is, we embedded a relevant impelling cue into the items (e.g., "If I only had a short distance to drive home, I would drive while intoxicated"). We found interactions between alcohol condition (sober, placebo, intoxicated) and question type (nonimpelling and impelling) that were consistent with alcohol myopia theory. For nonimpelling questions, sober/placebo and intoxicated participants reported equally negative attitudes and intentions toward drinking and driving. Presumably, both groups were able to access relevant cues (e.g., the possibility of being in a car accident) that would inhibit this behavior. In contrast, for the questions that contained an impelling cue, there was a difference between sober/placebo and intoxicated participants, such that intoxicated participants reported more favorable attitudes and intentions toward drinking and driving than did sober/placebo participants. Presumably, nonintoxicated participants who were exposed to the impelling cues still had the cognitive capacity to access relevant inhibiting cues (i.e., cues that emphasize the potential costs of risky behaviors), and so remained negative toward drinking and driving. In contrast, due to the decrease in cognitive capacity associated with alcohol, intoxicated participants may have focused on the impelling cues provided and doing so may have precluded them from accessing relevant inhibiting cues.

Similarly, in our research assessing the effects of alcohol on condom use (MacDonald et al., 1996), sober and intoxicated participants viewed a video vignette depicting a male and female undergraduate couple who are interested in having sexual intercourse, but no condom was available. Participants were asked what they would do if they were in a similar situation. Here we embedded impelling cues into the video vignette (e.g., the female character is very attractive; she discloses that she takes birth control pills). As expected, we found that males who were randomly assigned to the intoxicated condition reported more favorable intentions toward having unprotected sexual intercourse than did their sober and placebo counterparts.

To date, we have demonstrated that in the presence of salient impelling cues (i.e., cues that emphasize the benefits of risky behaviors), alcohol causes people to be more likely to report intentions to engage in risky behaviors (see also Gordon & Carey, 1996). Thus far, however, our findings cannot rule out the disinhibition hypothesis, *because both the disinhibition and alcohol myopia theories predict that in the presence of impelling cues, alcohol intoxication leads to greater intentions to engage in risky behaviors*. We believe that providing participants with impelling cues was an ecologically valid approach—in the real world, the impelling cues associated with a health-relevant behavior are often more salient or immediate than inhibiting cues. For example, consider a person who is deciding whether to have sexual intercourse without a condom. In this situation, it is likely that the relevant impelling cues (e.g., being sexually aroused, being in the presence of an attractive partner) will be more salient than the relevant inhibiting cues (e.g., the possibility of contracting a sexually transmitted disease, causing an unwanted pregnancy). In this way, the restriction of cognitive capacity associated with alcohol may cause an intoxicated person to focus on conspicuous impelling cues at the expense of attending to less vivid, but still very important, inhibiting cues. The fact that impelling cues are usually more prominent than inhibiting cues may explain why the belief that alcohol acts as a general disinhibitor is so prevalent and compelling: In the real world, people observe others who are intoxicated attend to and act on impelling cues in the environment.

In the studies we present in this article, we sought to extend our prior work assessing the effects of alcohol on intentions to engage in risky behaviors by assessing the effects of alcohol on decision making in the presence of *inhibiting cues*. This strategy allows a rigorous comparison between the two competing theories, disinhibition and alcohol myopia, to determine which theory best explains the effects of alcohol on decision making. Disinhibition theory predicts that alcohol will cause people to report greater intentions to engage in risky behaviors, regardless of the cues present in the environment (i.e., alcohol should *always* make a person behave in a less cautious manner).

In contrast, alcohol myopia theory predicts that the effects of alcohol will be *moderated* by the nature of cues that are salient to the person at the time of the decision. When impelling cues are sa-

lient, alcohol will cause a person to focus on impelling cues and subsequently report stronger intentions to engage in risky behaviors. But when inhibiting cues are salient, intoxicated people will focus on these inhibiting cues, perhaps shifting their attention from impelling cues in the environment. How strong will this effect be? One possibility is that the disinhibiting effect will be counteracted by these inhibiting cues and that this will lead to an elimination of disinhibition. A second, counterintuitive possibility is that inhibiting cues will actually lead to an inhibition effect; that is, in the presence of inhibiting cues, alcohol myopia theory suggests that the intoxicated person may actually have *weaker* intentions to engage in risky behaviors.

In summary, alcohol myopia theory predicts that in the presence of inhibiting cues, intoxicated people would not necessarily be more likely than sober people to report intentions to engage in risky health-related behaviors and might in fact be *even less likely* to do so. Therefore, providing participants with inhibiting cues allows a critical test of the two competing hypotheses: If, in the presence of inhibiting cues, intoxicated people report more cautious intentions than sober people, then we may rule out the disinhibition hypothesis, for disinhibition theory would never predict that alcohol would be associated with more cautious behavior.

We do recognize that in some situations, alcohol intoxication leads to disinhibition. However, we maintain that alcohol myopia theory provides a more parsimonious explanation of the effects of alcohol on the decision of whether to engage in risky behaviors than does disinhibition, because it can account for why alcohol leads to risky behavior in some situations and cautious behavior in others. It is important to note that the alcohol myopia and disinhibition theories are not necessarily contradictory. We contend that alcohol intoxication always causes a restriction in cognitive capacity and therefore causes people to be highly influenced by the cues in their environment. If impelling cues are highly salient, then disinhibition will occur. If inhibiting cues are salient, however, then inhibition will occur. Disinhibition is therefore subsumed by alcohol myopia theory.

In this series of studies, we presented impelling or inhibiting cues to participants who were either sober or intoxicated. Given that sober people possess the requisite cognitive capacity to access cues that are not in their immediate environment, we should find that cue type (impelling or inhibiting) will have little impact on intentions toward engaging in unprotected sexual intercourse for sober participants (or participants assigned to a placebo condition). On the other hand, given that alcohol myopia causes people to be greatly influenced by cues in their immediate environment, we should find that cue type has a strong effect on intentions toward engaging in unprotected sexual intercourse for participants who are intoxicated. When impelling cues are salient, intoxicated people should be more likely than sober people to report intentions to engage in risky behaviors; whereas when strong inhibiting cues are salient, intoxicated people should be less likely than sober people to report intentions to engage in risky behaviors. It could be, however, that the impelling cues in the situation are very strong or that the inhibiting cues are not potent enough to eliminate the focus on impelling cues. In these cases, the inhibiting cues may not reverse the direction of the effects of alcohol intoxication, but they may counteract the impelling cues that are present. Thus, a weaker form of the interaction consistent with alcohol myopia theory would be that when subtle inhibiting cues are made salient, intoxicated and sober people should be equally likely to report intentions to engage in risky behaviors.

In sum, we propose to demonstrate the "flip side" of alcohol myopia (which may in fact be the more important side): This will hold theoretical importance by demonstrating that alcohol can be associated with more prudent, rather than more risky, intentions. In addition, this finding would provide strong support for alcohol myopia theory. If alcohol merely acts as a disinhibitor, then under no circumstance would one expect that alcohol intoxication would cause people to report less risky intentions: Disinhibition theory would state that alcohol should always cause people to "throw caution to the wind."

Study 1: Laboratory Experiment— Questionnaire Manipulation

Method

PARTICIPANTS

Sixty-five male participants were recruited from introductory psychology classes in return for course credit and payment ($5 in the sober condition and $10 in the alcohol and placebo conditions). We chose not to recruit women for this experiment because of the potential negative health consequences of consuming alcohol while pregnant. We recruited only men who reported on a pretest that they were sexually active, between the ages of 18 and 25 (18 is the legal drinking age in Alberta), consumed alcohol at least once per month, were not in a romantic relationship of more than two years' duration, and, importantly, used condoms regularly.

PROCEDURE

Alcohol manipulation. Participants were called to the laboratory to participate in groups of two or three. Each group was randomly assigned to the sober, placebo, or intoxicated condition. Participants were escorted to separate rooms where they viewed a video that had been created for use by the researchers and has been used successfully in the past (see MacDonald et al., 1996). In this video, two attractive undergraduates named Mike and Rebecca meet, go out on a date, and go back to Rebecca's apartment. After talking, they begin to "make out" on the couch, and soon find themselves in a situation where they must decide whether to have sexual intercourse. In the video, it is made clear that Rebecca is interested in having intercourse and that she is taking birth control pills. On the other hand, it is also made clear that it would be very difficult to obtain a condom (neither Mike nor Rebecca has a condom, the corner store is closed, and the nearest 24-hour store would require a long walk). The video ends with a freeze frame as the characters try to resolve this dilemma. Participants complete the dependent measures in view of this freeze frame and are asked to report how they would behave if in a situation similar to that presented in the video.

Participants in the sober condition simply viewed the video and completed the dependent measures. Participants in the intoxicated condition were weighed at the beginning of the session and were given the requisite amount of alcohol in three drinks over an hour to increase their blood alcohol level (BAL) to .08%. At the end of the session, their BAL was assessed using a portable breathalyzer (Intoxilyzer 300, manufactured by CMI, Inc.). Participants in the placebo condition were led to believe, through a number of cues (e.g., the rims of the glasses they drank from were dipped in alcohol, so that the drink smelled as if it contained alcohol), that they were being given three alcoholic beverages, when in fact they were given only a minute dose of alcohol (i.e., the amount of alcohol that they received was not enough to register on a breathalyzer). We have used this placebo procedure in the past and have demonstrated that it is very effective (see MacDonald et al., 1995, 1996).

Cue manipulation. Cue type was manipulated by presenting participants with one of two versions of the questionnaire. In the impelling condition, participants responded to questions assessing the likelihood that they would engage in sexual intercourse. In the inhibiting condition, participants responded to questions assessing the likelihood that they would engage in sexual intercourse **without a condom** (bold type is as it appeared in the questionnaire). We manipulated cue type in this way because we believed that the inhibiting version would make salient the fact that sexual intercourse would be unprotected and therefore risky. In prior research (MacDonald et al., 1995), we have found that embedding different types of information into questionnaire items is an effective way to manipulate cues.

MEASURES

Intentions. Participants' intentions to engage in sexual intercourse without a condom were assessed using one item. In the impelling cue condition, the item read, "If I were in this situation, I would engage in sexual intercourse with Rebecca." In the inhibiting cue condition, the item read, "If I were in this situation, I would engage in sexual intercourse **without a condom**." Participants responded to the intentions item on a 9-point rating scale where 1 = *very unlikely* and 9 = *very likely*.

Justifications. Five items assessed participants' willingness to endorse justifications to engage in unprotected sexual intercourse if they were in a situation similar to the one presented in the video. In the impelling cue condition, these items were, "A situation like this only occurs once in a while, so it would be worth the risk involved for me to have intercourse," "Because Rebecca's on the pill and won't get pregnant, there's little for me to worry about if we have intercourse," "Because she

looks totally healthy, it's alright if we have intercourse," "Because I can tell that Rebecca is not the type who sleeps around, it's alright if we have intercourse," and "There's no reason for me to be worried about using a condom if she's not." In the inhibiting cue condition, the items were worded in such a way that emphasized that sexual intercourse in this situation would take place without a condom. For example, in the inhibiting cue condition, the first two justifications items read, "A situation like this only occurs once in a while, so it would be worth the risk involved for me to have intercourse **without** using a condom" and "Because Rebecca's on the pill and won't get pregnant, there's little for me to worry about if we have intercourse **without** using a condom." Participants responded to these items on 9-point rating scales where 1 = *strongly disagree* and 9 = *strongly agree*. These five items were highly correlated and were aggregated into one scale (Cronbach's $\alpha = .89$)

Results

MANIPULATION CHECK

Among participants in the intoxicated condition, the average BAL was .093 ($SD = .018$). Moreover, there were no differences in BAL between those in the impelling cue condition ($M = .091$, $SD = .043$) and those in the inhibiting cue condition ($M = .106$, $SD = .033$), $t(22) = 0.93$, *ns*.

INTENTIONS

Because preliminary analyses revealed that there were no differences between sober and placebo participants in either the impelling condition (sober $M = 3.15$, placebo $M = 2.71$), $t(18) = 0.49$, *ns*, or the inhibiting condition (sober $M = 3.33$, placebo $M = 3.00$), $t(18) = 0.32$, *ns*, we collapsed across these two conditions and analyzed the data in a 2 (intoxication condition: sober/placebo or intoxicated) × 2 (cue condition: impelling or inhibiting) analysis of variance (ANOVA). There was a significant interaction between intoxication condition and cue condition, $F(1, 61) = 5.32$, $p = .025$. A comparison within the impelling cue condition revealed that participants in the intoxicated condition ($M = 4.85$) were significantly more likely than participants in the sober/placebo condition ($M = 2.89$) to report intentions to engage in unprotected sexual intercourse, $t(61) = 3.63$, $p < .001$, thus replicating the findings of our prior research (MacDonald et al., 1996). Within the inhibiting cue condition, participants in the intoxicated condition ($M = 2.62$) were somewhat less likely than participants in the sober/placebo condition ($M = 3.20$) to report intentions to engage in unprotected sexual intercourse, although not significantly so, $t(61) = 1.09$, *ns*. Moreover, as expected, for intoxicated participants, those who were in the impelling cue condition reported more favorable intentions to engage in unprotected sexual intercourse than did participants in the inhibiting cue condition, $t(61) = 3.72$, $p < .001$. In contrast, for sober participants there was no difference between those who were in the impelling cue condition and those who were in the inhibiting cue condition, $t(61) = 0.63$, *ns*. These data are represented graphically in Figure. 9.1.

Although the means were in the predicted direction, there were no main effects of intoxication level or cue condition or interactions between these two independent variables for the justifications subscale.

Discussion

The results of Study 1 were consistent with alcohol myopia theory. In the impelling cue condition, participants in the intoxicated condition reported more positive intentions to engage in sexual intercourse without a condom than did those in the sober/placebo condition. The intoxicated participants may have been highly influenced by the impelling cues contained in the video. In contrast, within the inhibiting cue condition, participants in the intoxicated condition reported equally negative intentions to engage in sexual intercourse without a condom to their sober/placebo counterparts. In this condition, the very subtle manipulation of adding the words "without a condom" to the dependent measures was enough to offset the impelling cues contained in the video, and this led to an elimination of the disinhibition effect. Disinhibition theory cannot account for these findings.

Our next goal was to test this hypothesis in the "real world," to examine whether inhibiting cues could eliminate the disinhibition effect in places where people normally consume alcohol. A further advantage of field studies is that we are able to assess both males and females. In laboratory

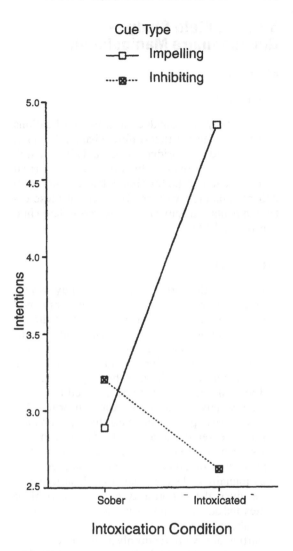

FIGURE 9.1 ■ Study 1: Mean reported intentions as a function of intoxication level and cue condition.

studies, we do not administer alcohol to females because of the potential negative health consequences of consuming alcohol while pregnant. In field studies, we are able to assess males and females because we do not administer alcohol or encourage people to drink alcohol. Instead, we assess individuals who are consuming alcohol in a naturalistic environment and whose decision to consume alcohol is not in any way related to their participation in our study.

Study 2: Field Study— Questionnaire Manipulation

Method

PARTICIPANTS

This study was conducted in two replications (1998 and 1999) at four different bars in Calgary, Alberta, and Lethbridge, Alberta. This research was conducted over eight different nights (two nights in each of the four bars). Participants were 325 patrons (130 women, 195 men) at these establishments. Participants' names were entered into a draw for $500.

PROCEDURE

Patrons in the bars were approached by two female experimenters. The experimenters explained that they were conducting a study about the effects of alcohol on social decision making. Patrons were told that if they wished to participate in the study, their participation would entail reading a short vignette, completing a brief questionnaire, and allowing their BAL to be assessed by a portable breathalyzer. Patrons were also informed that if they chose to participate in the study, their names would be entered into a draw for $500. If the patrons wished to participate in the study, written consent was obtained. After they completed the questionnaire and were breathalyzed, participants were given the opportunity to write down their names and addresses if they wished to receive feedback about the study.

Participants were randomly assigned to the impelling cue or the inhibiting cue condition. The following is the version given to female participants:

Imagine that you are single and that you run into a very attractive acquaintance while ordering a drink at the bar. The two of you begin to talk, and both of you find the conversation very enjoyable. He has a good sense of humor, and seems genuinely interested in what you are saying. It is clear that there is definite chemistry between you and that you are interested in this person. You continue to spend time together throughout the night. When the bar closes, he offers to walk you home. When you get home, he kisses you goodnight at the door. You decide to go inside and talk for a

while. After talking, you and he begin to make out on the couch. Things progress and you realize that you are both very interested in having sex with each other. You are on the pill, but neither of you have a condom. You discuss the possibility of going to a store, but there is not one nearby. You awkwardly discuss your sexual history, and he tells you that he does not sleep around.

The male version was identical, except for changes in the pronouns ("he" to "she") and reference to the birth control pill (i.e., "You are on the pill" in the female version was "She is on the pill" in the male version).

Cue type was manipulated by presenting participants with one of two versions of the questionnaire. In the impelling condition, participants responded to questions assessing the likelihood that they would engage in sexual intercourse. In the inhibiting condition, participants responded to questions assessing the likelihood that they would engage in sexual intercourse without a condom. This manipulation was on the second page of the questionnaire booklets that the participants completed; in this way, the experimenters were blind to condition as they administered the questionnaires.

MEASURES

Intentions. In Replications 1 and 2, participants' intentions to engage in sexual intercourse without a condom were assessed using one item, "If I were in this situation, I would have sex" (impelling condition) or "If I were in this situation, I would have sex **without a condom**" (inhibiting condition; bold type is as it appeared in the questionnaire). Participants responded to this item on a 9-point rating scale where 1 = *very unlikely* and 9 = *very likely*.

Justifications. In Replication 1 only, two items assessed participants' willingness to endorse justifications to engage in unprotected sexual intercourse if they were in the situation presented in the vignette. In the impelling cue condition, these items read, "A situation like this occurs only once in a while, so it would be worth the risk involved for me to have sex" and "Because I am (she is) on the pill, it is unlikely that I (she) will get pregnant." In the inhibiting cue condition, the items were the same, with the exception of "**without a condom**" added at the end of each sentence. Participants responded to these items on 9-point rating scales where 1 = *strongly disagree* and 9 = *strongly agree*. These two items were correlated, $r(162) = .39, p = .0001$, and were aggregated into one scale.

Demographic information. Participants were asked to report their ages, whether they were single, whether they were sexually active, whether they had been in a situation like the one described in the vignette, and the percentage of time that they use condoms when having sexual intercourse. In Replication 1, the demographic information was collected after participants completed the study, whereas in Replication 2, the demographic information was collected before participants read the vignette and completed the dependent measures. People who reported that they were currently single were included in the analyses, resulting in 265 participants (97 women, 168 men).

Results

Because this research was conducted in two different replications, we conducted preliminary analyses on the demographic information, using replication as a between-subjects factor. These results revealed that the participants in Replication 1 were significantly older (*M* age = 23.9) than those in Replication 2 (*M* age = 21.2), $t(256) = 5.67, p = .0001$. Moreover, the participants in Replication 1 reported using condoms more frequently (*M* = 70%) than did participants in Replication 2 (*M* = 58%), $t(264) = 2.56, p = .011$. Therefore, Replication (1 or 2) was entered as a between-subjects factor in the analyses.

For the analyses that follow, we divided participants into two groups, based on their BAL. Participants whose BAL was below .080 (the legal intoxication limit in Alberta) were classified as sober (mean BAL = .031, *SD* = .025, *n* = 148), and those whose BAL was at or above .080 were classified as intoxicated (mean BAL = .137, *SD* = .075, *n* = 117). There were no differences in BAL between those in the impelling cue condition and those in the inhibiting cue condition for the sober or intoxicated groups.

INTENTIONS

We conducted a 2 (intoxication level: sober or intoxicated) × 2 (cue condition: impelling or inhibiting) × 2 (gender: male or female) × 2 (repli-

cation: first or second) ANOVA on the intentions data. There was a main effect of gender, such that men (*M* = 4.45) were more likely to report intentions to have sexual intercourse without a condom than were women (*M* = 3.15), $F(1, 241) = 13.06, p = .0001$. There was also a main effect of cue condition, such that participants who responded to an impelling item (*M* = 4.50) were more likely to report intentions to have unprotected sexual intercourse than were those who responded to an inhibiting item (*M* = 3.42), $F(1, 241) = 11.63, p = .002$. There were no main effects of intoxication level or replication.

As hypothesized, there was a significant interaction between intoxication level and cue condition, $F(1, 241) = 5.90, p = .016$. A comparison within the impelling cue condition revealed that intoxicated participants (*M* = 5.36) were more likely than sober participants (*M* = 3.91) to report intentions to engage in unprotected sexual intercourse, $t(241) = 3.30, p < .001$. In contrast, within the inhibiting cue condition, intoxicated participants (*M* = 3.31) were less likely than sober participants (*M* = 3.51) to report intentions to engage in sexual intercourse, though not significantly so. Moreover, a comparison among intoxicated participants revealed that those in the impelling cue condition reported more favorable intentions to have sexual intercourse than did those in the inhibiting cue condition, $t(241) = 4.32, p < .001$. In contrast, a comparison among sober participants revealed that there was no difference between those in the impelling cue condition and those in the inhibiting cue condition, $t(241) = 0.98$, *ns*.

These data are represented graphically in Figure 9.2. There were no other two-way or higher order interactions.

JUSTIFICATIONS

We conducted a 2 (intoxication level: sober or intoxicated) × 2 (cue condition: impelling or inhibiting) × 2 (gender: male or female) ANOVA on the justifications data that were collected in Replication 1. Again, there was a main effect of gender, such that men (*M* = 4.29) were more likely than women (*M* = 2.97) to endorse justifications for doing so, $F(1, 95) = 9.28, p = .003$. There were no other main effects, and gender did not interact with the other independent variables.

There was a significant interaction between in-

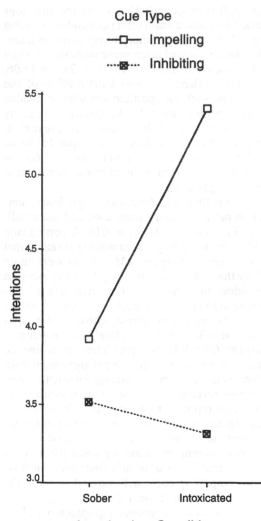

Cue Type

—□— Impelling

····▩···· Inhibiting

FIGURE 9.2 ■ Study 2: Mean reported intentions as a function of intoxication level and cue condition.

toxication level and cue condition, $F(1, 95) = 4.17$, $p = .044$. A comparison within the impelling cue condition revealed that intoxicated participants ($M = 4.62$) were marginally more likely than sober participants ($M = 3.37$) to endorse justifications to engage in unprotected sexual intercourse, $t(95) = 1.71$, $p < .10$. In contrast, within the inhibiting cue condition, intoxicated participants ($M = 3.29$) were less likely than sober participants ($M = 4.19$) to endorse justifications to engage in sexual intercourse, though not significantly so. Moreover, a comparison among intoxicated participants re-

vealed that those in the impelling cue condition were more likely to endorse justifications to have sexual intercourse than those in the inhibiting cue condition, $t(95) = 2.30$, $p < .05$. In contrast, among sober participants there was no difference between those in the impelling cue condition and those in the inhibiting cue condition, $t(95) = 1.38$, ns.

Discussion

There was a highly consistent pattern of results for the intentions and justifications data. As predicted, the cues that were provided in the question items affected the responses of intoxicated participants, but made little difference to those who were sober. Presumably, this is because sober participants could attend to inhibiting cues even when they were not highlighted in the question items, whereas intoxicated people were cognizant of inhibiting cues only when this information was made explicit.

Therefore, in a laboratory study and a field study, we found evidence consistent with alcohol myopia theory. The effects of alcohol were moderated by type of cue, a result that is inconsistent with disinhibition theory and consistent with alcohol myopia theory. The very subtle cue of adding the words **"without a condom"** to questionnaire items was enough to counteract impelling cues in the environment, thus eliminating differences between the intentions of sober and intoxicated participants. In both cases, however, the manipulations entailed the completion of a questionnaire.

An additional goal of the present research is to examine the effects of alcohol on the decision to engage in risky behaviors and eventually to provide information that can be applied to efforts to promote safer sexual behavior. In Study 3, we attempted to design a field study in which subtle inhibiting cues were manipulated in a way that would be applicable to the "real world" and could potentially be used in interventions aimed at decreasing the coincidence of alcohol intoxication and unprotected sexual intercourse.

Study 3: "Intervention" Field Study—Handstamp Manipulation

In this experiment, our goals were to make inhibiting or "safe sex" cues salient to participants as they were in a situation where alcohol was being consumed, to determine whether intoxicated people would be less likely to report intentions to have unprotected sex in the presence of such cues. There are a number of inhibiting cues relevant to the issue of unprotected sexual intercourse that could potentially be made salient to intoxicated participants and influence their intentions. Which type of inhibiting cue would be most effective when a person is intoxicated—cues that emphasize the benefits of using condoms or cues that emphasize the dangers of associated with unsafe sex? In his classic review of the literature of the effectiveness of fear communications, Leventhal (1970) suggested that fear-based appeals are effective to the extent that they provide specific recommendations about how to avoid the negative consequences present in the fear-arousing appeal, thus providing a "way out" of danger. On the other hand, Janis (1967) suggested that if fear-based appeals cause too much negative arousal, this may lead to rebound effects, because participants could become hypervigilant and defensive. We used both a mild cue (i.e., no fear) and a more powerful disease cue (i.e., moderate fear) in this study to allow a test of the effectiveness of both strategies in producing changes of intentions in intoxicated participants.

Method

PARTICIPANTS

This study was conducted at two different bars in Calgary, Alberta, over six different nights (three nights in each of the two bars). Participants were 452 patrons (167 women, 285 men) at these establishments. Participants' names were entered into a draw for $500 in return for their cooperation.

PROCEDURE

In this field study, cues were manipulated as patrons entered the bar. A research assistant (who did not identify herself as associated with the research) stood with the doorperson as patrons entered the bar. At bars it is common for patrons to get a stamp on their hands as they enter, to control reentry into the bar (i.e., people with handstamps do not have to line up again if they choose to leave and reenter the bar during the course of an evening). In this way, it did not seem unusual to

patrons that they might receive a handstamp at a bar. If patrons did ask about the messages on the handstamps, the research assistant merely said that the stamps were part of a "health awareness campaign being run by the bars in the area."

There were three stamps that were used. Each stamp was a circle, 1.1 inch in diameter, with a smaller circle within. In this way, the stamps could be construed as the outline of a condom. In the control stamp condition ($n = 163$), a drawing of a "smiley face" was inside the smaller circle.[1] In the inhibiting/mild cue condition ($n = 149$), the words "SAFE SEX" were written inside the smaller circle. In the inhibiting/moderate cue condition ($n = 138$), the words "AIDS KILLS" were written inside the smaller circle. These handstamps are shown in Figure 9.3. To avoid problems of contamination between the conditions, cue condition was assigned by night, not by patron (i.e., on a given night, all patrons received the same stamp).

Patrons in the bars were approached by two female experimenters (who were not associated with

FIGURE 9.3 ■ Study 3: Handstamps used for the cue manipulation.

---

[1]In Study 3, we compared the inhibiting cue conditions against a control stamp; that is, we did not actively manipulate impelling cues by providing further information that would be interpreted as promoting casual sexual intercourse. The vignette itself does contain impelling cues (e.g., it is specified that the acquaintance is attractive; birth control is mentioned), and there are a number of impelling cues that are naturally present in a bar environment, so the control condition can be seen as analogous to an impelling cue condition.

the person applying the handstamp). The experimenters explained that they were conducting a study about the effects of alcohol on social decision making. The experimenters made no mention of the handstamp. Patrons were told that if they wished to participate in the study, their participation would entail reading a short vignette, completing a brief questionnaire, and allowing their BAL to be assessed by a portable breathalyzer. They were also told that if they participated in the study, their names would be entered into a draw for $500. If the patrons wished to participate in the study, written consent was obtained. Participants read the vignette as described in Study 2 and completed dependent measures that were identical to those described in the impelling condition in Study 2.

MEASURES

Intentions. Participants' intentions to engage in sexual intercourse without a condom were assessed using one item, "If I were in this situation, I would have sex." Participants responded to this item on a 9-point rating scale where 1 = *very unlikely* and 9 = *very likely.*

Justifications. Two items assessed participants' willingness to endorse justifications to engage in unprotected sexual intercourse if they were in the situation presented in the vignette. These items read, "A situation like this occurs only once in a while, so it would be worth the risk involved for me to have sex" and "Because I am (she is) on the pill, it is unlikely that I (she) will get pregnant." Participants responded to these items on 9-point rating scales where 1 = *strongly disagree* and 9 = *strongly agree.* These two items were correlated, $r(443) = .40, p = .0001$, and thus were aggregated into one scale.

Demographic information. After the critical dependent measures were collected, participants were asked to report their ages, whether they were single, whether they were sexually active, whether they had been in a situation like the one described in the vignette, and the percentage of time that they use condoms when having sexual intercourse.

MANIPULATION CHECK

After the participants had completed the dependent measures and were breathalyzed, the experimenters covered the participants' hands and asked the participants to describe their handstamp. Most participants (83%) were able to report accurately the message on their handstamp. The experimenters recorded whether the participants had been able to recall the handstamp that they received. At this point, the experimenters mentioned that the handstamp was associated with the study, and participants were given the opportunity to write down their names and addresses if they wished to receive feedback about the study.

Results

Preliminary analyses revealed that there were no differences between the two bars on the demographic information or intoxication level, so we collapsed across bar on the analyses that follow. Only participants who were able to recall their handstamp were used in the analyses, resulting in 372 participants (147 women, 225 men).

Participants were divided into two groups, based on their BAL. As in Study 2, participants whose BAL was below .080 were classified as sober (mean BAL = .036, $SD = .024, n = 261$), and those whose BAL was at or above .080 were classified as intoxicated (mean BAL = .125, $SD = .045, n = 107$).

INTENTIONS

We conducted a 2 (intoxication level: sober or intoxicated) × 3 (cue condition: smiley face, "SAFE SEX," or "AIDS KILLS") × 2 (gender: male or female) ANOVA on the intentions data. There was a significant main effect for gender, such that men ($M = 4.68$) were more likely than women ($M = 2.88$) to report that they would engage in sexual intercourse if they were in a situation similar to the one presented in the vignette, $F(1, 351) = 36.74, p = .0001$. There were no other main effects, and there was not a significant interaction between intoxication level and cue condition when all three cue conditions were used.

We noticed, however, that the pattern of means suggested that there was a consistent pattern for the smiley face and the "SAFE SEX" cue condition, such that intoxicated participants ($M = 5.07$ for smiley face and $M = 4.30$ for "SAFE SEX") were more likely than sober participants ($M = 3.81$ for smiley face and $M = 3.35$ for "SAFE SEX") to report intentions to have sexual intercourse without a condom. In the more inhibiting/moderate

"AIDS KILLS" condition, however, the pattern of results suggested that intoxicated participants ($M = 3.75$) were somewhat *less* likely than sober participants ($M = 4.06$) to report intentions to engage in sexual intercourse without a condom.

To determine whether the "AIDS KILLS" stamp was an effective inhibiting cue, we compared this condition with the smiley face (control) condition, by conducting a 2 (intoxication level: sober or intoxicated) × 2 (cue condition: smiley face or "AIDS KILLS") × 2 (gender) ANOVA on the intentions data. Again, there was a main effect of gender, such that men ($M = 4.87$) were more likely than women ($M = 2.99$) to report intentions to engage in unprotected sexual intercourse, $F(1, 240) = 28.28$, $p = .0001$. There was a marginal interaction between intoxication level and cue type, $F(1, 240) = 2.97$, $p = .086$. A comparison within the "smiley face" condition revealed that there was an effect of intoxication level, such that intoxicated participants ($M = 5.07$) were more likely to report intentions to engage in unprotected sexual intercourse than were sober participants ($M = 3.81$), $t(240) = 2.55$, $p < .02$. In the "AIDS KILLS" condition, however, there were no differences between sober and intoxicated participants, $t(240) = 0.44$, *ns*. Moreover, a comparison among intoxicated participants revealed that there was a marginal effect of stamp, such that intoxicated participants with an "AIDS KILLS" stamp ($M = 3.75$) were less likely to report intentions to engage in unprotected sexual intercourse than were intoxicated participants with a smiley face (i.e., control) stamp ($M = 5.07$), $t(240) = 1.76$, $p < .09$.

There was also an interaction between intoxication level and gender, $F(1, 240) = 4.24$, $p = .041$, such that among women, intoxicated participants ($M = 4.19$) were more likely to report intentions to engage in unprotected sexual intercourse than were sober participants ($M = 2.77$), $t(240) = 2.01$, $p < .05$. Among men, however, the intoxicated participants ($M = 4.80$) and sober participants ($M = 4.90$) were equally likely to report intentions to engage in unprotected sexual intercourse, $t(240) = 0.21$, *ns*. There were no other two-way or higher order interactions.

Discussion

The results of Study 3 are encouraging in terms of developing real-world interventions to decrease the incidence of unsafe sexual activity. In this field study, we found that in the absence of inhibiting cues, intoxicated participants were more likely to express intentions to engage in sex without a condom than were sober people, presumably because they were influenced by the impelling cues in the scenario or in the bar environment. In contrast, introducing a simple cue manipulation "canceled out" the potentially dangerous impact of alcohol intoxication on participants' intentions (in fact, intoxicated participants were somewhat less likely to report intentions to engage in unprotected sexual intercourse than those who were sober). We found that a mild inhibiting cue (i.e., "SAFE SEX") was not sufficient to reduce the disinhibiting effect we found in the neutral cue (i.e., smiley face) condition. However, the inhibiting/moderate cue (i.e., "AIDS KILLS") was sufficiently powerful to counteract the disinhibition effect.

In terms of the debate about whether fear-arousing messages are effective inhibiting cues, our findings provide evidence consistent with Leventhal (1970), who theorized that powerful fear-arousing messages can motivate people, especially if targets receive information about how to avoid the negative consequences associated with the fear-arousing appeal. Although we did not provide explicit recommendations to participants in this study, they were given the opportunity to report intentions *not* to engage in unprotected sex, which may have been a convenient way to dispel the negative arousal caused by a powerful fear-based appeal. Moreover, it is important to consider the difficulties that may be encountered when attempting to make inhibiting cues salient in a real-world environment, such as a bar, where there are a great deal of stimuli competing for the attention of an intoxicated person. In these situations, it may be necessary to provide strong, vivid, and clear messages about the potential negative consequences of engaging in unsafe sexual activity to counteract persuasive impelling cues that might be present.

Therefore, in the laboratory study and the field studies, we demonstrated that subtle inhibiting cues could offset the impelling cues that are normally present when people are making the decision of whether to have unprotected sexual intercourse. In these three studies, we found the same pattern of results. Under conditions where impelling cues were salient, intoxicated participants reported more favorable intentions to engage in unprotected sexual intercourse than did sober participants. In these situations, participants were presumably attending to and reporting intentions consistent with the impelling cues contained in the video (Study 1) or the bar environment (Studies 2 and 3). When we introduced subtle inhibiting cues, however, the sober and intoxicated participants reported equally negative intentions to engage in unprotected sexual intercourse: Adding the words "without a condom" to the end of a questionnaire, or stamping participants' hands with an "AIDS KILLS" stamp neutralized the potentially dangerous effects of alcohol intoxication in situations where impelling cues are typically salient. These findings are consistent with alcohol myopia theory and inconsistent with disinhibition theory.

A better test of the two competing theories, however, would be to provide participants with even more powerful inhibiting cues. In this way, the inhibiting cues may not only counteract the impelling cues that are normally present in the environment, but may overcome them. Here, alcohol myopia theory would predict that in the presence of powerful inhibiting cues, alcohol intoxication should be associated with more prudent intentions. On the other hand, disinhibition theory would state that even in the presence of powerful inhibiting cues, alcohol should be associated with more risky intentions. In our next study, our goals were to emphasize inhibiting cues more strongly than in the preceding three studies, to determine whether alcohol intoxication can actually be associated with *more cautious* intentions.

Summary of Results

Recall that we had hypothesized that there would be an interaction between intoxication level and cue type, such that in the presence of impelling cues intoxicated people should be more likely to report intentions to have sexual intercourse without a condom, whereas in the presence of inhibiting cues intoxicated people should be less likely to report intentions to have sexual intercourse without a condom (strong form), or intoxicated and sober people should be equally likely to report intentions to have sexual intercourse without a condom (weak form). We conducted two laboratory studies and two field studies testing this hypothesis, and the four studies converge to show a

pattern of data that is consistent with our hypothesis. It is important to note that where this interaction was not statistically significant, the trends in the results were in the predicted direction.

We conducted a meta-analysis, using the expected interaction and main effects of intoxication level for each of the cue types on the intentions subscale, our main dependent variable. Using the method of weighted zs (Mosteller & Bush, 1954, as described in Rosenthal, 1978), we combined the four studies, and found that the 2 (alcohol condition: nonintoxicated or intoxicated) × 2 (cue condition: impelling or inhibiting) interaction was reliable for the intentions subscale, $z = 3.10$, $p = .001$. A chi-square analysis of the difference in significance among the four studies (Mullen & Rosenthal, 1985; Rosenthal & Rubin, 1979) revealed that any variation in the significance level of the interaction between intoxication level and cue type was due to chance, $\chi^2 (3) = 0.36$, ns.

We used the method of adding ts (Winer, 1971, as described in Rosenthal, 1978) to compare the nonintoxicated and intoxicated groups in both the impelling and inhibiting cue conditions. Within the impelling cue condition, we found that there was a highly reliable difference between nonintoxicated and intoxicated participants, $z = 5.43$, $p = .0001$, such that intoxicated participants were more likely to report intentions to engage in unprotected sexual intercourse than were their nonintoxicated counterparts (i.e., a disinhibition effect). A homogeneity test revealed that there was no difference in level of significance among the four studies, $\chi^2 (3) = 2.31$, ns. In contrast, within the inhibiting cue condition, we found that there was a reliable difference between nonintoxicated and intoxicated participants, $z = 2.06$, $p = .04$, such that intoxicated participants were less likely to report intentions to engage in unprotected sexual intercourse than were their nonintoxicated counterparts (i.e., an inhibition effect). Again, there was no difference in level of significance among the four studies, $\chi^2 (3) = 1.87$, ns.

General Discussion

The results of these four studies are consistent with alcohol myopia theory and cannot be explained by disinhibition theory. When sober (or placebo) and intoxicated participants were provided with cues that made either impelling or inhibiting reasons for having unprotected sex salient, cue type had no effect on sober or placebo participants. In contrast, cue type significantly affected intoxicated participants' intentions to engage in sexual intercourse without a condom.

One strength of this research is that we used different manipulations to make impelling or inhibiting cues salient to participants. In Studies 1 and 2, the words "without a condom" were used to provide inhibiting cues to some participants, but not others. In Study 3, cue condition was manipulated in a manner that was more ecologically valid: The regular business practices of popular bars were modified in a way that allowed us to introduce inhibiting cues into the environment. In Study 4, participants were asked questions designed to elicit different cues. In this way, participants themselves generated the impelling or inhibiting information. Although the individual studies may have limitations associated with the methodologies or dependent measures used, it is important to note that the overall pattern of findings converges to show a consistent interaction between alcohol intoxication level and cue condition. In addition, many plausible alternative explanations for our findings can be ruled out because we predicted and obtained interaction effects. For example, expectancy effects, social desirability effects, or demand characteristics are not plausible alternative explanations for our findings, because if intoxicated people felt compelled to report that they would act in a more risky fashion, this would have been equally true for intoxicated participants in the impelling cue condition and those who were in the inhibiting cue condition.

One limitation of this research, of course, is that we assessed intentions to engage in sexual intercourse without a condom and not actual condom use behavior. In these studies, ethical and practical considerations prevented us from assessing whether people did use a condom in sexual situations. However, recent research has shown that intentions to use condoms and condom use behavior are highly correlated: Sheeran, Abraham, and Orbell (1999) conducted a meta-analysis of 30 studies that assessed intentions to use condoms and actual condom use behavior and found a sample-weighted average correlation of .43. In fact, intentions to use condoms were among the strongest correlates of condom use behavior in both cross-sectional and longitudinal studies assessing correlates of condom use in heterosexuals. Therefore, we can be reasonably confident that intentions to use condoms are predictive of actual behavior.

Alcohol Myopia Versus Disinhibition

We believe that our findings hold great theoretical significance, in that we have demonstrated that the effects of alcohol intoxication on intentions to engage in unprotected sexual intercourse are moderated by the cues in the environment. In Studies 1–3, we found that the presence of subtle inhibiting cues eliminated, but did not reverse, the "risky" effects of alcohol intoxication on intentions to engage in sexual intercourse without a condom. Importantly, in Study 4, we found that the presence of strong inhibiting cues did reverse the potentially dangerous effects of alcohol intoxication: When inhibiting cues were salient, intoxicated participants were significantly less likely than their sober and placebo counterparts to report intentions to engage in unprotected sexual intercourse. These findings are consistent with alcohol myopia theory and are completely at odds with what would be expected by the notion that alcohol acts as a general disinhibitor. Therefore, it is clear that the disinhibition theory of alcohol does not provide a complete account of how alcohol affects intentions to engage in risky behaviors.

Alcohol myopia theory is inconsistent with prior conceptions of the effects of alcohol intoxication on behavior (e.g., Critchlow, 1986) and is incompatible with most casual observations about the effects of alcohol. As we have argued, disinhibition theory is widely accepted both by researchers and laypeople, perhaps due to the fact that alcohol is typically consumed in environments where impelling cues are highly salient. For example, in a typical bar, a person might dance with attractive potential sexual partners in an environment where music provides suggestive lyrics and videos provide seductive images. An intoxicated bar patron might be highly influenced by these impelling cues and be disposed to have sexual intercourse, even if a condom were unavailable.

What would alcohol myopia theory predict in the typical bar situation? It is important to note that when impelling cues are prominent, disinhibition and alcohol myopia would make the same prediction. In conditions where impelling cues are highly salient, alcohol myopia theory would predict that alcohol intoxication will act as a disinhibitor. However, when inhibiting cues are salient, alcohol myopia theory would predict that alcohol intoxication will act as an *inhibitor*. In this way, alcohol myopia theory offers a more complete and precise explanation of the effects of alcohol on decisions to engage in risky behaviors. Disinhibition theory is thus subsumed by alcohol myopia theory because it describes what will occur when impelling cues are salient. We have demonstrated, however, that the relationship between alcohol and intentions to engage in risky behaviors is more complex than disinhibition theory would suggest: Cue type (impelling or inhibiting) moderates the relationship between alcohol intoxication and intentions to engage in risky behaviors, as expected by alcohol myopia theory.

Practical Implications

Our findings may have implications for interventions designed to reduce the coincidence of alcohol intoxication and risky behaviors. We have demonstrated that alcohol intoxication does not always lead to increased intentions to engage in risky behaviors. Instead, alcohol intoxication causes people to be highly influenced by the cues in their environment. If cues that emphasize the potential benefits of risky behaviors are made salient, then alcohol may cause more positive intentions to engage in risky behaviors. On the other hand, if powerful cues that emphasize the potential costs of risky behaviors are made salient, then alcohol may cause more negative intentions to engage in risky behaviors. We believe that it is very worthwhile to apply these findings to negative behaviors that are associated with alcohol intoxication. Unprotected intercourse is a prime example of a costly behavior that is associated with alcohol intoxication (for a review, see Leigh and Stall, 1993). In the future, it may be possible to apply these hypotheses to other behaviors that hold powerful negative consequences, and are alcohol-induced, or alcohol-related, such as drinking and driving, relationship conflict (G. MacDonald, Holmes, & Zanna, 1998), or date rape.

We believe that the handstamp manipulation used in Study 3 could hold great promise for interventions. When the cues are placed on people's hands, not only will the cues be present in the context where alcohol is being consumed (i.e., the bar), but the cues will also be present in the context where the decision to engage in risky behaviors is made (i.e., a person's residence). In this way, handstamps (or keychains, etc.) may be more effective strategies for providing inhibiting reminders than merely placing posters around bars, because these cues will go home with the person to where the decision whether to engage in risky behaviors (e.g., having sexual intercourse without a condom) is made.

It is important to note, of course, that we are not implying that alcohol intoxication may be a feasible way to increase the persuasive impact of "safe sex" messages! On the other hand, we do believe that appeals designed to change certain behaviors, such as condom use, should incorporate strategies that will be effective when people are intoxicated. Prior research does suggest that alcohol intoxication and sexual behavior often coincide (Leigh & Morrison, 1991; Leigh & Stall, 1993). Moreover, our own research (MacDonald et al., 1995, 1996) demonstrates that when people are intoxicated and impelling cues are present, they are more likely to report intentions to engage in risky behaviors. It is our contention that if appropriate inhibiting cues are made salient, they may eliminate, or even reverse, the potentially tragic consequences of making health-relevant decisions under the influence of alcohol.

ACKNOWLEDGMENTS

This project was supported by Social Sciences and Humanities Research Council of Canada Grant 410-97-1576 and by a Population Health Investigator Fellowship from the Alberta Heritage Foundation for Medical Research awarded to Tara MacDonald. Partial reports of these data were presented at the annual meeting of the Society for Behavioral Medicine, San Diego, March 1999, and at the annual meeting of the Midwestern Psychological Association, Chicago, April 1999.

We wish to acknowledge the contribution of Geoff MacDonald, who helped to develop items for the manipulation used in Study 4. We thank Darlene Spencer for her excellent work on the video vignette that was used in Studies 1 and 4. We also thank Jennifer Bodmer, Jodie Bossenberry, Michaela Chatterson, Anna Ebel, Jacquie Ellice, Jennifer MacMillan, Bonnie MacPherson, Kim Poettcker, Paige Schwartzenberger, Vatonia Taylor, Jennifer Terpstra, and Glen Wright for their assistance with the data collection. Finally, we extend our appreciation for the support and cooperation that we received from the management and staff of the bars in Calgary, Alberta, and Lethbridge. Alberta, where the field studies were conducted.

REFERENCES

Critchlow, B. (1986). The powers of John Barleycorn: Beliefs about the effects of alcohol on social behavior. *American Psychologist, 41*, 751–764.

Gordon, C. M., & Carey, M. P. (1996). Alcohol's effects on requisites for sexual risk-reduction in men: An initial experimental investigation. *Health Psychology, 15*, 56–60.

Janis, I. L. (1967). Effects of fear arousal on attitude change: Recent developments in theory and experimental research. In L. Berkowitz (Ed.), *Advances in experimental social psychology* (Vol. 3, pp. 166–224). New York: Academic Press.

Leigh, B. C., & Morrison, D. M. (1991). Alcohol consumption and sexual risk-taking in adolescents. *Alcohol Health and Research World, 15*, 58–63.

Leigh, B. C., & Stall, R. (1993). Substance use and risky sexual behavior for exposure to HIV. *American Psychologist, 48*, 1035–1045.

Leventhal, H. (1970). Findings and theory in the study of fear communications. In L. Berkowitz (Ed.), *Advances in experimental social psychology* (Vol. 5, pp. 119–186). New York: Academic Press.

MacAndrew, C., & Edgarton, R. B. (1969). *Drunken comportment*. Chicago: Aldine.

MacDonald, G., Holmes, J. G., & Zanna, M. P. (1998, July). *Alcohol and relationship conflict*. Paper presented at the International Conference on Personal Relationships, Saratoga Springs, NY.

MacDonald, T. K., Zanna, M. P., & Fong, G. T. (1995). Decision making in altered states: Effects of alcohol on attitudes toward drinking and driving. *Journal of Personality and Social Psychology, 68*, 973–985.

MacDonald. T. K., Zanna, M. P., & Fong, G. T. (1996). Why common sense goes out the window: Effects of alcohol on intentions to use condoms. *Personality and Social Psychology Bulletin, 22*, 763–775.

MacDonald. T. K., Zanna, M. P., & Fong, G. T. (1998). Alcohol and intentions to engage in risky behaviors: Experimental evidence for a causal relationship. In J. G. Adair, D. Belanger, & K. Dion (Eds.), *Advances in psychological science: Vol. 1. Social, personal, and cultural aspects* (pp. 407–428). East Sussex, England: Psychology Press.

Mosteller, F. M., & Bush, R. R. (1954). Selected quantitative techniques. In G. Lindzey (Ed.), *Handbook of social psychology: Vol. 1. Theory and method*. Cambridge, MA: Addison-Wesley.

Mullen, B., & Rosenthal, R. (1985). *BASIC meta-analysis: Procedures and programs*. Hillsdale, NJ: Erlbaum.

Rosenthal, R. (1978). Combining results of independent studies. *Psychological Bulletin, 85*, 185–193.

Rosenthal, R., & Rubin, D. B. (1979). Comparing significance levels of independent studies. *Psychological Bulletin, 86*, 1165–1168.

Sheeran, P., Abraham, C., & Orbell, S. (1999). Psychosocial correlates of heterosexual condom use: A meta-analysis. *Psychological Bulletin, 125*, 90–132.

Steele, C. M., Critchlow, B., & Liu, T. J. (1985). Alcohol and social behavior: II. The helpful drunkard. *Journal of Personality and Social Psychology, 48*, 35–46.

Steele, C. M., & Josephs, R. A. (1990). Alcohol myopia: Its prized and dangerous effects. *American Psychologist, 45*, 921–933.

Steele, C. M., & Southwick, L. (1985). Alcohol and social behavior: I. The psychology of drunken excess. *Journal of Personality and Social Psychology, 48*, 18–34.

Winer, B. J. (1971). *Statistical principles in experimental design* (2nd ed.). New York: McGraw-Hill.

Social Influence and Health and Illness: Social Comparison and Social Norms

"A month has now passed since I quit smoking. It's been difficult and I've had to cope with a few lapses, but I haven't touched a cigarette for the past 14 days. Although I feel a bit better than I did right after I quit, I still get cravings. Is that okay or should I be worried? I wonder what the other people in the program who quit when I did are feeling?" These are thoughts of a female college student trying to stop smoking.

Assigning meaning to our feelings, our thoughts, and our actions is often difficult, and to do so we frequently rely on comparisons with other people. By engaging in social comparison (Festinger, 1954), we use the experiences and actions of others as a context or comparison standard against which to evaluate our own experiences (or actions). In the preceding example, the young woman is unsure how to think about her continued cravings. She would be reassured to discover that other quitters were still battling cravings, but would be concerned if she found that she alone was still experiencing the desire to smoke. The role of social comparison in the health domain has been of great interest to researchers and practitioners alike. Investigators have examined how comparisons with others affect the ability to cope with adverse outcomes, responses to threatening events, and willingness to engage in healthy and unhealthy patterns of behavior.

The manner in which people utilize social comparisons to cope with a serious health problem can be seen clearly in a classic study by Wood, Taylor, and Lichtman (1985). They examined the social comparison activity of a sample of women with breast cancer and, in particular, documented the extent to which each woman believed she was doing better, as well as, or worse than other women with breast cancer. They observed that almost regardless of their actual experiences, these women reported that they were doing better than others. This type of social comparison, which has been labeled downward social comparison, is thought to be a crucial way in which people cope with challenging experiences. Although people may feel reassured when they assert that others are not doing as well as they are, this does not mean that they want to spend time with people who are worse off than they are. People want to affiliate with others who are doing as well or better than themselves as these are the people who can provide them with the information or skills they need to continue to deal effectively with their health problem (Taylor & Lobel, 1989).

Social comparison activity can also affect how people prepare for and manage a threatening event such as major surgery. Kulik, Mahler, and Moore (1996) have shown that whom one is assigned as a preoperative roommate influences how patients, deal with and recover from major surgery. The right type of roommate (e.g., someone who has recently come out of surgery) can help people develop a clearer sense of what they are about to experience, and this understanding not only helps to reduce anxiety about the procedure but also dramatically shortens the length of the hospital stay. In fact, the authors observed that people without a room-mate—perhaps the rooming situation people often

think they would request—have the longest average stay in the hospital.

As people face decisions about whether to engage in a particular health-relevant behavior, they frequently consider what others might think and feel. According to the theory of reasoned action (Ajzen & Fishbein, 1980), people's perceptions of social norms are a primary determinant of their behavioral intention, which in turn predicts their behavior. Prentice and Miller (1993) demonstrate how college students' beliefs about the social norms regarding alcohol use on campus can affect their alcohol-related beliefs and behavior. Moreover, the authors illustrate how social norms persist even when they are in conflict with people's own private attitudes.

People not only consider what others think about a particular pattern of behavior, they also care about how individuals who engage in that pattern of behavior are perceived. In particular, adolescents and young adults are thought to perceive opportunities to engage in behaviors such as smoking and drinking as a way to take on the characteristics they ascribe to their image of the typical smoker or drinker. To the extent that these images are desirable, people will seek out opportunities to engage in the behavior. Across a range of risk behaviors, Gibbons and Gerrard (1995) examine this premise and illustrate the bidirectional relation between people's perceptions of the typical person engaged in a risk behavior (e.g., smoking) and their own willingness to engage in the behavior.

REFERENCES

Ajzen, I., & Fishbein, M. (1980). *Understanding attitudes and predicting social behavior.* Englewood Cliffs, NJ: Prentice-Hall.

Festinger, L. A. (1954). A theory of social comparison processes. *Human Relations, 7,* 117–140.

Gibbons, F. X., & Gerrard, M. (1995). Predicting young adults' health risk behavior. *Journal of Personality and Social Psychology, 69,* 505-517.

Kulik, J. A., Mahler, H. I. M., & Moore, P. J. (1996). Social comparison and affiliation under threat: Effects on recov-ery from major surgery. *Journal of Personality and Social Psychology, 71,* 967–979.

Prentice, D. A., & Miller, D. T. (1993). Pluralistic ignorance and alcohol use on campus: Some consequences of misperceiving the social norm. *Journal of Personality and Social Psychology, 64,* 243–256.

Taylor, S. E., & Lobel, M. (1989). Social comparison activity under threat: Downward evaluation and upward contacts. *Psychological Review, 96,* 569–575.

Wood, J. V., Taylor, S. E., & Lichtman, R. R. (1985). Social comparison in adjustment to breast cancer. *Journal of Personality and Social Psychology, 49,* 1169–1183.

Discussion Questions

1. Joanne Wood and her colleagues (1985) observed that nearly all women believed that they were coping "better than average." Of course, everyone cannot be above average. People may experience a range of psychological benefits from adopting this "irrational" mindset. What potential costs might there be to maintaining this perspective?
2. Preoperative patients benefited greatly from spending time with a roommate who had recently completed surgery. Because of the goals of their study, Kulik, Mahler, and Moore (1996) only followed the subsequent experiences of the preoperative patients. No one followed the experience of the postoperative roommate. Would you expect the roommates to have benefited—psychologically and physically—from the time they spent talking with the preoperative patient? Why or why not?
3. Given the ability of social norms to persist over time, even in the face of changes in individuals' private attitudes, what types of intervention strategies might one use to alter people's perceptions of the social norm?
4. In two separate studies, Prentice and Miller (1993) and Gibbons and Gerrard (1995) demonstrate how people's beliefs about the social norm or social image are related to unhealthy behavioral practices (e.g., alcohol consumption, smoking, unprotected sex). Would you expect social norms and/or social images to play a similar role in people's willingness to engage in health-promoting behaviors such as exercise, eating a well-balanced diet, and getting regular dental checkups? Why or why not?
5. In light of the articles you have read in this section, what are the negative and the positive effects that marketing and advertising can have on people's health practices?

Suggested Readings

Blanton, H., Stuart, A. E., & vandenEijnden, R. J. J. M. (2001). An introduction to deviance-regulation theory: The effect of behavioral norms on message framing. *Personality and Social Psychology Bulletin, 27,* 848–858.

A demonstration that people are particularly responsive to information about people who are engaging in non-normative behavior.

Buunk, B. P., & Gibbons, F. X. (1997). *Health, coping, and social comparison.* Hillsdale, NJ: Erlbaum.

An excellent edited collection of chapters that examine the numerous ways in which social comparison activity can impact health and health behavior.

Crandall, C. (1988). Social contagion and binge eating. *Journal of Personality and Social Psychology, 55,* 588–598.

A fascinating demonstration of how the norms within social groups shape people's behavior.

Taylor, S. E., & Lobel, M. (1989). Social comparison activity under threat: Downward evaluation and upward contacts. *Psychological Review, 96,* 569–575.

This paper provides a conceptual framework to explain why people coping with challenges want to compare themselves to those who are worse off, but spend time with people who are doing as well or better than them.

Social Comparison in Adjustment to Breast Cancer

Joanne V. Wood • State University of New York at Stony Brook
Shelley E. Taylor and Rosemary R. Lichtman
• University of California, Los Angeles

We investigated four theoretical perspectives concerning the role of social comparison (Festinger, 1954) in coping with a threatening event in a sample of breast cancer patients. According to the supercoper perspective, personal contact with comparison others is often unavailable to patients, and contact with media "supercopers"—fellow victims presented as adjusting very smoothly—may make patients feel inadequate by comparison. According to the similarity perspective, patients select comparison targets who are similar to themselves because those comparisons should be the most informative. The upward comparison perspective is predictive of comparisons to relatively advantaged or superior individuals. The downward comparison perspective leads to the prediction that under conditions of threat, individuals make comparisons to people who are inferior or less fortunate in order to enhance their self-esteem. We interviewed 78 breast cancer patients, and results of both closed-ended questions and spontaneously offered comparisons yielded a preponderance of downward comparisons. The results point to the value of using naturalistic methods for studying comparisons, and suggest a more active and cognitive role for social comparison than is usually portrayed.

Nearly all persons are confronted with serious illness in their lifetimes, either by becoming ill themselves or by being faced with the illness of someone they love. The difficulties wrought by serious illness include pain and disability, disruption of one's lifestyle, intense fears, and strains in close relationships (Cohen & Lazarus, 1979; Wortman, & Dunkel-Schetter, 1979). How do people adjust to these stressors? Social comparison (Festinger, 1954) may be important in adjustment through its two main functions: self-evaluation and self-enhancement.

Self-Evaluation and Adjustment

According to Festinger's (1954) theory, self-evaluation is the primary function of social comparison. He proposed that people have a drive to evaluate their opinions and abilities, and that they often do so by comparing themselves with others. Schachter (1959) extended the theory by proposing that individuals seek to clarify their emotional reactions in stressful situations, and this position has received laboratory support (Cottrell & Epley, 1977). Some writers have suggested that patients seek to evaluate their emotional reactions to illness (Mechanic, 1977; Wortman & Dunkel-Schetter, 1979). Wortman and Dunkel-Schetter, for example, wrote that

A person diagnosed with cancer is likely to be highly fearful and uncertain. The intensity of their feelings and anxieties may lead many patients to worry that they are coping poorly or losing their grip on reality. They experience a need to . . . learn whether their reactions are reasonable and normal. (p. 124)

Whether social comparison is important to this process of self-evaluation has not been studied directly. However, people grappling with crises want to express their feelings and to discuss them with others (Dunkel-Schetter & Wortman, 1982; Silver & Wortman, 1980). One function of such discussions may be to help individuals evaluate their reactions by comparing them with those of fellow victims.

Self-Enhancement and Adjustment

The desire for an accurate self-evaluation may clash at times with the desire to obtain a favorable self-evaluation (cf. Gruder, 1977; Singer, 1966), and self-enhancement has been identified as a motive for social comparison (e.g., Hakmiller, 1966). The results of laboratory studies suggest that a critical determinant of which motive is paramount seems to be a threat to self-esteem; under threat, individuals often opt for a self-enhancing strategy (Brickman & Bulman, 1977; Gruder, 1977). For example, they may avoid comparisons with others who appear to be superior.

Serious illness can pose great threats to self-esteem because it can bring many changes that are critical to one's identity: body image, occupation, valued activities, and close relationships (Cohen & Lazarus, 1979; Wortman & Dunkel-Schetter, 1979). Patients may be motivated, therefore, to enhance their self-esteem in a number of areas (Pearlin & Schooler, 1978; Taylor, 1983). Their self-enhancement goals may well be served by social comparison.

In summary, two hypothesized functions of so-cial comparison may be involved in adjustment to illness: Social comparison may be used to evaluate one's emotional reactions and may be used for self-enhancement. We examined four theoretical perspectives, each of which concerns one or both of the two motives for social comparison. These perspectives are called the *supercoper* perspective, the *similarity* perspective, the *upward comparison* perspective, and the *downward comparison* perspective.

The Supercoper Perspective

The supercoper perspective concerns how social comparison can affect a victim's self-evaluation of her adjustment. This perspective is drawn from Taylor and Levin's (1976) review of the breast cancer literature, in which they suggested that a range of comparison others is unavailable to many patients. Many women, for example, have no personal friends who have been through the same experience. One source of comparisons that may be more widely available is the media. However, Taylor and Levin (1976) observed that media coverage is often biased toward those who are adjusting very successfully. With respect to breast cancer, for example, well-known patients such as Marvella Bayh and Shirley Temple Black are often presented as being able to pick up their lives easily where they left off before their surgery. This media bias may not be unique to cancer; TV news coverage of many tragic events often seems to focus on victims who adjust well (cf. Wortman & Dunkel-Schetter, 1979). An unfortunate consequence of this media bias is that victims who are exposed to these "supercoper" models but who themselves are experiencing bouts of depression and self-doubt may feel inadequate.

Thus the supercoper perspective leads to two predictions: (a) Comparison others are generally unavailable to breast cancer patients, and, consequently, patients compare themselves with media figures; and (b) because the media disproportionately feature supercopers, comparisons with media figures make women feel worse about themselves. Whereas the supercoper perspective concerns the effects of comparisons, the remaining three perspectives concern selection of comparison others.

The Similarity Perspective

Like the supercoper perspective, the similarity perspective is concerned with self-evaluation of adjustment. Festinger (1954) maintained that in order for one to make an accurate self-evaluation, one must compare oneself with similar others. However, this similarity hypothesis is complicated by debate over what basis of similarity is important. According to some authors, it is similarity on the dimension under evaluation (see Goethals & Darley, 1977). In the context of self-evaluation of adjustment, such *dimension-specific* comparisons would involve comparisons with others who are adjusting similarly.

Other authors have contended that what Festinger (1954) meant was similarity on attributes related to the dimension under evaluation (e.g., Goethals & Darley, 1977), or what has been termed *related attributes* similarity (Wheeler & Zuckerman, 1977). Zanna, Goethals, and Hill (1975) provided this example to illustrate the distinction:

> A swimmer evaluating his [or her] ability would prefer comparing with another person who would have a similar time given his [or her] age, experience, and recent practice [all attributes related to swimming ability], rather than simply a person with a similar time [dimension-specific similarity]. (p. 87)

An informative comparison strategy, then, is to select a person who is similar on related dimensions, and then compare with that person in terms of the dimension under evaluation. Attributes that breast cancer patients consider to be related to adjustment—and therefore important to comparison selection—may include type of surgery, prognosis, and age. According to the similarity hypothesis, then, victims will compare themselves with women who are similar on the specific dimension in question or on attributes related to that dimension.

The Upward Comparison Perspective

Many laboratory studies have indicated that subjects often compare themselves with someone in the desirable direction—that is, someone who pos-

sesses a lot of a favorable attribute or very little of a negative attribute (Gruder, 1977). Upward comparison may serve either the purpose of self-evaluation or of self-enhancement. Breast cancer patients may, for example, attempt to measure their adjustment against that of someone who is better off, or they may feel better by identifying with her (cf. Brickman & Bulman, 1977). For either purpose, then, victims will compare themselves to other patients who are better off than they are, according to the upward comparison perspective.

The Downward Comparison Perspective

As discussed earlier, concerns for an honest self-evaluation are at times outweighed by a desire to preserve one's self-esteem (cf. Singer, 1966). Several studies have shown that comparisons with superior others are avoided when one's self-esteem has been threatened (e.g., Wilson & Benner, 1971). Moreover, under such conditions people may compare themselves with others who are inferior or less fortunate. Such "downward comparisons" have been reported in the experimental literature (e.g., Hakmiller, 1966; Wilson & Benner, 1971), and suggestive evidence has appeared in the coping literature (Pearlin & Schooler, 1978). Wills (1981) offered the first formal theoretical statement of downward comparison. He reviewed a large literature to support his thesis that under victimizing circumstances people often attempt to preserve their self-esteem through downward comparison.

The downward comparison idea is consistent with a more general conceptualization of victims' reactions that was recently proposed (Taylor, Wood, & Lichtman, 1983). When individuals become the victims of crime, illness, or natural disasters, Taylor et al. (1983) argued, they often seek to minimize their sense of victimization. Victims may use strategies of selective evaluation that attempt to limit their own and others' perceptions of how bad their situations are; downward comparison is one such strategy. Taylor et al. (1983) identified four additional strategies of selective evaluation: creating hypothetical, worse worlds (e.g., "It could have been worse"); construing benefit from the victimizing event (e.g., "I am a stronger person now"); manufacturing normative standards of adjustment, compared with which one's adjustment is good (e.g., "So many are just devastated, but I'm certainly not"); and selectively focusing on dimensions that make one appear advantaged, namely, "dimensional comparisons" (e.g., "At least I'm married—it must be so hard for these single women"). Of these four strategies, comparisons with normative standards and dimensional comparisons most clearly involve social comparison processes. Hence they are also examined in this study. According to the downward comparison perspective, victims will favor downward comparisons and these related selective evaluation strategies.

Method

Recruitment of Subjects

Subjects were obtained through a three-physician private oncology practice in Los Angeles. Thirty patients were screened out because of severity of illness or geographic inaccessibility. A letter describing the study was sent to the remaining 179 patients by the physicians' nurse, and 87 interested patients contacted the researchers, which yielded a response rate of 49%. Nine of these women eventually did not participate because of logistical problems.

Sample

The final sample included 78 women ranging in age from 29 to 78 (mean age was 53). Seventy-one percent were married. The mean level of education attained was one year of college. Overall, the economic distribution suggests a skew toward the middle and upper socioeconomic classes, and the sample had a somewhat disproportionate Jewish representation: Protestant (46%), Catholic (15%), Jewish (31%), other (4%), and no religion (4%).

All but 3 of the women had been treated surgically for their breast cancer. Thirty-five percent of those (26) had had a lumpectomy (removal of the malignant lump and some supportive tissue), 3% (2) had had a simple mastectomy (removal of the breast), 39% (29) had had a modified radical mas-

tectomy (removal of the breast and some adjacent lymph nodes), 12% (9) had had a Halsted radical mastectomy (removal of the breast, adjacent lymph nodes, and part of the pectoral muscles), and 12% (9) had had surgery on both breasts. Thirty-one percent of the patients were initially diagnosed as having Stage I cancers, 55% had Stage II cancers, and 14% had distant sites of metastases. Length of time since surgery ranged from 2 months to 16 years; the median was 25½ months. (For additional information about the sample, see Taylor, Lichtman, & Wood, 1984.)

Procedure

Respondents were telephoned and an interview was arranged, usually in the home. The interviewers were the authors and two other experienced female interviewers. The standardized, tape-recorded interview typically lasted between 1.5 and 2 hours and it covered (in order) demographic data, the woman's cancer experience and its treatment, attributions for cancer and beliefs about its controllability, life changes since cancer, changes in close relationships, specific fears about the cancer (e.g., death, finances), general emotional reactions (fear, anxiety, depression, and anger), social comparison processes, and compliance with medical regimen. Because the social comparison section of the interview was most critical to the present study, it is described after the remaining measures. The specific form of any other questions used in the analyses is covered in the Results section.

Questionnaire. A questionnaire was left with respondents, and the return rate was 90%. The only questionnaire measure involved in this study is the Locke-Wallace Scale of Marital Adjustment (Locke & Wallace, 1959).

Interviewer and physician ratings. Independent ratings of psychological adjustment to the illness were obtained from the interviewer and the physician on the Global Adjustment to Illness Scale (GAIS; Derogatis, 1975). Using interview and chart materials, interviewers also made a physical state rating for each patient. This 7-point scale ranged from 1 (*obviously deteriorating from metastatic cancer*) to 7 (*prognosis good*, e.g., a small tumor, no nodal involvement, symptom-free for at least 2 years).

Social Comparison Section of Interview

The social comparison questions tapped three general categories: (a) contacts with potential comparison others, (b) impressions about other patients' coping, and (c) comparisons made. First, several questions concerned the contacts the patients had with various media and social sources. Patients were asked how much contact they had had with cancer-related books, TV shows, and newspaper and magazine articles (these were coded on 4-point scales, from $1 = none$ to $4 = a lot$); other media sources ($1 = yes$, $2 = no$); other women and other breast cancer patients ($1 = none$, $4 = quite a few$); support groups ($1 = no$, $2 = yes, went once$, $3 = continued to go$); and Reach-to-Recovery volunteers ($1 = yes$, $2 = no$). In an effort to obtain an index of contacts that would be more reliable than the individual contact items, we created a contact composite through principal components analyses. This media composite consisted of books, TV shows, and newspaper and magazine articles. Its reliability, as measured via Cronbach's alpha, was .65.

Next, patients were asked what impressions they had formed of other women's coping as a result of their contacts and were asked, "Have you ever thought about how you have coped in comparison with any of these impressions? ($1 = yes$, $2 = no$); then, "In general, have you thought you were coping much better than other women with breast cancer, coping somewhat better, coping about the same, coping somewhat worse, or coping much worse?" Responses were coded on a 6-point scale from $1 = coping much better$ to $6 = coping much worse$ (the response "better than some, worse than others" was coded as 4). This scale is called the *coping-in-comparison rating*.

Free-Response Social Comparison Measures

Once data were collected and the interviews transcribed, it became clear that phenomena relevant to social comparison had occurred in instances other than the social comparison section of the interview. Throughout their interviews, most women spontaneously had made comparisons with other people. These comparative remarks offered us an opportunity to examine the theoretical perspectives through a measurement method different from the customary structured, closed-ended comparison questions. Their spontaneous quality suggests that the free-response comparisons occur naturally and may therefore be more central to the patients' experience than the comparisons elicited by investigator-designed questions.

Both descriptive and theoretical considerations guided the creation of the coding system for these free responses. In order to describe them fully, comparisons in different content domains—such as psychological adjustment and physical status—were kept separate. We also derived categories to address certain theoretical questions, as described later. To compute interrater agreement, the first author and a second coder each coded 24 randomly selected interview transcripts. Agreements were scored when particular quotations were selected and coded identically. All interrater agreements were computed as percentage of agreement on occurrences only.

Comparisons Relevant to the Supercoper Perspective

In order to examine the supercoper predictions, it is important to determine whether direct, personal contacts are available as comparison targets when one evaluates one's psychological adjustment. Hence the transcripts were coded for the presence of two responses, which are presented in Table 10.1. Descriptions of the emotional reactions or psychological adjustment of a seriously ill other with whom the patient had direct, personal contact were divided into two categories: *good copers* and *poor copers;* interrater agreements were .80 and 1.00, respectively.

Comparison in Adjustment

Comparisons Relevant to the Similarity Perspective

Because the similarity perspective concerns self-evaluation of psychological adjustment, several categories of comparisons involving relative adjustment were coded.

Others cope better, others cope worse, and others cope the same. Each quotation that involved a comparison on the dimension of psychological

TABLE 10.1. Free-Response Measures: Descriptions of Others' Adjustment

Category	Definition	Example	No. of comparisons made	Frequency	%[a]
Good coper	Description of patient reacting or adjusting well	She was very calm and cool and reassuring, and told me there was no pain afterwards.	0	50	68.5
			1	17	23.3
			2	3	4.1
			3	1	1.4
			4	1	1.4
			6	1	1.4
Poor coper	Description of patient reacting or adjusting poorly	I talked to the nurse, who had it just 2 weeks after I did, and she says, "I'm not making a good adjustment at all. I'm having a terrible time."	0	31	42.5
			1	29	39.7
			2	6	8.2
			3	4	5.5
			5	2	2.7
			6	1	1.4

[a]Percentages were computed from 73 interviews; 5 others were not transcribed because of equipment failure.

adjustment was coded as to whether the respondent explicitly stated that she was adjusting more poorly than, similarly to, or better than another. An example of *others cope better* is as follows:

> The girl across the street went in and had her breast removed. . . . A week later she was out working, cheerful, and seemed just fine. And look at me after all this time.

Others cope the same:

> There was a movie on about a young girl and how she coped with cancer. . . . I remember feeling the same way that she seemed to feel.

Others cope worse:

> I have never been like some of those people who have cancer and they feel well, this is it, they can't do anything, they can't go anywhere. . . . I just kept right on going.

In keeping with the nature of free-response comparisons, these three categories were not drawn from the interview questions in which we explicitly asked about comparisons. The interrater agreements for *others cope the same* and *others cope better* were both .50, and for *others cope worse* it was .86.

Related attributes. Related attributes were comparisons that involved the respondent's acknowledgment that adjustment may depend on such factors as marital status, age, physical status, and so on. The comment had to be descriptive of another person's psychological adjustment or emotional reactions, and had to strongly imply that a certain factor (such as age, marital status) influenced the other's adjustment. One woman, for example, said:

> I think maybe I'm coping a little better, but these other women were divorced. That makes a big difference in how you cope. I have a lot of stability and a lot of love, and that helps me cope.

The interrater agreement was .83.

Comparisons Relevant to the Upward and Downward Comparison Perspectives

The upward and downward comparison predictions may be tested by means of using some of the measures already described, such as the ratio of good copers to poor copers and the ratio of *others cope better* to *others cope worse*. Additional measures were coded also.

Manufacturing normative standards of adjustment. In one comparative strategy, the victim contrasts her own adjustment with a standard that seems to be based less on personal contact with fellow victims than on beliefs about hypothetical others (Taylor et al., 1983). She "manufactures a normative standard of adjustment," compared with which her adjustment is very good. An example is as follows:

> I have heard, secondhand, that some of them, many years down the road, are still not over

it. . . . There are women who don't ever reach this point [that I have].

To help ensure that the normative standards were not based on direct experience, we did not include statements that mentioned specific, known others. The interrater agreement was .80.

The measures discussed thus far involve comparisons made in the domain of psychological adjustment because the supercoper and similarity perspectives both involve self-evaluation of adjustment. However, the upward and downward comparison perspectives also involve self-enhancement, and self-enhancing comparisons may be made in many domains other than adjustment (e.g., physical and marital status). Hence other types of free responses were coded as well.

Physical comparisons. Descriptions of specific other cancer patients' physical condition were grouped into three categories, as described in Table 10.2. *Upward physical* and *downward physical* comparisons involved patients who were physically better off and physically worse off than the interviewee, respectively. Although generally downward comparisons are viewed as enabling one to feel better about one's situation, some comparisons in the downward direction were clearly threatening. Take the following example:

His wife had breast cancer, eventually cancer of the bone marrow, and I saw the wheelchairs. . . . I knew she was in the hospital and lost her hair. And I had my breast surgery by this time, and I'm suddenly thinking, oh my God, is this going to be me, this kind of future?

Such *threatening physical comparisons* were coded separately from other downward comparisons. Interrater agreements for upward, downward, and threatening physical comparisons were .73, .80, and .86, respectively.

Situational comparisons. Some free-response comparisons involved other cancer patients whose life situations, according to the respondent, were clearly worse or better than her own. Situational comparisons did not include physical state or psychological adjustment, which were coded elsewhere. Rather, they involved some other aspect of the target person's life, such as her family. An example of an *upward situational* comparison is as follows:

I was the only one that was working, everyone else had husbands to support them and take care of them. . . . I had to get out and get going when the rest of them could lay around.

A *downward situational* example is as follows:

TABLE 10.2. Free-Response Measures: Physical Comparisons

Category	Definition	Example	No. of comparisons made	Frequency	%[a]
Upward physical comparisons	Description of patient who is physically better off	She had a tumor the size of the end of her finger, which I would have been glad to trade her even.	0	70	95.9
			1	2	2.7
			2	1	1.4
Downward physical comparisons	Description of patient who is physically worse off	At first [the scar] was gross . . . Now I don't think it's so bad, especially after you've seen my friend; she just had two radiation implants put in.	0	34	46.6
			1	18	24.7
			2	10	13.7
			3	8	10.9
			4	2	2.7
			5	1	1.4
Threatening physical comparisons	Description of feeling scared or threatened by physically disadvantaged others	I went to a Cancer Society meeting one evening . . . and I realized how many women had *both* breasts removed. Until that time, it had never occurred to me. And I've never gone back to another meeting, because I had nightmares that night.	0	54	74.0
			1	14	19.2
			2	4	5.5
			3	1	1.4

[a] Percentages were computed from 73 interviews; 5 others were not transcribed because of equipment failure.

> I have heard stories where men walked out on their wives, couldn't accept it. My friend, her husband couldn't discuss it. He didn't want to hear anything about it.

The interrater agreement for upward situational responses was 1.00, and for downward situational responses it was .75.

Dimensional comparisons. Most of the categories identified so far involve selecting a comparison target who is relatively disadvantaged or advantaged. Taylor (1983) and Taylor et al. (1983), however, have identified a comparison strategy in which a comparison target is not selected. Rather, the comparer selects a comparison dimension and evaluates her own standing on the dimension, in relation to an alternative. For example, one breast cancer patient said:

> There are days when I look in the mirror and I am upset with the scar under my arm and I think to myself, "You are upset with that; how would you feel with a mastectomy scar?"

Note that the object of comparison is not a disadvantaged person, but a dimension of comparison (in this case, size of scar) on which the comparer is relatively better off. *Downward dimensional* and *upward dimensional* comparisons involved dimensions on which the respondent was advantaged or disadvantaged, respectively. An example of an upward dimensional comparison is as follows:

> They accept the woman like this, like I am now, when they're already married for years, or they already love her. . . . But I was single. . . . I don't have a man, and this is what really hurt me.

In order to be coded as a dimensional comparison, a statement had to be an explicitly made contrast between the patient's situation and that of others, and it could not involve specific individuals, so that the focus was on the dimension of comparison rather than on comparison targets. Interrater agreements were .89 for downward and 1.00 for upward dimensional comparisons.

Results

Representativeness of Sample

To examine the possibility of sample selectivity, we compared the 87 patients who volunteered to participate with the 92 who had not. Results of *t* tests revealed no significant differences between the two groups on demographic, disease, or treatment characteristics (see Taylor et al., 1984, for details) and on physicians' GAIS ratings. Thus it appears that the women who chose to participate did not differ in terms of physical status and psychological adjustment from those who did not. In addition, the respondents' GAIS scores ($M = 82$) fell within the range identified by other studies of cancer patients (Derogatis, Abeloff, & Melisaratos, 1979; J. L. Michela, personal communication, March, 1984).

Next we turn to the four theoretical perspectives. The results of the free-response coding are presented in two ways. First, we present the frequencies of each category, and the percentage of the sample of 73 who made each comparison. Second, chi-square analyses are reported when it is appropriate to compare the frequencies of categories (e.g., upward situational with downward situational). Rather than to compare the numbers of each comparison totaled across the sample, however, the chi-squares were used to compare the number of respondents who made each comparison. The rationale for this decision is that the total numbers would have included multiple comparisons made by single respondents. Hence the number of respondents making each comparison seems to be a more meaningful and conservative index of the use of comparisons.

The Supercoper Perspective

According to the supercoper perspective, comparison others are not widely available to patients, and consequently patients are forced to compare themselves with media figures. Because the media disproportionately feature supercopers, these comparisons may lead a woman to feel inadequate.

The results indicate that the first assumption of the supercoper perspective, that comparison others are not widely available to patients, is inaccurate. As one can see in Table 10.3, the overall degree of contact with both media and social sources was high. Most women had read at least one book on cancer, and over 90% said they had read newspaper or magazine articles. Eighty-five percent of the respondents said that they had discussed their cancer with other women, and over 66% said that they had spoken with "a few" or "quite a few" other breast cancer patients. Moreover, 49 women (67%) spontaneously described another patient's adjustment or emotional reactions (either good copers or poor copers, as described in Table 10.1). Taken together, these findings suggest that information about others' adjustment to cancer is more widely available than is assumed in the supercoper perspective, and that victims are not dependent on the media for comparison targets.

Despite this fact, our results supported the second prediction of the supercoper perspective, that the more contact a woman has with the media, the worse she thinks she is coping compared with other women: The media composite was negatively correlated with the coping-in-comparison rating ($r = -0.26$, $p < .03$).

The Similarity Perspective

According to the similarity perspective, individuals compare themselves with those who are similar on specific dimensions of evaluation or on related attributes. However, results suggest that comparisons with similar others are relatively infrequent.

Dimension-specific similarity. Only 12 (16.4%) of the women stated that another person (or persons) was adjusting in a similar manner (*others cope the same*). Although fewer (6, or 8.2%) said others were adjusting better (*others cope better*), the majority of the women (44, or 60.3%) indicated that others were coping more poorly (*others cope worse*). Of the 38 respondents who made any or all of these three comparisons, 3 women most often made "others cope better" comparisons (i.e., they made more comparisons with *others cope better* than with *others cope the same* and with *others cope worse*); 3 most often made *others cope the same* comparisons; and 32 most often made *others cope worse* comparisons. The chi-square analysis in which we compared these frequencies was highly significant, χ^2 (2, $N = 38$) = 44.26, $p < .001$.

On the coping-in-comparison rating, women were specifically asked to make a judgment in terms of dimension-specific similarity. Nearly half (28, or 46.6%) of the 60 who responded rated their adjustment as "much better than other women with breast cancer"; another third (20, or 33.3%) rated it as "somewhat better"; 8 (13.3%) said they were coping "about the same"; 2 (3.3%) said, "better

Table 10.3. Breast Cancer Patients' Media and Social Contacts

Contact source	Frequency	%
Media sources[a]		
Books		
None	27	36.5
One	17	23.0
Some	23	31.1
A lot	7	9.5
TV shows		
None	15	20.5
One	25	34.2
Some	27	37.0
A lot	6	8.2
Newspaper and magazine articles		
None	7	9.5
A few	30	40.5
Quite a few	27	36.5
Everything I can read	10	13.5
Other media[b]		
No	48	67.6
Yes	23	32.4
Social sources		
Other women		
None	11	14.7
Yes, 1 or 2	6	8.0
Yes, a few	54	72.0
Quite a few	4	5.3
Other breast cancer patients		
None	14	18.7
Yes, 1 or 2	11	14.7
Yes, a few	48	64.0
Quite a few	2	2.7
Support groups		
No	52	70.3
Went once	20	27.0
Continued to attend	2	2.7
Reach-to-Recovery volunteer		
No	38	53.5
Yes	33	46.5

[a] The media items specifically inquired about cancer-related material.
[b] "Other media" referred to pamphlets, radio programs, and so on.

than some, worse than others"; no one said, "somewhat worse"; and 2 (3.3%) said they were coping "much worse than other women with breast cancer." A goodness-of-fit test in which we compared this scale's distribution with a normal distribution indicated that they were significantly different, χ^2 (5, $N = 60$) = 568.40, $p < .001$. These results suggest that these patients do not typically compare with others who are close to themselves on the adjustment continuum.

Related attributes similarity. Over 60% of the 73 respondents mentioned "related attributes" in comparisons of psychological adjustment. Thirty-five women (47.9%) made one such comparison, and 9 (12.3%) made two. Several categories of related attributes were particularly common. A number of women (13, or 17.8%) mentioned the importance of marital status or support of loved ones. Other frequent related attributes were age (mentioned by 11 women, or 15.1%), type of surgery (9, or 12.3%), and prognosis (9, or 12.3%).

Overall, respondents frequently made comparisons in terms of proximity along the dimension of psychological adjustment (dimension-specific similarity) and in terms of attributes related to adjustment (related attributes similarity). However, close similarity does not seem to be critical to either type of comparison. Women rarely compared themselves with others who were similar on the dimension of adjustment, and they usually described related attributes on which they were very different from comparison others, as the example provided in the Method section illustrates.

Upward Versus Downward Comparison Perspectives

Two results already reported strongly suggest that the women were making many downward comparisons: Over 60% of respondents said that another patient was coping less well than she was (*others cope worse*), and when rating their adjustment relative to other women with breast cancer (coping-in-comparison rating), 80% said that they adjusted at least "somewhat better." We also examined additional free-response comparisons to test the upward and downward perspectives. With a few exceptions that we will note, in all chi-square analyses in which we compared upward comparisons to downward comparisons, we compared three frequencies: (a) the number of respondents who made more upward than downward comparisons; (b) the number who made an equal number of upward and downward comparisons; and (c) the number who made more downward than upward comparisons. The chi-squares are goodness-of-fit tests in which we compared the observed distribution with a distribution with equal frequencies in the three categories.

We first examined respondents' descriptions of others' coping. As shown in Table 10.1, about 31% of the sample gave an example of a good coper, whereas about 57% gave an example of a poor coper. The frequencies of respondents who described more good copers than poor copers ($n = 11$), who described an equal number of both ($n = 7$), and who described more poor than good copers ($n = 31$) were significantly different, $\chi^2(2, N = 49) = 20.2, p < .001$. Similarly, for manufacturing normative standards of adjustment, 20 women (27.4%) made a comparison with a downward normative standard; that is, they described a hypothetical standard in comparison with which their adjustment was exceptionally good. Only one woman (1.4%), in contrast, described most other women as adjusting better than she had. The difference between these two frequencies is highly significant, $\chi^2(1, N = 21) = 17.2, p < .001$. Clearly, then, several results suggest that patients were making many downward comparisons in the domain of psychological adjustment.

Physical comparisons. We compared the number of upward physical and downward physical comparisons and found a similar result. As shown in Table 10.2, only 4.1% of the sample mentioned another person who was physically better off than they were, whereas over half of the women described another person who was comparatively worse off. Of the 40 women who made either of these comparisons, 1 made an equal number of both, and 38 made more downward than upward comparisons, $\chi^2(2, N = 40) = 68.45, p < .001$.

However, some comparisons with physically worse off others may be threatening. A sizable number of women (26%) described threatening physical comparisons—that is, feeling threatened by comparing with physically disadvantaged others. Although these comparisons were voiced only about half as frequently as other downward physical comparisons, they illustrate that downward comparisons are not always self-enhancing.

Situational comparisons. Situational comparisons involve specific other cancer patients whose life circumstances (e.g., marital satisfaction and age) were better or worse than the respondent's. Fourteen women (19.2%) made at least one downward situational comparison (1 woman made two), whereas only 2 (2.7%) made an upward situational comparison. These two figures (no women made both comparisons) were significantly different, $\chi^2(1, N = 16) = 9.0, p = .003$.

Dimensional comparisons. In dimensional comparisons, the respondent emphasizes a dimension rather than a specific comparison person. Downward dimensional comparisons were found in 47 (64.4%) of the transcripts. Thirty-seven women (50.7% of the sample) made one such comparison, 8 (11.0%) made two, and 2 women (2.7%) made three. Upward dimensional comparisons were made much less frequently: only 7 women (9.6%) made these. Of the 48 women who made dimensional comparisons, 1 made more upward than downward, 3 made an equal number, and 44 made more downward than upward, $\chi^2(2, N = 48) = 73.62, p < .001$.

The most frequently occurring downward dimensional comparison (over 20% of them) involved type of surgery, such as the following example:

> I had just a comparatively small amount of surgery on the breast, and I was so miserable, because it was so painful. How awful it must be for women who have had a mastectomy. . . . I just can't imagine it, it would seem to be so difficult.

Nineteen percent of the downward dimensional comparisons involved older women comparing themselves favorably with younger women. Also frequent were statements made by mastectomy patients comparing their breast loss with greater disfigurements (15% of the downward dimensional comparisons), and comparisons involving chemotherapy (15%), marital status (10%), and other illnesses (8.5%).

In summary, these data from the domains of psychological adjustment, physical status, and life situations offer strong support for the downward comparison perspective: Downward comparisons were made much more frequently than were upward comparisons.

Totals of upward and downward comparisons. But what if this discrepancy between downward and upward comparisons is largely due to a small group of patients who make downward comparisons in every category? We created two summary comparison indices—upward and downward—by collapsing across free-response categories. The upward comparison index was the sum of the respondent's good coper, manufacturing normative standards of adjustment, upward physical, upward situational, and upward dimensional com-

parisons; the downward comparison index was the sum of the downward counterparts of each of these measures. (*Others cope better* and *others cope worse* were not included, so as not to overrepresent the adjustment domain.) Results of a chi-square analysis in which we used these indices support the conclusion that downward comparisons are prevalent across the entire sample. In this test we compared four groups: the numbers of respondents who (a) gave no free-response comparisons at all ($n = 4$), (b) made more upward than downward comparisons ($n = 1$), (c) made an equal number of both ($n = 5$), and (d) made more downward than upward comparisons ($n = 63$). The chi-square was highly significant, $\chi^2(3, N = 73) = 146.78, p < .001$. These data, then, offer resounding support for the downward comparison perspective.

Predictors of Downward Comparison

What factors contribute to making downward comparisons? One factor may be threat (Taylor et al., 1983; Wills, 1981). Several variables that may be indicators of stress or threat were correlated with the index of downward comparison described earlier.

Cancer- and treatment-related sources of threat. Type of surgery should be an indicator of threat; those women who have had more radical surgeries have presumably undergone more threat to their body image. Type of surgery was broken down into three groups (lumpectomy, simple and modified mastectomy, and Halsted radical), but it was not significantly related to the downward comparison index ($r = -.13$). Although poor prognoses are clearly threatening, prognosis (as measured by the physical state rating) was also unassociated with downward comparisons ($r = -.01$).

Social-situational sources of threat. Social support may help the patient feel less threatened, and hence should be negatively correlated with downward comparison. However, scores on the Locke-Wallace Marital Adjustment Scale (Locke & Wallace, 1959) and the patient's ratings of satisfaction, communication, and perceived support in her relationship with her significant other (each rated on 4-point scales) were uncorrelated with the downward comparison index (all $rs < .18$). Scores on one index, support from family suggested that the less the woman feels supported by her family, the more she makes downward comparisons ($r = -.37$, $p = .001$). However, the overall results for the cancer-related and social support sources of threat do not support the view that threat leads to downward comparison.

When do patients make downward comparisons? Downward comparisons may be seen as preliminary attempts at coping (Taylor et al., 1983) and may therefore be most important early in the adjustment process. As predicted, time since surgery was significantly negatively correlated with the downward comparison variable ($r = -.20$, $p < .05$), such that women closer in time to surgery are more likely than others to compare downward.

Discussion

Our major purpose was to test the predictions of four theoretical models concerning the social comparisons of victims, and to do so by using both closed-ended measures of social comparison and spontaneous responses. Both types of measures yielded results fruitful to the hypothesis testing.

The Supercoper Perspective

The supercoper perspective was largely disconfirmed. The results suggest that direct, personal contact with other breast cancer patients occurs more frequently than Taylor and Levin (1976) proposed. However, Taylor and Levin developed their ideas in 1974, when discussion of cancer was less open than it is today. The results may be an encouraging signal that now there is less stigma associated with cancer and that women now have more opportunities for contact with other patients. Hence today's cancer patient may also be less susceptible to media portrayals of supercopers. In fact, very few women even mentioned media figures during their interviews, and none of them appeared to feel comparatively inadequate. It is possible that well-known supercopers may be regarded as irrelevant to one's self-evaluation, which is consistent with the idea that potential comparison others may be ignored when they are dissimilar (Goethals & Darley, 1977). Brickman and Bulman (1977) noted that when a superior other is perceived as dissimilar, it

can "take some of the sting out of defeat or inferiority" (p. 162).

Although famous media supercopers may be ignored, contact with media sources was nonetheless associated with lower self-evaluations of adjustment. This finding has at least two plausible meanings. One is that women who are coping poorly seek information from the media and hence have more media contact. The second is that media contact results in lower self-evaluations. If the latter is true, perhaps the media affect self-evaluations not through their portrayals of prominent figures, but through their frequent depictions of "everyday" supercopers. Magazine stories about breast cancer often focus on "ordinary" women who are presented as strong and well-adjusted. Although many are described as having some anxiety, by the end of the article they have usually bounced back, even better adjusted than before their illness. These supercoping "ordinary" women may be less easily ignored than famous media figures because they are more similar to the patient. Because the media seem to have a general tendency to present victims who are adjusting easily, these results may well have implications for threatening events other than cancer (cf. Wortman & Dunkel-Schetter, 1979).

The Similarity and Upward Comparison Perspectives

Festinger (1954) initially proposed that individuals evaluate themselves against similar others. Our results contradict this hypothesis in some respects and support it in others. When comparing their psychological adjustment, respondents rarely compared themselves with others who were similarly adjusted or who were similar in related attributes. And they virtually never compared themselves with others who were similar in their physical status or life situations. At the same time, however, respondents' comparisons were almost always to fellow cancer patients. Although certain categories (e.g., good coper, *others cope worse*) permitted comparisons with victims of other physical illnesses, by far most comparisons were made to cancer patients specifically. About 19% of the respondents did make downward dimensional comparisons with people who did not have cancer, but even these are similar comparisons by virtue of their being with fellow victims of physical illness or disability. (Only two comparisons were not with fellow victims.) It seems likely that some reasonable range of similarity is required for a comparison to be relevant, but that within that context very similar others may or may not be favored, depending on one's comparison goals. In this study, although most comparisons were with cancer patients, very few were with very similar or with relatively advantaged cancer patients. In this sense, these results are consistent with those of studies that demonstrate a decline in similar or upward comparisons when there is a threat to self-esteem.

The Downward Comparison Perspective

Overwhelmingly, the comparison of choice of these breast cancer patients was a downward comparison. These findings would not be particularly interesting if the sample were unusually well adjusted, for there would be little chance of comparing upward. However, data reported earlier suggest that our sample's psychological and physical adjustment is typical of breast cancer patients, and therefore there should be available as many potential upward or similar comparisons as downward comparisons. That downward comparisons were so prevalent suggests that respondents were very selective in making comparisons. Downward comparisons may help the victim minimize her sense of victimization (Taylor et al., 1983; Wills, 1981).

Predictors of Downward Comparison

Wills (1981) and Taylor et al. (1983) proposed that threat leads to downward comparisons. However, several analyses were unsupportive of this position. A possible explanation is that the experience of breast cancer itself raises threat to a "ceiling." With a restriction on the variance of threat, it would be impossible to detect a covariation with the downward comparison index. A related explanation implies a ceiling on downward comparison: Downward comparisons may rise rapidly as threat increases, and may soon reach asymptote. Supporting this explanation are the very restricted ranges for each of the individual downward comparison variables, which were essentially dichotomous.

These predictions concerning the role of threat are somewhat paradoxical: As one's situation worsens, there may be less opportunity for downward comparison because the number of others who are more disadvantaged dwindles. This reasoning may explain why the threat hypothesis was not confirmed. However, contrary to this reasoning, the way in which respondents could conceive of a relatively disadvantaged other was at times quite impressive. For example, one woman who had metastatic disease considered herself lucky because she had found peace and meaning in her life, two things that many other people never achieve.

Lastly, it is possible that threat does not, in fact, prompt downward comparison. However, results of laboratory research persuasively demonstrate that upward comparisons are the norm, except when subjects are threatened (e.g., Hakmiller, 1966). Given this evidence and the plausible explanations listed earlier, it would be premature to conclude that threat is not important. Despite the lack of support for the threat hypothesis, our results strongly support the downward comparison perspective. Downward comparisons were much more frequent than other comparisons for each of the content domains examined, for each specific variable in the domains, and for the overwhelming majority of patients. These data from breast cancer patients bolster suggestive evidence of downward comparisons from rape victims (Burgess & Holmstrom, 1979) and disabled people (Schulz & Decker, 1985).

One predictor of downward comparison was identified: Downward comparisons seemed to be most important early in the adjustment process. Their function may be to prevent the victim from being overwhelmed by her new, frightening circumstances (cf. Taylor et al., 1983).

Implications for Social Comparison Theory and Research

The results of this study have several implications for research and theory in social comparison. First, this field study suggests that laboratory studies should be supplemented by more naturalistic investigations in order to capture fully the varied processes and purposes of comparison. Our content analysis of freely offered comparisons is a method that is new in the area. One may argue that such measures are only indirect indicators of social comparisons. However, one also may argue that free-response measures are more direct than the measures typically used: information seeking and the desire to affiliate. The construct validity of both of these measures has been seriously questioned because both information and affiliation may be sought for reasons other than social comparison (see, e.g., Dakin & Arrowood, 1981). In contrast, when our respondents made a comparative statement, there is no doubt that social comparison was involved.

Our content-analytic method also allows the texture of social comparison to emerge freely, unconstrained by structured, closed-ended measures. The emergent texture expands our knowledge about the types of comparisons people make, and identifies two types of comparisons not previously detailed in the literature. First, many women compared their adjustment with a normative standard of adjustment; they maintained that their own adjustment was very good compared with that of fellow sufferers. These comparisons seem to be made not to specific targets, but to a fabricated standard. Second, over 64% of the respondents spontaneously made downward dimensional comparisons, which allow one to choose any dimension one desires when drawing a comparison. Unlike the typical downward comparison, these two types of comparison do not depend on having a disadvantaged comparison target available, which suggests that the literature's emphasis on comparison targets may be misplaced. In fact, more women made downward dimensional comparisons than any type of comparison involving targets. Target-free comparisons allow the individual more flexibility in comparison making than researchers typically assume.

One may argue that dimensional comparisons are not necessarily self-selected. The victim's loved ones may point out to her the dimensions on which she is advantaged in order to lift her spirits. However, it is very unlikely that she is not already aware of the possible upward comparisons (e.g., mastectomees know about less disfiguring surgeries). Yet women in our study very rarely focused on these corresponding upward comparisons, which suggests that they were being selective. Nonetheless, it seems likely that social processes can contribute to the availability of downward comparisons.

Our findings also emphasize an active, cognitive nature to social comparison that may even involve construction. Although the literature has emphasized selection of comparison others, one's capacity to be selective is generally regarded to be constrained by the availability of comparison targets. In contrast, our findings suggest that availability of comparison others need not dictate choice of comparison. First, as described earlier, the respondents had many upward and similar comparisons available, yet they overwhelmingly made downward comparisons. Second, the respondents did not confine their comparisons to specific targets; at times they seemed to invent comparison targets, and they were able to arrive at comparison dimensions on which they appeared advantaged, even when other dimensions on which they were unfortunate loomed quite large. These results suggest that people may, at least under certain circumstances, manipulate the target or dimension to achieve the outcome they want. At times, then, social comparison may not be particularly "social" at all, in that one's comparisons may not necessarily involve actual comparisons with another real human being. Rather, individuals may construct their comparison world. These results portray social comparison as being more heavily cognitive than results of previous research have suggested.

Lastly, the respondents' spontaneous and frequent comparisons suggest that social comparison is a coping strategy of no small importance. Our results contrast with much of coping research, which tends to focus on victims' hardships, and suggest that more attention should be paid to victims' active attempts to rise above adverse circumstances.

ACKNOWLEDGMENTS

This article is based on the first author's doctoral dissertation, which was submitted to the University of California, Los Angeles (UCLA). She is grateful to Barry Collins, Chris Dunkel-Schetter, Oscar Grusky, Connie Hammen, David Wellisch, and especially John Michela for their advice and encouragement. We all thank Barbara Futterman and Patricia Loftus for their aid in data collection, Carol Wixom and Marlene Lukaszewski for their assistance in coding data, and Avrum Bluming, Robert Leibowitz, and Gary Dosik for permitting us to interview their patients. We are also grateful for the helpful contributions of two anonymous reviewers.

The research was supported by research funds from UCLA to all three authors, research funds from the National Institute of Mental Health (NIMH) to the second author (MH 34167), and by a Research Scientist Development Award (MH 00311) to the second author. The first author was also supported by an NIMH training grant and by a National Institutes of Health Biomedical Research Support Grant (SO7 RR0706720) at Stony Brook.

REFERENCES

Brickman, P., & Bulman, R. J. (1977). Pleasure and pain in social comparison. In J. M. Suls & R. L. Miller (Eds.), *Social comparison processes: Theoretical and empirical perspectives* (pp. 149–186). Washington, DC: Hemisphere.

Burgess, A. W., & Holmstrom, L. (1979). *Rape: Crisis and recovery*. Bowie, MD: Brady.

Cohen, F., & Lazarus, R. S. (1979). Coping with the stresses of illness. In G. C. Stone, F. Cohen, & N. E. Adler (Eds.), *Health psychology—A handbook* (pp. 217–254). San Francisco: Jossey-Bass.

Cottrell, N. B., & Epley, S. W. (1977). Affiliation, social comparison, and socially mediated stress reduction. In J. M. Suls & R. L. Miller (Eds.), *Social comparison processes: Theoretical and empirical perspectives* (pp. 43–68). Washington, DC: Hemisphere.

Dakin, S., & Arrowood, A. J. (1981). The social comparison of ability. *Human Relations, 34*, 89–109.

Derogatis, L. R. (1975). *The Global Adjustment to Illness Scale (GAIS)*. Baltimore: Clinical Psychometric Research.

Derogatis, L. R., Abeloff, M. D., & Melisaratos, N. (1979). Psychological coping mechanisms and survival time in metastatic breast cancer. *Journal of the American Medical Association, 242*, 1504–1508.

Dunkel-Schetter, C., & Wortman, C. B. (1982). The interpersonal dynamics of cancer: Problems in social relationships and their impact on the patient. In H. S. Friedman & M. R. Dimatteo (Eds.), *Interpersonal issues in health care* (pp. 69–100). New York: Academic Press.

Festinger, L. (1954). A theory of social comparison processes. *Human Relations, 7*, 117–140.

Frey, K. S., & Ruble, D. N. (1985). What children say when the teacher is not around: Conflicting goals in social comparison and performance assessment in the classroom. *Journal of Personality and Social Psychology, 48*, 550–562.

Goethals, G. R., & Darley, J. M. (1977). Social comparison theory: An attributional approach. In J. M. Suls & R. L. Miller (Eds.), *Social comparison processes: Theoretical and empirical perspectives* (pp. 259–278). Washington, DC: Hemisphere.

Gruder, C. L. (1977). Choice of comparison persons in evaluating oneself. In J. M. Suls & R. L. Miller (Eds.), *Social comparison processes: Theoretical and empirical perspectives* (pp. 21–42). Washington, DC: Hemisphere.

Hakmiller, K. L. (1966). Threat as a determinant of downward comparison. *Journal of Experimental Social Psychology, Supplement, 1*, 32–39.

Locke, H. J., & Wallace, K. M. (1959). Short marital adjustment and prediction tests: Their reliability and validity. *Marriage and Family Living, 21*, 251–255.

Mechanic, D. (1977). Illness behavior, social adaptation and the management of illness. *Journal of Nervous and Mental Disease, 165*, 79–87.

Pearlin, L. I., & Schooler, C. (1978). The structure of coping. *Journal of Health and Social Behavior, 19*, 2–21.

Schachter, S. (1959). *The psychology of affiliation*. Stanford, CA: Stanford University Press.

Schulz, R., & Decker, S. (1985). Long-term adjustment to physical disability: The role of social support, perceived control, and self-blame. *Journal of Personality and Social Psychology, 48*, 1162–1172.

Silver, R. L., & Wortman, C. B. (1980). Coping with undesirable life events. In J. Garber & M. E. P. Seligman (Eds.), *Human helplessness: Theory and application* (pp. 279–375). New York: Academic Press.

Singer, J. E. (1966). Social comparison—progress and issues. *Journal of Experimental Social Psychology, Supplement, 1*, 103–110.

Taylor, S. E. (1983). Adjustment to threatening events: A theory of cognitive adaptation. *American Psychologist, 38*, 1161–1173.

Taylor, S. E., & Levin, S. (1976). *The psychological impact of breast cancer: A review of theory and research*. San Francisco: West Coast Cancer Foundation.

Taylor, S. E., Lichtman, R. R., & Wood, J. V. (1984). Attributions, beliefs in control, and adjustment to breast cancer. *Journal of Personality and Social Psychology, 46*, 489–502.

Taylor, S. E., Wood, J. V., & Lichtman, R. R. (1983). It could be worse: Selective evaluation as a response to victimization. *Journal of Social Issues, 39*, 19–40.

Wheeler, L., & Zuckerman, M. (1977). Commentary. In J. M. Suls & R. L. Miller (Eds.), *Social comparison processes: Theoretical and empirical perspectives* (pp. 335–357). Washington, DC: Hemisphere.

Wills, T. A. (1981). Downward comparison principles in social psychology. *Psychological Bulletin, 90*, 245–271.

Wilson, S. R., & Benner, L. A. (1971). The effects of self-esteem and situation upon comparison choices during ability evaluation. *Sociometry, 34*, 381–397.

Wortman, C. B., & Dunkel-Schetter, C. (1979). Interpersonal relationships and cancer: A theoretical analysis. *Journal of Social Issues, 35*, 120–155.

Zanna, M. P., Goethals, G. R., & Hill, J. F. (1975). Evaluating a sex-related ability: Social comparison with similar others and standard setters. *Journal of Experimental Social Psychology, 11*, 86–93.

Predicting Young Adults' Health Risk Behavior

Frederick X. Gibbons and Meg Gerrard
Iowa State University

A prototype model of risk behavior is described and was tested in a longitudinal study of 679 college students, beginning at the start of their freshman year. Perceptions of the prototype associated with four health risk behaviors (smoking, drinking, reckless driving, and ineffective contraception) were assessed along with self-reports of the same behaviors. Results indicated that prototype perception was related to risk behavior in both a reactive and a prospective manner. That is, perceptions changed as a function of change in behavior, and perceptions predicted those behavior changes as well. This prospective relation was moderated by social comparison, as the link between perception and behavior change was stronger among persons who reported frequently engaging in social comparison.

Efforts to educate young adults with regard to the health consequences of their behavior have increased dramatically in the last decade. When measured in terms of increase in knowledge, these education programs appear to have been reasonably effective (Fisher & Misovich, 1990). This enhanced awareness among high school and college-age people has not been accompanied by an equally impressive decline in health risk behavior, however (Janus & Janus, 1993; Roscoe & Kruger, 1990; Rotheram-Borus & Koopman, 1991; U.S. Public Health Service, 1993). In fact, the lack of a (logical) relation between risk awareness and risk behavior has puzzled many researchers who have been trying to figure out why it is that young people often choose to engage in various activities that they know put them and their health at risk.

Much of the social psychological work in this area has been based on the general assumption that the best predictor of an adolescent's or an adult's behavior is simply intention to engage in that behavior (Ajzen & Fishbein, 1980; Fishbein & Ajzen, 1975). With this basic assumption in mind, most researchers have focused their efforts on identifying factors related to intentions to engage in health-promoting behaviors, such as physical exercise, or the use of condoms or seat belts (cf. Sheppard, Hartwick, & Warshaw, 1988). With one notable exception, researchers have been less interested in predicting health risk behaviors. The exception is substance use, especially adolescent smoking, which has received considerable empirical attention.

Images

A particularly successful approach to the study of smoking onset among adolescents has focused on the images they have of the behavior itself and of the type of person who does it. For example, in an extensive series of studies, Chassin and her colleagues have examined the relation between adolescents' images of smokers, their self-concepts, and their smoking behavior. The first study in this series (Chassin, Presson, Sherman, Corty, & Olshavsky, 1981) found that the self-concepts of adolescents who were currently smoking matched fairly closely the stereotypic image generally associated with smokers (see also Grube, Weir, Getzlaf, & Rokeach, 1984; McKennel & Bynner, 1969). Among the nonsmokers, those whose self-concepts matched the smoker image were more likely to report they intended to be smoking in a month and in a year (cf. Burton, Sussman, Hansen, Johnson, & Flay, 1989; Chassin, Presson, Sherman, McLOughlin, & Gioia, 1985). The same finding, but in reverse (i.e., a negative smoker image associated with the intention not to smoke) was reported by Barton, Chassin, Presson, and Sherman (1982). Similar results have also been obtained among adolescent boys with alcohol images (Chassin, Tetzloff, & Hershey, 1985).

The reasoning put forth in many of these studies suggests that young persons' decisions to engage in "adult-like" behaviors (cf. Jessor, Donovan, & Costa, 1991), such as smoking and drinking, are a reflection of their attempts to acquire the image that they associate with the behavior (Leventhal & Cleary, 1980) or with groups of individuals who engage in the behavior. In fact, a number of researchers have suggested that adolescents start smoking or using drugs in order to identify with, or perhaps gain membership in, a particular group or crowd (Brown & Lohr, 1987; Eiser, 1985; Mosbach & Leventhal, 1988; Sussman et al., 1990).

Prototypes

Results from the smoker image studies are consistent with those from the literature in social cognition suggesting that when people are considering joining a particular group they will often compare themselves with the prototype that they associate with that group. The closer the match between the self (concept) and the prototype, the greater the interest in joining the group. This has been demonstrated with preferences and intentions regarding college residence (Niedenthal, Cantor, & Kihlstrom, 1985), graduate school (Burke & Reitzes, 1981), and jobs or careers (Moss & Frieze, 1993).

Favorability

Consistent with the concept of image acquisition (Leventhal & Cleary, 1980), the prototypes in most of these matching studies represented what would be considered a goal state, or a positive identity or "possible self" (Markus & Nurius, 1986). An exception is a recent study by Niedenthal and Mordkoff (1991), in which preferences for different types of psychotherapists, along with perceptions of the "typical" patient associated with each therapist, were assessed within a nonclinical sample. In this case, the images of the typical patients were generally negative, and it was actually perceived dissimilarity or distance between the self and the patient prototype that predicted interest in the psychotherapist. Although the pattern of results in this study was complicated (patients distanced from the prototype on emotions but matched on personality characteristics), it does suggest that prototypes may influence intentions even when they are not favorable. That may also be the case with the smoker prototype. Although clearly related to smoking intention, the smoker images maintained by the adolescents in the more recent image studies were not very positive. Even among those who were smoking, the images generally ranged from ambivalent to negative (Barton et al., 1982; Chassin, Presson, et al., 1985; Cooper & Kohn, 1989).

Change

Gibbons, Gerrard, Lando, and McGovern (1991) looked at the prototype–behavior relation from the opposite perspective—what happens to the prototype over time as a function of change in behavior. These authors examined the "typical smoker" image among adults who were trying to quit smoking. Consistent with expectations, results indicated that these smokers did maintain clear and fairly "rich" or elaborate smoker images. In addition, those images did change over time, as expected, becoming less favorable and less similar to the self as the smokers tried to quit. That change was more pronounced among abstainers, but it also occurred among the relapsers. Once again, these images were generally not very favorable; they started off somewhat more favorable than a comparable group of nonsmokers but then ended up being even less favorable.

Distancing and Assimilation

In discussing results of Gibbons et al.'s (1991) study, Gibbons and Gerrard (1991) suggested that this change in prototype perception is an indication of an active effort on the part of smokers to distance themselves psychologically from the category or group that the prototype represents. Moreover, this distancing process is thought to involve social comparison by the smoker with the image he or she maintains (cf. Gibbons, 1985). More specifically, it is a motivated or directed type of comparison in which the comparer looks for evidence of distinction between the self and the image and facilitates this process (or search) by derogating the image. As a result of this "active downward comparison" (Wills, 1981), the image itself becomes both more negative and less similar to the self (for a more complete discussion, see Gibbons & Gerrard, 1995).

We suspect that a similar process, but in reverse, may occur among young people who are considering starting to smoke. Like the clinic smokers, young people have an image of what the typical smoker (their age) is like. Because the behavior is unusual, the image is likely to be quite salient (Skowronski & Carlston, 1989), and it is likely to prompt a social comparison. That should be more true among those who are thinking of smoking, but even those who aren't may engage in some comparison. Once again, that comparison is oriented in a particular direction, in this case, toward finding some evidence of similarity. In direct contrast to the distancing effect, this "assimilation" process should be reflected in a general improvement in prototype perception, over time, in terms of both similarity and favorability, as smoking behavior begins or increases.

Prototypes and Behavioral Prediction

The changes in prototype perception that occur during both distancing and assimilation are an indication of a more basic change in attitude toward the behavior itself. As the individual becomes more serious about either stopping or starting the behavior, his or her perception of the prototype is altered in a favorable or an unfavorable direction. In this sense, the prototype effect is reactive. We also believe that prototypes have a prospective relation with behavior, however, which is an assumption that other researchers have shared but never tested. That is, the nature of the image associated with a particular behavior may be an indication of impending behavior change. For example, the nondrinking teen who has a relatively favorable image of the typical teenage drinker, and who engages in some social comparison with that image, is more likely to start or increase his or her drinking than is another teen who has a less favorable image.

As the smoking image research discussed earlier has indicated, part of this prospective effect is a reflection of behavioral intention. When it comes to risky behavior, however, we believe there is more to the prototype construct than simply a report of (expected) future actions. For young people, in particular, these are very social behaviors; they are also very public behaviors with clear associated images. The prototype, then, is a representative of a visible and easily identifiable group of people—those who smoke or those who drink, for example. The more favorable and similar to the self the individual's image of that representative is, the more willing the person is to be included in that category of people and to convey that image to others—which is what will happen if he or she does perform the behavior (Gibbons & Gerrard, 1995). When asked directly, a young adult may not respond that he is planning to do something that may very well jeopardize his health, and, in fact, he may not actually be intending to do the behavior (Brooks-Gunn & Furstenberg, 1989), though it is likely that he has at least considered it. By the same token, that young person may not have a very favorable image of the prototype. If he does not have a negative image of the group or category, however, then the chances are greater that he would engage in the behavior if given the opportunity.

The Current Research

The current study examined, once again, the relation between risk images and risk behavior. Although based on previous image research, however, the approach taken in this study is somewhat different from that characteristic of most studies in this area. First, we did not view the images or the groups they represent as goal states for the participants in the current sample. One reason for this is simply that these participants were older (i.e., college students, whereas previous studies have dealt with adolescents) and therefore are less likely to be seeking an identity. A second, more important reason has to do with the nature of the images themselves. Although it may not have been true 20 years ago, the images associated with many health risk behaviors today, especially smoking (Goldstein, 1991), are not very favorable. The question, then, is not how appealing is the image to these young adults, but rather how acceptable is it. Thus, we did not expect the images to be very favorable. We also did not expect that a prototype-self match would predict better than prototype favorability and similarity. The match is more appropriate for assessing aspiration, or desire for membership in, a particular group (i.e., a goal state), especially if that membership is likely to include considerable contact (e.g., graduate school or a job). In short, the young adults in our study probably are not trying to become "Marlboro men" or women, but they are concerned—to varying extents—about how others will view them if they are seen with a cigarette in their mouths or a drink in their hands.

Overview

Previous research has demonstrated that the images adolescents associate with different risk behaviors, primarily smoking, are related to their intentions to engage in those behaviors. Although establishing the importance of this factor, this research has raised a number of questions about the relation between behavioral images and behavior, and it has left a number of other questions unanswered. We attempted to answer some of those questions in this study.

The first, and simplest, of the questions is whether risk behavior images are, in fact, responsive to risk behavior. Our assumption is that these images will become more favorable among young adults who have reported an increase in the behavior, just as they have been shown to decrease among smokers who are trying to quit. Thus, we expected to find evidence of both distancing and assimilation in prototype perception.

Although previous research has established a link between image perception and intention, and between self-prototype match and aspiration, none of these studies has been longitudinal. Thus, there is no way to determine if the images they have assessed are actually related to behavior change (cf. Fiske & Taylor, 1991, p. 514), or if they are just alternative indicators of interest or intention (Sussman et al., 1990). It is possible, for example, that adolescents may first decide they are interested in a behavior and then, as a result of that decision, alter their perception of the type of person who engages in that behavior. From an education or intervention perspective, that is a very different process from what we are suggesting, which is that prototype favorability and similarity do predict behavior independent of intention.

Although the images in which we are interested are common and most likely recognized by virtually all young adults, we didn't expect those images to be equally influential for all of our sample. Our assumption is that risk images influence behavior through a process of social comparison (Gibbons & Gerrard, 1991, 1995). If that is the case, then we would expect that those who are most likely to socially compare are also most likely to be influenced by the images. Thus, we predicted that social comparison tendencies would moderate the prototype-behavior link: Those prone to engage in comparison should show more relation than those less inclined to compare.

Almost all of the extant image research has concerned smoking behavior. There is no reason to assume that the process is unique to smoking, however, or even to substance use. Theoretically, the same process should work with any risk behavior, as long as the behavior does have a reasonably clearly defined image associated with it. In the current study, we examined reckless driving, drinking, and ineffective contraception, in addition to smoking. We assumed that the prototypes would predict associated behaviors and that that process would be moderated by social comparison tendencies for all four behaviors. Finally, there is reason to expect that some images may be more influential for men than for women (Brown, Clasen, & Eicher, 1986). Consequently, we included gender as a factor, although it was not a main focus of the study.

Method

PARTICIPANTS

Letters were sent to approximately 1,100 incoming college freshmen 3 weeks before they arrived on campus, inviting them and their parents to participate in a research project that concerned health attitudes and behavior of this group; 679 completed the first questionnaire. By the beginning of the spring semester, 33 had dropped out of school, and 18 could not be scheduled or declined to return for the second session, leaving a total of 628 (97% of those who were still on campus) who completed the Time 1 (T1) and the Time 2 (T2) scales. There were no differences between participants who dropped out and those who did not on any of the T1 behaviors (all $ps > .10$). The final sample was 55% female, with a mean age of 18.0; it comprised 15% of the entire freshman class and was representative of that group on a variety of dimensions (e.g., age, income, high school grade point average [GPA]).

PROCEDURE

Approximately 80% of the sample completed the T1 questionnaire in their homes 1 to 2 weeks before coming on campus. The others completed the questionnaire in our laboratory within 3 weeks of their arrival on campus. There were no differences between these two groups on any of the behavior or prototype measures. On arrival, participants were greeted by a graduate student of the same sex who served as an interviewer. Although all of the items for the current study were completed on paper, the interviewer did precede and follow the scale completion with an explanation of the study and some of the specific questions. The primary role of the interviewer, however, was to be available to answer any questions the students might have during the completion of the scale. The interviewer emphasized confidentiality and privacy. The same procedure was used for the second interview, which occurred in our lab 6–7 months after the first. The two interviews lasted

about 75 min each; in return, participants were paid $20 for each interview.

MEASURES

Background and behavior. First, a number of standard demographic items were completed (e.g., age, sex). The behavioral measures included reckless driving, which was assessed with a 5-item scale created specifically for this project. The items included speeding, disobeying traffic signals and signs, driving under the influence, horsing around (e.g., drag racing), and driving without a seat belt (each followed by a 7-point scale that ranged from *never* to *frequently*). These were combined into a single scale (as: T1 = .68, T2 = .67). Smoking included items on current smoking ("How often do you smoke now?" followed by a 5-point scale that ranged from *not at all* to *regularly*) and lifetime smoking ("How many times have you smoked cigarettes?" followed by a 5-point scale that ranged from *never* to *regularly*). These two were added together to form a single index (as: T1 = .87, T2 = .89). Alcohol included a frequency item ("How many times in the last 6 months have you had a whole drink of alcohol?" followed by a 5-point scale that ranged from *never* to *regularly* [*at least two or three times a week*]) plus a problem-drinking item ("How often in the last 6 months have you had too much to drink or gotten drunk?" followed by a 5-point scale that ranged from *never* to *4 or more times*). These two items also were combined (as: T1 = .88, T2 = .87). Finally, participants were asked two questions about their sexual behavior. If they had had sex, and, if so, what type of birth control they had used the last time they had intercourse. Ineffective contraception was operationalized as the *typical* failure rate (Hatcher et al., 1990) of the method they used during the last time they had intercourse. This measure reduces the social desirability bias associated with self-reports of preventive practices (cf. Loftus, Smith, Klinger, & Fiedler, 1992) and has been shown to provide accurate information on actual contraceptive use (Gerrard & Warner, 1990). At T2, participants were asked the same set of questions, including if they had performed the behaviors, and how often, during the preceding 6 months.

Intention. Intention to engage in the behaviors in the next year was assessed at T1 by asking the following questions, each rated on a 7-point Likert-type scale: "Do you think you will . . . smoke/drive recklessly (if you're going to be driving) in the next year?" (e.g., from *definitely will not* to *definitely will*), and "How often do you think you will drink alcohol?" (from *never* to *often* [*at least 4 or 5 times/week*]). Birth control intention was assessed by asking, "If you were to have sex . . . how likely do you think it is that you (or your partner) would use the following kinds of birth control?" This was followed by a list including oral contraceptive pills, condoms, and then other methods, such as rhythm and withdrawal (from *not at all likely* to *extremely likely*). Very few participants reported intention to use any method other than the pill and condom, and so analyses were performed only on these two methods.

Prototype perception. A general definition of a prototype was provided (see Gibbons, Gerrard, & Boney-McCoy, 1995), and then the four specific prototypes were presented separately in the following manner: "the 'typical' young adult (your age) who . . . smokes cigarettes . . . drinks alcohol . . . drives recklessly . . . gets (gets a woman) pregnant . . ." (same-sex target for the pregnancy prototype only). Participants were asked to describe their image of that typical person in terms of 12 adjectives (*smart, confused, popular, immature, "cool" [sophisticated], self-confident, independent, careless, unattractive, dull [boring], considerate, and self-centered*; each was accompanied by a 7-point scale that ranged from *not at all* to *extremely*). These items were chosen because they were thought to reflect a general risk image (i.e., across all four behaviors) appropriate to young adults (cf. Gibbons, Helweg-Larsen, & Gerrard, 1995). Subsequent analyses of college students' open-ended responses (i.e., "Describe in your own words the typical . . .") have supported this assumption. Each list was followed by a question asking how similar participants thought they were to that typical person (same scale). Finally, to allow for a self-prototype comparison, participants were asked to evaluate themselves on the same 12 adjectives. This self-rating preceded the four prototype ratings.

We created a prototype perception scale by multiplying the mean of the 12 adjectives by the similarity item. We then conducted analyses on this product, rather than the individual components, for several reasons. The primary reason was our contention that the two variables do relate to risk be-havior in an interactive fashion. Put another way, with regard to the decision to engage in risk behavior, a favorable prototype image means something different (is more impactful) for individuals who believe they are quite similar to that image than it does for people who do not think they are similar. Also, previous research has suggested that the product of the favorability and similarity components is the most appropriate representation of prototype perception (Gibbons, Gerrard, & Boney-McCoy, 1995). Finally, given that we were examining four different behaviors, for reasons of parsimony and data reduction, we chose not to report all of the separate results for the two measures even though those results were virtually identical to those reported here using the product term (see below).

Social comparison. We assessed social comparison tendencies at T2 with a scale created for the project. A general description of social comparison was provided, followed by 12 questions (e.g., "How often do you compare your test scores with those of other persons?" "How often do you compare what you are like now with what you used to be like in the past?"), each accompanied by a 130-cm line (e.g., from *never* to *a lot*). Participants placed a slash on the line at the point that best reflected their self-assessment. We then performed a principal-components analysis with varimax rotation on these items. This analysis identified four factors with eigenvalues greater than 1.0, explaining a total of 59% of the variance in the scale. The four factors, in order of magnitude of eigenvalue, were labeled Temporal Comparison, Social Behavior Comparison, Level of Comparison, and Temporal Versus Social Comparison (information on the results of the analysis are presented in the Appendix). The factor that we were most interested in (a priori) was the second one, because it concerned the extent to which participants compared themselves with others in terms of their social behavior (e.g., "How often do you compare yourself with other people in terms of social behavior [i.e., social skills, popularity, etc.]?"). Even though the process in which we were interested involves social comparison with an image, the measure we used assessed comparison with other individuals. We did this because we believe that the two processes are closely related and because we thought that participants would find a series of questions pertaining to social comparison with several different images difficult to interpret. Thus, the sum of the three items was used as the moderating variable in the regression analyses ($\alpha = .65$).

Results

OVERVIEW

Results are presented in three sections. The first section includes prevalence figures on the risk behaviors and change in those behaviors. The second section concerns the reactive hypothesis and presents results on the change in prototype perception as a function of change in risk behavior. The third section presents results from a series of hierarchical regressions testing the prospective hypothesis.

PART 1: BEHAVIOR AND BEHAVIOR CHANGE

The percentage of students who reported having engaged in each behavior at T1 and at T2, and also the change in behavior over time, are presented in Table 11.1. Specifically, participants were assigned to one of the following four categories according to the amount that their risk behavior had changed from T1 to T2: not engaging in risk behavior at either T1 or T2 (i.e., having smoked, driven recklessly, or drunk alcohol no more than once or twice, or having used a birth control method at last intercourse with a typical failure

rating of 12% [condom] or less); no change in risk behavior (i.e., engaging in more than a minimal amount of the behavior at T1 and approximately the same level at T2); and an increase, or a decrease, in behavior. To be classified in the increase or the decrease categories, participants had to report more than just a slight change in behavior (i.e., at least a 2-point change on the 5-point scale) over the 6-month period. For example, if they moved from *never smoked* to *smoked a few times* or from *smoked once or twice* to *smoked more than a few times*, they were classified as increasers. For increase and decrease in ineffective contraception, participants had to report a change from a method less effective than a condom (e.g., withdrawal) to a condom or pill, or from use of pill or condom (or virgin status) to a less effective method.

Change. In absolute terms, there was a significant increase from T1 to T2 in the amount of smoking and drinking that was reported (both $ps < .001$) but not in risky driving or ineffective contraception. Men reported more smoking ($p < .01$) and reckless driving ($p < .001$) overall than did women. The men also increased their smoking more than women, whereas women *decreased* their use of ineffective contraception (became safer) more than did men (both $ps < .05$). There were no other gender effects. The figures these students reported are roughly comparable to national norms for their age group; that is, they are slightly below the norm for smoking and slightly above the norm for alcohol consumption (U.S. Public Health Service, 1991).

TABLE 11.1. Percentage of Participants Reporting Risk Behavior, Prevalence Estimates, and Behavior Change by Gender

	Behavior[a]							
	Reckless driving		Smoking		Drinking		Ineffective contraception[b]	
	M	F	M	F	M	F	M	F
Engaging in behavior at T1	51	28	16	16	57	60	25	33
Engaging in behavior at T2	51	26	23	14	81	81	30	23
Change category								
No risk[c]	37	60	74	80	21	17	39	41
Risk decrease	17	6	3	6	7	9	6	13
Risk increase	10	6	12	7	37	34	12	8
Same risk	36	27	11	7	34	40	7	8

Note. Ns: men, T1 = 303, T2 = 265–276; women, T1 = 376, T2 = 335–348. M = male; F = female.
[a] Percentage who reported doing the behavior more than once or twice during the preceding period.
[b] Percentage of participants who reported using either relatively ineffective or no contraception at last intercourse (see text); does not include participants who were virgins at T1 (45% of men and 36% of women).
[c] No risk = not engaging in risk behavior at T1 (Time 1) and T2 (Time 2); decrease = decline in risk behavior from T1–T2; etc.

PART 2: CHANGE IN PROTOTYPE PERCEPTION

Correlations of the behavioral reports and the prototype indexes (hereafter referred to as the *prototypes*) with each other and with intention are presented in Table 11.2 (alphas for the four sets of prototype adjectives ranged from .73 to .81 at each time period; mean correlation of similarity and favorability across the four prototypes was .41). These correlations indicate that the four prototypes and the four risk behaviors are related to one another (as is typically the case for risk behaviors; Jessor et al., 1991), but they are certainly not redundant (mean *r* among prototypes = .28, among behaviors = .30).

To assess the effect of behavior change on change in prototype perception, we performed 2 × 4 × 2 (gender × change category × time) repeated measures analyses of variance (ANOVAs) on the prototypes. The repeated measures analyses provide the clearest picture of the relative mean values across change category, as well as magnitude of change in those values over time. To account for possible categorical differences in initial responses, however, we also performed analyses of covariance (ANCOVAs) on the T2 data, using the T1 prototypes as covariates. Because there was only one main effect involving gender (see below) and no interactions, the prototype means presented in Table 11.3 are collapsed across gender.

Reckless driving. For reckless driving, as well as the other three risk behaviors, participants who were engaging in the behavior had more favorable images than did those who were not engaging (all $ps < .001$). Consistent with their behavior, men had a more favorable impression of the typical reckless driver than did women at both time periods, overall $F(1, 610) = 21.02$, $p < .001$. In addition, the anticipated Time × Change interaction was significant, $F(3, 610) = 5.50$, $p < .001$. Simple effects analyses across time indicated that prototype perception changed as expected; specifically, it improved among increasers and declined among decreasers, $rs(610) = 2.16$ and 3.17, $ps < .05$ and .002, respectively. Consistent with the ANOVA, the ANCOVA revealed a significant effect of change category ($p < .001$) and a significant difference between the increasers and decreasers, $t(609) = 2.96$, $p < .004$. Finally, participants whose driving behavior stayed at the same level (i.e., no risk or same risk) reported no change in prototype perception.

Smoking. Even though there wasn't a lot of change in smoking behavior over time, the Change Category × Time interaction was significant, $F(3, 601) = 17.07$, $p < .001$, and the pattern of means was as predicted. Participants who reduced their smoking behavior lowered their evaluations of the prototype (cf. Gibbons et al., 1991), whereas the opposite occurred among those students who reported an increase in smoking over the time pe-

TABLE 11.2. Correlations Among All Relevant Measures at Time 1

Variable	1	2	3	4	5[a]
Prototypes, behavior, and social comparison[b]					
1. Driving	.40	.23	.27	.20	.04
2. Smoking	.35	.51	.45	.31	.00
3. Drinking	.48	.53	.59	.25	.14
4. Ineffective contraception	.12	.15	.16	.14	.03
5. Social comparison	.08	−.05	.09	.02	—
Intention with[c]					
Prototype	.29	.49	.55	.22	
Behavior	.41	.73	.76	.13	

Note. For *r*s (676) = .08, .10, and .12, *p*s = .05, .01, and .001, respectively.
[a] Social comparison index (at Time 2) correlated with the four prototypes (column) and four behaviors (row) at Time 1.
[b] Correlations among prototypes, behaviors, and SC index: those above the diagonal are correlations among the four prototypes; those on the diagonal are correlations between prototypes and their associated behaviors; those below the diagonal are correlations among the four behaviors.
[c] Correlations of behavioral intention with associated prototypes and behavior.

TABLE 11.3. Change in Prototype Perception (T1–T2) as a Function of Change in Risk Behavior

Risk behavior	Change category				All participants
	No risk	Increase	Decrease	Same risk	
Reckless driving					
T1	9.78	14.00	16.45	13.90	12.15
T2	9.08	15.94	13.99	14.32	11.77
Difference	−.70	1.94*	−2.46*	.45	−.38
Adjusted T2	10.79$_a$	15.72$_b$	12.66$_c$	14.16$_b$	
N	309	51	68	190	618
Smoking					
T1	7.44	9.78	17.13	15.40	8.75
T2	7.64	14.48	11.09	16.19	9.19
Difference	.20	4.70**	−6.04**	.79	.44
Adjusted T2	9.81$_a$	15.63$_b$	9.06$_a$	14.91$_b$	
N	472	58	26	52	609
Drinking					
T1	9.40	16.62	21.64	18.78	16.43
T2	10.44	20.52	16.34	18.95	17.62
Difference	1.04	3.90**	−5.30**	.17	1.19
Adjusted T2	14.06$_a$	20.51$_b$*	13.81$_a$	17.86$_c$	
N	118	215	51	233	617

Note. Adjusted T2 = Time 2 mean adjusted for Time 1 (T1) mean; adjusted means without common subscripts differ at $p \le .05$. Entries with different subscripts are significantly different from each other.
*$p < .05$. **$p < .01$.

riod, $ts(600) = 5.83$ and 5.03, $ps < .001$. The ANCOVA again revealed a significant effect of category ($p < .001$) as well as a significant difference between the adjusted means of the increasers and the decreasers, $t(600) = 4.79$, $p < .001$. Perceptions of the no-risk and continued-risk groups remained at the same (relatively low and relatively high) levels from T1 to T2.

Drinking. The Category × Time interaction was significant on the drinking prototype, $F(3, 609) = 23.13$, $p < .001$, with the pattern of means again being as expected. The increase and the decrease among the two relevant groups were both significant, $ts(610) = 7.67$ and 5.08, $ps < .001$, respectively. The ANCOVA also was significant ($p < .001$), and the adjusted mean of the increase group was greater than that of the decrease group, $ts(608) = 6.86$, $p < .001$. Again, there was no prototype change in the no-risk and the same-risk categories.

Ineffective contraception. To assess change in sexual prototype as a function of change in contraceptive behavior, we divided participants into five groups on the basis of their most recent birth control use. The five consisted of the same four

categories as above, plus a fifth category consisting of people who were virgins at both T1 and T2. In fact, there was relatively little change in efficacy during the 6-month period (only 19% of participants were in either the increase or the decrease categories). Those who were using ineffective contraception at T1 did have more favorable prototype perceptions than did either those who were virgins or those who were using relatively effective contraception, $ts(659) = 4.54$ and 2.10, $ps < .001$ and $.05$. The pattern for the rest of the participants was not consistent with our hypotheses, however, and the interaction between category and time was not significant ($p > .25$).

Self versus prototype. To determine how prototype perception compared with self-perception, and also to check whether self-perception varied as a function of risk behavior, we repeated the prototype analyses including self-evaluations on the (same) 12 adjectives as an additional within-subjects variable (i.e., change category × self vs. prototype × time). Alpha for the self index was .72. Because self-evaluations did not differ as a function of behavior or behavior change, this new analysis did not differ from the original at all. In other words, it was prototype perception and not self-perception that changed over time. In addition, evaluations of the prototype were significantly more negative than were self-evaluations for participants in all of the change categories, at both time periods, on all four prototypes (all $ts > 4.9$, $ps < .0001$; in fact, this was the case for each one of the 12 adjectives). Thus, although participants who were doing the behavior did have more favorable prototype images than those who were not, risk images for all participants were much more negative than were their self-images.

PART 3: PREDICTING CHANGE IN BEHAVIOR

To determine whether prototype perception did predict change in risk behavior, we performed a series of hierarchical regressions in which T1 behavior was entered first, followed, in order, by gender (coded such that a negative beta indicates behavior increase by the men), behavioral intention, and then (T1) prototype. Because we assumed this process would be moderated by social comparison tendencies, we also entered a Prototype × SC term (centered) into the equation after all main effects had been entered. This was followed by the Prototype × Gender and then the Prototype × SC × Gender interaction terms. These last two terms are reported only when they are significant. Results of the final regression equations (including betas and associated t values) are presented in Table 11.4 and in Figure 11.1.

Reckless driving. The beta weight associated with the prototype variable was marginally significant for reckless driving ($p < .08$). The beta associated with primary interaction of prototype with social comparison was significant, however ($p < .04$). Moreover, the pattern of this interaction, depicted in Figure 11.1, was as anticipated. That is, the predictive power of the prototype was significantly greater for participants who were high (as opposed to low) in SC tendencies. No other interaction terms were significant. Also, social comparison was positively related to increase in behavior, and there was a tendency for men to report more of an increase in this behavior than women ($p < .08$).

Smoking. Both gender and intention were significant predictors of change in smoking behavior over time, as men and those intending to smoke reported the greatest increases ($ps < .005$). In addition, the beta for the prototype variable was not significant, and the beta for the Prototype × SC index interaction was of marginal significance ($p < .08$). The three-way interaction involving gender was significant, however ($p < .003$). As can be seen in Figure 11.1, the pattern of this interaction was such that the prototype was most predictive of change in smoking behavior for male participants with higher SC scores. Thus, the expected pattern held, but only among male participants. In addition, the two-way Prototype × Gender interaction was significant, reflecting the fact that the prototype was predictive of change in behavior for men but not for women. In fact, the slopes of the

TABLE 11.4. Hierarchical Regression Analyses Predicting Time 2 Risk Behavior

	Risk behavior							
	Reckless driving		Smoking		Drinking		Ineffective contraception	
Variable	β	t	β	t	β	t	β	t
Time 1 behavior	.71	22.88*	.75	22.48**	.43	9.13**	.26	5.13**
Gender	−.04	−1.80	−.06	2.86**	−.00	−0.06	−.15	2.95**
Intention	.04	−1.41	.11	3.25**	.29	6.35**	−.01	−0.23
SC	.06	2.15*	.00	−0.00	.05	1.81	.07	1.36
Prototype	.05	1.77	.01	0.43	.05	1.34	.17	3.28**
Prototype × SC	.06	2.15*	.04	1.76	.02	0.80	.11	2.13*
Prototype × Gender	—		−.04	−2.07*	−.04	−1.50	−.11	−2.19*
Prototype × SC × Gender	—		−.06	−3.02**	−.06	−1.94*	−.11	−2.09*
Final R^2	.59**	.72**	.50**	.15**				

Note. $N = 617$–623; for ineffective contraception, $N = 347$ (nonvirgins). SC = social comparison.
* $p \leq .05$. ** $p < .01$.

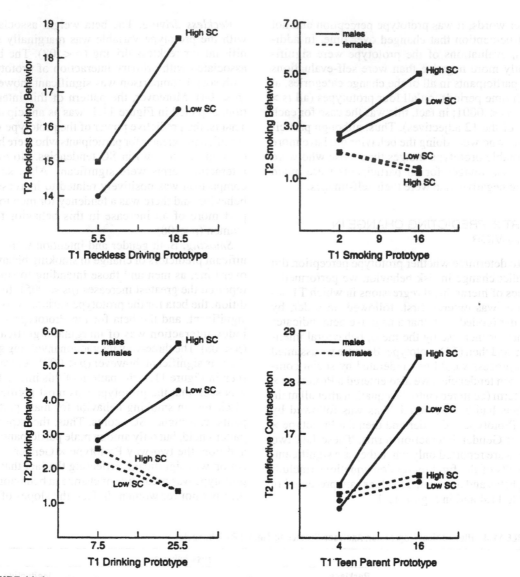

FIGURE 11.1 ■ Time 2 (T2) risk behaviors as a function of Time 1 (T1) prototype, social comparison (SC), and gender.

regression lines for both the high- and low-SC women did not differ from 0 (*p*s > .40).

Drinking. Analyses on the measure of drinking behavior produced results that were very similar to those on the smoking measure. That is, intention was significant, but neither the prototype main effect nor the Prototype × SC interaction terms were. The Prototype × SC × Gender interaction was significant, however (*p* = .05), as the men's responses, once again, fit the expected pattern. As

with smoking, the slopes of the regression lines for the women were not significantly different from zero.

Ineffective contraception. Several variables predicted change in self-reports of ineffective contraception. First, men reported a greater increase in this risk behavior than did women. Second, the prototype variable did predict an increase in ineffective contraception by itself (*p* < .002) and in interaction with both gender and social comparison (both $ps < .04$). Finally, the three-way interaction term also was significant ($p < .04$), as the high-SC men, once again, were most likely to demonstrate a relation between prototype perception and change in risk behavior.

Additional analyses. We conducted two additional sets of regression analyses for exploratory purposes. First, the prototype measures were replaced by prototype matching measures (i.e., means of the 12 self–prototype difference scores for each of the four sets of adjectives). A comparison of the result of the prototype-matching analyses with those of the prototype analyses revealed that the final R^2 was higher in the equations including just the prototype, as opposed to the matching measure, on all four behaviors, although not by much. In addition, the prototype entered prior to the matching index in three of four stepwise regressions that included both measures (the exception being alcohol). Thus, the prototype does appear to be somewhat better than the matching measure at predicting risk behavior for this age sample, though it is not significantly better (which is not surprising, given that the two measures correlate $> .70$ on all four behaviors).

Second, we conducted a series of hierarchical regression analyses in which the two components of the prototype measure (similarity and favorability) were entered separately as main effects, prior to the interaction (product) term. The results were very similar to those reported here. The primary interaction terms—either the SC × Prototype or SC × Prototype × Gender (actually the SC × [Favorability × Similarity] three-way and then the SC × Gender × [Favorability × Similarity] four-way interactions)—remained significant for three of the four behaviors. The four-way interaction was not significant for alcohol ($p = .20$; the three-way interaction was significant for the men on this measure, however). Also, in two cases—driving and smoking—similarity entered significantly, and favorability did not, whereas the opposite pattern occurred for ineffective contraception. In sum, although it is clear from the correlations that the favorability and similarity components are not redundant, it also appears that the product of the two is the best single predictor of behavior (cf. Gibbons, Gerrard, & Boney-McCoy, 1995).

Summary. The predictive power of the prototype measures varied across behaviors, ranging from significant on contraception to insignificant on smoking. As expected, however, the relation between prototype perception and change in risk behavior was moderated by SC tendencies. Specifically, the Prototype × SC interaction term was significant for all participants for reckless driving and ineffective contraception, and marginally significant for smoking. In addition, that moderation pattern was stronger for men on three of the four behaviors (alcohol, smoking, and ineffective contraception). In short, the moderation of the prototype effect was demonstrated among either the entire sample, or the men, on each one of the four behaviors.

Discussion

SUMMARY OF RESULTS

Perceptions of the prototype "tracked" behavior quite closely for three of the four risk behaviors. The correlation between the two was substantial at T1 and remained so at T2. Moreover, participants whose self-reports of behavior increased also tended to report more positive (and more similar) prototype perception, as expected, whereas the opposite occurred among those whose risk behavior declined. If behavior remained steady, so did the index. These results are consistent with those of previous studies that have examined smoker images among adolescents, and they also extend that research to include other types of risk behaviors. Similarly, the results are consistent with the distancing research among smokers by Gibbons et al. (1991) but add to that research by demonstrating the reverse process, what we have called *assimilation*, among young adults whose smoking and other risk behaviors have increased.

An important question raised by previous work in this area is whether prototype perception is an indicator of imminent behavior change or is simply a reflection of change that has already occurred—perhaps a form of dissonance reduction. The fact that previous research has demonstrated that the smoker image is more negative among smokers who have decided to quit, but are still smoking at a high rate, than it is among smokers who have not yet made the decision to stop (Gibbons et al., 1991), suggests that image change may precede behavior change. That hypothesis received further support from the current data, as prototype perception at T1 did predict T2 behavior. Moreover, it did so after T1 behavior and intention had both been entered into the regression equation. This latter point is important to keep in mind for two reasons: (a) there was a considerable amount of stability across time (i.e., T1 behavior predicted T2 behavior very well), and (b) for three of the behaviors, behavioral intentions were also very highly correlated with subsequent behavior. Thus, there wasn't a lot of variance in T2 behavior "left over" to be explained after these two variables had been accounted for, and yet the prototype construct (by itself or in interaction with social comparison) did explain that additional variance significantly.

THE PROTOTYPE

Acquiring an image. In an absolute sense, the prototype images in this study were neither very favorable nor very similar to the self (cf. Gibbons, Gerrard, & Boney-McCoy, 1995; Gibbons, Helweg-Larsen, & Gerrard, 1995). That was true even for students who were engaging in the behavior at a fairly high rate (drinking was the only prototype that received an overall evaluation above the midpoint of the scale, and that was only slightly above). This puts a somewhat different perspective on the prototype than that proposed by earlier researchers, who have argued that adolescents intending to smoke are trying to acquire a particular image that they believe is stereotypically associated with the behavior (Leventhal & Cleary, 1980). There are two reasons why it appears unlikely that the college students in this sample were motivated strongly by a desire to acquire any of these behavioral images. First, and most obvious, it is doubtful that they would want to acquire an image that they considered to be much more negative than the one they currently had (it is possible that this tendency might be moderated by self-esteem, but that hypothesis was not supported by the current data). Second, it seems likely that if these young adults were trying to acquire an image through these behaviors, then the self-images of those who did start or who increased the behavior would have changed somewhat over time. That was not the case.

A significant portion of the predictive power of the prototype exists independent of intention. Using smoking as an example, for some adolescents,

a favorable image is a reflection of a decision they have made to begin or to increase smoking. For others, however, the same favorable image is an indication that their smoking will be largely situationally determined; they aren't intending to smoke, but they might if the opportunity presents itself. Conversely, a negative image among those already smoking suggests the individual has either made the decision to cut down or will make that decision soon. Thus, some adolescents and young adults engage in "premeditated" comparison with the image because they are considering the behavior. Others compare with the image more spontaneously, because the situation in which they happen to be—that is, an opportunity to perform the behavior—has made the image relevant to them. Its relevance comes from the fact that they realize they will assume the image themselves if they decide to engage in the behavior. In short, there are two pathways from prototype to behavior: one through intention, the other through willingness (cf. Gibbons, Gerrard, Blanton, & Russell, 1995).

Prototype favorability versus matching. When the behavioral images are considerably more negative than self-perception, as was the case with all four risk prototypes, a measure of self-image match is problematic for two reasons. First, people with high self-esteem will necessarily have greater self–other discrepancies (even though self-esteem may not be linked at all to the behavior, as was the case in our data for all of the behaviors except smoking, which did show a weak but significant relation; $p < .05$). Second, the match confounds image favorability and similarity to the self (i.e., it is not possible to have a favorable image that is not similar to the self). As our results indicated, using the favorability and similarity terms as distinct elements, combined as a product term, enhances the predictive power of the image. It also captures the interactive nature of their relationship. Specifically, the results indicated that participants with images that were relatively favorable and similar to the self were most likely to increase their risk behavior.

Limits on prediction. The predictive power of the image is limited by several factors. One has to do with the image itself—to what extent is the prototype generally recognized? It is doubtful, for example, that an individual's image of the typical user (or nonuser) of radon test kits would have much influence on that person's decision to buy or not buy a kit. On the other hand, a vivid image, such as that of a rock climber or whitewater rafter, may have a greater behavioral impact than any of the images that we used, albeit for a smaller number of people. A second possible limiting factor has to do with the behavior being predicted. For example, it is unlikely that the image of the unmarried college-age parent has a lot of influence on a college student's choice of birth control for a single act of intercourse. Perhaps a "risky sex" or even a "promiscuity" image might be more influential. On the other hand, the parent image may have an effect on a series of contraceptive decisions. By the same token, we suspect the image may lose some of its predictive power among older adolescents whose substance use is primarily a stress reaction (cf. Vaccaro & Wills, 1994; Wills, 1986). When the behavior serves more of a coping than a recreational function, then the social image associated with it is likely to become less important.

THE COMPARISON PROCESS

Our description of how the prototype influences behavior is based on two assumptions: (a) individuals do compare with the image, although some do it more than others, and (b) the images are most influential among those who are most likely to socially compare. Evidence in support of both assumptions can be found in the data set. First, in a subsequent assessment, we asked a subset of the same group if they had ever thought about the prototype or the type of person we had described in the study. For each one of the four risk behaviors, more than 80% of the students indicated they had previously thought about the typical person who engages in the behavior. Moreover, participants high in social comparison tendencies (based on a median split of the SC index) reported significantly more consideration than did those low in comparison tendencies ($p < .001$, across the four prototypes).

Second, social comparison tendencies did moderate the impact of the prototypes on risk behavior. In fact, separate regression analyses on participants above and below the median on the SC index indicated that the latter group had virtually no relation between the favorability of their images and their behaviors. What this means is that a young person might have a reasonably favorable image of the type of person who drinks alcohol, but that image may not influence his or her drinking behavior because he or she does not typically engage in much social-behavior comparison. By the same token, someone who has a negative image and is prone to socially compare should be more motivated to quit than someone less inclined toward comparison. In short, a tendency toward relatively frequent social comparison appears to be a prerequisite for the relevant prototype to have a strong impact on behavior.

GENDER

Men reported significantly greater increases in smoking and in ineffective contraception than did women. In addition, for three behaviors—smoking, drinking, and ineffective contraception—the predictive pattern of the prototype–SC combination was significantly stronger among the men. This gender difference is not a reflection of SC habits, as the women actually reported more social-behavior SC than did the men ($p < .05$). One reason for the difference could be simply the fact that there was more variability (to be predicted) in the men's behavior. In addition, it would also appear that some risk images—smoking and drinking, for example—are just not as important to women as they are to men (see similar results by Brown et al., 1986, and Chassin et al., 1985; but see also Burton et al., 1989). As one reviewer pointed out, this may be due in part to the environment in which the behaviors occur. Specifically, college students may view these risk behaviors, and therefore the corresponding images, as more masculine in nature, or more appropriate for men. If so, it would be expected that men would be both more aware of and more responsive to them. This interesting gender difference seems to be a logical target for future research with other samples. A detailed discussion, however, is beyond the scope of this chapter.

DEVELOPMENTAL DIFFERENCES

Comparing this study, conducted with young adults, with most previous studies of health risk behavior, which have been conducted with adolescents, raises a number of developmental issues, some of which have intervention implications.

First, it may very well be that for younger adolescents, risk images do represent goal states of one kind or another, at least more than they do for young adults. In contrast, the latter group may be more likely to aspire to (and also "match" with) certain professional or career images (cf. Moss & Frieze, 1993). Second, the fact that prototypes predicted risk behavior more so among those who were high in social comparison tendencies suggests that image influence may actually be more pronounced among adolescents than it is among young adults (Gibbons & Gerrard, 1995). The reason is that social influence, as reflected in conformity behavior (Berndt, 1979; Bronfenbrenner, 1970; Brown et al., 1986) and social comparison (cf. Suls & Mullen, 1982), tends to be more impactful during that younger age period, especially with regard to risk behavior (Krosnick & Judd, 1982).

Finally, results of the repeated measures analysis, together with those of the regressions, suggest that the images and behaviors may interact with or even promote one another. That is, having a favorable image increases the likelihood that the behavior will be performed; performing the behavior, in turn, increases the favorability of the prototype. What this reciprocal relation suggests is that intervention efforts intended to interrupt the link between image perception and risk behavior should be directed at younger age groups. One reason for this suggestion is simply because younger children are most prone to comparison behavior. A second reason is that, even though risk behavior does affect risk images, we suspect formation of these images precedes onset of behavior for most adolescents—children as young as third or fourth grade have fairly well-defined smoker and drinker images, for example (Bland, Bewley, Banks, & Pollard, 1975; Chassin, Tetzloff, & Hershey, 1985). To effectively alter these images, interventions must begin at a fairly young age.

Of course, SC behavior does not stop at adolescence or even college age (Ruble & Frey, 1991). There is reason to believe that the process we have described here may continue well into adulthood but may very well be manifested differently among persons who are older. A middle-aged woman's decision to drive recklessly, for example, may not be influenced by her image of the typical reckless driver her age (though her decision to drive after drinking might be more noticeably affected). On the other hand, results of our research with adult smokers suggest that comparison with a negative smoker image is a motivating factor even for clinic participants who are much older. Moreover, desire to quit a particular behavior is likely to prompt social comparison (with the prototype) among most adults, which means that SC tendencies or dispositions may be less of a prerequisite for image influence among older people. One hypothesis to be tested in future research, then, is that distancing from a prototype is a "strategy" used by adults to help them overcome a behavioral problem, whereas assimilation, moderated by SC tendencies, is more common among young adults, and especially adolescents, whose risk behavior patterns and habits are still being formed. When examined, these hypotheses should provide useful information about effective intervention techniques for persons of all ages.

ACKNOWLEDGMENTS

This research was supported by National Institute of Mental Health Grant 1 P50 MH48165-01 and National Institute on Drug Abuse Grant R03 DA07534. We thank Dan Russell, Sue Boney-McCoy, Fred Lorenz, and Jan-Fekke Ybema for their comments on the article.

REFERENCES

Ajzen, I., & Fishbein, M. (1980). *Understanding attitudes and predicting social behavior.* Englewood Cliffs, NJ: Prentice-Hall.

Baron, R. M., & Kenny, D. A. (1986). The moderator-mediator variable distinction in social psychological research: Conceptual, strategic, and statistical considerations. *Journal of Personality and Social Psychology, 51,* 1173–1182.

Barton, J., Chassin, L., Presson, C. C., & Sherman, S. J. (1982). Social image factors as motivators of smoking initiation in early and middle adolescence. *Child Development, 53,* 1499–1511.

Berndt, T. J. (1979). Developmental changes in conformity to peers and parents. *Developmental Psychology, 15,* 608–616.

Bland, J. M., Bewley, B. R., Banks, M. H., & Pollard, V. (1975). School children's beliefs about smoking and disease. *Journal of Health Education, 34,* 71–78.

Bronfenbrenner, U. (1970). Reaction to social pressure from adults versus peers among Soviet day school and boarding school pupils in the perspective of an American sample. *Journal of Personality and Social Psychology, 15,* 179–189.

Brooks-Gunn, J., & Furstenberg, F. F. (1989). Adolescent sexual behavior. *American Psychologist, 44,* 249–257.

Brown, B. B., Clasen, D. N., & Eicher, S. A. (1986). Perceptions of peer pressure. peer conformity dispositions, and self-reported behavior among adolescents. *Developmental Psychology, 22,* 521–530.

Brown, B. B., & Lohr, M. J. (1987). Peer-group affilation and adolescent self-esteem: An integration of ego-identity and symbolic-interaction theories. *Journal of Personality and Social Psychology, 52,* 47–55.

Burke, P. J., & Reitzes, D. C. (1981). The link between identity and role performance. *Social Psychology Quarterly, 44,* 83–92.

Burton, D., Sussman, S., Hansen, W. B., Johnson, C. A., & Flay, B. R. (1989). Image attributions and smoking intentions among seventh grade students. *Journal of Applied Social Psychology, 19,* 656–664.

Busemeyer, J. R., & Jones, L. E. (1983). Analysis of multiplicative combination rules when the causal variables are measured with error. *Psychological Bulletin, 93,* 549–562.

Chassin, L., Presson, C., Sherman, S. J., Corty, E., & Olshavsky, R. W. (1981). Self-images and cigarette smoking in adolescence. *Personality and Social Psychology Bulletin, 7,* 670–676.

Chassin, L., Presson, C., Sherman, S. J., McLaughlin, L., & Gioia, D. (1985). Psychosocial correlates of adolescent smokeless tobacco use. *Addictive Behaviors, 10,* 431–435.

Chassin, L., Tetzloff, C., & Hershey, M. (1985). Self-image and social-image factors in adolescent alcohol use. *Journal of Studies in Alcohol, 46,* 39–47.

Cooper, W. H., & Kohn, P. M. (1989). The social image of the young female smoker. *British Journal of Addiction, 84,* 935–941.

Eiser, J. R. (1985). Smoking: The social learning of an addiction. Special Issue: The emergence of research at the interface of social, clinical, and developmental psychology. *Journal of Social and Clinical Psychology, 3,* 446–457.

Fishbein, M., & Ajzen, I. (1975). *Belief, attitude, intention and behavior: An introduction to theory and research.* Reading, MA: Addison-Wesley.

Fisher, J. D., & Misovich, S. (1990). Social influence and AIDS-preventive behavior. In J. Edwards, R. S. Tindale, L. Heath, & E. J. Posavac (Eds.), *Social influence processes and prevention* (pp. 39–70). New York: Plenum.

Fiske, S. T., & Taylor, S. E. (1991). *Social cognition* (2nd ed.). New York: McGraw-Hill.

Gerrard, M., & Warner, T. D. (1990). Antecedents of pregnancy among women Marines. *Journal of the Washington Academy of Sciences, 80,* 1–15.

Gibbons, F. X. (1985). Social stigma perception: Social comparison among mentally retarded persons. *American Journal of Mental Deficiency, 90,* 98–100.

Gibbons, F. X., & Gerrard, M. (1991). Downward social comparison and coping with threat. In J. M. Suls & T. A. Wills (Eds.), *Social comparison: Contemporary theory and research* (pp. 317–345). Hillsdale, NJ: Erlbaum.

Gibbons, F. X., & Gerrard, M. (1997). Health images and their effects on behavior. In B. P. Buunk & F. X. Gibbons (Eds.), *Health coping, and well-being* (pp. 63–94). Hillsdale, NJ: Erlbaum.

Gibbons, F. X., Gerrard, M., Blanton, H., & Russell, D. W. (1995). *Reason or reaction? Two paths to health risk.* Manuscript in preparation, Iowa State University.

Gibbons, F. X., Gerrard, M., & Boney-McCoy, S. (1995). Prototype perception predicts (lack of) pregnancy prevention. *Personality and Social Psychology Bulletin, 21,* 84–92.

Gibbons, F. X., Gerrard, M., Lando, H. A., & McGovern, P. G. (1991). Social comparison and smoking cessation: The role of the "typical smoker." *Journal of Experimental Social Psychology, 27,* 239–258.

Gibbons, F. X., Helweg-Larsen, M., & Gerrard, M. (1995). Prevalence estimates and adolescent risk behavior: Cross-cultural differences in social influence. *Journal of Applied Psychology, 80,* 107–121.

Goldstein, J. (1991). The stigmatization of smokers: An empirical investigation. *Journal of Drug Education, 21,* 167–182.

Grube, J. W., Weir, I. L., Getzlaf, S., & Rokeach, M. (1984). Own value system, value images, and cigarette smoking. *Personality and Social Psychology Bulletin, 10,* 306–313.

Hatcher, R. A., Stewart, F., Trussel, J., Kowal, D., Guest, F., Stewart, G. K., & Cates, W. (1990). *Contraceptive technology: 1990–1992.* New York: Irvington.

Janus, S., & Janus, C. (1993). *Janus report on sexual behavior.* New York: Wiley.

Jessor, R., Donovan, J. E., & Costa, F. M. (1991). *Beyond adolescence: Problem behavior and young adult development.* Cambridge, England: Cambridge University Press.

Krosnick, J. A., & Judd, C. M. (1982). Transitions in social influence at adolescence: Who induces cigarette smoking? *Developmental Psychology, 18,* 359–368.

Leventhal, H., & Cleary, P. D. (1980). The smoking problem: A review of the research theory in behavioral risk modification. *Psychological Bulletin, 88,* 370–405.

Loftus, E. F., Smith, K. D., Klinger, M. R., & Fiedler, J. (1992). Memory and mismemory for health events. In J. M. Tanur (Ed.), *Questions about questions: Inquiries into the cognitive bases of surveys* (pp. 102–137). New York: Russell Sage Foundation.

Markus, H. R., & Nurius, P. (1986). Possible selves. *American Psychologist, 41,* 954–969.

McKennel, A. C., & Bynner, J. M. (1969). Self images and smoking behavior among school boys. *British Journal of Educational Psychology, 39,* 27–39.

Mosbach, P., & Leventhal, H. (1988). Peer-group identification and smoking: Implications for intervention. *Journal of Abnormal Psychology, 97,* 238–245.

Moss, A. K., & Frieze, I. H. (1993). Job preferences in the anticipatory socialization: A comparison of two matching models. *Journal of Vocational Behavior, 42,* 282–297.

Niedenthal, P. M., Cantor, N., & Kihlstrom, J. F. (1985). Prototype matching: A strategy for social decision making. *Journal of Personality and Social Psychology, 48,* 575–584.

Niedenthal, P. M., & Mordkoff, J. T. (1991). Prototype distancing: A strategy for choosing among threatening situations. *Personality and Social Psychology Bulletin, 17,* 483–493.

Roscoe, B., & Kruger, T. L. (1990). AIDS: Late adolescents' knowledge and its influence on sexual behavior. *Adolescent, 25,* 38–48.

Rotheram-Borus, M. J., & Koopman, C. (1991). Sexual risk behaviors, AIDS knowledge, and beliefs about AIDS among runaways. *American Journal of Public Health, 81,* 206–208.

Ruble, D. N., & Frey, K. S. (1991). Changing patterns of comparative behavior as skills are acquired: A functional model of self-evaluation. In J. M. Suls & T. A. Wills (Eds.), *Social comparison: Contemporary theory and research* (pp. 79–113). Hillsdale, NJ: Erlbaum.

Sheppard, B. H., Hartwick, J., & Warshaw, P. R. (1988). The theory of reasoned action: A meta-analysis of past research with recommendations for modifications and future research. *Journal of Consumer Research, 15*, 325–343.

Skowronski, J. J., & Carlston, D. E. (1989). Negativity and extremity biases in impression formation: A review of explanations. *Psychological Bulletin, 105*, 131–142.

Stacy, A. W., Widaman, K. F., Hays, R., & DiMatteo, M. R. (1985). Validity of self-reports of alcohol and other drug use: A multitrait-multimethod assessment. *Journal of Personality and Social Psychology, 49*, 219–232.

Suls, J., & Mullen, B. (1982). From the cradle to the grave: Comparison and self-evaluation across the life span. In J. Suls (Ed.), *Psychological perspectives on the self* (Vol. 1, pp. 97–125). Hillsdale, NJ: Erlbaum.

Sussman, S., Dent, C. W., Stacy, A. W., Burciaga, A. R., Turner, G. E., Charlin, V., Craig, S., Hansen, W. B., Burton, D., &

Flay, B. R. (1990). Peer group association and adolescent tobacco use. *Journal of Abnormal Psychology, 99*, 349–352.

U.S. Public Health Service. (1991). *National household survey on drug abuse* (DHHS Publication No. ADM 91–1788). Washington, DC: U.S. Government Printing Office.

U.S. Public Health Service. (1993). *Prevention: Federal programs and progress 91/92*. Washington, DC: Office of Disease Prevention.

Vaccaro, D., & Wills, T. A. (1994). *Stress-coping factors in adolescent substance use: Ethnic differences*. Manuscript submitted for publication.

Wills, T. A. (1981). Downward comparison principles in social psychology. *Psychological Bulletin, 90*, 245–271.

Wills, T. A. (1986). Stress and coping in early adolescence: Relationships to substance use in urban school samples. *Health Psychology, 5*, 503–529.

APPENDIX: Structure and Loadings From Principal-Components Analysis of the Social Comparison Scale

How often do you compare with:	Component 1: Temporal comparison	Component 2: Social-behavior comparison[a]	Component 3: Level of comparison	Component 4: Temporal versus social comparison
Academic self in future?	.79			
Self in future (general)?	.76			
Self in past (general)?	.71			
Academic self in past?	.68			
Others on social behavior?		.76		
Others in general (personally)?		.75		
At what level of social behavior?		.68		
At what level of academic (absolute)?			.85	
At what level of academic (relative to you)?			.84	
Others versus past self (academics)?				.76
Others versus current self (academics)?				.72
Others (academics)?				.54

Note. The analysis was conducted with varimax (orthogonal) rotation; all component eigenvalues >1.0.
[a] Used as the social comparison index moderator in the regression analyses.

Pluralistic Ignorance and Alcohol Use on Campus: Some Consequences of Misperceiving the Social Norm

Deborah A. Prentice and Dale T. Miller • Princeton University

Four studies* examined the relation between college students' own attitudes toward alcohol use and their estimates of the attitudes of their peers. All studies found widespread evidence of pluralistic ignorance: Students believed that they were more uncomfortable with campus alcohol practices than was the average student. Study 2 demonstrated this perceived self–other difference also with respect to one's friends. Study 3 tracked attitudes toward drinking over the course of a semester and found gender differences in response to perceived deviance: Male students shifted their attitudes over time in the direction of what they mistakenly believed to be the norm, whereas female students showed no such attitude change. Study 4 found that students' perceived deviance correlated with various measures of campus alien- ation, even though that deviance was illusory. The implications of these results for general issues of norm estimation and responses to perceived deviance are discussed.

F̲ew issues have fascinated social psychologists as much or for as long as the relation between private attitudes and social norms. Conventional wisdom has it that when individuals perceive their attitudes to be different from the normative atti- tudes of their social group, they will experience discomfort and will resolve the discrepancy, usu- ally by changing their attitudes in the direction of the norm. This analysis rests on an assumption that has gone largely unexamined by social psy- chologists: that people can accurately identify the social norm. In this article, we report four stud-

ies that challenge the generality of this assump- tion and document the consequences of its vio- lation.

Although social influence has been a major topic of research for the past century (see Moscovici, 1985; Turner, 1991), the question of how people identify the social norm has scarcely arisen. Labo- ratory investigators have typically created situa- tions in which the norm either is formed by sub- jects as part of the experimental task or is given unambiguously by the experimental procedure. For example, subjects in Sherif's (1936) auto-kinetic experiments were in a situation in which no norm existed. As part of the judgment task, they jointly (or individually) developed perceptual norms.

---

*Four studies were reported in the original article; three have been included here. Study 4 has been removed.

Subjects in Asch's (1951) conformity studies, on the other hand, were in a situation with a strong and unambiguous norm: They were asked to give a judgment after hearing numerous "other subjects" give the same (objectively incorrect) answer. Sherif's subjects were free to negotiate the norm; Asch's subjects were provided with a clear, consensual group norm. In neither of these prototypical cases was it the subject's task to identify a preexisting norm.

Field research on social influence might logically be expected to have more to say about how people identify the social norm. However, most field studies have focused primarily on the effects of norms to the exclusion of considerations about how people locate those norms. For example, in Newcomb's (1943) study of attitude change among students at Bennington College, the fact that the prevailing norms of the college were liberal was presented as an unambiguous property of the social context. Presumably, the newcomer to Bennington found enough evidence of liberal views in the outward behavior of the residents to ascertain that these views were, in fact, the norm. Similarly, Festinger, Schachter, and Back's (1950) investigation of pressures toward uniformity in the Westgate and Westgate West housing projects examined adherence to prevailing norms without providing any evidence of how those norms were established or communicated. More recent investigations have shown a similar tendency to focus on the effects, rather than on the identification, of norms (e.g., Cialdini, Kallgren, & Reno, 1991; Crandall, 1988).

Despite the dearth of direct evidence regarding how people identify existing norms, the classic influence studies do suggest two general properties of norms that determine how they are perceived and communicated. First, social norms are defined by people's public behavior. The negotiated reality of Sherif's subjects, the public judgments of Asch's confederates, the liberal views expressed by Bennington students, and the attitudes expressed by the residents of Westgate and Westgate West all were public statements that defined the social norm. To the extent that public statements accurately reflect the private attitudes and judgments of their proponents, the subjective norm that they instantiate will coincide with the actual norm of the group. To the extent that they misrepresent people's private views, the subjective norm will diverge from the actual norm.

In addition to their public nature, norms are imbued with an impression of universality: People assume that all members of a group endorse that group's social norms (Allport, 1924), and, in turn, the power of norms to affect an individual's attitudes and behavior is heavily dependent on their perceived universality. As consensus (or the appearance of consensus) breaks down, the norm loses its influence. The Asch (1951) studies provide clear evidence of the importance of universality: When just one confederate deviated from the normative response (even by giving an alternative wrong answer), conformity dropped to nearly zero.

Pluralistic Ignorance

Although the social psychological literature offers little evidence of how people identify social norms, it does provide some striking examples of systematic errors in norm estimation. Many of these examples come from research on pluralistic ignorance. *Pluralistic ignorance* is a psychological state characterized by the belief that one's private attitudes and judgments are different from those of others, even though one's public behavior is identical (Miller & McFarland, 1991). It develops most commonly under circumstances in which there is widespread misrepresentation of private views. In these cases, people's tendency to rely on the public behavior of others to identify the norm leads them astray, for the social norm that is communicated misrepresents the prevailing sentiments of the group. If participants understood this state of affairs, the situation would be self-correcting. However, they typically make the mistake of assuming that even though others are acting similarly, they are feeling differently. Their own behavior may be driven by social pressure, but they assume that other people's identical behavior is an accurate reflection of their true feelings.

Although many studies have demonstrated pluralistic ignorance, both in and out of the laboratory (see, e.g., Breed & Ktsanes, 1961; Miller & McFarland, 1987; O'Gorman, 1975; Packard & Willower, 1972; Schanck, 1932), little research has addressed the question of how victims of pluralistic ignorance respond to the perceived discrepancy between their private attitudes and the social norm.

These individuals have several strategies available to them for reducing the discrepancy: They can move their private attitudes closer to the (perceived) norm, bring the norm closer to their attitudes, or reject the group altogether. Given that the last two of these options will often appear too costly or too difficult to effect, at least in the short run, the simplest way for individuals to eliminate the discrepancy is to change their private attitudes. This internalization of the norm will most often occur in situations in which private attitudes or judgments are not well established (see Kelman, 1958). One such situation is the classic case of the unresponsive bystander. In seeking to explain why bystanders fail to help a victim of an emergency, Latané and Darley (1970) suggested that pluralistic ignorance is at the root of this inaction. They argued that individual bystanders fail to act because they are unsure about the seriousness of the situation; however, these same bystanders often assume that the inaction of others reflects a high degree of confidence that the situation is not serious. In this case, pluralistic ignorance is easily resolved through internalization of the social norm: Bystanders will adopt a consensual (if erroneous) definition of the situation as a nonemergency.

In other cases of pluralistic ignorance, private attitudes and judgments are well established; here, individuals will be unable to internalize the normative position. One such case is a classroom dynamic investigated by Miller and McFarland (1987, 1991). The situation is as follows: A professor who has just presented difficult material will typically ask students if they have any questions. This request for students to acknowledge their confusion often fails to elicit a response, even though confusion is widespread. The students' inaction is driven by pluralistic ignorance: Individual students are inhibited from raising their hands out of fear of asking a stupid question, but they interpret their classmates' identical behavior as an indication that everyone else understands the material. In this situation, pluralistic ignorance will not be resolved by students deciding that they actually do understand the material. They have ample and irrefutable evidence that they do not understand it. Instead, pluralistic ignorance will likely persist, leaving students feeling deviant and alienated from each other.

The research reported in this article was designed to explore these consequences of pluralistic ignorance. In all four studies, we examined pluralistic ignorance in the context of students' attitudes toward alcohol drinking on campus. We chose this particular issue because attitudes toward drinking are currently in a period of transition at Princeton, as the university becomes more sensitive to the negative effects of alcohol use on academic and social life. Many theorists have argued that pluralistic ignorance frequently accompanies such periods of social change, with private attitudes changing more quickly than social norms (see Breed & Ktsanes, 1961: Fields & Schuman, 1976; Miller & McFarland, 1991). Thus, we expected the issue of alcohol use to provide an excellent context for our empirical studies.

Alcohol Use on Campus

Alcohol use by college undergraduates has become a major concern of university administrators and public health officials across the country (Berkowitz & Perkins, 1986; Maddox, 1970; Straus & Bacon, 1953). A recent survey revealed that whereas the use of other recreational drugs has dropped significantly over the past 2 decades, alcohol use has declined more slowly (Barringer, 1991). According to the College Health Association, alcohol is the single greatest risk to the health of university students. One powerful predictor of adolescent alcohol use, and of other forms of substance use, is peer influence (e.g., Graham, Marks, & Hansen, 1991; Kandel, 1980; Perkins, 1985; Stein, Newcomb, & Bentler, 1987). Moreover, the impact of peers appears to increase, rather than decrease, as adolescents mature (Huba & Bentler, 1980; Zucker & Noll, 1982).

The alcohol situation at Princeton is exacerbated by the central role of alcohol in many of the university's institutions and traditions. For example, at the eating clubs, the center of social life on campus, alcohol is on tap 24 hours a day, 7 days a week. Princeton reunions boast the second highest level of alcohol consumption for any event in the country after the Indianapolis 500 (Clitherow, 1991). The social norms for drinking at the university are clear: Students must be comfortable with alcohol use to partake of Princeton social life.

In the face of these strong norms promoting alcohol use, we suspected that students' private attitudes would reveal substantial misgivings about drinking. Within their first few months at college, students are exposed to vivid and irrefutable evidence of the negative consequences of excessive alcohol consumption: They nurse sick roommates, overlook inappropriate behavior and memory losses, and hear about serious injuries and even deaths that result from drinking. They may have negative experiences with alcohol themselves and may notice its effects on their academic performance. This accumulating evidence of the ill effects of alcohol is likely to affect their private attitudes but not the social norm: Indeed, believing that others are still comfortable with alcohol, students will perpetuate that norm by continuing to adopt a nonchalant demeanor that masks their growing concerns. If this analysis is, in fact, correct, we should find clear evidence of pluralistic ignorance regarding students' comfort with alcohol use on campus.

The present studies sought to document the existence of pluralistic ignorance regarding alcohol use and to investigate some of its consequences for individuals' attitudes and behavior. Study 1 was designed to demonstrate pluralistic ignorance by showing a divergence between private attitudes and the social norm as well as a belief in the universality of that norm. Study 2 extended this effect by showing a similar divergence between private attitudes and perceptions of the attitudes of one's friends. Study 3 explored the extent to which individuals respond to pluralistic ignorance by internalizing the social norm over time. The three studies focused on comfort with alcohol use; the fourth study examined attitudes toward the university's policy banning beer kegs on campus.

Study 1

In our first study, we tested the assumption that students' attitudes toward alcohol drinking on campus are characterized by a divergence between private attitudes and perceptions of the social norm. We also examined the extent to which social norms are imbued with an illusion of universality by asking subjects to estimate the variability, as well as the central tendency, of other students' attitudes.

Method

Subjects. Subjects were 132 undergraduates, who voluntarily attended a mass testing session in which they participated in this and other short studies for pay. The sample included 69 women and 63 men, with approximately even distribution of women and men across the 1st- through 4th-year classes.

Procedure. Subjects responded to a brief, one-page questionnaire that was included in a large booklet. The questionnaire was preceded by a page of instructions on how to use the response scales. The first question asked the following:

1. How comfortable do you feel with the alcohol drinking habits of students at Princeton?

Subjects indicated their own comfort by circling a number on the corresponding 11-point scale (1 = *not at all comfortable* and 11 = *very comfortable*). Then they were asked to estimate the comfort of other students:

2. How comfortable does the average Princeton undergraduate feel with the alcohol drinking habits of students at Princeton? (Please circle the average student's response and then bracket the two values between which the attitudes of 50% of students fall.)

Again, subjects indicated the average student's comfort by circling a number on the corresponding 11-point scale and then bracketing the two numbers on the same scale within which they believed the attitudes of 50% of students fall.

Results and Discussion

We expected that students would vary in their own comfort with alcohol drinking on campus but that they would believe other students to be uniformly more comfortable than they are. Means and standard deviations for the two comfort questions are presented in Table 12.1. Subjects' ratings indicated a sharp divergence between their own comfort and their subjective estimates of the comfort of others. A 2 (sex) × 2 (target) analysis of variance (ANOVA) revealed a highly significant main effect of target, $F(1, 130) = 55.52$, $p < .0001$: Respondents were much less comfortable with the alcohol drinking habits of Princeton undergraduates than they believed the average student to be. This main effect of target was qualified by a significant Sex × Target interaction, $F(1, 130) = 9.96$, $p < .005$, indicating that the gap between ratings of own and others' comfort was substantially larger for women than for men. Nevertheless, the self–other difference was significant for both male, $F(1, 62) = 10.35$, $p < .005$, and female subjects, $F(1, 68) = 51.95$, $p < .0001$.

A closer analysis of the distributions of comfort ratings indicated that students' perceptions of the attitudes of others converged on a highly consistent norm. Although their own comfort ratings spanned the entire 11-point scale in a relatively uniform distribution, their estimates of the average student's comfort assumed an almost perfectly normal distribution, with high agreement on an average of approximately 7. A statistical comparison of the variances of the two distributions revealed a highly significant difference, $F(131, 131) = 2.99$, $p < .0001$.

In addition, subjects' estimates of the variability of others' attitudes provided strong evidence for the illusion of universality. The median estimate of the range within which the attitudes of 50% of students fell (i.e., the interquartile range) was 4, with a lower bound of 5 and an upper bound of 9. (We use medians here to facilitate comparison with the actual distribution. The means are very close to the medians in all cases.) Thus, students' subjective distributions of attitudes toward drinking on campus had a mean of approximately 7,

with an interquartile range from 5 to 9. By contrast, the actual distribution of attitudes, as reflected by subjects' own comfort ratings, had a mean of 5.33, with an interquartile range from 3 to 8. These distributions demonstrate the two defining features of pluralistic ignorance: A divergence of subjective from actual norms and an illusion of universality.

Study 2

The results of Study 1 provided strong support for our expectation that students' attitudes toward campus alcohol practices would be characterized by pluralistic ignorance. However, two methodological features of the study allowed for alternative interpretations of the results. First, our question about the social norm asked students to rate the comfort of the average Princeton undergraduate with alcohol drinking on campus. Although we believed that ratings of the average student would provide a good indication of the perceived norm, it is also possible that the category "average student" lacked psychological reality for our subjects. Second, we asked the two comfort questions in a fixed order, with the question about the self always preceding the question about the average student. It is possible that subjects rated the average student as more comfortable simply because they made that rating second.

To preclude these alternative explanations for the findings of Study 1, we conducted a second study, in which we manipulated the order of the self and other questions and included an additional question that assessed the comfort of the respondent's friends with alcohol drinking on campus. Unlike ratings of the average student, ratings of friends were certain to be made with a group of real people in mind.

Method

Subjects. Subjects were 242 undergraduates, who voluntarily attended a mass testing session in which they filled out this and other questionnaires for pay. The sample included 145 women and 97 men, with an approximately even distribution of women and men across the 1st- through 4th-year classes.

TABLE 12.1. Ratings of Own and Average Student's Comfort With Alcohol Drinking in Study 1

Measure	Self	Average student
Women		
M	4.68	7.07
SD	2.69	1.68
Men		
M	6.03	7.00
SD	2.76	1.57
Total		
M	5.33	7.04
SD	2.73	1.63

Note. All ratings were made on 11-point scales (1 = *not at all comfortable* and 11 = *very comfortable*).

Procedure. Subjects answered the two questions asked in Study 1 (minus the variability estimates) and a third question that asked them to rate how comfortable their friends feel with the alcohol drinking habits of students at Princeton. Half of the subjects (77 women and 44 men) rated themselves first and the average student second; the other half (68 women and 53 men) rated the average student first and themselves second.

Results and Discussion

Means and standard deviations for the three comfort questions are shown in Table 12.2. A 2 (sex) × 3 (target) × 2 (question order) ANOVA revealed a highly significant effect of target, $F(2, 476) = 54.52, p < .0001$. Pairwise comparisons of the three means indicated that ratings of own comfort were significantly lower than ratings of friends' comfort or of the average student's comfort (using Tukey tests, with $p < .05$). The main effect of target was qualified by a significant Target × Order interaction. $F(2, 476) = 3.45, p < .05$, indicating that the differences between comfort ratings for the three targets were greater when the question

TABLE 12.2. Ratings of Own and Others' Comfort With Alcohol Drinking in Study 2

Measure	Self	Friend	Average student
Self-question first			
Women			
M	5.84	6.49	6.96
SD	2.69	2.42	1.41
Men			
M	6.02	6.82	7.11
SD	2.66	2.12	1.20
Total			
M	5.91	6.61	7.01
SD	2.68	2.32	1.34
Other-question first			
Women			
M	5.06	6.13	7.16
SD	2.47	2.34	1.72
Men			
M	5.87	6.94	7.47
SD	2.54	2.12	1.37
Total			
M	5.41	6.49	7.30
SD	2.50	2.24	1.57

Note. All ratings were made on 11-point scales (1 = *not at all comfortable* and 11 = *very comfortable*).

about the average student came first. However, separate pairwise comparisons within each form of the questionnaire showed that ratings of own comfort were significantly lower than ratings of the other two targets for both question orders. Friends' comfort was rated as intermediate between own comfort and the average student's comfort in all cases, but the difference between ratings of friends and of the average student was significant only when the average student question came first (for all reported differences, $p < .05$).

Students' perceptions of the comfort of the average student again converged on a highly consistent norm. Ratings of the average student were significantly less variable than ratings of the self, $F(241, 241) = 3.14, p < .0001$, and of friends. $F(241, 241) = 2.46, p < .0001$. Not surprisingly, ratings of friends' comfort showed considerable variability across subjects, although still not quite as much variability as self-ratings.

These results, especially concerning perceptions of friends, raise some interesting questions about the relation between local (friend) and global (campus) norms and about the role of these norms in producing pluralistic ignorance. In the case of alcohol use on campus, both types of norms are on the side of greater comfort with alcohol than students privately feel, and thus it is difficult to disentangle them. In theory, however, local and global norms may be quite distinct and may contribute independently to producing the perceived self–other differences. Misestimation of the local norm may occur because, as in the bystander and classroom cases, students base their estimates on observations of their friends' public behavior and erroneously assume that that behavior is diagnostic of their private attitudes. Misestimation of the global norm may be driven, in part, by a similar process but may also be influenced by the collective representation of Princeton as a drinking campus and by the importance of a liberal position on alcohol to the college student identity. We return to a consideration of the mechanisms underlying pluralistic ignorance in the general discussion.

In summary, the results of Studies 1 and 2 confirmed our intuition that students' comfort with alcohol use on campus would manifest the classic characteristics of pluralistic ignorance. Although the subjects in these studies were volunteers and thus may not have been representative of the student body (a weakness we remedy in the next study), we believe that the phenomenon demonstrated here is quite general: Undergraduates believe that everybody is more comfortable with drinking than they are themselves (see also Perkins & Berkowitz, 1986). The situation of drinking on campus shares much in common with the classic examples of pluralistic ignorance cited in the introduction. In all cases, individuals assume that others' outward display of comfort and ease reflects their actual feelings, even though those individuals' own identical behavior is some what at odds with their internal states.

Study 3

Armed with evidence for the validity of our assumptions about the alcohol issue, we designed the next study to explore some of the consequences of pluralistic ignorance. Study 3 addressed the question of how individuals respond to pluralistic ignorance over time. One prediction is that when individuals perceive their attitudes to be different from the normative attitudes of their social group, they will gradually change their attitudes in the direction of the group norm, either because they are persuaded by the group's position or because they internalize the sentiments that they originally expressed inauthentically. This conformity prediction has considerable precedent in the social influence literature, which has always placed a heavy emphasis on conformity as a means of resolving self–group discrepancies (see Moscovici, 1985). However, in the case of alcohol use on campus, the presence of irrefutable evidence of the ill effects of excessive drinking might make it very difficult for students to decide that they are, in fact, comfortable with the drinking norms. If students are unable to internalize the (perceived) normative position, we should observe no reduction in pluralistic ignorance over time.

To examine the extent to which students would change their attitudes to reduce pluralistic ignorance, we surveyed a random sample of college sophomores at two time points: Initially, in September, when they had just returned from summer vacation and had had little recent exposure to college drinking norms, and then again in December, after they had spent several months as active members of the college community. We assumed that 8 to 9 weeks between interviews would be sufficient

to observe internalization effects, if such effects existed. In addition, we asked two questions to assess their recent and typical levels of alcohol consumption. Although we expected no gross changes in drinking habits over the course of the semester, we were interested in the relation of drinking behavior to both private attitudes and estimates of the norm. These behavioral questions were included in both interviews.

We tested for internalization effects in two ways. Our first expectation was that students would increasingly adopt the normative position toward alcohol use on campus over the course of the semester. Thus, we predicted that their private attitudes would show a change in the direction of greater comfort over time. Our second expectation was that internalization would result in greater consistency among private attitudes, estimates of the norm, and drinking behavior. Thus, we predicted that the correlations among these variables would increase over time.

Method

Subjects. Fifty 2nd-year undergraduates (25 women and 25 men) participated in this study. We chose 2nd-year students because we assumed that they would be familiar with student culture and, in particular, with norms for drinking but that they would still be new enough at the university to be concerned about fitting in. Subjects were selected at random from the student telephone directory and were each interviewed twice over the telephone.

Procedure. Subjects were contacted for the first interview during the 2nd or 3rd week of the fall term. They were asked to participate in a telephone survey of students' attitudes toward the university's alcohol policies. The interviewer explained that their telephone numbers had been chosen at random from the telephone directory and that their responses would be completely anonymous. Over 90% of the students contacted agreed to participate.

The interview began with several questions about the university's alcohol policies that are irrelevant to the present investigation. The critical questions regarding their own attitudes toward drinking and their estimates of the average student's attitude were as follows:

1. Now, I'd like to know how you feel about drinking at Princeton more generally. How comfort-

able do you feel with the alcohol drinking habits of students here? I'd like you to use a 0-to-10 scale, where 0 means you're not at all comfortable and 10 means you're very comfortable.

2. How comfortable would you say the average Princeton undergraduate feels with the alcohol drinking habits of students here at Princeton, where 0 means not at all comfortable and 10 means very comfortable?

Subjects responded to each question by giving the interviewer a number from 0 to 10. Finally, subjects were asked about their own drinking habits. After reassuring them of their anonymity, the interviewer asked two open-ended questions:

3. How many alcoholic drinks have you had in the last week?

4. How many alcoholic drinks do you have in a typical week during the semester?

Subjects estimated their weekly alcohol intake. At the conclusion of the interview, subjects were informed that we would be calling back later in the term to find out whether people's attitudes had changed over time. The interviewer explained that "When we do [call back], we would like to talk to you again, so if you could let your roommates know that you're the survey person, we'd really appreciate it."

Approximately 8 weeks after the first interview, subjects were recontacted for the second interview. All 50 students again agreed to participate. They were asked the same questions as in the first survey, including the questions about their own comfort with drinking, the average student's comfort with drinking, and their recent and typical alcohol intake.

Results

Attitudes and norms. The social psychological literature contains many compelling demonstrations of the power of social influence to move individual attitudes in the direction of the social norm. We tested the prediction that people will internalize what they perceive to be the social norm by examining changes in subjects' ratings of their own comfort and the average student's comfort with alcohol drinking over the course of the semester. Means and standard deviations for the two comfort questions are shown in Table 12.3. (We added 1 point to each observation to make the scales comparable with those used in Study 1.) Inspection of the means suggests that in the face of relatively stable social norms, men, but not women, did indeed bring their own attitudes into line.

Inferential statistics confirmed this observation. A 2 (sex) × 2 (target) × 2 (time) ANOVA revealed a significant three-way interaction, $F(1, 48) = 3.92$, $p = .05$. Female subjects rated themselves as significantly less comfortable with alcohol drinking than the average Princeton undergraduate across both interviews: for target main effect, $F(1, 24) = 11.94$, $p < .005$; Target × Time interaction, $F < 1$. Male subjects showed a similar self–other difference in the first interview, $F(1, 24) = 8.24$, $p < .01$; by the second interview, the difference was

TABLE 12.3. Ratings of Own and Others' Comfort With Alcohol Drinking in Study 3

Group	September		December	
	Self	Average student	Self	Average student
Women				
M	6.08	7.16	5.94	7.74
SD	2.47	1.55	3.10	1.20
Men				
M	5.84	7.48	7.08	7.58
SD	3.01	1.45	2.70	1.27
Total				
M	5.96	7.32	6.51	7.66
SD	2.75	1.50	2.91	1.24

Note. All ratings were made on 11-point scales (0 = *not at all comfortable* and 10 = *very comfortable*). We added 1 point to each observation to make the scale comparable with the scale used in Studies 1 and 2.

eliminated, $F(1, 24) = 1.69, p > .10$; Target × Time interaction, $F(1, 24) = 3.92, p = .06$. Thus, men behaved in the way social influence theorists would expect: They changed their own attitudes toward drinking in the direction of the social norm. Women, on the other hand, showed no change in attitudes over time.

Correlational analyses provided further evidence of internalization among male, but not among female, subjects. If individuals respond to perceived deviance by bringing their attitudes into line with their perceptions of the norm, we would expect the correlation between attitudes and norms to increase over time. Male subjects showed just such an increase. Correlations between attitudes and norms are presented in the top line of Table 12.4. For men, the correlation between attitudes and norms increased from .34 in the first interview to .76 after 8 weeks. For women, the attitude–norm correlation showed a substantial decrease from .60 in the first interview to –.08 in the second interview.

Again, as in Studies 1 and 2, estimates of the comfort of the average Princeton student with alcohol were much less variable than subjects' own comfort ratings. A statistical comparison of the variances of the two distributions yielded a highly significant difference at both time points, $Fs(49, 49) = 3.36$ and 5.51 for the first and second interviews, respectively, $ps < .0001$.

Drinking behavior. We examined the relation of private attitudes and social norms to drinking behavior as well. Subjects' estimates of the number of drinks they had had in the past week and the number of drinks they had in a typical week correlated highly ($r = .78$ for the first interview and .93 for the second interview) and so we averaged them to form a single index of drinking behavior at each interview. Means and standard deviations for this index are shown in Table 12.5. We expected drinking habits to be reasonably

stable among our sophomore subjects, and indeed an initial ANOVA revealed a significant gender difference in drinking ($M = 2.69$ for women and 6.16 for men), $F(1, 46) = 5.17, p < .05$, but no change in drinking over time ($F < 1$) nor any Sex × Time interaction, $F(1, 46) = 1.61, p > .10$. However, correlational analyses provided some indirect evidence of increased consistency of attitudes, norms, and behavior again among male, but not among female, subjects.

Correlations of behavior with attitudes and norms are shown in the last two lines of Table 4. For female subjects, both sets of correlations remained fairly stable over time. The attitude–behavior correlation was around .5 at both interviews, and the norm–behavior correlation was not significantly different from zero at either time point. For male subjects, both the attitude–behavior and the norm–behavior correlations increased over the course of the semester: The attitude–behavior correlation went from .28 at the first interview to .59 at the second interview, and the norm–behavior correlation went from –.11 at the first interview to .34 at the second interview. Of course, we can draw no causal inferences on the basis of these results. Still, the pattern of correlations for men is quite consistent with the operation of conformity pressures to bring attitudes, norms, and behavior into line.

One final set of analyses lent further support to this conclusion. We performed separate multiple regression analyses for men and women within interviews to test a model of individual attitudes as a joint function of drinking behavior and social norms. The results of these analyses are shown in Table 12.6. For women, their own comfort with drinking was predicted quite well from their drinking habits and their estimates of others' comfort with drinking at the start of the term; that prediction grew substantially worse over time. For men, the opposite was true: Their alcohol drinking habits and their estimates of others' comfort with drink-

Table 12.4. Correlations Among Drinking Behavior, Own Attitudes, and Estimates of Others' Attitudes

Measure	Women		Men	
	September	December	September	December
Own and others' attitudes	.60**	–.08	.34†	.76***
Behavior and own attitudes	.56**	.45*	.28	.59**
Behavior and others' attitudes	.13	–.16	–.11	.34†

† $p < .05$, one-tailed. *$p < .05$, two-tailed. **$p < .01$, two-tailed. ***$p < .001$, two-tailed.

TABLE 12.5. Self-Reported Drinking Behavior

Group	September	December
Women		
M	3.60	1.79
SD	5.28	2.92
Interquartile range	0–5	0–3
Men		
M	5.74	6.44
SD	8.74	7.26
Interquartile range	0–9	1–9

Note. Drinking behavior was measured by averaging subjects' estimates of the number of alcoholic drinks they had in the past week and the number they had in a typical week.

ing provided a relatively poor prediction of their own comfort at the start of the term, but that prediction became much better over time. Again, these results for men are consistent with theorizing about conformity pressures in social groups; the results for women, on the other hand, suggest increasing alienation over the course of the semester.

Discussion

The pattern of results in this study clearly indicates internalization on the part of men and alienation on the part of women. The obvious question raised by these results is why men and women responded to pluralistic ignorance so differently. Because these gender differences were not predicted, we have no ready-made explanation for them. However, one potential explanatory factor is suggested by the finding that male subjects reported an alcohol consumption rate over double that reported by female subjects. One interpretation of this difference is that alcohol consumption is a more central or integral aspect of male social life than of female social life. If so, men might be expected to feel greater pressures to learn to be

TABLE 12.6. Predicting Own Attitudes From Drinking Behavior and Estimates of Others' Attitudes

Group	Adjusted R	Adjusted R²
Women		
September	.75**	.56
December	.36†	.13
Men		
September	.44*	.20
December	.85**	.73

† p < .05, one-tailed. * p < .05, two-tailed. ** p < .001, two-tailed.

comfortable with alcohol. By contrast, women, and particularly women at historically male institutions, may be accustomed to finding themselves at odds with the social norm concerning alcohol. As a result, they may have come to view that norm as less relevant to their behavior than to the behavior of men.

Another possibility is that men are simply more inclined to react to feeling deviant from the norm with conformity, whereas women react to deviance with alienation. Although this suggestion that men conform more readily than women runs contrary to previous theorizing about gender differences in influenceability (see Eagly, 1978), there is some supporting evidence for it in the literature on gender differences in ego defenses. Considerable research suggests that in the face of ego threat, men react with externalizing defenses, such as projection and displacement, whereas women react with internalizing defenses, such as repression and reaction formation (Cramer, 1987; Levit, 1991). In the case of pluralistic ignorance, these differences in ego defenses may translate into a greater tendency of men to internalize the norm: Whereas women turn against themselves for being deviant, men take constructive steps to be less deviant.

One final point deserves consideration. Although men appear to have been able to resolve pluralistic ignorance through internalization, it is important to note that at the beginning of their 2nd year in college, both men and women were experiencing pluralistic ignorance in equal measure. Furthermore, Studies 1 and 2 provided evidence of pluralistic ignorance in a cross-section of the male population, including older as well as younger students. These findings suggest that internalization of the norm may provide only a temporary resolution of the perceived self–other discrepancy in comfort with alcohol; when social pressures are less immediate (e.g., during school breaks) or when those pressures change (e.g., as they do in students' 3rd and 4th years at Princeton), men may experience recurring concerns about students' excessive drinking habits.

General Discussion

In pursuit of an answer to the question of how people respond to perceived differences between themselves and the group, social psychologists have largely ignored the more preliminary questions of how, and with what degree of accuracy, people identify social norms. In most laboratory investigations of social influence, the task of identifying group norms is eliminated by fiat of experimental design. (If the norm is measured at all, it is only done so as a manipulation check.) In real-world social groups, however, the task of identifying the group norm can be highly complex and demanding, so much so that members' estimates of the norm are often seriously in error. The present studies documented significant errors in college students' estimates of social norms relating to comfort with alcohol. Especially interesting was the systematic nature of the errors: Students erred by overestimating their fellow students' support for the status quo. Indeed, they assumed that the average other student was more in favor of the status quo than they themselves were. In short, students were victims of pluralistic ignorance: They believed that the private attitudes of other students were much more consistent with campus norms than were their own.

Norm Misperception: Possible Interpretations

The reported discrepancy between students' own attitudes and those they attribute to their friends and peers may have many sources. The least interesting interpretation, from a psychological standpoint, is that the reported discrepancy is merely that: a reported discrepancy that does not reflect true perceptions. By this impression management account, students may not actually think they are deviant but only portray themselves as such. Their descriptions of themselves as deviating from the status quo could simply constitute strategic attempts to present themselves as nonconformists, as people who are less supportive of their group's norm than the average group member. By presenting themselves in this way, the students might have hoped to convey the impression (if they assumed that the researcher disapproved of the group's norm) that they were more mature, more progressive, or more enlightened than their peers.

An impression management account could be applied to virtually all the studies that have reported erroneous perceptions of one's own attitudinal or behavioral deviance. The form that pluralistic ignorance takes in these studies is almost always the same: Subjects report that they are more sympathetic to the positions or concerns of some out-group than are their peers. For example, whites portray themselves as more sympathetic to blacks than their fellow whites (Fields & Schuman, 1976), teachers portray themselves as more sympathetic to students than their fellow teachers (Packard & Willower, 1972), and prison guards portray themselves as more sympathetic to prisioners than their fellow guards (Kauffman, 1981).

Although it is possible that students in the present studies were motivated to portray themselves as more sympathetic to the position of the university administration than their fellow students, there are a number of reasons to doubt this self-presentational account. First, the anonymous nature of the data collection provided subjects with very little incentive to self-present. Even more problematic for the self-presentational account is the finding in Study 3 that male subjects moderated their perception of their deviance over time by shifting their attitudes toward their estimates of the social norm. If these subjects were attempting to present themselves as being more progressive or enlightened than their peers, it is unlikely that they would have reported their attitudes to be closer to the norm at one time than another. In short, the present findings are much more consistent with the view that the pluralistic ignorance observed in the present studies represented authentic perceptions of deviance and not just ones offered for public consumption.

Another possible interpretation of students' perceived deviance focuses on the representativeness of the public data from which they inferred others' attitudes. These data may have been skewed in the direction of the perceived norm. For example, campus publications may have tended to express more pronorm opinions than antinorm opinions. Similarly, students who strongly supported campus norms may have expressed their attitudes more vociferously than those who only weakly supported them or who disapproved of them. Korte (1972) offered the following general summary of this process:

> The side of an issue representing a cultural (or subcultural) value is more prominent, more frequently and loudly advocated by its adherents. From the point of view of the individual, this source of bias constitutes an unrepresentative sampling of the relevant population. (p. 586)

Through an accurate reading of a biased distribution of publicly expressed opinions, students may have been led to erroneous perceptions of their peers' attitudes. Interestingly, this account implies that pluralistic ignorance could arise without students misrepresenting their true opinions. It suggests that pluralistic ignorance may require a silent majority but not a dissembling one.

We cannot rule out the biased sample hypothesis, but it has difficulty accounting for the data on friends' attitudes in Study 2. There, we found that subjects revealed pluralistic ignorance not just when estimating the attitudes of the average Princeton student but also when estimating the attitudes of their friends. It seems implausible that students would use the public expressions of their vocal friends to infer the private attitudes of their silent friends. Inferences concerning the population of a campus must be estimated from a sample of that population, but inferences concerning the population of one's friends need not depend on sample-to-population generalization.

Two other possible accounts of the pluralistic ignorance observed in these studies focus on students' interpretation and encoding of their own and others' behavior. The first of these accounts, which we call the *differential interpretation hypothesis*, suggests that students display pluralistic ignorance in their reactions to alcohol issues because they (a) present themselves as being more supportive of campus norms than they are and (b) fail to recognize that others are also misrepresenting their true feelings. The first of these points is well documented: Many authorities have noted that group members often display more public support for group norms than they privately feel (Goffman, 1961; Matza, 1964; Schanck, 1932). As Goffman (1961) stated, "when the individual presents himself before others, his performance will tend to incorporate and exemplify the officially accredited values of the society, more so, in fact, than does his behavior as a whole" (p. 35).

Comfort with alcohol and opposition to alcohol restrictions may not be "officially accredited" campus values, but they may serve a similar function. Alcohol on most college campuses, and certainly on the Princeton campus, is not simply a critical feature of social life: It is also an important source of in-group-out-group polarization. Nothing is more central to the power struggle between students and the administration, faculty, and larger community than campus alcohol policy. Thus, even if students do not privately support the student position on alcohol, they may feel compelled to do so publicly out of a sense of group loyalty. Acknowledging that the other side has a point, or is not all bad, can carry a stiff social penalty.

There may be many reasons for students to exaggerate publicly their support for campus alcohol norms, but why do they not assume that their peers' public behavior is similarly inauthentic? One possibility, suggested by Miller and McFarland (1987, 1991), is that people hold a general belief that they are more fearful of appearing deviant than is the average person. Thus, students may be disposed to accept as authentic the public pronorm behaviors of their peers, despite recognizing that their own public pronorm behaviors are inauthentic.

A final explanation for the observed pluralistic ignorance points to potential differences in the way students encode their own and others' behavior. According to this differential encoding account, students may fail to recognize how pronorm their public behavior actually is, mistakenly believing that their private discomfort with alcohol practices is clear from their words and deeds. If students do suffer from an *illusion of transparency* (Miller & McFarland, 1991), they might reasonably assume that because the words and deeds of others signal more comfort than they themselves feel (and supposedly express), they must be alone in their discomfort.

Although both the differential interpretation and differential encoding hypotheses are plausible accounts of pluralistic ignorance in the present context, we have no direct evidence to support or to distinguish between them. It is quite possible that the two operate in parallel, along with other biases, to make pluralistic ignorance an overdetermined phenomenon. Future research could shed light on these accounts by determining whether students do (a) misrepresent their private attitudes in their public pronouncements or (b) generate different interpretations for what they saw as similar public behavior in themselves and others.

Before leaving our analysis of pluralistic ignorance effects, we should comment briefly on the apparent inconsistency between this phenomenon and the well-documented *false consensus effect*:

people's tendency to overstimate their similarity to others (Marks & Miller, 1987; Ross, Greene, & House, 1977). The two phenomena are different but are not incompatible (see Suls, 1986). The norm misperception that arises in cases of pluralistic ignorance is most appropriately operationalized as a mean difference between the actual group norm and the perceived group norm; false consensus, on the other hand, is most appropriately operationalized as a positive correlation between ratings of the self and ratings of others. Theoretically, it is possible for there to be both a positive correlation between people's judgments of self and others and a mean difference in self–other ratings. Indeed, we found precisely this pattern of results in Study 1 (for the self–other correlation, $r = .37$, $p < .001$) and in Study 2 ($r = .27$, $p < .01$). Thus, although students anchored their estimates of the average student's level of comfort on their own (hence the positive correlation), they also perceived there to be a systematic difference between their comfort level and the comfort of others. Nisbett and Kunda (1985) provided numerous other examples in which subjects displayed both false consensus effects and systematic biases in central tendency estimates.

Norm Misperception: Social and Psychological Consequences

What are the consequences of mistakenly assuming that the views of one's peers are different from one's own? Although illusory norms may not have the force of overt social pressure behind them, they still can have powerful social and psychological consequences.

Social consequences. Pluralistic ignorance has traditionally been linked to two consequences: the social construction of emergency situations as nonemergencies and the perpetuation of unsupported social norms. Defined broadly, the pluralistic ignorance found in the present studies may have had both of these consequences. Consider emergency nonintervention first. We obviously did not focus on emergency situations directly in these studies, but it is quite possible that most of our subjects had witnessed situations involving alcohol abuse that they viewed as potentially serious. If so, we can surmise that the pluralistic ignorance dynamic described by Latané and Darley (1970) may have been replicated frequently on the

Princeton campus, resulting in (a) the withholding of assistance to inebriated students about whom all members of groups were concerned and (b) increased confidence on the part of nonacting, but nonetheless concerned, bystanders that they were much less cool about the consequences of excessive drinking than were their friends and fellow bystanders.

The role of pluralistic ignorance in perpetuating unsupported or weakly supported social norms in the present context is also easy to sketch. Alcohol may have continued to play a central role in campus life not because students wanted it that way but because they thought that everyone else wanted it that way. For example, students themselves might often, or even generally, be indifferent to the availability of alcohol at a party, but they may assume that most other students have a strong perference for parties at which alcohol is present. This logic could have many consequences, the most obvious of which is that students, assuming that more people will come to parties that serve alcohol, will seek out parties with alcohol. It also suggests that students hosting parties will assume that they must provide alcohol to satisfy their guests. In short, attempts to institute alcohol-free social activities or institutions may fail to generate support because students mistakenly (and self-fulfillingly) assume they will not be widely supported.

One additional social consequence illustrated by the present findings is that individuals may actually conform to their mistaken estimates of the group norm. Previous research on substance use has shown that people's estimates of the prevalence of drug use among their peers influences their own use, whether these estimates are accurate or inaccurate (Kandel, 1980; Marks, Graham, & Hansen, 1992; Sherman, Presson, Chassin, Corty, & Olshavsky, 1983). Similarly, in Study 3, male subjects modified their private attitudes over time in the direction of the position they mistakenly assumed was held by the average student. In effect, they achieved a level of comfort that few students initially felt simply because they thought that everyone felt that way. This analysis highlights the fact that the norms of a social group may be largely independent of norms of the group members (Turner & Killian, 1972). The desire to be correct and to fit in may lead people to conform, even without social pressure, to what they (mis)perceive to be the norm of the group. In these cases, pluralistic ignorance will be highly ephemeral. If people come to believe what they mistakenly attribute to everyone else, then an originally erroneous perception of the situation will become accurate at the private, as well as the public, level. Misjudgments of others will drive out correct judgments of the self.

Psychological consequences. Our discussion suggests that the social consequences of pluralistic ignorance are significant. However, as the present research indicates, pluralistic ignorance has powerful psychological consequences as well. As documented in our studies, many of the consequences of mistakenly perceiving oneself as deviant are not much different from the consequences of accurately perceiving oneself as deviant. Discomfort, alienation, and an inclination to move in the direction of the majority appear to characterize the phenomenology of illusory deviants as well as real deviants. Indeed, because victims of pluralistic ignorance will typically be involuntary deviants, they may experience the pain of their deviance quite acutely. They may lack the comforting belief that they chose to march to the beat of a different drummer.

Whether victims of pluralistic ignorance do or do not experience their deviance more acutely than voluntary deviants, we have evidence that they manifest real symptoms. For the male subjects in Study 3, for example, the pain of perceiving themselves as deviant may have been a critical factor motivating them to conform to the (illusory) norm of their social group. Moreover, the present findings suggest that people may be much less inclined to conform to majority influence, real or imagined, than is generally assumed by social psychologists. Female subjects in Study 3 retained their (self-perceived) deviant attitudes. These results raise the possibility that conformity may not play as dominant a role in resolving self–group discrepancies as most psychological equilibrium models have posited.

Conclusions

The reported studies illustrate a number of important points about the relation between private attitudes and social norms. Taken together, they indicate that people can often err considerably in situating their attitudes in relation to those of their peers and that these errors have real consequences, both for the individual and for the group. Because little research attention has been given to questions of norm estimation, we know very little about the processes through which individuals identify and represent the norms of their social groups. The present results suggest that further attention to these questions may lead to a better understanding of the ways in which norms can perpetuate social problems, like alcohol use, and can inhibit social change.

The findings of these studies have practical implications as well. In particular, our analysis of the role of pluralistic ignorance in perpetuating dysfunctional social norms has clear implications for programs designed to effect social change. Programs aimed at the individual, such as informational campaigns or individual counseling sessions, may change private attitudes, but they are likely to leave social norms, and in many cases public behavior, untouched. Indeed, our research suggests that recent attempts by universities to raise consciousness about alcohol abuse on campus may have been effective at changing the attitudes of individual students (see also Trice & Beyer, 1977) but not at changing their perceptions of the attitudes of their peers. A more effective way to facilitate social change may be to expose pluralistic ignorance in a group setting and to encourage students to speak openly about their private attitudes within the group. Such an approach would promote social change by demonstrating that it has, in effect, already occurred at the individual level and simply needs to be acknowledged at the social level.

ACKNOWLEDGMENTS

The preparation of this article was facilitated by National Institute of Mental Health Grant MH44069 to Dale T. Miller. We thank Jenifer Lightdale and Carolyn Oates for their assistance with data collection and analysis.

REFERENCES

Allport, F. H. (1924). *Social psychology*. Boston: Houghton Mifflin.

Asch, S. E. (1951). Effects of group pressure upon the modification and distortion of judgments. In H. Guetzkow (Ed.), *Group leadership and men* (pp. 177–190). Pittsburgh, PA: Carnegie Press.

Barringer, F. (1991, June 23). With teens and alcohol, it's just say when. *New York Times*, p. 1.

Berkowitz, A. D., & Perkins, H. W. (1986). Problem drinking among college students: A review of recent research. *Journal of American College Health, 35*, 21–28.

Breed, W., & Ktsanes, T. (1961). Pluralistic ignorance in the process of opinion formation. *Public Opinion Quarterly, 25*, 382–392.

Cialdini, R. B., Kallgren, C. A., & Reno, R. R. (1991). The focus theory of normative conduct: A theoretical refinement and reevaluation of the role of norms in human behavior. In M. P. Zanna (Ed.), *Advances in experimental social psychology* (Vol. 24, pp. 201–234). San Diego, CA: Academic Press.

Clitherow, R. (1991, March). What is to be done? Alcohol abuse at Princeton. *The Princeton Tory, 7*, 8–13.

Cramer, P. (1987). The development of defenses. *Journal of Personality, 51*, 79–94.

Crandall, C. (1988). Social contagion and binge eating. *Journal of Personality and Social Psychology, 55*, 588–598.

Eagly, A (1978). Sex differences in influenceability. *Psychological Bulletin, 85*, 86–116.

Festinger, L., Schachter, S., & Back, K. (1950). *Social pressure in informal groups*. New York: Harper & Row.

Fields, J. M., & Schuman, H. (1976). Public beliefs and the beliefs of the public. *Public Opinion Quarterly, 40*, 427–448.

Goffman, E. (1961). *Asylums: Essays on the social situation of mental patients and other inmates*. Garden City, NJ: Anchor Books.

Graham, J. W., Marks, G., & Hansen, W. B. (1991). Social influence processes affecting adolescent substance use. *Journal of Applied Psychology, 76*, 291–298.

Huba, G. J., & Bentler, P. M. (1980). The role of peer and adult models for drug taking at different stages in adolescence. *Journal of Youth and Adolescence, 9*, 449–465.

Huitema, B. E. (1980). *The analysis of covariance and alternatives*. New York: Wiley.

Kandel, D. B. (1980). Drug and drinking behavior among youth. In A. Inkeles, N. J. Smelser, & R. Turner (Eds.), *Annual review of sociology* (Vol. 6, pp. 235–285). Palo Alto, CA: Annual Reviews.

Kauffman, K. (1981). Prison officer attitudes and perceptions of attitudes. *Journal of Research in Crime Delinquency, 18*, 272–294.

Kelman, H. (1958). Compliance, identification, and internalization: Three processes of attitude change. *Journal of Conflict Resolution, 2*, 51–60.

Korte, C. (1972). Pluralistic ignorance about student radicalism. *Sociometry, 35*, 576–587.

Latané, B., & Darley, J. (1970). *The unresponsive bystander: Why doesn't he help?* New York: Appleton-Century-Crofts.

Levit, D. B. (1991). Gender differences in ego defenses in adolescence: Sex roles as one way to understand the differences. *Journal of Personality and Social Psychology, 61*, 992–999.

Maddox, G. L. (Ed.). (1970). *The domesticated drug: Drinking among collegians*. New Haven, CT: College and University Press.

Marks, G., Graham, J. W., & Hansen, W. B. (1992). Social projection and social conformity in adolescent alcohol use: A longitudinal analysis. *Personality and Social Psychology Bulletin, 18*, 96–101.

Marks, G., & Miller, N. (1987). Ten years of research on the false-consensus effect: An empirical and theoretical review. *Psychological Bulletin, 102*, 72–90.

Matza, D. (1964). *Delinquency and drift*. New York: Wiley.

Miller, D. T., & McFarland, C. (1987). Pluralistic ignorance: When similarity is interpreted as dissimilarity. *Journal of Personality and Social Psychology, 53*, 298–305.

Miller, D. T., & McFarland, C. (1991). When social comparison goes awry: The case of pluralistic ignorance. In J. Suls & T. Wills (Eds.), *Social comparison: Contemporary theory and research* (pp. 287–313). Hillsdale, NJ: Erlbaum.

Moscovici, S. (1985). Social influence and conformity. In G. Lindzey & E. Aronson (Eds.), *The handbook of social psychology* (3rd ed., Vol. 2, pp. 347–412). New York: Random House.

Newcomb, T. M. (1943). *Personality and social change*. New York: Holt, Rinehart & Winston.

Nisbett, R. E., & Kunda, Z. (1985). Perceptions of social distributions. *Journal of Personality and Social Psychology, 48*, 297–311.

Noelle-Neumann, E. (1986). *The spiral of silence*. Chicago: University of Chicago Press.

O'Gorman, H. J. (1975). Pluralistic ignorance and White estimates of White support for racial segregation. *Public Opinion Quarterly, 39*, 313–330.

Packard, J. S., & Willower, D. J. (1972). Pluralistic ignorance and pupil control ideology. *Journal of Education Administration, 10*, 78–87.

Perkins, H. W. (1985). Religious traditions, parents, and peers as determinants of alcohol and drug use among college students. *Review of Religious Research, 27*, 15–31.

Perkins, H. W., & Berkowitz, A. D. (1986). Perceiving the community norms of alcohol use among students: Some research implications for campus alcohol education programming. *International Journal of Addictions, 21*, 961–976.

Ross, L., Greene, D., & House, P. (1977). The "false consensus effect": An egocentric bias in social perception and attributional processes. *Journal of Experimental Social Psychology, 13*, 279–301.

Schanck, R. L. (1932). A study of community and its group institutions conceived of as behavior of individuals. *Psychological Monographs, 43*(2), 1–133.

Sherif, M. (1936). *The psychology of social norms*. New York: Harper.

Sherman, S. J., Presson, C. C., Chassin, L., Corty, E., & Olshavsky, R. (1983). The false consensus effect in estimates of smoking prevalence: Underlying mechanisms. *Personality and Social Psychology Bulletin, 9*, 197–207.

Stein, J. A., Newcomb, M. D., & Bentler, P. M. (1987). An 8-year study of multiple influences on drug use and drug use consequences. *Journal of Personality and Social Psychology, 53*, 1094–1105.

Straus, R., & Bacon, J. M. (1953). *Drinking in college*. New Haven, CT: Yale University Press.

Suls, J. (1986). Notes on the occasion of social comparison theory's thirtieth birthday. *Personality and Social Psychology Bulletin, 12*, 289–296.

Trice, H. M., & Beyer, J. M. (1977). A sociological property of drugs: Acceptance of users of alcohol and other drugs among university undergraduates. *Journal of Studies on Alcohol, 33*, 58–74.

Tukey, J. (1977). *Exploratory data analysis*. Reading, MA: Addison-Wesley.

Turner, J. (1991). *Social influence*. Pacific Grove, CA: Brooks/Cole.

Turner, R., & Killian, L. (1972). *Collective behavior* (2nd ed.). Englewood Cliffs, NJ: Prentice-Hall.

Zucker, R. A., & Noll, R. B. (1982). Precursors and developmental influences on drinking and alcoholism: Etiology from a longitudinal perspective. *Alcohol consumption and related problems* (Alcohol and Health Monograph No. 1, pp. 289–327). Rockville, MD: National Institute on Alcohol Abuse and Alcoholism.

Social Comparison and Affiliation Under Threat: Effects on Recovery From Major Surgery

James A. Kulik • University of California, San Diego

Heike I. M. Mahler • California State University, San Marcos, and University of California, San Diego

Philip J. Moore • University of California, San Francisco

This study extends stress and affiliation research by examining the effects of preoperative roommate assignments on the affiliation patterns, preoperative anxiety, and postoperative recovery of 84 male coronary-bypass patients. Patients were assigned preoperatively to a room alone or to a semiprivate room with a roommate who was either cardiac or noncardiac and either preoperative or postoperative. Patients assigned to a roommate who was postoperative rather than preoperative were less anxious, were more ambulatory postoperatively, and had shorter postoperative stays. Independently, patients were more ambulatory postoperatively and were discharged sooner if assigned to a roommate who was cardiac rather than noncardiac. No-roommate patients generally had the slowest recoveries. Affiliations reflecting cognitive clarity concerns, emotional comparison, and emotional support were examined. Theoretical implications for research involving social comparison and affiliation under threat are considered.

Social psychologists have long been interested in the affiliation tendencies of people who are faced with a novel, threatening situation. The theoretical cornerstone of this stress and affiliation research stems from Festinger's (1954) social comparison theory. Festinger argued that people have a basic need to have accurate appraisals of their opinions and abilities and that lacking an objective standard for a reference, individuals will evaluate their opinions and abilities in comparison with other people. Festinger (1954) proposed further in his "similarity hypothesis" that people prefer particularly to compare themselves with others of relatively similar ability or opinion. Purportedly, similar others provide a more accurate gauge of one's relative standing than do people of very different ability or opinion.

As Taylor, Buunk, and Aspinwall (1990) noted, implicit in Festinger's (1954) original formulation was the potential relevance of social comparison processes for efforts to cope with stressful situations. That is, as a part of coping with a novel, threatening, or challenging situation, individuals are likely to have a need to evaluate the nature of the situation, their resources, and their emotional reactions. It was Schachter (1959), however, who explicitly extended social comparison theory and the similarity hypothesis to the domain of stress and emotion, by proposing that people facing novel threats will experience an increased desire to affiliate with others, particularly with others who are currently facing the same threat, that is, who are presumably of similar emotional status. As Schachter (1959) so deftly put it, "misery doesn't love just any kind of company, it loves only miserable company" (p. 24).

The reasons that individuals under threat might experience an increased desire to affiliate with similarly threatened others have been the subject of considerable theoretical interest. Schachter (1959) considered various possibilities but, in an extension of basic social comparison theory, clearly favored a self-evaluation explanation. According to this view, novel threats evoke uncertainty regarding resultant bodily arousal. This uncertainty purportedly motivates us to affiliate specifically with similarly threatened others, because such individuals are thought to provide the best gauge for evaluating the intensity, nature, or appropriateness of our emotional state. Thus Schachter (1959) proposed an "emotional similarity hypothesis," wherein needs for emotional self-evaluation are induced by a novel threat and are met through social comparison or, more specifically, through emotional comparison with similarly threatened others.

Schachter (1959) also considered briefly the possibility that affiliation with similar others under threat may be motivated additionally by a desire for emotional support and reassurance for purposes of anxiety reduction, but this possibility received relatively little empirical study until recently (Helgeson & Mickelson, 1995). Finally, Schachter (1959) considered the possibility that a desire to increase "cognitive clarity" for the impending threat, that is, to reduce uncertainty regarding the nature and dangerousness of the situation, might motivate affiliation with similarly threatened others. In doing so, he acknowledged that emotional comparison can be viewed as a special case of cognitive clarity efforts (i.e., part of reducing uncertainty about a novel threat situa-

tion may involve reducing uncertainty about how one should respond emotionally).

This line of stress and affiliation work more recently has been both challenged and expanded considerably in several respects. First, as Kulik and Mahler (1990) noted, eliciting an affiliate-choice preference while experimentally removing any chance for one's desire for cognitive clarity to operate does not rule out the possibility that a desire for cognitive clarity is normally a significant motivator of affiliation under threat (cf. Kirkpatrick & Shaver, 1988). Thus, what the Zimbardo and Formica (1963) results actually suggest is that when the motivation for cognitive clarity is presumably blocked, affiliation choices in the face of threat may be determined by desires for emotional comparison. This clearly is not the same as saying affiliation choices under threat are motivated principally or generally by desires for emotional comparison, particularly when one considers how infrequently threat-relevant affiliation is likely prohibited in real-world contexts.

The role that one's desire for cognitive clarity plays in motivating affiliation in the face of threat is also interesting to consider in the light of recent theoretical expansions of basic social comparison theory. It is now generally believed, for example, that people engage in social comparison processes for several reasons, including self-evaluation (Festinger, 1954); self-enhancement, that is, striving to feel better about themselves (e.g., Hakmiller, 1966; Thornton & Arrowood, 1966; Wills, 1981); and self-improvement (cf. Brickman & Bulman, 1977; Festinger, 1954; Wood, 1989; Wood & Taylor, 1991; see also Helgeson & Mickelson, 1995, for additional possible motivations). In an important refinement, Taylor and Lobel (1989) proposed that although threat may lead people in general to prefer to compare themselves cognitively to others worse off for purposes of self-enhancement (cf. Wills, 1981), threat also may lead people to seek upward comparison information and affiliation (i.e., information or contact with others who are better off) for purposes of self-improvement, that is, in order to gain information that will enable them to improve their situation (cf. Helgeson & Taylor, 1993; Molleman, Pruyn, & van Knippenberg, 1986). Social comparison for self-improvement can be viewed as a close cousin, if not a direct descendant, of the original concept of cognitive clarity in that what is at issue fundamentally is the seeking of threat-relevant information.

The vast majority of stress and affiliation work has relied on the affiliate choice paradigm, that is, on respondents' stated desires for waiting in the presence of others, or on summary statements indicating with whom one generally affiliates (see review by Buunk, 1994). Still relatively lacking are examinations of how people under threat actually interact with others when face to face and, more specifically, the extent to which emotional comparison, emotional support, or cognitive clarity concerns are indicated in such interactions. Stated preferences for affiliation under threat provide at best only part of the stress-affiliation picture, because much as attitudes and behavior toward an object are often divergent (Ajzen & Fishbein, 1977), the correspondence between a stated desire to be in the presence of another person (which is essentially an attitude) may not necesarily predict actual affiliation levels (behavior) once with that person. Thus, regardless of the factors that may lead a threatened individual to desire initially to be in the presence of another person, a separate issue concerns the patterns and causes of affiliations that occur once the threatened individual is in the presence of others.

The first major goal of the present study was to expand on this more naturalistic line of work by considering in more detail the affiliations that patients facing imminent threat of (coronary-bypass) surgery have with their roommates. It seems likely that someone who faces such a severe threat will have various needs, including information about the specific experiences to expect, assurances that the procedure is survivable and tolerable, and perhaps assurances that their feelings and actions are appropriate. Thus, we were interested particularly in the extent to which, as a function of the similarity of the roommate's surgical problem and operative status, patients would report affiliations that involved emotional comparison, emotional support, or efforts to obtain cognitive clarity for the (surgery) threat. Given the absence of previous relevant work, our hypotheses were necessarily somewhat tentative. First, because a roommate who has already been through the same surgery may be perceived as affording the greatest opportunity for obtaining cognitive clarity for the threat (Kulik & Mahler, 1989), we expected that cogni-

tive clarity affiliations would be greatest for patients paired with postoperative cardiac roommates. This could occur as an additive function, or as an interactive function of the roommate's characteristics. That is, all else being equal, we might expect that for the coronary-bypass patient, a roommate who is likewise cardiac rather than noncardiac and, separately, who is postoperative rather than preoperative is more apt to have information about likely postoperative sensations and about what one needs to do after major surgery (e.g., walk, perform deep-breathing exercises). If so, and if such differential affordances lead to differential amounts of cognitive clarity affiliation in an additive fashion, the upshot would be the greatest cognitive clarity affiliation with a roommate who was both cardiac and postoperative. An alternative (not mutually exclusive possibility) is that such a roommate is perceived as disproportionately (or perhaps uniquely) valuable from a cognitive clarity standpoint and, therefore, prompts disproportionately high levels of cognitive clarity affiliation, that is, an interaction effect.

With respect to more emotion-focused affiliations, Schachter's (1959) previously described emotional similarity hypothesis seems to predict that patients might demonstrate the greatest evidence of emotional comparison before surgery with a roommate who is currently facing the same threat, that is, is similarly preoperative and cardiac. The hypothesis that threatened individuals also may prefer the company of others faced with the same threat in order to receive emotional support and reassurance (Schachter, 1959) suggests the possibility that supportive affiliations also might be greatest for patients assigned to a fellow preoperative cardiac roommate. The lack of relevant prior work in a face-to-face, acute threat situation rendered this our most speculative hypothesis, however.

In addition to examining the foregoing aspects of patients' affiliations in the face of imminent threat, our second major goal was to explore whether there is any evidence that such affiliations actually mediate hospital recovery. Relevant to this issue are the results of a small, preliminary study in which coronary-bypass patients were found to experience less anxiety before surgery, to walk more after surgery, and to have shorter lengths of stay after surgery if assigned preoperatively to a roommate who was postoperative rather than pre-operative (Kulik & Mahler, 1987). Although provocative, that preliminary study had several important limitations. First, the small sample size ($N = 27$) rendered the results tentative and in need of replication. Second, the study did not include a no-roommate condition, making it unclear whether exposure to a roommate who was postoperative was beneficial or whether exposure to a fellow preoperative roommate was harmful in an absolute sense. Finally, and most important for the present study, the earlier study included no assessment of affiliation. It was therefore unclear exactly how affiliation might have been involved, if at all.

How might affiliation before surgery with a hospital roommate influence hospital recovery? A sizable literature suggests that provision by hospital staff of information about the sensations and procedures to expect after surgery can sometimes reduce patients' preoperative anxiety and postoperative lengths of stay (see Devine, 1992; Mumford, Schlesinger, & Glass, 1982; Suls & Wan, 1989, for relevant reviews). Such information may enable patients to interpret postoperative events as more normal and less threatening and to spend less energy worrying and more on performing activities that benefit recovery (for more extensive discussions of these issues, see Johnson, 1984; Johnson, Christman, & Stitt, 1985; Leventhal & Johnson, 1983). An interesting possibility, then, is that affiliation with certain types of hospital roommates before surgery can serve as an adjunct to professional information preparations. Patients who, through affiliation with their roommate, feel they are better informed about what to expect and do after surgery ultimately may have better hospital recoveries. An additional major goal of this study, then, was to explore this mediational hypothesis.

To examine the foregoing issues, we assigned patients who were scheduled for coronary-bypass surgery to a room alone or to a roommate who was either similar or dissimilar in type of operation (cardiac vs. noncardiac) and either similar or dissimilar in operative status (preoperative vs. postoperative). With the assistance of the nursing staff, who were kept unaware of the hypotheses, study patients were assigned strictly on the basis of bed availability. Logistical constraints precluded implementation of a pure random assignment procedure, but supporting data (described later) suggest that the procedure we used was in fact effectively random. Patient affiliations with their roommate that were relevant to cognitive clarity, emotional comparison, and emotional support were assessed in addition to preoperative anxiety levels and postoperative recovery rates.

Method

Participants

Participants were men who underwent first-time, nonemergency coronary-bypass surgery at the San Diego Veterans Affairs Medical Center. Patients who had serious, concomitant medical problems (e.g., valve disease, cancer) were not eligible to participate. A total of 94 patients who met the inclusion criteria were asked to participate; of these, 91 (97%) agreed. Seven patients who had serious perioperative complications (e.g., death, stroke, bleeding requiring reopening) were not included in the analyses. The final sample was 81% white, 8% black, 7% Hispanic, and 4% Asian. Classifying occupational backgrounds of the sample according to a modification of Warner (1960), we found that 17% were professional or self-employed workers, 16% were managers, 20% were sales or clerical workers, 24% were skilled laborers, and 23% were semiskilled or unskilled laborers. Fifty-seven percent were married, 37% were divorced or separated, and 6% had never married. Age ranged from 41 to 70 years ($M = 58.3$, $SD = 7.3$), and education ranged from 8 to 24 years ($M = 12.8$, $SD = 3.0$).

Procedure

Most patients were recruited to the study by telephone shortly before hospital admission, but when this was not possible, patients were recruited shortly after admission. The study was described as concerned with determining the factors that may be important for recovery from surgery for the potential benefit of future patients. The same surgical team and nursing staff cared for all study patients. Patients who agreed to participate were asked the night before surgery to complete a brief questionnaire containing items relevant to their current anxiety level and, unless assigned a room alone, to their interactions with their roommate (described later). Questionnaires were completed in a private room with P. Moore, who was kept unaware of experimental conditions.

Several of the major indexes of preoperative cardiac functioning (ejection fraction, left ventricular end-diastolic pressure, number and severity of wall motion abnormalities) were coded directly from patients' cardiac catheterization reports (Braunwald, 1980). Diabetes, hypertension, and smoking histories, as well as patient age and number of bypass grafts performed, also were coded from patients' medical charts to monitor randomization and potentially to serve as covariates. Preliminary analyses revealed that the preoperative physical indexes were generally nonpredictive of the outcome measures, with the exception that a positive history of diabetes was associated with a longer postoperative length of stay, $r(82) = .30$, $p < .01$. Diabetes history, however, was not significantly related to experimental condition ($Fs < 1.38$).

Experimental Conditions

Seventy-four of the study patients were assigned preoperatively to a male roommate who was either similar (preoperative) or dissimilar (postoperative) in *operative status* and who was either similar (cardiac) or dissimilar (noncardiac) in *operation type*. (Noncardiac roommates were heterogeneous but involved primarily pulmonary, abdominal, and general surgery patients.) An additional 10 patients (no-roommate condition) were assigned to the same hospital rooms, but without any roommate, to enable secondary comparisons. All study patients received the same routine preoperative preparation from the hospital staff.

Separate Roommate Operative Status (preoperative vs. postoperative) × Roommate Operation Type (cardiac vs. noncardiac) analyses of variance (ANOVAs), which were performed on each of the preoperative physical status measures, revealed only one significant effect: Patients assigned a roommate who was preoperative had somewhat higher (better) ejection fraction values than those assigned a roommate who was postoperative ($Ms = 58.81$ vs. 56.47), $F(1, 68) = 3.90$, $p = .052$). However, in that ejection fraction was unrelated to the outcome measures ($ps > .40$), this

difference cannot account for any of the results that follow. More generally, these analyses suggest that patients were effectively randomized to conditions. Means and standard deviations for the indexes of preoperative physical status are presented in Table 13.1.

Dependent Measures

Preoperative anxiety. Considerable research indicates that people differ in how they express anxiety and that intercorrelations between different measures as a result tend not to be high (e.g., Lang, Melamed, & Hart, 1970; Martin & Stroufe, 1970). Because a single indicator of anxiety therefore could be misleading (Lacey, 1967), we felt it important to use multiple measures of preoperative anxiety, consisting of self-reports, nurse observations, and medication usage, respectively (cf. Melamed & Siegel, 1980).

Self-reported anxiety was obtained from a preoperative questionnaire administered the evening before surgery. Patients completed a short (10-item) form of the State version of the State-Trait Anxiety Inventory (STAI; Spielberger, Gorsuch, & Lushene, 1970). Such short forms of the STAI have been shown elsewhere to provide valid measures of state anxiety (O'Neil, Spielberger, &

TABLE 13.1. Preoperative Physical Status Indexes of Sample

Variable	M	SD
Ejection fraction	57.28	13.89
LVEDP	17.59	8.64
Abnormal wall motion areas	1.87	1.53
Severity of wall abnormalities	1.24	0.89
Number of prior MIs	1.05	1.07
Number of grafts	3.73	1.03
Diabetes	0.33	0.47
Hypertension	0.70	0.46
Current smoker	0.33	0.47

Note. N = 84. Ejection fraction is a widely accepted measure of left ventricular function that indicates the percentage of blood in the left ventricle that is ejected per beat (normal = 67% ± 9%), effectively, how well the heart is working as a pump (Cheitlin, Sokolow, & McIlroy, 1993). LVEDP (left ventricular end-diastolic pressure) measures ventricular filling pressure (normal 4–12 mm Hg) and, in combination with consideration of wall motion abnormalities, can index the contractility of the heart. Wall motion abnormalities in the left ventricle can be present in 0–5 regions, each to varying degrees of severity (0 = none, 1 = hypokinetic, 2 = akinetic, 3 = dyskinetic; Braunwald, 1980). MIs = myocardial infarctions. For diabetes, hypertension, and current smoker, 0 = no and 1 = yes.

Hansen, 1969). Nurse observations of preoperative anxiety (present or absent) were coded directly from the patient charts. Statements coded as indicating anxiety were generally very straightforward (e.g., "Patient appears very anxious about his surgery"). We also coded directly from the chart the number of anxiolytic and sedative medications (e.g., Valium, Ativan, Dalmane) that patients requested the night before surgery.

Patient affiliation. The actual recording of conversations between patients would presumably provide the most accurate record of interactions, but for ethical reasons this was not an option. We also had to contend with the severity of the situation faced by patients, limitations on patient access necessitated by hospital routines, and the fact that no existing affiliation instrument was suitable for our goals. It therefore was necessary to assess exposure and to develop a brief self-report patient interaction questionnaire (PIQ), designed to assess affiliations relevant to cognitive clarity or information seeking, emotional comparison, and emotional support, respectively. Accordingly, to assess exposure, patients were asked to estimate the number of hours they had spent in the room with their roommate and the total number of minutes they had spent talking to their roommate. Relevant to cognitive clarity, patients were asked to indicate on separate 4-point scales that ranged from *not at all* (1) to *very much so* (4) the extent to which they had (a) discussed with their roommate how it would feel after surgery, (b) discussed ways to make recovery easier, (c) learned things by watching their roommate that would be helpful for their own recovery, (d) learned things by talking to their roommate that would be helpful for their own recovery, and (e) felt they had "a better idea of what to expect after surgery" because of their roommate. In an effort to assess emotional comparison activity, we also asked patients to indicate the extent to which they (a) had mentioned to their roommate how they felt emotionally about their operation (e.g., how calm or nervous), (b) had thought about how nervous their roommate seemed compared with themselves, and (c) had been told by their roommate how he felt emotionally about his operation (e.g., how calm or nervous). Finally, to assess emotional support affiliations, we asked patients to indicate the extent to which (a) their roommate had said things to them in an effort to make them feel better about their operation (e.g.,

"things will be all right"), (b) they had said things to their roommate in an effort to make him feel better about his operation, and (c) they liked joking with their roommate about their operations. The foregoing PIQ items were presented in a random order to patients assigned roommates.

With respect to the exposure judgments, which are relatively objective in nature, previous work with similar populations has shown reasonable interpatient agreement ($rs = .75–.87$; Kulik et al., 1993). Most of the PIQ items, however, involve patients' interpretations of their roommate affiliations and therefore could not be objectively verified (e.g., "have a better idea of what to expect after surgery because of roommate"; "learned useful things by watching roommate"; "learned useful things by talking to roommate"; "said things to make roommate feel better or roommate said things to make patient feel better"). We were able, however, to get some idea of the construct and discriminative validity of the a priori subscales by performing a principal-components factor analysis with varimax rotation on the PIQ items. The results indicated that a two-factor solution accounted for 62% of the variance. The first factor alone, which corresponded directly to our intended cognitive clarity subscale, accounted for 48.6% of the variance (eigenvalue = 5.34). The second factor, which essentially merged the items intended to measure emotional support and emotional comparison, respectively, accounted for an additional 13.4% of variance (eigenvalue = 1.47). There was a modest correlation between these two factors (.34). The only PIQ item that did not load on either of these factors was the question related to joking about the operation. It therefore was dropped from further consideration. For purposes of data reduction, the five cognitive clarity items indicated above were averaged to form a single index of cognitive clarity or information-seeking affiliation ($\alpha = .91$). Likewise, the items intended to measure emotional support and emotional comparison were combined (absent the joking item) to form a five-item, overall index of emotion-focused affiliation ($\alpha = .74$).

Postoperative ambulation. Postoperative ambulation is routinely encouraged in surgery patients to prevent various complications (e.g., atelectisis, phiebitis). We therefore sought to measure this important recovery behavior in two ways. First, patients were asked around dinner time on Postoperative Days 3–5 to recall where, if any-

TABLE 13.2. Patient Affiliation as a Function of Operation Type and Operative Status of Roommate

Affiliation index	Roommate's operation type		Roommate's operative status	
	Cardiac	Noncardiac	Preoperative	Postoperative
Cognitive clarity	2.40 (0.17)	1.55 (0.13)***	1.73 (0.17)	2.22* (0.15)
Emotion focused	2.24 (0.13)	1.77 (0.12)**	1.96 (0.18)	2.05 (0.11)

Note. Values are means, with standard errors of mean in parentheses (S-). ns = 36, 37, 24, and 49 for the cardiac, noncardiac, preoperative, and postoperative conditions, respectively.
*p < .05. **p < .01. ***p < .001.

where, they had walked that day (e.g., four trips to the bathroom and two round trips to the television room). The total distance walked for each day was calculated subsequently by referring to a floor plan of the hospital.

In addition to these self-reports of ambulation, patients were asked to wear an Integrated Motor Activity Monitor, a lightweight 1-square-in. (2.5-square-cm) device that counts movements by means of a miniature mercury switch that is sensitive to 10° of tilt off horizontal.[1] Several studies have indicated that this device provides an objective, highly reliable, and valid measure of physical activity (e.g., Foster, McPartland, & Kupfer, 1978; LaPorte, Kuller, McPartland, Matthews, & Casperson, 1979). Each recording day, the activity monitor was attached over the surgical stocking, laterally on the ankle of the nonoperated leg of the patient. The activity monitor was worn from approximately 9:30 a.m. until 6:30 p.m. each recording day ($M = 8.71$ hr, $SD = 0.93$ hr). Patients were told simply that the device measured "muscle activity," that they should not get it wet, and that they otherwise should just do what they normally would do.

Speed of recovery. The number of hours between the end of the operation and the patient's release to the general ward from the surgical intensive care unit (SICU), converted to days, provided an indicator of initial recovery rate. The total number of postoperative hours until hospital release, converted to days, provided a second, overall measure of postoperative length of stay. This information was coded directly from patient charts.

---

[1] Because the activity monitors were introduced to the protocol after data collection had begun, data are available on this measure only for a subset ($n = 56$) of the sample. This subset, however, was essentially random across conditions.

Results

Primary Analyses

Patient affiliation. To first assess opportunity for affiliation, we subjected the amount of time patients were actually in the room with their roommate to a Roommate Operative Status (preoperative vs. postoperative) × Roommate Operation Type (cardiac vs. noncardiac) ANOVA. The results revealed that opportunity did not differ by condition (all Fs < 1) and that patients generally had a reasonable opportunity to affiliate with their roommates before they participated in the study (sample $M = 12.91$ hr, $SD = 14.34$). A similar ANOVA that was performed on patients' estimates of the total number of minutes they had spent talking to their roommate indicated that on average, patients spent over 3 hr talking (sample $M = 192.23$ min, $SD = 353.92$), and that these estimates did not differ significantly by condition.

Turning then to the specifics of patient affiliations, we performed separate Roommate Operative Status (preoperative vs. postoperative) × Roommate Operation Type (cardiac vs. noncardiac) ANOVAs on the cognitive clarity and emotion-focused affiliation indexes, respectively. (The data of 1 patient who did not complete any of the affiliation questions were necessarily deleted from all affiliation analyses.) As shown in Table 13.2, the results indicated first that patients engaged in significantly more cognitive clarity affiliation if their roommate was cardiac rather than noncardiac, $F(1, 69) = 14.04$, $p < .001$. Independent of this effect, patients also engaged in significantly more cognitive clarity affiliation if their roommate was postoperative rather than preoperative, $F(1, 69) = 4.64$, $p < .04$ (see Table 13.2). Finally, there was some tendency for cognitive clarity affiliation to be especially high when patients had a roommate who was postoperative and cardiac ($M = 2.84$)

relative to the other conditions ($Ms = 1.50$ to 1.97), but the overall interaction effect did not reach significance ($p < .10$).

Table 13.2 also indicates the results of parallel analyses of the emotion-focused affiliation index. Here we found that patients were more likely to engage in affiliation that explicitly involved emotions when a roommate was likewise cardiac rather than noncardiac, $F(1, 69) = 6.99, p < .01$. No other effect of this analysis was significant ($ps > .25$).

Preoperative anxiety. An initial Roommate Operative Status (preoperative vs. postoperative) × Roommate Operation Type (cardiac vs. noncardiac) multivariate analysis of variance (MANOVA) also was performed on the indexes of preoperative anxiety. The results revealed a significant effect of operative status, $F(3, 66) = 8.26, p < .001$, so that patients generally exhibited less anxiety before surgery if assigned a roommate who was postoperative rather than preoperative. Subsequently performed 2 (roommate operative status) × 2 (roommate operation type) ANOVAs indicated that this difference was significant with respect to the number of anxiety or sedative medications requested by patients, $F(1, 70) = 6.38, p < .02$, and the number of nurse notes of preoperative anxiety, $F(1, 70) = 18.14, p < .001$, respectively, but was not significant for self-reported anxiety ($F < 1$; see Table 13.3). Additional comparisons performed with Student's t tests indicated that anxiety, measured by medications requested and nurse notes of anxiety, for patients assigned to the no-roommate condition was intermediate between that of patients assigned postoperative roommates and patients assigned postoperative roommates, respectively, but did not differ significantly from either.

Postoperative ambulation. A Roommate Operative Status (preoperative vs. postoperative) ×

Roommate Operation Type (cardiac vs. noncardiac) ANOVA that was performed on postoperative ambulation levels also revealed significant differences as a function of preoperative roommate assignment. Activity monitor readings, averaged across Postoperative Days 3–5, were greater for patients who had been assigned preoperatively to a cardiac rather than noncardiac roommate, $F(1, 44) = 5.62, p < .03$. Independent of this effect, activity monitor readings also were greater for patients who had been assigned to a roommate who was postoperative rather than preoperative, $F(1, 44) = 6.25, p < .02$. Patients assigned to the no-roommate condition generally had activity monitor readings that were intermediate and not significantly different (see Table 13.4). Self-reported daily ambulation, averaged across Postoperative Days 3–5, also was greater for patients who had been assigned preoperatively to a roommate who was cardiac rather than noncardiac, $F(1, 69) = 7.12, p < .01$. Self-reported ambulation of patients who had been assigned a cardiac roommate was also higher than for patients who had no roommate preoperatively ($p < .01$, Student's t test). No other effects involving ambulation were significant.

Speed of recovery. A 2 (roommate operative status) × 2 (roommate operation type) ANOVA that was performed on SICU time indicated that patients tended to have shorter SICU stays if they had been assigned preoperatively to roommates who were postoperative rather than preoperative or cardiac rather than noncardiac, respectively, but that these differences did not reach significance ($ps = .12$).

A 2 (roommate operative status) × 2 (roommate operation type) ANOVA performed on the total postoperative length of stay, however, did reveal several significant effects. Specifically, we found

---

TABLE 13.3. Means for Preoperative Anxiety as a Function of Roommate's Operative Status

	Roommate		
Anxiety measure	Preoperative	Postoperative	No
Nurse notes	0.63 (0.10)	0.20 (0.06)	0.44 (0.17)
Medications[a]	0.88 (0.18)	0.35 (0.07)	0.40 (0.13)
STAI—State version (self-report)[b]	21.72 (1.25)	22.22 (0.92)	23.90 (1.98)

Note. Standard errors of the mean are presented in parentheses. *ns* = 24, 49, and 10 for preoperative, postoperative, and no-roommate conditions, respectively. STAI = State–Trait Anxiety Inventory.
[a]Number of anxiolytics and sedatives requested by patients the night before surgery.
[b]Values on the 10-item STAI—State version (self-report) can range from 10 to 40.

significant effects both of roommate operative status $F(1, 70) = 5.09$, $p < .03$, and roommate operation type, $F(1, 70) = 4.07$, $p < .05$. As can be seen in Table 13.4, a patient, on average, was able to leave the hospital 1.3 days sooner if assigned before surgery to a roommate who was postoperative rather than preoperative. Independent of this effect, a patient who had been assigned before surgery to a cardiac roommate averaged a postoperative length of stay that was approximately 1.1 days shorter than that of a patient who had been assigned a noncardiac roommate. These effects were additive in that there was no Operative Status × Operation Type interaction ($F < 1$). It is interesting that additional comparisons performed by Student's t tests indicated that the postoperative stays of patients assigned to a roommate who was cardiac ($p < .03$) or who was postoperative ($p < .03$) were also significantly shorter than those of patients who had no roommate before surgery. Patients assigned no roommate also averaged longer postoperative stays than did patients who had been assigned to roommates who were noncardiac or preoperative, respectively, but these differences were not significant (see Table 13.4).

Mediational Analyses

The effects of roommate conditions on postoperative length of stay are clearly of greatest interest from a practical standpoint. Therefore, in an effort to better understand the nature of these effects, we conducted a final series of analyses to determine whether there was any evidence that patients assigned a postoperative or a cardiac roommate had relatively short postoperative stays because of their differential roommate affiliations—that is, whether patients' affiliations might have served directly as mediators. According to Baron and Kenny (1986), a variable is considered to function as a mediator to the extent that it accounts for the relationship between a given independent and dependent variable. Further, they argue that mediation is best tested by means of a set of three regression equations in which the proposed mediator (affiliation) is first regressed on the independent variables (roommate operation type and operative status conditions); the second equation involves regressing the dependent variable (length of stay) on the independent variables; and the key third equation involves regressing the dependent variable simultaneously on both the independent and mediator variables. Mediation is suggested when all of the following occur: The independent variable significantly affects the mediator in the first equation, the independent variable significantly predicts the dependent variable in the second equation, and the mediator significantly predicts the dependent variable while reducing to nonsignificance the previously significant relationship between the independent and dependent variables.

We first examined the hypothesis that the roommate effects on postoperative length of stay were mediated by cognitive clarity affiliations. To do this, we first regressed the index of cognitive clarity affiliation on roommate operation type and roommate operative status, which were entered simultaneously after being dummy coded ($0 = cardiac$, $1 = noncardiac$; $0 = preoperative$, $1 = postoperative$). Given the previous ANOVA results

TABLE 13.4. Effects of Roommate Condition on Postoperative Ambulation and Length of Stay

| Measure | Roommate's operation type | | Roommate's operative status | | No roommate |
	Cardiac	Noncardiac	Preoperative	Postoperative	
Ambulation self-report (yards)					
M	269.90 (40.51)	124.46 (25.82)	140.73 (25.10)	223.84 (30.70)	126.17 (25.92)
N	36	37	23	50	8
Ambulation activity monitor					
M	96.19 (12.27)	48.47 (10.84)	47.17 (9.28)	97.49 (10.95)	86.12 (27.87)
N	26	22	15	33	7
Postoperative length of stay (days)					
M	8.04 (0.34)	9.17 (0.36)	9.24 (0.49)	7.97 (0.30)	9.96 (0.98)
N	37	37	24	50	10

Note. Standard errors of the mean are presented in parentheses.

(presented in Table 13.2), the results of this first regression analysis not surprisingly again indicated that both the roommate's operation type (β coefficient = $-.50$, SE_b = $.19$, $p < .0001$) and operative status (β coefficient = $.22$, SE_b = $.20$, $p = .04$) were significantly related to cognitive clarity affiliation. When postoperative length of stay was regressed simultaneously on roommate operation type and roommate operative status, the results likewise paralleled previous ANOVA results (presented in Table 13.4) by revealing significant effects of both roommate's operation type (β coefficient = $-.26$, SE_b = $.52$, $p < .03$) and operative status (β coefficient = $-.27$, SE_b = $.56$, $p < .03$). The critical test, then, was the third regression, in which postoperative length of stay was regressed simultaneously on both cognitive clarity affiliation and the experimental conditions. The results revealed first that the more cognitive clarity affiliation patients engaged in with their roommate before surgery, the shorter was their postoperative length of stay (β coefficient = $-.26$, SE_b = $.32$, $p = .04$). Moreover, the effect of affiliation substantially reduced the effect of the roommate's operation type (β coefficient = 0.13, SE_b = $.58$, $p > .30$) and, to a lesser extent, the effect of the roommate's operative status (β coefficient = $-.21$, SE_b = $.56$, $p > .08$). This overall pattern is consistent with the notion that the benefits for postoperative length of stay of having a roommate before surgery who was cardiac rather than noncardiac and postoperative rather than preoperative, respectively, were due at least in part to the relatively greater informational value of such roommates.

Discussion

Patient Affiliations

We found that faced with the imminent threat of major (coronary-bypass) surgery, patients engaged in more cognitive clarity affiliation with a roommate who had a similar rather than dissimilar surgical problem and, independently, with a roommate who was postoperative rather than preoperative. Affiliations concerned more directly with emotions, that is, emotional support and emotional comparison, also were greater when patients had a roommate who had a similar rather than dissimilar surgical problem.

In contrast, we found no evidence that the total amount of time patients spent talking to their roommates differed as a function of roommate condition. This null result appears at odds with a previous study, which found that patients reported spending more total time talking to a roommate who was preoperative rather than postoperative (Kulik et al., 1993). There are several possible explanations for the divergence. First, the studies involved very different surgical populations. Another possibility is that there was more noise in the measurement of the total time spent talking in the current study, and therefore, actual differences were masked. This might have occurred as a result of much longer average exposure times in the current study (almost 13 hr) compared with the earlier study (about 2.5 hr). Third, and a bit more subtle, there may have been important differences in the opportunity for affiliation in the respective studies. That is, Kulik et al. (1993) proposed that patients might have talked less overall with postoperative than preoperative roommates in that postoperative roommates were more apt to be temporarily noncommunicative because of their physical condition (e.g., pain, nausea, sleeping). Within a brief exposure time, any such obstacles could have a substantial effect on the total affiliation that occurred. With the longer exposure time available in the present study, however, there would presumably be a greater likelihood of some period during which the postoperative roommate was reasonably receptive. Given that patients do not spend the majority of their time together actually talking anyway, a few such opportunities may be sufficient to yield similar total verbal affiliation levels. At present, we favor this last interpretation, particularly given that a recent laboratory analogue study, which also used a very different population (college students) and minimized measurement error by recording verbal affiliations verbatim, produced results similar to those of the present study, namely, differences by condition for threat-related affiliation but not for total affiliation (Kulik et al., 1994). Clearly, however, these speculations must await further tests.

Health-Related Outcomes

The present study also found several interesting results relevant to health outcomes. Patients assigned preoperatively to a roommate who was postoperative rather than preoperative were on average less anxious before surgery, walked more after surgery, and, most important, had shorter postoperative stays. Independently of these effects, we also found that patients assigned to a roommate with a similar (cardiac) rather than dissimilar (noncardiac) surgical problem walked more after surgery and had shorter postoperative stays. Whereas the foregoing effects of the roommate's operative status replicate results of an initial pilot study (Kulik & Mahler, 1987), the independent effects of the similarity of the roommate's type of operation had not been found previously. We believe the explanation lies in the fact that the pilot study involved a substantially smaller sample size and therefore had less statistical power. In any event, these separate effects on postoperative stays were additive. As a result, the average length of stay for patients assigned to the "best" combination—that is, a roommate who was cardiac and postoperative—was approximately 25% shorter (7.27 vs. 9.68 days) than that of patients assigned to the "worst" combination—that is, a preoperative, noncardiac roommate.

The current results appear unlikely to be attributable to preexisting differences between experimental conditions prior to surgery. The lack of significant differences by condition across a broad array of demographic and preoperative physical status variables suggests that patients were effectively randomized. The results also appear not to be attributable to any confounding effect of roommate assignments made after surgery. Postoperative assignments were unrelated to preoperative roommate assignments and could not have caused the preoperative anxiety differences.

An interesting question is whether preoperative assignment to a roommate with a similar surgical problem was helpful, or whether a dissimilar roommate was harmful, in an absolute sense. The same question of relativity applies to the observed effects of assigning patients to a roommate who was postoperative as opposed to preoperative (independent of surgical problem). The auxiliary comparisons with the group of patients that was assigned no roommate are especially relevant to this issue. Interpretations here must be made with caution inasmuch as the no-roommate group was quite small because of logistical constraints (bed availability in the study hospital rarely allows a room alone). With this caveat in mind, however, we note that the no-roommate group generally did not differ reliably from the other conditions in terms of preoperative anxiety. No-roommate patients did, however, report postoperative ambulation levels that were comparable to those of patients who had been assigned a noncardiac roommate and lower than those of patients who had been assigned a cardiac roommate. More interesting, the average length of stay for the no-roommate group was not significantly longer than that of patients assigned roommates who were preoperative or noncardiac but was significantly longer than that of patients assigned a roommate who was postoperative or cardiac. This pattern suggests, in terms of length of stay at least, that it is more likely that assignment to a roommate who has a similar surgical problem or who is postoperative is actually beneficial than that there is a harmful effect of exposure to a roommate who differs in type of surgery or who is preoperative.

What might account for such benefits? We can offer no definitive explanation at this stage, but one key may be the degree to which the patient's uncertainty was reduced by affiliation with the roommate before surgery. Consistent with this view, the cognitive clarity value of the roommate condition before surgery was monotonically related to length of postoperative recovery, with the situation that produced the greatest cognitive clarity affiliation (postoperative cardiac roommate) producing the quickest recovery, the lowest cognitive clarity situation (no roommate) producing the slowest recovery, and intermediate cognitive clarity situations producing intermediate recovery rates. It is interesting that the roommate condition that ostensibly would afford the lowest cognitive clarity (preoperative, noncardiac) produced recovery rates that were most comparable to the no-roommate condition (9.68 days vs. 9.96 days). Even more impressive, explicit mediational analyses provided relatively direct support for the idea that the roommate effects on recovery rates stemmed from differences in cognitive clarity gained from affiliation with the roommate before surgery. These findings thus suggest that affiliation with fellow patients may serve as an unrecognized adjunct to professionally delivered, preoperative preparations that are aimed at reducing recovery time by providing a better conception of what to expect and do postoperatively (see Devine, 1992; Mumford, Schlesinger, & Glass, 1982; Suls & Wan, 1989, for relevant reviews).

Theoretical Considerations

From a theoretical standpoint, the results of primary interest involve the patients' affiliations with their roommates before the threat posed by major surgery. As outlined earlier, Schachter's (1959) emotional similarity hypothesis, in its stronger form, would predict that overall affiliation under threat should be greatest with someone currently facing the same threat or, in its weaker form, that affiliation under threat for purposes of emotional comparison at least should be greatest with such a person. Our results provide no support for the stronger prediction (based on total time spent talking), but we did find some support for the idea that under threat, people will engage in more emotional comparison affiliation with a similar (cardiac) other than they will with a dissimilar (noncardiac) other. We believe that this may be the most direct evidence to date that under threat, there is indeed greater emotional comparison affiliation with a similar other in a face-to-face situation. It should be noted, however, that the observed effect was only marginally significant, and perhaps more important, there was no indication that emotional comparison affiliations were greater specifically with a roommate who was currently facing the same threat (and therefore presumably was more similar emotionally) than with one who had already experienced the same threat. It may be the case, of course, that our measure of emotional comparison affiliation was not sensitive enough to detect such specificity. A more interesting possibility, however, is that the importance of an affiliate's emotional similarity is less critical for enabling emotional comparison than has been generally assumed. After all, a potential affiliate who has already experienced a similar threat presumably can still provide a relevant reference for judging one's own emotional response by indicating how he or she had felt emotionally before the threat. It may be that the tendency of many previous stress and affiliation choice studies to prohibit verbal affiliation has contributed inadvertently to an overemphasis on the similarity of the affiliate's current emotional state. That is, with verbal affiliation restricted, those who are currently threatened can likely still communicate nonverbally how they are feeling more readily than those who have experienced the same threat can communicate nonverbally how they felt when they were in a similar position. Thus, if verbal affiliation is prohibited, threatened individuals seeking emotional comparison may show a more specific preference for affiliation with someone who currently faces the same threat. However, so long as potential affiliates have first-hand experience with the same threat and are free to discuss their emotional experiences, they may be viewed as capable of reducing uncertainties relevant to emotional reactions and thereby motivate comparable discussion of one's emotional status.

The additional findings that cognitive clarity and emotional support affiliations were greater for patients whose roommates had similar, compared with dissimilar, health problems also are interesting from a theoretical standpoint. As noted previously, Schachter (1959) originally considered the possibility that threat increases the desire to affiliate with others who face a similar threat because of desires for emotional comparison, emotional support, and cognitive clarity. However, he (and most affiliate-choice research) focused largely on the importance of emotional comparison as the primary determinant of affiliation under threat. It has been argued elsewhere that methodological problems and faulty reasoning may have led to an overemphasis on the importance of emotional comparison and to an underestimation of the importance of the desire for cognitive clarity as a motivation for affiliation choices under threat (Kulik & Mahler, 1990). Comprehensive reviews of this early literature appear, at least implicitly, to reach the same conclusions (see Cottrell & Epley, 1977; Rofe, 1984; Shaver & Klinnert, 1982).

The present results, which involved not single affiliation choices, but rather face-to-face affiliation patterns, further suggest that the narrow emphasis on threat and affiliation for purposes of emotional comparison was misplaced. Cognitive clarity, emotional comparison, and emotional support affiliations all were influenced by the similarity of the other's situation, suggesting that there are indeed multiple reasons why people affiliate under threat. Given that differential measurement error can account for differences in strength of effects, we are not in a position to conclude definitively that one aspect of affiliation with a similar other is predominant under threat. Indeed, a related point worth noting is that there is likely to be a certain amount of overlap in these affiliations, because affiliations directed primarily toward one goal may also at least indirectly influence other affiliations and goals. For example, information provided by just seeing that someone made it through the operation may provide a modicum of reassurance (e.g., "he made it through so I should too"). More interesting, if under threat, one indicates to another person how he or she is feeling emotionally, doing so may increase the likelihood that the other person will do the same and thus provide an explicit basis for emotional comparison; mentioning one's emotions may also make it more likely that the other person will say something reassuring (i.e., provide emotional support) than if one had not. Such interactive processes may have contributed in the present study to the finding that items devised a priori to tap emotional support and emotional comparison affiliations, respectively, empirically warranted combination into a more general, "emotion-focused" index of affiliation. The important point is that any such tendency for types of affiliation to overlap, which seems more likely the more complex and interactive the situation, is likely to foil efforts to determine in any conclusive fashion which type of affiliation is most prevalent under threat (cf. Kulik et al., 1994).

Although we may not want to draw the lines between these different types of affiliation too sharply, two aspects of our results provide important evidence that they also should not be considered isomorphic. First, mediation analyses provided direct (and we think remarkable) evidence that cognitive clarity affiliations mediated the roommate condition effects on postoperative lengths of stay. No such mediational evidence was found for emotion-focused affiliations. Thus although both types of affiliation were greater with a roommate who had a similar rather than dissimilar health problem, there were important functional differences between the types of affiliation. Additional discriminative evidence is suggested by the finding of an independent effect of the roommate's operative status on cognitive clarity but not on emotion-focused affiliations.

This finding is of interest in its own right in that as a main effect, it indicates that patients were more likely to gain information about what to expect about their own surgery from someone recovering from surgery than from someone awaiting surgery, even when the other's surgery was dissimilar to theirs. An interesting point implied here is that the usual, dichotomized way in which the similarity or dissimilarity of an affiliate's threat situation is conceptualized in this area may be a bit misleading. Presumably, the ideal comparison other for gaining cognitive clarity information is someone who already has been through the exact same procedure and is similar in other related attributes, such as age and prior physical health (cf. Goethals & Darley, 1977); however, such an ideal is rarely available in practice, and holding out for cognitive clarity affiliation only with such an individual may be nonadaptive. As a result, even if the other person is recovering from a threat experience that is somewhat dissimilar to the threat the patient currently faces, the patient may engage in a social comparison process as a part of efforts to achieve cognitive clarity. That is, a patient may discuss the other's recovery, consider the similarity of threat situations, and essentially extrapolate as best he can to his own situation. In the present context, for example, a patient with a roommate who is already recovering from brain surgery conceivably could discuss the roommate's recovery process and infer something like, "he had brain surgery, which is worse than heart surgery, so if he feels X amount of pain or fatigue 3 days after surgery, I should probably feel less than X at the same point."

That said, there may be a level of dissimilarity where experience no longer matters. In the present study, all roommates who were postoperative had undergone reasonably major surgeries, and there are numerous aspects of recovery that are common across major surgeries (e.g., nausea; gas pains; incision pains; and requisite recovery tasks, such as ambulating and performing deep-breathing exercises). It remains possible that if our postoperative, dissimilar roommates had been more extremely dissimilar (e.g., recovering from very minor procedures that involved no general anesthesia), their cognitive clarity value would have been negligible. Under such circumstances, the trend we observed for cognitive clarity affiliation to be especially pronounced among patients assigned a roommate who was postoperative and similar (cardiac) might well have reached significance. These fundamentally parametric issues remain to be explored.

Finally, the current affiliation results represent an important extension of the stress and affiliation literature from the domain of single acts of affiliation choice or stated preferences to the domain of face-to-face affiliations under acute, real-world threat. The sort of mediational results we obtained would not even be possible in an affiliate choice paradigm. It is important to recognize, however, that an even broader view will be needed ultimately to understand more completely how and why people affiliate with each other in acute threat situations. Although not assessed directly in the present study, the possibility that under threat, more verbal affiliation is directed toward threat-irrelevant than threat-relevant issues has been suggested by several studies (Kulik, Mahler, & Earnest, 1994; Kulik, Moore, & Mahler, 1993; Morris et al., 1976). Thus, a variety of factors that are likely to be important in mundane, nonthreatening situations also may influence affiliation patterns in threat situations. A study by Miller and Zimbardo (1966), for example, suggested that affiliation choices under threat may be determined more by the interpersonal similarity than by the emotional similarity of potential affiliates. Individual-differences factors, such as general extraversion or need for affiliation, also may play a role (e.g., McAdams & Constantian, 1983).

Ultimately, the motivations of both affiliates will need to be considered if researchers are to obtain a complete understanding of actual affiliative behavior in acute threat situations. It is interesting to consider, for example, the possibility that patients engaged in relatively more affiliation for cognitive clarity with postoperative roommates at least in part because of the desires of the roommates. Perhaps threat-experienced individuals in effect assume a role in relation to a threat-inexperienced individual, one in which there is some sense of obligation to impart their knowledge to "help this person through." Perhaps if such role obligations exist, they are felt more strongly when one has already experienced what the other person faces. These are interesting issues that await direct study.

For the present, the important point is that the restricted manner in which affiliation under threat typically has been studied, that is, through trying to identify the singular cause of one-time, stated affiliate choices, likely has led to overly simplistic if not misleading conclusions regarding the nature of stress and affiliation relationships generally and the role of emotional comparison specifically. Our results indicate that as this line of work expands to include actual affiliation patterns in acute threat situations, it will become impor-

tant to consider multiple, partially overlapping aspects of affiliations. Although much more complicated, by considering basic stress and affiliation relationships more naturalistically (cf. Kulik & Mahler, 1990), richer results and new questions are likely to be generated. Given that affiliation patterns apparently can have a significant, direct bearing on something so important as length of hospital stay, such investigations may yield important practical benefits as well.

ACKNOWLEDGMENTS

This research was supported by Grant HS06348 from the Agency for Health Care Policy and Research of the Public Health Service. We thank Nicko Christenfeld for his helpful comments and Margaret Hill for her technical assistance. We also would like to thank Jennifer N. Bloomquist, R.N., M.N., Riyad Y. Tarazi, M.D., Verna Nickle, R.N., Mary Kushner, Cathy Petravich, Cathy Verkaaik, Dorothy Torrence, and all of the nursing and support staff on 5-North and in the Surgical Intensive Care Unit at the San Diego Veterans Administration Medical Center for their assistance. Finally, we thank the patients, whose generosity at an extremely difficult time made the project possible.

REFERENCES

Ajzen, I., & Fishbein, M. (1977). Attitude–behavior relations: A theoretical analysis and review of empirical research. *Psychological Bulletin, 84,* 888–918.

Baron, R. M., & Kenny, D. A. (1986). The moderator–mediator variable distinction in social psychological research: Conceptual, strategic, and statistical considerations. *Journal of Personality and Social Psychology, 51,* 1173–1182.

Braunwald, E. (1980). Assessment of cardiac performance. In E. Braunwald (Ed.), *Heart disease: A textbook of cardiovascular medicine* (pp. 472–492). Philadelphia: W. B. Saunders.

Brickman, P., & Bulman, R. J. (1977). Pleasure and pain in social comparison. In J. M. Suls & R. L. Miller (Eds.), *Social comparison processes: Theoretical and empirical perspectives* (pp. 149–186). Washington, DC: Hemisphere.

Buunk, B. P. (1994). Social comparison processes under stress: Towards an integration of classic and recent perspectives. In W. Stroebe & M. Hewstone (Eds.), *European Review of Social Psychology* (Vol. 5, pp. 211–241). New York: Wiley.

Cheitlin, M. D., Sokolow, M., & McIlroy, M. B. (1993). *Clinical cardiology.* East Norwalk, CT: Appleton & Lange.

Cliff, N. (1987). *Analyzing multivariate data.* San Diego, CA: Harcourt Brace Jovanovich.

Cohen, F., & Lazarus, R. S. (1979). Coping with the stresses of illness. In G. C. Stone, F. Cohen, & N. E. Adler (Eds.), *Health psychology—A handbook* (pp. 77–112). San Francisco: Jossey-Bass.

Cohen, F., & Lazarus, R. S. (1983). Coping and adaptation in health and illness. In D. Mechanic (Ed.), *Handbook of health, health care, and the health professions* (pp. 608–635). New York: Free Press.

Cohen, J., & Cohen, P. (1975). *Applied multiple regression/correlation analyses for the behavioral sciences* (pp. 299–300, 332). Hillsdale, NJ: Erlbaum.

Cottrell, N. B., & Epley, S. W. (1977). Affiliation, social comparison and socially mediated stress reduction. In J. M. Suls & R. L. Miller (Eds.), *Social comparison processes: Theoretical and empirical perspectives* (pp. 43–68). Washington, DC: Hemisphere.

Darley, J. M. (1966). Fear and social comparison as determinants of conformity behavior. *Journal of Personality and Social Psychology, 4*, 73–78.

Darley, J. M., & Aronson, E. (1966). Self-evaluative vs. direct anxiety reduction as determinants of the fear–affiliation relationship. *Journal of Experimental Social Psychology, 1*(Suppl. 1), 66–79.

Devine, E. C. (1992). Effects of psychoeducational care for adult surgical patients: A meta-analysis of 191 studies. *Patient Education and Counselling, 19*, 129–142.

Festinger, L. A. (1954). A theory of social comparison processes. *Human Relations, 7*, 117–140.

Firestone, I. J., Kaplan, K. J., & Russell, J. C. (1973). Anxiety, fear, and affiliation with similar-state versus dissimilar-state others: Misery sometimes loves nonmiserable company. *Journal of Personality and Social Psychology, 26*, 409–414.

Foster, F. G., McPartland, R. J., & Kupfer, D. J. (1978). Motion sensors in medicine: Part I. A report on reliability and validity. *Journal of Inter-American Medicine, 3*, 4–8.

Goethals, G. R., & Darley, J. M. (1977). Social comparison theory: An attributional approach. In J. M. Suls & R. L. Miller (Eds.), *Social comparison processes: Theoretical and empirical perspectives* (pp. 259–278). Washington, DC: Hemisphere.

Hakmiller, K. L. (1966). Threat as a determinant of downward comparison. *Journal of Experimental Social Psychology, 2*(Suppl. 1), 32–39.

Helgeson, V. S., & Mickelson, K. D. (1995). Motives for social comparison. *Personality and Social Psychology Bulletin, 21*, 1200–1209.

Helgeson, V. S., & Taylor, S. E. (1993). Social comparisons and adjustment among cardiac patients. *Journal of Applied Social Psychology, 23*, 1171–1195.

Johnson, J. E. (1984). Psychological interventions and coping with surgery. In A. Baum, S. E. Taylor, & J. E. Singer (Eds.), *Handbook of psychology and health* (Vol. 4, pp. 167–187). Hillsdale, NJ: Erlbaum.

Johnson, J. E., Christman, N. J., & Stitt, C. (1985). Personal control interventions: Short- and long-term effects on surgical patients. *Research in Nursing and Health, 8*, 131–145.

Kirkpatrick, L. A., & Shaver, P. (1988). Fear and affiliation reconsidered from a stress and coping perspective: The importance of cognitive clarity and fear reduction. *Journal of Social and Clinical Psychology, 7*, 214–233.

Kulik, J. A., & Mahler, H. I. M. (1987). Effects of preoperative roommate assignment on preoperative anxiety and postoperative recovery from coronary-bypass surgery. *Health Psychology, 6*, 525–543.

Kulik, J. A., & Mahler, H. I. M. (1989). Stress and affiliation in a hospital setting: Preoperative roommate preferences. *Personality and Social Psychology Bulletin, 15*, 183–193.

Kulik, J. A., & Mahler, H. I. M. (1990). Stress and affiliation

research: On taking the laboratory to health field settings. *Annals of Behavioral Medicine, 12*, 106–111.

Kulik, J. A., Mahler, H. I. M., & Earnest, A. (1994). Social comparison and affiliation under threat: Going beyond the affiliate-choice paradigm. *Journal of Personality and Social Psychology, 66*, 301–309.

Kulik, J. A., Moore, P., & Mahler, H. I. M. (1993). Stress and affiliation: Hospital roommate effects on preoperative anxiety and social interaction. *Health Psychology, 12*, 119–125.

Lacey, J. I. (1967). Somatic response patterning and stress: Some revisions of activation theory. In M. H. Appley & R. Trumbull (Eds.), *Psychological stress: Issues in research* (pp. 14–37). New York: Appleton-Century-Crofts.

Lang, P. J., Melamed, B., & Hart, J. (1970). Automating the desensitization procedure: A psychophysiological analysis of fear modification. *Journal of Abnormal Psychology, 76*, 220–234.

LaPorte, R. E., Kuller, L. H., McPartland, R. J., Matthews, G., & Casperson, C. (1979). An objective measure of physical activity for epidemiologic research. *American Journal of Epidemiology, 109*, 158–168.

Lazarus, R. S., & Folkman, S. (1984). *Stress, appraisal, and coping.* New York: Springer.

Leventhal, H., & Johnson, J. E. (1983). Laboratory and field experimentation: Development of a theory of self-regulation. In P. J. Wooldridge, M. H. Schmitt, J. K. Skipper, & R. C. Leonard (Eds.), *Behavioral science and nursing theory* (pp. 189–262). St. Louis, MO: Mosby.

Martin, B., & Stroufe, L. A. (1970). Anxiety. In C. G. Castello (Ed.), *Symptoms of psychopathology: A handbook* (pp. 216–259). New York: Wiley.

McAdams, D. P., & Constantian, C. A. (1983). Initimacy and affiliation motives in daily living: An experience sampling analysis. *Journal of Personality and Social Psychology, 45*, 851–861.

Melamed, B. G., & Siegel, L. J. (1980). *Behavioral medicine: Practical applications in health care.* New York: Springer.

Miller, N., & Zimbardo, P. G. (1966). Motives for fear-induced affiliation: Emotional comparison or interpersonal similarity? *Journal of Personality, 34*, 481–503.

Molleman, E., Pruyn, J., & van Knippenberg, A. (1986). Social comparison processes among cancer patients. *British Journal of Social Psychology, 25*, 1–13.

Morris, W. N., Worchel, S., Bois, J. L., Pearson, J. A., Rountree, C. A., Samaha, G. M., Wachtler, J., & Wright, S. L. (1976). Collective coping with stress: Group reactions to fear, anxiety, and ambiguity. *Journal of Personality and Social Psychology, 33*, 674–679.

Mumford, E., Schlesinger, H. J., & Glass, G. V. (1982). The effects of psychological intervention on surgery and heart attacks: An analysis of the literature. *American Journal of Public Health, 72*, 141–151.

O'Neil, H. F., Spielberger, C. D., & Hansen, D. N. (1969). The effects of state-anxiety and task difficulty on computer-assisted learning. *Journal of Educational Psychology, 60*, 343–350.

Rofe, Y. (1984). Stress and affiliation: A utility theory. *Psychological Review, 91*, 235–250.

Schachter, S. (1959). *The psychology of affiliation.* Stanford, CA: Stanford University Press.

Shaver, P., & Klinnert, M. (1982). Schachter's theories of affiliation and emotions: Implications of developmental research. In L. Wheeler (Ed.), *Review of personality and social psychology* (Vol. 3, pp. 37–71). Beverly Hills, CA: Sage.

Spielberger, C. D., Gorsuch, R. L., & Lushene, R. E. (1970). *Manual for the State-Trait Anxiety Inventory*. Palo Alto, CA: Consulting Psychologists Press.

Suls, J., & Wan, C. K. (1989). Effects of sensory and procedural information on coping with stressful medical procedures and pain: A meta-analysis. *Journal of Consulting and Clinical Psychology, 57*, 372–379.

Taylor, S. E., Buunk, B., & Aspinwall, L. (1990). Social comparison, stress, and coping. *Personality and Social Psychology Bulletin, 16*, 74–89.

Taylor, S. E., & Lobel, M. (1989). Social comparison activity under threat: Downward evaluation and upward contacts. *Psychological Review, 96*, 569–575.

Thornton, D. A., & Arrowood, A. J. (1966). Self-evaluation, self-enhancement, and the locus of social comparison. *Journal of Experimental Social Psychology, 2*(Suppl. 1), 40–48.

Warner, W. L. (1960). *Social class in America: A manual of procedure for the measurement of social status*. New York: Harper & Row.

Wills, T. A. (1981). Downward comparison principles in social psychology. *Psychological Bulletin, 90*, 245–271.

Wood, J. V. (1989). Theory and research concerning social comparisons of personal attributes. *Psychological Bulletin, 106*, 231–248.

Wood, J. V., & Taylor, K. L. (1991). Serving self-relevant goals through social comparison. In J. Suls & T. A. Wills (Eds.), *Social comparison: Contemporary theory and research* (pp. 23–50). Hillsdale, NJ: Erlbaum.

Zimbardo, P. G., & Formica, R. (1963). Emotional comparison and self-esteem as determinants of affiliation. *Journal of Personality, 31*, 141–162.

Social Support and Health and Illness

Of the many benefits that come from having strong social ties and a network of personal relationships, one of the most important is their effect on physical health. In fact, a famous study conducted among 7,000 residents of Alameda County in California revealed that people who have a large number of social and community ties live longer than do those who have fewer ties to other members of their community (Berkman & Syme, 1979).

Social support is the term used to represent the experience, emanating from other people, that one is valued, respected, cared about, and loved. Social support can come from many sources—spouses or lovers, family, friends, or even community contacts such as social and religious groups to which one might belong. Other people can help us by providing tangible assistance when we need it, appraising difficult situations, modeling effective coping responses, or merely providing emotional support (Sarason, Sarason, & Gurung, 1997; Wills, 1991). Taken together, social support is thought to reduce the total amount of stress a person experiences (the direct effect hypothesis) as well as help one to cope better when stressed (the buffering hypothesis).

Social support has been shown to affect health in a myriad of ways. Social support can have positive influences on the operational efficiency of the immune system and the reactivity of the cardiovascular system, especially when support comes from close friends (Christenfeld et al., 1997; Uchino, Cacioppo, & Kiecolt-Glaser, 1996). In addition, we are more likely to engage in healthy behaviors (and avoid bad habits) when we have support from other people (Lewis & Rook, 1999).

The lead article in this section by medical sociologist James House and his colleagues was one of the first to document systematically that social support can lower the incidence of illness, reduce the risk of mortality from illness, and speed illness recovery (House, Landis, & Umberson, 1988). They start with the long-standing observation that people who are socially isolated, or in other ways not well integrated into their communities, are more likely to die at younger ages than other people and suffer from a host of mental and physical disorders. House and his colleagues summarize the data from many different epidemiological studies to try to understand this relationship. Although it is possible that people who are sick and dying might lose their social connections, these authors show by reviewing prospective studies (studies that follow people over a period of

time) that indeed the causality is in the opposite direction: People who have few social relationships and/or have social relationships of low quality are at greater risk for death than the average person.

In his article, Sheldon Cohen, a social psychologist, pays careful attention to various pathways that provide explanations for *how* social support influences health. He focuses on the various biological and psychological mechanisms—from immune and cardiovascular functioning to health beliefs, emotions, health behaviors, and tangible assistance—that might account for the positive consequences of social support (and the negative consequences of not having enough of it). Cohen pays particular attention to studies that help us to understand the aspects of social support that might be related to the onset of disease, its severity and progression, and recovery from it. He concludes with avenues for further research, some of which have begun to be explored in the time since this article was written (see list of suggested readings).

REFERENCES

Berkman, L. F., & Syme, S. L. (1979). Social networks, host resistance, and mortality: A nine-year followup study of Alameda County residents. *American Journal of Epidemiology, 109,* 186–204.

Christenfeld, N., Gerin, W., Linden, W., Sanders, M., Mathur, J., Deich, J. D., & Pickering, T. G. (1997). Social support effects on cardiovascular reactivity: Is a stranger as effective as a friend? *Psychosomatic Medicine, 59,* 388–398.

Cohen, S. (1988). Psychosocial models of the role of social support in the etiology of physical disease. *Health Psychology, 7,* 269–297.

House, J. S., Landis, K. R., & Umberson, D. (1988). Social relationships and health. *Science, 241,* 540–545.

Lewis, M. A., & Rook, K. S. (1999). Social control in personal relationships: Impact on health behaviors and psychological distress. *Health Psychology, 18,* 63–71.

Sarason, B. R., Sarason, I. G., & Gurung, R. A. R. (1997). Close personal relationships and health outcomes: A key to the role of social support. In S. Duck (Ed.), *Handbook of personal relationships* (pp. 547–573). New York: Wiley.

Uchino, B. N, Cacioppo, J. T., & Kiecolt-Glaser, J. K. (1996). The relationship between social support and physiological processes: A review with emphasis on underlying mechanisms and implications for health. *Psychological Bulletin, 119,* 488–531.

Wills, T. A. (1991). Social support and interpersonal relationships. In M. S. Clark (Ed.), *Prosocial behavior* (pp. 265–289). Newbury Park, CA: Sage.

Discussion Questions

1. Imagine the last time you were seriously ill. Did you receive social support from another person or group of people? In what ways did it affect the progression of your illness?
2. Prospective studies follow people over a period of time, but they are difficult and expensive to conduct. Cross-sectional studies look at a large group of people at one point in time. In both kinds of studies, investigators can observe correlations between social support and health outcomes. What are the advantages of prospective over cross-sectional studies that justify their added costs?
3. Can you imagine a particular type of person or a particular kind of situation for whom or in which social support has negative consequences?
4. Both articles in this section of the book suggest multiple pathways by which social support influences health. For which of these pathways do you think the evidence is strongest? Weakest?

Suggested Readings

Cohen, S. (2002). Psychosocial stress, social networks, and susceptibility to infection. In H. G. Koenig, & H. J. Cohen (Eds.), *The link between religion and health: Psychoneuroimmunology and the faith factor* (pp. 101–123). London: Oxford University Press.
This volume is devoted to examining why participating in organized religion seems to have positive health consequences. The chapter by Cohen examines the role social support may play and provides an update on how social support from this and other sources reinforces the immune system's ability to fend off disease.

Cohen, S., Underwood, L. G., & Gottlieb, B. H. (2000). *Social support measurement and intervention: A guide for health and social scientists.* London: Oxford University Press.
Everything and anything you might want to know about measuring social support.

Cunningham, M. R., & Barbee, A.P. (2000). Social support. In C. Hendrick & S. S. Hendrick (Eds.), *Close relationships: A sourcebook* (pp. 273–285). Thousand Oaks, CA: Sage.
A broader view of social support and social support networks ranging from romantic partners to health care providers. Provides some attention to the potential evolutionary origins of social support systems.

Durkheim, E. (1897). *Suicide.* New York: Free Press.
A sociological classic demonstrating that those people who lose their connections to other people and to social institutions and thus become alienated from society suffer greatly by, for example, being at greater risk for suicide.

Uchino, B. N, Cacioppo, J. T., & Kiecolt-Glaser, J. K. (1996). The relationship between social support and physiological processes: A review with emphasis on underlying mechanisms and implications for health. *Psychological Bulletin, 119,* 488–531.
This is a nice follow-up to the article by Cohen with a bit more of an emphasis on underlying physiological mechanisms that connect social support to health and illness.

READING 14

Social Relationships and Health

James S. House and Karl R. Landis • University of Michigan
Debra Umberson • University of Texas, Austin

Recent scientific work has established both a theoretical basis and strong empirical evidence for a causal impact of social relationships on health. Prospective studies, which control for baseline health status, consistently show increased risk of death among persons with a low quantity, and sometimes low quality, of social relationships. Experimental and quasi-experimental studies of humans and animals also suggest that social isolation is a major risk factor for mortality from widely varying causes. The mechanisms through which social relationships affect health and the factors that promote or inhibit the development and maintenance of social relationships remain to be explored.

. . . my father told me of a careful observer, who certainly had heart-disease and died from it, and who positively stated that his pulse was habitually irregular to an extreme degree; yet to his great disappointment it invariably became regular as soon as my father entered the room.—Charles Darwin (1965/1872)

Scientists have long noted an association between social relationships and health. More socially isolated or less socially integrated individuals are less healthy, psychologically and physically, and more likely to die. The first major work of empirical sociology found that less socially integrated people were more likely to commit suicide than the most integrated (Durkheim, 1951[1817]). In subsequent epidemiologic research age-adjusted mortality rates from all causes of death are consistently higher among the unmarried than the married (Carter & Glick, 1970; Kitigawa & Hauser, 1973; Kraus & Lilienfeld, 1959). Unmarried and more socially isolated people have also manifested higher rates of tuberculosis (Holmes, 1956), accidents (Tillman & Hobbs, 1949), and psychiatric

disorders such as schizophrenia (Faris, 1934; Kohn, & Clausen, 1955). And as the above quote from Darwin suggests, clinicians have also observed potentially health-enhancing qualities of social relationships and contacts.

The causal interpretation and explanation of these associations has, however, been less clear. Does a lack of social relationships cause people to become ill or die? Or are unhealthy people less likely to establish and maintain social relationships? Or is there some other factor, such as a misanthropic personality, which predisposes people both to have a lower quantity or quality of social relationships and to become ill or die?

Such questions have been largely unanswerable before the last decade for two reasons. First, there was little theoretical basic causal explanation. Durkheim (1951[1897]) proposed a theory of how social relationships affected suicide, but this theory did not generalize to morbidity and mortality from other causes. Second, evidence of the association between social relationships and health, especially in general human populations, was almost entirely retrospective or cross-sectional before the late

1970s. Retrospective studies from death certificates or hospital records ascertained the nature of a person's social relationships after they had become ill or died, and cross-sectional surveys of general populations determined whether people who reported ill health also reported a lower quality or quantity of relationships. Such studies used statistical control of potential confounding variables to rule out third factors that might produce the association between social relationships and health, but could do this only partially. They could not determine whether poor social relationships preceded or followed ill health.

In this article, we review recent developments that have altered this state of affairs dramatically: (a) emergence of theoretical models for a causal effect of social relationships on health in humans and animals; (b) cumulation of empirical evidence that social relationships are a consequential predictor of mortality in human populations; and (c) increasing evidence for the causal impact of social relationships on psychological and physiological functioning in quasi-experimental and experimental studies of humans and animals. These developments suggest that social relationships, or the relative lack thereof, constitute a major risk factor for health—rivaling the effects of well-established health risk factors such as cigarette smoking, blood pressure, blood lipids, obesity, and physical activity. Indeed, the theory and evidence on social relationships and health increasingly approximate that available at the time of the U.S. Surgeon General's 1964 report on smoking and health (U.S. Surgeon General's Advisory Committee, 1964), with similar implications for future research and public policy.

The Emergence of "Social Support" Theory and Research

The study of social relationships and health was revitalized in the middle 1970s by the emergence of a seemingly new field of scientific research on "social support." This concept was first used in the mental health literature (Caplan, 1974; President's Commission on Mental Health, 1978), and was linked to physical health in separate seminal articles by physician-epidemiologists Cassel (1976) and Cobb (1976). These articles grew out of a rapidly developing literature on stress and psychosocial factors in the etiology of health and illness (Cassel, 1970). Chronic diseases have increasingly replaced acute infectious diseases as the major causes of disability and death, at least in industrialized countries. Consequently, theories of disease etiology have shifted from ones in which a single factor (usually a microbe) caused a single disease, to ones in which multiple behavioral and environmental as well as biologic and genetic factors combine, often over extended periods, to produce any single disease, with a given factor often playing an etiologic role in multiple diseases.

Cassel (1976) and Cobb (1976) reviewed more than 30 human and animal studies that found social relationships protective of health. Recognizing that any one study was open to alternative interpretations, they argued that the variety of study designs (ranging from retrospective to experimental), of life stages studied (from birth to death), and of health outcomes involved (including low birth weight, complications of pregnancy, self-reported symptoms, blood pressure, arthritis, tuberculosis, depression, alcoholism, and mortality) suggested a robust, putatively causal, association. Cassel and Cobb indicated that social relationships might promote health in several ways, but emphasized the role of social relationships in moderating or buffering potentially deleterious health effects of psychosocial stress or other health hazards. This idea of "social support," or something that maintains or sustains the organism by promoting adaptive behavior or neuroendocrine responses in the face of stress or other health hazards, provided a general, albeit simple, theory of how and why social relationships should causally affect health (House, 1981).

Publications on "social support" increased almost geometrically from 1976 to 1981. By the late 1970s, however, serious questions emerged about the empirical evidence cited by Cassel and Cobb and the evidence generated in subsequent research. Concerns were expressed about causal priorities between social support and health (since the great majority of studies remained cross-sectional or retrospective and based on self-reported data), about whether social relationships and supports buffered the impact of stress on health or had more direct effects, and about how consequential the effects of social relationships on health really were (Heller, 1979; Reed et al., 1983; Thoits, 1982). These concerns have been addressed by a continuing cumulation of two types of empirical data: (a) a new series of prospective mortality studies in human populations and (b) a broadening base of laboratory and field experimental studies of animals and humans.

Prospective Mortality Studies of Human Populations

Just as concerns began to surface about the nature and strength of the impact of social relationships on health, data from long-term, prospective studies of community populations provided compelling evidence that lack of social relationships constitutes a major risk factor for mortality. Berkman and Syme (1979) analyzed a probability sample of 4,775 adults in Alameda County, California, who were between 30 and 69 in 1965 when they completed a survey that assessed the presence or extent of four types of social ties—marriage, contacts with extended family and friends, church membership, and other formal and informal group affiliations. Each type of social relationship predicted mortality through the succeeding 9 years. A combined "social network" index remained a significant predictor of mortality (with a relative risk ratio for mortality of about 2.0, indicating that persons low on the index were twice as likely to die as persons high on the index) in multivariate analyses that controlled for self-reports in 1965 of physical health, socioeconomic status, smoking, alcohol consumption, physical activity, obesity, race, life satisfaction, and use of preventive health services. Such adjustment or control for baseline health and other risk factors provides a conservative estimate of the predictive power of social relationships, since some of their impact may be mediated through effects on these risk factors.

The major limitation of the Berkman and Syme study was the lack of other than self-reported data on health at baseline. Thus, House et al. (1982) sought to replicate and extend the Alameda County results in a study of 2,754 adults between 35 and 69 at their initial interview and physical examinations in 1967 through 1969 by the Tecumseh (Michigan) Community Health Study. Composite indices of social relationships and activities (as well as a number of the individual components) were inversely associated with mortality during the succeeding 10- to 12-year follow-up period,

with relative risks of 2.0 to 3.0 for men and 1.5 to 2.0 for women, after adjustment for the effects of age and a wide range of biomedically assessed (blood pressure, cholesterol, respiratory function, and electrocardiograms) as well as self-reported risk factors of mortality. Analyzing data on 2,059 adults in the Evans County (Georgia) Cardiovascular Epidemiologic Study, Schoenbach et al. (1986) also found that a social network index similar to that of Berkman and Syme (1979) predicted mortality for an 11- to 13-year follow-up period, after adjustment for age and baseline measures of biomedical as well as self-reported risk factors of mortality. The Evans County associations were somewhat weaker than those in Tecumseh and Alameda County, and as in Tecumseh were stronger for males than females.

Studies in Sweden and Finland have described similar results. Tibblin (1986), Welin (1985), and associates studied two cohorts of men born in 1913 and 1923, respectively, and living in 1973 in Gothenburg, Sweden's second largest city. After adjustments for age, baseline levels of systolic blood pressure, serum cholesterol, smoking habits, and perceived health status, mortality in both cohorts through 1982 was inversely related to the number of persons in the household and the men's level of social and outside home activities in 1973. Orth-Gomer and Johnson (1987) analyzed the mortality experience through 1981 of a random sample of 17,433 Swedish adults aged 29 to 74 at the time of their 1976 or 1977 baseline interviews. Frequency of contact with family, friends, neighbors, and co-workers in 1976–77 was predictive of mortality through 1981, after adjustment for age, sex, education, employment status, immigrant status, physical exercise, and self-reports of chronic conditions. The effects were stronger among males than among females, and were somewhat nonlinear, with the greatest increase in mortality risk occurring in the most socially isolated third of the sample. In a prospective study of 13,301 adults in predominantly rural eastern Finland, Kaplan et al. (1996) found a measure of "social connections" similar to those used in Alameda County, Tecumseh, and Evans County to be a significant predictor of male mortality from all causes during 5 years, again after adjustments for other biomedical and self-reported risk factors. Female mortality showed similar, but weaker and statistically nonsignificant, effects.

These studies manifest a consistent pattern of results, as shown in Figures 14.1 and 14.2, which show age-adjusted mortality rates plotted for the five prospective studies from which we could extract parallel data. The report of the sixth study (Orth-Gomer & Johnson, 1987) is consistent with these trends. The relative risks (*RR*) in Figures 14.1 and 14.2 are higher than those reported above because they are only adjusted for age. The levels of mortality in Figures 14.1 and 14.2 vary greatly across studies depending on the follow-up period and composition of the population by age, race, and ethnicity, and geographic locale, but the patterns of prospective association between social integration (i.e., the number and frequency of social relationships and contacts) and mortality are remarkably similar, with some variations by race, sex, and geographic locale.

Only the Evans County study reported data for blacks. The predictive association of social integration with mortality among Evans County black males is weaker than among white males in Evans County or elsewhere (Fig. 14.1), and the relative risk ratio for black females in Evans County, although greater than for Evans County white females, is smaller than the risk ratios for white females in all other studies (Fig. 14.2). More research on blacks and other minority populations is necessary to determine whether these differences are more generally characteristic of blacks compared to whites.

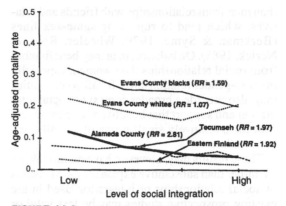

FIGURE 14.2 ■ Level of social integration and age-adjusted mortality for females in five prospective studies. *RR*, the relative risk ratio of mortality at the lowest versus highest level of social integration.

Modest differences emerge by sex and rural as opposed to urban locale. Results for men and women are strong, linear, and similar in the urban populations of Alameda County (i.e., Oakland and environs) and Gothenburg, Sweden (only men were studied in Gothenburg). In the predominantly small-town and rural populations of Tecumseh, Evans County, and eastern Finland, however, two notable deviations from the urban results appear: (a) female risk ratios are consistently weaker than those for men in the same rural populations (Figs. 14.1 and 14.2), and (b) the results for men in more rural populations, although rivaling those in urban populations in terms of risk ratios, assume a distinctly nonlinear, or threshold, form. That is, in Tecumseh, Evans County, and eastern Finland, mortality is clearly elevated among the most socially isolated, but declines only modestly, if at all, between moderate and high levels of social integration.

Explanation of these sex and urban–rural variations awaits research on broader regional or national populations in which the same measures are applied to males and females across the full rural–urban continuum. The current results may have both substantive and methodological explanations. Most of the studies reviewed here, as well as others (Gove, 1972; Helsing & Szklo, 1981; Stroebe & Stroebe, 1983), suggest that being married is more beneficial to health, and becoming widowed more detrimental, for men than for women. Women, however, seem to benefit as much or more

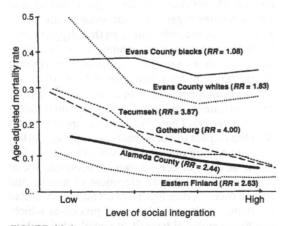

FIGURE 14.1 ■ Level of social integration and age-adjusted mortality for males in five prospective studies. *RR*, the relative risk ratio of mortality at the lowest versus highest level of social integration.

than men from relationships with friends and relatives, which tend to run along same-sex lines (Berkman & Syme, 1979; Wheeler, Rice, & Nezlek, 1983). On balance, men may benefit more from social relationships than women, especially in cross-gender relationships. Small communities may also provide a broader context of social integration and support that benefits most people, except for a relatively small group of socially isolated males.

These results may, however, have methodological rather than substantive explanations. Measures of social relationships or integration used in the existing prospective studies may be less valid or have less variance in rural and small-town environments, and for women, thus muting their relationship with mortality. For example, the data for women in Figure 14.2 are similar to the data on men if we assume that women have higher-quality relationships and hence that their true level of social integration is moderate even at low levels of quantity. The social context of small communities may similarly provide a moderate level of social integration for everyone except quite isolated males. Thus measures of frequency of social contact may be poorer indices of social integration for women and more rural populations than for men and urban dwellers.

Variations in the results in Figures 14.1 and 14.2 should not, however, detract from the remarkable consistency of the overall finding that social relationships do predict mortality for men and women in a wide range of populations, even after adjustment for biomedical risk factors for mortality. Additional prospective studies have shown that social relationships are similarly predictive of all-cause and cardiovascular mortality in studies of people who are elderly (Blazer, 1982; Seeman et al., 1987; Zuckerman, Kasl, & Ostfeld, 1984) or have serious illnesses (Orth-Gomer et al., 1986; Ruberman et al., 1984).

Experimental and Quasi-Experimental Research

The prospective mortality data are made more compelling by their congruence with growing evidence from experimental and clinical research on animals and humans that variations in exposure to social contacts produce psychological or physi-

ological effects that could, if prolonged, produce serious morbidity and even mortality. Cassel (1976) reviewed evidence that the presence of a familiar member of the same species could buffer the impact of experimentally induced stress on ulcers, hypertension, and neurosis in rats, mice, and goats, respectively; and the presence of familiar others has also been shown to reduce anxiety and physiological arousal (specifically secretion of free fatty acids) in humans in potentially stressful laboratory situations (Back & Bogdonoff, 1967; Wrightsman, 1960). Clinical and laboratory data indicate that the presence of or physical contact with another person can modulate human cardiovascular activity and reactivity in general, and in stressful contexts such as intensive care units (Lynch, 1979, pp. 122–141). Research also points to the operation of such processes across species. Affectionate petting by humans, or even their mere presence, can reduce the cardiovascular sequelae of stressful situations among dogs, cats, horses, and rabbits (Lynch, 1979, pp. 163–180). Nerem et al. (1980) found that human handling also reduced the arteriosclerotic impact of a high fat diet in rabbits. Recent interest in the potential health benefits of pets for humans, especially the isolated aged, is based on similar notions, although the evidence for such efforts is only suggestive (Goldmeier, 1986).

Bovard (1985) has proposed a psychophysiologic theory to explain how social relationships and contacts can promote health and protect against disease. He reviews a wide range of human and animal studies suggesting that social relationships and contacts, mediated through the amygdala, activate the anterior hypothalamic zone (stimulating release of human growth hormone) and inhibit the posterior hypothalamic zone (and hence secretion of adrenocorticotropic hormone, cortisol, catecholamines, and associated sympathetic autonomic activity). These mechanisms are consistent with the impact of social relationships on mortality from a wide range of causes and with studies of the adverse effects of lack of adequate social relationships on the development of human and animal infants (Bowlby, 1973). This theory is also consistent with sociobiological processes which, due to the survival benefit of social relationships and collective activity, would promote genetic selection of organisms who find social contact and relatedness rewarding and the lack of such contact and relatedness aversive (Mendoza, 1984).

The epidemiologic evidence linking social relationships and supports to morbidity in humans is limited and not fully consistent. For example, although laboratory studies show short-term effects of social relationships on cardiovascular functioning that would, over time, produce cardiovascular disease, and prospective studies show impacts of social relationships on mortality from cardiovascular disease, the link between social relationships and the incidence of cardiovascular morbidity has yet to be firmly demonstrated (Cohen, 1988; Reed et al., 1983). Overall, however, the theory and evidence for the impact of social relationships on health are building steadily (Berkman, 1985; Broadhead et al., 1983).

Social Relationships as a Risk Factor for Health: Research and Policy Issues

The theory and data reviewed above meet reasonable criteria for considering social relationships a cause or risk factor of mortality, and probably morbidity, from a wide range of diseases (Broadhead et al., 1983; Lilienfeld & Lilienfeld, 1980, pp. 289–321; U.S. Surgeon General's Advisory Committee, 1964). These criteria include strength and consistency of statistical associations across a wide range of studies, temporal ordering or prediction from cause to effect, a gradient of response (which may in this case be nonlinear), experimental data on animals and humans consistent with nonexperimental human data, and a plausible theory (Bovard, 1985) of biopsychosocial mechanisms explaining the observed associations.

The evidence on social relationships is probably stronger, especially in terms of prospective studies, than the evidence which led to the certification of the Type A behavior pattern as a risk factor for coronary heart disease (National Heart, Lung, and Blood Institute, 1982). The evidence regarding social relationships and health increasingly approximates the evidence in the 1964 Surgeon General's report (U.S. Surgeon General's Advisory Committee, 1964) that established cigarette smoking as a cause or risk factor for mortality and morbidity from a range of diseases. The age-adjusted relative risk ratios shown in Figures 14.1 and 14.2 are stronger than the relative risks for all cause mortality reported for cigarette smoking (U.S. Surgeon General's Advisory Committee, 1964). There is, however, less specificity in the associations of social relationships with mortality than has been observed for smoking, which is strongly linked to cancers of the lung and respiratory tract (with age-adjusted risk ratios between 3.0 and 11.0). Better theory and data are needed on the links between social relationships and major specific causes of morbidity and mortality.

Although a lack of social relationships has been established as a risk factor for mortality, and probably morbidity, three areas need further investigation: (a) mechanisms and processes linking social relationships to health, (b) determinants of levels of "exposure" to social relationships, and (c) the means to lower the prevalence of relative social isolation in the population or to lessen its deleterious effects on health.

Mechanisms and Processes Linking Social Relationships to Health

Although grounded in the literature on social relationships and health, investigators on social support in the last decade leaped almost immediately to the interpretation that what was consequential for health about social relationships was their supportive quality, especially their capacity to buffer or moderate the deleterious effects of stress or other health hazards (Cassel, 1976; Cobb, 1976). Many recent studies have reported either a general positive association between social support and health or a buffering effect in the presence of stress (Cohen & Syme, 1985), but these studies are problematic because the designs are largely cross-sectional or retrospective and the data usually self-reported. The most compelling evidence of the causal significance of social relationships on health has come from the experimental studies of animals and humans and the prospective mortality studies reviewed above—studies in which the measures of social relationships are merely the presence or absence of familiar other organisms, or relative frequency of contact with them, and which often do not distinguish between buffering and main effects. Thus, social relationships appear to have generally beneficial effects on health, not solely or even primarily attributable to their buffering effects, and there may be aspects of social relationships other than their supportive quality that account for these effects.

We now need a broader theory of the bio-psychosocial mechanisms and processes linking social relationships to health than can be provided by extant concepts or theories of social support. That broader theory must do several things. First, it must clearly distinguish between (a) the existence or quantity of social relationships, (b) their formal structure (such as their density or reciprocity), and (c) the actual content of these relationships such as social support. Only by testing the effects on health of these different aspects of social relationships in the same study can we understand what it is about social relationships that is consequential for health.

Second, we need better understanding of the social, psychological, and biological processes that link the existence, quantity, structure, or content of social relationships to health. Social support—whether in the form of practical help, emotional sustenance, or provision of information—is only one of the social processes involved here. Not only may social relationships affect health because they are or are not supportive, they may also regulate or control human thought, feeling, and behavior in ways that promote health, as in Durkheim's (1951[1897]) theory relating social integration to suicide. Current views based on this perspective suggest that social relationships affect health either by fostering a sense of meaning or coherence that promotes health (Antonovsky, 1979) or by facilitating health-promoting behaviors such as proper sleep, diet, or exercise, appropriate use of alcohol, cigarettes, and drugs, adherence to medical regimens, or seeking appropriate medical care (Umberson, 1987). The negative or conflictive aspects of social relationships need also to be considered, since they may be detrimental to the maintenance of health and of social relationships (Rook, 1984).

We must further understand the psychological and biological processes or mechanisms linking social relationships to health, either as extensions of the social processes just discussed (e.g., processes of cognitive appraisal and coping [Lazarus & Folkman, 1984]) or as independent mechanisms. In the latter regard, psychological and sociobiological theories suggest that the mere presence of, or sense of relatedness with, another organism may

have relatively direct motivational, emotional, or neuroendocrine effects that promote health either directly or in the face of stress or other health hazards but that operate independently of cognitive appraisal or behavioral coping and adaptation (Bowlby, 1973; Lynch, 1979, pp. 87–180; Mendoza, 1974; Zajonc, 1965).

Determinants of Social Relationships: Scientific and Policy Issues

Although social relationships have been extensively studied during the past decade as independent, intervening, and moderating variables affecting stress or health or the relations between them, almost no attention has been paid to social relationships as dependent variables. The determinants of social relationships, as well as their consequences, are crucial to the theoretical and causal status of social relationships in relation to health. If exogenous biological, psychological, or social variables determine both health and the nature of social relationships, then the observed association of social relationships to health may be totally or partially spurious. More practically, Cassel (1976), Cobb (1976), and others became interested in social support as a means of improving health. This, in turn, requires understanding of the broader social, as well as psychological or biological, structures and processes that determine the quantity and quality of social relationships and support in society.

It is clear that biology and personality must and do affect both people's health and the quantity and quality of their social relationships. Research has established that such factors do not, however, explain away the experimental, cross-sectional, and prospective evidence linking social relationships to health (House, Umberson, & Landis, in press). In none of the prospective studies have controls for biological or health variables been able to explain away the predictive association between social relationships and mortality. Efforts to explain away the association of social relationships and supports with health by controls for personality variables have similarly failed (Cohen, Sherrod, & Clark, 1986; Schultz & Decker, 1985). Social relationships have a predictive, arguably causal, association with health in their own right.

The extent and quality of social relationships experienced by individuals is also a function of broader social forces. Whether people are employed, married, attend church, belong to organizations, or have frequent contact with friends and relatives, and the nature and quality of those relationships, are all determined in part by their positions in a larger social structure that is stratified by age, race, sex, and socioeconomic status and is organized in terms of residential communities, work organizations, and larger political and economic structures. Older people, blacks, and the poor are generally less socially integrated (House, 1987), and differences in social relationships by sex and place of residence have been discussed in relation to Figures 14.1 and 14.2. Changing patterns of fertility, mortality, and migration in society affect opportunities for work, marriage, living and working in different settings, and having relationships with friends and relatives, and can even affect the nature and quality of these relations (Watkins, Menken, & Bongaarts, 1987). These demographic patterns are themselves subject to influence by both planned and unplanned economic and political change, which can also affect individuals' social relationships more directly—witness the massive increase in divorce during the last few decades in response to the women's movement, growth in women's labor force participation, and changing divorce law (Cherlin, 1981; Weitzman, 1985).

In contrast with the 1950s, adults in the United States in the 1970s were less likely to be married, more likely to be living alone, less likely to belong to voluntary organizations, and less likely to visit informally with others (Veroff, Douvan, & Kulka, 1981). Changes in marital and childbearing patterns and in the age structure of our society will produce in the 21st century a steady increase of the number of older people who lack spouses or children—the people to whom older people most often turn for relatedness and support (Watkins, Menken, & Bongaarts, 1987). Thus, just as we discover the importance of social relationships for health, and see an increasing need for them, their prevalence and availability may be declining. Changes in other risk factors (e.g., the decline of smoking) and improvements in medical technology are still producing overall improvements on health and longevity, but the improvements might be even greater if the quantity and quality of social relationships were also improving.

ACKNOWLEDGMENTS

J. S. House is professor and chair of sociology and a research scientist in the Survey Research Center of the Institute for Social Research, Institute of Gerontology, and Department of Epidemiology at the University of Michigan, Ann Arbor, MI 48109. K. R. Landis is a doctoral candidate in the Department of Sociology and research assistant in the Survey Research Center. D. Umberson is a postdoctoral fellow in the Survey Research Center at the University of Michigan and assistant professor–designate of sociology at the University of Texas, Austin.

REFERENCES

Antonovsky, A. (1984). *Health, stress and coping.* San Francisco: Jossey-Bass.

Back, K. W., & Bogdanoff, M. D. (1967). Buffer conditions in experimental stress. *Behavioral Science, 12,* 384–390.

Berkman, L. F. (1985). The relationship of social support networks and social support to morbidity and mortality. In S. Cohen & S. L. Lyme (Eds.), *Social support and health* (pp. 241–262). New York: Academic Press.

Berkman, L. F., & Syme, S. L. (1979). Social networks, host resistance, and mortality: A nine-year follow-up study of Alameda County residents. *American Journal of Epidemiology, 109,* 186–204.

Blazer, D. (1982). Social support and mortality in an elderly community population. *American Journal of Epidemiology, 115,* 684–694.

Bovard, E. W. (1985). Brain mechanisms in effects of social support on viability. In R. B. Williams, *Perspectives on behavioral medicine* (Vol. 2, pp. 103–109). New York: Academic Press.

Bowlby, J. (1973). Affectional bonds: Their nature and origin. In R. S. Weiss (Ed.), *Loneliness: The experience of emotional and social isolation* (pp. 38–52). Cambridge, MA: MIT Press.

Broadhead, W. E., Kaplan, B. H., James, S. A., Wagner, E. H., Schoenbach, V. J., Grimson, R., Heyden, S., Tibblin, G., & Gehlbach, S. H. (1983). The epidemiologic evidence for a relationship between social support and health. *American Journal of Epidemiology, 117,* 521–537.

Caplan, G. (1974). *Support systems and community mental health.* New York: Behavioral Publications.

Carter, H., & Glick, P. C. (1970). *Marriage and divorce: A social and economic study.* Cambridge, MA: Harvard University Press.

Cassel, J. (1970). Physical illness in response to stress. In S. Levine & N. A. Scocch (Eds.), *Social stress* (pp. 189–209). Chicago: Aldine.

Cassel, J. (1976). The contribution of the social environment to host resistance. *American Journal of Epidemiology, 104,* 107–123.

Cobb, S. (1976). Social support as a moderator of life stress. *Psychosomatic Medicine, 38,* 300–314.

Cohen, S. (1988). Psychosocial models of the role of social support in the etiology of physical disease. *Health Psychology, 7,* 269–297.

Cohen, S., & Syme, S. L. (1985). *Social support and health.* New York: Academic Press.

Cohen, S., Sherrod, D. R., & Clark, M. S. (1986). Social skills and the stress-protective role of social support. *Journal of

Personality and Social Psychology, 50, 963–973.

Darwin, C. (1965[1872]). *Expression of the emotions in man and animals.* Chicago: University of Chicago Press.

Durkheim, E. (1951[1897]). *Suicide.* New York: Free Press.

Faris, R. E. L. (1934). Cultural isolation and the schizophrenic personality. *American Journal of Sociology, 40,* 155–164.

Goldmeier, J. (1986). Pets or people: Another research note. *Gerontologist, 26,* 203–206.

Gove, W. R. (1972). The relationship between sex-roles, marital status, and mental illness. *Social Forces, 51,* 34–44.

Heller, K. (1979). In A. P. Goldstein & F. H. Kanter (Eds.), *Maximizing treatment gains: Transfer enhancement in psychotherapy* (pp. 353–382). New York: Academic Press.

Helsing, K. J., & Szklo, M. (1981). Mortality after bereavement. *American Journal of Epidemiology, 114,* 41–52.

Holmes, T. H. (1956). In P. J. Sparer (Ed.), *Personality, stress, and tuberculosis* (pp.). New York: International Universities Press.

House, J. S. (1981). *Work stress and social support.* Reading, MA: Addison-Wesley.

House, J. S. (1987). Social support and social structure. *Sociological Forum, 2,* 135–146.

House, J. S., Robbins, C., & Metzner, H. M. (1982). The association of social relationships and activities with mortality: Prospective evidence from the Tecumseh Community Health Study. *American Journal of Epidemiology, 116,* 123–140.

House, J. S., Umberson, D., & Landis K. (1988). Structures and processes of social support. *Annual Review of Sociology, 14,* 293–318.

Kaplan, G. A., Strawbridge, W. J., Cohen, & Hungerford, L. R. (1996). Natural history of leisure-time physical activity and its correlates: Associations with mortality from all causes of cardiovascular disease over 28 years. *American Journal of Epidemiology, 144,* 793–797.

Kitigawa, E. M., & Hauser, P. H. (1973). *Differential mortality in the United States: A study in socio-economic epidemiology.* Cambridge, MA: Harvard University Press.

Kohn, M. L., & Clausen, J. A. (1955). Social isolation and schizophrenia. *American Sociological Review, 20,* 265–273.

Kraus, A. S., & Lilienfeld, A. N. (1959). Some epidemiological aspects of the high mortality rate in the young widowed group. *Journal of Chronic Diseases, 10,* 207–217.

Lazarus, R. S., & Folkman, S. (1984). *Stress, appraisal and coping.* New York: Springer.

Lilienfeld, A. M., & Lilienfeld, D. E. (1980). *Foundations of epidemiology.* New York: Oxford University Press.

Lynch, J. J. (1979). *The broken heart.* New York: Basic Books.

Mendoza, S. P. (1984). The psychology of social relationships. In P. R. Barchas & S. P. Mendoza (Eds.), *Social cohesion: Essays toward a sociophysiological perspective* (pp.). Westport, CT: Greenwood Press.

Nerem, R. M., Levesque, M. J., & Cornhill, J. F. (1980). Social environment as a factor in diet-induced atherosclerosis. *Science, 208,* 1475–1476.

Orth-Gomer, K., & Johnson, J. (1987). Social network interaction and mortality. *Journal of Chronic Diseases, 40,* 949–957.

Orth-Gomer, K.(1986). In S. O. Isacsson & L. Janzon (Eds.), *Social support: Health and disease* (pp. 21–31). Stockholm, Sweden: Almqvist & Wiksell.

President's Commission on Mental Health. (1978). *Report to*

the president (Vols. 1–5). Washington, DC: Government Printing Office.

Reed, D., McGee, D., Yano, K., & Feinleib, M. (1983). Social networks and coronary heart disease among Japanese men in Hawaii. *American Journal of Epidemiology, 117,* 384–396.

Rook, K. (1984). The negative side of social interaction. *Journal of Personality and Social Psychology, 46,* 1097–1108.

Ruberman, W. E., Weinblatt, E., Goldberg, J. D., & Chaudhory, B. S. (1984). Psychosocial influences on mortality after myocardial infarction. *New England Journal of Medicine, 311,* 552–559.

Schoenbach, V. J., Kaplan, B. H., Fredman, L., & Kleinbaum, D. G. (1986). Social ties and mortality in Evans County, Georgia. *American Journal of Epidemiology, 123,* 577–591.

Schultz, R. & Decker, S. (1985). Long-term adjustment to disability. *Journal of Personality and Social Psychology, 48,* 1162–1172.

Seeman, T. E., Kaplan, G. A., Kundson, L., Cohen, R., & Guralnik, J. (1987). Social network ties and mortality among the elderly in the Alameda County study. *American Journal of Epidemiology, 126,* 714–723.

Stroebe, M., & Stroebe, W. (1983). Who suffers more? Sex differences in health risks of the widowed. *Psychological Bulletin, 93,* 279–301.

Thoits, P. A. (1982). Conceptual, methodological, and theoretical problems in studying social support as a buffer against life stress. *Journal of Health and Social Behavior, 23,* 145–159.

Tibblin, G. (1986). In S. O. Isacsson & L. Janzon (Eds.), *Social support: Health and disease* (pp. 11–19). Stockholm, Sweden: Almqvist & Wiksell.

Tillmann, W. A., & Hobbs, G. E. (1949). The accident-prone automobile driver. *American Journal of Psychiatry, 106,* 321–331.

U.S. Surgeon General's Advisory Committee on Smoking and Health. (1964). *Smoking and health.* Washington, DC: U.S. Public Health Service.

Umberson, D. (1987). Family status and health behaviors. *Journal of Health and Social Behavior, 28,* 306–319.

Veroff, J., Douvan, B., & Kulka, R. A. (1981). *The inner American: A self-portrait from 1957 to 1976.* New York: Basic Books.

Watkins, S. C., Menken, J. A., & Bongaarts, J. (1987). Demographic foundations of family change. *American Sociological Review, 52,* 346–358.

Weitzman, L. J. (1985). *The divorce revolution.* New York: Free Press.

Welin, L., Tibblin, G., Svardgudd, K., Tibblin, B., Ander-Peciva, S., Larsson, B., & Wilhelmsen, L. (1985). Prospective study of social influences on mortality. *The Lancet, i,* 915–918.

Wheeler, L., Reis, H., & Nezlek, J. (1983). Loneliness, social interaction, and sex-roles. *Journal of Personality and Social Psychology, 45,* 943–953.

Wrightsman, L. S., Jr. (1960). Effects of waiting with others on changes in levels of felt anxiety. *Journal of Abnormal Social Psychology, 61,* 216–222.

Zajonc, R. B. (1965). Social facilitation. *Science, 149,* 269–274.

Zuckerman, D. M., Kasl, S. V., & Ostfeld, A. M. (1984). Psychosocial predictors of mortality among the elderly poor. *American Journal of Epidemiology, 119,* 410–423.

Psychosocial Models of the Role of Social Support in the Etiology of Physical Disease

Sheldon Cohen • Carnegie Mellon University

Although there has been a substantial effort to establish the beneficial effects of social support on health and well-being, relatively little work has focused on *how* social support influences physical health. This article outlines possible mechanisms through which support systems may influence the etiology of physical disease. I begin by reviewing research on the relations between social support and morbidity and between social support and mortality. I distinguish between various conceptualizations of social support used in the existing literature and provide alternative explanations of how each of these conceptualizations of the social environment could influence the etiology of physical disease. In each case, I address the psychological mediators (e.g., health relevant cognitions, affect, and health behaviors) as well as biologic links (e.g., neuroendocrine links to immune and cardiovascular function). I conclude by proposing conceptual and methodological guidelines for future research in this area, highlighting the unique contributions psychologists can make to this inherently interdisciplinary endeavor.
Key words: social support, physical disease, psychosocial models

Social support has been prospectively associated with mortality (Berkman & Syme, 1979; Blazer, 1982; House, Robbins, & Metzner, 1982; Schoenbach, Kaplan, Fredman, & Kleinbaum, 1986) and has been implicated in the etiology of both physical illness and psychological distress (see reviews by Berkman, 1985; Broadhead et al., 1983; S. Cohen & Wills, 1985; Kessler & McLeod, 1985; Leavy, 1983; Wallston, Alagna, DeVellis, & DeVellis, 1983). Although there has been a tremendous effort to establish the beneficial effects of support on health and well-being, relatively little work has focused on *how* social support influences health (cf. Heller, Swindle, & Dusenbury, 1986).

I believe that differentiation between various conceptions of social support and specification of the processes by which each conceptualization influences health and well-being are requisite for further progress in understanding the role of support in the maintenance of health and prevention of disease (see early call for such distinctions by Kaplan, Cassel, & Gore, 1977). In service of this goal, I suggest some distinctions in social support based on existing research, selectively review studies of the role of social support in the etiology of physical disease, and propose a series of models linking different conceptualizations of social support to physical health. My discussion is limited

227

to the etiology of physical illness (onset and progression but not recovery) and focuses on disease endpoints (morbidity and mortality) rather than on illness behaviors such as symptom reporting and use of medical services.

Differentiating Social Support

There is little agreement among the scientific community in regard to a precise definition of social support (S. Cohen & Syme, 1985; Shumaker & Brownell, 1984; Wilcox & Vernberg, 1985). Moreover, existing studies apply the term to a broad range of conceptualizations of social networks and the functions they provide. Rather than attempt an all-encompassing definition, I propose broad categorical classifications of the concepts commonly included under the social support rubric and define some specific concepts that I believe may be linked with physical disease.

Several investigators have proposed typologies of social support measures to help provide organization to the field. For example, House and Kahn (1985; also Turner, 1983) suggested three categories of support measures: social networks, social relationships, and social supports. Social networks refer to measures deriving from formal network theory, including measures of network size, density, multiplexity, reciprocity, durability, intensity, frequency, dispersion, and homogeneity. Social relationship measures assess the existence, quantity, and type of existing relationships. Finally, social support measures assess resources provided by others with various measures assessing type (e.g., emotional, informational), source, quantity, or quality of resource.

Cohen and his colleagues (S. Cohen & Syme, 1985; S. Cohen & Wills, 1985) proposed a distinction between structural and functional support measures. Structural refers to measures describing the existence of and interconnections between social ties (e.g., marital status, number of relationships, or number of relations who know one another). Functional measures assess whether interpersonal relationships serve particular functions (e.g., provide affection, feelings of belonging, or material aid). House and Kahn's (1985) social network and social relationship categories would be classified as structural, whereas their social support category would be classified functional.

As discussed in the following review, only a small sample of possible conceptions of social support have been used with any frequency in studies of morbidity and mortality. The most common measure is a structural index of social ties that is often termed *social integration* (SI). A prototypic SI index includes marital status, close family and friends, participation in group activities, and church/religious affiliations. Functional measures used in the physical disease literature include network satisfaction and perceived availability of material aid or psychological support.

Research Suggesting a Link Between Social Support and the Etiology of Physical Disease

I now present a select review of the studies linking various conceptions of social support to the etiology of disease. (See an earlier review by Berkman, 1985.) My review focuses on social support conceptions that are examined across several studies. As a whole, the data are suggestive of important links among social environment, disease, and mortality but provide only clues as to the processes by which such links occurs.

Mortality Studies

The best-documented effects in this literature are of the role of social integration on total mortality. In general, after controlling for traditional risk factors such as blood pressure, cigarette smoking, and serum cholesterol levels, *healthy* persons with higher SI scores are at lower risk for mortality than their more isolated counterparts (Berkman & Syme, 1979; House et al., 1982; Schoenbach et al., 1986). Although there is evidence that SI decreases risk only or primarily for men (House et al., 1982; Schoenbach et al., 1986), some studies have found social integration effects for both men and women (Berkman & Syme, 1979; Orth-Gomer & Johnson, 1986). Even studies that have failed to find effects for women in analyses of total mortality reported SI–mortality associations for women in secondary analyses. Hence, House et al. (1982) reported that women with lower SI scores were at higher risk of deaths due to ischemic heart disease, and Schoenbach et al. (1986) found an SI–

total mortality effect for elderly women (70 to 80 years old). Associations between SI and mortality in this literature are generally weaker for nonwhites than for whites (Berkman, 1986).

There is also evidence that SI predicts mortality for persons who are *unhealthy* at the onset of the study, namely, for male survivors of acute myocardial infarctions or MIs (Ruberman, Weinblatt, Goldberg, & Chaudhary, 1984). These men were followed for 1 to 3 years after their MIs. After controlling for traditional risk, relatively isolated survivors were found to have more total deaths and more sudden cardiac deaths than their less isolated counterparts.

Three of the mortality studies assessed satisfaction with social networks. Marital satisfaction (Berkman & Syme, 1979) and satisfaction with social activities (House et al., 1982) were both unrelated to mortality. In a study of older adults, however, perceived adequacy of support was associated with decreased risk of mortality (Blazer, 1982). Unfortunately, the limited number of studies and the lack of conceptual consistency across these studies makes it difficult to draw any firm conclusions about the role of support satisfaction.

Limits in interpretation of mortality data. Studies predicting mortality in healthy populations do not provide direct evidence in regard to the role of social support in the etiology of disease. First, mortality can be caused by factors other than disease (e.g., accidents or natural deterioration with age). In the case of support, however, studies breaking mortality down by cause indicate an association between social integration and deaths attributed to disease (e.g., Berkman & Breslow, 1983; House et al., 1982). Second, even if mortality is attributable to disease, mortality studies of initially healthy persons do not clarify the stage of the disease process at which support acts. Hence, greater mortality for those with fewer social contacts may be accounted for by increased incidence (onset) of disease, increased severity of disease, faster progression of disease, or reduced recovery from disease. Some specificity is provided by the single study reporting SI prediction of mortality for persons *with* serious disease (MI survivors; Ruberman et al., 1984). Because this study predicts mortality after disease onset, it suggests that support plays a role in disease progression and/or recovery. These results do not, however, eliminate the possibility of SI influences on disease onset.

Morbidity Studies

Although there are strong suggestions that various conceptions of social support are associated with disease onset, the results of the morbidity studies are less consistent and generally more difficult to interpret. The majority of this evidence examines the association of support to coronary heart disease (CHD), although there are also scattered studies of support and cancer, support and pregnancy complications, and so forth.

CHD. There is evidence from two studies of Japanese-American men that SI measures are associated with prevalence of MI, angina pectoris (AP), and CHD (Joseph, 1980; Reed, McGee, Yano, & Feinleib, 1983). Due to the possibility that structures and/or functions of social networks differ across subcultures, caution is urged in generalizing these results to other populations.

More culturally diverse samples were used in two recent studies of the relation between support and the prevalence of coronary artery disease (CAD). T. E. Seeman and Syme (1987) studied men and women undergoing angiography in six San Francisco Bay Area hospitals. They reported that persons with greater instrumental support available from their networks and persons who felt loved had less atherosclerosis than their unsupported counterparts. Atherosclerosis was unrelated to SI, to its structural components, or to emotional support from family or friends. A similar study, focusing on emotional support in a sample of men and women undergoing angiography at Duke University, was reported by Blumenthal et al. (1987). Like T. E. Seeman and Syme (1987), they found no main effect of emotional support on atherosclerosis. However, they did find an interaction between emotional support and the Type A behavior pattern. Greater occlusion of the coronary arteries was related to less emotional support among Type As but to more emotional support among Type Bs. Although T. E. Seeman and Syme (1987) also tested the interaction between emotional support and the Type A behavior pattern, they did not find this effect. These studies suggest that support may play a role in CAD, but they are inconsistent in regard to the nature of this role. Moreover, sample biases in angiography studies suggest cautious interpretation (S. Cohen & Matthews, 1987). Because angiography samples are limited to symptomatic patients, these studies attempt to discriminate between those patients with symptoms who have CAD and those patients with symptoms who do not. This is quite different from distinguishing between the diseased and healthy in the general population.

One of the studies of CHD in Japanese-American men, the Honolulu Heart Study, examined SI as a predictor of the onset (incidence) of CHD, as well as the concurrent (prevalence) relations between SI and disease (Reed, McGee, & Yano, 1984; Reed et al., 1983). These incidence data only partly support a relation between SI and CHD. Total CHD rates were higher among more isolated men when an SI scale developed through factor analysis was used. This effect was accounted for primarily through the prediction of nonfatal MIs. However, this scale was not associated with the incidence of AP or of fatal MIs, and a conceptually developed SI scale failed to predict any of these outcomes.

A different conceptualization of support—perception of social support received from a supervisor—was addressed in an analysis of data from working women participating in the Framingham Heart Study (Haynes & Feinleib, 1980). Working women who perceived that their supervisors were nonsupportive had an increased risk of developing CHD over an 8-year period. Interpretation of these data is muddied by the possibility that the perception of supervisor support may be a proxy for job stress rather than an independent assessment of support level.

Three morbidity studies that have examined the possible role of social support as a *buffer* (moderator) of the increased risk associated with high levels of stress also vary in support measurement and results. Johnson (1986) found that degree of interaction with coworkers buffered the effects of work stress on CHD prevalence for both men and women. Medalie and Goldbourt (1976) found that men who reported that their wives loved and supported them were buffered from the effects of high anxiety on the incidence of AP. However, the Honolulu Heart Study (Reed et al., 1984) found no stress-buffering effect of an SI-like index for men in predicting CHD incidence.

Other outcomes. The Honolulu Heart Study data set was also analyzed for evidence of social support relations to cancer (Joffres, Reed, & Nomura, 1985). None of the eight items tested (assessing marital status, number of contacts, and frequency of activities) showed the predicted positive impact

of support. In another analysis of these data, four structural support measures—closeness of parents, marital status, number of children, and number of persons in the household — were used to predict incidence of CHD, stroke, cancer, and all diseases (Reed et al., 1984). The inverse relation found between this index and CHD incidence is presented earlier in this article. None of the other outcomes was related to the total SI score.

An SI measure was also used to predict pregnancy complications in a recent prospective study of Navajo women (Boyce et al., 1986). SI was marginally related to complications, with greater complications occurring among the relatively isolated group. Again, the possible importance of culture in support effects suggests caution in generalizing this result.

Two studies have found that psychosocial assets—a single index including personal characteristics, health, and social support—acted as a stress buffer. The first reported increased pregnancy complications among persons with high stress and low assets (Nuckolls, Cassel, & Kaplan, 1972); the second found increased dosage of adrenocorticosteroids (medication used to control asthma) among high-stress, low-assets asthma sufferers (deAraujo, van Arsdel, Holmes, & Dudley, 1973). Unfortunately, it is unclear whether these effects are attributable to social support or to some other aspect of the assets measure. (See methodological and statistical critique of these studies in S. Cohen & Edwards, 1989.)

Suggestion of a stress-buffering effect more clearly attributable to support is provided by a pregnancy complication study by Norbeck and Tilden (1983). Support measures in this study included perceived availability of emotional and tangible support. Women's perceptions of tangible support acted as a buffer of the stress occurring during pregnancy in the prediction of two of three categories of complications but not for total complications. However, neither the four interactions between life stress and emotional support nor any of the eight interactions between life stress during the prior year and support were consistent with the hypothesis that support operates as a stress buffer.

Summary

In sum, there is reasonable evidence for a tie between social integration and mortality and a suggestion of such an effect in the morbidity (specifically CHD) studies. Although less consistent in both conceptualization and results, the morbidity studies also suggest that perceived availability of support may operate as a stress buffer. A major weakness in the morbidity work is the lack of evidence of support effects in studies that prospectively predict the onset (incidence) of disease. (For example, only the Honolulu Heart Study provided incidence data for a link between social integration and CHD in an initially healthy sample.) As a result, this work is similar to the mortality work in that it is unclear whether support influences onset, progression, or recovery from disease. Moreover, prevalence studies are also open to an interpretation of reverse causation—illness resulting in smaller and/or less accessible social networks.

The morbidity literature is also weak from another perspective. The vast majority of existing studies focus on CHD. Because heart disease is the major cause of death in the United States, CHD (and CAD in particular) is an important disease to study. The widely accepted model of CAD pathogenesis attributes MIs to atherosclerosis, a relatively unique (among diseases) pathogenic process. Development of atherosclerosis, however, is presumed to be facilitated by psychologically mediated neuroendocrine response, particularly the release of the catecholamines epinephrine and norepinephrine, and by standard behavioral risks such as smoking and poor diet (Glass, 1977). Because neuroendocrine and behavioral mediators are thought to be involved in the development of a wide range of diseases (e.g., infectious diseases, cancer, and stroke), evidence implicating social support in CHD suggests the likelihood that support may play a role in other diseases as well.

Models Linking Social Support to the Onset of Illness

The models to be presented address the hypothetical roles of social support in *onset, severity,* and *progression* of disease. Although much of what is discussed could also be applied to recovery, there is enough difference between these stages and recovery to require additional assumptions. For example, adequate models of recovery require a focus on support influences on disease symptoms, rehabilitative behaviors, availability and quality of caretaking, and so forth. The interested reader is referred to reviews and discussions of recovery in DiMatteo and Hays (1981), Wallston et al. (1983), and Wortman and Conway (1985).

I discuss three levels of analysis for modeling the possible influence of social support on the etiology of disease: generic models, stress-centered models, and psychosocial process models. This categorization of levels is in some ways arbitrary but provides a tool for illustrating the incremental development that has occurred in the conceptualization of the relation between social support and disease. The generic and stress-centered models represent early and relatively simple approaches; the psychosocial process models build on these early models by specifying the complexity of psychosocial processes in greater detail. Specificity of support conception occurs only in the context of the psychosocial process models. The models I present all focus on either a lack of support (e.g., isolation as a cause of illness) or on support as a promoter of health. These models are recursive in nature (i.e., they move in one direction, from support to health, without addressing alternative directions and feedback loops). Exclusion of these alternative paths is not intended to reflect any hypotheses about their existence. Finally, models within each category are not considered mutually exclusive. That is, it is possible (and even likely) that support influences health through more than one mechanism.

Generic Models

At the most elementary level, it can be posited that social support is linked to illness either through its influence on behavioral patterns that increase or decrease risk for disease (Model 1) or through effects on biological responses that influence disease (Model 2). These models are depicted in Table 15.1.

Examples of *health behaviors* that may be influenced by social support include diet, exercise, smoking, and alcohol intake. Depending on social norms and on the nature of information provided by one's social network, support may increase or decrease these behaviors. Poor health habits could put persons at risk for practically any disease. For example, smoking is a major risk factor for stroke,

TABLE 15.1. Generic Models Linking Social Support to Physical Disease

Model 1: support → behavior → disease
Model 2: support → biological response → disease
Model 3: support → behavior → biological response → disease

heart disease, and lung cancer. *Biological processes* presumed to be influenced directly or indirectly by social support include neuroendocrine response, immune response (either directly or as a reaction to neurendocrine reactivity), and hemodynamic responses. Increased support is presumed to result in suppression of neuroendocrine and hemodynamic response and in increased immune competence. Diseases associated with immune functioning include infectious diseases, allergies, autoimmune diseases, and cancer (see Ader, 1981; Ader & N. Cohen, 1984; Jemmott & Locke, 1984). Neuroendocrine response may modulate immune response (e.g., Laudenslager, 1988), but elevated neuroendocrine response may also directly damage artery walls and facilitate other pathogenic processes presumed to be involved in CAD (e.g., Glass, 1977; Krantz & Manuck, 1984). Finally, hemodynamic responses (e.g., sheer turbulence in blood flow) are also associated with CAD pathogenesis (e.g., Manuck, Kaplan, & Matthews, 1986).

Models 1 and 2 converge when the effects of behavior on disease are mediated by biological response (Model 3). Behaviors may be linked to the same biological processes proposed in Model 2. For example, active forms of coping result in increased neuroendocrine response that may be directly or indirectly (through the immune system) linked to disease (e.g., Manuck, Harvey, Lechleiter, & Neal, 1978; Obrist, 1981; Solomon, Holmes, & McCaul, 1980). Alternatively, behaviors may influence other biological processes. For example, poor diet may be associated with elevated serum cholesterol levels (which may promote CAD), and excessive alcohol intake may result in direct damage to the liver.

Stress-Centered Models

The next level of analysis addresses whether social support is only important for persons under stress or whether it is potentially beneficial irre-spective of stress level. The stress-buffering model proposes that support is related to well-being only (or primarily) for persons under stress (see early discussion by Cassel, 1976). This is termed the *stress-buffering model* because it posits that support "buffers" (protects) persons from the potentially pathogenic influence of stressful events. The alternative model proposes that social resources have a beneficial effect irrespective of whether persons are under stress. Because the evidence for this model derives from the demonstration of a statistical main effect of support with no Stress × Support interaction, this is termed the *main-effect model*. Implied (but not specified) in both stress-buffering and main-effect models is that support is linked to disease endpoints through behavioral and/or biological processes discussed earlier.

In the case of the stress-buffering model, support presumably operates by short-circuiting or preventing behavioral and biological responses to stress that are inimical to health. The possible stress-buffering mechanisms of social support are depicted in Table 15.2. As indicated by the table, support may play a role at two different points in the causal chain linking stress to illness (cf. S. Cohen & McKay, 1984; Gore, 1981; House, 1981; also see discussion of coping and appraisal process in Lazarus & Folkman, 1984). First, support may intervene between the potentially stressful event (or expectation of that event) and a stress reaction by attenuating or preventing a stress appraisal response. That is, the perception that others can and will provide necessary resources may redefine the potential for harm posed by a situation and/or bolster one's perceived ability to cope with imposed demands and hence may prevent a particular situation from being appraised as highly stressful. Second, adequate support may intervene between the experience of stress and the onset of the pathological outcome by reducing or eliminating the affective reaction, by directly dampening physiologic processes, or by altering maladaptive behavior responses. Support may alleviate the impact of stress appraisal by providing a solution

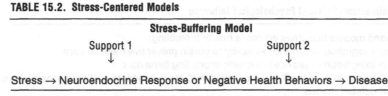

TABLE 15.2. Stress-Centered Models

Stress-Buffering Model

Support 1   Support 2
↓   ↓

Stress → Neuroendocrine Response or Negative Health Behaviors → Disease

Support 1 refers to benign appraisal of stressful events due to support.
Support 2 refers to dampening of endocrine response due to reappraisal, adjustive counterresponse, inhibition of maladjustive response.

to the problem, by reducing the perceived importance of the problem, by providing a distraction from the problem, by tranquilizing the neuroendocrine system so that people are less reactive to perceived stress, or by facilitating healthful behaviors such as exercise, personal hygiene, proper nutrition, and rest (cf. S. Cohen & Wills, 1985; House, 1981).

Psychosocial Process Models

A final category of models includes those that provide elaborate descriptions of the nature of psychosocial mediation of the social support–health relation. These models specify the psychological and biological processes implied in the generic models and separately address main and stress-buffering effects.

The models proposed in this section rely on hypothesized links between specific conceptions of support and specific psychosocial and biological processes. It is theoretically possible to derive different models for each of the multiple conceptions of social support proposed and/or measured in the literature. However, I felt it would be more useful and less cumbersome to model only those relations that are substantially supported by existing empirical work. Such a basis is provided by combining the conclusions of this review of studies of the role of support in physical disease with earlier reviews of studies of the role of support in psychological distress (S. Cohen & Wills, 1985; Kessler & McLeod, 1985). These reviews suggest that social integration is the primary cause of main effects of social support and that perceived availability of support is the primary cause of stress-buffering effects. As a result, the models discussed here focus on how social integration and perceived availability of support are linked to disease out-

comes. This choice should not be interpreted as my conclusion that these are the only relevant conceptualizations of support in this context. I am merely using existing empirical work to help determine a focus that merits detailed analysis at this time.

Main-Effect Models

Recall that the main-effect model predicts that the influence of support on health is independent of current stress level and that main effects of support have been primarily found when support is defined as social integration. Hence, our main-effect models focus on plausible links between *social integration* and health. Social integration has been conceptualized by Thoits (1983) as having multiple identities (i.e., ties to network members with different roles). Table 15.3 summarizes several psychological pathways through which social integration may influence the susceptibility to and recovery from disease.

Information-based models. Having a wide range of network ties presumably provides multiple sources of information and hence an increased probability of having access to an appropriate information source. Information could influence health-relevant behaviors or could help one to avoid stressful or other high-risk situations. For example, network members could provide information regarding access to medical services or information regarding the benefits of behaviors that positively influence health and well-being. Appropriate information could also aid in avoiding stressful life events or in avoiding exposure to infectious or carcinogenic agents (Berkman, 1985; S. Cohen & Syme, 1985). It is noteworthy, however, that integration in a social network could also operate to the detriment of health: discouraging use of medical services, providing inadequate alter-

TABLE 15.3. Main-Effect Models of Psychological Influence

Information-based models (assumes advice is health promoting)
    Social integration → (advice) → ability to obtain preventive medical care
    Social integration → (advice) → health-promoting behaviors
    Social integration → (advice) → information to avoid stressors and other health risks
Identity and self-esteem models
    Social integration (role identity) → sense of identity + evaluative basis for sense of mastery →
        meaning to one's life → less despair and anxiety → health-promoting behaviors
    Social integration → self-esteem and perceived control → greater motivation to care for oneself →
        health-promoting behaviors
    Social integration → increased positive affect, sense of well-being, control over environment →
        suppressed neuroendocrine reactivity and enhanced immune function or → health-promoting
        behaviors
    Isolation → increased negative affect, sense of alienation, lack of perceived control → elevated
        neuroendocrine response and immune suppression or → negative health behaviors
    Lacking ties → stress → negative affective state → . . .
Social influence models
    Social integration → social controls and peer pressures, constraints to behave as others do → health-
        enhancing behaviors (assumes pressures toward health-promotive behaviors)
Tangible-resource models
    Social networks → aid and tangible and economic services → network taking better care of
        members → limited exposure to risk factors

native care, or influencing people to adopt behaviors inimical to health (e.g., McKinlay, 1973; Sanders, 1982; Seeman, Seeman, & Sayles, 1985).

Identity and self-esteem models. There are several theoretical perspectives suggesting that social support increases feelings of self-esteem, of self-identity, and of control over one's environment—feelings that result in better health. Social integration is presumed to provide a source of generalized positive affect, a sense of predictability and stability in one's life, and a recognition of self-worth due to demonstrated ability to meet normative role expectations (Cassel, 1976; Hammer, 1981; Thoits, 1983; Wills, 1985). These positive psychological states are presumed to be facilitative because they lessen psychological despair (Thoits, 1985), result in greater motivation to care for oneself (e.g., S. Cohen & Syme, 1985), or result in suppressed neuroendocrine response and enhanced immune function (Bovard, 1959; Cassel, 1976).

A popular model in this category assumes that it is *isolation* that causes disease rather than social integration that enhances health. This approach assumes that isolation increases negative affect and sense of alienation and decreases sense of control. Alternatively, one can merely view isolation as a stressor. In any case, as noted earlier, these negative psychological states could induce increases in neuroendocrine response, suppress immune function, and interfere with performance of health behaviors.

Social influence models. A socially integrated person is subject to social controls and peer pressures that influence normative health behaviors. To the extent that these pressures promote healthful behaviors (e.g., exercise, better diet, not smoking, moderating alcohol intake), social integration would promote better health. To the extent that normative behaviors within a social network promote behaviors that are deleterious to health, social integration would result in poorer health and well-being.

Tangible-resource models. A network may operate to prevent disease by providing aid and tangible and economic services that result in better health and better health care for network members. For example, network members could provide food, clothing, and housing that operate to prevent disease and limit exposure to risk factors. Networks may also provide (nonprofessional) health care that prevents minor illness from developing into more serious disease.

Stress-Buffering Models

Recall that the stress-buffering model posits that support "buffers" (protects) persons from the potentially pathogenic influence of stressful events. As suggested earlier, the following models focus on the *perceived availability of social support* because this conception has been found to result in stress-buffering effects. S. Cohen and McKay (1984) and S. Cohen and Wills (1985) have also proposed that stress-buffering occurs only when there is a match between the needs elicited by the stressful event and the functions of support that are perceived to be available. For example, having someone who would loan you money may be useful in the face of a temporary job loss but useless in the face of the death of a friend. A matching of support with need is implied, although not specified, in many of the models to be discussed. S. Cohen and Wills also argued that certain types of support may be useful in coping with all or many

stressors. Specifically, having people to talk to about problems (appraisal support) and having people who make you feel better about yourself (self-esteem support) may be generally useful because these are coping requirements elicited by most stressors. The stress-buffering models are depicted in Table 15.4.

Information-based models. Stress may elicit network provision of information about the nature of the potential stressful events or about ways of coping with those events (see discussion of social comparison under stress by S. Cohen & McKay, 1984; Wills, 1983). To the extent that this information reduces the evaluation of potential threat or harm in the context of existing coping resources, the event would be appraised as less threatening and/or harmful and hence the risk of illness decreased. It is also likely that in many cases the perception of available support operates *without any actual support being provided.* That is, knowing (or at least believing) that others will provide

---

TABLE 15.4. Stress-Buffering Models of Psychological Influence

Information-based models
    Stress → network provision of stress-buffering information (or perception of the availability of that information) resulting in benign appraisal of stressful events or enhanced ability to cope with stressful events or their affective consequences
        → prevention of stress-induced biological and behavioral responses inimical to health
        → health maintenance

Identity and self-esteem models
    Stress → network-assisted or -enhanced coping
        → increased control and/or self-esteem
        → suppression of neuroendocrine response, enhanced immune function, and/or health-enhancing behaviors
        → health maintenance
    Stress → network-assisted or -enhanced coping (or perceived availability of network assistance)
        → increased control and/or self-esteem
        → suppression of neuroendocrine response, enhanced immune function, and/or health-enhancing behaviors
        → health maintenance

Social influence models
    Stress → network pressures (or expected pressures) to adopt particular modes of coping with stressors resulting in benign appraisal of stressful events or (when coping strategies are appropriate) enhanced ability to cope with stressful events and the emotional effects of stress appraisal
        → prevention of stress-induced biological and behavioral responses inimical to health
        → health maintenance

Tangible-resource models
    Stress → network provision of aid and tangible and economic services resulting in benign appraisal of stressful events or enhanced ability to cope with stressful events
        → prevention of stress-induced biological and behavioral responses inimical to health
        → health maintenance

needed information if it becomes necessary can similarly result in a potentially stressful event or events being appraised as benign (e.g., Wethington & Kessler, 1986). In both cases, a reduction in stress appraisal would be presumed to reduce negative affect, negative health behaviors, and concomitant physiological reactivity.

Emotional responses to stressful events may also elicit network provision of information. In this case, the information would be health enhancing if it helped to control undesirable feelings (Thoits, 1985). The reduction of negative affect produced by a stress appraisal is presumed to influence health outcomes in the same ways as already discussed—that is, by reducing negative health behaviors and physiological reactivity.

Identity and self-esteem models. These models are minor twists on the information models already described. They suggest that others' willingness to help and/or the enhanced ability to cope that results from receiving help increase feelings of personal control and self-esteem. As noted earlier, such feelings may influence health through increased motivation to perform health behaviors or through suppression of neuroendocrine responses and enhanced immune function. Again, the mere perception that help is available may similarly trigger these processes.

Social influence models. Social controls and peer pressures could influence persons to cope with stressors in particular normative manners. Such influence processes would promote health to the extent that the normative coping behaviors were effective in reducing perceptions of stress, nonadjustive behavioral adaptations, and negative affective responses. Inappropriate norms, however, could lead to less effective coping and hence greater risk of stress-elicited disease. To the extent that social coping norms were internalized, or that persons expected others to pressure them to cope in a particular manner, the mere perception of availability could influence stress–disease process in the same manner as actually receiving support.

Tangible-resource models. Network contribution of aid or of tangible or economic services could reduce the probability of potentially stressful events being appraised as threatening or harmful and hence could reduce the behavioral and affective concomitants of such an appraisal. Again, the mere perception of the availability of aid may operate without actual receipt of help. Tangible resources could also help resolve specific (tangible-related) problems after a stress appraisal is made.

Evidence for Separate Links in the Psychosocial Models

There is only a handful of studies that provide evidence for the individual links (separate paths) in the proposed psychosocial models. Unfortunately, in many cases, the conceptualizations of support do not match up well with those proposed in this article, and the results are not always directly relevant. However, a short review is presented to provide a summary of what we know about the potential links.

Social support and health behaviors. In their prospective analysis of the Alameda County data, Berkman and Syme (1979) found that health practices were positively associated with SI. Their health practice measure equally weighted smoking, drinking alcohol, eating breakfast, eating between meals, sleeping 7 or 8 hr a night, participation in regular physical activity, and weight (adjusted for height). These health practices explained only a small amount of the association between SI and mortality (Berkman & Breslow, 1983), and the SI–mortality association remained after they were partialed out. This small mediating effect is tempered by the fact that the health practice measure used in these analyses was assessed only at the beginning of the study and thus may not accurately reflect health practice changes that occurred over the course of the study.

In a prospective study of adults 65 years old and older, Blazer (1982) also found evidence for a relation between support and health practices. All three support measures—an SI-type measure, a frequency-of-interaction measure, and a perceived-availability-of-support measure—were associated with relatively beneficial changes in self-care over the course of the 30-month study. The self-care instrument assessed various instrumental and physical (or body care) tasks that permit individuals to live independently.

The possibility that social networks and social supports influence health behaviors is also suggested by recent research on quitting smoking. Successful quitting has been linked to positively supportive behaviors from one's spouse (Abrams et al., 1985; Lichtenstein, Glasgow, & Abrams,

1986; Mermelstein, Cohen, Lichtenstein, Kamarck, & Baer, 1986), and the ability to maintain smoking abstinence over 30 to 60 days has been linked to perceived availability of social support, especially to perceived availability of persons to talk to about one's problems (Mermelstein et al., 1986). Negative influences of social networks on smoking have also been found when one's network is made up primarily of other smokers. Initiating, quitting, and staying off cigarettes have been tied to the proportion of smokers in a person's social network (see review in S. Cohen et al., 1988). The more smokers, the greater the chance of smoking.

A final study examined the influence of perceived availability of support *in times of illness* for performance of preventive health behaviors. In a community sample, M. Seeman et al. (1985) found that the perceived availability of instrumental support is unrelated to preventive health behavior, whereas the perceived ability to consult with friends and relatives in times of illness is *negatively* related to health practices. This work is interesting but difficult to interpret in this context. It is possible that support in times of illness is somewhat independent of support processes that operate during more representative healthy periods. For example, family members may provide support in time of illness but not provide support for coping with the more usual life strains and hassles. The latter form of support is what is proposed earlier—see Stress-Buffering Models—as a predictor of health practices.

Social support and affect. Relatively higher levels of social support have been clearly linked with less negative affect (see reviews by S. Cohen & Wills, 1985; Kessler & McLeod, 1985). The strongest ties have been shown in both prospective and cross-sectional studies of depressed affect and social integration (e.g., Schaefer, Coyne, & Lazarus, 1981; Surtees, 1980; Williams, Ware, & Donald, 1981), confidant relationships (e.g., Dean & Ensel, 1982; Henderson, 1981), and perceptions of informational and emotional support (e.g., S. Cohen & Hoberman, 1983; Schaefer et al., 1981). Perceived availability of support has also been shown to protect persons from the psychological distress usually associated with high levels of stressful life events (e.g., S. Cohen & Hoberman, 1983; Henderson, Byrne, & Duncan-Jones, 1981; Wilcox, 1981).

There is less evidence in regard to the association between social support and positive affect. Positive morale has been found to be positively associated with tangible, emotional, and informational support (Schaefer et al., 1981), number of friends and relatives who could be counted on (Eckenrode, Kruger, & Cerkovnik, 1986), number of friends and relatives who had provided help with problems in the previous year (Eckenrode et al., 1986), and neighborhood cohesion (P. Cohen et al., 1982). Schaefer et al. (1981), however, did not find a relation between SI and positive morale.

Social support, self-esteem, and personal control. In a study of the stress-buffer model, increased self-esteem and personal control were found among stressed persons with a confidant (Pearlin, Menaghan, Lieberman, & Mullan, 1981). This work suggests the possibility that control and self-esteem mediate stress-buffering effects. A study of the main-effect model found evidence for an association between control and health but not for control as a mediator of the relation between support and health (M. Seeman et al., 1985). Health locus of control and generalized feelings of control were both positively associated with perceived overall health status and preventive care. This study found, however, only minimal correlations between instrumental support in response to illness and general and health-specific control and between availability of someone to talk to about an illness and these control measures. Because this work assessed support in times of illness and did not address the possibility that support operated as a stress buffer—both measures assess perceived availability—it does not provide a direct test of any of the proposed models.

Social support and neuroendocrine response. Support influences on neuroendocrine response have been suggested as possible mediators of relations between support and CAD and between support and immune functioning. At this point, the only study addressing a support–neuroendocrine link provides rather mixed results. Fleming, Baum, Gisriel, and Gatchel (1982) found that perceived availability of emotional support was related to decreased norepinephrine both among persons living near the Three Mile Island nuclear plant and among those living in a control area. Emotional support, however, was not related to epinephrine levels, and the authors failed to find the stress-buffering interaction (effectiveness of support only for those living near Three Mile Island) that they (and I) expected.

Social support and immune function. Suggestive evidence of a link between support and immune function is provided by two recent studies of the relations between loneliness and immune modulation (Glaser, Kiecolt-Glaser, Speicher, & Holliday, 1985; Kiecolt-Glaser et al., 1984). If we assume that loneliness is roughly equivalent to the social isolation pole of SI, then these data can be viewed as suggestive for our purpose (see Rook, 1985, for limitations of this assumption). Specifically, both medical students and psychiatric patients with high scores on a loneliness scale had higher levels of latent viral activity (as indicated by elevated antibody titers to herpes viruses) than those who described themselves as less lonely. An elevation of latent viral activity is considered an indication of a relatively suppressed cellular immune response.

Where Do We Go From Here?

A Role for Psychologists?

Sophisticated studies of the relations between social supports and physical health are by nature interdisciplinary. To address models proposing social influences on infection, atherosclerosis, and other pathogenic processes, it is necessary to collaborate with medical scientists with expertise in the specific disease under consideration and in state-of-the-art techniques for assessing pathogenic process and disease. However, the role of psychologists in this work is as important as that of medical scientists. Psychologists are *uniquely* qualified to provide insight into the mechanisms through which social environments influence cognition, affect, behavior, and physiologic response (cf. Taylor, 1978). In short, psychology has the theory, data, and perspective necessary to propose plausible models that suggest *when and why* social networks and/or perceptions of support influence health. Psychologists also have the technical skills necessary to develop psychometrically sound measures of social support and of the psychological states and behaviors proposed as important mediators of support–disease links.

Research Priorities

The thrust of this article is an attempt to influence the form of the questions researchers ask when designing studies of the relations between social support and health. The general message is to enter this work with clear hypotheses regarding *both* the psychosocial and pathogenic processes by which specific conceptualizations of support influence specific outcomes. Choices of social support concepts and of disease outcomes should be driven by theory or theories specifying the psychological and biological pathways by which such outcomes could occur.

This orientation calls for a rather different approach to research design and analysis than has been traditionally applied in this area. First, much of the existing work involves post hoc analyses of data sets that were not designed to test hypotheses regarding social support. In most cases, the choice of support measures has been dictated by the questions about the social environment that happened to be available in an existing data set. Instead, social support measures used in future studies should be chosen because they represent appropriate concepts for predicting the etiology of the diseases under consideration. Second, existing work often measures traditional risk factors for the disease under consideration (e.g., smoking, diet, serum cholesterol) and controls for these factors in the data analyses. In other words, the question being asked up to now is whether social support influences disease outcomes independent of traditional risk. Several models proposed in this article, however, suggest that support may have its influence on morbidity and mortality *through its influence on behavioral risk factors.* Hence, in these cases, these factors should not be treated as controls but rather as mediators (Berkman, 1985). It may be that previous studies controlling for risk underestimated the influence of support on health by subtracting effects on risk that were actually attributable to support. Finally, existing work seldom looks at the role of psychological states, behavior, and concomitant physiological states in mediating the influence of support on health. Instead, hypothesized psychological (e.g., affect, self-esteem, personal control), behavioral (e.g., smoking, diet, health service utilization), and biological (e.g., neuroendocrine and immune function) mediators should be assessed whenever possible.

What social support concepts do we study? Existing evidence suggests that social integration and perceived availability of support are predictive of disease and mortality. Hence, modeling (as in this article) and testing the role of these concepts in disease development and progression are relatively good strategies at this time. However, these models reflect only two of many possible conceptualizations of the social environment, and it would be a mistake to limit our theory and research to these concepts merely because they have been used successfully in the past. Other social support concepts that may play a role in disease etiology include the various structural components derived from social network theory (e.g., density, reciprocity, dispersion, and the qualitative aspects of perceived or received functional support; House & Kahn, 1985).

What diseases do we study? Most models linking psychosocial factors to disease, including the majority of those proposed in this article, assume that the primary link between the psychosocial and biological systems is provided either by *health practices* or by affect-mediated *neuroendocrine response*. Because health practices and neuroendocrine response may have implications for a wide range of diseases, insufficient social support (and stress) are often thought to be potential precursors of a variety of disorders (cf. Cassel, 1976; Selye, 1956). For example, negative affective responses could influence cancer and infectious diseases through neuroendocrine-elicited immunosuppression and CHD through neuroendocrine-elicited facilitation of coronary artery occlusion. Similarly, cigarette smoking provides a good example of a health practice that has been implicated in multiple diseases, including CHD, stroke, lung cancer, and upper respiratory infection.

It is clear, however, that some diseases are more likely to be influenced by social support than others and that each disease (or possibly, each category of disease) should be considered separately. Two questions should be addressed in deciding whether a particular disease is susceptible to support influence. First, is it plausible that behavioral and biological processes presumed to be influenced by social support are important precursors of the disease? For example, although modulations of neuroendocrine response and/or changes in health

practices are assumed to play a role in the pathogenesis of some diseases (e.g., CAD), their influence on others (e.g., Hodgkin's disease) is less clear. Second, is the conception of support under study temporally stable enough to provide an exposure that is long enough to influence the pathogenesis of the disease under consideration (S. Cohen & Matthews, 1987)? The answer to this question depends on the relation between the temporal stability of a particular conception of support and the developmental course of the disease under study. Plausible models assume either (a) that the support conception under examination is relatively stable over the period of disease development or (b) that a short-term exposure to a particular level of social support is sufficient to influence the disease process.

An example of the importance of matching the stability of the support measure and temporal characteristics of disease pathogenesis is provided by the relation between social integration and CAD. Social integration is a temporally stable conceptualization of social support, and CAD has a very long and slow course of development (clinical disease generally requiring many years). Hence, there is a reasonable match here between stability of the support measure and the temporal characteristics of disease pathogenesis. That is, exposure to relatively lower levels of social integration lasts over the period of disease development. Conceptualizations of social support with much shorter temporal stabilities such as support satisfaction or perceived availability (see S. Cohen & Matthews, 1987) would *not* be plausible predictors of CAD pathogenesis, although they may be plausible predictors of disease with short-term developments—diseases such as colds and influenza.

It is possible, however, to propose plausible models of slowly developing diseases that focus on support measures with shorter stabilities. For example, we have been discussing support processes that may influence the development of atherosclerosis. As noted earlier, this disease develops over many years. However, clinically significant progressions in CAD can occur over relatively short periods. Consider, for example, modeling MI incidence. Assume that persons with undetected CAD are more likely to manifest this disease in an MI if they experience stress (e.g., Glass, 1977). A severe stressor might trigger the onset of the detectable disease. In this case, perceived available support, a support concept with less temporal stability, may be important if it is stable over the course of stressor exposure and operates to buffer persons from stress at *the trigger point*. Hence, perceived availability of support might protect such a person from stress-triggered disease progression.

Finally, there are plausible support–disease models in which short-term exposures to a particular support level triggers the *onset of the development* of a disease with a long (slow) developmental course. Take, for example, the possibility that sudden and severe breaches in social support—such as those produced by divorce or bereavement—may be associated with immunologic changes that set a given disease in motion. Hence, a short term without support may hit with sufficient impact to produce a dramatic but short-lived compromise in immune functioning—triggering the onset of a disease like cancer, which may then be self-perpetuating.

In sum, the question of whether a particular disease is susceptible to support influence depends on (a) whether the conceptualization of support under consideration affects processes that influence disease pathogenesis, (b) the temporal stability of the support concept, and (c) the nature and time course of the pathogenesis of the disease. As noted earlier, existing work on morbidity is almost totally limited to CAD. It is clear, however, that stable conceptions of support like social integration are plausibly related to the onset and progression of diseases with both long-term and short-term pathogeneses and that less stable support conceptions like perceived availability are plausibly related both to diseases with short-term developments and to diseases for which stressors may act as triggers of progression or onset. Future work on diseases with plausible links to both stable and unstable conceptualizations of support is a high priority at this time. High-prevalence diseases such as infectious diseases (ranging from common upper respiratory infections to AIDS) and cancer provide opportunities in this area that have the potential for both theoretical and practical contributions.

What mediators do we study? The models proposed in this article are neither mutually exclusive nor independent. For example, it is likely that the positive influence of social integration on health is mediated *both* through social influences improving health practices and through psychological states, such as control and self-esteem, triggering biological processes. Hence, the simultaneous measurement of behavioral and psychological links seems optimal. There are no human studies tying self-esteem and personal control to biologically verified disease, and hence these often-discussed mediators provide an untapped area for exploration. Finally, because the assumption that support triggers neuroendocrine response is critical to several possible mediating paths, further investigation of this link is essential.

Other variables to consider. Access to, and the meaning of, social support may vary across other social and psychological dimensions. Sources and forms of support may differ among cultures or social classes and between the sexes (Berkman, 1986; S. Cohen & Syme, 1985; Schoenbach et al., 1986). For example, information provided by a network may be less accurate and hence less helpful to persons with lower educational levels. Support may also be useful to persons with some social skills and personality factors but not with others. One possible moderator is personal control. That is, persons with control may be more able to make use of their networks than those who feel they cannot control their outcomes (Lefcourt, Martin, & Saleh, 1984; Sandler & Lakey, 1982; M. Seeman et al., 1985). Future empirical work and theoretical modeling should be sensitive to these differences. Initially, it will be useful to stratify samples by subgroups and to examine the relative efficacy of different types of support for different populations. As the data base increases, it may be necessary to develop unique models for unique populations.

The need for biological verification of disease. Although the influence of social support on sensitivity to symptoms, reporting of symptoms, and utilization of health services are interesting issues, it is imperative to understand that these outcomes do not necessarily involve the same mechanisms that influence disease processes. Certainly, the development of models of symptom reporting and health utilization is a worthwhile pursuit and one especially appropriate for psychologists (cf. Leventhal, Meyer, & Nerenz, 1980; Pennebaker, 1982). If our goal is to understand disease, however, it is necessary to focus on "hard," biologically verifiable (as opposed to self-reported symptoms) disease endpoints.

Studies of biologically documented atherosclerosis, MI, and cancer meet the "hard" outcome criterion, although these diseases involve long-term development and hence are expensive and difficult to study prospectively. One strategy for pursuing such questions would be to "piggyback" sophisticated social support measures and measures of psychological and physiological mediators onto ongoing studies designed to examine other (often biological) issues in disease risk. Alternatively, those interested in infectious diseases (e.g., upper respiratory infections) have a more accessible opportunity to develop and test models of the social etiology of disease as measured by "hard" outcomes. This approach allows for a prospective design and for monitoring of changes in antibodies, virus shedding, and other disease-relevant biological changes over the course of diseases with very short developmental periods (days).

Development of psychometrically valid measures. Psychologists' methodological skills are critically needed to improve the quality of work on support and disease. The primary area for contribution is measurement. Psychometric examination of empirically derived scales used in earlier studies would help clarify the reliability of the early measures and aid in appropriate interpretation of study results. Moreover, it is imperative that future studies employ psychometrically reliable and valid measures of support. Several scales are available at this time (see, e.g., review by House & Kahn, 1985; Sarason, Shearin, Pierce, & Sarason, 1987), and a priori scale construction is a worthy pursuit for those who are unhappy with available instruments or for those who need instruments to assess different support concepts.

The need for prospective data on risk onset and disease onset. Although there is a consistent database in regard to the relation between SI and mortality, there is little work on support and morbidity, and existing studies tend to suffer from inadequate conception and measurement. Moreover, even though we know that SI influences disease-related mortality, we know little about when in the course of the disease support operates. As a consequence, future prospective studies of the incidence of morbidity with adequate controls for disease state at study onset are imperative. Such designs help eliminate causal alternatives and aid in differentiating between the influence of

social support on onset, course, and recovery from disease.

Possibly more important is the total lack of evidence in regard to the role of social support in the *onset* of biologic and behavioral disease risk. Prospective studies of the relation of support to smoking, alcohol abuse, diet change, physical inactivity, and biologic risk such as (in the case of CHD) hypertension, elevated serum cholesterol, and triglycerides would provide some clear evidence for the plausibility of support–disease models presumed to be mediated by health practices and biologic risk.

Summary

The early years of research on the social support concept have resulted in an almost uniform enthusiasm for its importance in the development of disease and maintenance of health (S. Cohen & Syme, 1985). It is only now, after the concept has generated some credibility, that its complexities have become apparent. Shotgun approaches and reanalysis of data sets that were not designed to test links between social support and health will no longer add significantly to our understanding of the construct. Studies need to be designed to test hypotheses about the psychological and biological processes that link social environments and their psychologic representations to health. Psychologists are uniquely qualified to contribute to this effort. They can provide theory and data on the influence of social environments on the behaviors and psychological states that are presumed to influence health, and they have the skills necessary to develop the psychometrically sound measures needed to test proposed links between support and physical well-being.

This article outlines a series of models linking two conceptions of support—social integration and perceived availability of support—to disease onset and progression. Other representations of these specific processes are possible. Moreover, I have addressed only two of the multiple conceptions of social networks and social supports. It is likely that other characteristics of social networks (e.g., density, range, and multiplicity) and of social supports (e.g., actual support received, adequacy, and source) play an important role in disease etiology. I hope that this work will stimulate others to propose alternative models and that future work will focus on specifying the psychological and biological cal processes that link the social environment to disease onset, severity, progression, and recovery.

ACKNOWLEDGMENTS

Preparation of this article was supported by a Research Scientist Development Award to the author from the National Institute of Mental Health (K02 MH00721) and by a grant from the National Institute of Allergies and Infectious Diseases (AI23072). The author is indebted to Sally Shumaker and Tom Wills for their comments on an earlier draft.

REFERENCES

Abrams, D. B., Pinto, R. P., Monti, P. M., Jacobus, S., Brown, R., & Elder, J. P. (1985, March). *Health education vs. cognitive stress management vs. social support training for relapse prevention in worksite smoking cessation.* Paper presented at the annual convention of the Society for Behavioral Medicine, New Orleans.

Ader, R. (1981). *Psychoneuroimmunology.* New York: Academic Press.

Ader, R., & Cohen, N. (1984). Behavior and the immune system. In W. Doyle Gentry (Ed.), *Handbook of behavioral medicine* (pp. 117–173). New York: Guilford.

Berkman, L. F. (1985). The relationship of social networks and social support to morbidity and mortality. In S. Cohen & S. L. Syme (Eds.), *Social support and health* (pp. 241–262). New York: Academic Press.

Berkman, L. F. (1986). Social networks, support, and health: Taking the next step forward. *American Journal of Epidemiology, 123,* 559–562.

Berkman, L. F., & Breslow, L. (1983). *Health and ways of living.* New York: Oxford University Press.

Berkman, L. F., & Syme, S. L. (1979). Social networks, host resistance, and mortality: A nine-year follow-up study of Alameda County residents. *American Journal of Epidemiology, 109,* 186–204.

Blazer, D. G. (1982). Social support and mortality in an elderly community population. *American Journal of Epidemiology, 115,* 684–694.

Blumenthal, J. A., Burg, M. M., Barefoot, J., Williams, R. B., Haney, T., & Zimet, G. (1987). Social support, Type A behavior, and coronary artery disease. *Psychosomatic Medicine, 49,* 331–339.

Bovard, E. (1959). The effects of social stimuli on the response to stress. *Psychological Reviews, 66,* 267–277.

Boyce, W. T., Schaefer, C. H., Harrison, R. H., Haffner, W. H. J., Lewis, M., & Right, A. L. (1986). Social and cultural factors in pregnancy complications among Navajo women. *American Journal of Epidemiology, 124,* 242–253.

Broadhead, W. E., Kaplan, B. H., James, S. A., Wagner, E. H., Schoenbach, V. J., Grimson, R., Heyden, S., Tibblin, G., & Gehlbach, S. H. (1983). The epidemiologic evidence for a relationship between social support and health. *American Journal of Epidemiology, 117,* 521–537.

Cassel, J. C. (1976). The contribution of the social environment to host resistance. *American Journal of Epidemiology, 104,* 107–123.

Cohen, P., Struening, E. L., Muhlin, G. L., Genevie, L. E., Kaplan, S. R., & Peck, H. B. (1982). Community stressors, mediating conditions, and well being in urban neighborhoods. *Journal of Community Psychology, 10,* 377–391.

Cohen, S., & Edwards, J. R. (1989). Personality characteristics as moderators of the relationship between stress and disorder. In R. W. J. Neufeld (Ed.), *Advances in the investigation of psychological stress* (pp. 235–283). New York: Wiley.

Cohen, S., & Hoberman, H. (1983). Positive events and social supports as buffers of life change stress. *Journal of Applied Social Psychology, 13,* 99–125.

Cohen, S., Lichtenstein, E., Mermelstein, R., Kingslover, K., Baer, J. S., & Kamarck, T. W. (1988). Social support interventions for smoking cessation. In B. H. Gottlieb (Ed.), *Marshalling social support: Formats, processes and effects* (pp. 211–240). New York: Sage.

Cohen, S., & Matthews, K. A. (1987). Editorial: Social support, Type A behavior and coronary artery disease. *Psychosomatic Medicine, 49,* 325–330.

Cohen, S., & McKay, G. (1984). Social support, stress and the buffering hypothesis: A theoretical analysis. In A. Baum, S. E. Taylor, & J. E. Singer (Eds.), *Handbook of psychology and health* (pp. 253–267). Hillsdale, NJ: Lawrence Erlbaum.

Cohen, S., & Syme, S. L. (1985). Issues in the study and application of social support. In S. Cohen & S. L. Syme (Eds.), *Social support and health* (pp. 3–22). New York: Academic Press.

Cohen, S., & Wills, T. A. (1985). Stress, social support, and the buffering hypothesis. *Psychological Bulletin, 98,* 310–357.

Dean, A., & Ensel, W. M. (1982). Modeling social support, life events, competence, and depression in the context of age and sex. *Journal of Community Psychology, 10,* 392–408.

deAraujo, G., van Arsdel, P. P., Holmes, T. H., & Dudley, D. L. (1973). Life change, coping ability and chronic intrinsic asthma. *Journal of Psychosomatic Research, 17,* 359–363.

DiMatteo, M. R., & Hays, R. (1981). Social support and serious illness. In B. H. Gottlieb (Ed.), *Social networks and social support* (pp. 117–148). Beverly Hills, CA: Sage.

Eckenrode, J., Kruger, G., & Cerkovnik, M. (1986, August). *Positive and negative affect: Life events and social support as predictors.* Paper presented at the annual meeting of the American Psychological Association, Washington, DC.

Fleming, R., Baum, A., Gisriel, M. M., & Gatchel, R. J. (1982). Mediating influences of social support on stress at Three Mile Island. *Journal of Human Stress, 8,* 14–22.

Glaser, R., Kiecolt-Glaser, J. K., Speicher, C. E., & Holliday, J. E. (1985). Stress, loneliness, and changes in herpesvirus latency. *Journal of Behavioral Medicine, 8,* 249–260.

Glass, D. C. (1977). *Behavior patterns, stress, and coronary disease.* Hillsdale, NJ: Lawrence Erlbaum.

Gore, S. (1981). Stress-buffering functions of social supports: An appraisal and clarification of research models. In B. S. Dohrenwend & B. P. Dohrenwend (Eds.), *Stressful life events and their contexts* (pp. 202–222). New York: Prodist.

Hammer, M. (1981). "Core" and "extended" social networks in relation to health and illness. *Social Science and Medicine, 17,* 405–411.

Haynes, S., & Feinleib, M. (1980). Women, work and coronary heart disease: Prospective findings from the Framingham Heart Study. *American Journal of Public Health, 70,* 133–141.

Heller, K., Swindle, R. W., Jr., & Dusenbury, L. (1986). Component social support processes: Comments and integration. *Journal of Consulting and Clinical Psychology, 54,* 466–470.

Henderson, S. (1981). Social relationships, adversity and neurosis: An analysis of prospective observations. *British Journal of Psychiatry, 138,* 391–398.

Henderson, S., Byrne, D. G., & Duncan-Jones, P. (1981). *Neurosis and the social environment.* New York: Academic Press.

House, J. S. (1981). *Work stress and social support.* Reading, MA: Addison-Wesley.

House, J. S., & Kahn, R. L. (1985). Measures and concepts of social support. In S. Cohen & S. L. Syme (Eds.), *Social support and health* (pp. 83–108). New York: Academic Press.

House, J. S., Robbins, C., & Metzner, H. L. (1982). The association of social relationships and activities with mortality: Prospective evidence from the Tecumseh Community Health Study. *American Journal of Epidemiology, 116,* 123–140.

Jemmott, J. B., III, & Locke, S. E. (1984). Psychosocial factors, immunologic mediation, and human susceptibility to infectious diseases: How much do we know? *Psychological Bulletin, 95,* 78–108.

Joffres, M., Reed, D. M., & Nomura, A. M. Y. (1985). Psychosocial processes and cancer incidence among Japanese men in Hawaii. *American Journal of Epidemiology, 121,* 488–500.

Johnson, J. V. (1986). *The impact of workplace social support, job demands and work control upon cardiovascular disease in Sweden* (Rep. No. 1). Stockholm, Sweden: University of Stockholm, Division of Environmental and Organizational Psychology, Department of Psychology.

Joseph, J. (1980). *Social affiliation, risk fact status and coronary heart disease: A cross-sectional study of Japanese-American men.* Unpublished doctoral dissertation, University of California, Berkeley.

Kaplan, B. H., Cassel, J. C., & Gore, S. (1977). Social support and health. *Medical Care, 15,* 47–58.

Kessler, R. C., & McLeod, J. D. (1985). Social support and mental health in community samples. In S. Cohen & S. L. Syme (Eds.), *Social support and health* (pp. 219–240). New York: Academic Press.

Kiecolt-Glaser, J. K., Garner, W., Speicher, C. E., Penn, G. M., Holliday, J., & Glaser, R. (1984). Psychosocial modifiers of immunocompetence in medical students. *Psychosomatic Medicine, 46,* 7–14.

Krantz, D. S., & Manuck, S. B. (1984). Acute psychophysiologic reactivity and risk of cardiovascular disease: A review and methodologic critique. *Psychological Bulletin, 96,* 435–464.

Laudenslager, M. L. (1988). The psychobiology of loss: Lessons from humans and nonhuman primates. *Journal of Social Issues, 44,* 19–36.

Lazarus, R. S., & Folkman, S. (1984). *Stress, coping, and adaptation.* New York: Springer.

Leavy, R. L. (1983). Social support and psychological disorder: A review. *Journal of Community Psychology, 11,* 3–21.

Lefcourt, H. M., Martin, R. A., & Saleh, W. E. (1984). Locus of control and social support: Interactive moderators of stress. *Journal of Personality and Social Psychology, 47,* 378–389.

Leventhal, H., Meyer, D., & Nerenz, D. (1980). The common sense representation of illness danger. In S. Rachman (Ed.), *Contributions to medical psychology* (Vol. 2, pp. 7–30). New York: Pergamon.

Lichtenstein, E., Glasgow, R. E., & Abrams, D. (1986). Social support in smoking cessation: In search of effective interventions. *Behavioral Therapy, 17,* 607–619.

Manuck, S. B., Harvey, A., Lechleiter, S., & Neal, K. (1978). Effects of coping on blood pressure responses to threat of aversive stimulation. *Psychophysiology, 15,* 544–549.

Manuck, S. B., Kaplan, J. R., & Matthews, K. A. (1986). Behavioral antecedents of coronary heart disease and atherosclerosis. *Arterio Sclerosis, 6,* 2–14.

McKinlay, J. B. (1973). Social networks, lay consultation and help-seeking behavior. *Social Forces, 51,* 275–292.

Medalie, J. H., & Goldbourt, U. (1976). Angina pectoris among 10,000 men: II. Psychosocial and other risk factors as evidenced by a multivariate analysis of a five year incidence study. *American Journal of Medicine, 60,* 910–921.

Mermelstein, R., Cohen, S., Lichtenstein, E., Kamarck, T., & Baer, J. S. (1986). Social support and smoking cessation and maintenance. *Journal of Consulting and Clinical Psychology, 54,* 447–453.

Norbeck, J. S., & Tilden, V. P. (1983). Life stress, social support and emotional disequilibrium in complications of pregnancy: A prospective, multi-variant study. *Journal of Health and Social Behavior, 24,* 30–45.

Nuckolls, K. B., Cassel, J., & Kaplan, B. H. (1972). Psychosocial assets, life crisis and the prognosis of pregnancy. *American Journal of Epidemiology, 95,* 431–441.

Obrist, P. A. (1981). *Cardiovascular psychophysiology.* New York: Plenum.

Orth-Gomer, K., & Johnson, J. V. (1986). *Social network interaction and mortality in Sweden.* Stockholm, Sweden: National Institute for Psychosocial Factors and Health and Karolinska Institute.

Pearlin, L. I., Menaghan, E. G., Lieberman, M. A., & Mullan, J. T. (1981). The stress process. *Journal of Health and Social Behavior, 22,* 337–356.

Pennebaker, J. W. (1982). *The psychology of physical symptoms.* New York: Springer-Verlag.

Reed, D., McGee, D., & Yano, K. (1984). Psychosocial processes and general susceptibility to chronic disease. *American Journal of Epidemiology, 119,* 356–370.

Reed, D., McGee, D., Yano, K., & Feinleib, M. (1983). Social networks and coronary heart disease among Japanese men in Hawaii. *American Journal of Epidemiology, 117,* 384–396.

Rook, K. S. (1985). The functions of social bonds: Perspectives from research on social support, loneliness and social isolation. In I. G. Sarason & B. R. Sarason (Eds.), *Social support: Theory, research and applications* (pp. 243–268). Boston: Martinus Nijhoff.

Ruberman, W., Weinblatt, E., Goldberg, J. D., & Chaudhary, B. S. (1984). Psychosocial influences on mortality after myocardial infarction. *New England Journal of Medicine, 311,* 552–559.

Sanders, G. S. (1982). Social comparison and perceptions of

health and illness. In G. S. Sanders & J. Suls (Eds.), *The social psychology of health and illness* (pp. 129–157). Hillsdale, NJ: Lawrence Erlbaum.

Sandler, I., & Lakey, B. (1982). Locus of control as a stress moderator: The role of control perceptions and social support. *American Journal of Community Psychology, 8,* 41–52.

Sarason, B. R., Shearin, E. N., Pierce, G. R., & Sarason, I. G. (1987). Interrelations of social support measures: Theoretical and practical implications. *Journal of Personality and Social Psychology, 52,* 813–832.

Schaefer, C., Coyne, J. C., & Lazarus, R. S. (1981). The health-related functions of social support. *Journal of Behavioral Medicine, 4,* 381–406.

Schoenbach, V. J., Kaplan, B. H., Fredman, L., & Kleinbaum, D. G. (1986). Social ties and mortality in Evans County, Georgia. *American Journal of Epidemiology, 123,* 577–591.

Seeman, M., Seeman, T. E., & Sayles, M. (1985). Social networks and health status: A longitudinal analysis. *Social Psychology Quarterly, 48,* 237–248.

Seeman, T. E., & Syme, S. L. (1987). Social networks and coronary artery disease: A comparison of the structure and function of social relations as predictors of disease. *Psychosomatic Medicine, 49,* 340–353.

Selye, H. (1956). *The stress of life.* New York: McGraw-Hill.

Shumaker, S. A., & Brownell, A. (1984). Toward a theory of social support: Closing conceptual gaps. *Journal of Social Issues, 40,* 11–36.

Solomon, S., Holmes, D. S., & McCaul, K. D. (1980). Behavioral control over aversive events: Does control that requires effort reduce anxiety and physiological arousal? *Journal of Personality and Social Psychology, 39,* 729–736.

Surtees, P. G. (1980). Social support, residual adversity and depressive outcome. *Social Psychiatry, 15,* 71–80.

Taylor, S. E. (1978). A developing role for social psychology in medicine and medical practice. *Personality and Social Psychology Bulletin, 4,* 515–523.

Thoits, P. A. (1983). Multiple identities and psychological well-being: A reformulation and test of the social isolation hypothesis. *American Sociological Review, 48,* 174–187.

Thoits, P. A. (1985). Social support processes and psychological well-being: Theoretical possibilities. In I. G. Sarason & B. Sarason (Ed.), *Social support: Theory, research and applications* (pp. 51–72). The Hague, Netherlands: Martinus Nijhoff.

Turner, R. J. (1983). Direct, indirect and moderating effects of social support upon psychological distress and associated conditions. In H. B. Kaplan (Ed.), *Psychosocial stress: Trends in theory and research* (pp. 105–156). New York: Academic Press.

Wallston, B. S., Alagna, S. W., DeVellis, B. M., & DeVellis, R. F. (1983). Social support and physical health. *Health Psychology, 4,* 367–391.

Wethington, E., & Kessler, R. C. (1986). Perceived support, received support, and adjustment to stressful events. *Journal of Health and Social Behavior, 27,* 78–89.

Wilcox, B. L. (1981). Social support, life stress, and psychological adjustment: A test of the buffering hypothesis. *American Journal of Community Psychology, 9,* 371–386.

Wilcox, B. L., & Vernberg, E. (1985). Conceptual and theoretical dilemmas facing social support research. In I. G. Sarason & B. R. Sarason (Eds.), *Social support: Theory, research and application* (pp. 3–20). The Hague, Netherlands: Martinus Nijhoff.

Williams, A. W., Ware, J. E., Jr., & Donald, C. A. (1981). A model of mental health, life events, and social supports applicable to general populations. *Journal of Health and Social Behavior, 22,* 324–336.

Wills, T. A. (1983). Social comparison in coping and help-seeking. In B. M. DePaulo, A. Nadler, & J. D. Fisher (Eds.), *New directions in help seeking* (Vol. 2, pp. 109–141). New York: Academic Press.

Wills, T. A. (1985). Supportive functions of interpersonal relationships. In S. Cohen & S. L. Syme (Eds.), *Social support and health* (pp. 61–82). New York: Academic Press.

Wortman, C. B., & Conway, T. L. (1985). The role of social support in adaptation and recovery from physical illness. In S. Cohen & S. L. Syme (Eds.), *Social support and health* (pp. 281–302). New York: Academic Press.

Changing Behavior

A social psychological analysis of health behavior provides an opportunity to specify factors that shape the ongoing series of decisions that people make about their health. Although structural factors such as access to health insurance and other health care resources, taxes on alcohol and tobacco, and opportunities for physical activity have a substantial impact on people's health, how people think and reason about their health remains a potent determinant of their health practices and an important opportunity for intervention (Salovey, Rothman, & Rodin, 1998). In this section, we examine a range of factors that determine whether providing people with information relevant to their health will lead to increases in health-promoting behavior. Specifically, we consider experimental investigations that have examined the manner in which information is presented, the specific information that is emphasized, and to whom the information is targeted.

Efforts to communicate health information have traditionally involved the delivery of an explicit message; for example, the not especially effective anti-drug slogan, "Just say no." The intent or goal of a message such as this is unambiguous. However, people who are the intended targets of the message may find it easy to discredit and/or may resist being told how to think or act. In a sense, the message may fall on deaf ears. Stone and his colleagues (1994) have proposed an alternative approach to delivering health information that may minimize some of these threats to intervention effectiveness. Rather than telling people directly that they must change their behavior (in this case, use condoms), the intervention is designed to elicit feelings of hypocrisy from people about their prior failures to take care of their health. By allowing people to draw their own inferences about the wisdom of their behavior, they may feel less resistance to the conclusions that are drawn (i.e., it would be wise to adopt a safer pattern of behavior).

The premise that the effectiveness of an informational intervention is contingent on the specific information presented is not controversial. Models of behavioral decision making differ in the particular beliefs that are emphasized, and stage models go so far as to state that the specific type of information that should be presented to a person is contingent on where they are in the decision-making process (see Part 2). However, demonstrations of the differential impact of different types of health information are rare. The premise that people in different stages of the decision process have different informational needs was tested by Weinstein, Lyon, Sandman, and Cuite (1998) in the area of home radon testing. Specifically, they examined whether people who have decided to test for household radon gas, a lung cancer risk, would be more responsive to information about how to purchase and conduct a test, whereas those who have yet to decide whether to test would be more

responsive to information about the personal risks posed by home radon.

Decisions regarding the information to include in an intervention message are likely to be successful when grounded in a theoretical framework, as a theory specifies how and under what conditions specific informational content will affect people's judgments and behavior. Two different interventions by Rothman and his colleagues (Rothman et al., 1993; Rothman et al., 1999) illustrate how theoretical frameworks such as prospect theory (Tversky & Kahneman, 1981) and attribution theory (Kelly & Michela, 1980) can be used to guide intervention development. In one study, Rothman and his colleagues (1999) examine the relative impact of emphasizing either the benefits or the costs of engaging in a particular pattern of behavior. Although informational interventions have typically focused on the costs or dangers associated with either engaging in a risky behavior (e.g., unprotected sex) or failing to perform a healthy behavior (e.g., regular mammograms), Rothman et al. (1999) delineate when it is and when it is not best to emphasize potential costs or losses. In the second study, Rothman and his colleagues (1993) examine the benefits of encouraging people to take responsibility for their health and not just to wait for directions or guidance from a health professional.

REFERENCES

Kelley, H. H., & Michela, J. L. (1980). Attribution theory and research. *Annual Review of Psychology, 31,* 457–501.

Rothman, A. J., Martino, S. C., Bedell, B. T., Detweiler, J. B., & Salovey, P. (1999). The systematic influence of gain- and loss-framed messages on interest in and use of different types of health behavior. *Personality and Social Psychology Bulletin, 25,* 1355–1369.

Rothman, A. J., Salovey, P., Turvey, C., & Fishkin. S. A. (1993). Attributions of responsibility and persuasion: In-

creasing mammography utilization among women over 40 with an internally oriented message. *Health Psychology, 12,* 39–47.

Salovey, P., Rothman, A. J., & Rodin, J. (1998). Health behavior. In D. Gilbert, S. Fiske. & G. Lindzey (Eds.), *Handbook of social psychology* (4th ed.. Vol 2., pp. 633–683). New York: McGraw-Hill.

Stone, J., Aronson, E., Crain, A. L., Winslow, M. P., & Fried, C. B. (1994). Inducing hypocrisy as a means of encouraging young adults to use condoms. *Personality and Social Psychology Bulletin, 20,* 116–128.

Tversky, A., & Kahneman, D. (1981). The framing of decisions and the rationality of choice. *Science, 221,* 453–458.

Weinstein, N. D., Lyon, J. E., Sandman, P. M., & Cuite, C. L. (1998). Experimental evidence for stages of health behavior change: The precaution adoption process model applied to home radon testing. *Health Psychology, 17,* 445–453.

Discussion Questions

1. In the study conducted by Stone and colleagues, the people who were led to draw the inference that they were being hypocritical purchased the most condoms. Would you expect a similar effect on behavior if people were told by another person that they were being hypocritical?

2. It is unlikely that any single intervention strategy will be effective in all contexts. Under what conditions would you expect a message that is explicit about its goal (e.g., "Just say no to drugs") to be most effective?

3. Weinstein and colleagues have provided strong evidence that people are most responsive to interventions that target the stage they are at in the decision-making process. Despite this empirical demonstration, why might it be unwise for interventions to adopt a stage-matched approach?

4. Judgments regarding the effectiveness of an intervention strategy depend to a large degree on the outcome measure investigators choose to focus on. For example, Rothman and colleagues (1993) demonstrated that women were more likely to obtain mammograms if they had viewed a message that emphasized their own responsibility for their health. However, no data were collected following the mammogram. Although the intervention was able to increase utilization rates, is it possible that there could be negative consequences associated with making women feel responsible for obtaining a mammogram (e.g., might women who learn they have breast cancer feel worse under these conditions)?

Suggested Readings

Kreuter, M. W., Strecher, V. J ., & Glassman, B. (1999). One size does not fit all: The case for tailored print materials. *Annals of Behavioral Medicine, 21,* 276–283.
A discussion of the potential benefits and costs of tailoring materials to an individual's background and needs.

Leventhal, H. (1970). Findings and theory in the study of fear communications. In L. Berkowitz (Ed.), *Advances in experimental social psychology* (Vol. 5, pp. 119–186). New York: Academic Press.
A comprehensive review of research on the influence of fear appeals on health behavior.

McGuire, W. J. (1991). Using guiding-idea theories of the person to develop educational campaigns against drug abuse and other health-threatening behavior. *Health Education Research, 6,* 173–184.

A provocative discussion of the broad range of theoretical perspectives that could be used to elicit health behavior change.

McCaul, K. D., Glasgow, R. E., & O'Neill, H. K. (1992). The problem of creating habits: Establishing health-protective dental behaviors. *Health Psychology, 11,* 101–110.

An examination of the challenges associated with eliciting health behavior change and their implications for the evaluation of intervention effectiveness.

National Institute of Mental Health Multisite HIV Prevention Trial Group. (2001). Social-cognitive theory mediators of behavior change in the National Institute of Mental Health multisite HIV prevention trial. *Health Psychology, 20,* 369–376.

An example of a large-scale clinical trial designed to test the impact of social cognitive factors on HIV risk behavior.

Rothman, A. J. (2000). Toward a theory-based analysis of behavioral maintenance. *Health Psychology, 19,* 64–69.

An examination of the decision-making processes that guide the initiation and maintenance of ongoing health practices.

Experimental Evidence for Stages of Health Behavior Change: The Precaution Adoption Process Model Applied to Home Radon Testing

Neil D. Weinstein and Judith E. Lyon

Rutgers, The State University of New Jersey

Peter M. Sandman • Newton, Massachusetts

Cara L. Cuite • Rutgers, The State University of New Jersey

Hypotheses generated by the precaution adoption process model, a stage model of health behavior, were tested in the context of home radon testing. The specific idea tested was that the barriers impeding progress toward protective action change from stage to stage. An intervention describing a high risk of radon problems in study area homes was designed to encourage homeowners in the model's *undecided* stage to decide to test, and a low-effort, how-to-test intervention was designed to encourage homeowners in the *decided-to-act* stage to order test kits. Interventions were delivered in a factorial design that created conditions matched or mismatched to the recipient's stage ($N = 1,897$). Both movement to a stage closer to testing and purchase of radon test kits were assessed. As predicted, the risk treatment was relatively more effective in getting undecided people to decide to test than in getting decided-to-act people to order a test. Also supporting predictions, the low-effort intervention proved relatively more effective in getting decided-to-act people to order tests than in getting undecided people to decide to test.
Key words: health promotion, stage theories, radon, precaution adoption process model

Most current theories of individual health behavior consist of a set of variables thought to be important and a rule (or equation) prescribing how these variables should be combined (Conner & Norman, 1996; Weinstein, 1993). How-

ever, a number of researchers have questioned whether reactions to health hazards can be represented adequately by a single prediction rule. Instead, they describe the adoption of precautions in terms of a series of stages (Baranowski, 1992–

1993; Horn, 1976; Janis & Mann, 1977; Prochaska & DiClemente, 1983; Weinstein, 1988; Weinstein & Sandman, 1992).

The most distinctive and potentially useful feature of stage theories is the idea that the determinants of progress toward protective action vary from stage to stage. The factors most important in getting someone to first pay attention to a risk, for example, may not be the ones that are most important in determining whether he or she eventually decides to take action. Thus, stage theories imply that treatments need to be matched to the stage of the audience, focusing on the specific barriers that inhibit movement to the next stage and changing over time as the audience progresses from stage to stage (DiClemente, Carbonari, & Velasquez, 1992). By suggesting how to tailor interventions to audiences, stage theories offer the prospect of more effective and more efficient behavior change efforts.

Most non-stage theories, in contrast, are based on a single theoretically or empirically derived equation (e.g., Ajzen & Madden, 1986; Fishbein & Ajzen, 1975; Ronis, 1992). This equation generates a numerical value for each person, and this value is interpreted as the likelihood that the person will take action. The prediction equation thus places each person along a continuum, and the goal of interventions is to move people along the continuum. Such an approach acknowledges quantitative differences among people, but it does not admit the possibility of qualitative changes in the barriers that interfere with progress. The notion of matching interventions to people is either incidental or completely missing in this approach.

The Precaution Adoption Process Model (PAPM)

This present article describes an experimental test of a particular stage theory, the *precaution adoption process model* (Weinstein, 1988; Weinstein & Sandman, 1992). The PAPM distinguishes among seven stages: (1) unaware of the health action; (2) aware but not personally engaged; (3) engaged and trying to decide what to do; (4) decided not to act (a step *out* of the sequence toward action); (5) decided to act but not yet having acted; (6) acting; and (7) maintaining the new health-protective behavior (Weinstein & Sandman, 1992).

Thus, the proposed sequence of stages leading to action is 1-2-3-5-6-7. The model asserts that people usually pass through this sequence in order, without skipping any stage, although there is no minimum length of time that must be spent in any one stage. Movement backward toward an earlier stage can also occur.

Some data have been published pertaining to the PAPM (e.g., Blalock et al., 1996; Weinstein & Sandman, 1992) and a much larger amount pertaining to another stage theory, the *transtheoretical model* (for an overview, see Prochaska et al., 1994). The great majority of these data come from cross-sectional surveys and compare the attributes of people in different stages. Although substantial between-stages differences are often found, differences among people in different stages can be present even if behavior change is actually a continuous process (Weinstein, Rothman, & Sutton, 1998). Cross-sectional data provide only weak support for stage models.

A few experiments based on stage ideas have been conducted (Campbell et al., 1994; Prochaska, DiClemente, Velicer, & Rossi, 1993; Skinner, Strecher, & Hospers, 1994). However, they tend to compare a highly personalized, stage-based intervention with a standardized intervention, so it is not clear whether it is the content of the stage-based intervention or simply its personalization that makes it more successful.

Still, rigorous experimental tests of stage theories are possible (Weinstein et al., 1998). Experiments can directly test the prediction that Treatment I is better than Treatment II for moving people from stage A to stage B, whereas Treatment II is better than Treatment I for moving people from stage B to stage C. The 2 (preintervention stage) × 2 (interventions) design suggested by this example is the simplest experimental test or the fundamental idea that different issues are important at different stages. Crossing two transitions with two properly selected interventions creates two conditions in which the interventions and stages are matched and two in which they are mismatched. This is the core of the design adopted for our experiment, although we add a control condition (no treatment) and a combination intervention (Treatment I + Treatment II), leading to a 2 (preintervention stage) × 2 (presence or absence of Treatment I) × 2 (presence or absence of Treatment II) design.

Examining the PAPM in the Context of Home Radon Testing

The PAPM is a framework that claims to identify important stages along the route to action. Experimental support for a stage framework requires one to find treatments that have different effects at different stages. It should be kept in mind, however, that transitions at each stage may be influenced by several variables (Weinstein, 1988) and that the variables that are important will depend, to some extent, on the nature of the health behavior.

The health behavior examined in our investigation was home radon testing. Radon is a radioactive gas produced by the decay of small amounts of naturally occurring uranium in soil. Radon in homes is the second leading cause of lung cancer after smoking (National Academy of Sciences, 1988; U.S. Environmental Protection Agency [EPA], 1992a), causing an estimated 7,000 to 30,000 deaths a year in the United States (Puskin, 1992). Radon concentrations exceeding the EPA's recommended action level are present in about 6% of homes in the United States (EPA, 1991, 1992b). At present, reducing radon in existing homes is left largely to voluntary action. Individuals must decide on their own that testing is desirable and, if excessive radon is found, that radon reduction is needed.

Testing for radon does not involve ingrained habits or arduous and repetitive procedures. A positive radon test does not mean that one is afflicted with a fatal illness. For these reasons, a brief intervention might be enough to change people's decisions and actions.

In this experiment we focused on two transitions relevant to radon testing: from being undecided about testing one's home (stage 3) to deciding to test (stage 5), and from deciding to test (stage 5) to actually ordering a test (stage 6). Two interventions were needed, one matched to each transition. We did not study the transition from never having thought about testing to thinking about testing because merely participating in a radon study and answering questions about testing would probably be sufficient to produce this change. We excluded people who had decided not to test because a brief intervention would probably be unable to reverse that decision.

Previous surveys and experiments (Sandman & Weinstein, 1993; Weinstein, Sandman, & Roberts, 1990) suggested that increasing homeowners' perceptions of personal risk—that is, increasing the perceived likelihood of having unhealthy home radon levels in their own homes—is an important factor in getting undecided people to decide to test. This was chosen as the focus of one intervention.

Interventions focusing on risk have not been effective, however, in getting people to order tests (Weinstein et al., 1990; Weinstein, Sandman, & Roberts, 1991). Instead, several studies have found that increasing the ease of testing increases the number of test orders (Doyle, McClelland, & Schulze, 1991; Weinstein et al., 1990, 1991). Thus, for people who had already decided to test, we developed an intervention that would lower the barriers to action by providing information about do-it-yourself test kits and a test order form.

The basic hypothesis examined here was that interventions matched to stage would be more effective than interventions that were mismatched. In other words, the crucial test was for an interaction between stage and intervention. Additional hypotheses accompany the data analysis. We did not investigate how many stages exist or whether people pass through the stages in the specified sequence. Comparisons of stage predictions with the predictions of other theories of health behavior will be reported elsewhere.

Method

Overview of Study Design

Pilot interviews and focus groups revealed that people in the study area knew relatively little about radon. Their beliefs appeared to reflect vague recollections of the issue as it had appeared in the media years earlier. Because their stated testing stage and testing intentions might be weakly held and unstable, all participants viewed a general informational video before receiving any experimental treatment. Their stage of testing was assessed by questionnaire after this first video (preintervention measurement). Only people in the undecided or decided-to-act stages with respect to radon testing took part in the succeeding experiment.

Within a week after the questionnaire had been returned and eligibility to continue had been determined, the experimental interventions were delivered to participants. One intervention (High Likelihood) focused on increasing the perceived likelihood of having a home radon problem. The second (Low Effort) focused on decreasing the perceived and actual effort required to test. These two treatments were combined factorially to create four conditions: Control (no intervention), High Likelihood, Low Effort, and Combination (High Likelihood + Low Effort). Study participants were assigned at random to one of these four experimental conditions, creating a 2 (preintervention stage: undecided or decided-to-test) × 2 (High Likelihood treatment: present or absent) × 2 (Low Effort treatment: present or absent) factorial design. Beliefs about radon were assessed by questionnaire after the experimental treatment (postintervention measurement), and a follow-up interview was used to determine final stage and actual test orders.

Site Selection

A site was sought that had both elevated levels of radon (so that messages claiming high risk would be justified) and limited previous attention to radon (so that residents would be receptive to new information on this issue). Columbus, Ohio, met these criteria. Radon levels there were high (64–75% of homes were above the EPA's suggested action level [EPA, 1991; Grafton, 1990; H. E. Grafton, personal communication, April 1995]), and no major attempts to encourage radon testing had occurred since a campaign 8 years earlier.

Participation Criteria

People with listed telephone numbers in the Columbus, Ohio, area were screened on several variables. Telephone interviewers asked to speak to "the man or woman in your household who is most likely to make decisions about home environmental hazards, such as asbestos or lead-based paint." Screening criteria were as follows: (a) Owns a single-family house or townhouse; (b) has heard of radon; (c) has not tested for radon; (d) has never thought about testing, is undecided, or plans to test; (e) has no plans to move in the next year; (f) owns a videocassette recorder; and (g) is 65 years of age or less. (Pilot studies showed that older people were less likely to test, claiming, with some valid-

ity, that reducing radon after many years of exposure would probably have little effect.)

Materials

Three different videos were developed for the experiment, using student ratings, focus groups of Columbus residents, and finally a large-scale pilot study in Columbus to refine the messages and their presentation.

Initial educational message. All participants viewed a 6-min tape titled "Basic Facts About Radon," which provided a brief overview of the topic. It explained what radon is, how it causes illness, how it gets into houses, and how radon problems can be solved. The narrator stated that elevated radon levels have been found throughout the United States, but no details were provided about the risk in any particular location. The video noted that "the Surgeon General and the American Medical Association join the EPA in strongly recommending home radon testing." It further stated that "kits that homeowners can use themselves are also available and are easy to use. A wide range of test kits are on the market." However, no information was provided about the advantages of specific types of tests, their cost, how to use the test kits, or how to obtain them.

High Likelihood condition. This treatment consisted of a 5-min video, "Radon Risk in Columbus Area Homes," and an accompanying cover letter. The goal of the video was to convince people that they have a moderate to high chance of finding unhealthy radon levels in their own homes. Results of radon studies indicating high local levels, pictures of actual local homes with high levels, and testimony by a local homeowner and a city health official all presented evidence of the problem. The geological explanation for the high regional levels was illustrated with maps, and myths about radon levels that had been identified in past research were presented and refuted. Radon testing was briefly mentioned in one 11-s segment: "Fortunately, it is much easier than you may suppose to find out whether your home has a radon problem. Low-cost test kits are readily available and simple to use."

Low Effort condition. Participants in this condition received a 5-min video, "How to Test Your Home for Radon," an accompanying cover letter, and a form to order test kits through the American Lung Association (ALA). The video described how to select a kit type (making an explicit recommendation in order to reduce uncertainty), locate and purchase a kit, and conduct a test. The process was represented as simple and inexpensive. The order form was developed in collaboration with the National Safety Council and the ALA of Mid-Ohio and bore their emblems. It offered the short-term test kits recommended in the video at $7 each, and long-term test kits at $16 each. These were the same prices that the ALA and the National Safety Council charged the general public. This video said nothing about the frequency or seriousness of high radon levels.

Combination condition. People in this condition received a 10-min video that was simply a combination of the "Radon Risk in Columbus Area Homes" and "How to Test Your Home for Radon" video segments, in that order. They received the same letter and order form as people in the Low Effort condition.

Control condition. Participants in this group received a letter stating that their assistance in viewing a second video was not needed (they had already screened "Basic Facts About Radon").

Cover letters. Letters accompanying each experimental condition video (but not the "Basic Facts" video) provided limited information about obtaining home test kits. All letters stated, "More information about radon can be obtained from the American Lung Association of Mid-Ohio, which is listed in the white pages. The American Lung Association office also sells inexpensive home radon kits." In the Low Effort and Combination conditions, the letters added, "For your convenience, a form for ordering a kit is enclosed." The letter received by participants in the Control condition contained the same statement about the availability of information and tests from the ALA as the cover letter accompanying the High Likelihood video.

Video response questionnaires. Accompanying all videos was a questionnaire made up of three parts. Part A focused on the organization of the video content. It also asked participants, "On what two topics [from a list of eight] would you be most interested in having more information?" There were two choices relating to each of four issues: the health effects of radon; the likelihood of finding high levels in one's home; radon testing; and radon reduction. Part B focused on the visual and sound quality of the video. Part B and the video organization questions of Part A were included to be consistent with our request for respondents' reactions to the videos and are not discussed further.

Part C asked respondents for their thoughts about radon after having viewed the video. Among the questions in Part C was a sequence designed to assess stage of testing: "What are your thoughts about testing your home for radon?": (a) "I have already completed a test, have a test in progress, or have purchased a test" [tested stage]; (b) "I have never thought about testing my home" [not-engaged stage]; (c) "I'm undecided about testing" [undecided stage]; (d) "I've decided I *don't* want to test" [decided-not-to-test stage]; or (e) "I've decided I *do* want to test" [decided-to-test stage]." People who selected the last response were then asked, "Is testing something you plan to do soon or just something you'll do someday when you have a chance?" Intentions to test were assessed with the question, "How likely would you say it is that you will test your home for radon in the next few months?" The response options were 0 (*definitely won't*), 1 (*probably won't*), 3 (*50–50 chance*), 4 (*probably will*), and 5 (*definitely will*).

One set of additional questions asked participants about risk issues: the likelihood of finding radon problems in their own homes (1 = *very unlikely*, 5 = *very likely*); the same issue in percentage terms (1 = *less than 10%*, 5 = *greater than 90%*); and the percentage of homes in the Columbus area with radon problems (1 = *less than 10%*, 5 = greater than 90%). A second set of questions referred to the ease of testing: "How easy do you think it would be for you to locate and buy a do-it-yourself kit . . . ?" (1 = *very difficult*, 4 = *very easy*); "How easy do you think it would be for you to use a radon test kit?" (1 = *very difficult*, 4 = *very easy*); and "What do you think is the typical cost of a home radon test kit?" (1 = *under $10*, 5 = *over $100*). Participants were also asked about the difficulty of reducing home radon levels (1 = *very difficult*, 4 = *very easy*).

Follow-up interview. This brief telephone interview assessed participants' final stage, whether they had ordered and conducted a radon test in their home, and what radon topics they wanted more information about. To detect possible false reports of testing, those who said they had tested were asked what type of kit they had purchased, where they obtained the kit, how long it remained in place, and so on.

Procedure

Recruitment interviews were completed with 24,484 Columbus-area residents. A total of 41.5% screened out because they were not homeowners, not in the desired age range, because of other factors unrelated to radon, or a combination of these. Of the remaining, 3.8% had never heard of radon, 20.6% had never thought about testing, 20.4% were undecided, 18.1% had decided not to test, 7.9% had decided to test, and 29.2% had already tested. When those eligible at this point in the study (those who had never thought about testing, were undecided, or had decided to test) were invited to react to the videos about radon that we had developed, 65.0% agreed.

Those consenting ($N = 4,706$) were mailed the video, "Basic Facts About Radon," and a questionnaire assessing their reactions. Those individuals who were either in the undecided stage or decided-to-test stage after watching "Basic Facts About Radon" were assigned at random to one of the four experimental conditions and were mailed the materials appropriate for that condition. To enhance the impact of the interventions, participants were asked to watch each video twice: once for content and once for style. The response rate to the second video was 73.2%, with no significant differences among conditions.

Follow-up telephone interviews (completion rate = 94.5%) were carried out 9–10 weeks after respondents returned the second video questionnaire, allowing them ample time to have ordered a test. All those who completed the follow-up interview were mailed a thank-you letter and a radon test kit order form.

Results

Study Sample

Participants were dropped from the data analysis if they were missing important data ($n = 18$), said that someone else in the household had watched the experimental video ($n = 15$), said they had no role in "making decisions about things like radon testing" ($n = 1$), or could not answer questions about the test they claimed to have purchased ($n = 2$). This left a sample of 1,897 (58.8% women and 41.2% men). Preintervention (i.e., after "Basic Facts About Radon"), the division among stages of those retained in the study was 28.8% undecided and 71.2% decided-to-test.

The median length of residence was 7 years, and 52.5% of the sample was between 36 and 50 years of age. College graduates comprised 77.1% of the group. The racial distribution was 91.3% white and 5.4% African American, with smaller portions in other groups. A comparison of the sample with the population from which it was drawn was not possible because demographic data restricted to owners of single-family homes were not available.

Although age, sex, education, years of residence in their present home, presence of children under age 10 in the home, and smoking status were all assessed, only education proved to be appreciably correlated with subsequent test orders. More education was associated with greater testing ($r = .10$, $p < .0001$). None of the interactions between demographic variables and stage, experimental condition, or intentions affected testing, so demographic variables are not discussed further, although analyses were conducted while controlling for education.

Manipulation Checks and Preintervention Differences Between Stages

As would be expected from random assignment, there were no significant differences among conditions on any preintervention variable.

Perceived radon risk. Preintervention and postintervention means were examined to see whether the High Likelihood intervention had produced the effect intended. The three risk questions (perceived likelihood in own home, percentage chance in own home, and percentage prevalence in community) were combined to form a Perceived Risk scale ($\alpha = .83$; range = 1–5). The High Likelihood intervention produced highly significant and nearly identical increases in perceived risk in the High Likelihood and Combination conditions: from 2.28 to 3.39, $t(471) = 29.3$, $p < .0001$, and from 2.33 to 3.49, $t(468) = 30.5$, $p < .0001$, respectively. There was a slight decline in perceived risk in the Low Effort condition: from 2.19 to 2.09, $t(445) = 3.8$, $p < .002$.

Supporting the idea that deciding to test is partly determined by perceptions of personal risk, mean perceived risk before the intervention was 1.97 and 2.40 in the undecided and decided-to-test groups, respectively, $F(1, 1885) = 130.4$, $p < .0001$, with stage accounting for 6.5% of the variance in the risk variable. In contrast, stage accounted for only 0.0%–0.8% of the variance in the questions about finding test kits, using test kits, fixing radon problems, and the cost of testing.

The effects of the interventions on perceived risk were independent of respondents' preintervention stage, and there were no Preintervention Stage × Treatment interactions (ps > .4).

Perceived ease of testing. As intended, the Low Effort intervention succeeded in convincing people that testing is quite easy (combined ease of finding a test kit and ease of using a test kit: $\alpha = .62$; range = 1–4). The increases in the Low Effort and Combination conditions were nearly identical: from 3.34 to 3.77, $t(445) = 17.9$, $p < .0001$, and from 3.27 to 3.75, $t(468) = 16.0$, $p < .0001$, respectively. There was a very slight decrease in the High Likelihood condition: from 3.40 to 3.35, $t(471) = 2.4$, $p < .02$. The perceived cost of testing, another indicator of ease, declined in the Low Effort and Combination conditions: from $26.46 to $17.40, $t(398) = 10.3$, $p < .0001$, and from $25.87 to $17.85, $t(424) = 9.3$, $p < .0001$, respectively, with negligible change in the High Likelihood condition (from $25.85 to $26.41, *ns*). (Dollar values were calculated using the midpoint of the range for each scale choice, with *over $100* interpreted as $125.)

The effects of the interventions on perceived ease of testing were independent of respondents' preintervention stage, and there were no Preintervention Stage × Treatment interactions (ps > .4).

Reported desire for information. Both pre- and postintervention, participants indicated the topics about which they would like more information. Variables were created to indicate whether they had expressed an interest in the likelihood of radon problems in local homes (*risk*), testing (*testing*), health effects (*health*), and home radon reduction (*reduction*).

There were no preintervention differences between conditions in the proportion of the sample interested in any topic. As expected, after treatment there were highly significant between-conditions differences on all four information topics, $F(2, 1414) = 133, 238, 26$, and 54, for risk, testing, health, and reduction information, respectively (all ps < .0001), but there were no differences by Preintervention Stages or Preintervention Stage × Condition interactions (ps > .1). Collapsing across preintervention stage, the High Likelihood intervention was found to decrease desire for risk information (from 79% to 16% and from 76% to 18% in the High Likelihood and Combination conditions, respectively). In a similar vein, interest in testing information decreased in the Low Effort and Combination conditions (from 33% to 3% and from 29% to 5%, respectively). Thus, as intended, the High Likelihood treatment appeared to satisfy respondents' needs for information about personal risk, and the Low Effort treatment appeared to satisfy respondents' needs for information about how to test.

Although participants in both stages showed a high level of interest in information about the local prevalence of radon problems after viewing the "Basic Facts" video, this interest was higher among undecided (80.8%) than decided-to-test (74.2%) participants, $F(1, 1895) = 9.4$, $p < .003$. Undecided participants also showed greater interest in information about health effects, 45.6% vs. 36.1%, $F(1, 1895) = 14.8$, $p < .0001$. In contrast, decided-to-test participants showed greater interest in information about testing: 33.0% versus 21.6%, $F(1, 1895) = 24.5$, $p < .0001$; and about radon reduction, 23.3% versus 18.9%, $F(1, 1895) = 4.5$ $p < .05$. Of course, showing that interest in information varies with stage is not the same as showing that receiving this information will lead to a change in stage.

Predicting Progress Toward Action

From a stage perspective, interventions are successful if they move people to any stage closer to action, so action is not the only or even the most appropriate measure of the effectiveness of an intervention. First, we examine progress toward testing as the dependent variable, then we examine test orders themselves.

Table 16.1 shows the percentage of people from

each preintervention stage who progressed *one or more* stages toward testing. We chose this outcome criterion for several reasons. First, even though the lack of some specific information may prevent people from moving to the next stage, they might already possess the information needed to go from the next stage to the one following. Consequently, when people stuck at a particular stage are helped by an intervention to advance to the next stage, some of these people may proceed to additional stages without further assistance. Second, all participants in our study received some information that could lower barriers to carrying out a decision to test. The "Basic Facts" video briefly informed them about the existence of easy-to-use, do-it-yourself tests, and the cover letters sent to participants in all conditions told them where to obtain inexpensive test kits. Thus, the High Likelihood treatment might help people decide to test, and the information given about testing, although limited, might be sufficient to allow some of these people to proceed to the next stage and order tests.

The upper half of Table 16.1 indicates the percentage of people at follow-up who had moved from the undecided stage to either the decided-to-test or the testing stage. The lower half of the table shows the percentage of decided-to-test people who had moved on to the testing stage. Although the table has each of the four conditions in a separate column, the analysis of variance used a $2 \times 2 \times 2$ statistical model that included pretreatment stage, High Likelihood treatment, Low Effort treatment, and their interactions.

The analysis showed more people progressing from the undecided stage than from the decided-to-test stage, $F(1, 1886) = 61.6$, $p < .0001$, and more progress from those who received the High Likelihood treatment than from those who did not,

$F(1, 1886) = 31.5$, $p < .0001$. Most important, as predicted, there was a significant Stage × High Likelihood Treatment interaction, $F(1, 1886) = 18.5$, $p < .0001$, indicating that the High Likelihood treatment was much more effective for undecided participants than for decided-to-act participants.

There was also a large main effect of the Low Effort treatment, $F(1, 1886) = 89.4$, $p < .0001$. The Stage × Low Effort Treatment interaction, $F(1, 1886) = 5.9$, $p < .02$, indicated that, as hypothesized, the Low Effort treatment in the Low Effort and Combination conditions had a relatively bigger effect on the people already planning to test than on people who were undecided. The High Likelihood × Low Effort interaction and the three-way interaction were not significant.

Predicting Test Orders

Follow-up interviews indicated that radon tests were ordered by 342 study participants or 18.0% of the sample. Of this total, 63.4% were ordered from the ALA of Mid-Ohio; the rest were obtained from various stores, government offices, and private testing companies.

The experimental data concerning test orders are presented in Table 16.2. For people initially planning to test, *progress* means actually testing according to the PAPM, so the data in the lower half of Table 16.2 are the same as those in the lower half of Table 16.1. As expected, there was more testing from the decided-to-test stage than from the undecided stage, $F(1, 1887) = 42.3$, $p < .0001$. In addition, there was much more testing from people exposed to a Low Effort treatment than from those who did not receive this treatment, $F(1, 1887) = 87.9$, $p < .0001$. The High Likelihood treat-

TABLE 16.1. Progress Toward Acting of One Stage or More

	Condition			
Preintervention stage	Control	High Likelihood	Low Effort	Combination
Undecided				
%	18.8	41.7	36.4	54.5
n	138	144	130	139
Decided to test				
%	8.0	10.4	32.5	35.8
n	339	338	329	345

Note. n = number of people in each experimental group.

TABLE 16.2. Test Orders

Preintervention stage	Condition			
	Control	High Likelihood	Low Effort	Combination
Undecided	(a) 5.1	(b) 3.5	(c) 10.1	(d) 18.7
Decided to test	(e) 8.0	(f) 10.4	(g) 32.5	(h) 35.8

Note. Values in table are percentages.

ment effect and the Low Effort × High Likelihood interaction were not significant (*ps* > .1). Most important was the highly significant interaction between Stage and Low Effort treatment, $F(1, 1887) = 18.2$, $p < .0001$. The other interactions (Stage × High Likelihood and Stage × Low Effort × High Likelihood) were not significant (*ps* > .1).

Next, a series of more detailed tests examined the cell-by-cell contrasts that are predicted by the PAPM. Each of these predictions about test orders can be viewed as a planned comparison. In subsequent paragraphs, the predictions are presented in brackets, with experimental groups labeled by letters that refer to the cells in Table 16.2.

Test order rates of both undecided and decided-to-test participants in the Control condition were expected to be quite low because both groups were viewed as lacking information needed to progress to action [(a) ≈ (e), both small]. The main problems facing people who had decided to test were hypothesized to be the difficulties in choosing, purchasing, and using radon test kits. Thus, the Low Effort treatment was expected to be much more helpful than the High Likelihood treatment in getting people in this stage to actually order tests [(g) > (f)]. In fact, past research (Weinstein et al., 1990, 1991) suggested that the High Likelihood treatment would be ineffective in eliciting testing from people planning to test [(f) ≈ (e)], and, more obviously, unable to elicit test orders from undecided people [(b) ≈ (a)]. Furthermore, because it was anticipated that people in the decided-to-test stage did not need further information about risk, we predicted that testing in the Combination condition would not be significantly greater than testing in the Low Effort condition [(h) ≈ (g)].

According to the PAPM, people who are undecided have to decide to test before acting, so a Low Effort intervention alone was not expected to produce test orders from this group [(c) ≈ (a)]. However, undecided people in the Combination condi-

tion received both High Likelihood information (seen as important in deciding to test) and Low Effort assistance (seen as important for carrying out action intentions). Some of these people might be able to make two stage transitions [(d) > (c)], but not as many as decided-to-test people in the Combination condition who only needed to advance only one stage [(d) < (h)].

We conducted *t* tests to compare the means of the cells mentioned in the preceding eight hypotheses. These demonstrated that none of the pairs predicted to be approximately the same were significantly different (*ps* > .3), but all pairs predicted to be different were significantly different: all *ps* < .0001, except for the hypothesis that (d) > (c), $p = .03$. We return to this last hypothesis in the next section.

Calculations of Two-Stage Transitions

The cell-by-cell hypotheses just presented had been based on the expectation that our interventions were completely stage specific. In particular, our initial expectation about the rate of testing from undecided people in the Low Effort condition (cell c) was based on the expectation that this treatment would not persuade anyone that they should test. Yet Table 16.1 shows that the Low Effort treatment did get many undecided people to decide to test. Given this new knowledge, how should we revise our predictions? According to the precaution adoption process model, in order to test, undecided people have to make two separate stage transitions. If these transitions are viewed as independent, sequential steps, the probability of a person moving forward two steps (from undecided to testing) should be the product of the two separate probabilities involved: the probability that undecided people move toward testing (and thus get at least to the decided-to-test stage) times the probability that people who get to the decided-to-test stage carry out this decision. According to this reasoning, the predicted rate of testing by undecided people in the Low Effort condition should be $.364 \times .325 = .118$ or 11.8% (see Table 16.1 for the separate probabilities). This is very close to the observed value of 10.1% in Table 16.2. This same argument can be used to calculate testing rates for undecided people in the Combination condition. The expected rate of testing in this cell is $.545 \times .358 = .195$ or 19.5%. This is, again, extremely close to the observed value of 18.7% in Table 16.2.

Discussion

This research was stimulated by the belief that the adoption of new health-protective behaviors is usually too complex to be explained by a single prediction equation, no matter how many variables that equation contains. We suggested, instead, that there are relatively distinct stages along the path to action and offered the precaution adoption process model to summarize these stage notions. For health promotion, the most important contribution of a stage perspective is the idea that the obstacles inhibiting movement vary from one stage to the next. In this investigation we focused on two stage transitions, from *undecided* to *decided to act* and from *decided to act* to *acting*.

Perhaps the first point that should be emphasized in this discussion is the magnitude of the effects produced by our interventions. When viewed in terms of odds ratios—for example, the three-fold difference in test orders between the undecided and decided-to-test stages in the Low Effort condition or the 10-fold difference between cells with the highest and lowest testing rates—the effects observed here were quite large.

Predictions of the Precaution Adoption Process Model

Not only were the predicted Stage × Intervention interactions associated with progress toward testing supported but so too were all eight detailed hypotheses about test orders. Risk vulnerability was, as expected, more important in getting people to decide to act than in getting them to carry out this decision. In fact, risk information had no ap-

parent value in producing action among people who had already decided to test. The Low Effort intervention, in contrast, greatly aided people who had decided to act but was relatively less important among people who were undecided.

No prediction equation from any current theory of health behavior can produce this pattern of results. The theory of planned behavior (Ajzen, 1985, 1991; Ajzen & Madden, 1986), which proposes a positive interaction between intentions and control, can explain an increase in the effectiveness of the Low Effort intervention among people closer to action, but it cannot explain why increasing perceived risk led people to decide to test (i.e., increased testing intentions) but did not increase testing.

The interaction observed between stage and the High Likelihood intervention might have been even stronger if the intervention had been more effective in raising risk perceptions. Despite our attempts to counter the myths people use to deny their risk, there was evidence that participants tended to resist the risk message. People in the High Likelihood and Combination conditions were told that 73% of the homes in their community had high radon levels, but they estimated their own chances at only 54%. Optimistic bias—the tendency to rate one's own risk as lower than peers' risk—actually increased after exposure to the risk information. (Although people in these conditions increased their estimates of their own risk, they increased their estimates of their neighbors' risks still more.) In the conditions receiving risk information, the own risk minus others' risk difference score changed from 4.7% preintervention to 8.7% postintervention, demonstrating an increase in optimistic bias, $t(911) = 5.01, p < .0001$. The postintervention optimistic bias was greater among undecided than among decided-to-test participants, -10.52 versus -5.74, $F(1, 1371) = 18.1, p < .0001$.

The interaction between stage and the Low Effort intervention might also have been stronger if that intervention had been less effective in persuading undecided people to test. We can imagine study participants who were reluctant to test nevertheless telling themselves, "If it is really that simple and inexpensive, I might as well do it." Many other health behaviors are not nearly so easy, and in other situations similar low-effort interventions may be insufficient to convince undecided people that they should act.

The unexpected success of the Low Effort intervention among undecided people led us to use a calculation predicated on the notion of a sequential stage model—the idea that the probability of moving forward two stages is the product of the probabilities of moving through each transition separately—to calculate the testing rates of undecided people who received the Low Effort treatment. The agreement between the calculated and observed rates (11.8% and 10.1%, respectively, in the Low Effort condition and 19.5% and 18.7%, respectively, in the Combination condition) was quite impressive, providing further support for the presence of a stage process.

The Combination Condition

Because the combination treatment was effective among both undecided and decided-to-test participants, one might be tempted to conclude that the PAPM has not provided any new treatment ideas. "Just use the combination treatment," someone might say. There are several flaws in this reasoning.

First, the combination treatment was approximately twice as long as each of its two components. Media time is expensive; speakers usually have a fixed length of time for their presentations; and audiences have a limited attention span. Thus, attempting to replace the Low Effort or High Likelihood interventions with their combination would involve substantial costs.

Second, people are likely to be more engaged by the treatment that matches their stage. For example, when not participating in a research study, people who are undecided about taking a precaution may not pay attention to the detailed procedural information they might need later to carry out that precaution. The data presented earlier concerning interest in information provide some support for this claim.

Third, among people who had decided to act, the superiority of the combination intervention was actually negligible. The Low Effort treatment produced just as many test orders; the risk information was superfluous. As we suggested in the introduction, and as our data suggest, stage models offer the prospect of more effective and efficient interventions than a scattershot, one-size-fits-all approach. Nevertheless, if only a single message can be given to a mixed-stage audience, the combination intervention would probably be the most appropriate.

Conclusion

Predictions derived from stage models are undoubtedly more accurate in some situations than in others. For example, when people are asked for their decisions concerning new hazards or new precautions (topics to which they have given little thought), their responses may say little about their eventual actions. In fact, we may have been fortunate in this investigation that a brief video designed to remind participants about a topic that had received little local attention in the past 8 years elicited reactions that could predict their subsequent behavior. Stage models of health behavior (and probably most other models of health behavior) are likely to be most accurate among people who have been exposed to the health issue recently in their daily lives.

Have we proved that people pass through distinct stages as they come to adopt precautions? No. Neither have we demonstrated that applying treatments in the sequence suggested by the PAPM is better than applying them in another sequence, the gold standard test for a stage theory (Weinstein et al., 1998). It is still possible that precaution adoption can be explained by a continuous equation, although this equation would have to be quite complex if some variables increase in importance and some decrease in importance depending on the values of still other variables.

Even if behavior is eventually explainable by a complex prediction equation, stages can still be extremely useful. They can help us by identifying regions in the multidimensional space of independent variables where specific variables are particularly influential. By categorizing people who had not yet acted into distinct subgroups, the precaution adoption process model helped us to identify important barriers to action. Furthermore, it suggested how to match interventions to individuals and successfully predicted the effects of such matching. Although the evidence for stages may be limited at this time, the idea certainly deserves further attention.

ACKNOWLEDGMENTS

This study was supported with funding from the National Cancer Institute (CA60890), the Environmental Protection Agency (X824392-01-0), and the New Jersey Agriculture Experiment Station (Project 26101).

We wish to thank Margot Ogé, David Rowson, and Dennis

Wagner of the Environmental Protection Agency; Leyla McCurdy of the American Lung Association; Jane Ann Page and Cheryl Cooper of the American Lung Association of Mid-Ohio; Michael Pompili and Harry Grafton of the Columbus, Ohio, Health Department; Nyki Brandon Palermo of the National Safety Council; Fred Rehbein of Reel Resources; Daniel West of Insul-Tech Radon; Mark Schulman and Adrienne Viviano of Schulman, Ronca, & Bucuvalas; and Sharon Johnson for their cooperation and assistance. We also thank Paul Lehrer, Ann O'Leary, Barbara McCrady, Mark Conner, Meg Gerrard, Alex Rothman, Stephen Sutton, and anonymous reviewers for suggestions during the planning of the research and the preparation of this article.

REFERENCES

Ajzen, I. (1985). From intentions to actions: A theory of planned behavior. In J. Kuhl & J. Beckmann (Eds.), *Action control: From cognition to behavior* (pp. 11–40). Berlin, Germany: Springer-Verlag.

Ajzen, I. (1991). The theory of planned behavior. *Organizational Behavior and Human Decision Processes, 50,* 179–211.

Ajzen, I., & Madden, T. J. (1986). Prediction of goal-directed behavior: Attitudes, intentions, and perceived behavioral control. *Journal of Experimental Social Psychology, 22,* 453–474.

Baranowski, T. (1992–1993). Beliefs as motivational influences in stages in behavior change. *International Quarterly of Community Health Education, 13,* 3–29.

Blalock, S. J., DeVellis, R. F., Giorgino, K. B., DeVellis, B. M., Gold, D., Dooley, M. A., Anderson, J. B., & Smith, S. L. (1996). Osteoporosis prevention in premenopausal women: Using a stage model approach to examine the predictors of behavior. *Health Psychology, 15,* 84–93.

Campbell, M. K., DeVellis, B. M., Strecher, V. J., Ammerman, A. S., DeVellis, R. F., & Sandler, R. S. (1994). Improving dietary behavior: The effectiveness of tailored messages in primary care settings. *American Journal of Public Health, 84,* 783–787.

Conner, M., & Norman, P. (1996). *Predicting health behavior.* Philadelphia: Open University Press.

DiClemente, C. C., Carbonari, J. P., & Velasquez, M. M. (1992). Alcohol treatment mismatching from a process of change perspective. In R. R. Watson (Ed.), *Drug and alcohol abuse reviews* (Vol. 3, pp. 115–142). Totowa, NJ: Humana Press.

Doyle, J. K., McClelland, G. H., & Schulze, W. D. (1991). Protective responses to household risk: A case study of radon mitigation. *Risk Analysis, 11,* 121–134.

Fishbein, M., & Ajzen, I. (1975). *Belief, attitude, intention and behavior: An introduction to theory and research.* Reading, MA: Addison-Wesley.

Grafton, H. E. (1990). Indoor radon levels in Columbus and Franklin County, Ohio residences, commercial buildings, and schools. In *The 1990 International Symposium on Radon and Radon Reduction Technology* (EPA No. 600/9–90/00a, v. 1-Preprints, A-I-1).

Horn, D. (1976). A model for the study of personal choice health change. *International Journal of Health Education, 19,* 88–97.

Janis, I. L., & Mann, L. (1977). *Decision making: A psychological analysis of conflict choice, and commitment.* New York: Free Press.

National Academy of Sciences. (1988). *Health effects of radon and other internally deposited alpha-emitters: BEIR IV.* Washington, DC: National Academy Press.

Prochaska, J. O., & DiClemente, C. C. (1983). Stages and processes of self-change in smoking: Toward an integrative model of change. *Journal of Consulting and Clinical Psychology, 51,* 390–395.

Prochaska, J. O., DiClemente, C. C., Velicer, W. F., & Rossi, J. S. (1993). Standardized, individualized, interactive, and personalized self-help programs for stages of smoking cessation. *Health Psychology, 12,* 399–405.

Prochaska, J. O., Velicer, W. F., Rossi, J. S., Goldstein, M. G., Marcus, B. H., Rakowski, W., Fiore, C., Harlow, L. L., Redding, C. A., Rosenbloom, D., & Rossi, S. R. (1994). Stages of change and decisional balance for 12 problem behaviors. *Health Psychology, 13,* 39–46.

Puskin, J. S. (1992). An analysis of the uncertainties in estimates of radon-induced lung cancer. *Risk Analysis, 12,* 277–285.

Ronis, D. L. (1992). Conditional health threats: Health beliefs, decisions, and behaviors among adults. *Health Psychology, 11,* 127–134.

Sandman, P. M., & Weinstein, N. D. (1993). Predictors of home radon testing and implications for testing promotion programs. *Health Education Quarterly, 20,* 1–17.

Skinner, C. S., Strecher, V. J., & Hospers, H. (1994). Physicians' recommendations for mammography: Do tailored messages make a difference? *American Journal of Public Health, 84,* 43–49.

U.S. Environmental Protection Agency, Radon Division, Office of Radiation and Indoor Air. (1991, Sept.). *EPA's map of radon zones, Ohio.* Washington, DC: Author.

U.S. Environmental Protection Agency, Office of Radiation Programs, & U.S. Department of Health and Human Services Centers for Disease Control. (1992a). *A citizen's guide to radon* (2nd ed.). Washington, DC: Author.

U.S. Environmental Protection Agency, Office of Radiation Programs. (1992b, May). *Technical support document for the citizen's guide to radon* (EPA 400-R-92-011). Washington, DC: Author.

Weinstein, N. D. (1988). The precaution adoption process. *Health Psychology, 7,* 355–386.

Weinstein, N. D. (1993). Testing four competing theories of health-protective behavior. *Health Psychology, 12,* 324–333.

Weinstein, N. D., Rothman, A. M., & Sutton, S. R. (1998). Stage theories of health behavior: Conceptual and methodological issues. *Health Psychology, 17,* 290–299.

Weinstein, N. D., & Sandman, P. M. (1992). A model of the precaution adoption process: Evidence from home radon testing. *Health Psychology, 11,* 170–180.

Weinstein, N. D., Sandman, P. M., & Roberts, N. E. (1990). Determinants of self-protective behavior: Home radon testing. *Journal of Applied Social Psychology, 20,* 783–801.

Weinstein, N. D., Sandman, P. M., & Roberts, N. E. (1991). Perceived susceptibility and self-protective behavior: A field experiment to encourage home radon testing. *Health Psychology, 10,* 25–33.

READING 17

Attributions of Responsibility and Persuasion: Increasing Mammography Utilization Among Women Over 40 With an Internally Oriented Message

Alexander J. Rothman, Peter Salovey, Carolyn Turvey, and Stephanie A. Fishkin • Yale University

One hundred ninety-seven women over 40 years old and not adhering to national guidelines for screening mammography viewed persuasive messages varying in attributional emphasis (internal, external, or information-only). Internal attributions of responsibility for health-promoting behavior were expected to motivate the greatest change in women's attitudes and behaviors in relation to breast cancer and mammography. Attitudes about breast cancer and mammography were measured immediately and 6 months after the presentation. Twelve months later, women who viewed the internal message were more likely to have obtained a screening mammogram than women assigned to the other two conditions. The attributions of responsibility encouraged by the persuasive messages were associated with whether viewing the presentation led to behavior change.

Key words: attributions, breast cancer, mammography, persuasion

Behavioral choices can account for substantial variance in illness (reviewed by Rodin & Salovey, 1989). As a result, how best to influence decisions to adopt healthy behaviors is an important psychological question. This experiment investigated the influence of one social psychological variable, attribution of responsibility, on persuasion and the subsequent adoption of a health-protective behavior. Specifically, we compared the influence of persuasive messages varying in emphasis on internal versus external attri-

butions of responsibility for the early detection of breast cancer on attitudes about and actual use of regular screening mammography.

Attributions of Responsibility and Health Behaviors

A potentially important characteristic of persuasive health messages is their relative emphasis on who is responsible for maintaining one's health. Often, health messages attempt to persuade people to take charge of their life and to be more responsible for their health. Smokers are urged to stop smoking, passengers are instructed to buckle up, alcoholics are told to stop drinking, and women are advised to perform early-detection behaviors for breast cancer, such as breast self-examination. To induce people to change their habits, these health messages encourage them to take a more active role in their health care and to attribute responsibility to themselves for their health-related behavior.

Research on attributions has generally addressed one of two questions: *Attribution* theories have examined the cognitive antecedents of attributions, and *attributional* theories have examined the attitudinal and behavioral consequences of attributions (Forsterling, 1985, 1986; Harvey & Weary, 1984; Kelley & Michela, 1980; see Michela & Wood, 1986, for a review of this framework within the health domain). Previous examinations of attributions and health have focused primarily on explanations for unfortunate events or illnesses. In these investigations, an attribution operates as an explanation for an event that has already occurred and serves as the basis on which to assess controllability, blame, or meaning (Janoff-Bulman, 1979; Shaver, 1985; Taylor, Lichtman, & Wood, 1984; Wortman, 1976; but see Downey, Cohen-Silver, & Wortman, 1990). This article, however, focuses on whether internal and external attributions differentially influence attitudes about, and the performance of, a health-protective behavior.

In comparison with research on the relationship between attribution and adjustment, the premise that attributions have a differential influence on health behavior has been examined only selectively. There is research to suggest that attributional orientation, the way in which a person perceives the causes or motives for changes in beliefs and actions, affects attitude and behavior change. External attributions for the causes of a behavior change are associated with poorer adherence to recommendations and poorer maintenance of new behaviors (e.g., Davison & Valins, 1969; Storms & Nisbett, 1970). Internal attributions for the motives for behavior change, however, are positively correlated with the adoption of health behaviors such as fluoride mouth rinsing (Lund & Kegeles, 1984), smoking cessation (Colletti & Kopel, 1979; Fisher, Levenkron, Lowe, Loro, & Green, 1982), and high blood pressure screening

(King, 1982). Similarly, research on health locus of control (Wallston & Wallston, 1981, 1982) has suggested that an internal locus of control is associated with health information seeking, although perhaps only for those people who place great importance on their health (e.g., Quadrel & Lau, 1989; Wallston, Maides, & Wallston, 1976).

In an extensive study on attribution and behavior change, Harackiewicz, Sansone, Blair, Epstein, and Manderlink (1987) manipulated internal and external attributions for participation in a smoking cessation program. Subjects who entered the program were randomly assigned to treatments that differed in the externality of the cessation strategy (self-help manual vs. nicotine gum) and in motivational orientation (intrinsic vs. extrinsic). Although initial cessation of smoking was partially associated with external attributions for behavior change, long-term behavior change was predicted best by internal attributions for the success of the treatment program. However, the participants in the extrinsic and intrinsic conditions who made the appropriate attributions for their behavior change, external and internal respectively, successfully quit smoking.

The latter finding is consistent with the framework proposed by Brickman et al. (1982), who suggested that for an intervention to be successful, the causal attributions promoted by the program should correspond to those causal attributions made by people about the health problem and its alleviation. Although Brickman et al. emphasized the importance of the match between the attributions made by a person and an intervention, they also suggested that holding people responsible for their health behavior produces long-term change.

It seems, then, that attributions of responsibility to oneself for the performance of health-related behaviors are positively associated with the execution of these behaviors. However, this conclusion is based primarily on assessments of correlations between self-reported attributions and behavior change (e.g., Colletti & Kopel, 1979; Fisher et al., 1982; King, 1982). In the present study, we manipulated the attributional emphasis for performing health-protective behaviors in a persuasive message about breast cancer and mammography. We predicted that a message that attributed responsibility to the self (internal) as compared with one that attributed responsibility to a health care provider (external) for initiating health-protecting behaviors would lead women to increase their perceived responsibility for breast cancer prevention and would encourage them to obtain a screening mammogram.

Prevention and Early Detection of Breast Cancer: The Use of Screening Mammography

One out of every nine American women will get breast cancer at some point in her life. Each year, over 100,000 women are diagnosed with breast cancer in the United States, one third of whom die of the disease. Breast cancer is the most common cancer found in women and, after lung cancer, is the second leading cancer killer (American Cancer Society, 1990; National Cancer Institute, 1989). Screening mechanisms such as breast self-examination, clinical breast examination by a health professional, and mammography are thought to be highly effective in detecting breast cancer early when treatment options are maximized. Presently, the American Medical Association, the American Cancer Society, and the National Cancer Institute all recommend that asymptomatic women between 40 and 49 years of age have a mammogram every 1 to 2 years and then annually after age 50 (Fox, Klos, & Tsou, 1988).

Mammography is the most controversial, least studied, and least used breast cancer screening device. Despite long-standing guidelines, before 1987, only 15–20% of women over 50 reported having had a mammogram in the past year (Howard, 1987). Similarly, about 19% of all women between the ages of 35 and 49 had ever had a single screening mammogram (Fox, Baum, Klos, & Tsou, 1985). However, more recent data suggest that mammography use is increasing (Centers for Disease Control, 1989a, 1989b; Rimer, Keintz, Kessler, Engstrom, & Rosan, 1989). For example, a recent nationwide study reported that 31% of women were adhering to the mammography guidelines (Centers for Disease Control, 1990). Still, these adherence rates are lower than those for breast self-examination (50–70%) and clinical breast examination (70–80%; Fox, Baum, Klos, & Tsou, 1985).

The underuse of mammography is shocking when one considers that mammography is "the most sensitive and reliable method of early detection" (Gold, 1988, p. 517). In the Breast Cancer Detection Demonstration Project (Baker, 1982), 42% of detected breast cancers were found by mammography alone as compared with 9% for clinical breast examination alone. In addition, several studies have shown that mammography may be associated with lowered cancer mortality (Baker, 1982; Eddy, Hasselblad, McGivney, & Hendee, 1988; Newell, Dodd, & Fink, 1988; Shapiro, Vanet, Strax, Vanet, & Roeser, 1982; see Miller, 1991, for a review), although the specific impact of mammography on mortality remains controversial.

The reason most often suggested for the underuse of mammography is that doctors do not recommend it to their patients (Fox et al., 1988). Consequently, systematic efforts to address the low rates of mammography use have focused almost exclusively on interventions aimed at changing referral practices among health care providers (Fox, Tsou, & Klos, 1985a, 1985b). Only recently has attention been paid to influencing the behavior of patients (Reynolds, West, & Aiken, 1990; Rimer et al., 1989).

The Present Experiment

This experiment examined how altering attributions of responsibility for maintaining one's health affected women's attitudes and behaviors regarding screening mammography. We presented persuasive educational programs about breast cancer and mammography to women 40 years old and over who were not adhering to the national guidelines for mammography. Women viewed a video that emphasized either internal (self) or external (health care provider) attributions of responsibility for performing early-detection behaviors. A similar group of women viewed a program that emphasized neither self nor health care provider attributions of responsibility but contained the same information about breast cancer and mammography. Women's attitudes about breast cancer and mammography and their perceptions of responsibility for getting a mammogram were measured after the presentation. We assessed whether participants obtained a screening mammogram 6 and 12 months later. We predicted that women in the internal condition would show greater attitude and behavior change than women in the external or information-only conditions. The external and information-only messages were not expected to differ significantly from each other in their effectiveness in promoting mammogram use.

Method

Subjects

Women age 40 or over were recruited from a large Northeastern utility company to attend an information session on breast cancer and mammography by a tear-off coupon placed in company and union newsletters. Of the 350 women who responded, 250 were eligible for the study. Women were deemed eligible if they were 40 or over and had not had more than 50% of the number of screening mammograms recommended for someone their age, although they were not told that they had been selected on the basis of this criterion. Women were paid $10 for their participation and, in turn, donated their compensation to the American Cancer Society.

Subjects in this study were assigned to one of three conditions: internal, external, and information-only. Two hundred fifty eligible women signed up to participate in the study, 197 of whom completed and returned the two required questionnaire packets (79% response rate). After a subject was deemed eligible, she selected one of five viewing times to attend the information session. When every subject had selected a viewing time, experimental conditions were randomly assigned to each of the time slots. Because there were only five viewing times, the information-only condition was shown just once. Overall, there were 90 subjects in the internal condition, 44 subjects in the external condition, and 63 in the information-only condition. The unequal number of subjects in each condition was primarily due to differences in preferences for the five viewing times.

Persuasive Message Presentation

Women who were eligible for the videotaped information session viewed one of the three programs (internal, external, or information-only). The three messages varied solely in their attribu-

tion of responsibility for preventing and detecting breast cancer.

The internal tape emphasized a woman's own responsibility for getting a mammogram and detecting breast cancer (e.g., "Eight out of 10 lumps that *you* might find will not be breast cancer," and "While it is not known yet how to prevent breast cancer, the value and benefits of *your* finding it early are well-known").

The external tape emphasized a doctor's responsibility for detecting breast cancer, using mammography (e.g., "Eight out of 10 lumps that a doctor might find will not be breast cancer," and "While it is not known yet how to prevent breast cancer, the value and benefits of a doctor finding it early are well-known").

The information-only tape was designed to communicate information without any singular emphasis on internal or external attributions of responsibility (e.g., "Eight out of 10 lumps that are found will not be breast cancer," and "While it is not yet known how to prevent breast cancer, the value and benefits of finding it early are well-known").

The "Facts About Mammography" videotape was designed by a collaborative team from the Yale Department of Psychology and the Yale Cancer Prevention Research Unit at the Department of Epidemiology and Public Health. The presentation covered general information about breast cancer, risk factors, and preventive measures. The presentation was videotaped slide show with an accompanying audiotape that was dubbed onto videotape by professional television technicians. "Facts About Mammography" was written to be understood by individuals reading at the sixth-grade level to ensure comprehension by all subjects. All three conditions of "Facts About Mammography" were the same length and contained exactly the same factual material.

Measures

PREPRESENTATION

General health background. This form contained 22 items concerning demographic characteristics as well as cancer-related health history (e.g., family history of cancer, frequency of medical visits, personal breast problems, frequency of mammograms, frequency of breast self-examination).

POSTPRESENTATION

Attitudes about breast cancer and mammography. Twelve questions addressed a woman's perception of the effectiveness and importance of mammography (e.g., "How effective do you think mammography is for finding lumps in a woman's breast?") as well as her perceptions of the experience of having a mammogram (e.g., "How painful do you feel mammography is?"). In addition, a woman's perceptions of her own and her doctor's responsibility for keeping herself healthy and detecting breast cancer were measured (e.g., "How responsible do you feel your doctor is for keeping you healthy?" and "How responsible do you feel you are for finding breast cancer?"). All questions were coded on a scale ranging from *not at all* (1) to *very much* (5).

Reactions to the presentation. Ten questions assessed reactions to the videotaped educational session on the same 5-point scale (e.g., "How relieved did the slide show make you feel?" and "How interesting was the slide show?").

Knowledge about breast cancer and mammography. Subjects were presented with seven multiple-choice questions concerning facts about breast cancer covered in the presentation (e.g., "How many women in the United States do you think will get breast cancer at some point in their lives?"). Knowledge scores were determined by summing correct responses.

Future behavior related to breast cancer. After the presentation, subjects were asked whether they intended to have a mammogram during the next 12 months.

BEHAVIORAL FOLLOW-UP

Six and 12 months after the presentation, subjects were recontacted to determine whether they had obtained a mammogram. During the 6-month follow-up, subjects also answered a short series of questions on their attitudes about mammography.

Procedure

Before attending the educational presentation on breast cancer and mammography, women who were eligible for the study were asked to complete a packet including consent forms and the General Health Background Questionnaire. Using the company's closed-circuit television network, women then viewed a 20-minute presentation entitled "Facts About Mammography" at one of five presentation times during the day. After the presentation of either the internal, external, or information-only videotape, subjects completed a sealed packet of measures that they had received in the mail. This packet included the postpresentation measures described above. On completion of the measures, subjects were asked to mail all forms to the investigators in a stamped, self-addressed envelope. Once the forms were received, subjects were sent a letter thanking them for their participation as well as an additional pamphlet containing information about the Yale Mobile Mammography Unit. Each pamphlet contained a slogan relevant to the subject's assigned condition. The internal pamphlet stated, "It's your responsibility: Get a mammogram," the external pamphlet stated, "Doctors recommend: Get a mammogram," and the information-only pamphlet stated, "Get a mammogram."

Six months after viewing the program, all subjects were recontacted by telephone and were asked whether they had obtained a mammogram during the prior 6 months. At that time, subjects also answered several questions concerning their attitudes about mammography and their perceptions of responsibility for performing preventive health behaviors related to breast cancer. Any subject who had not yet obtained a mammogram or could not be reached at 6 months was recontacted 12 months after the presentation. The persuasive intervention was conducted in January 1990, and 6- and 12-month behavioral measures were collected in July 1990 and January 1991, respectively.

Results

Subject Demographics

Subjects in the three conditions were compared on an extensive series of non-health-related and health-related demographic variables, and condition differences were not found on these measures.

Scoring of Scales

The scales eliciting reactions to the videotape and the attitudes about breast cancer and mammography questionnaire were expected to be multidimensional. To extract these factors, each scale was submitted to a principal-components analysis with varimax rotation.

Reaction to the videotape. Two components accounting for 55% of the total variance were extracted in a principal-components analysis on these items. Items with loadings greater than or equal to .40 were retained, so long as their second-highest loadings were not within .10 of their highest loading. (This criterion was used for all principal-components analyses.) The first component contained six items reflecting how interesting, hopeful, and relieving the presentation made the women feel and was labeled *positive reactions* (eigenvalue = 3.36; accounted for 34% of the total variance). The second component contained four items reflecting how sad and afraid the videotape made subjects feel and was labeled *negative reactions* (eigenvalue = 2.06; accounted for 21% of the total variance). The inter-correlation of the two factor scores was .03.

Attitudes about breast cancer and mammography questionnaire. Four components were extracted from the attitudes about breast cancer and mammography questionnaire, accounting for 55% of the total variance. The first component contained five items that reflected the importance of mammography (e.g., "How important is it for you to have a mammogram?") and was labeled *value of mammography* (eigenvalue = 2.68; accounted for 22% of the total variance). The second component contained two items that reflected a health care provider's responsibility for keeping a person healthy, and it was labeled *responsibility of a health care provider for health* (eigenvalue = 1.69; accounted for 14% of the total variance). Two items loaded on the third component, reflecting the perceived danger of mammography, which was labeled *fear of mammography* (eigenvalue = 1.21; accounted for 10% of the total variance). Finally, three items reflecting a person's own responsibility for keeping himself or herself healthy loaded on a fourth component, called *responsibility of self for health* (eigenvalue = 1.06; accounted for 9% of the total variance). The intercorrelations among the four factor scores ranged from –.17 to .29.

Reactions to the Video Presentation

All three educational videotapes were designed to differ only in the attributional stance emphasized. To ensure that there were no other relevant differences among the tapes, we elicited subjects' reactions to the presentations. Table 17.1 contains the means for these measures. Subjects' positive and negative affective reactions to the presentation did not differ by condition, $F(2, 194) < 1$, *ns*, and $F(2, 192) = 2.38$, *ns*, respectively. In addition, subjects in the three experimental conditions did not differ significantly in the amount of knowledge about breast cancer and mammography they acquired from the presentation, $F(2, 194) < 1$.

Attributions of Responsibility and Breast Cancer

The presentations were designed to emphasize different attributions of responsibility for preventing and detecting breast cancer. We hypothesized that women in the internal condition would be more likely to attribute responsibility to the self and that women in the external condition would be more likely to attribute responsibility to health care providers.

Subjects separately rated their perceptions of responsibility for both themselves and a health care provider for maintaining a person's health.[1] An overall responsibility score was calculated for each subject by subtracting the perceived responsibility for health care providers from the perceived responsibility of oneself. Table 17.2 contains these responsibility scores. An analysis of variance (ANOVA) with contrast weights set at 1, –1, and 0 (internal, external, and information-only conditions, respectively) confirmed that subjects in the internal condition attributed more responsibility to themselves in relation to health care providers than subjects in the external condition, $F(1, 194) = 5.15$, $p < .02$. To understand the nature of this effect more completely, we separately analyzed subjects' attributions of responsibility to themselves and health care providers. Although women

---

[1]Before viewing the presentation, there were no differences across experimental condition in women's perceptions of responsibility for either themselves or a health care provider for maintaining health.

TABLE 17.1. Means and Standard Deviations for Reactions to the Videotape Presentations and Knowledge by Condition

	Condition					
	Internal		External		Information	
Variable	M	SD	M	SD	M	SD
Positive reactions	3.48	0.80	3.46	0.78	3.50	0.86
Negative reactions	1.52	0.75	1.33	0.44	1.63	0.71
Knowledge about breast cancer	4.72	1.28	4.86	1.44	4.76	1.43

in the internal and external conditions did not differ in their attributions of responsibility to themselves, $F(1, 194) < 1$, women in the external condition attributed significantly more responsibility to their health care providers than women in the internal condition, $F(1, 194) = 6.33, p < .01$. This pattern of attributions could be found, albeit more weakly, even 6 months after the women viewed the presentation. Subjects in the internal condition continued to attribute relatively greater responsibility to the self ($M = .25$), and subjects in the external condition attributed relatively greater responsibility to a health care provider ($M = -.72$); $F(1, 191) = 2.60, p < .10$.

General Attitudes About Breast Cancer and Mammography

Subjects' attitudes about mammography were examined in the light of our experimental manipulation. An inspection of the means in Table 17.3 showed that there were no differences among conditions in how much women valued mammography, $F(2, 194) < 1$, nor in how much they feared mammography, $F(2, 194) < 1$. Contrary to some

findings (e.g., Howard, 1987), women appeared not to be afraid of mammography and in fact expressed extremely positive regard for the procedure. These attitudes were well represented in subjects' expressed intentions to get a mammogram in the following year (92.8% of women in the internal condition, 88.1% of women in the external condition, and 89.6% of women in the information-only condition).

Obtaining Mammograms After the Presentation

Subjects were contacted 6 and 12 months after the presentation. Subjects were not contacted at 12 months if they reported having obtained a mammogram at the 6-month interview. After we completed the 12-month follow-up, mammogram data for 185 of the original 197 subjects were available. None of the 185 women who were contacted reported obtaining a mammogram because of a diagnosed breast problem. We had hypothesized that women in the internal condition were more likely to obtain a mammogram than women in either the external or the information-only condi-

TABLE 17.2. Means and Standard Deviations for Attitudes About Breast Cancer and Mammography and Attributions of Responsibility for Health by Condition

	Condition					
	Internal		External		Information	
Variable	M	SD	M	SD	M	SD
Postpresentation value of mammography	4.62	0.41	4.64	0.36	4.67	0.38
Postpresentation fear of mammography	1.57	0.80	1.65	0.87	1.73	0.94
Postpresentation responsibility of self minus health care provider	0.75	1.00	0.34	0.98	0.64	0.96
6-month follow-up responsibility of self minus health care provider	0.25	3.53	−0.72	2.88	−0.18	3.10

TABLE 17.3. Twelve-Month Behavioral Follow-Up: Mammography

Obtained mammogram	Condition		
	Internal$_a$	External$_b$	Information$_b$
% yes	65.9	57.1	55.2
% no	34.1	42.9	44.8

Note. Conditions with different subscripts differ reliably from each other at $p < .01$.

tions. Of women in the internal condition, 65.9% reported obtaining a mammogram during the 12 months after the presentation, and 57.1% and 55.2% of the women in the external and information-only conditions, respectively, reported having obtained a mammogram. Haberman's (1974) analysis of frequency data using the FREQ program, a form of log-linear analysis, was used to test our hypothesis. We tested the fit to the data presented in Table 17.3 of two alternative models: (a) a model that assumed no difference among the three conditions in the use of mammography and (b) a model that assumed that mammography use in the internal condition was different from use in the external and information-only conditions. A model is said to fit when the residual likelihood ratio chi-square is nonsignificant. The model predicting no difference among conditions did not reliably fit the data, $L^2(2) = 10.77$, $p < .01$. However, the model testing that mammography use rates in the internal condition were different from the rates in the external and information-only conditions fit the data quite well, $L^2(1) = 2.88$, *ns*. Furthermore, the improvement in goodness of fit from Model 1 to Model 2 was reliable, $\Delta L^2(1) = 7.89$, $p < .01$. Women who viewed the internal presentation were significantly more likely to obtain a mammogram than women in either of the other two conditions.

To evaluate further the effectiveness of our intervention, the percentage of women who had a mammogram in each condition was compared with a baseline percentage of women in the state of Connecticut who annually obtained a mammogram. Presently, Connecticut has one of the highest mammography use rates in the United States; in 1989, 48.5% of all eligible women age 40 or over obtained a mammogram (Adams, personal communication, July 16, 1991; Connecticut Department of Health Services, 1990). This baseline is consistent with data from 1987–1988 reporting

that 45% of women age 40 or over had a mammogram in the past year (Sackmary, 1989). A comparison of the utilization rates in each condition showed that consistent with hypotheses, women in the internal condition were more likely to obtain a mammogram than the average women in Connecticut, $\chi^2(1) = 12.10$, $p < .005$. However, women in both the external and the information-only conditions were not reliably more likely to get a mammogram, $\chi^2(1) = 2.96$, *ns*, and $\chi^2(1) = 1.78$, *ns*, respectively.

Discussion

We hypothesized that persuasive messages varying in attributions of responsibility would differentially affect women's attitudes and subsequent behavior concerning the prevention of breast cancer. Women who viewed a presentation that emphasized internal attributions of responsibility for health were then expected to attribute greater responsibility for health to themselves and to be more likely to obtain a mammogram during the ensuing year than women in either of the other two conditions.

There were no differences in affective responses to the three presentations, nor were there any differences in the knowledge that the three presentations conveyed. Furthermore, women in each presentation condition reported no difference in their value or fear of mammography, indicating that the three conditions did not differ in the emotions they aroused or in the information about breast cancer and mammography communicated. However, there was a difference among conditions in whether a woman obtained a mammogram during the 12 months after the presentation. Women who viewed the presentation that emphasized internal attributions of responsibility for health were more likely to describe themselves as responsible for the prevention of cancer and then to obtain a mammogram than women who viewed either the external or the information-only presentation. Furthermore, only women who viewed the internal presentation were reliably more likely to obtain a mammogram than the average eligible woman in Connecticut. This increase was particularly impressive given that the women who participated in our study previously had not complied with guidelines for mammography, whereas the comparative baseline percentage for Connecticut was computed on a random sample that included both compliant and noncompliant women.

Women were recruited for this study with the assistance of the utility company's health education program. Although we would have preferred to have recruited a no-intervention control group from the same pool of women who participated in our three experimental conditions, the company would not allow us to withhold information about breast cancer from any interested employee, for obvious ethical considerations. The option of merely delaying the transmission of information about breast cancer for 1 year was unacceptable to both the experimenters and the company both because of the possible development of breast cancer in any woman during those 12 months and because such a "wait list" group quite likely would receive additional breast cancer information through contact with study participants and the media.

The finding that the internal-attribution condition was most effective in promoting mammography is generally compatible with previous studies. Perhaps this message of responsibility enables people to feel in control of their life and therefore encourages them to take an active role in monitoring their health. Unfortunately, at the present time, these mediating variables have not been measured.

The framework proposed by Brickman et al. (1982) suggests that behavior is facilitated if there is a match between the attributions made by the individual about some behavior and the attributions promoted by the intervention. However, the present experiment did not provide support for this hypothesis. Women who were internally oriented in their attributional style before the video were not more likely to obtain a mammogram after viewing the internally oriented presentation. Likewise, women who were externally oriented in their attributional style before the video were not more likely to obtain a mammogram after viewing the externally oriented presentation.

The findings presented in this article, if replicated, have important implications for public health campaigns designed to promote mammography. Our results suggest that when presenting information about breast cancer and mammography, emphasizing a woman's responsibility for taking care of her health will significantly increase the likelihood that she will obtain a mammogram.

However, in assessing the public health implications of this study, one needs to consider characteristics of the sample of women who participated. The women in this sample were educated, relatively affluent, and predominantly white. Unfortunately, the percentage of nonwhite women was too small to investigate whether there were any differences that were due to race or ethnicity in the effectiveness of the messages. Previous research, however, has demonstrated that the use of mammography can vary depending on culture and ethnicity (e.g., Bastani, Marcus, & Hollatz-Brown, 1991; Rimer et al., 1989; Stein, Fox, & Murata, 1991).

Finally, the differential effect of attributions of responsibility demonstrated in this experiment is noteworthy, given that the manipulation of attributional orientation was subtly imbedded in an involving persuasive message about a serious health concern. Although the role that attributions play in coping processes has recently been challenged (Downey et al., 1990), this experiment affirms the importance of attributions of responsibility for influencing actions taken to minimize a potential health problem.

Conclusion

The relationship between attributions of responsibility and health behavior is complex (Michela & Wood, 1986). In a large field experiment, we examined whether women obtained a screening mammogram after viewing an educational presentation that emphasized attributing responsibility for performing health behaviors to either themselves or to health care providers. An analysis of the number of women who obtained a mammogram during the year after the presentation strongly suggests that a persuasive presentation that emphasizes one's own responsibility for maintaining health is most effective in promoting mammogram use.

ACKNOWLEDGMENTS

We would like to thank Robert P. Abelson, Mahzarin R. Banaji, Michael Baron, Christine Dunkel-Schetter, Susan Greener, Nina Sayer, and three anonymous reviewers for their comments on drafts of this article. Robert P. Abelson also suggested the specific analysis of frequency data reported here. Carol Antone, Michael Baron, Chloé Drake, Maree Hampton, and Kelli Keough's assistance in the implementation of this study is also appreciated. We gratefully acknowledge the help of Lorraine Mattei, the staff of the Reach Out for Health Program, the Television Production Team of the Southern New England Telephone Company, and Martine Skoog and the Connecticut Union of Telephone Workers, without whom this study would not have been possible. Finally, we would like to thank Mary L. Adams of the Connecticut Department of Health Services for providing us with state mammography utilization data.

Research reported in this article was funded by National Cancer Institute Grant P01-CA42101 (Project 9). Preparation of this article was also facilitated by the following grants to Peter Salovey: National Institute of Health Biomedical Research Support Grant S07-RR07015, National Center for Health Statistics Contract 200-88-7001, and Presidential Young Investigator Award BNS-9058020 from the National Science Foundation.

Portions of this study were presented at the 1991 annual meeting of the Eastern Psychological Association in New York.

REFERENCES

American Cancer Society. (1990). *1990 Cancer facts and figures*. New York: Author.

Baker, L. H. (1982). Breast Cancer Detection Demonstration Project: 5-year summary report. *Cancer, 32*, 194–225.

Bastani, R., Marcus, A. C., & Hollatz-Brown, A. (1991). Screening mammography rates and barriers to use: A Los Angeles County survey. *Preventive Medicine, 20*, 350–363.

Brickman, P., Rabinowitz, V. C., Karuza, J., Coates, D., Cohn, E., & Kidder, L. (1982). Models of helping and coping. *American Psychologist, 37*, 368–384.

Centers for Disease Control. (1989a). *Trends in screening mammograms for women 50 years of age and older—Behavioral risk factor surveillance system, 1987*. Atlanta, GA: Author.

Centers for Disease Control. (1989b). *Use of mammography for breast cancer screening: Rhode Island, 1987*. Atlanta, GA: Author.

Centers for Disease Control. (1990). *Use of mammography—United States, 1990*. Atlanta, GA: Author.

Colletti, G., & Kopel, S. A. (1979). Maintaining behavior changes: An investigation of three maintenance strategies and the relationship of self-attribution to the long-term reduction of cigarette smoking. *Journal of Consulting and Clinical Psychology, 47*, 614–617.

Connecticut Department of Health Services. (1990). *Connecticut behavioral health risks: 1989 results*. Hartford, CT: Author.

Davison, G. C., & Valins, S. (1969). Maintenance of self-attributed and drug-attributed behavior change. *Journal of Personality and Social Psychology, 11*, 25–33.

Downey, G., Cohen-Silver, R. C., & Wortman, C. B. (1990). Reconsidering the attribution–adjustment relation following a major negative event: Coping with the loss of a child. *Journal of Personality and Social Psychology, 59*, 925–940.

Eddy, D. M., Hasselbald, V., McGivney, W., & Hendee, W. (1988). The value of mammography screening in women under age 50 years. *Journal of the American Medical Association, 259*, 1512–1519.

Fisher, E. B., Levenkron, J. C., Lowe, M. R., Loro, A. D., & Green, L. (1982). Self-initiated self-control in risk reduction. In R. B. Stuart (Ed.), *Adherence, compliance, and generalization in behavioral medicine* (pp. 169–191). New York: Brunner/Mazel.

Forsterling, F. (1985). Attributional retraining: A review. *Psychological Bulletin, 98*, 495–512.

Forsterling, F. (1986). Attributional conceptions in clinical psychology. *American Psychologist, 41*, 275–285.

Fox, S., Baum, J. K., Klos, D. S., & Tsou, C. V. (1985). Breast cancer screening: The underuse of mammography. *Radiology, 156*, 607–611.

Fox, S., Klos, D. S., & Tsou, C. V. (1988). Underuse of screening mammography by family physicians. *Radiology, 166*, 432–433.

Fox, S., Tsou, C. V., & Klos, D. S. (1985a). Increasing mammography screening: An application of general principles of CME methodology. *Journal of Psychosomatic Obstetrics and Gynecology, 4*, 95–104.

Fox, S., Tsou, C. V., & Klos, D. S. (1985b). An intervention to increase mammography screening by residents in family practice. *Journal of Family Practice, 20*, 467–471.

Gold, R. H. (1988). Painless mammography. *Archives of Internal Medicine, 148*, 517.

Haberman, S. (1974). *The analysis of frequency data*. Chicago: University of Chicago Press.

Harackiewicz, J. M., Sansone, C., Blair, L. W., Epstein, J. A., & Manderlink, G. (1987). Attributional processes in behavior change and maintenance: Smoking cessation and continued abstinence. *Journal of Consulting and Clinical Psychology, 55*, 372–378.

Harvey, J. H., & Weary, G. (1984). Current issues in attribution theory and research. *Annual Review of Psychology, 35*, 427–459.

Howard, J. (1987). Using mammography for cancer control: An unrealized potential. *Cancer, 37*, 33–48.

Janoff-Bulman, R. (1979). Characterological versus behavioral self-blame: Inquiries into depression and rape. *Journal of Personality and Social Psychology, 37*, 1798–1809.

Kelley, H. H., & Michela, J. L. (1980). Attribution theory and research. *Annual Review of Psychology, 31*, 457–501.

King, J. B. (1982). The impact of patients' perceptions of high blood pressure on attendance at screening: An extension of the health belief model. *Social Science and Medicine, 16*, 1079–1092.

Lund, A. K., & Kegeles, S. S. (1984). Rewards and adolescent health behavior. *Health Psychology, 3*, 351–369.

Michela, J. L., & Wood, J. V. (1986). Causal attributions in health and illness. In P. H. Kendall (Ed.), *Advances in cognitive-behavioral research and therapy* (Vol. 5, pp. 179–235). San Diego, CA: Academic Press.

Miller, A. (1991). Early detection of breast cancer. In J. R. Harris, S. Hellman, I. C. Henderson, & D. W. Kinne (Eds.), *Breast diseases* (2nd ed., pp. 215–228). Philadelphia: Lippincott.

National Cancer Institute. (1989). *What you need to know about breast cancer* (DHHS Publication No. NIH 89-1556). Washington, DC: U.S. Government Printing Office.

Newell, G. R., Dodd, G. D., & Fink, D. J. (1988). Screening mammography: A public health practice. *Cancer Bulletin, 40*, 56–58.

Quadrel, M. J., & Lau, R. R. (1989). Health promotion, health locus of control, and health behavior: Two field experiments. *Journal of Applied Social Psychology, 19*, 1497–1521.

Reynolds, K. D., West, S. G., & Aiken, L. S. (1990). Increasing the use of mammography: A pilot program. *Health Education Quarterly, 17*, 429–441.

Rimer, B. K., Keintz, M. K., Kessler, H. B., Engstrom, P. F., & Rosan, J. R. (1989). Why women resist screening mammography: Patient related barriers. *Radiology, 172*, 243–246.

Rodin, J., & Salovey, P. (1989). Health psychology. *Annual Review of Psychology, 40*, 533–579.

Rothman, A. J. (1990). *Attributions of responsibility and persuasion: Women's attitudes about breast cancer and mammography*. Unpublished master's thesis, Yale University, New Haven, CT.

Sackmary, B. (1989). *Attitudes and behavior about cancer and its prevention: A survey of adults in Connecticut*. Hartford: Cancer Control Program, Department of Health Services.

Shapiro, S., Vanet, W., Strax, P., Vanet, L., & Roeser, R. (1982). Ten to fourteen-year effect of screening on breast cancer mortality. *Journal of National Cancer Institute, 69*, 349–355.

Shaver, K. (1985). *The attribution of blame: Causality, responsibility, and blameworthiness*. New York: Springer-Verlag.

Stein, J. A., Fox, S. A., & Murata, P. J., (1991). The influence of ethnicity, socioeconomic status, and psychological barriers on use of mammography. *Journal of Health and Social Behavior, 32*, 101–113.

Storms, M. D., & Nisbett, R. E. (1970). Insomnia and the attribution process. *Journal of Personality and Social Psychology, 16*, 319–328.

Taylor, S. E., Lichtman, R. R., & Wood, J. V. (1984). Attributions, beliefs about control, and adjustment to breast cancer. *Journal of Personality and Social Psychology, 46*, 489–502.

Wallston, K. A., Maides, S., & Wallston, B. S. (1976). Health-related information seeking as a function of health-related locus of control and health value. *Journal of Research in Personality, 10*, 215–222.

Wallston, K. A., & Wallston, B. S. (1981). Health locus of control scales. In H. Lefcourt (Ed.), *Advances and innovations in locus of control research* (pp. 65–95). San Diego, CA: Academic Press.

Wallston, K. A., & Wallston, B. S. (1982). Who is responsible for your health? The construct of health locus of control. In G. Sanders & J. Suls (Eds.), *Social psychology of health and illness* (pp. 189–243). Hillsdale, NJ: Erlbaum.

Wortman, C. B. (1976). Causal attributions and personal control. In J. H. Harvey, W. J. Ickes, & R. F. Kidd (Eds.), *New directions in attribution research* (Vol. 1, pp. 23–52). Hillsdale, NJ: Erlbaum.

Inducing Hypocrisy as a Means
of Encouraging Young Adults to Use Condoms

Jeff Stone, Elliot Aronson, A. Lauren Crain,
Matthew P. Winslow, and Carrie B. Fried
University of California at Santa Cruz

This experiment applied a new twist on cognitive dissonance theory to the problem of
AIDS prevention among sexually active young adults. Dissonance was created after a
proattitudinal advocacy by inducing hypocrisy—having subjects publicly advocate the
importance of safe sex and then systematically making the subjects mindful of their own
past failures to use condoms. It was predicted that the induction of hypocrisy would
motivate subjects to reduce dissonance by purchasing condoms at the completion of the
experiment. The results showed that more subjects in the hypocrisy condition bought
condoms and also bought more condoms, on average, than subjects in the control
conditions. The implications of the hypocrisy procedure for AIDS prevention programs
and for current views of dissonance theory are discussed.

At this writing, more than 100,000 deaths in the United States are attributed to the human immunodeficiency virus (HIV) that causes AIDS. The Centers for Disease Control estimates that approximately 40,000 new cases of HIV infection are developing each year, and unless effective prevention techniques are discovered soon, these numbers could rise dramatically during the next 10 years.

Initially, the AIDS epidemic moved through high-risk groups such as the gay and intravenous-drug-using communities. Research evidence suggests that gay males responded with risk-reduction behavior (Coates, Stall, & Hoff, 1990), and there is also evidence of behavior change among intravenous-drug-using samples (see Des Jarlais & Friedman, 1990). Behavior change among sexually active heterosexual adolescents and young adults, however, has been more difficult to achieve

(e.g., Kegeles, Adler, & Irwin, 1988). A recent congressional report announced that the number of active AIDS cases among adolescents climbed 77% between the years 1989 and 1991. Clearly, effective intervention techniques targeted for sexually active teens and young adults are needed because, once again, a new high-risk group appears to be emerging from those who were less at risk only 2 years ago (Baum & Temoshok, 1990).

Adopting safer sexual behavior (e.g., condom use) is still the most efficient way to prevent the transmission of HIV among sexually active teens and young adults. To encourage safer sex, most intervention efforts have relied on educating these groups about AIDS and how to prevent it. The assumption of this approach seems to be that simply providing young people with information about AIDS should be enough to motivate behavior change. The motivation, however, is based on the element of fear. Educational campaigns seem to rely on scaring young people with the dire consequences of unsafe sex as a means of encouraging safer sexual behavior.

Unfortunately, the solution is not that simple. Over the past several years, systematic research by social psychologists has shown that fear does not always trigger rational, problem-solving behavior. When people are frightened, they tend to go into denial—to convince themselves that such a frightening thing as AIDS is unlikely to happen to them (Fisher & Misovich, 1990). As a result, people might underestimate their vulnerability (e.g., the "illusion of invulnerability"; Fisher, Misovich, & Kean, 1987) or overestimate how much they practice safer sexual behaviors (e.g., Aronson, Adler, & McDougall, 1988). These distortions are not easy to counteract, because simply presenting people with actuarial data proving vulnerability does not dispel this fallacious thinking (Snyder, 1978). Such reactions may account for otherwise puzzling behavior, such as the commonly reported unprotected sexual behavior among uninfected partners of individuals who have been diagnosed as HIV positive (Weisse, Nesselhof-Kendall, Fleck-Kandath, & Baum, 1990).

Currently, there are few AIDS interventions that reliably motivate changes in sexual behavior. Recent reviews suggest that most techniques are atheoretical or, because of their research design, provide only a best guess about what aspect of the program caused the observed results (e.g., Becker & Joseph, 1988; O'Keeffe, Nesselhof-Kendall, & Baum, 1990; see Fisher & Fisher, 1992). In recognition of this problem, a recent science directorate from the American Psychological Association encouraged AIDS behavioral researchers (a) to employ more experimental or quasi-experimental designs to investigate their interventions and (b) to "capitalize" on the fundamentals of "social marking techniques" that have successfully motivated behavior change in other health domains (Coates & Sanstad, 1992).

The research reported in this article is responsive to both recommendations. Marketing techniques, to the degree that they are based on principles of persuasion, constitute a major area of study in social psychology. One of the most powerful and relatively permanent persuasion techniques has come from social psychological theory and research on cognitive dissonance (Festinger, 1957). The effect of dissonance motivation on "self-persuasion" has been used successfully to change attitudes and behavior in such domains as energy conservation (Gonzales, Aronson, & Costanzo, 1988; Pallack, Cook, & Sullivan, 1980), weight reduction (Axsom & Cooper, 1981), and the cessation of adolescent smoking (Chassin, Presson, & Sherman, 1990).

Our application of dissonance and self-persuasion to the prevention of AIDS takes advantage of an existing hypocrisy—the fact that most college students believe they should systematically use condoms to prevent AIDS but do not always behave according to this belief. As a means of encouraging condom use, our procedure attempts to create feelings of hypocrisy by inducing subjects to make a public commitment to the systematic use of condoms. By itself, this commitment would not be expected to cause much dissonance, because advocating safer sex is helpful to others and is consistent with positive self-expectations for decent and reasonable behavior. But suppose subjects are then made mindful of the fact that they themselves do not use condoms regularly; the resulting inconsistency between their public commitment and the increased awareness of their current risky sexual behavior should cause dissonance. To reduce dissonance, subjects are expected to begin to practice what they preach—that is, to change their sexual behavior, effectively bringing their practice of safe sex in line with their preachings about the importance of condom use for AIDS prevention (see Thibodeau & Aronson, 1992).

In the initial investigation of the induction of hypocrisy, Aronson, Fried, and Stone (1991) used self-reported intentions as a measure of condom use. The results showed that the induction of hypocrisy made subjects more aware of their past failures to use condoms, effectively cutting through the denial processes that most people use to avoid acknowledging their risk for AIDS. But there was a ceiling effect on the measure of future condom use—all subjects in the experiment pledged relatively high intentions to use condoms in the future. It seems that, after exposure to AIDS information, pledging high intentions to use condoms more frequently in the future is too easy and socially desirable. As a result, almost everyone in the first experiment was able to claim high intentions regardless of experimental condition. Interestingly enough, despite the apparent ceiling effect on the measure of future intentions, the data from follow-up interviews suggested that subjects from the hypocrisy condition were using condoms more often 3 months after the experiment than subjects in the three control conditions.

On the basis of this result, Aronson et al. (1991) speculated that the future intentions reported by the subjects in the hypocrisy condition might have been more realistic or indicative of behavior than the intentions reported by the subjects in the other three experimental groups. That is, when subjects in the hypocrisy condition said they would use condoms in the future, they meant it; subjects in the other three conditions were somewhat less likely to follow through on their intentions. The current investigation of hypocrisy was designed to directly examine the effects of the procedure on AIDS-related behaviors.

AIDS researchers, however, cannot measure condom use in the most direct manner; that is, we cannot crawl into bed with our subjects during their lovemaking. This limitation led us to develop an intermediate measure of condom use. Specifically, subjects were given an opportunity to purchase condoms at the completion of the experiment. Thus, if the induction of hypocrisy motivated subjects to change their sexual behavior, we predicted that subjects in the hypocrisy condition would be more likely to take advantage of the opportunity to buy condoms. Purchasing condoms is not identical to using condoms, but it is a crucial step between holding positive attitudes toward condom use and the practice of safer sex.

Method

Overview

Our model of hypocrisy required the manipulation of two factors: the knowledge that one has publicly preached a firmly held belief and the stark realization that one does not live up to that belief. In a 2 × 2 factorial design, we varied whether or not subjects made a public commitment to the use of condoms and the degree to which they were made mindful of their past failures to use condoms. The combination of these two factors created four conditions: (a) mindful and committed (hypoc-

risy), (b) commitment only, (c) mindful only, and (d) unmindful and uncommitted (an information-only control group). After participating in one of the conditions, subjects were interviewed about their past and future condom use and then were given an opportunity to purchase condoms and acquire AIDS information pamphlets.

Subjects

Subjects were recruited from a psychology subject pool advertisement for a study on "health and persuasion." The advertisement explicitly asked for students between the ages of 18 and 25 who had been heterosexually active within the previous 3 months. These criteria were specified to systematically eliminate subjects who were less at risk for AIDS and might have little use for condoms. Categorically, we screened out students who were not sexually active, students who were married, and female students who were having lesbian relationships. Subjects were reminded of these criteria during scheduling, and the information was also collected in a sexual behavior survey administered at the completion of the experiment.

In addition, we screened out subjects who had had their blood tested for HIV, because (a) it was likely that HIV-tested subjects had already been made mindful of their past risky sexual behavior, thus preexposing them to one of our experimental factors, and (b) HIV-tested subjects might have already experienced dissonance about their AIDS-related behaviors. The final sample consisted of 32 male and 40 female non-HIV-tested undergraduates between ages 18 and 25 ($M = 19.20$). The ethnicity of the sample was 70% Caucasian, 21% Asian, and 9% Hispanic. The entire sample reported having been heterosexually active within the 3 months prior to participating, and all reported their marital status as single. All subjects participated for partial course credit and were promised an additional $4 during scheduling, ostensibly because the experiment "sometimes runs a little more than one hour." The extra money was actually related to the dependent measure, as explained in detail below.

Procedure

All subjects were assigned randomly to condition before they arrived in the lab. When they entered the "AIDS Research Program" office, the purpose of the study was introduced as "the development of an AIDS prevention and education program to be used at the high school level." The experimenter explained that the target of the prevention campaign was those students who were just becoming sexually active but were not yet knowledgeable about AIDS. Subjects were told that because high school students might be exposed to misinformation from their peers about sex and AIDS, it was important to teach sexually active students that "condoms are the easiest and most reliable way for them to prevent the transmission of AIDS during intercourse." All subjects were then introduced to one of the levels of the commitment manipulation.

Commitment Manipulation

To induce public commitment toward condom use, half of the subjects were asked to develop a persuasive speech about AIDS and safer sex and deliver it in front of a videocamera. These subjects, those in the *commitment* condition, were led to believe that the experimenter was interested in finding the best communicator to get the message about safe sex to high school students. The experimenter explained that celebrities or athletes would not be effective communicators when it came to persuading high school students about a serious topic like AIDS. This belief was based on the "fact" that high school students knew that celebrities "like Madonna" were paid for endorsements and "did not really drink Pepsi." Consequently, the experimenter "thought" college students would be more credible with high school students because college students would be seen as "a little older and more experienced, yet not so different that they would lose their credibility." Subjects in the commitment condition were then told that the main purpose of the AIDS prevention program was to make a videotape of college students discussing AIDS and safer sex. Subjects developed their own presentation, using a standardized menu of facts about AIDS, and were encouraged to outline the speech on paper. Subjects were then led to an adjoining room to rehearse and videotape the advocacy. After the videotaping, subjects returned with the experimenter to the research office, where they filled out a short AIDS knowledge questionnaire.

The other half of the subjects (*no commitment*) were induced to develop a persuasive message using the same menu of information, but these subjects did not deliver the speech to a videocamera. Subjects in the no-commitment condition were led to believe that the purpose of developing their speech was to test a hypothesis about the relationship between developing persuasive material and memory for content-related information. After outlining their speech, these subjects completed a short AIDS knowledge questionnaire, ostensibly to see whether the procedure helped them remember more facts about the AIDS epidemic.

Mindfulness Manipulation

After completing their respective levels of commitment, subjects were introduced to the levels of the mindful manipulation. Subjects in the *mindful* condition were told that to make the program completely effective, it would be helpful to know more about why condoms are difficult for most people to use. The experimenter explained that if more were known about the circumstances that made condom use difficult or impossible, this information could be included in the prevention program to "help high school students deal more effectively with these situations." Subjects were then given a list of "some circumstances that we came up with that might make it difficult to use condoms." Actually, this list consisted of the top 10 responses generated by subjects in the earlier hypocrisy experiment by Aronson et al. (1991). Subjects were directed to read the list carefully and then make a separate list of the circumstances surrounding their own past failure to use condoms. Subjects were instructed to use the examples from the experimenter's list and "any other examples you can think of that are not on our list but may have occurred for you in the past."

Subjects in the *unmindful* condition were not exposed to the list of circumstances. These subjects went directly from the commitment manipulation to the dependent measures without any direct reference to their past condom use.

Dependent Measures

To test the effectiveness of our manipulations, we employed both self-report and behavioral measures of condom use. The self-report measures were two interview questions, asked by the experimenter, designed to measure subjects' past use and future intent to use condoms. The two questions were "In the past how often did you use condoms to protect yourself from the AIDS virus during intercourse?" (scale anchors were *not enough* and *enough*) and "In the future what percentage of the time will you use condoms to protect yourself from the AIDS virus during intercourse?" (scale anchors were *0%* and *100%*). For each question, subjects were handed a slip of paper that contained a 17-cm horizontal line and asked to mark a vertical line between the anchors that best represented their response to the interview question.

To collect the behavioral evidence required to test the hypothesis, it was necessary to channel subjects' dissonance-reducing behavior into a measurable route while they were in our laboratory. If subjects were experiencing dissonance because they were confronted with the reality that, in the past, they had not taken their own good advice about using condoms, we suspected that one way for them to reduce the dissonance would be to obtain condoms immediately. However, simply giving subjects free condoms would be too easy; we feared that most subjects would simply grab a handful of condoms because it is hard to pass up a free gift. Therefore, it was necessary to provide subjects with an opportunity to obtain condoms at some cost—but not at so great a cost as to inhibit purchase. We accomplished this by having subjects purchase condoms ostensibly provided by a third party with the $4 they earned for participating in the research.

After the short interview questions, subjects were told that the session was completed. The experimenter signed the participants' credit slip and gave them four $1 bills for participating. Subjects were asked to fill out a receipt for the social science business office, but before they had an opportunity to begin, the experimenter said:

> Before you start that, let me tell you that the AIDS educators from the Health Center sent over some condoms and pamphlets on AIDS when they heard about our prevention program. They wanted us to give our subjects an opportunity to buy condoms for the same price they are sold at the health center—10 cents—and this way you don't have to go across campus and stand in a long line.

I need to go next door and prepare for the next subject, so go ahead and finish this receipt; you can leave it here on the table. And if you want to buy some condoms or take some pamphlets, just help yourself to anything on that desk; that dish has some spare coins so you can make change. OK? Thanks again for coming in today.

The experimenter then left the room and entered an adjoining room, closing the office door to leave the subject alone in the lab.

The condoms were located on a desk across the room, in a clear plastic container. For each subject, the container held 140 condoms, 10 each of 14 brands. A sign on the container reminded subjects that the condoms were 10 cents each; a bowl of loose change and an envelope of $1 bills were clearly available next to the condom "fishbowl." To assess the number of condoms taken, the condom "fishbowl" was recounted and refilled after each subject left the office. Next to the condoms were 10 different informational pamphlets on AIDS (e.g., information on HIV testing, modes of transmission, etc.). The pamphlets were organized in stacks of 10 with each stack holding 5 copies of one pamphlet (for a total of 50 pamphlets). A sign on the wall read, "Due to dwindling supplies, please only take 1 from each stack." Similar to the condom fishbowl, the stacks of pamphlets were recounted after each subject left the office to determine how many of each pamphlet were taken.

Leaving subjects alone in the office and closing the door served two purposes: (a) It allowed the procurement of condoms and pamphlets in total privacy so that subjects could buy condoms and take pamphlets without the presence of the experimenter to impede or enhance this behavior, and (b) when subjects opened the office door to leave, that served as a signal for the waiting experimenter to continue the procedure.

As each subject was leaving, the experimenter appeared in the hallway, claiming to have forgotten to have subjects complete one questionnaire. With subjects' permission (no one refused), both reentered the office, and subjects completed a survey of their recent sexual behavior.

The sexual behavior survey contained items designed to measure the frequency of subjects' sexual activity during the previous year. Specifically, the survey questions asked for categorical responses concerning the frequency of sexual intercourse during the last year, number of sexual partners during the last year, frequency of sexual intercourse during the last month, and number of partners during the last month. Subjects were also asked to estimate how frequently they used condoms and to estimate how many condoms they had used during the last month. Following the questions concerning sexual behavior, a question asked, "Has your blood ever been medically or officially tested for the HIV (the AIDS virus)?" Finally, subjects completed some demographic questions concerning their age, ethnic identity, sexual lifestyle, and marital status (reported above). After subjects placed the confidential questionnaire in an envelope, the experimenter began the debriefing session.

Follow-Up Interviews

To further examine the effectiveness of the experimental treatments on subsequent sexual behavior, we conducted telephone interviews with the subjects approximately 90 days after the experiment. The interviews were conducted by two female research assistants who were unaware of the subjects' experimental condition. In greeting subjects, the interviewer introduced herself as a research assistant with the "University of California AIDS Research Program." The interviewer then reminded subjects of their participation in the study and gently asked whether they could answer some brief questions concerning their sexual behavior since the study (no subject who was contacted refused, although some requested that the interview take place at a more convenient time). The survey instrument was the same one used to collect the sexual behavior information immediately at the completion of the experiment. However, to increase the sensitivity of the measures, the response formats for some questions were changed from categorical to continuous. For example, subjects were asked to estimate the number of times they had had intercourse, the number of partners, and the number of condoms they had used since the study. At the completion of the survey, subjects were thanked for their time, and the interviewer answered any questions about the experiment or the follow-up survey.

Results and Discussion

Behavioral Effects of Hypocrisy

The primary measure of the induction of hypocrisy was the condom-purchasing behavior of our subjects. First, we examined the percentage of subjects in each condition who purchased condoms. A Gender × Commitment × Mindful loglinear ANOVA revealed a significant main effect for the mindfulness factor, $\chi^2 (64) = 5.87, p < .02$, and a significant Commitment × Mindfulness interaction; $\chi^2 (64) = 3.79, p < .05$. The interaction showed that significantly more subjects in the hypocrisy condition bought condoms (83%) compared with subjects who only made the commitment (33%), $\chi^2 (64) = 9.28, p < .003$, subjects who were only made mindful of past risky behavior (50%), $\chi^2 (64) = 4.23, p < .04$, and subjects who only learned AIDS information (44%), $\chi^2 (64) = 5.94, p < .01$.

In addition to purchasing more often, a significant Commitment × Mindfulness interaction, $F(1, 64) = 3.80, p < .05$, revealed that subjects in the hypocrisy condition bought more condoms, on average ($M = 4.95$), than subjects who made the commitment ($M = 2.28$), $F(1, 64) = 4.18, p < .04$, and subjects who were only made mindful ($M = 2.40$), $F(1, 64) = 3.65, p < .05$. Although the means were in the predicted direction, subjects in the information-only condition ($M = 3.50$) purchased only slightly fewer condoms than subjects in the hypocrisy condition, $F(1, 64) = 1.87, p < .23$.

The condom-purchasing data strongly supported the hypothesis—subjects in the hypocrisy condition were more likely to buy condoms at the completion of the experimental session. Furthermore, when they purchased condoms, subjects in the hypocrisy condition bought more condoms, on average, than subjects in the three control conditions. Importantly, there were no gender differences: The purchasing behavior of males and females was not significantly different.

In addition to the purchase of condoms, subjects were given the opportunity to take AIDS information pamphlets. This measure was included to determine whether subjects in the hypocrisy condition were motivated to learn more about AIDS than subjects in the other experimental conditions. Few subjects took the AIDS pamphlets (only 25% of the total sample), and a Gender × Commitment × Mindfulness log-linear ANOVA revealed only a very marginal Gender × Commitment interaction for the percentage of subjects who took pamphlets, $\chi^2 (64) = 2.36, p < .11$. The interaction indicated that females who made a commitment were more likely to take pamphlets (35%) than males who made a commitment (19%), but males who did not make a commitment were more likely to take pamphlets (31%) than females who did not make a commitment (15%).

A significant Gender × Commitment interaction was found for the number of pamphlets acquired, $F(1, 64) = 0.99, p < .05$. Females who made a commitment obtained more pamphlets ($M = 1.5$) than males who made a commitment ($M = 0.39$), but males who made no commitment obtained more pamphlets ($M = 0.94$) than females who made no commitment ($M = 0.30$). Overall, pamphlets were acquired by only a small percentage of subjects, and mostly by females who made the public commitment and by males who did not make the public commitment.

When viewed together, the measures of condom purchasing and pamphlet acquisition can be seen as an indication of the preventive effectiveness of each treatment. That is, if the experimental treatments motivated subjects to take their risk for AIDS more seriously, subjects would be more likely to take preventive action by purchasing condoms or at least acquiring more information about AIDS. Condom purchasing is more clearly related to adopting safer sexual practices and perhaps also reflects a very high level of concern about risk for AIDS. At the same time, acquiring additional AIDS information may also reflect a realistic intention by subjects to make behavioral changes eventually. The hypothesis would predict that subjects in the hypocrisy condition should demonstrate the most concern about their AIDS-related behaviors. Overall, more subjects in the hypocrisy condition should therefore have been planning preventive action, as indicated either by taking pamphlets, by purchasing condoms, or by acquiring both condoms and pamphlets at the completion of the experiment.

To examine this hypothesis, the data were categorized to reflect those subjects in each condition who either (a) only purchased condoms, (b) only acquired AIDS information pamphlets, or (c) acquired both condoms and pamphlets. These three

categories were combined to derive a composite index of concern for AIDS preventive action. A Gender × Commitment × Mindfulness log-linear ANOVA on the concern index revealed a main effect for the mindfulness condition, $\chi^2(64) = 6.46$, $p < .01$, and the predicted Commitment × Mindfulness interaction, $\chi^2(64) = 4.37, p < .04$. Figure 18.1 indicates that fully 94% of the subjects in the hypocrisy condition showed some concern about their risk for AIDS—only 1 subject out of 18 in the hypocrisy condition did *not* make an effort to acquire either condoms or pamphlets. Significantly more concern was shown by subjects in the hypocrisy condition than by subjects who only made a public commitment to use condoms (44%), $\chi^2(64) = 7.28, p < .007$; subjects who were only made mindful of their past risky sexual behavior (61%), $\chi^2(64) = 4.39, p < .03$; and subjects who only learned AIDS information for a test (56%), $\chi^2(64) = 5.31, p < .02$. This pattern was not qualified by the gender of the subjects.

Why would 17 of 18 subjects in the hypocrisy condition expend the time and effort at the end of the experiment to take preventive action? We believe this occurred because the hypocrisy manipulation produced cognitive dissonance (Festinger, 1957). In this situation, subjects experienced dissonance because although their public commitment

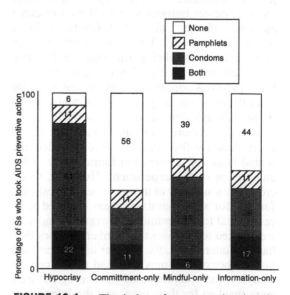

FIGURE 18.1 ■ The index of concern, showing the percentage of subjects in each condition who bought condoms, took pamphlets, or did both.

about the importance of safe sex was consistent with their beliefs, the advocacy was inconsistent with their past risky sexual behavior. The contradiction between their beliefs and behavior caused subjects to examine a firmly held belief about themselves—their self-view as competent and moral people with integrity, the kind of people who generally live up to their own positive standards for behavioral conduct (Aronson, 1968, 1992; Thibodeau & Aronson, 1992). The realization that they had violated the standards for sexual conduct with respect to AIDS prevention aroused dissonance, and subjects were motivated to reduce the discomfort. In this case, there was a clear route to dissonance reduction—behavior change through the adoption of safer sexual practices, such as condom use. Thus, in our view, the induction of hypocrisy motivated subjects to buy condoms because this behavior was the most efficient way to reduce the discrepancy between a positive self-concept and the standards for behavioral conduct.

Self-Reports of Future Intent to Use Condoms

Before they were given the opportunity to purchase condoms, subjects were interviewed by the experimenter about their past and future condom use. For the subjects' estimates of their future intentions to use condoms, a Gender × Commitment × Mindfulness ANOVA revealed a main effect for the commitment factor, $F(1, 64) = 8.70, p < .004$. Subjects who made the public commitment gave higher estimates of future intent to use condoms ($M = 15.1$ cm on the 17-cm line) than subjects who did not make the public commitment ($M = 12.1$). As can be seen in Table 18.1, estimates of future condom use were slightly higher for subjects in the hypocrisy condition ($M = 15.50$) than for those in the commitment-only condition ($M = 14.80$), although the difference was not significant, $F < 1$. The intentions of the subjects in the hypocrisy condition, however, were significantly higher than the intentions reported by subjects in the mindful-only ($M = 12.40, F = 4.61, p < .03$) and information-only conditions ($M = 11.80, F = 6.24, p < .01$). This main effect for public commitment replicates the pattern of data for the future intentions of subjects in the initial hypocrisy experiment reported by Aronson et al. (1991).

The relationship between subjects' reported intentions to use condoms and their actual purchase of condoms has implications for an important issue in AIDS prevention research. Many interventions have to rely on self-reported changes in sexual behavior as the primary measure of the effectiveness of the program. As has been discussed recently (see Catania, Gibson, Chitwood, & Coates, 1990), there are many reasons for questioning the validity of self-report measures of sexual behavior. The current data suggest that the validity of such measures may vary with the nature of the intervention. For example, although subjects who made the public commitment reported the highest intentions to use condoms in the future, only subjects in the hypocrisy condition (those who made the public commitment *and then* were reminded of their past condom use) actually followed through on their pledges by purchasing condoms (83% of subjects in the hypocrisy condition vs. 33% of subjects in the commitment-only condition purchased an average of 4.95 vs. 2.28 condoms, respectively). These data confirm the speculations by Aronson et al. (1991)—future intentions were more indicative of subsequent behavior for subjects in the hypocrisy condition than for subjects in the control conditions. More generally, these data show that high behavioral intentions to use condoms may not reliably predict whether people will expend the effort to acquire condoms for use during sex. Consequently, we encourage AIDS prevention researchers to use both self-report and behavioral measures to assess the effectiveness of any intervention technique.

Acknowledging Risk: Self-Reports of Past Condom Use

A second important issue to AIDS prevention is how people assess their risk for acquiring HIV (e.g., Bauman & Siegel, 1987; Catania, Kegeles, & Coates, 1990). Modification of sexual behavior, such as using condoms regularly, may depend on how well the intervention technique causes subjects to objectively examine their risk for AIDS. Aronson et al. (1991) reported that subjects in the hypocrisy condition gave significantly lower estimates of past condom use than subjects in the three control conditions. The relatively high mindfulness of subjects in the hypocrisy condition led the authors to conclude that the hypocrisy manipula-

TABLE 18.1. Estimates of Past and Future Condom Use Collected During the Experiment

	Experimental condition			
	Commitment		No commitment	
Interview question	Mindful (Hypocrisy)	Nonmindful (Commitment-only)	Mindful (Mindful-only)	Nonmindful (Information-only)
Estimates of past condom use				
Females	8.00	8.60	10.00	8.50
Males	14.00	11.13	6.13	11.63
Future intent to use condoms				
Females	15.10	14.50	12.00	10.00
Males	16.00	15.25	13.00	14.00
Improvement[a]				
Females	7.10	5.90	2.00	1.50
Males	2.00	4.13	6.88	2.38

Note. Higher numbers indicate higher estimates of past and future use of condoms and more indication of improvement.
[a]The index of improvement is the difference between estimates of past use and future intent to use condoms.

tion may cut through the denial mechanisms that prevent people from acknowledging their risk for acquiring HIV. The current experiment allowed us to replicate and extend this finding by comparing it with the observed behavioral data.

A Gender × Commitment × Mindfulness ANOVA for the estimates of past condom use revealed only a marginally significant three-way interaction, $F(1, 64) = 3.27, p < .07$. The nature of the omnibus interaction is highlighted by the simple crossover interaction between estimates of past condom use reported by males and females in the hypocrisy and mindful-only groups (see Table 18.1). Hypocrisy males reported a very high level of past condom use ($M = 14.00$) relative to hypocrisy females, who reported a moderate level ($M = 8.00$). Mindful-only females reported moderately high levels of past condom use ($M = 10.00$) relative to mindful-only males, who reported very low estimates of past condom use ($M = 6.13$). Thus, whereas hypocrisy females reported the lowest estimates of past condom use, replicating the findings of Aronson et al. (1991), males in the hypocrisy condition were significantly less mindful of their past risks for the HIV.

The differences between males and females on estimates of past condom use also affected the index of improvement reported by Aronson et al. (1991). In the current study, the difference between estimates of past and future condom use was analyzed by a 2 × 2 × 2 × 2 ANOVA, in which gender, commitment, and the mindful manipulation were treated as between-groups factors and the ques-

tions measuring past and future condom use were treated as a within-subjects repeated measure. A significant Gender × Commitment × "Improvement" Interaction, $F(1, 64) = 5.66, p < .02$, revealed that making the commitment caused females to think more seriously about increasing their use of condoms (difference between past and future estimates; $M = 6.50$) relative to males who made the commitment ($M = 3.06$), whereas males who did not make the commitment reported more improvement ($M = 4.63$) than females who did not make the commitment ($M = 1.75$).

Although these findings may imply that the effect of hypocrisy on denial is not as general as Aronson et al. suggested, the apparent lack of replication could also be due to an important difference between the two experiments. In the first experiment, subjects were made mindful of their past sexual behavior *before* they were introduced to the commitment variable; in the current experiment, subjects were made mindful of their past behavior *after* they had been introduced to the commitment variable. As a result, the inability of the current experiment to replicate the effect on denial reported by Aronson et al. could be due to an order effect for whether the mindful manipulation was introduced before or after the commitment manipulation.

To further investigate how the procedures affected the subjects' perceptions of their past sexual behavior, we analyzed their responses to the sexual behavior survey collected after they had the opportunity to purchase condoms. After responses to each survey question were converted to a 5-point scale, a Gender × Commitment × Mindfulness MANOVA showed a significant effect for the commitment condition, Wilks's lambda $F(7, 55) = 2.19$, $p < .04$. Pairwise comparisons of the means presented in Table 18.2 revealed that subjects in the mindful-only condition reported significantly longer sexual relationships, more sexual activity during the year and month prior to the experiment, and less frequent condom use than in both the hypocrisy and commitment-only conditions (all protected Fisher LSD $ts = 1.99, p < .05$). Importantly, these estimates for the information-only group were not significantly different from the estimates of *any* of the other treatment groups. Taking these findings together, it appeared that subjects in the hypocrisy, commitment-only, and mindful-only conditions were reconstructing their memories of past sexual behavior to be consistent with their activities during the experiment.

One implication of these data is that the procedures led subjects to justify their past sexual behavior in such a way as to downplay their risk. For example, after exposure to AIDS information, subjects made mindful of their past failures to use condoms reported slightly longer past monogamous relationships and slightly fewer partners during the year and month prior to the experiment. Although these responses were not significantly different from those of the information-only group, the mindful-only group may have adjusted the recall of their sexual behavior to justify past failures to practice safe sex.

Similarly, subjects in the hypocrisy and commitment-only conditions may have adjusted their estimates of past sexual behavior to fit the content of their speeches. The means indicate that subjects who made the commitment slightly downplayed their risk for AIDS on the survey by reporting shorter monogamous sexual relationships, less sexual activity during the year and month prior to the study, and more frequent condom use. It is not difficult to understand why subjects who advocated the importance of safe sex to an impressionable audience might want to see themselves as shining examples of such behavior. In doing so, subjects who made the commitment slightly underestimated their risk by seeing themselves as monogamous but less sexually active and as using condoms more frequently.

Our procedures appear to have caused subjects to search for a way to avoid recognizing their own risk for AIDS—a somewhat disheartening possibility. However, denying their risk for AIDS was clearly not the case for the hypocrisy condition, where the manipulation encouraged 83% of the subjects to purchase significantly more condoms. The most compelling interpretation of the data is that our procedures caused subjects in the commitment and mindful conditions to seek some justification for their past risky sexual behavior but that the hypocrisy manipulation apparently provided subjects with the motivation to face their risk head-on and take preventive behavioral action at the completion of the experiment.

Follow-Up Interviews

The behavioral data clearly showed that the induction of hypocrisy encouraged subjects to ac-

TABLE 18.2. Sexual Behavior Survey Collected at the Completion of the Experiment

	Experimental Condition			
Question	Hypocrisy ($n = 17$)	Commitment-only ($n = 17$)	Mindful-only ($n = 18$)	Information-only ($n = 17$)
Current sexual relationship	2.65ₐ	2.82ₐ	2.55ₐ	2.65ₐ
Average length of sexual relationships	3.17ₐ	3.82ₐ	4.61_b	4.29_ab
Sex during the last year	4.00ₐ	4.00ₐ	4.83_b	4.17_ab
Partners during the last year	1.76ₐ	1.88ₐ	1.44ₐ	1.47ₐ
Sex during the last month	2.12ₐ	2.35ₐ	3.44_b	2.82_ab
Partners during the last month	1.05ₐ	1.05ₐ	1.00ₐ	1.05ₐ
Frequency of condom use	3.06ₐ	2.71ₐ	1.72_b	2.12_ab
Condoms used during the last month	1.82ₐ	2.12ₐ	1.83ₐ	1.94ₐ

Note. Scale values range from 1 to 5; larger numbers indicate more sexual activity or more frequency for each question. Means with different subscripts are significantly different at the .05 level.

quire condoms at the completion of the experiment. This measure, however, could be indicating more about condom purchasing than about condom use (e.g., Catania, Gibson, Chitwood, & Coates, 1990). From an AIDS prevention standpoint, the important question is, did these subjects subsequently use the condoms that they purchased? To examine this possibility, we conducted interviews with our subjects by telephone about their sexual behavior 3 months after they participated in the experiment.

The interviewers contacted 64 (89%) of the original 72 subjects, and 52 (81% of those contacted) reported having been sexually active since the study. In addition, the responses from 3 subjects proved to be highly influential outliers in the data; all reported having sexual intercourse over 90 times since the study and also reported using over 90 condoms during that time. We chose to drop the data from these 3 subjects because their scores were more than 5 standard deviations from the grand mean for each variable. As a result, the follow-up data reported here are based on 68% ($n = 49$) of the original sample that participated in the experiment.

The means for all the follow-up questions are presented in Table 18.3. Of most interest to the current analysis are the condom use data. A loglinear Gender × Commitment × Mindful ANOVA of the percentage of subjects who reported using condoms during the 3 months after the study revealed a marginally significant Commitment × Mindful interaction, $F(1, 48) = 2.45, p < .12$. Fully 92% of the subjects in the hypocrisy condition—11 of the 12 contacted—reported using condoms in the 3 months following the study. Although this frequency of condom use was significantly higher than the frequency reported by subjects in the commitment-only condition (55%, $F = 4.07, p < .04$), the hypocrisy group was not more likely to be using condoms than the mindful-only (71%, $F = 1.36$, ns) and information-only (75%, $F < 1$, ns) groups.

As a more direct measure of condom use, subjects were asked to estimate how often they used condoms and how many condoms they had used since participating in the study. Subjects in the hypocrisy condition reported a slightly higher frequency of condom use, although not a significantly higher frequency than any of the control groups, all $Fs < 1$. For number of condoms used since the study, the analysis revealed a marginally significant main effect for the mindful factor, $F(1, 48) = 2.59, p < .11$. Subjects who were made mindful reported using slightly more condoms ($M = 7.54$) than subjects who were not made mindful of their past failure to use condoms ($M = 5.74$). Again, none of the observed differences between the experimental groups were significant, all $Fs < 1$.

Finally, to adjust for the differences in sexual activity across the experimental groups, subjects' estimates of the number of condoms used were divided by their estimates of how much sexual intercourse they had had since participating in the study. This calculation produced a measure of the percentage of the time subjects had used condoms when having intercourse. A similar $2 \times 2 \times 2$ ANOVA revealed only a marginal Commitment × Mindful interaction, $F(1, 48) = 2.58, p < .11$. Although hypocrisy subjects reported somewhat more condom use per act of intercourse ($M = 63\%$ of the time) than commitment-only ($M = 46\%$, $F < 1$, ns) and mindful-only ($M = 44\%$, $F = 1.21$, ns)

TABLE 18.3. Self-Reports of Sexual Behavior Collected 3 Months After Participation in the Study

Question	Experimental condition			
	Hypocrisy ($n = 12$)	Commitment-only ($n = 11$)	Mindful-only ($n = 14$)	Information-only ($n = 12$)
Percentage of subjects reporting condom use	92%	55%	71%	75%
Average amount of sexual intercourse since the study	13.6	9.1	24.2	18.4
Average number of sexual partners	1.2	1.5	1.1	1.4
Frequency of condom use since the study	2.75	1.82	2.00	2.08
Number of condoms used since the study	5.83	3.91	9.00	7.41
Percentage of time condoms were used during intercourse	63%	46%	44%	65%

Note. Higher numbers indicate higher frequency of activity for each item.

subjects, information-only subjects ($M = 65\%$) also reported a high frequency of condom use as a percentage of acts of intercourse.

In sum, the follow-up interviews provided very little indication that subjects in the hypocrisy condition were using condoms more regularly than subjects in the control conditions 3 months after the experiment. The data showed that 92% of the subjects in the hypocrisy condition reported using condoms and that they reported a slightly higher frequency of condom use than subjects in the three control conditions. Nonetheless, the observed differences between the hypocrisy group and the control groups were not very strong and, given their self-report nature, should be interpreted with caution.

Alternative Explanations and Theoretical Implications

We have suggested that the observed effects of hypocrisy on condom purchasing were caused by dissonance motivation. It is conceivable, however, that the effect of hypocrisy on condom purchasing might also be accounted for by a simple learning or priming explanation. That is, our experimental treatments might be viewed as systematically varying the amount of persuasive information subjects received. For example, subjects in the information-only condition received one source of persuasive material—the AIDS information. Subjects in the commitment-and-mindful-only conditions were exposed to two sources of persuasion: Both groups learned AIDS information, and the commitment-only group used the information to persuade a high school audience, while the mindful-only group were then made mindful of their past failures to use condoms (cf. central-route persuasion; see Petty & Cacioppo, 1986). Subjects in the hypocrisy condition were supplied with three sources of influence—the AIDS information, the public commitment, and the personal reminder of their own risky behavior. Thus the model is additive rather than interactive—a linear model, based on priming or learning, would predict that the more persuasive appeals people are exposed to, the more likely they are to comply.

The obtained pattern of data, however, may not be additive. One way to examine the additive influence of the variables is through statistical procedures. If the effect of hypocrisy is due to the additive effect of the commitment and mindful factors, then the variance attributed to the main effect for each variable will account for most of the variance in the purchasing behavior (Cohen & Cohen, 1983). This is not the case. Subjects who were provided with two sources of influence (i.e., the commitment-only and mindful-only groups) were no more likely to buy condoms than subjects who received only one source of influence (i.e., information only, both Fs < 1). Evidently, adding together two sources of influence was no more effective than simply educating subjects with facts and figures about AIDS. In sum, "more" was not necessarily "better"; a simple learning or priming explanation for the combined effect of the commitment and mindfulness factors does not offer a more parsimonious account of the condom-purchasing data.

Furthermore, it could be argued that the hypocrisy manipulation makes attitudes about AIDS and condom use more accessible, which leads subjects to purchase more condoms (e.g., Fazio, 1986). We cannot empirically rule out this explanation; in fact, we believe that making the link between an attitude and behavior (or, more specifically, between the self-concept and behavior) accessible is a necessary component of the hypocrisy effect. In our view, however, it is the motivation that results from this connection that causes subjects to take behavioral action. This supposition is not directly supported by the current data, but it has been demonstrated in a recent experiment by Fried and Aronson (1992).

Fried and Aronson manipulated hypocrisy by having subjects make a public commitment to the importance of recycling and then reminding them that they do not always recycle. In the important control conditions, half the subjects in the hypocrisy condition were allowed to misattribute their dissonance arousal to characteristics of the laboratory (e.g., lighting, temperature, noise level) and then were asked to donate their time to a local recycling center. If the hypocrisy manipulation aroused dissonance motivation, then subjects who were allowed to misattribute their arousal to something about the laboratory would not be expected to volunteer time for the recycling center (e.g., Zanna & Cooper, 1974). The data supported this prediction; 68% of subjects in the hypocrisy condition volunteered for the recycling center, but only

32% of hypocrisy subjects volunteered when they were allowed to misattribute their dissonance arousal. Thus, although the current hypocrisy experiment on AIDS and condom use does not provide direct evidence of dissonance arousal, the study by Fried and Aronson (1992) clearly suggests that motivation is an important component of the effect of hypocrisy on behavior.

As a new twist on the forced-compliance paradigm, the hypocrisy hypothesis also has interesting implications for the causes of dissonance recently discussed in Cooper and Fazio's "New Look" formulation (Cooper & Fazio, 1984; Scher & Cooper, 1989). According to Cooper and Fazio, dissonance has little to do with the subject's self-concept; it occurs because subjects assume responsibility for an unwanted aversive outcome. In the hypocrisy twist on the forced-compliance paradigm, subjects are induced to assume responsibility for producing a positive consequence—that is, subjects make a speech that clearly has positive consequences for the audience. When subjects are made aware of their past failure to live up to their own good advice, dissonance is aroused because the hypocrisy causes them to question their self-view as competent and moral people with integrity. The hypocrisy paradigm suggests that aversive consequences, although sufficient to cause dissonance, are not a necessary condition for dissonance to occur. Rather, any action that violates an important self-view has the potential to cause feelings of dissonance (Aronson, 1968, 1992; Thibodeau & Aronson, 1992).

Practical Implications

Although the follow-up data provided only suggestive evidence for long-term behavior change, the condom-purchasing data indicate that the induction of hypocrisy can encourage people to take steps toward practicing safer sex. As an intervention technique, we believe these procedures could be applied in many public educational environments. One approach that lends itself to the induction of hypocrisy is the use of "cooperative learning groups" in health or biology courses (e.g., the jigsaw technique; see Aronson, Blaney, Stephan, Sikes, & Snapp, 1978). To illustrate, students in groups could start by brainstorming on reasons for why it is important to practice safe sex or abstain from sex completely. This activity would

be similar to the public commitment factor in hypocrisy. Next, making students mindful of their own sexual behavior could be accomplished by having a small discussion group work together to generate a list of the circumstances that make the use of condoms or sexual abstinence difficult. This method could produce active involvement in the learning process, along with increased awareness of risky sexual activity, which parallels our experimental procedures nicely. Needless to say, the effects of such an application have yet to be determined.

ACKNOWLEDGMENT

This research was supported by grant #R90SC006 to Elliot Aronson from the University of California Universitywide AIDS Research Program. The authors would like to express their indebtedness to Staci Emerson, who served as an experimenter for the duration of the project, and to Christine Lilly, Maria S. Ramirez, and Trisha Strasser for their help in collecting the data. Also, special thanks to Anthony R. Pratkanis for his suggestions concerning the condom-purchasing measure. A. Lauren Crain is now a graduate student at the University of Kansas and Matthew P. Winslow is in graduate studies at the University of Minnesota. Correspondence about this article should be addressed to Jeff Stone, Department of Psychology, Princeton University, Princeton, NJ 08544 or to Elliot Aronson, Department of Psychology, Kerr Hall, University of California, Santa Cruz, CA 95064.

REFERENCES

Aronson, E. (1968). Dissonance theory: Progress and problems. In E. Aronson, R. Abelson, W. McGuire, T. Newcomb, M. Rosenberg, & P. Tannenbaum (Eds.), *Theories of cognitive consistency: A sourcebook* (pp. 5–27). Chicago: Rand McNally.

Aronson, E. (1992). The return of the repressed: Dissonance theory makes a comeback. *Psychological Inquiry, 3*(4), 303–311.

Aronson, E., Adler, N. E., & McDougall, K. (1988). *The prediction of interventions to use condoms as a function of beliefs, norms, control, and past experience.* Unpublished manuscript, University of California at Santa Cruz.

Aronson, E., Blaney, N., Stephan, C., Sikes, J., & Snapp, M. (1978). *The jigsaw classroom.* Beverly Hills, CA: Sage.

Aronson, E., Fried, C. B., & Stone, J. (1991). Overcoming denial and increasing the intention to use condoms through the induction of hypocrisy. *American Journal of Public Health, 81,* 1636–1638.

Axsom, D., & Cooper, J. (1981). Reducing weight by reducing dissonance: The role of effort justification in inducing weight loss. In E. Aronson (Ed.), *Readings about the social animal* (pp. 180–193). New York: W. H. Freeman.

Baum, A., & Temoshok, L. (1990). Psychosocial aspects of the acquired immunodeficiency syndrome. In L. Temoshok

& A. Baum (Eds.), *Psychological perspectives on AIDS: Etiology, prevention, and treatment* (pp. 1–16). Hillsdale, NJ: Lawrence Erlbaum.

Bauman, L. J., & Siegel, K. (1987). Misperception among gay men of the risk for AIDS associated with their sexual behavior. *Journal of Applied Social Psychology, 17,* 329–350.

Becker, M. H., & Joseph, J. G. (1988). AIDS and behavior change to reduce risk: A review. *American Journal of Public Health, 78,* 394–410.

Catania, J. A., Gibson, D. R., Chitwood, D. D., & Coates, T. J. (1990). Methodological problems in AIDS behavioral research: Influences on measurement error and participation bias in studies of sexual behavior. *Psychological Bulletin, 108,* 339–362.

Catania, J. A., Kegeles, S., & Coates, T. (1990). Towards an understanding of risk behavior: An AIDS risk reduction model (ARRM). *Health Education Quarterly, 17,* 53–72.

Chassin, L., Presson, C. C., & Sherman, S. J. (1990). Social psychological contributions to the understanding and prevention of adolescent cigarette smoking. *Personality and Social Psychology Bulletin, 16,* 133–151.

Coates, T. J., & Sanstad, K. H. (1992, March/April). Preventing HIV disease: An agenda for behavioral science. *Psychological Science Agenda,* pp. 10–11.

Coates, T. J., Stall, R. D., & Hoff, C. C. (1990) Changes in sexual behavior among gay and bisexual men since the beginning of the AIDS epidemic. In L. Temoshok & A. Baum (Eds.), *Psychological perspectives on AIDS: Etiology, prevention, and treatment* (pp. 103–138). Hillsdale, NJ: Lawrence Erlbaum.

Cohen, J., & Cohen, P. (1983). *Applied multiple regression/correlation analysis for the behavioral sciences* (2nd ed.). Hillsdale, NJ: Lawrence Erlbaum.

Cooper, J., & Fazio, R. H. (1984). A new look dissonance theory. In L. Berkowitz (Ed.), *Advances in experimental social psychology* (Vol. 17, pp. 229–262). New York: Academic Press.

Des Jarlais, D. C., & Friedman, S. R. (1990). Target groups for preventing AIDS among intravenous drug users. In L. Temoshok & A. Baum (Eds.), *Psychological perspectives on AIDS: Etiology, prevention, and treatment* (pp. 35–50). Hillsdale, NJ: Lawrence Erlbaum.

Fazio, R. H. (1986). How do attitudes guide behavior? In R. M. Sorrentino & E. T. Higgins (Eds.), *Handbook of motivation and cognition: Foundations of social behavior* (pp. 204–243). New York: Guilford.

Festinger, L. (1957). *A theory of cognitive dissonance.* Stanford, CA: Stanford University Press.

Fisher, J. D., & Fisher, W. A. (1992). Changing AIDS-risk behavior. *Psychological Bulletin, 111,* 455–474.

Fisher, J. D., & Misovich, S. J. (1990). Social influence and AIDS-preventive behavior. In J. Edwards, R. S. Tinsdale, L. Heath, & E. J. Posavac (Eds.), *Applying social influence processes in preventing social problems* (pp. 39–70). New York: Plenum.

Fisher, J. D., Misovich, S. J., & Kean, K. (1987). *Fear of AIDS, AIDS-knowledge, and AIDS preventive behavior among college students, gay men, and medical personnel.* Unpublished manuscript, University of Connecticut.

Fried, C. B., & Aronson, E. (1992). *Hypocrisy, misattribution, and dissonance reduction.* Manuscript submitted for publication.

Gonzales, M. H., Aronson, E., & Costanzo, M. (1988). Using social cognition and persuasion to promote energy conservation: A quasi-experiment. *Journal of Applied Social Psychology, 18,* 1049–1066.

Kegeles, S. M., Adler, N. E., & Irwin, C. E. (1988). Sexually active adolescents and condoms: Changes over one year in knowledge, attitudes, and use. *American Journal of Public Health, 78,* 460–461.

O'Keeffe, M. K., Nesselhof-Kendall, S., & Baum, A. (1990). Behavior and prevention of AIDS: Bases of research and intervention. *Personality and Social Psychology Bulletin, 16,* 166–180.

Pallack, M. S., Cook, D. A., & Sullivan, J. J. (1980). Commitment and energy conservation. In L. Bickman (Ed.), *Applied social psychology annual.* New York: Plenum.

Petty, R. E., & Cacioppo, J. T. (1986). The elaboration likelihood model of persuasion. In L. Berkowitz (Ed.), *Advances in experimental social psychology* (Vol. 19, pp. 123–205). New York: Academic Press.

Scher, S. J., & Cooper, J. (1989). Motivational basis for dissonance: The singular role of behavioral consequences. *Journal of Personality and Social Psychology, 56,* 899–906.

Snyder, C. R. (1978). The "illusion of uniqueness." *Journal of Humanistic Psychology, 19,* 33–41.

Thibodeau, R., & Aronson, E. (1992). Taking a closer look: Reasserting the role of the self-concept in dissonance theory. *Personality and Social Psychology Bulletin, 18,* 591–602.

Weisse, C. S., Nesselhof-Kendall, S., Fleck-Kandath, C., & Baum, A. (1990). Psychosocial aspects of AIDS prevention among heterosexuals. In L. Bickman (Ed.), *Applied social psychology annual.* New York Plenum.

Zanna, M. P., & Cooper, J. (1974). Dissonance and the pill: An attribution approach to studying the arousal properties of dissonance *Journal of Personality and Social Psychology, 29,* 703–709.

READING 19

The Systematic Influence of Gain- and Loss-Framed Messages on Interest in and Use of Different Types of Health Behavior

Alexander J. Rothman and Steven C. Martino • University of Minnesota
Brian T. Bedell, Jerusha B. Detweiler, and Peter Salovey • Yale University

Framing health messages systematically in terms of either gains or losses influences the behaviors that people adopt. Rothman and Salovey proposed that the relative influence of gain- and loss-framed messages is contingent on people's perception of the risk or uncertainty associated with adopting the recommended behavior. Specifically, loss-framed messages are more effective when promoting illness-detecting (screening) behaviors, but gain-framed messages are more effective when promoting health-affirming (prevention) behaviors. Two experiments* provide a direct test of this conceptual framework.. In Experiment 1, participants' willingness to act after reading about a new disease was a function of how the information was framed and the type of behavior promoted. Experiment 2 replicated and extended these findings with a real health concern—gum disease. Gain-framed pamphlets heightened interest in a plaque-fighting mouth rinse, whereas loss-framed pamphlets heightened interest in a plaque-detecting disclosing rinse. Research on message framing provides a theoretically based guide for the development of effective health messages.

There is little question that persuading people to make healthier behavioral choices would provide substantial reductions in illness morbidity and premature mortality (Department of Health and Human Services, 1991). Yet the development of effective persuasive appeals has proved to be rather difficult. Even when a persuasive intervention has

been shown to be effective in a particular health domain, more often than not it has been developed in the absence of a theoretical framework that could guide the application of the intervention more generally (Salovey, Rothman, & Rodin, 1998). Are there specific strategies that can be adopted to maximize the effectiveness of messages designed to promote healthy behavior?

Over the past 10 years, researchers have focused on the relative effectiveness of messages that emphasize the benefits of performing a behavior

*The original article contained 2 studies, only study 2 is included here.

(gain-framed messages) and messages that emphasize the costs of not performing a behavior (loss-framed messages) (e.g., Meyerowitz & Chaiken, 1987; Rothman, Salovey, Antone, Keough, & Martin, 1993; see Rothman & Salovey, 1997, for a review). Although aspects of this approach can be traced back to earlier research on fear appeals (Leventhal, 1970), this particular line of research has been grounded in the basic tenets of Kahneman and Tversky's (1979; Tversky & Kahneman, 1981) prospect theory. The framing postulate of prospect theory states that people's decisions are sensitive to how information is presented. Specifically, people are risk-seeking in their preferences when considering loss-framed information but are risk-averse in their preferences when considering gain-framed information.

Consistent with the underlying tenets of prospect theory, Rothman and Salovey (1997) provided a taxonomy of situations that afford predictions as to when gain- or loss-framed health appeals are maximally persuasive. They proposed that when people are considering a behavior that they perceive involves some risk or uncertainty (e.g., it may detect a health problem), loss-framed appeals are more persuasive, but when people are considering a behavior that they perceive involves a relatively certain outcome (e.g., it prevents the onset of a health problem), gain-framed appeals are more persuasive. Current support for this framework is based on comparisons of the relative effectiveness of gain- and loss-framed appeals that have been drawn across studies conducted in different health domains. In this article, we describe two experiments that provide the first systematic tests of these predictions within the same health domain.

Integrating Message Framing and Health Promotion

Meyerowitz and Chaiken (1987) were the first investigators to examine the relative influence of gain- and loss-framed information on health behavior. They modified a pamphlet that promoted breast self-examination (BSE) so that it provided a series of either loss- or gain-framed statements about breast cancer and BSE. Consistent with their predictions, women who had received the loss-framed pamphlet were more likely to have performed the behavior over a 4-month follow-up period as compared to women who had read the gain-framed pamphlet. Several subsequent studies have similarly observed that providing people with loss-framed information is an effective way to promote the performance of or preferences for mammography (Banks et al., 1995), HIV testing (Kalichman & Coley, 1995), amniocentesis (Marteau, 1989), skin cancer examinations (Block & Keller, 1995; Rothman, Pronin, & Salovey, 1996), and blood cholesterol screening (Maheswaran & Meyers-Levy, 1990). However, investigators also have found that providing people with gain-framed information is a more effective way to promote healthy behavioral practices, such as requests for a free sample of sunscreen (Detweiler, Bedell, Salovey, Pronin, & Rothman, 1999; Rothman et al., 1993), the use of infant car seats (Christophersen & Gyulay, 1981), and intentions to use condoms (Linville, Fischer, & Fischhoff, 1993).

How might these diverging findings be reconciled? Rothman and Salovey (1997) have proposed that the relative effectiveness of a gain- or loss-framed appeal is contingent on the type of behavior that is promoted. Loss-framed messages should be an effective means to promote behavior but only if engaging in that behavior is perceived to be risky or uncertain. Recall that Meyerowitz and Chaiken (1987) predicted an advantage for loss-framed messages because women reported that engaging in BSE was a risky behavior. In fact, a subsequent study (Meyerowitz, Wilson, & Chaiken, 1991) revealed that a loss-framed message about breast cancer promoted BSE only among those women who previously reported that they perceived BSE to be a risky behavior. If people perceived all health behaviors as risky, one would expect a consistent advantage for loss-framed appeals. However, not all health behaviors are perceived as risky or uncertain.

An important distinction between health behaviors can be made based on the function that they serve. Detection behaviors such as BSE or mammography serve to detect the presence of a health problem and because they can inform people that they may be sick, initiating the behavior may be considered a risky decision. Although detection behaviors such as mammography provide critical long-term benefits, characterizing them as risky accurately captures people's subjective assessment of these behaviors (e.g., Hill, Gardner, & Rassaby, 1985; Mayer & Solomon, 1992; Meyerowitz & Chaiken, 1987). In contrast, prevention behaviors such as the regular use of sunscreen or condoms forestall the onset of an illness and maintain a person's current health status. In fact, these behaviors are risky only to the extent that one chooses not to take action. This distinction is important because it provides a useful heuristic to predict which behaviors people tend to perceive as risky and which behaviors people tend to perceive as relatively certain or safe (for a discussion of these issues, see Rothman & Salovey, 1997). Moreover, it suggests that loss-framed appeals would be more effective in promoting detection behaviors but gain-framed appeals would be more effective in promoting prevention behaviors.

To date, conclusions concerning the relative effectiveness of gain- and loss-framed appeals have had to rely on comparisons drawn across studies and across health domains. That these effects have been obtained across a variety of health threats is encouraging with respect to the generalizability of this approach to health promotion. However, the numerous differences between the health domains and health behaviors studied make it difficult to assert unequivocally that the relative influence of gain- and loss-framed appeals is contingent on the function of the behavior. Even within a single health domain, prevention and detection behaviors (e.g., condoms and HIV testing) can differ on dimensions such as cost, familiarity, difficulty, frequency, and the need for trained personnel to perform the behavior. These substantial differences leave open the possibility of alternative explanations for the observed pattern of findings. Studies are needed that experimentally manipulate both the framing of a health message and the function of a specific health behavior.

The following two experiments provide the empirical evidence needed to support the theoretical framework proposed by Rothman and Salovey (1997). Experiment 1 tested the proposed framework in the context of a hypothetical disease. The use of a hypothetical disease afforded the opportunity to construct a single health behavior that could be presented as either a prevention or a detection behavior. Of course, there are limitations to any study that relies on a hypothetical, and consequently unfamiliar, health problem. Experiment

2 complemented and extended the findings obtained in Experiment 1 by testing the proposed framework in the context of real health problems, tooth decay and gum disease, and using real health behaviors that differed only in terms of their described function (prevention vs. detection).

Experiment 2: Dental Health and Gum Disease

Are there any real health behaviors that can be understood to differ only in terms of the function they serve? In the area of dental hygiene, the answer is yes. People regularly use mouth rinses to prevent the buildup of dental plaque and the development of gum disease (Adams & Addy, 1994). However, other mouth rinses—called disclosing rinses—are used to detect the presence of dental plaque and the onset of gum disease.[1] In either case, the behavior can be easily incorporated into someone's regular dental hygiene habits. All one has to do is place a small amount of the rinse in one's mouth, swish it around, and then spit it out. In the case of prevention, the mouth rinse inhibits plaque from developing on a person's teeth. In the case of detection, the disclosing rinse identifies those areas of one's teeth where plaque has accumulated and indicates the areas at risk that need to be targeted for a thorough brushing.

In Experiment 2, participants were provided with either a gain- or a loss-framed pamphlet about plaque and gum disease that recommended an oral hygiene behavior that was said to either prevent plaque (a mouth rinse) or detect plaque (a disclosing rinse). By focusing on a familiar health problem and real health behaviors, this experiment addressed concerns that the findings obtained in Experiment 1 could not be generalized beyond a hypothetical disease. Because most, if not all, people are concerned about the accumulation of plaque and the development of cavities and gum disease, we expected that our participants would be motivated to attend to and process the framed material. Attention to the framed information also should be heightened by the fact that it was pre-

---

[1]Generally, people chew on disclosing tablets to detect plaque accumulation. However, it is possible to dissolve these tablets in water to produce a rinse that serves the same function. We included the latter form of the behavior in our pamphlets so that it would be consistent with the mouth rinse behavior.

sented in a professionally designed pamphlet that was purportedly developed by the University of Minnesota Dental Health Communications Project. Finally, the use of real behaviors allowed us to offer participants the opportunity to mail in a postage-paid postcard to request a free sample of the recommended product. The rate at which people requested free samples provides a strong test of participants' interest in the product.

Not only did Experiment 2 test the framework outlined by Rothman and Salovey (1997) in the context of a real health issue but it also extended previous research in this area in several ways. Prior studies have provided people with gain- and loss-framed information, but there has been little attempt to include any assessment of the framing manipulation (but see Block & Keller, 1995). In this study, framing manipulation checks were included to ensure that the two framing conditions were correctly perceived as having emphasized gains or losses.

Immediately after reading the pamphlet, participants provided a complete list of the thoughts and feelings that they had had while reading the pamphlet. Investigators have routinely used thought listings to assess the extent to which participants have processed a persuasive communication (Eagly & Chaiken, 1993). This task provided an opportunity to examine whether exposure to gain- and loss-framed information elicits a similar degree of message elaboration. Some investigators have suggested that people may be less likely to process gain-framed information systematically (Maheswaran & Meyers-Levy, 1990; Smith & Petty, 1996). The thought-listing task also enabled us to test whether participants' cognitive responses to the information mediated the effect that the gain- and loss-framed messages had on interest in the recommended health behavior. Although investigators have successfully identified when gain- and loss-framed messages should be effective, they have had difficulty identifying the constructs that mediate their impact on behavior.

Method

Overview

The present experiment tested the relative effectiveness of gain- and loss-framed messages to pro-mote the performance of detection and prevention behaviors in a 2 (message frame: gain, loss) × 2 (behavior: prevention, detection) between-participants design. Participants read a gain- or loss-framed pamphlet that described an oral hygiene behavior that either prevents or detects dental health problems. Subsequently, participants indicated their own attitudes and intentions concerning the behavior and were provided an opportunity to request a free sample of the recommended product.

Participants

Participants included 120 undergraduates (89 women, 31 men) from the University of Minnesota who responded to an advertisement for a study on communication and health behavior. Participants received $5 as compensation for completing the experiment.

Dental Hygiene Pamphlets

The dental health information was presented in a four-page pamphlet that was designed to appear professional and was attributed to the University of Minnesota Dental Health Communications Project. Four different versions of the pamphlet were developed. Two pamphlets promoted the use of a prevention behavior (mouth rinse) and two pamphlets promoted the use of a detection behavior (disclosing rinse). The two behaviors were operationalized such that they required the same actions (i.e., swishing liquid in one's mouth and spitting it out).

Of the participants who read about a standard mouth rinse, half read gain-framed information about the behavior (e.g., "People who use a mouth rinse daily are taking advantage of a safe and effective way to reduce plaque accumulation") and half read loss-framed information (e.g., "People who do not use a mouth rinse daily are failing to take advantage of a safe and effective way to reduce plaque accumulation"). Likewise, of the people who read about disclosing rinse, half read gain-framed information (e.g., "Using a disclosing rinse before brushing enhances your ability to detect areas of plaque accumulation") and half read loss-framed information (e.g., "Failing to use a disclosing rinse before brushing limits your ability to detect areas of plaque accumulation").

Care was taken to ensure that the gain- and loss-framed versions of the pamphlets provided the same information. Aside from specific details about the particular behavior promoted, all pamphlets presented the same general information about dental health. The pamphlet was divided into five sections: (a) how plaque is formed and how a cavity develops, (b) the development of gum disease, (c) proper oral hygiene behavior, (d) how mouth rinse (disclosing rinse) works, and (e) a recommendation to use mouth rinse (disclosing rinse).

Measures

Premanipulation measures. There were three groups of premanipulation measures.

1. *Demographics.* A series of items assessed general demographic information, including participants' age, gender, ethnic background, and educational background.

2. *Dental history.* A series of items assessed participants' dental hygiene practices and dental health background. These items included questions about how often participants brushed their teeth, flossed, and visited a dentist for routine examinations. Participants also reported their history of dental procedures as well as the number of cavities they recalled having had filled. Finally, participants were asked if they had ever suffered from any form of gum disease.

3. *Perception of risk and severity of gum disease.* Participants rated how likely they were to develop some form of gum disease if they continued their current dental hygiene practices. This rating was made on a 9-point scale ranging from 1 (*extremely unlikely*) to 9 (*extremely likely*). Participants also reported how worried they were about developing gum disease and how serious a problem developing gum disease would be. Each rating was made on a 9-point scale ranging from 1 (*not at all*) to 9 (*extremely*).

Postmanipulation measures. There were six groups of postmanipulation measures and one behavioral measure.

1. *Thought-listing task.* Participants were asked to list the thoughts that they had while reading the pamphlet. Participants were instructed to list only one thought per box and that they need not use all of the boxes provided.

Two judges, who were blind to framing condi-

tion, independently coded the thoughts listed on two different dimensions. First, judges coded the thoughts as either favorable (i.e., a statement expressing a positive reaction to the information contained in the pamphlet), unfavorable (i.e., a statement expressing a negative reaction to the information contained in the pamphlet), neutral (i.e., a statement about the information in the pamphlet expressing a reaction that was neither clearly positive nor clearly negative), or unrelated (i.e., a statement not associated with the information presented in the pamphlet). Interrater agreement on this dimension was high ($r = .85$), and disagreements were resolved through discussion.

The judges also coded each statement as to whether it indicated feelings of concern about the participant's own dental health (e.g., "My gums have been feeling sore lately") or feelings of reassurance about one's health (e.g., "I'm glad I take good care of my teeth"). Thoughts about dental health that expressed neither concern nor reassurance were classified as neutral, and thoughts not about dental health were classified as unrelated. Interrater agreement on this second dimension was acceptable ($r = .79$), and disagreements were resolved through discussion.

2. *Affective reactions to the pamphlet.* On a series of seven positive (assured, calm, cheerful, happy, hopeful, relaxed, relieved) and seven negative (anxious, afraid, discouraged, disturbed, sad, troubled, worried) adjective scales, participants indicated how they felt while reading the pamphlet. Ratings were made on a 7-point scale ranging from 1 (*not at all*) to 7 (*extremely*). Ratings of the negative items were reverse scored and an affective reaction index was constructed ($\alpha = .86$).

3. *Perceptions of risk and severity of gum disease.* The three items included in the premanipulation measures were repeated in the postmanipulation questionnaire.

4. *Attitude toward the behavior.* Four questions assessed participants' attitude toward performing the behavior about which they had read. Participants rated the effectiveness of the behavior, how important it is to perform the behavior, how beneficial it is to perform the behavior, and how favorable they felt toward engaging in the behavior. Ratings were made on a 9-point scale ranging from 1 (*not at all*) to 9 (*extremely*). These questions were combined into a single index ($\alpha = .83$).

5. *Behavioral intentions.* Three questions assessed participants' intentions regarding the behavior about which they had read. Using a 9-point scale ranging from 1 (*I have no intention of doing this*) to 9 (*I am certain that I will do this*), participants indicated how likely it was that they would buy the product within the next week and how likely it was that they would use the product in the next week. Using an open-ended response format, participants indicated how much they would pay for a 12-ounce bottle of the product.

6. *Evaluations of the pamphlet.* A series of five questions assessed participants' evaluation of the pamphlet. Participants indicated how interesting, involving, and informative they found the pamphlet. In each case, ratings were made on a 9-point scale ranging from 1 (*not at all*) to 9 (*extremely*). These three ratings were collapsed into a single index representing participants' evaluation of the quality of the pamphlet ($\alpha = .82$).

Two questions provided a check on the framing manipulation. Participants judged the tone of the information included in the pamphlet on a 9-point scale ranging from –4 (*mostly negative*) to +4 (*mostly positive*), with the midpoint labeled *neutral*. Participants also indicated whether the pamphlet emphasized the benefits associated with doing the behavior or the costs associated with not doing the behavior. This rating was made on a 9-point scale ranging from –4 (*costs*) to +4 (*benefits*), with the midpoint labeled *equally emphasized*.

7. *Behavioral measure: Request for free sample of product.* At the end of the experiment, participants were given a postage-paid postcard that they could mail in to receive a free sample of the promoted product (mouth rinse or disclosing rinse).

Procedure

Participants were scheduled individually or in groups of two to five individuals. The experimenter explained that the purpose of the experiment was to evaluate the effectiveness of pamphlets promoting proper dental hygiene. After signing a consent form, participants completed a packet of measures and were randomly given one of four pamphlets to read. Participants were instructed to take as much time as they wanted reading the pamphlet. When a participant was finished reading, the pamphlet was collected and the postmanipulation measures were distributed. At the close of the experiment, participants were given a postcard to mail in for a free sample of the product about which they had read.

Results

An initial set of analyses were conducted to determine whether any of the demographic or dental history variables moderated the effect of message frame and behavior on the postmanipulation measures. Because no moderating effects were obtained, all analyses are presented collapsed over these factors.

Evaluation of the Pamphlet and Manipulation Checks

Participants' evaluations of the pamphlet were examined to confirm that the pamphlets differed only in terms of how the health information was framed (see Table 19.1). Analyses revealed that participants' ratings of the quality of the pamphlet were unaffected by the framing manipulation, $F(1, 116) = 1.50$, $p > .20$, by the type of behavior promoted in the pamphlet ($F < 1$), or by the interaction between these two factors ($F < 1$).

To assess whether the framing manipulation was perceived as intended, participants rated whether the pamphlet placed more emphasis on the benefits associated with doing the behavior or the costs associated with not doing the behavior. Participants in the loss-framed condition judged the pamphlet as emphasizing costs more than benefits, whereas participants in the gain-framed condition judged the pamphlet as emphasizing benefits over costs, $F(1, 116) = 27.14$, $p < .001$. An examination of participants' ratings of the tone of the pamphlet revealed a similar pattern of results. Participants who read loss-framed information judged the tone of the pamphlet to be significantly more negative than did those who read gain-framed information, $F(1, 116) = 6.19$, $p < .05$. Finally, participants' affective reaction to the pamphlet was consistent with their perception of its tone. Participants reported having a more positive affective reaction to the gain-framed pamphlet than to the loss-framed pamphlet, $F(1, 116) = 8.39$, $p < .01$. No other effects on these measures approached significance, all $Fs < 1.88$.

TABLE 19.1. Evaluations of and Reactions to the Pamphlet as a Function of Message Frame, Experiment 2

	Message frame			
	Gain		Loss	
	M	**SD**	**M**	**SD**
Evaluation of the pamphlet				
Quality of the pamphlet	5.97	(1.69)	6.32	(1.47)
Tone of the pamphlet	0.37	(1.67)	−0.42**	(1.74)
Emphasis on benefits versus costs	1.65	(1.89)	−0.25****	(2.12)
Reaction to the pamphlet				
Affective reaction to the pamphlet	4.59	(0.85)	4.13***	(0.85)
Perceived risk for contracting gum disease[a]	4.15	(1.91)	5.27****	(1.88)
Worry about developing gum disease[a]	4.72	(2.13)	5.54***	(2.03)
Perceived seriousness of gum disease[a]	6.83	(1.70)	7.26*	(1.03)

Note. For the emphasis on benefits versus costs, positive values indicate a greater emphasis on benefits and negative values indicate a greater emphasis on costs. For all other measures, higher values indicate more positive tone, more positive affect, higher quality, and greater risk or concern.
a. Mean is adjusted for its covariate (i.e., value measured prior to the experimental manipulation).
*$p < .10$. **$p < .05$. ***$p < .01$. ****$p < .001$.

Perceptions of Risk and Severity

Several items assessed participants' perceptions of the likelihood that they would develop some form of gum disease and the perceived severity of its development. Analyses of each of these measures controlled for participants' responses prior to reading the pamphlet. Participants first estimated the likelihood that they would develop some form of gum disease if they continued their current dental hygiene practices. An analysis of covariance controlling for participants' initial perceptions revealed a main effect of message frame, $F(1, 114) = 13.90, p < .001$. Participants who read loss-framed pamphlets felt more at risk for developing some form of gum disease provided they continued their current hygiene practices than did those who read gain-framed pamphlets. Participants in the loss-framed condition similarly reported that they were more worried about developing gum disease, $F(1, 114) = 7.41, p < .01$, and that the development of gum disease was a more serious problem, $F(1, 114) = 3.28, p < .08$. There were no other significant effects on any of these measures, Fs < 1.

Thought Reactions to the Pamphlet

The total number of issue-relevant thoughts listed by participants was examined to determine whether there were differences across conditions in amount of cognitive responding to the pamphlet. Partici-

pants listed the same number of thoughts in response to the pamphlet regardless of which behavior was promoted or how the information was framed (all Fs < 1).

We also examined the types of thoughts that participants had while reading the pamphlet. The overall valence of the thoughts that participants listed was determined by subtracting the number of unfavorable thoughts from the number of favorable thoughts. Participants who read the loss-framed pamphlet listed somewhat more favorable responses to the message than did participants who read the gain-framed pamphlet, $F(1, 116) = 3.46, p = .06$ (see Table 19.2 for relevant means). The effect of behavior and the interaction between message frame and behavior were both not significant, Fs < 1. Further analyses were conducted separately on the number of favorable and unfavorable reactions that participants had listed. Although participants in the loss-framed condition listed more favorable reactions to the pamphlet than did those in the gain-framed conditions, $F(1, 116) = 3.42, p = .06$, there was no difference across conditions in the number of unfavorable reactions listed by participants, $F(1, 116) = 1.56, p > .20$.

To determine the valence of the thoughts that participants had about their own dental health, the number of negative thoughts about dental health that had been listed was subtracted from the number of positive thoughts listed. An analysis of this index revealed that participants who read loss-framed pamphlets listed more negative thoughts

TABLE 19.2. Thought Reactions to the Pamphlet as a Function of Message Frame, Experiment 2

	Message frame			
	Gain		Loss	
	M	*SD*	*M*	*SD*
Total number of thoughts listed	4.60	(2.04)	4.77	(1.82)
Overall valence of thoughts[a]	0.03	(3.32)	1.05*	(2.60)
Number of favorable thoughts	1.60	(1.93)	2.22*	(1.73)
Number of unfavorable thoughts	1.57	(2.02)	1.17	(1.43)
Overall valence of dental health thoughts[b]	0.52	(1.67)	−0.47***	(1.95)
Number of positive dental health thoughts	0.98	(1.30)	0.63*	(0.92)
Number of negative dental health thoughts	0.47	(.93)	1.10***	(1.54)

[a]Overall valence of thoughts equals the number of favorable thoughts minus the number of unfavorable thoughts.
[b]Overall valence of dental health thoughts equals the number of positive dental health thoughts minus the number of negative dental health thoughts.
*$p < .10$. ***$p < .01$.

about their current dental health than did those who read gain-framed pamphlets, $F(1, 116) = 8.78$, $p < .005$. The effect of behavior and the interaction between message frame and behavior were both not significant, $Fs(1, 116) = 1.34$ and 0.73, $ps > .25$. Separate analyses of positive and negative statements about dental health also were conducted. Participants in the loss-framed conditions listed more thoughts expressing concern about their teeth and gums than did those in the gain-framed conditions, $F(1, 116) = 7.47$, $p < .01$. Although there was a tendency for people in the loss-framed condition to express fewer favorable thoughts about their dental health, this comparison was only marginally significant, $F(1, 116) = 2.88$, $p < .10$.

Attitude Toward the Behavior

Participants evaluated the behavior about which they had read on a series of four dimensions, and these ratings were combined into a single index. Participants' attitudes toward the behavior were found to be affected by both the type of behavior recommended, $F(1, 116) = 9.21$, $p < .01$, and how the information about the behavior was framed, $F(1, 116) = 13.46$, $p < .0001$. Participants reported holding more favorable attitudes toward the prevention behavior (mouth rinse) ($M = 7.13$, $SD = 1.58$) than toward the detection behavior (disclosing rinse) ($M = 6.11$, $SD = 1.55$). Participants who had read a loss-framed pamphlet held more favorable attitudes toward performing the behavior ($M = 7.04$, $SD = 1.48$) than did those who had

read a gain-framed pamphlet ($M = 6.20$, $SD = 1.69$), regardless of which behavior was promoted in the pamphlet. The interaction between message frame and behavior was not significant, $F < 1$.

Behavioral Intentions

Several indicators assessed participants' intentions regarding the dental hygiene product about which they had read. We predicted that participants who read a gain-framed pamphlet that promoted mouth rinse would report stronger intentions to purchase and make use of the product than would participants who read a loss-framed version of the pamphlet. In contrast, for participants who read about disclosing rinse, we predicted that those who had read the loss-framed pamphlet would report stronger intentions regarding the product than would those who had read the gain-framed pamphlet.

Participants first reported their intentions to buy the product within the next week. Consistent with predictions, the interaction between message frame and behavior was significant, $F(1, 116) = 7.22$, $p < .01$. When participants read a pamphlet promoting the use of mouth rinse, those individuals who read gain-framed information reported stronger intentions to purchase the product ($M = 6.67$, $SD = 3.01$) than did those who read loss-framed information ($M = 5.33$, $SD = 2.81$). Conversely, when participants read about disclosing rinse, those individuals who read loss-framed information reported stronger intentions to purchase the product ($M = 4.43$, $SD = 2.58$) than did those who read gain-framed information ($M = 3.10$, $SD =$

2.44). There was also a main effect of behavior such that participants who read about mouth rinse reported stronger intentions to purchase the product ($M = 6.00$, $SD = 2.96$) than did those who read about disclosing rinse ($M = 3.77$, $SD = 2.58$), $F(1, 116) = 20.24$, $p < .001$.

Participants' intentions to use the product about which they had read within the next week revealed a similar, albeit marginally, significant interaction between message frame and behavior, $F(1, 116) = 3.50$, $p = .06$. The pattern of the interaction was as predicted. In the prevention behavior condition, participants who read gain-framed information reported greater intentions to use mouth rinse within the next week ($M = 6.63$, $SD = 2.79$) than did those who read loss-framed information ($M = 5.83$, $SD = 2.70$), whereas in the detection behavior condition, participants who read loss-framed information reported greater intentions to use disclosing rinse within the next week ($M = 3.87$, $SD = 2.73$) than did those who read gain-framed information ($M = 2.87$, $SD = 2.30$). Overall, participants reported greater intentions to use mouth rinse within the next week ($M = 6.23$, $SD = 2.75$) than disclosing rinse ($M = 3.37$, $SD = 2.55$), $F(1, 116) = 35.48$, $p < .001$.

Finally, participants reported how much they would be willing to pay for a 12-ounce bottle of the product. The ANOVA yielded the predicted interaction between message frame and behavior, $F(1, 116) = 4.24$, $p < .05$. Participants who read gain-framed pamphlets promoting the use of mouth rinse indicated that they were willing to pay more for the product ($M = \$3.23$, $SD = 1.72$) than did participants who read loss-framed pamphlets ($M = \$2.89$, $SD = 1.10$). Conversely, participants who read loss-framed pamphlets about disclosing rinse were willing to pay more for the product ($M = \$3.56$, $SD = 1.96$) than did participants who read gain-framed pamphlets ($M = \$2.67$, $SD = 1.59$). No other effects were significant ($Fs < 1$).

Requests for Product Samples

All participants received a postcard that they could mail in to request a free sample of the recommended product. We predicted that participants would be more likely to request a sample of mouth rinse if they had read a gain-framed pamphlet than if they had read a loss-framed pamphlet but that participants would be more likely to request a

sample of disclosing rinse if they had read a loss-framed pamphlet than if they had read a gain-framed pamphlet. Because the behavioral data were categorical, log-linear analysis was used. As predicted, the saturated model that contained the three-way interaction between message frame, behavior, and request provided the best fit of the data; moreover, removing the three-way interaction from the model significantly reduced the fit of the model, $\Delta L^2(1) = 8.83$, $p < .005$. Of those participants who read pamphlets promoting the use of mouth rinse, a greater percentage of participants in the gain-framed condition returned postcards requesting free samples (67%) than did those in the loss-framed condition (47%). Conversely, of those participants who read pamphlets promoting the use of disclosing rinse, a significantly greater percentage of participants in the loss-framed condition requested a sample of the product (73%) than did those in the gain-framed condition (37%, see Figure 19.1).

Mediational Analyses

Although there is substantial empirical evidence that the manner in which health information is framed influences behavioral decisions, little is known about the factors that mediate framing effects. Rothman and Salovey (1997) suggested several potential mediators that were assessed in this experiment: participants' affective reactions to the

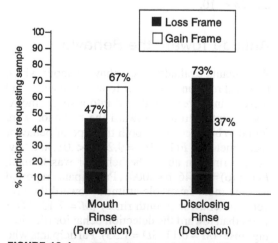

FIGURE 19.1 ■ The influence of message frame and behavior on requests for a free sample of the recommended dental product, Experiment 2.

framed material, their cognitive responses to the material, their attitudes toward the recommended behavior, and their perceptions of risk and concern about the health threat. Mediational analyses were conducted to examine the effect of message frame on participants' behavioral intentions and their requests for a free sample of the recommended product. Because of the interaction between message frame and behavior, analyses were conducted separately for each behavior.

Detection behavior (disclosing rinse). To test for mediation, the message framing manipulation must have influenced the outcome variable and the potential mediator must be both affected by the framing manipulation and related to the outcome variable (Baron & Kenny, 1986). Our analyses first focused on participants' behavioral intentions. To simplify the analysis, the three measures of behavioral intention were standardized and combined into a single index ($\alpha = .78$). Regression analysis revealed that participants' behavioral intentions were stronger after having read a loss-framed pamphlet than after having read a gain-framed pamphlet, $\beta = .27$, $t(58) = 2.16$, $p < .05$. Furthermore, participants' attitude toward the product and the overall valence of their thoughts about the material were each significantly affected by the framing manipulation (βs = .36 and .26, ps < .05, respectively) and significantly related to the behavioral intention index (βs = .65 and .47, ps < .0001, respectively).

To test for mediation, participants' behavioral intentions were first regressed onto the potential mediator and then message frame (coded −1 [gain-frame], 1 [loss-frame]) was entered into the regression model. When participants' attitudes toward the recommended product were included in the regression, there was a significant reduction in the effect that message frame had on behavioral intentions, $\beta = .04$, $t(57) = .41$, $p = .68$; $z = 4.25$, $p < .0001$. Similar, albeit somewhat weaker, findings were obtained when the valence of participants' thoughts about the framed material was included as a mediator, $\beta = .17$, $t(57) = 1.46$, $p = .15$; $z = 1.63$, $p < .05$.

Mediational analyses also were conducted to test the relation between message frame and participants' request for a free sample of the recommended product (coded 0 [no], 1 [yes]). However, analyses revealed no significant relation between any of the potential mediators and requests for a

free sample. Even the relation between behavioral intention and sample requests was only marginally significant, $\beta = .18$, $t(58) = 1.43$, $p < .16$. This pattern of findings precluded any further tests of a mediational model with respect to the sample requests.

Prevention behavior (mouth rinse). Separate mediational analyses were conducted for participants' behavioral intentions and their requests for a free sample. Unexpectedly, none of the potential mediators satisfied the criteria necessary for testing a mediational model for the relation between message frame and behavioral intentions concerning mouth rinse. However, participants' behavioral intentions did satisfy the criteria necessary to test its role as a mediator for the influence of message frame on requests for a free sample of mouth rinse. When card requests were regressed on behavioral intention and message frame, there was a marginally significant reduction in the effect of message frame on card requests, $\beta = -.13$, $t(57) = 1.08$, $p = .28$; $z = 1.26$, $p < .10$, whereas the relation between behavioral intention and card request remained significant, $\beta = .34$, $t(57) = 2.74$, $p < .01$.

Discussion

The results obtained in Experiment 2 not only replicated those of Experiment 1 but also revealed the predicted relation between message frame and behavior in the context of a real health concern. When the use of mouth rinse was promoted, it was more effective to have participants read a gain-framed than a loss-framed pamphlet about gum disease. However, the loss-framed pamphlet was more effective when the use of disclosing rinse was promoted. This pattern of results provides strong empirical evidence in support of our conceptual framework.

Prior tests of the influence of framed information on attitudes and behavior have generally failed to confirm that the framed appeals were perceived to differ in their relative emphasis on benefits and costs (Rothman, Martino, & Jeffery, 1997). In the current experiment, participants' perception of the framed material was assessed. Although participants perceived all four versions of the pamphlet to be of equal quality, they correctly identified the tone and emphasis that the pamphlets were designed to convey.

The gain- and loss-framed pamphlets also elicited different cognitive responses from participants. Although people reported a similar number of thoughts, the loss-framed pamphlets elicited more favorable thoughts from participants, perhaps indicating that people are more familiar, and thus more comfortable with, health materials that focus on potential losses. However, regarding specific thoughts about their own dental health, the loss-framed pamphlets elicited more negative thoughts about participants' teeth and gums, whereas the gain-framed pamphlets elicited more reassuring thoughts about one's teeth and gums.

Participants' thoughts about the persuasive message and their attitudes toward the recommended behavior were more favorable when they had read the loss-framed as compared to the gain-framed pamphlet. The discrepancy between these results and the differential effect of frame on subsequent behavior is striking but is consistent with prior research (e.g., Banks et al., 1995; Rothman et al., 1993; but see Meyerowitz & Chaiken, 1987). This pattern of findings constrained attempts to identify the processes that underlie the persuasive influence of message framing on behavior. Analyses indicated that the influence of loss-framed messages on behavioral intentions was mediated by participants' attitude toward the behavior and the valence of their thoughts about the pamphlet. However, participants' behavioral intentions did not mediate the effect of message frame on requests for a free sample of disclosing rinse. Conversely, although none of the variables measured in this study mediated the effect of gain-framed information on intentions regarding mouth rinse, there was some evidence that participants' reported behavioral intentions mediated the influence of message frame on requests for a free sample of mouth rinse. Given the strong and consistent pattern of behavioral findings, the consistently weak evidence for mediation is a clear indication that a more systematic account of how framed information influences behavior is needed.

General Discussion

A number of investigators have asserted that framing messages systematically in terms of either benefits or costs can provide an effective way to promote health behaviors (e.g., Banks et al., 1995;

Kalichman & Coley, 1995; Meyerowitz & Chaiken, 1987; Rothman et al., 1993). Perhaps because of its similarity to a traditional fear appeal, it was initially assumed that loss-framed appeals would consistently be more effective than gain-framed appeals. However, based on a review of the empirical literature, Rothman and Salovey (1997) argued that the relative influence of gain- and loss-framed messages is contingent on how people perceive the behavior promoted. Specifically, do they perceive performing the behavior to be risky or uncertain? Because people tend to perceive choosing to perform a detection behavior to be risky but choosing to perform a prevention behavior to be safe, the observed advantage for loss- and gain-framed messages should depend on the type of behavior promoted. The two experiments reported in this article provided the first direct test of this conceptual model by using an experimental paradigm in which the frame of the message and the type of behavior were manipulated. Each experiment provided empirical evidence consistent with predictions: gain-framed appeals proved to be more effective in promoting a prevention behavior, whereas loss-framed appeals proved to be more effective in promoting a detection behavior.

The Distinction Between Prevention and Detection Behaviors

Although the relation between message frame and behavior type has proved quite robust, the predictions laid out by Rothman and Salovey (1997) do not rest on features that are intrinsic to prevention and detection behaviors. The finding that loss-framed appeals are a more effective way to promote detection behaviors relies on the fact that society consistently teaches people to perceive behaviors such as BSE and mammography as illness detecting.[2] However, it is possible for these behaviors to be reframed as health-affirming behaviors (i.e., a woman could get a mammogram to affirm that her breasts are healthy). In fact, people

---

[2]The general tendency to construe detection behaviors in terms of their ability to detect the presence rather than the absence of a problem is consistent with research that has shown that people have an easier time processing and reasoning about the presence rather than the absence of features (McGuire & McGuire, 1991).

who regularly follow a set of preventive behaviors (e.g., brush and floss their teeth) should have little reason to be concerned about a screening exam. To the extent that people perceive performing a detection behavior to be a safe, health-affirming practice, a gain-framed rather than a loss-framed appeal should be more persuasive. Consistent with this outlook, two studies that assessed how people perceived a detection behavior found that the predicted advantage for a loss-framed appeal was limited to those people who believed that engaging in the behavior would be risky (Meyerowitz et al., 1991; Rothman et al., 1996).

A further distinction also could be made among detection behaviors. Research has consistently focused on behaviors that screen for health problems (e.g., HIV, cancer). With advances in fields such as genetic testing, tests may be developed that identify factors that are health promoting. Given the tendency to construe detection behaviors in terms of what they are designed to detect, people may not perceive behaviors that screen for healthy attributes as risky (i.e., one no longer runs the risk of finding something wrong). Under these conditions, a gain-framed appeal should be more effective.

What about the prediction that gain-framed messages should be used to promote prevention behaviors? To the extent that adopting a prevention behavior is not perceived as a safe or certain option, gain-framed appeals should become less effective. Consistent with this proposition, Block and Keller (1995, Experiment 1) found that a loss-framed appeal heightened participants' attitude toward and interest in a prevention behavior when the behavior was said to be only 20% effective. The perceived effectiveness of a prevention or a detection behavior may contribute to whether choosing to perform the behavior is considered a risky or safe proposition.

How Do Gain- and Loss-Framed Messages Influence Behavior?

There is little question that providing people with either gain- or loss-framed health information influences the decisions they make and the behaviors they choose to perform. Moreover, framed information has been shown to influence behaviors taken both soon after the information has been

presented and up to 12 months after participants have viewed a framed presentation (e.g., Banks et al., 1995). In contrast to the behavioral findings, investigators have had difficulty identifying the psychological processes that mediate the influence of framed information on behavior. Although some evidence of mediational processes was obtained in Experiment 2, the findings were inconsistent across the two behavior conditions. Why would participants' intentions and behavior be more closely linked for a prevention behavior compared to a detection behavior? Perhaps the feelings of concern and anxiety that people associate with adopting a detection behavior undermines their determination to act on their intentions. Although investigators have long been interested in the premise that too much fear will undermine behavior (e.g., Janis, 1967), this perspective has received minimal empirical support (Sutton, 1982). In fact, in the current study, participants in the detection behavior condition who received loss-framed information reported the highest proportion of card requests. Of course, we have no information as to the proportion of participants across the experimental conditions who actually used the product that they were mailed.

Some researchers have suggested that a message-processing approach may help elucidate the influence that message framing has on behavior (e.g., Maheswaran & Meyers-Levy, 1990; Smith & Petty, 1996). Specifically, any observed advantage for either gain- or loss-framed messages may rest on the fact that people have processed one version of the message more extensively than the other. Smith and Petty (1996, Experiment 2) found that information that is framed in an unexpected manner (e.g., people expect a loss-framed but are given a gain-framed message) is processed more extensively than information framed in an expected manner, and consequently had a stronger influence on people's attitudes and intentions. However, this effect was limited to those people who were otherwise not motivated to process the message (i.e., people low in NFC). People who were dispositionally motivated to process the message were unaffected by the expectancy manipulation. It is not clear how a differential processing perspective could account for the fact that framing effects on behavior have been obtained with people who were highly involved in a health issue and therefore likely to have systematically processed the information they received regardless of how it was framed (e.g., Banks et al., 1995; Detweiler et al., 1999; Rothman et al., 1993). Moreover, in Experiment 2, participants appeared to process the gain- and loss-framed pamphlets in a similar manner, although in the predicted behavior condition, each frame was shown to be more effective than the other. However, comparisons of the total amount of cognitive responding provide only a general assessment of cognitive elaboration (Smith & Petty, 1996). Measures of participants' responses to strong and weak framed arguments provide a more sophisticated assessment of message processing, and including these measures in subsequent research should help to clarify these issues.

Conclusion

Rothman and Salovey (1997) proposed a conceptual framework designed to assist investigators in developing interventions to promote healthy behavior. Although a number of field experiments had revealed findings consistent with this framework, the studies reported in this article provide the first direct confirmation of the predicted relation between message frame and behavior. Despite the fact that we have developed an increasingly sophisticated understanding of when gain- and loss-framed messages are likely to be effective, the processes through which framed messages influence decision making and behavior are still not well understood. Identifying these processes will improve both the theoretical bases of message framing effects and the ability to provide people with health information that is maximally persuasive.

ACKNOWLEDGMENTS

We thank the members of the Minnesota Health Judgment Lab; the Yale Health, Emotion, and Behavior Lab; and Duane Wegener for their comments on the experiments presented here. We also thank the John O. Butler Company and the Colgate-Palmolive Company for providing free samples of dental hygiene products. Preparation of this article was facilitated by a University of Minnesota Summer Faculty Fellowship, a University of Minnesota Grant-in-Aid, and support from the American Cancer Society (RPG-93-028-05-PBP), the National Cancer Institute (R01 CA68427-01A2), and the National Institute of Mental Health (P01 MH/DA56826). Portions of this research were presented at the 1997 annual convention of the American Psychological Association, Chicago, Illinois.

REFERENCES

Adams, D., & Addy, M. (1994). Mouthrinses. *Advanced Dental Research, 8,* 291–301.

Banks, S. M., Salovey, P., Greener, S., Rothman, A. J., Moyer, A., Beauvais, J., & Eppel, E. (1995). The effects of message framing on mammography utilization. *Health Psychology, 14,* 178–184.

Baron, R. M., & Kenny, D. A. (1986). The moderator-mediator variable distinction in social psychological research: Conceptual, strategic, and statistical considerations. *Journal of Personality and Social Psychology, 51,* 1173–1182.

Block, L. G., & Keller, P. A. (1995). When to accentuate the negative: The effects of perceived efficacy and message framing on intentions to perform a health-related behavior. *Journal of Marketing Research, 32,* 192–203.

Cacioppo, J. T., Petty, R. E., Feinstein, J. A., Jarvis, W., & Blair, G. (1996). Dispositional differences in cognitive motivation: The life and times of individuals varying in need for cognition. *Psychological Bulletin, 119,* 197–253.

Cacioppo, J. T., Petty, R. E., & Kao, C. F. (1984). The efficient assessment of need for cognition. *Journal of Personality Assessment, 48,* 306–307.

Christophersen, E. R., & Gyulay, J. E. (1981). Parental compliance with car seat usage: A positive approach with long-term follow-up. *Journal of Pediatric Psychology, 6,* 301–312.

Department of Health and Human Services. (1991). *Healthy people 2000: National health promotion and disease prevention objectives.* Washington, DC: Government Printing Office.

Detweiler, J. B., Bedell, B. T., Salovey, P., Pronin, E., & Rothman, A. J. (1999). Message framing and sunscreen use: Gain-framed messages motivate beach-goers. *Health Psychology, 18,* 189–196.

Eagly, A. H., & Chaiken, S. (1993). *The psychology of attitudes.* Fort Worth, TX: Harcourt Brace Jovanovich.

Hill, D., Gardner, G., & Rassaby, J. (1985). Factors predisposing women to take precautions against breast and cervix cancer. *Journal of Applied Social Psychology, 15,* 59–79.

Janis, I. L. (1967). Effects of fear arousal on attitude change: Recent developments in theory and experimental research. In L. Berkowitz (Ed.), *Advances in experimental social psychology* (Vol. 3, pp. 166–224). San Diego, CA: Academic Press.

Kahneman, D., & Tversky, A. (1979). Prospect theory: An analysis of decisions under risk. *Econometrica, 47,* 263–291.

Kalichman, S. C., & Coley, B. (1995). Context framing to enhance HIV-antibody-testing messages targeted to African American women. *Health Psychology, 14,* 247–254.

Leventhal, H. (1970). Findings and theory in the study of fear communications. In L. Berkowitz (Ed.), *Advances in experimental social psychology* (Vol. 5, pp. 119–186). San Diego, CA: Academic Press.

Linville, P. W., Fischer, G. W., & Fischhoff, B. (1993). AIDS risk perceptions and decision biases. In J. B. Pryor & G. D. Reeder (Eds.), *The social psychology of HIV infection* (pp. 5–38). Hillsdale, NJ: Lawrence Erlbaum.

Maheswaran, D., & Meyers-Levy, J. (1990). The influence of message framing and issue involvement. *Journal of Marketing Research, 27*, 361–367.

Marteau, T. M. (1989). Framing of information: Its influence upon decisions of doctors and patients. *British Journal of Social Psychology, 28*, 89–94.

Mayer, J. A., & Solomon, L. (1992). Breast self-examination skill and frequency: A review. *Annals of Behavioral Medicine, 14*, 189–196.

McGuire, W. J., & McGuire, C. V. (1991). The content, structure, and operation of thought systems. In R. S. Wyer, Jr., & T. K. Srull (Eds.), *Advances in social cognition* (Vol. 4, pp. 1–78). Hillsdale, NJ: Lawrence Erlbaum.

Meyerowitz, B. E., & Chaiken, S. (1987). The effect of message framing on breast self-examination attitudes, intentions, and behavior. *Journal of Personality and Social Psychology, 52*, 500–510.

Meyerowitz, B. E., Wilson, D. K., & Chaiken, S. (1991, June). *Loss-framed messages increase breast self-examination for women who perceive risk.* Paper presented at the annual convention of the American Psychological Society, Washington, DC.

Rothman, A. J., Martino, S. C., & Jeffery, R. W. (1997). *Predicting preferences in the domains of gains and losses: The importance of knowing when a gain is a gain and a loss is a loss.* Unpublished manuscript, University of Minnesota, Minneapolis.

Rothman, A. J., Pronin, E., & Salovey, P. (1996, October). *The influence of prior concern on the persuasiveness of loss-framed messages about skin cancer.* Paper presented at the annual meeting of the Society of Experimental Social Psychology, Sturbridge, MA.

Rothman, A. J., & Salovey, P. (1997). Shaping perceptions to motivate healthy behavior: The role of message framing. *Psychological Bulletin, 121*, 3–19.

Rothman, A. J., Salovey, P., Antone, C., Keough, K., & Martin, C. D. (1993). The influence of message framing on intentions to perform health behaviors. *Journal of Experimental Social Psychology, 29*, 408–433.

Salovey, P., Rothman, A. J., & Rodin, J. (1998). Health behavior. In D. Gilbert, S. Fiske, & G. Lindzey (Eds.), *Handbook of social psychology* (4th ed., Vol. 2, pp. 633–683). New York: McGraw-Hill.

Smith, S. M., & Petty, R. E. (1996). Message framing and persuasion: A message processing analysis. *Personality and Social Psychology Bulletin, 22*, 257–268.

Sobel, M. E. (1982). Asymptotic confidence intervals for indirect effects in structural models. In S. Leinhardt (Ed.), *Sociological methodology 1982* (pp. 290–312). San Francisco: Jossey-Bass.

Sutton, S. R. (1982). Fear-arousing communications: A critical examination of theory and research. In J. R. Eiser (Ed.), *Social psychology and behavioral medicine* (pp. 303–337). New York: John Wiley.

Tversky, A., & Kahneman, D. (1981). The framing of decisions and the rationality of choice. *Science, 221*, 453–458.

Wegener, D. T., Petty, R. E., & Klein, D. J. (1994). Effects of mood on high elaboration attitude change: The mediating role of likelihood judgments. *European Journal of Social Psychology, 24*, 25–43.

Weinstein, N. D., Rothman, A. J., & Nicolich, M. (1998). Use of correlational data to examine the effects of risk perceptions on precautionary behavior. *Psychology & Health, 13*, 479–501.

Personality and Health

Personality is the idea that people have observable character traits that are relatively stable across different kinds of situations and over time. For many years, psychologists and health professionals have tried to link these stable styles with the propensity to develop different diseases. For example, the Type A personality style—characterized by aggressiveness, competitiveness, and feeling time pressured—was thought to be linked to the development of heart disease (Friedman & Rosenman, 1974). A different personality style, termed Type C, was thought to make one prone to cancer. Type C individuals were described as having difficulty expressing anger or tension and generally responding to stressful situations by withdrawing and feeling depressed or hopeless (Bahnson, 1981; Temoshok, 1987). People with high blood pressure have been described as chronically angry (Jonas & Lando, 2000) and cynical (Williams, 1984). People who are depressed but who tend to complain a lot about their negative feelings are described as having a pain-prone personality (Johansson & Lindberg, 2000). Is there any truth to the idea that certain kinds of personality characteristics predispose one to different diseases? Well, the evidence for blanket generalizations like the ones described above is pretty weak. But the articles in this section of the book make the case that there are some connections between personality and illness worthy of exploration.

Howard Friedman and Stephanie Booth-Kewley (1987) ask whether there is a general personality style that is connected to all kinds of illness. Using a statistical procedure called a meta-analysis, in which the data from many different studies are combined, they find evidence for a kind of generic disease-prone personality type. It seems that individuals who experience a lot of depression, anger, and anxiety tend to be more likely to report asthma, arthritis, ulcers, headaches, and heart disease. The strongest relationship they discovered was between these negative emotional styles and heart disease.

And that brings us to the second article in this section of the book, Tim Smith's review of the literature on hostility and health (1992). His review confirms that Friedman and Booth-Kewley are likely correct: People who are prone to heart disease do experience more negative emotion than other people, especially anger and hostility. Smith's review is quite important as it suggests that only one part of the original Type A idea has any validity. Although it is true that people who experience and express a lot of anger and hostility are more likely to have heart attacks, other aspects of the Type A personality style such as being competitive, hard-driving, and time pressured do not seem to be related to heart disease (as long as one can be this kind of high achiever with a smile on his or her face). However, researchers are still struggling to specify the underlying processes: What is it that links anger and hostility to heart disease and other outcomes? Smith describes several possibilities ranging from increased physiological reactivity, greater degrees of interpersonal conflict and reduced social support, to unhealthy habits like drinking and smoking.

On the flip side, Michael Scheier and his

collaborators (1989) demonstrate in a study of 51 middle-aged men that being optimistic leads to a faster and more pleasant recovery from coronary artery bypass surgery. Optimism—seeing desired outcomes as attainable—allows people to exert effort even when faced with setbacks, and this attitude seems to help people get out of the hospital more quickly and return to presurgical activities. Even after 6 months, individuals who had been more optimistic prior to their surgery were more likely to report that their lives had returned to normal.

Yet, it is not the case that expressing negative emotions is always harmful. In fact, doing so in certain contexts can actually have a positive impact on health. For nearly 2 decades, James Pennebaker has been studying how the expression of troubling emotions, especially through writing (such as in a journal) regularly, can reduce reports of illness and use of the health care system. In his article, Pennebaker (1997) provides a brief review of all the ways his studies have shown that writing about emotional experiences brings about significant improvements in physical health. These effects seem quite robust, although, again, the processes that are responsible for these effects have yet to be well-specified. Does writing about emotional experiences "release" pent-up feelings in a kind of cathartic way, or does writing about these difficult times allow one to develop a new understanding of them and to integrate one's thoughts and feelings more adaptively? We would put our money on the second mechanism, but the verdict, as you will see, is still out.

REFERENCES

Bahnson, C. B. (1981). Stress and cancer: The state of the art. *Psychosomatics, 22,* 207–220.

Friedman, H. S., & Booth-Kewley, S. (1987). The "disease-prone personality": A meta-analytic view of the construct. *American Psychologist, 42,* 539–555.

Friedman, M., & Rosenman, R. H. (1974). *Type A behavior and your heart.* New York: Knopf.

Johansson, E., & Lindberg, P. (2000). Low back pain patients in primary care: Subgroups based on the multidimensional pain inventory. *International Journal of Behavioral Medicine, 7,* 340–352.

Jonas, B. S., & Lando, J. F. (2000). Negative affect as a prospective risk factor for hypertension. *Psychosomatic Medicine, 62,* 463–471.

Pennebaker, J. W. (1997). Writing about emotional experi-ences as a therapeutic process. *Psychological Science, 8,* 162–166.

Scheier, M. F., Matthews, K. A., Owens, J. F., Magovern, G. J., Sr., Lefebvre, R. C., Abbott, R. A., & Carver, C. S. (1989). Dispositional optimism and recovery from coronary artery bypass surgery: The beneficial effect on physical and psychological well-being. *Journal of Personality and Social Psychology, 57,* 1024–1040.

Smith, T. W. (1992). Hostility and health: Current status of a psychosomatic hypothesis. *Health Psychology, 11,* 139–150.

Temoshok, L. (1987). Personality, coping style, emotion, and cancer: Towards an integrative model. *Cancer Surveys, 6,* 545–567.

Williams, R. B. (1984). An untrusting heart. *The Sciences, 24,* 31–36.

Discussion Questions

1. What is the difference between saying that certain personality styles are associated with physical health outcomes and saying that certain emotional experiences are associated with physical health outcomes? Is there a difference between personality tendencies and emotional tendencies?
2. Is anger a double-edged sword? Is it the case that if you express a lot of anger you are more prone to heart disease, but if you suppress your anger you are more prone to cancer? What is the healthy way to deal with anger?
3. Do you accept our belief that the only strong evidence for connections between personality and illness concerns anger and heart disease?
4. What are the implications of the articles in this section of the book for the design of illness prevention programs? Should, for example, health insurance companies pay for anger management classes for hostile individuals?
5. Can you imagine a "health-prone" personality style? What it would be like?

Suggested Readings

Contrada, R. J., Cather, C., & O'Leary, A. (1999). Personality and health: Dispositions and processes in disease susceptibility and adaptation to illness. In L. Pervin & O. P. John (Eds.), *Handbook of personality* (2nd edition, pp. 576–604). New York: Guilford Press.

An excellent and thorough overview of all the evidence connecting personality, health, and disease.

Miller, S. M., Fang, C. Y., Diefenbach, M. A., & Bales, C. B. (2001). Tailoring psychosocial interventions to the individual's health information-processing style: The influence of monitoring versus blunting in cancer risk and disease. In A. Baum & B. L. Andersen

(Eds.), *Psychosocial interventions for cancer* (pp. 343–362). Washington, DC: American Psychological Association.

Another personality characteristic that might influence health and illness is monitoring/blunting, the tendency to seek out versus avoid health information.

Norman, P., Bennett, P., Smith, C., & Murphy, S. (1998). Health locus of control and health behavior. *Journal of Health Psychology, 3,* 171–180.

Another popular personality characteristic thought to be related to health outcomes is health locus of control, the belief that one's health is caused either by one's own actions, powerful others, or luck. This article reports a large-scale survey of nearly 12,000 people who completed a standard health locus of control inventory. Respondents with an internal health locus of control were more likely than others not to smoke cigarettes or drink heavily and were more likely to exercise and eat a healthy diet.

Taylor, S. E. (1989). *Positive illusions*. New York: Basic Books.

Is maintaining a positive view of oneself and the world—even in the face of objective evidence to the contrary—the key to a healthy life? Shelley Taylor argues that it might be.

The "Disease-Prone Personality": A Meta-Analytic View of the Construct

Howard S. Friedman and Stephanie Booth-Kewley
University of California, Riverside

This article examines the notion that personality plays a causal role in the development of disease. In particular, this article develops the heuristic strategy of simultaneously comparing several emotional aspects of personality and several diseases, with close attention to the strength of the links between personality and disease. The published literature on personality correlates of five diseases with so-called "psychosomatic" components—asthma, arthritis, ulcers, headaches, and coronary heart disease—is reviewed and discussed, with a focus on construct validity. The statistical technique of meta-analysis is used to provide an easily viewed comparative summary. The results point to the probable existence of a generic "disease-prone" personality that involves depression, anger/hostility, anxiety, and possibly other aspects of personality. However, except in the case of coronary heart disease, the evidence is weak. Nevertheless, there is sufficient evidence to argue for a key role for psychological research on the prevention and treatment of disease. Specific directions for future research are described.

Many people seem to believe that there is solid evidence linking personality to the development of particular diseases. We often hear, for example, about worriers getting ulcers or about anxious people developing migraine headaches. We might blame a heart attack on a "workaholic" personality or asthma on emotional repression. But what exactly is known about the relationship between personality and disease?

In ancient times, Hippocrates proclaimed the four bodily humors (blood, black bile, yellow bile, and phlegm) as the basis of personality, and these elements were extended by Galen to refer not only to temperament but also to the causes of disease

(Allport, 1961). The predominant humor in a person was thought to produce the dominant temperament, and an excess of a humor led to disease. For example, an excess of black bile would produce a melancholic personality, eventual depression, and associated physical illness. Today, we have replaced humors with hormones, but the basic typology lives on: the hopeless, depressed "melancholic"; the angry, hostile "choleric"; the apathetic, alexithymic "phlegmatic"; and the ruddy, optimistic "sanguine." The fact that links among emotion, personality, and health have been written about for 2,000 years suggests both that there may be some truth to these conceptions and that the framework is sufficiently flexible to accommodate almost any observations.

In modern times, the question of personality and illness received a great deal of attention from Sigmund Freud and the psychoanalysts that followed. Using hypnosis and related psychodynamic techniques, Freud was able to cure hysterical paralysis and related conditions (Freud, 1955). Today, there is no doubt that many illnesses have a significant psychological component, whether it is impotence resulting from fear after a heart attack, functional paralysis resulting from psychological trauma, or anorexia resulting from depression. In such cases, however, no organic condition is necessarily involved—when the psychological problems are eliminated, the patient is often cured. But the more puzzling question is whether mental disturbance leads to organic disease (cf. Dunbar, 1943). On the basis of clinical observation, Alexander (1950) answered affirmatively, suggesting that various diseases are caused by specific unconscious emotional conflicts. For example, he linked ulcers to oral conflicts, migraines to repressed hostility, and asthma to separation anxiety. Although these ideas are suggestive, little controlled empirical research has been performed to test them.

Taking a more biological perspective, there is no doubt that psychological stress is closely linked to some illnesses. There are many sorts of evidence for this relationship. Most simple to observe are the immediate bodily "illness" responses such as fainting or nausea in response to the sight of blood or mutilation. Further, there are ample animal studies showing harmful physiological effects resulting from stress (e.g., Levy, 1985; Selye, 1976; Weiss, 1971). Also interesting are studies showing human illness following loss or bereavement (cf. Engel, 1967; Schmale, 1958). Perhaps most convincing are the "life change" studies, which find an increased likelihood of disease following objectively quantifiable life stresses (Dohrenwend & Dohrenwend, 1974; Holmes & Rahe, 1967). However, many people experience life changes and do not become ill. The effects of a stressor may be buffered by appropriate coping mechanisms (Cohen & Lazarus, 1983) and may affect different types of people to different degrees. That is, this research on stress does not, in itself, elucidate an association between particular personalities and particular diseases.

Possible Links Between Personality and Disease

Disease-Caused Personality Changes

If personality is associated with disease, it may be because certain aspects of personality are the *result* of disease processes. For example, some (though not all) patients with serious illnesses such as cancer become fearful or depressed (e.g., Dunkel-Schetter & Wortman, 1982). So, clinicians may notice that ill people appear psychologically disturbed; for example, oncologists may see (or even elicit) what they believe to be a "cancer personality," and so on. Furthermore, harmful biological processes may induce certain chronic mental disorders. For example, it has been suggested that hypoxia can bring about depression (Katz, 1982). However, what about the possibility that personality sometimes plays a causal role in disease?

Unhealthy Habits

Personality could be a causal factor in disease through a variety of very different types of mechanisms. First of all, personality could lead to disease through unhealthy behaviors. For example, if anxiety leads people to overeat and if obesity contributes to the development of diabetes, then anxiety is a causal factor for diabetes. In such cases of indirect causation, of course, curing the anxiety would not necessarily cure or prevent the diabetes unless the obesity was also affected. Studies investigating the links between personality and disease should control for unhealthy behaviors (such as cigarette smoking, various influences of diet, etc.), but most do not, possibly because there are so many potentially relevant behaviors. As future research becomes more focused, it may be easier to take these influences into account.

Direct Influences of Personality

Personality could affect disease directly through some physiological mechanisms. For example, if the so-called Type A personality leads to hypertension or artery damage (a controversial issue), and if these states encourage the development of coronary heart disease, then the Type A personality would be a cause of heart disease; eliminating the Type A personality would then presumably reduce the likelihood of heart disease. This type of model combines Selye's (1976) notion of a general adaptation response to a noxious stimulus with the idea of individual coping mechanisms (Cohen & Lazarus, 1979). In other words, depending on a person's view of the world, typical pattern of emotional responding, and psychological resources (Kobasa, 1979), he or she would be more or less likely to experience certain physiological responses when confronted by environmental challenge. Therefore, personality would play a causal role in disease. This model is what people generally mean when they refer to a "coronary-prone personality," an "asthma-prone personality," and so on.

It is important to note that this model does not suggest that personality is the only cause of the disease (Weiner, 1977). Most disease processes are likely "multifactorial," meaning that a genetic predisposition to the disease, invading stressors such as viruses or traumas, developmental processes (age), hormonal differences, and other factors may be involved in the etiology of disease. Thus, according to this model, many people prone to disease X will not develop disease X, but on the other hand, relatively few people who are not prone to disease X will develop it.

Biological Third Variables

Another theoretically interesting possibility is that personality is related to disease through an underlying biological third variable. For example, if a hyper-responsive nervous system is an underlying factor in the development of an anxious personality and if a hyper-responsive nervous system is an underlying factor in the development of heart disease, then chronic anxiety would be a marker for heart disease; but the anxiety per se would not necessarily play a causal role in the development of heart disease, depending on the nature of the mechanisms involved (cf. Kahn, Kornfeld, Frank, Heller, & Hoar, 1980; and Krantz & Durel, 1983, regarding hyperreactivity and Type A behavior). Prominent theories and research in this area—relating the nervous system, personality, and health—involve the concepts of emotional expression, extraversion, and the "internalizing/externalizing" dimension. Examples date from Pavlov's (1927) writings on strong versus weak nervous

systems and include Eysenck's (1967) theory of introversion/extraversion. This work has been summarized by Ross Buck (1984), who developed a general, if preliminary, model of relationships among nervous system activity, emotional expression, personality, and health. Simply put, a main conclusion of this approach is that inhibition of emotional expression is likely to be a correlate and may be a cause of poor health. Another area of thought along these lines concerns the idea that facial expressions of emotion serve to regulate the flow of blood to the brain, thus linking chronic moods to nervous system function (Zajonc, 1985). Biological third-variable models are not necessarily inconsistent with personality-causing-disease models of the biological models allow for feedback to and changes in the nervous system as a function of personality-influenced emotional responding.

Illness Behaviors

Medical social psychology and sociology have demonstrated the necessity of distinguishing organic disease from "illness" (DiMatteo & Friedman, 1982; Mechanic, 1978). Illness is partly a socially defined state that involves being diagnosed by a physician and entering the sick role. Social factors may thus sometimes artifactually produce or inflate a link between personality and disease. For example, if backaches, chest pains, choking feelings, and so on produce a diagnosis of disease but are also closely related to diagnoses of anxiety or depression, then the resulting personality–disease link does not really fall into the category of direct personality influence on organic disease. It is a method artifact. Of course, the distinction is not perfectly clear-cut; contrary to the thinking of the traditional medical model of disease, there is no absolute definition of disease that excludes social factors. Still, most researchers will want (at some point) to distinguish between "chest pain" and "death due to coronary occlusion," between "stiff joints" and "destruction of articular cartilage," and so on.

Multiple Influences: The Body as a System

In many cases, it is likely that a variety of different causal influences and feedback loops will be at work in the relationship between personality and disease. For example, excessive anxiety may lead to smoking, drinking, and/or insomnia, which will set in motion a series of physiological processes (influenced partly by genetic makeup), which will in turn affect both various aspects of health and the anxiety itself, and so on. It is an oversimplification to say that any single factor is the cause of disease that results. Nevertheless, personality dimensions having potentially deleterious effects on health should be investigated. Even without conclusive evidence, a common goal for individuals or their clinicians is to try to prevent or affect disease by changing personality (e.g., "Don't work so hard," "Let out your feelings," "Don't worry so much"; or workshops on "How to change your Type A personality"). Because effective psychological interventions are an important ultimate goal, it is worthwhile to focus directly on the relationship between personality and disease.

Physiological Mechanisms

In research on personality and disease, people cannot be randomly assigned to a given personality and then followed. So, no single study could ever "prove" a causal link. Some of the strongest evidence of such a link will have to come from physiological research that identifies disease mechanisms and shows how they may be affected by psychological factors. However, this task is more difficult than it first appears. First, most serious chronic disease processes are not well understood (especially in terms of etiology), and there is no reason to assume they will be fully understood any time in the near future. Second, psychological constructs such as stress, personality, and coping are not readily operationalized by physiologists; there are differences between the electrical shocks administered to a dog or a pig and the emotional shocks administered to a recently bereaved widow. Whether these different types of disturbances act on identical underlying physiological processes remains unknown. Third, physiological and biochemical systems of the human body are interrelated and often interdependent. As one system is thrown out of equilibrium, others may be affected, and so simple causal links are difficult to uncover. In short, physiologists are not likely to resolve this matter in the foreseeable future. Nevertheless,

physiological processes are the boundary conditions for psychological understanding: It is silly to postulate a psychological model of disease causation that is physiologically impossible.

Is it reasonable to postulate an effect of personality on the development or progression of disease? What are the known links between psychological responses and disease-relevant physiological processes? Are the processes disease-specific? Considerable attention is currently being focused on the immune system, often in the context of psychological depression, anxiety, and repressed affect (see reviews by Ader, 1981; Jemmott & Locke, 1984; Levy, 1985; Solomon, 1985). Although many questions concerning mechanisms remain unanswered, there is little doubt that psychological stress can result in decreased immune system function. Asthma and arthritis are two diseases often mentioned in this regard. The second area to which attention is being paid is that of anger and hostility (Chesney & Rosenman, 1985) and their physiological consequences. Coronary heart disease, hypertension, and headaches are often mentioned in this context. Both of these syndromes, anger/hostility and depression/anxiety/repression, have been associated with elevated levels of corticosteroids (such as cortisol) and catecholamines (such as epinephrine). Interestingly, elevation of either corticosteroid or catecholamine levels may result in immunosupression and metabolic abnormalities (cf. Goodkin, Antoni, & Blaney, 1986; Krantz, Baum, & Singer, 1983).

There is also increasing evidence that immune system functioning is not autonomous but instead is closely tied to psychophysiological processes and subject to modulation by the brain (Ader & Cohen, 1985). This field of study is thus termed *psychoneuroimmunology*. One additional recent development is the discovery of an "anxiety peptide" (a small molecule that increases anxiety) in the brain (Marx, 1985). Together with increasing evidence that immune system function can be classically conditioned—that is, brought under control of the central nervous system (Ader & Cohen, 1985)—such developments mean that it makes sense to think in terms of long-term, stable changes in resistance to disease. Such stability is of course necessary for us to think in terms of personality (as opposed to transient environmental stressors).

It is important to note that these processes are

not specific to a particular disease in the way that the tubercle bacillus is specific to tuberculosis. There is no clear evidence that a specific pattern of psychological responses leads to a specific set of physiological reactions that in turn lead to a specific disease. A key question for research and a main focus of this article is the extent to which future research should be looking for personalities that lead to particular diseases, as opposed to studying a general disease-prone personality.

Construct Validity

To reach a solid understanding of the relationship between personality and disease, it is necessary to consider simultaneously various aspects of personality and various diseases. To speak sensibly of a particular disease-proneness (such as a "coronary-prone personality"), we need to determine whether a certain type of personality is related to only one or to many diseases, and similarly we must discover whether a given disease is related to only one or to many aspects of personality. Although this broad approach to construct validation may seem obvious when stated in this way, *it has almost never been followed in practice.* Researchers typically pick a single disease such as heart disease and look for its personality correlates. Even worse for purposes of construct validation, a researcher may pick only a single aspect of personality and try to relate it to a single disease. For example, a researcher may try to see whether hard-drivingness relates to heart disease or whether repression leads to cancer. Historically, this narrow approach to construct validity has developed out of work in clinical settings. Physicians may notice that many of their patients seem to have a certain type of personality, and they may then explore that relationship without placing it into the necessary broader context.

Insufficient attention to construct validity has left the field of personality and disease unfocused and confusing. Perhaps as a result, some physicians and health researchers refuse to believe that psychology plays any significant role in causing disease. An editorial in the *New England Journal of Medicine* asks, "What about heart attacks, peptic ulcers, asthma, rheumatoid arthritis, and inflammatory bowel disease? Are they caused by stress in certain personality types, and will changing the personality change the course of the disease?" (Angell, 1985, p. 1570). The answer given is that "it is time to acknowledge that our belief in disease as a direct reflection of mental state is largely folklore" (Angell, 1985, p. 1572).

Not relying on folklore, we have, in this article, endeavored to provide an empirically based framework for future research on the relationship between personality and disease. We have taken several theoretically important and commonly studied aspects of personality—depression, anxiety, anger/hostility, and extraversion—and reviewed their relationships to five chronic diseases. To aid in simplifying this mass of data, we have combined results using the quantitative techniques of meta-analysis.

Psychosomatic Diseases?

The five diseases selected for study—asthma, headaches, ulcers, arthritis, and heart disease—are all widespread chronic diseases whose etiology is not well understood. In many primitive societies, such diseases were blamed on demons (Murdock, 1980). Demons are psychologically appealing culprits for two reasons. First, they account for the unpredictable onset and course of chronic illness; and second, they allow for some blaming of the victim, who must have been immoral to allow such possession. It can, of course, be argued that mental illness is the modern replacement for demons; therefore, according to this argument, psychological explanations for chronic illness merely involve collective rationalization and victim blaming. There is certainly some truth to this point of view. Indeed, tuberculosis was seen as caused by the character of those afflicted until the tubercle bacillus was discovered (Sontag, 1974). Although it often does seem that the search for psychological causes of disease is a search for evanescent demons, here we rely on the published scientific literature.

The following paragraphs briefly summarize the relevant aspects of what seems to be generally believed (on the basis of theoretical speculation and traditional reviews) about the personalities and pathophysiologies associated with the five diseases under consideration. This information serves as an orientation to and basis of comparison with our meta-analysis. Furthermore, it is important to note that those in the field of medicine actually know relatively little about the etiology of these diseases. A diagnosis of "coronary heart disease" or "migraine" or "asthma" is much more descriptive than explanatory.

Bronchial asthma affects about 1 in 20 Americans. It is characterized by obstruction of air exchange in the lungs. Muscle spasms and tissue swelling narrow the bronchial tubes, sometimes for days. Although it is often triggered by allergens, psychological factors have long been implicated in this disease. In traditional reviews, anxiety seems to be the most commonly mentioned psychological cause, although it is hard to imagine that anyone choking and gasping for air would not become anxious as a result. The asthmatic personality is supposedly also dependent, aggressive, and neurotic, although the empirical evidence is weak (Creer, 1978; Weiner, 1977). Many asthmatics also suffer from other immunologic disorders (e.g., eczema, allergic rhinitis, food allergies), making plausible the idea that immune system function plays a key role in asthma.

Headache—muscular contraction and migraine headache—is one of the most common medical problems and accounts for tens of millions of medical visits yearly. Muscle contraction headaches (involving the muscles of the head and neck) are almost always attributed to psychological factors. Migraine, which involves abnormally dilated blood vessels in the head (and which is often treated by drugs that reduce this dilation), is also often attributed to psychological conflicts. Some migraines seem to be caused by allergies, but migraine is often classed as a cardiovascular disorder. The "migraine personality" is usually thought to involve anger, repressed hostility, and/or emotional tension, but the evidence is mixed (Adams, Feuerstein, & Fowler, 1980). There is clearer evidence that migraine (and probably other headache) attacks are often precipitated by psychological stress (Bakal, 1977). As distinct from the other diseases under consideration, diagnosis of headache depends heavily on the self-report of the patient.

Peptic ulcer, a lesion of the stomach or duodenum, affects 1% or 2% of the general U.S. population, often causing a burning sensation and severe pain. Ulcers seem to be caused by excessive levels of hydrochloric acid and/or problems with the protective lining of the gastrointestinal tract.

Psychoanalytic theorists, including Alexander (1950), have posited a link between emotional conflict and various gastrointestinal disorders (perhaps captured in such expressions as "I'm fed up with you"; "You make me want to vomit"). One study of army recruits (Weiner, Thaler, Reiser, & Mirsky, 1957) evidently gave rise to the general perception of a link between personality and ulcers, but no well-controlled, large-scale followups have been conducted in the 30 years since. There is evidence that gastric lesions in rats (personality unknown) can be brought about by psychological stress (Weiss, 1968, 1971), but there is no accepted view of whether this generally occurs in humans or what the physiological mechanism might be (Soll & Isenberg, 1983).

Rheumatoid arthritis is a common inflammatory disease, affecting over 2 million Americans, which often causes severe pain and disability. It has long been believed that psychological factors play a role in the development of arthritis; and it is known that psychological problems are present in those who have the disease (see reviews by Anderson, Bradley, Young, McDaniel, & Wise, 1985; Moos, 1964). The so-called "arthritic personality" is viewed as depressed, perfectionistic, and unable to express anger. But the research in this area too is limited by a full range of methodological weaknesses. Anderson et al. (1985) did conclude that arthritis is associated with a relatively high degree of psychological stress. Furthermore, because arthritis seems to involve the immune system, psychological factors are likely to be important in the progression of arthritis, regardless of how the disease begins. In other words, even if arthritis is of genetic or infectious origin, its course and clinical manifestation are likely to be influenced by psychological factors. This point may be relevant to the other slow-developing diseases under consideration as well.

Coronary heart disease (CHD; and the associated condition of arteriosclerosis) is the greatest cause of premature death in the United States. Arteriosclerosis, a disease process not well understood, involves the forming of fatty plaques in the arteries throughout the body. When this plaque formation becomes advanced in the coronary arteries of the heart, insufficient oxygen is supplied to the heart muscle, which contributes to angina pectoris (chest pain), coronary insufficiency, and/ or myocardial infarction (heart attack). The same physiological processes that can depress the immune system (i.e., activation of the adrenal-medullary and the pituitary-cortical systems) can also interfere in the metabolism of lipids and cholesterol and may also cause direct arterial damage (Krantz, Baum & Singer, 1983). There is a large literature on the so-called "coronary-prone personality." According to Friedman and Rosenman (1974), Type A people, who are aggressively involved in a chronic incessant struggle to achieve more and more in less and less time, are prone to CHD. There are many studies showing a link between the Type A personality pattern and CHD, but there also have been several significant failures to replicate (cf. Shekelle et al., 1985). In recent years, attention has turned more toward the possible role of hostility in the development of CHD (Chesney & Rosenman, 1985). From a construct validity viewpoint, this movement is a good one, because hostility, but not the Type A behavior pattern, has often been studied in relation to other diseases.

Cancer (or the progression of cancer) is another disease that has been examined in terms of its psychological correlates (e.g., Levy, 1985). However, research on cancer has a number of special difficulties, including the key problems that "cancer" is actually a number of very different diseases and that the stigma of cancer makes its study especially susceptible to issues of "victim blaming" and other unscientific influences. For these reasons, cancer is not included in our analysis.

It is interesting to note that none of these "disease-prone" personalities describes a happy, satisfied, laid-back, and sociable individual who brings illness on himself or herself by a casual disregard for the meaningful and moral issues of humanity. Is an emotionally troubled person really at higher risk for developing disease? A particular disease?

Meta-Analysis

The method of quantitative integration, or "meta-analysis" (Glass, McGaw, & Smith, 1981; Light & Pillemer, 1984; Rosenthal, 1984), is a useful tool for combining the results of independent studies so that they may be more easily viewed. Like any statistical technique, meta-analysis does not work miracles but merely helps us organize and understand the information we already have. It has advantages and drawbacks, and like any technique, its value depends in large part on the quality of the data used. Meta-analysis cannot perform magic when the appropriate controlled studies have not been conducted, but it can reveal specific patterns deserving of further investigation. Concerning the possibility of a causal link between personality and disease, meta-analysis is useful in addressing three basic questions: First, is the bulk of the evidence encouraging, or should the matter be dropped and our attention turned elsewhere? Second, what is the size of any relationships being uncovered? This information is very important for designing research studies of adequate statistical power, for evaluating failures to replicate, and for ascertaining the possible economic savings that could be produced by large-scale interventions. Third, meta-analysis draws our attention to discriminant validity—namely, the question of whether there are different patterns associated with different diseases or whether there is a more global or general "disease-prone" personality.

In meta-analysis, the results of weaker studies are combined with those of stronger ones; this combination helps avoid selection biases on the part of the reviewer and keeps attention focused on the broader issues. Meta-analysis also involves averaging over studies with somewhat different independent variables (e.g., two measures of anxiety), dependent variables (e.g., partial coronary artery occlusion and myocardial infarction), and samples (e.g., of different ages and health status). From a construct validity viewpoint, this diversity is exactly what is needed; when enough research has been completed, subanalyses that use statistical blocking on variables of interest can be done. The study of personality and disease is an immature field in which most researchers are still nurturing their own pet theories; it is hoped that this review can provide a fresh perspective on what we know now and where we should go from here.

Here we provide a caveat: Finer distinctions involving the different subcategories of the five diseases considered in this review can and should be made in any comprehensive attempts to explain the precise links between personality and disease. Furthermore, possible mediating physiological mechanisms should be examined in detail before any specific model is accepted. Finally, additional work is needed on reliability issues of all sorts, especially in the defining and measuring of the relevant personalities and diseases. Such matters are, however, beyond the scope of the present article, whose goal is to show what is known in broad terms and to point out logical directions for future study.

Method

Literature Search

First, extensive manual searches of the medical and psychological literature were performed, covering a time span from 1945 to 1984. *Psychological Abstracts* was searched using the following key words or phrases: "disorders," "psychosomatic disorders," "cardiovascular disorders," "myocardial infarction," "asthma," "gastrointestinal ulcers," "headache," and "migraine headache." (*Psychological Abstracts* does not include "arthritis" as a topic listing.) *Index Medicus* was searched using the following key words or phrases: "personality," "arteriosclerosis," "coronary disease," "myocardial infarction," "asthma," "peptic ulcer," "rheumatoid arthritis," "headache," and "migraine." Second, additional articles were located using the bibliographies of the articles already located. Third, those journals that yielded the largest number of suitable articles in the first two steps of the literature search were manually searched from cover to cover. These journals were *Journal of Behavioral Medicine, Journal of Chronic Disease, Journal of Psychosomatic Research*, and *Psychosomatic Medicine*.

Criteria for Inclusion in the Meta-Analysis

The literature search yielded a preliminary database of 229 studies. To qualify for inclusion in the meta-analysis, the studies had to meet each of the following criteria. First, the study had to have used at least one of the following aspects of personality as an independent variable: anger, hostility, aggression, depression, anxiety, or extraversion. These personality variables were selected because they are of theoretical interest and have been extensively studied in relation to disease. The first four variables are thought to be related to illness, and the last (extraversion) is thought to be related to ner-

vous system function. Second, the study had to have investigated at least one of the following targeted disease variables: coronary heart disease, asthma, peptic ulcer, rheumatoid arthritis, or headache. A third criterion for inclusion in the meta-analysis was that a study had to have used quantifiable variables and could not have been purely descriptive or anecdotal in nature (such as a case study).

A fourth criterion for inclusion in the meta-analysis was that a study had to contain enough information to allow the estimation of an effect size and significance level. (Effect size tells us how large an effect is, disregarding sample size.) In addition, the result had to be representable as that of a focused statistical test (i.e., a test with one degree of freedom) of the relationship between a personality variable and a disease criterion. When results of focused statistical tests were not provided in an article, they were calculated whenever possible from means and standard deviations or raw data provided in the article. When statistical errors in the original analyses were detected, they were corrected before the study was included in the meta-analysis.

Of the 229 studies yielded by the literature search, 101 studies met all of the above requirements for inclusion and thus were used in the meta-analysis. These studies are listed in the Appendix. Of the 128 studies discarded, 37 were editorial or literature reviews only, 29 lacked sufficient information for estimation of effect sizes and significance levels, 24 had not investigated one of the personality attributes selected as the focus of the present study, 22 were purely descriptive or anecdotal and provided no quantifiable data, and 16 had not investigated one of the disease endpoints selected for focus in the present study.

Personality Variables

Separate meta-analyses were performed for anxiety, depression, and extraversion and for two combinations of personality variables that appeared highly similar—namely, anger/hostility and anger/hostility/aggression. These latter multiple categories were formed for a variety of reasons. In the literature, there is much theoretical confusion regarding the constructs of anger, hostility, and aggression. Whereas many investigators seem to view these three attributes as highly interrelated or even synonymous, others view them as different. However, even among those who distinguish among these constructs, there is a lack of agreement regarding how each should be defined. We tried to classify measures as tapping either anger, hostility, or aggression by using the names and content or descriptions of the measures as a guide. But there were still some measures for which classification was ambiguous, because some measures seemed to assess anger and hostility and some seemed to assess anger, hostility, and aggression. Thus we decided to form two categories: one combining results for anger and hostility and one combining results for anger, hostility, and aggression. In making these classifications, we defined anger as an emotion involving pronounced autonomic arousal, which is precipitated by some real or perceived wrong; hostility as an enduring attitude involving negative feelings and evaluations of other people; and aggression as the actual or intended harming of others.

Thus analyses were performed for the following five personality variables:

1. *Anger/hostility*. This category consists of results obtained for all assessments of anger or hostility—31 of the studies used in the meta-analysis fall into this category.
2. *Anger/hostility/aggression*. This category consists of results obtained for all assessments of anger, hostility, and aggression—42 of the studies in the meta-analysis fall into this category.
3. *Depression*. This category consists of results obtained for all measures of depression—45 of the studies in the meta-analysis fall into this category.
4. *Extraversion*. This category consists of results obtained for all measures of extraversion or sociability—39 of the studies in the meta-analysis fall into this category.
5. *Anxiety*. This category consists of results obtained for all measures of anxiety—43 of the studies in the meta-analysis fall into this category.

Disease Outcomes

The disease outcome categories for which meta-analyses were performed were (a) coronary heart disease (CHD), (b) asthma, (c) ulcers, (d) rheumatoid arthritis, and (e) headaches. The CHD cat-

egory includes myocardial infarction (MI), angina, cardiac death, and global CHD (some combination of MI, angina, coronary insufficiency, and electrocardiographic abnormalities). Diagnosis of MI was based primarily on electrocardiographic findings and history; diagnosis of angina was based primarily on self-report; and diagnosis of cardiac death was based on autopsy findings. The ulcer category includes peptic ulcers only and not, for example, skin ulcers. Ulcer diagnosis was based on X-ray findings and history. The arthritis category includes rheumatoid arthritis only and not, for example, osteoarthritis. Diagnosis of rheumatoid arthritis was based on established medical criteria such as presence of the rheumatoid serum factor, radiological findings, and the presence of symmetrical joint swelling. The headache category includes tension, migraine, and cluster headaches, as well as combinations thereof. Diagnosis of headache was based on self-report.

Of the 101 studies retained in the meta-analysis, 41 studies investigated CHD, 15 investigated asthma, 16 investigated ulcers, 14 investigated arthritis, 10 investigated headaches, 2 investigated asthma, ulcers, and arthritis, 2 investigated asthma and headaches, and 1 investigated asthma and ulcers. In 90 of the 101 studies included in this meta-analysis, the personality–disease relationship was investigated by comparing a group of subjects who had, or later developed, the disease in question with a group of subjects who did not have the disease. In the 11 studies that did not use this case-control approach, a sample of subjects who had the disease in question was identified, and disease severity was related to one or more personality measures.

Ninety of the 101 studies included in this meta-analysis were cross-sectional in design; the other 11 studies were prospective. Ten of the 11 prospective studies investigated CHD, and the other one investigated ulcers.

Meta-Analytic Techniques Used

In the present study, the product-moment correlation coefficient (r) was used as the effect size estimate because it is easily interpretable and is readily computed from either chi-square, t, F, d, or standard normal deviate Z. Combined or average effect sizes, indexed by the correlation coefficient, were computed by (a) transforming each r into a

Fisher's z coefficient, (b) summing these Fisher's zs, (c) dividing the sum by the number of studies (or "raw" effect sizes used), and (d) transforming the resulting Fisher's z back into an r (Rosenthal, 1984). For combining significance levels, the Stouffer method of adding standard normal deviate Zs (Mosteller & Bush, 1954) was used. This method was selected because it is both routinely applicable and simple.

Indices (rs and Zs) were given positive signs when they were in the predicted direction and negative signs when in the opposite direction. For each personality variable, we predicted (for the sake of simplicity) that individuals who had "more" of the personality attribute in question would have a greater extent of, or be more likely to have, each of the illnesses being considered. For example, subjects scoring higher on depression, anxiety, and so forth were predicted to have a greater extent of, or be more likely to have, asthma, ulcers, and so forth than those who scored lower on these variables.

In addition to computing Pearson rs, Zs, and probability levels, for each analysis a "fail-safe N" (Rosenthal, 1984) was also computed. The fail-safe N was devised by Rosenthal as a protection against the bias introduced by the fact that studies obtaining nonsignificant findings are less likely to be published than those with significant findings. The fail-safe N is an estimate of the number of unpublished, nonsignificant studies that would have to exist for the obtained probability value to be rendered nonsignificant (p > .05).

Of the 101 studies used in the meta-analysis, 9 failed to report the actual effect size or probability value obtained but indicated that the results were statistically significant at a certain probability level (typically .05). In these cases, the effect size used in the meta-analysis was the smallest value that was statistically significant at the specified level. This is a conservative approach because, on the average, the actual effect sizes would have been larger than the assumed values that were used. Another 14 studies failed to report the effect size or probability value obtained but stated that the results were not statistically significant. In one set of analyses, we simply excluded these studies; in a second set of analyses, we assumed these effect sizes to be equivalent to a zero correlation. Again, the latter approach is conservative.

Some of the studies selected for inclusion in the meta-analysis reported results for more than one personality measure, personality variable, or disease. Because, strictly speaking, the procedures of meta-analysis rest on the assumptions of independence of effect sizes and probability levels (Rosenthal, 1984), in this review we allowed each sample to contribute only one effect size per personality variable. In cases in which a study reported different effect sizes based on different measures of the same personality variable (e.g., different measures of anxiety) for the same sample, we used the mean of the relevant effect sizes. In the few articles in which results for a personality variable were reported for more than one independent sample, we allowed each sample to contribute an effect size.

Results

The quantitative summary results are presented in Tables 20.1 and 20.2. Table 20.1 shows the results obtained when studies with unspecified, nonsignificant effect sizes were excluded; Table 20.2 includes those studies, giving them zero effect size, a very conservative approach. The personality and disease categories are listed in the leftmost column, followed by the combined correlation coefficient (r), the number of published studies, the number of independent samples, the Z statistic, the significance level, and the fail-safe N.

Overall, the average magnitude of the relationship between personality problems (depression, anxiety, hostility) and disease appears to be in the range of about .10 to .25 when stated in terms of the correlation coefficient r. Because of unreliabilities in measuring both personality and disease, the true relationship may be somewhat higher. Although the magnitude of this relationship is small when compared to those found in certain realms of experimental psychology, it is moderate or high when compared to other medical risk factors. For example, in the well-known prospective Framingham and Western Collaborative Group studies of heart disease, the correlations between cholesterol and CHD, and between smoking and CHD, were all under .15. (Greater amounts of variance explained sometimes result when synergistic interactive effects occur.)

It would be a mistake to dismiss these relationships as accounting for "only 4% of the variance"

TABLE 20.1. Results of Meta-Analysis of Personality and Disease Relationships With Assumed Effect Sizes of Zero Not Included

Disease and personality variable	Combined r	No. of articles	No. of samples	z	p	Fail-safe N
CHD and anxiety	.136	14	14	5.58	<.0000001	148
CHD and depression	.238	12	10	6.35	<.0000001	140
CHD and anger/hostility/aggression	.143	20	24	7.09	<.0000001	422
CHD and anger/hostility	.167	15	17	7.26	<.0000001	315
CHD and extraversion	.078	11	14	3.01	.0013	33
Asthma and anxiety	.362	9	13	12.66	<.0000001	757
Asthma and depression	.167	6	8	3.98	.00003	39
Asthma and anger/hostility/aggression	.224	8	10	4.46	.000004	64
Asthma and anger/hostility	.258	6	9	5.35	<.0000001	87
Asthma and extraversion	−.132	5	5	−1.89	.0297	2
Ulcer and anxiety	.186	7	7	4.71	.000001	51
Ulcer and depression	.079	7	7	2.85	.0022	15
Ulcer and anger/hostility/aggression	−.031	7	8	−.09	.4623	—
Ulcer and anger/hostility	−.014	6	7	.15	.4410	—
Ulcer and extraversion	−.174	6	7	−2.62	.0044	11
Arthritis and anxiety	.200	7	9	5.83	<.0000001	105
Arthritis and depression	.156	9	11	7.08	<.0000001	193
Arthritis and anger/hostility/aggression	.147	2	3	3.26	.0006	9
Arthritis and anger/hostility	.158	2	3	3.77	.00008	13
Arthritis and extraversion	−.175	4	4	−2.54	.0056	6
Headache and anxiety	.205	3	5	3.89	.00005	23
Headache and depression	.187	7	9	5.49	<.0000001	92
Headache and anger/hostility/aggression	.052	1	2	.52	.3016	—
Headache and anger/hostility	−.013	1	2	−.13	.4502	—
Headache and extraversion	.089	6	9	2.02	.0216	5

Note. CHD = coronary heart disease.

(Rosenthal & Rubin, 1982). In a population of hundreds of millions of people, a true causal factor accounting for 4% of the variance refers to thousands of lives yearly. For example, a relative risk of two—meaning that those with the risk factor are twice as likely to suffer the disease than those without it—would typically translate into a correlation coefficient of just about this magnitude. Or, stated differently, assuming that there are equal numbers of people with and without the predictor (risk factor) in question, then an effect size of "only" .20 could mean the difference between a 60% incidence of the disease (in people with the predictor) versus only 40% incidence (in those without the predictor; Rosenthal & Rubin, 1982). In short, the risks associated with the personality factors investigated in this review seem to be of meaningful size and of the same order of magnitude as more well-established risk factors such as cigarette smoking in CHD.

The size of the relationships revealed in our analyses helps explain in part why the links between personality and disease are such elusive phenomena. For a correlation of .15, a sample size of 300 is necessary for the effect to be significant at the .01 level. Traditional, relatively small-sample studies in psychology are therefore inappropriate for studying these links. Their statistical power is too low. Rather, large-scale studies such as those traditionally done by epidemiologists will be necessary for the detection of these modest but probably important associations.

Specific Findings

As can be seen in Tables 20.1 and 20.2, all five personality variable categories were found to have positive and reliable associations with coronary heart disease. Higher levels of anxiety, depression, anger, hostility, aggression, and extraversion are

TABLE 20.2. Results of Meta-Analysis of Personality and Disease Relationships With Assumed Effect Sizes of Zero Included

Disease and personality variable	Combined r	No. of articles	No. of samples	z	p'	Fail-safe N
CHD and anxiety	.115	14	14	4.90	.0000005	111
CHD and depression	.217	13	11	6.06	<.0000001	139
CHD and anger/hostility/aggression	.136	21	25	6.78	<.0000001	400
CHD and anger/hostility	.162	16	18	7.10	<.0000001	318
CHD and extraversion	.067	11	14	2.69	.0035	24
Asthma and anxiety	.317	11	15	12.72	<.0000001	882
Asthma and depression	.149	7	9	3.75	.00009	38
Asthma and anger/hostility/aggression	.201	11	14	5.13	.0000002	123
Asthma and anger/hostility	.234	7	10	5.07	.0000002	85
Asthma and extraversion	−.095	7	7	−1.59	.0555	—
Ulcer and anxiety	.163	8	8	4.41	.000005	50
Ulcer and depression	.069	8	8	2.66	.0039	13
Ulcer and anger/hostility/aggression	−.027	8	9	−.09	.4640	—
Ulcer and anger/hostility	−.013	7	8	.14	.4447	—
Ulcer and extraversion	−.136	8	9	−2.31	.0104	9
Arthritis and anxiety	.200	7	9	5.83	<.0000001	105
Arthritis and depression	.137	11	14	6.75	<.0000001	222
Arthritis and anger/hostility/aggression	.111	3	4	2.82	.0024	8
Arthritis and anger/hostility	.158	2	3	3.77	.00008	13
Arthritis and extraversion	−.103	8	9	−2.10	.0180	6
Headache and anxiety	.205	3	5	3.89	.00005	23
Headache and depression	.180	8	11	5.54	<.0000001	114
Headache and anger/hostility/aggression	.052	1	2	.52	.3016	—
Headache and anger/hostility	−.013	1	2	−.13	.4502	—
Headache and extraversion	.063	8	12	1.39	.0828	—

Note. CHD = coronary heart disease.

associated with a greater likelihood of heart disease. Moreover, the combined effect sizes for anxiety, anger/hostility, anger/hostility/aggression, and depression are of similar magnitude to that observed between Type A behavior and CHD (Booth-Kewley & Friedman, 1987).

Regarding asthma, the variables of anxiety, depression, and anger/hostility/aggression are again positively and reliably associated with disease, but higher levels of introversion are associated with asthma. The pattern of results that emerged for rheumatoid arthritis is similar to that found for asthma, but the correlations are some what weaker. For ulcers, associations with anger, hostility, and aggression are not significant. For headaches, anxiety and depression show positive and reliable associations with illness.

Overall Findings

Overall, the degree of consistency across diseases is quite remarkable. If there were an "arthritic per-sonality," a "coronary-prone personality," and so on, then we would expect clear evidence of independent association between particular aspects of personality and the particular diseases. For example, a casual reader of the current medical literature might expect CHD to be related to hostility but not depression, and arthritis to be related to depression but not hostility. Such differences were not generally found. These findings do not rule out the possibility that such illness-specific disease-prone personalities will eventually be discovered, but such a direction for research does not seem promising at present. The consistency of the findings presented here also argues against the idea that specific diseases cause specific personality problems through direct physiological mechanisms (which is one version of a somatopsychic hypothesis).

Perhaps the most striking single relationship is the apparent association between depression and disease (in particular, depression and the four diseases other than ulcers). In recent years, a great deal of attention has been directed to anger and hostility, but perhaps insufficient attention has been given to depression.

One deviation from the generally consistent pattern concerns extraversion. Small associations were found between CHD and headaches and being extraverted, whereas asthma, ulcers, and arthritis tended to be associated with being introverted.

The most intensive research has been directed at coronary heart disease, including some prospective studies. A breakdown of prospective versus concurrent studies is shown in Table 20.3. As can be seen, the prospective evidence through 1984 is almost as strong as the concurrent evidence. In many ways, the CHD research is the most reliable and believable, having received serious attention during the past 25 years. Yet the pattern of relationships between personality and CHD shows sufficient resemblance to that between personality and the other diseases to suggest the tentative conclusion that these other relationships are also real. Unfortunately, there is not yet enough published research to allow further statistical blocking analyses on the other diseases.

Illness Behaviors

If personality is correlated with disease because of artifacts associated with the way that disease is assessed, then we should find stronger associations where there is a greater degree of shared method variance. For example, diagnosis of headaches and, to some extent, of asthma depends on interviews and self-report measures, as does the assessment of personality. However, the results show that the other diseases also show substantial (and comparable) associations with personality.

In the case of coronary heart disease, both kinds of assessment apply—"soft" and "hard" criteria. Diagnosis of angina relies heavily on patients' reports, whereas diagnosis of myocardial infarction (heart attack) relies very little on the patients' reports. Costa and McRae (1985) argued that neuroticism predicts angina but not MI; however, they did not include all of the relevant studies in their analysis and, more important, did not compute average effect sizes. We therefore analyzed relationships separately for angina and MI; these analyses are presented in Table 20.4. (The MI category includes cardiac death for the prospective studies.) As can be clearly seen, the associations between personality and CHD certainly do not disappear when MI is used as the endpoint. Thus, the associations between personality and CHD are not due to this type of measurement artifact.

A second, more subtle, type of artifact (that could inflate personality-to-disease associations) could arise as a function of the control group used in a study. Basically a subject selection bias, this artifact can occur if certain people are more likely than others to enter the health care system. For example, if patients at a headache clinic are more depressed than the population as a whole (i.e., than the norm groups), an artificial personality-to-disease correlation will result if there are many people with headaches who are not depressed, do not enter the headache clinic, and so are not included in the study. However, in addition to being difficult to evaluate, such artifacts are not readily subjected to meta-analysis due to the wide variety of research designs employed. Nevertheless, because of the potential importance of this issue, we evaluated those non-CHD studies in our sample that measured depression, anxiety, or anger/hostility/aggression in terms of the nature of the subject samples.

TABLE 20.3. Combined Correlations Between Personality and Coronary Heart Disease for Prospective Versus Concurrent Studies

Personality variable	Prospective studies			Concurrent studies		
	Combined r	No. of samples	p	Combined r	No. of samples	p
Anxiety	.136	2	<.0000001	.122	13	.0002
Depression	.203	2	.0001	.204	11	<.0000001
Anger/hostility/aggression	.101	6	.0024	.135	19	<.0000001
Anger/hostility	.101	6	.0024	.169	15	<.0000001
Extraversion	—	—	—	.078	14	.0013

TABLE 20.4. Meta-Analysis of Personality and Myocardial Infarction (MI) Versus Angina

CHD category and personality variable	Combined r	No. of articles	No. of samples	z	p	Fail-safe N
With assumed effect sizes of zero not included						
MI and anxiety	.179	10	9	4.07	.00002	47
MI and depression	.259	9	7	5.24	<.0000001	65
MI and anger/hostility/aggression	.120	13	13	3.65	.0001	51
MI and anger/hostility	.151	10	11	4.22	.00001	62
MI and extraversion	.099	8	11	3.39	.0004	36
Angina and anxiety	.100	2	2	5.49	<.0000001	21
Angina and depression	.165	4	3	4.29	.000009	18
Angina and anger/hostility/aggression	.280	2	2	3.59	.0002	8
Angina and anger/hostility	.280	2	2	3.59	.0002	8
Angina and extraversion	−.137	2	2	−2.38	.0087	3
With assumed effect sizes of zero included						
MI and anxiety	.179	10	9	4.07	.00002	47
MI and depression	.259	9	7	5.24	<.0000001	65
MI and anger/hostility/aggression	.114	14	14	3.47	.0003	49
MI and anger/hostility	.143	11	12	4.02	.00003	60
MI and extraversion	.099	8	11	3.39	.0004	36

Note. There were no studies of angina with assumed effect sizes of zero. CHD = coronary heart disease.

Studies in which the cases and controls were both in or out of the medical care system were compared to studies in which the cases were in the medical care system but the controls were not. In some studies there was not enough information given to permit classification, and in general, the number of studies in each group was quite small, precluding formal meta-analysis. However, the results of this rough comparison were consistent overall in indicating that the correlations between personality and disease were somewhat smaller when cases and controls were both either inside or outside the medical care system. For example, the combined correlation between asthma and anxiety was about .35 when the cases were in the medical system and the controls were not, but this decreased to a correlation of about .31 when cases and controls were both in or both out of the medical system. Although this sort of comparison is very rough and the number of studies is very small, it appears that this type of artifact may sometimes be occurring. Therefore, future reviews and future research designs should take this factor into account.

Discussion

Chronic diseases such as asthma, migraines, arthritis, ulcers, and CHD afflict millions of Americans, cost billions of dollars in medical expenses and missed work, and cause untold suffering. To the extent that these diseases are "psychosomatic"—that is, caused or catalyzed in part by psychological factors—tremendous opportunity exists for improving the health of the population. Is the relationship between personality and disease fact or folklore? Is the size of any such relationship comparable to that of other disease risk factors? Where should future research be most profitably directed?

A meta-analytic review helps bring the critical issues into focus. Different studies have used different personality measures, different disease criteria, different populations, and different control groups. These variations make simple meta-analytic interpretation problematic, but they do provide a degree of external validity uncommon in psychological research. Furthermore, meta-analysis directs our attention to the data, to the size of the relationships being uncovered, and to the questions needing additional attention. Meta-analysis makes any single finding (or failure to replicate) less important. It reminds us that Type I and Type II errors do exist, in which a single study can find a relationship that is not real or can fail to uncover a relationship that is real. Several very reliable findings *did* emerge from our review and raise specific questions for future research.

As Rosenthal (1984) has noted, generalizing across studies is in some ways analogous to generalizing across persons ("subjects"). When we find a significant influence of a psychological variable in a single experiment, there is always error variance—which means that not everyone in the study responded in the same way. Still, we are satisfied with the significant relationship discovered, and we believe that future research will explain some more of the error variance. With meta-analysis, there is also "error" variance—not all of the studies show the same result. Yet readers of a meta-analysis sometimes seem unduly bothered by these discrepancies. There is a tendency to want to go back and look at the particular deviant studies and try to explain why they differ. Such an analysis is fine *if it means additional empirical research.* Unfortunately, excessive desire for closure may result in post hoc rationalization in a hasty search for clarity. For example, examination may reveal that discrepant studies may differ on age factors, diet factors, employment factors, socialization factors, or many other factors that may affect health. Excessive speculation, unaccompanied by new empirical work, defeats the purpose of meta-analysis. We fervently hope that the questions raised by the present review and analysis will be answered with well-designed new research and not with speculations about old studies.

The Disease-Prone Personality

An important question influencing future research in psychology and health is whether or not various diseases seem to be associated with particular personalities. Based on the existing evidence, it does *not* appear that different diseases have different personality traits linked with them. If this finding holds up in future research, then constructs such as the asthma-prone personality, the coronary-prone personality, and so on will have to be revised. However, there may well exist a generic "disease-prone personality."

Although our analysis suggests that personality may play some causal role in the development or progression of coronary heart disease and perhaps in other diseases as well, the existing evidence is relatively weak. Most of the studies are retrospective, and many have insufficiently large sample sizes. The interrelationships among personality predictors are not known, and the possible moderating role played by unhealthy behaviors has not been much studied. No detailed physiological process linking personality and disease has been established.

On the other hand, the accumulated evidence is definitely not inconsistent with a causal role for personality. The empirical evidence is consistent across research domains, across diseases, and across a wide variety of methods. The size of the relationships between personality and disease was found to be comparable to that which exists between many well-known risk factors and disease. The idea of a generic disease-prone personality is also supported by a recent cluster analysis of the relationship of MMPI scores and illness (Stanwyck & Anson, 1986), which found that patients having heart disease, arthritis, asthma, cancer, and headaches score as moderately but not extremely neurotic (i.e., high on the MMPI Hypochondriasis, Depression, and Hysteria scales). Overall, the data seem much too consistent to warrant dismissing the link between personality and disease as "folklore."

One additional source of evidence supporting the probability of some sort of a causal role for personality comes from an intervention study regarding heart disease. In that study, over 800 victims of myocardial infarction were randomly assigned to receive or not to receive psychological counseling to reduce Type A characteristics (Friedman et al., 1984). Over a 3-year period, those receiving the counseling had a significantly reduced rate of recurrence of nonfatal MIs. Although Type A behavior is often summarized as "hurry sickness," it is instructive to examine the nature of the psychological intervention used in this study. It consisted of extensive instruction in progressive muscle relaxation, modification of exaggerated emotional reactions, self-management, and establishment of new values and goals. It seems likely that such counseling would also have been effective in dealing with anxiety, hostility, and depression (in addition to Type A personality). Although this study yielded valuable evidence concerning the role of personality in causing heart attacks, it would have been even better if other aspects of personality had been measured and if other diseases had also been included. Perhaps attention should be focused less on changing the Type A personality style of heart attack victims and more on promoting psychological well-being in the broader population.

It is also interesting to note that there is no good evidence that the personality-to-disease link is created by disease-caused personality changes. Given the bulk of the evidence, it is not sensible to make too much of any single study's failure to show an association between personality and the subsequent development of a particular disease, as Angell (1985) and others have done. Rather, our analysis points out the type of evidence that would be necessary to interpret the disease-prone personality as "folklore." Relevant evidence would include (a) studies that intervene to reduce psychological dysfunction but show no improvement in health over the long term (compared to a control group); (b) population survey studies (with representative samples) that show no association between personality and disease; (c) biological studies that show it to be unlikely that chronic psychological state could affect disease-relevant physiological processes; and (d) prospective studies that show that disease produces predictable changes in personality.

In sum, given existing evidence, it may be that Selye's (1976) general adaptation syndrome is closer to the truth than the sundry psychosomatic formulations that have been advanced over the past century. Personality may function like diet: Imbalances can predispose one to all sorts of diseases. Such a conclusion is supported by the considerable evidence emerging from physiological studies. Although the precise physiological pathways appear to be complex, psychological disturbance seems to produce systemic effects on immune system function and on metabolic processes, rather than effects on particular organs. However, we simply do not know enough at present to answer certain key questions about causality; but we do know enough to direct our efforts in certain promising directions.

Future Research

Because most studies do not examine more than one or two aspects of personality, it is impossible to tell whether each aspect acts independently of, interactively with, or redundantly with the other aspects. For example, there has been speculation about the deleterious physiological effects of chronic anger and the deleterious physiological effects of chronic depression. Are disease-prone people both angry and depressed or angry but not depressed, or is either of these states sufficient? This is a question that deserves immediate attention.

Analogously, attention should be addressed to the relationships among various chronic diseases, with an eye toward underlying third variables. For example, there is an association between migraines and irritable bowel syndrome (IBS; Schuster, 1983). When we have a firmer understanding of how various aspects of personality relate to various diseases, it will become easier to theorize about likely physiological processes that underlie these relationships.

Regardless of the direction of causality, there is strong evidence of a reliable association between illness and chronic psychological distress. Hence, treatment of medical patients by health psychologists and clinical psychologists seems prudent and worthwhile. At the very least, such interventions may improve the psychological adjustment among a high-risk population. Such interventions may also have a beneficial effect on the progression or recurrence of serious chronic illness. Of course, it is equally important to avoid exaggerating the existing evidence. Only vigorous and sustained research can ultimately establish the utility of psychological interventions in preventing and alleviating chronic illness.

ACKNOWLEDGMENTS

This research was supported in part by a University of California, Riverside intramural research grant. We wish to thank John Ashe, Robert Kaplan, James Kulik, Tracey Revenson, Carrie Saetermoe, and Miriam Schustack for helpful comments.

REFERENCES

Adams, H. E., Feuerstein, M., & Fowler, J. (1980). Migraine headaches: Review of parameters, etiology, and intervention. *Psychological Bulletin, 87,* 217–237.

Ader, R. (Ed.). (1981). *Psychoneuroimmunology*. New York: Academic Press.

Ader, R., & Cohen, N. (1985). CNS–immune system interaction: Conditioning phenomena. *Behavioral and Brain Sciences, 8,* 379–394.

Alexander, F. (1950). *Psychosomatic medicine*. New York: Norton.

Allport, G. W. (1961). *Pattern and growth in personality*. New York: Holt, Rinehart & Winston.

Anderson, K. O., Bradley, L. A., Young, L. D., McDaniel, L. K., & Wise, C. M. (1985). Rheumatoid arthritis: Review of psychological factors related to etiology, effects, and treatment. *Psychological Bulletin, 98,* 358–387.

Angell, M. (1985). Disease as a reflection of the psyche. *New England Journal of Medicine, 312*, 1570–1572.

Bakal. D. A. (1977). Headache: A biopsychological perspective. *Psychological Bulletin, 82*, 369–382.

Bihldorf, J. P., King, S. H., & Parnes, L. R. (1971). Psychological factors in headache. *Headache, 11*, 117–127.

Booth-Kewley, S., & Friedman, H. S. (1987). Psychological predictors of heart disease: A quantitative review. *Psychological Bulletin, 101*, 343–362.

Buck, R. (1984). *The communication of emotion.* New York: Guilford Press.

Cattell, R. B., & Scheier, I. H. (1961). *The meaning and measurement of neuroticism and anxiety.* New York: Ronald Press.

Chesney, M. A., & Rosenman, R. H. (Eds.). (1985). *Anger and hostility in cardiovascular and behavioral disorders.* New York: Hemisphere.

Cohen, F., & Lazarus, R. S. (1979). Coping with the stresses of illness. In G. C. Stone, F. Cohen, & N. E. Adler (Eds.), *Health psychology: A handbook* (pp. 217–254). San Francisco: Jossey-Bass.

Cohen, F., & Lazarus, R. S. (1983). Coping and adaptation in illness. In D. Mechanic (Ed.), *Handbook of health, health care, and the health professions* (pp. 608–635). New York: Free Press.

Costa, P. T., & McCrae, R. R. (1985). Hypochondriasis, neuroticism, and aging: When are somatic complaints unfounded? *American Psychologist, 40*, 19–28.

Creer, T. (1978). Asthma: Psychological aspects and management. In E. Middleton, C. Reed, & E. Ellis (Eds.), *Allergy: Principles and practice* (Vol. 2, pp. 796–811). St. Louis, MO: Mosby.

DiMatteo, M. R., & Friedman, H. S. (1982). *Social psychology and medicine.* Cambridge, MA: Oelgeschlager, Gunn, & Hain.

Dohrenwend, B. S., & Dohrenwend, B. P. (1974). *Stressful life events: Their nature and effects.* New York: Wiley.

Dunbar, F. H. (1943). *Psychosomatic diagnosis.* New York: Harper.

Dunkel-Schetter, C., & Wortman, C. (1982). The interpersonal dynamics of cancer: Problems in social relationships and their impact on the patient. In H. S. Friedman & M. R. DiMatteo (Eds.), *Interpersonal issues in health care.* New York: Academic Press.

Engel, G. L. (1967). The concept of psychosomatic disorder. *Journal of Psychosomatic Research, 11*, 3–9.

Eysenck, H. J. (1967). *The biological basis of personality.* Springfield, IL: Charles C. Thomas.

Freud, S. (1955). *Collected works: Vol. 2. Studies on hysteria.* New York: Hogarth Press.

Friedman, M., & Rosenman, R. H. (1974). *Type A behavior and your heart.* New York: Knopf.

Friedman, M., Thoresen, C., Gill, J., Powell, L., Ulmer, D., Thompson, L., et al. (1984). Alteration of Type A behavior and reduction in cardiac occurrences in postmyocardial infarction patients. *American Heart Journal, 108*, 237–248.

Glass, G. V., McGaw, B., & Smith, M. L. (1981). *Meta-analysis in social research.* Beverly Hills, CA: Sage.

Goodkin, K., Antoni, M. H., & Blaney, P. H. (1986). Stress and hopelessness in the promotion of cervical intrapithelial neoplasis to invasive squamous cell carcinoma of the cervix. *Journal of Psychosomatic Research, 30*, 67–76.

Holmes, T. H., & Rahe, R. H. (1967). The social readjustment rating scale. *Journal of Psychosomatic Research, 11*, 213–218.

Jemmott, J. B., & Locke, S. E. (1984). Psychosocial factors, immunological mediation, and human susceptibility to infectious diseases: How much do we know? *Psychological Bulletin, 95*, 78–108.

Kahn, J. P., Kornfeld, D. S., Frank, K. A., Heller, S. S., & Hoar, P. F. (1980). Type A behavior and blood pressure during coronary artery bypass surgery. *Psychosomatic Medicine, 42*, 407–414.

Kanter, V. B., & Sandler, J. (1955). Studies in psychopathology using a self-assessment inventory. *British Journal of Medical Psychology, 28*, 157–166.

Kasl, S. V., & Cobb, S. (1969). The intrafamilial transmission of rheumatoid arthritis. *Journal of Chronic Diseases, 22*, 239–258.

Katz, I. R. (1982). Is there a hypoxic affective syndrome? *Psychosomatics, 23*, 846–853.

Kiviniemi, P. (1977). Emotions and personality in rheumatoid arthritis. *Scandanavian Journal of Rheumatology, 6*(Suppl. 18), 1–132.

Kobasa, S. (1979). Stressful life events, personality and health: An inquiry into hardiness. *Journal of Personality and Social Psychology, 37*, 1–11.

Krantz, D. S., Baum, A., & Singer, J. E. (Eds.). (1983). *Handbook of psychology and health: Vol. 3. Cardiovascular disorders and behavior.* Hillsdale, NJ: Erlbaum.

Krantz, D. S., & Durel, L. (1983). Psychobiological substrates of the Type A behavior pattern. *Health Psychology, 2*, 393–411.

Levy, S. (1985). *Behavior and cancer.* San Francisco: Jossey-Bass.

Light, R. J., & Pillemer, D. B. (1984). *Summing up: The science of reviewing research.* Cambridge, MA: Harvard University Press.

Marshall, S. (1960). Personality correlates of peptic ulcer patients. *Journal of Consulting Psychology, 24*, 218–223.

Marx, J. (1985). "Anxiety peptide" found in brain. *Science, 227*, 934.

Mason, J. H., Weener, J. L., Gertman, P. M., & Meenan, R. F. (1983). Health status in chronic disease: A comparative study of rheumatoid arthritis. *Journal of Rheumatology, 10*, 763–768.

Mechanic, D. (1978). *Medical sociology* (2nd ed.). New York: Free Press.

Moos, R. H. (1964). Personality factors associated with rheumatoid arthritis. *Journal of Chronic Diseases, 17*, 41–55.

Mosteller, F. M., & Bush, R. R. (1954). Selected quantitative techniques. In G. Lindzey (Ed.), *Handbook of social psychology: Vol. 1. Theory and method* (pp. 289–334). Reading, MA: Addison-Wesley.

Murdock, G. P. (1980). *Theories of illness: A world survey.* Pittsburgh, PA: University of Pittsburgh Press.

Pavlov, I. P. (1927). *Conditioned reflexes: An investigation of the physiological activity of the cerebral cortex.* Oxford, England: Oxford University Press.

Rosenthal, R. (1984). *Meta-analytic procedures for social research.* Beverly Hills, CA: Sage.

Rosenthal, R., & Rubin, D. B. (1982). A simple, general purpose display of magnitude of experimental effect. *Journal of Educational Psychology, 74*, 166–169.

Schmale, A. H. (1958). Relationship of separation and depression to disease. *Psychosomatic Medicine, 20*, 259–277.

Schuster, M. M. (1983). Irritable bowel syndrome. In M. H. Sleisenger & J. S. Fortran (Eds.), *Gastrointestinal diseases: Pathophysiology, diagnosis, and management* (3rd ed., pp. 880–895). Philadelphia: W. B. Saunders.

Selye, H. (1976). *The stress of life* (rev. ed.). New York: McGraw-Hill.

Shekelle, R. B., Hulley, S. B., Neaton, J. D., Billings, J. H., Borhani, N. O., Gerace, T. A., Jacobs, D. R.. Lasser, N. L., Mittlemark, M. B., & Stamler, J. for the Multiple Risk Factor Intervention Trial Research Group. (1985). The MRFIT behavior pattern study. II. Type A behavior and incidence of coronary heart disease. *American Journal of Epidemiology, 122,* 559–570.

Siltanen, P., Lauroma, M., Nirkoo, O., Punsar, S., Pyorala, K., Tuominen, H., & Vanhala, K. (1975). Psychological characteristics related to coronary heart disease. *Journal of Psychosomatic Research, 19,* 183–195.

Soll, A. H., & Isenberg, J. I. (1983). Duodenal ulcer diseases. In M. H. Sleisenger & J. S. Fortran (Eds.), *Gastrointestinal diseases: Pathophysiology, diagnosis, and management* (3rd ed., pp. 625–672). Philadelphia: W. B. Saunders.

Solomon, G. F. (1985). The emerging field of psychoneurimmunology. *Advances: Journal of the Institute for the Advancement of Health, 2,* 6–19.

Sontag, S. (1974). *Illness as metaphor.* New York: Farrar, Straus & Giroux.

Stanwyck, D., & Anson, C. (1986). Is personality related to illness: Cluster profiles of aggregated data. *Advances, Institute for the Advancement of Health, 3,* 4–15.

Thomas, C. B., Ross, D. C., & Duszynski, K. R. (1975). Youthful hypercholesteremia: Its associated characteristics and role in premature myocardial infarctions. *The Johns Hopkins Medical Journal, 136,* 193–208.

van Dijl, H. (1979). Myocardial infarction patients and sociability. *Journal of Psychosomatic Research, 23,* 3–6.

van Dijl, H. (1982). Myocardial infarction patients and heightened aggressiveness/hostility. *Journal of Psychosomatic Research, 26,* 203–208.

Weiner, H. (1977). *Psychobiology and human disease.* New York: Elsevier.

Weiner, H., Thaler, M., Reiser, M. F., & Mirsky, I. A. (1957). Etiology of duodenal ulcer. *Psychosomatic Medicine, 19,* 1–10.

Weiss, J. M. (1968). Effects of coping response of stress. *Journal of Comparative and Physiological Psychology, 65,* 251–260.

Weiss, J. M. (1971). Effects of coping behavior in different warning signal conditions on stress pathology in rats. *Journal of Comparative and Physiological Psychology, 77,* 1–13.

Zajonc, R. B. (1985). Emotion and facial efference: A theory reclaimed. *Science, 228,* 15–21.

APPENDIX: STUDIES USED IN THE META-ANALYSIS

Aaron, N. S. (1967). Some personality differences between asthmatic, allergic and normal children. *Journal of Clinical Psychology, 23,* 336–340.

Agarwal, K., & Sethi, J. P. (1978). A study of psychogenic factors in bronchial asthma. *Journal of Asthma Research, 15,* 191–198.

Aitken, R. C. B., Zealley, A. K., & Rosenthal, S. V. (1969). Psychological and physiological measures of emotion in chronic asthmatic patients. *Journal of Psychosomatic Research, 13,* 289–297.

Alp, M. H., Court, J. H., & Grant, A. K. (1970). Personality pattern and emotional stress in the genesis of gastric ulcer. *Gut, 11,* 773–777.

Apter, A., & Hurst, L. A. (1973). Personality and duodenal ulcer. *South African Medical Journal, 47,* 2131–2133.

Arrowood, M. E., Uhrich, K., Gomillion, C., Popio, K. A., & Raft, D. (1982). New markers of coronary prone behavior in a rural population. *Psychosomatic Medicine, 44,* 119. (Abstract)

Bakker, C. B., & Levenson, R. M. (1967). Determinants of angina pectoris. *Psychosomatic Medicine, 29,* 621–633.

Barefoot, J. C., Dahlstrom, W. G., & Williams, R. B. (1983). Hostility, CHD incidence, and total mortality: A 25-year follow-up study of 255 physicians. *Psychosomatic Medicine, 45,* 59–64.

Barendregt, J. T. (1957). A cross-validation study of the hypothesis of psychosomatic specificity with special reference to bronchial asthma. *Journal of Psychosomatic Research, 2,* 109–114.

Barolin, G. S. (1976). Brief report: Headache and depression. *Headache, 16,* 252–253.

Bendien, J., & Groen, J. (1963). A psychological-statistical study of neuroticism and extraversion in patients with myo-

cardial infarction. *Journal of Psychosomatic Research, 7,* 11–14.

Bengtsson, C., Hallstrom, T., & Tibblin, G. (1973). Social factors, stress experience, and personality traits in women with ischemic heart disease, compared to a population sample of women. *Acta Medica Scandinavica, 549*(Supplement), 82–92.

Benjamin, S. (1977). Is asthma a psychosomatic illness? II. A comparative study of response impairment and mental health. *Journal of Psychosomatic Research, 21,* 471–481.

Bianchi, G., Fergusson, D., & Walshe, J. (1978). Psychiatric antecedents of myocardial infarction. *Medical Journal of Australia, 1,* 297–301.

Bihldorff, J. P., King, S. H., & Parnes, L. R. (1971). Psychological factors in headache. *Headache, 11,* 117–127.

Blumenthal, J. A., Thompson, L. W., Williams, R. B., & Kong, Y. (1979). Anxiety-proneness and coronary heart disease. *Journal of Psychosomatic Research, 23,* 17–21.

Bourestom, N. C., & Howard, M. T. (1965). Personality characteristics of three disability groups. *Archives of Physical Medicine and Rehabilitation, 46,* 626–632.

Bruhn, J. G., Chandler, B., & Wolf, S. (1969). A psychological study of survivors and nonsurvivors of myocardial infarction. *Psychosomatic Medicine, 31,* 8–19.

Cleveland, S. E., & Johnson, D. L. (1962). Personality patterns in young males with coronary disease. *Psychosomatic Medicine, 24,* 600–611.

Couch, J. R., Ziegler, D. K., & Hassanein, R. S. (1975). Evaluation of the relationship between migraine headache and depression. *Headache, 15,* 41–50.

Crisp, A. H., Kalucy, R. S., McGuinness, B., Ralph, P. C., & Harris, G. (1977). Some clinical, social, and psychological characteristics of migraine subjects in the general population. *Postgraduate Medical Journal, 53,* 691–697.

Croog, S. H.. Koslowsky, M., & Levine. S. (1976). Personality self-perceptions of male heart patients and their wives: Issues of congruence and "coronary personality." *Perceptual and Motor Skills, 43,* 927–937.

Crown. J. M., & Crown, S. (1973). The relationship between personality and the presence of rheumatoid factor in early rheumatoid disease. *Scandinavian Journal of Rheumatology, 2,* 123–126.

Dimsdale, J. E., Hutter, A. M., Hackett. T. P., & Block, P. (1981). Predicting extensive coronary artery disease. *Journal of Chronic Diseases, 34,* 513–517.

Gardiner, B. M. (1980). Psychological aspects of rheumatoid arthritis. *Psychological Medicine, 10,* 159–163.

Garvey, M. J., Schaffer. C. B., & Tuason, V. B. (1983). Relationship of headaches to depression. *British Journal of Psychology, 143,* 544–547.

Gillum, R., Leon, G. R., Kamp, J., & Becerra-Aldama, J. (1980). Prediction of cardiovascular and other disease onset and mortality from 30-year longitudinal MMPI data. *Journal of Consulting and Clinical Psychology, 48,* 405–406.

Haynes, S. G.. Feinleib. M., & Kannel, W. B. (1980). The relationship of psychosocial factors to coronary heart disease in the Framingham study: III. Eight year incidence of coronary heart disease. *American Journal of Epidemiology, 111,* 37–58.

Henryk-Gutt. R., & Rees, W. L. (1973). Psychological aspects of migraine. *Journal of Psychosomatic Research, 17,* 141–153.

Herbert. M. (1965). Personality factors and bronchial asthma. *Journal of Psychosomatic Research, 8,* 353–364.

Jacobs, M. A., Spilken, A. Z., Norman, M. M., & Anderson, L. S. (1970). Life stress and respiratory illness. *Psychosomatic Medicine, 32,* 233–242.

Jenkins, C. D., Stanton, B., Klein, M. D., Savageau, J. A., & Harken, D. E. (1983). Correlates of angina pectoris among men awaiting coronary bypass surgery. *Psychosomatic Medicine, 45,* 141–153.

Kanter, V. B., & Hazelton, J. E. (1964). An attempt to measure some aspects of personality in young men with duodenal ulcer by means of questionnaires and a projective test. *Journal of Psychosomatic Research, 8,* 297–309.

Kanter, V. B., & Sandler, J. (1955). Studies in psychopathology using a self-assessment inventory. *British Journal of Medical Psychology, 28,* 157–166.

Kasl, S. V., & Cobb, S. (1969). The intrafamilial transmission of rheumatoid arthritis. *Journal of Chronic Diseases, 22,* 239–258.

Kiviniemi, P. (1977). Emotions and personality in rheumatoid arthritis. *Scandinavian Journal of Rheumatology. 6*(Suppl. 18), 1–132.

Krasner, L. (1953). Personality differences between patients classified as psychosomatic and nonpsychosomatic. *Journal of Abnormal and Social Psychology, 48,* 190–198.

Kudrow. L. (1974). Physical and personality characteristics in cluster headache. *Headache, 13,* 197–202.

Kudrow. L., & Sutkus, B. J. (1979). MMPI pattern specificity in primary headache disorders. *Headache, 19,* 18–24.

Lebovitz, B. Z.. Shekelle, R. B.. Ostfeld, A. M., & Paul, O. (1967). Prospective and retrospective psychological studies of coronary heart disease. *Psychosomatic Medicine, 29,* 265–272.

Leigh, D., & Marley, E. (1956). A psychiatric assessment of adult asthmatics: A statistical study. *Journal of Psychosomatic Research, 1,* 128–136.

Lewinsohn, P. M., (1956). Personality correlates of duodenal ulcer and other psychosomatic reactions. *Journal of Clinical Psychology, 12,* 296–298.

Liang, M. H., Rogers, M., Larson, M., Eaton, H. M., Murawski, B. J., Taylor, J. E., Swafford. J., & Schur, P. H. (1984). The psychosocial impact of systemic lupus erythematosis and rheumatoid arthritis. *Arthritis and Rheumatism, 27,* 13–19.

Lucas, R. N. (1977). Migraine in twins. *Journal of Psychosomatic Research, 21,* 147–156.

Lyketsos, G., Arapakis, G., Psaras, M., Photiou, I., & Blackburn, I. M. (1982). Psychological characteristics of hypertensive and ulcer patients. *Journal of Psychosomatic Research, 26,* 255–262.

Maggini, C., Guazzelli, M., Castrogiovanni, P., Mauri, M., De Lisio, G. F., Chierchia, S., & Cassano, G. B. (1976/1977). Psychological and physiopathological study on coronary patients. *Psychotherapy and Psychosomatics, 27,* 210–216.

Marshall, S. (1960). Personality correlates of peptic ulcer patients. *Journal of Consulting Psychology, 24,* 218–223.

Mason, J. H., Weener, J. L., Gertman, P. M., & Meenan, R. F. (1983). Health status in chronic disease: A comparative study of rheumatoid arthritis. *Journal of Rheumatology, 10,* 763–768.

Matthews, K. A., Glass, D. C., Rosenman, R. H., & Bortner, R. W. (1977). Competitive drive, Pattern A and coronary heart disease: A further analysis of some data from the Western Collaborative Group Study. *Journal of Chronic Diseases, 30,* 489–498.

Medalle, J. H., Snyder, M., Groen, J. J., Neufeld, H. N., Goldbourt, U., & Riss, E. (1973). Angina pectoris among 10,000 men: 5 year incidence and univariate analysis. *American Journal of Medicine, 55,* 583–594.

Miles, H. H., Waldfogel, S., Barrabee, E. L., & Cobb, S. (1954). Psychosomatic study of 46 young men with coronary artery disease. *Psychosomatic Medicine, 16,* 455–477.

Miller, C. K. (1965). Psychological correlates of coronary artery disease. *Psychosomatic Medicine, 27,* 257–265.

Minski, L., & Desai, M. M. (1955). Aspects of personality in peptic ulcer patients. *British Journal of Medical Psychology, 28,* 113–134.

Moldofsky, H., & Rothman, A. I. (1971). Personality, disease parameters and medication in rheumatoid arthritis. *Journal of Chronic Diseases, 24,* 363–372.

Moos, R. H., & Solomon, G. F. (1965). Psychologic comparisons between women with rheumatoid arthritis and their nonarthritic sisters. *Psychosomatic Medicine, 27,* 135–149.

Mordkoff, A. M., & Golas, R. M. (1968). Coronary artery disease and response to the Rosenzweig Picture-Frustration Study. *Journal of Abnormal Psychology, 73,* 381–386.

Mueller. A. D., & Lefkovits. A. M. (1975). Personality structure and dynamics of patients with rheumatoid arthritis. *Journal of Clinical Psychology, 13,* 143–147.

Mueller, A. D., Lefkovits, A. M., Bryant, J. E., & Marshall, M. L. (1961). Some psychosocial factors in patients with rheumatoid arthritis. *Arthritis and Rheumatism, 4,* 275–282.

Ostfeld, A. M., Lebovitz, B. Z., Shekelle, R. B., & Paul, O. (1964). A prospective study of the relationship between personality and coronary heart disease. *Journal of Chronic Diseases, 17,* 265–276.

Paffenbarger, R. S., Wing, A. L., & Hyde, R. T. (1974). Chronic disease in former college students. XIII: Early precursors of peptic ulcer. *American Journal of Epidemiology, 100*, 307–315.

Pancheri, P., Teodori, S., & Aparo, U. L. (1978). Psychological aspects of rheumatoid arthritis vis-à-vis osteoarthritis. *Scandinavian Journal of Rheumatology, 7*, 42–48.

Philip. A. E., & Cay, E. L. (1972). Psychiatric symptoms and personality traits in patients suffering from gastro-intestinal illness. *Journal of Psychosomatic Research, 16*, 47–51.

Philips, C. (1976). Headache and personality. *Journal of Psychosomatic Research, 20*, 535–542.

Pierloot, R. A., & Van Roy, J. (1969). Asthma and aggression. *Journal of Psychosomatic Research, 13*, 333–337.

Piper, D. W., Greig, M., Thomas, J., & Shinners, J. (1977). Personality pattern of patients with chronic gastric ulcer. *Gastroenterology, 73*, 444–446.

Plutchik, R., Williams, M. H., Jerrett, I., Karasu, T. B., & Kane, C. (1978). Emotions, personality and life stresses in asthma. *Journal of Psychosomatic Research, 22*, 425–431.

Purcell, K., Turnbull, J. W., & Bernstein, L. (1962). Distinctions between subgroups of asthmatic children: Psychological test and behavior rating comparisons. *Journal of Psychosomatic Research, 6*, 283–291.

Rees, L. (1956). Physical and emotional factors in bronchial asthma. *Journal of Psychosomatic Research, 1*, 98–114.

Rees, L. (1964). The importance of psychological, allergic, and infective factors in childhood asthma. *Journal of Psychosomatic Research, 7*, 253–262.

Rime, B., & Bonami, M. (1973). Specificité psychosomatique et affections cardiaques coronariennes: Essai de vérification de la théorie de Dunbar au moyen du MMPI [Psychosomatic specificity and coronary heart disease: Testing Dunbar's theory using the MMPI]. *Journal of Psychosomatic Research, 17*, 345–352.

Rime, B., & Bonami, M. (1979). Overt and covert personality traits associated with coronary heart disease. *British Journal of Medical Psychology, 52*, 77–84.

Robinson, H., Kirk, R. F., & Frye, R. L. (1971). A psychological study of rheumatoid arthritis and selected controls. *Journal of Chronic Diseases, 23*, 791–801.

Rothstein, C., & Cohen, I. S. (1958). Hostility and dependency conflicts in peptic ulcer patients. *Psychological Reports, 4*, 555–558.

Sainsbury, P. (1960). Neurosis and psychosomatic disorders in outpatients. *Advances in Psychosomatic Medicine, 1*, 259–269.

Schucman, H., & Thetford, W. N. (1970). A comparison of personality traits in ulcerative colitis and migraine patients. *Journal of Abnormal Psychology, 76*, 443–452.

Scodel, A. (1953). Passivity in a class of peptic ulcer patients. *Psychological Monographs, 67*(10, whole No. 360).

Segers, M. J., & Mertens, C. (1977). Personality aspects of coronary heart disease related behavior. *Journal of Psychosomatic Research, 21*, 79–85.

Segraves, R. T. (1971). Personality and family history of disease. *British Journal of Psychiatry, 119*, 197–198.

Shekelle, R. B.. Gale, M., Ostfeld, A. M., & Oglesby, P. (1982). Hostility, risk of coronary heart disease, and mortality. *Psychosomatic Medicine, 45*, 109–114.

Siltanen, P., Lauroma, M., Nirkko, O., Punsar, S., Pyorala, K., Tuominen, H., & Vanhala, K. (1975). Psychological

characteristics related to coronary heart disease. *Journal of Psychosomatic Research, 19*, 183–195.

Smith, T. W., Follick, M. J., & Korr. K. S. (1984). Anger, neuroticism, Type A behaviour and the experience of angina. *British Journal of Medical Psychology, 57*, 249–252.

Stevens, J. H., Turner, C. W., Rhodewalt, F., & Talbot, S. (1984). The TABP and carotid artery atherosclerosis. *Psychosomatic Medicine, 46*, 105–113.

Storment, C. T. (1951). Personality and heart disease. *Psychosomatic Medicine, 13*, 304–313.

Teiramaa, E. (1978). Psychosocial and psychic factors in the course of asthma. *Journal of Psychosomatic Research, 22*, 121–125.

Teiramaa, E. (1979). Psychic factors and the inception of asthma. *Journal of Psychosomatic Research, 23*, 253–262.

Theorell, T. (1973). Psychosocial factors in myocardial infarction—why and how? *Advances in Cardiology, 8*, 117–131.

Theorell, T., DeFaire, U., Schalling, D., Adamson, U., & Askevold, F. (1979). Personality traits and psychophysiological reactions to a stressful interview in twins with varying degrees of coronary heart disease. *Journal of Psychosomatic Research, 23*, 89–99.

Theorell, T., Lund, E., & Floderus, B. (1975). The relationship of disturbing life-changes and emotions to the early development of myocardial infarction and other serious diseases. *International Journal of Epidemiology, 4*, 281–293.

Thiel, H. G., Parker, D., & Bruce, T. A. (1973). Stress factors and the risk of myocardial infarction. *Journal of Psychosomatic Research, 17*, 43–57.

Thomas, C. B., & Greenstreet, R. L. (1973). Psychobiological characteristics in youth as predictors of five disease states: Suicide, mental illness, hypertension, CHD, and tumor. *Johns Hopkins Medical Journal, 132*, 16–43.

Thomas, C. B., Ross, D. C., & Duszynski, K. R. (1975). Youthful hypercholesteremia: Its associated characteristics and role in premature myocardial infarctions. *Johns Hopkins Medical Journal, 136*, 193–208.

van Dijl, H. (1979). Myocardial infarction patients and sociability. *Journal of Psychosomatic Research, 23*, 3–6.

van Dijl, H. (1982). Myocardial infarction patients and heightened aggressiveness/hostility. *Journal of Psychosomatic Research, 26*, 203–208.

Ward, D. (1971). Rheumatoid arthritis and personality: A controlled study. *British Medical Journal, 2*, 297–299.

Wardwell, W. I., Bahnson, C. B., & Caron, H. S. (1963). Social and psychological factors in coronary heart disease. *Journal of Health and Social Behavior, 4*, 154–165.

Weiner, H., Thaler, M., Reiser, M. F., & Mirsky, I. A. (1957). Etiology of duodenal ulcer. *Psychosomatic Medicine, 19*, 1–10.

Wiener, D. H. (1952). Personality characteristics of selected disability groups. *Genetic Psychology Monographs, 45*, 175–255.

Williams, R. B., Haney, T. L., Lee, K. L., Kong, Y., Blumenthal, J. A.. & Whalen, R. E. (1980). Type A behavior, hostility, and coronary atherosclerosis. *Psychosomatic Medicine, 42*, 539–549.

Wretmark, G., (1953). The peptic ulcer individual. *Acta Psychiatrica et Neurologica Scandinavica* (Suppl. 84). 1–183.

Zyzanski, S. J., Jenkins, C. D., Ryan, T. J., Flessas, A., & Everist, M. (1976). Psychological correlates of coronary angiographic findings. *Archives of Internal Medicine, 136*, 1234–1237.

READING 21

Hostility and Health: Current Status of a Psychosomatic Hypothesis

Timothy W. Smith • University of Utah

Recent research has renewed interest in the potential influence of hostility on physical health. This review indicates that the evidence available from prospective studies, although not entirely consistent, suggests that hostile persons may be at increased risk for subsequent coronary heart disease and other life-threatening illnesses. Further, several plausible mechanisms possibly linking hostility and health have been articulated and subjected to initial evaluation. Hostile individuals display heightened physiological reactivity in some situations, report greater degrees of interpersonal conflict and less social support, and may have more unhealthy daily habits. Additional research is needed, and it must address a variety of past conceptual and methodological limitations. Perhaps the most central of these concerns are the assessment of individual differences in hostility and the role of social contexts in the psychosomatic process.

Key words: hostility, coronary heart disease (CHD), personality, physiological reactivity, psychosomatics

Recent developments in health psychology and behavioral medicine have revitalized a centuries-old psychosomatic hypothesis: Chronic anger and hostility may contribute to the etiology of coronary heart disease (CHD) and other life-threatening illnesses. Early medical writers suggested that hostile people were more likely to develop coronary disease than nonhostile people and that episodes of anger could precipitate coronary events (for a review, see Dembroski, MacDougall, Herd, & Shields, 1983). Previously in the 20th century, psychoanalytic theorists also identified anger, hostility, and associated intrapsychic conflicts as potential causes of CHD and essential hypertension (Diamond, 1982). In the past decade, attempts to identify the important elements within the broadly

defined Type A behavior pattern have focused on hostility (Dembroski & Costa, 1987).

This most recent period of interest in hostility has produced a far more thorough and rigorous evaluation of the basic psychosomatic hypothesis than appeared previously. Pooling the relevant prospective tests, a tentative confirmation of this hypothesis emerged (Matthews, 1988). However, as is the case for the general literature on personality and health (Holroyd & Coyne, 1987), troubling inconsistencies have appeared. Further, formidable methodological and conceptual problems must be addressed before more definitive conclusions can be reached. These inconsistencies and problems provide the outlines for a continuing research agenda, but they could also contribute to the premature abandonment of research efforts without resolution or heuristic reformulation of the original questions. Current research on hostility and health has come to a crossroads of this sort.

The purpose of this review is to discuss the findings concerning hostility and health that have accumulated in recent years and to outline issues and questions for future research. Three main topics are covered: (a) adequacy of procedures for assessing hostility, (b) evidence of an association between measures of hostility and objective health outcomes, and (c) potential mechanisms linking hostility and health. The less extensive literature on the development of hostility is also briefly reviewed.

Definitions of Key Concepts

Many authors have noted that research on hostility and health suffers from ambiguity surrounding basic concepts. The constructs of anger, aggression, and hostility are closely related but are often incompletely distinguished. The distinctions among affect, cognition, and behavior provide a useful framework in this regard (Buss, 1961; Spielberger et al., 1985). From this perspective, *anger* refers to an unpleasant emotion ranging in intensity from irritation to rage, usually in response to perceived mistreatment or provocation. Further, anger can be seen as both an emotional state and an enduring personality trait. In the latter case, it refers to individual differences in the frequency and intensity of this affect (Spielberger et al., 1985). Although often associated with the emotion of anger, *aggression* refers to overt behavior. Motivated by many possible factors and taking a variety of forms, aggression is typically defined as attacking, destructive, or hurtful actions.

Historically there has been less agreement about the conceptual definition of *hostility*. With the distinctions among affect, behavior, and cognition blurred to some extent, hostility has been defined as the tendency to wish to inflict harm on others or the tendency to feel anger toward others (Chaplin, 1982). Hostility can also be defined as a set of negative attitudes, beliefs, and appraisals concerning others. In this approach, hostility connotes a view of others as frequent and likely sources of mistreatment, frustration, and provocation, and, as a result, a belief that others are generally unworthy and not to be trusted.

In a recent discussion of this issue, Barefoot (1992) suggested that, because hostility often but not always involves affect, behavior, and cognition, these aspects of hostility should be articulated and assessed separately. In this conceptual approach, the affective component of hostility includes a variety of related emotions, including anger, annoyance, resentment, and contempt. The cognitive component includes negative beliefs about human nature in general (i.e., cynicism) and the belief that disagreeable behavior of others is intentionally directed at the self (i.e., hostile attributions). Finally, the behavioral component includes aggression and a variety of often subtle forms of antagonism, insult, and uncooperativeness.

Assessment of Hostility

If existing or future studies of hostility and health are to be interpreted as relevant to the basic psychosomatic hypothesis, it must be demonstrated that the personality measures they employ actually assess individual differences in hostility. That is, regardless of the robustness of the statistical association between measures of hostility and subsequent health, the basic conceptual hypothesis cannot be evaluated convincingly unless the assessment devices are valid measures of the construct of hostility.

To date, two measures of hostility have been used most—the Cook and Medley (1954) Hostility (Ho) scale and ratings of the potential for hostility derived from the Type A structured interview (Dembroski & Costa, 1987). In the following sections, evidence of the construct validity of these measures is discussed. Although used in far fewer studies, the two aspects of hostility measured by the Buss–Durkee Hostility Inventory (BDHI; Buss & Durkee, 1957) are potentially important and warrant discussion.

Interview Methods: Potential for Hostility

Several systems have been developed to measure individual differences in hostility in the context of the Type A interview (Barefoot, 1992; Dembroski, MacDougall, Costa, & Grandits, 1989; Hecker, Chesney, Black, & Frautschi, 1988). Although these systems may initially appear quite similar, there are important differences among them. The earliest procedure was a component rating system developed by Matthews, Glass, Rosenman, and Bortner (1977) and used in re-analyses of CHD in the Western Collaborative Group Study (WCGS). A variety of specific behaviors were assessed, including several conceptually related to hostility (e.g., frequent anger, irritation). Although clearly influential in the development of subsequent hostility measures, this large set of specific ratings has not been used in additional studies of cardiovascular disease endpoints.

A system developed and refined by Dembroski and his colleagues has received wider use (Dembroski & Costa, 1987). *Potential for hostility (PH)* is defined as the tendency to experience anger, irritability, and resentment in daily life and/or the tendency to react to aggravating events with expressions of antagonism, rudeness, and uncooperativeness. In the early uses of this system, a 5-point rating scale was used to evaluate PH after auditors listened to an entire interview. More recently, separate ratings of the subcomponents of hostile content, hostile intensity, and hostile style have been used, in addition to the overall hostility rating (Dembroski & Costa, 1987). *Hostile content* refers to the respondents' descriptions of anger and hostility. *Intensity* refers to reports or displays of emphatic hostile responses. *Style* refers to disagreeable and uncooperative behavior displayed during the interview itself.

Ratings of PH and its subcomponents have been made reliably with this system (e.g., Dembroski, MacDougall, R. B. Williams, Haney, & Blumenthal, 1985; Musante, MacDougall, Dembroski, & Costa, 1989). However, evaluations of the construct validity of PH ratings have been relatively sparse. Some evidence of convergent validity is reflected in modest but significant correlations between PH ratings and Ho scores, with *r*s ranging from .29 (Swan, Carmelli, & Rosenman, 1990) to .37 (Dembroski et al., 1985). In a study of children and adolescents, PH ratings were significantly correlated with self-reported anger expression among boys but not among girls (Woodall & Matthews, 1989). However, these ratings were not related to scores on a modified version of the Ho scale for either group. PH ratings have also been found to be correlated with self-reports of characteristically antagonistic interactions with

others but not with peer ratings on the trait of agreeableness versus antagonism (Costa, McCrae, & Dembroski, 1989). PH ratings are more strongly and consistently related to expressive aspects of hostility than to experiential aspects (Musante et al., 1989). *Expressive hostility* refers to overt behaviors such as assaultiveness, verbal aggression, rudeness, and disagreeableness. In contrast, *experiential hostility* refers to cognitive and affective processes, such as resentment, suspicion, anger, and contempt.

Although these correlations provide some evidence of convergent validity, complete evaluations of construct validity require demonstrations of convergent and discriminant validity. In one of two samples of college students, PH was sigificantly correlated with self-reported neuroticism; in the other sample, it was inversely correlated with self-reports and peer ratings of the trait of openness to experience (Costa et al., 1989). Thus, additional and more thorough evaluations of the validity of this central assessment procedure are needed.

Recent interview-based ratings of hostility have employed more involved rating procedures. Hecker et al. (1988) developed a system to code 14 dimensions in structured-interview responses, one of which is hostility. In contrast to the Dembroski system, the Hecker et al. system uses ratings made after each question in the interview. Interrater reliabilities are high, but little formal evidence of construct validity has been provided to date.

Barefoot (1992) also developed a refined rating system, based on the previous work by Hecker and Dembroski, for use with the Type A structured interview. Following each question, four specific types of hostile behavior are rated, including hostile evasion of the question, indirect challenge of the interviewer, direct challenge, and displays of irritation. These behaviors are also combined to form an overall hostile-behavior index. In its initial use, high levels of reliability have been achieved. However, as with the Hecker et al. (1988) system, formal evaluations of construct validity are yet to appear.

Ho Scale

The Ho scale displays relatively high levels of internal consistency, with Cronbach's alphas averaging about .80 (T. W. Smith & Frohm, 1985). However, previous factor analyses of the Ho scale have suggested the presence of two factors, labeled *Cynicism* and *Paranoid Alienation* (Costa, Zonderman, McCrae, & R. B. Williams, 1986). Barefoot, Dodge, B. L. Peterson, Dahlstrom, and R. B. Williams (1989) also proposed a conceptually—rather than an empirically—derived set of content clusters of Ho scale items. Thus, heterogeneity of the Ho scale items may contribute to the inconsistent association between total-scale scores and health outcomes. Nonetheless, to interpret studies using the total Ho scale, psychometric properties of the 50-item set must be evaluated, and the trait or traits assessed by the scale must be identified.

Evidence regarding the temporal consistency of Ho scores is mixed. In samples of medical students and middle-aged adults, the 1- and 4-year test–retest correlations were found to be greater than $r = .80$ (Barefoot, Dahlstrom, & R. B. Williams, 1983; Shekelle, Gale, Ostfeld, & Paul, 1983). However, the Ho scores were considerably less stable over a 22-year period in a recent study of college students (Siegler et al., 1990), with a test–retest correlation of $r = .39$. In a study of children and adolescents, a modified version of the Ho scale was found to have a test–retest correlation over a 4-year period of $r = .56$—although scores were more stable for girls ($r = .65$) than for boys ($r = .29$; Woodall & Matthews, 1991). These studies suggest that the predictive utility of the Ho scale may be compromised by reduced temporal consistency of the scores when younger samples are studied over long periods.

Several studies have indicated that the Ho scale is significantly correlated with self-reports of anger and hostility (Barefoot et al., 1989; T. W. Smith & Frohm, 1985; T. W. Smith, Pope, Sanders, Allred, & O'Keeffe, 1988; Woodall & Matthews, 1989). Further, some evidence indicates that the Ho scale is somewhat more closely correlated (T. W. Smith & Frohm, 1985) with experiential aspects of hostility (e.g., resentment or suspicion) than it is with expressive aspects (e.g., assaultiveness or verbal aggression). Evaluations of the discriminant validity of the Ho scale have produced mixed evidence. T. W. Smith and Frohm (1985) found that the Ho scale was significantly more closely correlated with reported anger proneness than with anxiety or depression. Similarly, Barefoot et al. (1989) found in one of two samples that Ho scores were more closely correlated with

the trait of antagonism versus agreeableness than with the traits of neuroticism, openness to experience, extraversion, or conscientiousness. Other studies, however, have indicated that the Ho scale is highly correlated with measures of neuroticism or general emotional distress (e.g., Barefoot et al., 1989, Sample 2). To the extent that neuroticism or emotional distress is unrelated to objective health outcomes (Watson & Pennebaker, 1989), the overlap of the Ho scale with this broad dimension is likely to weaken its predictive utility.

As noted previously, the Ho scale has been found to be significantly correlated with behavioral ratings of PH (Dembroski et al., 1985; Swan et al., 1990). Further, high Ho scores have also been found to be associated with greater levels of overt hostile behavior during married couples' discussions of areas of disagreement, although this association was considerably weaker for women than for men (T. W. Smith, Sanders, & Alexander, 1990).

The cognitive correlates of hostility as measured by the Ho scale have been examined in several studies as well. Ho scores have been found to be significantly more closely correlated with reports of daily angry and suspicious thoughts than with depressed or anxious thoughts (Pope, T. W. Smith, & Rhodewalt, 1990). Moreover, high Ho scores are associated with the tendency to view unrelated others and spouses as intentionally provoking, although the latter association is true for husbands but not for wives (Pope et al., 1990; T. W. Smith et al., 1990). Further, a recent study using an incidental-recall measure of cognitive processes found that high Ho scores were associated with enhanced recall of hostile-trait adjectives (e.g., rude, unfriendly) after an antagonistic interpersonal interaction (Allred & T. W. Smith, 1991). This result suggests that people with high Ho scores maintain a negative schema or set of stable expectations that facilitates processing of disparaging information about others.

BDHI

A variety of factor-analytic studies support a distinction between experiential and expressive hostility as measured by the BDHI (e.g., Buss & Durkee, 1957; Musante et al., 1989). The Experiential Hostility factor is primarily defined by the BDHI Resentment and Suspicion subscales, and the Expressive Hostility factor is primarily defined by the BDHI Assaultiveness and Verbal Aggression subscales (Bushman, Cooper, & Lemke, 1991). The construct validity of this distinction is also supported by a study examining correlations of the Experiential Hostility and Expressive Hostility factors with self-reports and peer ratings of the personality traits of neuroticism and antagonism (Costa et al., 1989). *Neuroticism* is primarily characterized by the tendency to experience negative emotions, including anxiety, depression, and anger. *Antagonism* refers to an interpersonal style consisting of callousness, uncooperativeness, criticality, cynicism, and mistrust. At the other end of this dimension is *agreeableness*, characterized by a polite, courteous, sympathetic, trusting, and cooperative interpersonal style. Experiential hostility was correlated with both neuroticism and antagonism, although somewhat more closely with the former. In contrast, expressive hostility was correlated with antagonism and was unrelated to neuroticism. Thus, the limited evidence available supports the typical interpretation of the Experiential Hostility factor versus the Expressive Hostility factor.

General Issues in Assessment

The assessment research accumulating to date supports the interpretation of PH ratings, the Ho scale, and the BDHI as reflecting the construct of hostility, although additional evaluations of construct validity are certainly needed. However, it is also clear that these measures are not interchangeable and should be interpreted as reflecting the same construct only with caution. The related but distinct aspects of hostility they assess may not represent equally important influences on health or may be related through different mechanisms.

The findings of the measurement studies reveal a potential dilemma for researchers in this area, particularly in the case of the Ho scale. Heterogeneous item content and overlap with neuroticism may limit the value of this scale as a measure of hostility. However, its (inconsistent) association with objective health outcomes in prospective studies makes this scale more immediately relevant to psychosomatic research than more psychometrically sound instruments that are as of yet untested in prospective studies. This conflict between known health relevance and psychometric limita-

tions underscores the importance of additional prospective studies.

Evidence of an Association Between Hostility and Health

The relation between individual differences in hostility and a variety of health outcomes has been examined in both cross-sectional and prospective studies. Due to their quite different nature, these two groups of studies are reviewed separately.

Cross-Sectional Studies

In one of the earliest studies of hostility and coronary disease, R. B. Williams et al. (1980) examined the independent association between (a) interview-based ratings of Type A behavior and Ho scores and (b) coronary atherosclerosis in a sample of 424 patients undergoing coronary angiography. Multivariate analyses indicated that both Type A behavior and hostility scores were significantly associated with the presence of clinically significant coronary artery disease (CAD), although hostility was the stronger predictor.

Subsequent studies of patients undergoing angiography have failed to replicate the association between Ho scores and CAD. In a sample of 131 patients, Dembroski et al. (1985) did not find a significant correlation between Ho scores and either the number of diseased coronary arteries or an index of total CAD severity. Similar nonsignificant results were reported by Helmer, Ragland, and Syme (1991) in a sample of 158 patients.

Two studies have compared Ho scores in samples of CHD patients and matched controls. Friedman and Booth-Kewley (1987) found no differences in average Ho scores between groups of 50 patients and 50 controls. Similarly, Fontana et al. (1989) found that the average Ho scores were not significantly different in groups of 23 CHD patients and 41 medical and surgical patients without a history of CHD. However, when Ho scores were dichotomized, high hostility was significantly associated with CHD diagnosis.

In a random sample of more than 4,000 male veterans ranging in age from 31 to 46 years, Joesoef, Wetterhall, DeStefano, Stroup, and Fronek (1989) found a small but significant association between Ho scores and the prevalence of peripheral artery disease. In a sample of more than 3,700 Finnish male twins ages 40 to 59 years, scores on a self-report measure of anger proneness, irritability, and argumentiveness were associated with increased prevalence of angina (Koskenvuo et al., 1988).

In two studies by Dembroski and his colleagues, interview ratings of PH were found to be associated with CAD. The first study found that ratings of hostility and an anger-in coping style were both associated with increased severity of CAD in a sample of 131 patients (Dembroski et al., 1985). These variables also had an interactive association with CAD such that hostility was associated with disease severity among patients who scored high, but not with those who scored low, on ratings of the anger-in style. In the second study, ratings of hostility and anger-in were both related to increased severity of CAD in a sample of 125 patients (MacDougall, Dembroski, Dimsdale, & Hackett, 1985). However, the interactive effect of these variables was not replicated.

Helmer et al. (1991) failed to find an association between CAD severity and hostility as rated with the Hecker et al. (1988) system. In contrast, recent research by Barefoot and his colleagues (see Barefoot, 1992, for a review) has indicated that ratings of hostility from their refined interview rating system are associated with the severity of CAD among angiography patients.

The association between different aspects of hostility (as measured by the BDHI) and CAD was examined in a study of 72 angiography patients (Siegman, Dembroski, & Ringel, 1987). Experiential hostility was inversely related to severity of CAD. In contrast, expressive hostility displayed a significant positive association with CAD. These findings were limited to patients younger than 60 years; the associations were not significant in older patients.

Implications and limitations of cross-sectional studies. The results of these studies provide some evidence of a concurrent association between hostility and cardiovascular disease. This evidence is apparently more consistent when hostility is assessed with behavioral ratings of hostility than with the Ho scale, but the small number of studies precludes firm conclusions.

Cross-sectional studies are of course limited by their concurrent design; causal hypotheses cannot be tested. These designs also suffer from a variety of other limitations that reduce their value in evaluating the basic psychosomatic hypothesis (Matthews, 1988). For example, the range of severity of cardiovascular disease is often restricted, such as in angiography samples in which the majority of patients display significant coronary occlusions. As a result, statistical tests of risk factor–disease associations may be weakened.

The findings reported by Siegman et al. (1987) suggest another potential limitation of clinical samples for tests of the health consequences of hostility. Although expressive aspects of hostility were positively associated with CAD severity, experiential aspects were inversely related. Scores on a measure of neuroticism were also inversely associated with CAD in this study. This latter result has been demonstrated in several previous studies (for a review, see T. W. Smith & P. G. Williams, 1992). It is possible that people with characteristically high levels of anxiety or negative emotionality complain of chest pain and other symptoms to the extent that they undergo invasive diagnostic tests. As a result, angiography samples would include several patients—perhaps as many as 25%—who are free of CAD but score high on measures of trait anxiety or neuroticism. This selection process would produce the apparent yet spurious inverse association between negative emotionality and CAD. Aspects of hostility that are strongly correlated with neuroticism, such as the Experiential Hostility factor in the Siegman et al. (1987) study, may also display an artifactual inverse relation. Further, measures of hostility that assess both experiential and expressive aspects of hostility may be unrelated or weakly related to CAD in angiography samples due to the opposing associations of neuroticism and hostility with CAD.

Thus, although cross-sectional studies of hostility and cardiovascular disease have produced some suggestive findings, methodological limitations preclude definitive conclusions. Future investigations of this type must be sensitive to the compound problems in selection, measurement, and statistical hypothesis testing inherent in such designs, especially when they include clinical populations.

Prospective Studies

Behavioral ratings of hostility have been used in three prospective studies of CHD. In the previously mentioned reanalysis of the WCGS, Matthews et al. (1977) compared 62 initially healthy cases who developed CHD during the follow-up period and 124 matched controls on a variety of different aspects of Type A behavior as assessed at baseline through the structured interview. The variables providing the best discrimination between cases and controls included ratings of PH, anger directed outward, frequent experience of anger, and irritation while waiting in lines. In a subsequent, similar reanalysis of baseline Type A components in the WCGS, Hecker et al. (1988) compared 250 initially healthy CHD cases and 500 matched controls. In multivariate analyses controlling traditional risk factors and simultaneously testing 12 Type A components, interview-rated hostility was the only significant component that discriminated cases and controls.

Component scoring of Type A structured interviews was also employed in a reanalysis of the Multiple Risk Factor Intervention Trial (MRFIT) data concerning Type A behavior and subsequent CHD (Dembroski et al., 1989). Intake levels of PH and its three subcomponents—hostile content, intensity of hostility, and hostile interpersonal style—along with other Type A components were compared in a sample of 192 CHD cases and 384 matched controls. Only overall ratings of PH and the hostile interpersonal style subcomponent were significant predictors of CHD. These associations were independent of other risk factors and occurred in younger but not older subjects.

To date, six published prospective studies have examined the association between hostility (as measured by the Ho scale) and health outcomes. In a study of 1,877 men enrolled in the Western Electric Study (WES), Shekelle et al. (1983) found that Ho scores were significantly associated with increased risk of major coronary events (i.e., myocardial infarction [MI] or CHD death) over a 10-year follow-up, even after the scores were adjusted for traditional risk factors. In analyses of 20-year follow-up data, Ho scores were significantly associated with increased risk of CHD death, cancer death, and all-cause mortality, again despite adjustments for traditional risk factors. A recent reanalysis of the WES indicated that scores on the Minnesota Multiphasic Personality Inventory (MMPI) Cynicism factor, which overlaps considerably with the Ho scale, were independently predictive of coronary death and total mortality in

multivariate analyses (Almada et al., 1991). Scores on the MMPI Neuroticism factor were not independently predictive of these outcomes.

In a study of 255 men who had taken the MMPI during medical school, Barefoot et al. (1983) found that higher levels of hostility were associated with increased risk of coronary events (i.e., MI or CHD death) and all-cause mortality over a 25-year follow-up. In a similar follow-up study of 118 lawyers, Barefoot et al. (1989) found that high Ho scores were associated with reduced survival over a 28-year period. This increased mortality risk was associated with subsets of Ho scale items reflecting cynicism, hostile affect, and aggressive behavior but not of items reflecting hostile attributions, social avoidance, or miscellaneous content.

Three studies have failed to find a prospective association between Ho scores and health outcomes. McCraine, Watkins, Brandsma, and Sisson (1986) examined the association between Ho scores and health outcomes in a sample of more than 450 physicians who completed the MMPI in the process of applying to medical school. Ho scores were unrelated to CHD and total mortality over the 25-year follow-up. However, given the testing conditions, the medical school applicants may have understandably presented themselves in a positive light. Thus, invalid Ho scores could account for the lack of significant effects. However, two other studies not open to this criticism have also failed to find significant prospective associations using the Ho scale. Leon, Finn, Murray, and Bailey (1988) failed to find an association in a 30-year follow-up of 280 men, as did Hearn, Murray, and Luepker (1989) in a 33-year follow-up of almost 1,400 men.

As previously noted, conceptual definitions of hostility include negative attitudes and beliefs about others. In this vein, two studies have examined the association between self-reported suspiciousness and health outcomes. Also studying the WES, Ostfeld, Lebouits, Shekelle, and Paul (1964) found that suspiciousness was associated with increased risk of CHD over a 4½-year follow-up. In a study of 500 older adults, Barefoot et al. (1987) found that suspiciousness was associated with increased risk of death over a 15-year follow-up.

Although it did not use common measures of hostility, another study reported relevant findings. Koskenvuo et al. (1988) assessed hostility with a three-item scale reflecting reported argumentiveness, irritation, and anger proneness. In prospective analyses including men who were initially healthy and men with previous CHD ($N = 3,000$), hostility was associated with increased risk of cardiovascular mortality as well as death from all natural causes. High hostility scores were associated with increased risk of recurrent coronary events (i.e., CHD death or hospitalization) in a subsample of 300 men with previous cardiovascular illness (i.e., CHD and hypertension). However, hostility was not related to risk of subsequent CHD events in previously healthy subjects.

Implications of prospective studies. Although several negative studies have appeared, the majority of studies indicate that hostile people are at increased risk of subsequent CHD or other life-threatening illnesses. In a recent meta-analysis of four available studies, Matthews (1988) concluded that hostility was a significant risk factor for CHD. Although other negative studies have been reported (i.e., Hearn et al., 1989; Leon et al., 1988), additional positive studies have appeared as well (Barefoot et al., 1989; Barefoot et al., 1987; Dembroski et al., 1989; Hecker et al., 1988). Thus, it is unlikely that Matthews's conclusions would be modified in light of recent reports. The inconsistency of effects may, in part, be due to the various assessment devices. In particular, the results of prospective studies using the Ho scale have been mixed. Nonetheless, the available evidence generally supports the basic psychosomatic hypothesis.

Mechanisms Linking Hostility and Health

The apparent association between the construct of hostility and subsequent health raises the obvious question of mechanisms underlying this relation. Several plausible mechanisms have been articulated, each of which posits at least one set of intervening variables.

Psychophysiological Reactivity Model

R. B. Williams, Barefoot, and Shekelle (1985) proposed that hostility contributes to cardiovascular and perhaps other diseases through its association with heightened cardiovascular and neuroendo-

crine reactivity. Briefly, this model suggests that hostile people display larger increases in blood pressure (BP), heart rate (HR), and stress-related hormones in response to potential stressors. Given their anger proneness, hostile people experience anger more frequently and intensely than their more agreeable counterparts. Given their mistrust, hostile people may also be "on guard" more frequently, scanning their social environments for indications of impending mistreatment. More frequent or pronounced episodes of anger and vigilant observation of the social environment are hypothesized to produce heightened psychophysiological reactivity. Exaggerated reactivity, in turn, is hypothesized to initiate and hasten the development of CAD and the symptoms of CHD. Further, neuroendocrine responses could also impair immune functioning, increasing vulnerability to other diseases.

Results of the studies examining the association between individual differences in hostility and psychophysiological reactivity have been somewhat inconsistent. In what follows, studies using the primary measures of hostility are discussed.

PH. Dembroski, MacDougall, and their colleagues have reported several studies examining the association between interview-derived ratings of hostility and cardiovascular reactivity. PH is consistently related to increased BP responses to some laboratory stressors (e.g., reaction-time tasks) in these studies (e.g., Dembroski, MacDougall, Shields, Petitto, & Lushene, 1978; MacDougall, Dembroski, & Krantz, 1981). The results of these studies, however, do not demonstrate increased reactivity among hostile subjects to the structured interview itself.

Studies of reactivity and ratings of hostility by other researchers have produced more varied findings. Diamond et al. (1984) found no association between ratings of hostility and cardiovascular reactivity to stressors involving competition, frustration, or harassment. Glass, Lake, Contrada, Kehoe, and Erlanger (1983) found that ratings of hostility were inversely correlated with average systolic BP (SBP) and diastolic BP (DBP) responses to cognitive tasks. In contrast, Anderson et al. (1986) found that various PH aspects (e.g., hostile style and intensity of hostile answers) were associated with heightened SBP responses during the structured interview in a sample of working black women. In a sample of Swedish working men and women, Lundberg, Hedman, Melin, and Frankenhaeuser (1989) found that hostility ratings were associated with larger increases in SBP, epinephrine, and norepinephrine averaged over a series of laboratory stressors. Hostility ratings were also associated with increased HR, SBP, and cortisol reactivity at work (i.e., relative to values obtained at home during a day off). However, these associations were significant for men but not women. Finally, in a study of adolescent males and females, McCann and Matthews (1988) found that PH ratings were associated with larger SBP and DBP increases during an isometric hand-grip task but not during arithmetic or tracing stressors. Thus, when hostility is operationalized with interview-based ratings, support for the psychophysiologic model is mixed at best.

Ho scale. Studies of psychophysiologic correlates of the Ho scale are also mixed, but the inconsistencies appear more interpretable. Three studies of nonsocial stressors (i.e., mental arithmetic, cold pressor, Stroop color–word task) have all indicated that Ho scores are unrelated to cardiovascular reactivity (Kamarck, Manuck, & Jennings, 1990; Sallis, Johnson, Trevorrow, Kaplan, & Melbourne, 1987; M. A. Smith & Houston, 1987).

Studies of interpersonal stressors have generally produced expected results. Hardy and T. W. Smith (1988) found that males with high Ho scores displayed larger DBP responses to a role-playing task involving interpersonal conflict than did males with low Ho scores. Ho scores were unrelated to reactivity during low-conflict interactions. Similarly, Suarez and R. B. Williams (1989) found that Ho scores of college-age men were associated with increased cardiovascular reactivity to a stressful word-identification task when combined with harassment but not to the word-identification task alone. T. W. Smith and Allred (1989) found that, among male undergraduates, high Ho scores were associated with larger SBP and DBP responses during a current-events debate with another subject. In a related study, Christensen and T. W. Smith (1990) found that high Ho scores were associated with increased BP reactivity in a social interaction task involving high levels of self-disclosure. Hostility was unrelated to reactivity during a nondisclosing interaction, perhaps indicating that self-disclosure is particularly stressful for mistrusting, hostile people. Finally, T. W. Smith and Brown (1991) found that, among husbands attempting to

influence or control their wives in a marital interaction task, high Ho scores were associated with greater BP reactivity. When husbands were engaged in simple discussions with their wives, Ho scores were inversely related to reactivity. Ho scores were unrelated to cardiovascular reactivity among the wives in both experimental conditions.

Two studies involving interpersonal stressors failed to find expected cardiovascular correlates of the Ho scale. Kamarck et al. (1990) found that Ho scores were unrelated to BP responses to the Type A structured interview. Similarly, Allred and T. W. Smith (1991) found that high and low Ho groups did not differ in their cardiovascular responses to a discussion task involving high or low levels of disagreement.

Although not entirely consistent, the results of laboratory studies using the Ho scale suggest that hostility is generally associated with heightened BP reactivity to relevant interpersonal stressors but not to nonsocial tasks. Ho scores have also been related to physiological responses outside the laboratory. Pope and T. W. Smith (1991) found that, compared with male undergraduates with low Ho scores, male undergraduates with high Ho scores displayed significantly higher daytime levels of urinary cortisol. The groups did not differ in waking urinary cortisol levels, and the waking-to-daytime increase among subjects with high Ho scores was three times as large as that observed among subjects with low Ho scores. In a recent ambulatory BP monitoring study of paramedics, Jamner, Shapiro, Goldstein, and Hug (1991) reported that high Ho scores were associated with increased DBP levels while subjects were at the hospital but not while they were in the ambulance or at the ambulance station between emergency calls. The authors suggested that stressful interactions with hospital personnel may elicit enchanced reactivity among hostile subjects. Thus, results of studies using the Ho scale are generally consistent with the psychophysiological model of hostility and health.

BDHI. The BDHI has been used in far fewer studies of psychophysiologic reactivity. Biaggio, Supplee, and Curtis (1981) found that BDHI total scores were unrelated to BP responses to a role-playing task involving anger-provoking situations. However, the multicomponent nature of the BDHI may have precluded significant effects. In a re-analysis of their study of the Ho scale and cardiovascular reactivity, Suarez and R. B. Williams (1990) used the BDHI and other scales to form Expressive Hostility and Experiential Hostility factors. The former dimension was more closely related to cardiovascular reactivity than the latter, and the associations were observed primarily in the harassment condition. Thus, although more research is clearly needed, the Experiential Hostility and Expressive Hostility factors may be differentially related to physiological reactivity.

Conclusions regarding the psychophysiological model. A variety of observations consistent with this model have been reported, but inconsistent findings have emerged as well. Particularly troublesome are the results obtained with the interview-based measure of PH. That this measure is apparently unrelated to responses during relevant interpersonal stressors is curious and somewhat problematic for the model. The social stressors used in studies involving PH have primarily consisted of the structured interview itself. Examination of other interpersonal stressors might be useful, although negative findings with a harassment stressor have already been reported (Diamond et al., 1984). Again, clearly more research is needed in this regard. Although results with the Ho scale are more consistent with the model and with typical conceptualizations of the construct of hostility, discrepant results occur in these studies as well. The pool of relevant findings with the BDHI is too small at present to permit firm conclusions.

One factor possibly underlying some of the inconsistent results in these studies involves interactions between the trait of hostility and the social psychology of laboratory experiments. Houston (1986) suggested that hostile subjects may adopt an oppositional attitude toward the experiment or the experimenter. As a result, hostile subjects may be less involved or engaged in the tasks presented in the experiment and, as a result, may display less reactivity than is observed in involving situations. Appropriate interpersonal laboratory stressors may be more likely to engage hostile subjects.

An additional avenue for future psychophysiological research on hostility involves patients with established CHD. Animal research suggests that the arousal of anger can precipitate myocardial ischemia in the presence of coronary occlusions (Verrier, Hagestad, & Lown, 1987). It is possible, then, that hostility in coronary patients may be associated with greater succeptability to stress-induced myocardial ischemia. Thus, the psychophysiological model of hostility and health could also be applied to the question of precipitation of acute coronary events. Given the evidence that hostility may also contribute to cancer and other causes of death (e.g., Shekelle et al., 1983), it may also be fruitful to explore the immunological correlates of hostility.

Psychosocial Vulnerability Model

A second potential mechanism linking hostility and health involves psychosocial factors. Given the conceptual and empirical descriptions of hostile individuals previously outlined, one would expect these individuals to experience a more taxing interpersonal environment (T. W. Smith & Frohm, 1985). Several studies have supported this view of the psychosocial correlates of hostility. High Ho scores have been found to be associated with generally high levels of interpersonal conflict and low levels of social support (Barefoot et al., 1983; Hardy & T. W. Smith, 1988; Houston & Kelly, 1989; Scherwitz, Perkins, Chesney, & Hughes, 1991; T. W. Smith & Frohm, 1985; T. W. Smith et al., 1988). Further, Houston and Kelly (1989) and T. W. Smith et al. (1988) also found these associations in the context of work, marriage, and family origin, although they found one curious exception to this otherwise consistent pattern: Hostility is associated with marital distress and conflict for men but not for women. High Ho scores have also been associated with reports of more frequent and severe daily hassles and increased levels of major negative life events (Hardy & T. W. Smith, 1988; Scherwitz, Perkins, Chesney, & Hughes, 1991; T. W. Smith & Frohm, 1985; T. W. Smith et al., 1988). This psychosocial profile could make hostile persons more vulnerable to disease.

Although these findings are consistent with the psychosocial vulnerability model, several limitations of this research are noteworthy. First, relevant studies have relied on the Ho scale, and, as a result, little is known about the psychosocial correlates of other measures of hostility. Second, low levels of social support and high levels of interpersonal conflict, daily hassles, and negative life events are potentially correlated with neuroticism. The psychosocial correlates of hostility as measured by the Ho scale could reflect overlap with this third variable. Finally, shared method variance stemming from similar item content on hostility scales and psychosocial measures could inflate the observed associations. Additional observational studies or ratings by family members and coworkers would provide important information about the stresses and strains of daily life for hostile persons.

Transactional Model

A third view of the link between hostility and health represents an extension and integration of the psychophysiological and psychosocial models. Briefly, from this perspective, hostile people are not seen simply as responding to daily stressors with greater and more prolonged episodes of cardiovascular and neuroendocrine reactivity as compared with nonhostile individuals. Rather, they are seen as creating—through their thoughts and actions—more frequent, severe, and enduring contacts with stressors (T. W. Smith & Pope, 1990; see also Suls & Sanders, 1989). By anticipating provocation and mistreatment from others, by interpreting the actions of others as reflecting hostile intent, by behaving overtly antagonistically, and by mistrusting prevasively, hostile people are likely to elicit and exacerbate interpersonal conflict in their daily lives. This cognitive and behavioral style would also be likely to undermine the available levels of social support. Once created, this more taxing and less supportive social environment would tend to reinforce and maintain the hostile person's characteristic thoughts and behaviors.

In this perspective, the pathogenic physiological reactivity linking hostility and health reflects responses to two classes of daily events—increased reactivity to the unavoidable irritants experienced by both hostile and nonhostile people and the additional irritants created by the stress-engendering, hostile style of interaction. The psychosocial vulnerability associated with hostility previously described is seen as reflecting a reciprocal interaction between hostile people and their social environments. The net result of this reciprocal interaction pattern is increased frequency, magnitude, and duration of episodes of physiological reactivity.

Several of the findings discussed earlier are consistent with this model. The cognitive and interpersonal correlates of hostility demonstrated in previous studies support this view, as do the typical psychosocial correlates and physiological reactions to interpersonal stressors. However, no studies to date have provided a direct test of the active interactional or transactional aspects of the model. Although tests of this model in the laboratory may be difficult, laboratory studies and studies monitoring activities and concomitant physiological responses outside the laboratory could evaluate the impact of hostility on the social environment and associated reactivity. Through studies of this type, the transactional model may provide a description of the biopsychosocial process through which hostile people come to be at greater risk of disease.

Health Behavior Model

The preceding models all share a common assumption: Physiological aspects of the stress response comprise the final common pathway between hostility and health. Recently, a different model was proposed. Leiker and Hailey (1988) suggested that hostile people may be at greater risk of disease at least in part due to poor health habits. In a study of male and female undergraduates, Leiker and Hailey found that high Ho scores were associated with reports of less physical exercise, less self-care (e.g., dental hygiene and adequate sleep), and more alcohol use (including drinking while driving). Similarly, Houston and Vavak (1991) found that high Ho scores were associated with greater alcohol use, more frequent driving after drinking, and greater body mass index values. Shekelle et al. (1983) reported significant associations with cigarette smoking and alcohol consumption. Koskenvuo et al. (1988) found that hostile people reported heavier smoking and alcohol consumption and less leisure-time physical activity. Hostility was not related to body mass in this study. Scherwitz, Perkins, Chesney, Hughes, Sidney, and Manolio (1991) recently reported that, among young adults, high Ho scores were associated with tobacco use, alcohol consumption, and greater caloric intake. Siegler, G. L. Peterson, Barefoot, and R. B. Williams (1991) also found that Ho scores of college students were positively associated with caffeine intake, body mass index, and smoking 20 years later. Finally, Dembroski et al. (1989) found that interview-based ratings of PH were associated with cigarette smoking.

These findings are intriguing and offer a potentially valuable alternative or complement to other models. However, the results are purely descriptive. Although a variety of conceptual models of health behavior are potentially relevant, to date no studies have tested possible explanations of the association between hostility and health habits.

Thus far, the health behavior model has been examined exclusively in terms of traditional behavioral risks, such as smoking, alcohol use, and exercise. Hostility is also potentially related to other dangerous behaviors. For example, due to an oppositional, a mistrusting, or a generally cynical style, hostile people may delay seeking medical treatment or may fail to comply with prescribed treatments (Suls & Sanders, 1989). Delays and noncompliance could be life threatening if, for example, someone is in the early phases of MI or has noticed a possible early warning sign of cancer.

Constitutional Vulnerability Model

Several authors have suggested that the apparent association between personality and health may actually reflect the effects of a third variable—an underlying constitutional or structural weakness (Krantz & Durel, 1983; Suls & Sanders, 1989). Rather than exerting a causal influence on health, the personality dimension may simply be associated with an underlying, health-relevant biological factor. For example, individual differences in hostility may be caused by genetically determined differences in autonomic lability. This lability, rather than hostility itself, may contribute to disease.

As discussed later, several studies have suggested that hostility may be determined in part by genetic factors. This genetic factor could also be related to vulnerability. Thus, rather than evaluating a mechanism underlying the causal influence of hostility on health, examinations of the physiological correlates of hostility may reveal a more basic and central risk factor.

If this underlying factor involves physiological reactivity, the correlated personality trait may still be relevant to health. For example, as in the preceding discussion of the transactional model, the cognitive and behavioral aspects of hostility may increase exposure to social stressors. As a result, by virtue of their thoughts and actions, biologically vulnerable persons would be exposed to what is, for them, a particularly unhealthy enviornment.

Common Issues in Models Linking Hostility and Health

From the preceding discussion, it is clear that several plausible and heuristically valuable models of the impact of hostility on health have been developed. The models are not mutually exclusive. To the contrary, the psychophysiological, psychosocial, and transactional models are clearly closely related and even complementary. The health behavior model suggests an alternative pathway but does not necessarily contradict the others. Further, each of these mechanisms could function as a complement to constitutional vulnerability.

Testing mechanism models. The proposed models are all essentially mediational approaches, identifying one or more factors mediating the statistical association between hostility and health. However, only portions of these models have been tested. Research has evaluated the association between hostility and the mediating mechanisms, although additional studies of this type are needed. Ultimately, complete path-analytic tests of the models are possible and would involve assessment of hostility, intervening variables, and health outcomes.

In developing more complete tests of the association between hostility and health, it is important to note that in several cases these models identify relevant situational stressors as an important factor in the psychosomatic process. That is, they identify moderating factors as well as mediating mechanisms. For example, the psychophysiological reactivity model and much of the related research suggest that hostility is associated with increased reactivity only in the presence of relevant social stressors. Thus, a more sensitive and complete test of hostility as a risk factor would evaluate hostility, relevant environmental variables, and their interactive association with disease rather than the main effect of the personality variable alone. The predictive utility of the construct may be enhanced by consideration of social contexts and related moderating variables in epidemiological studies.

The problem of correlated risk factors. These models are also relevant to the design and interpretation of statistical tests of the association between hostility and health. For example, the common practice in such studies is to assess and statistically control the traditional risk factors in order to evaluate the unique predictive utility of hostility. Smoking, exercise, and other risk factors are implicitly construed as potential confounds in such analytic procedures. This practice may lead to an underestimate of the health effects of hostility. Used differently, such procedures can provide more complete tests of the models. For example, if in a prospective study a significant univariate association between hostility and subsequent health is eliminated or significantly attenuated when health behaviors are statistically controlled, the health behavior model may be at least partially supported. If hostility is associated with health outcomes even when a comprehensive set of risk factors is controlled, the health behavior model may not provide a complete explanation of the association between hostility and health. The multivariate tests of this type reported to date (e.g., Dembroski et al., 1989; Hecker et al., 1988; Koskenvuo et al., 1988; Shekelle et al., 1983) suggest that the health behavior model does not provide an adequate explanation. However, the comprehensiveness and validity of risk-factor assessments may not have been sufficient to provide a definitive test, and the implied path model was not explicitly evaluated.

It is also common in these epidemiological studies to control baseline plasma cholesterol values if they are available. Although some negative findings have been reported (Scherwitz, Perkins, Chesney, Hughes, Sidney, & Manolio, 1991), hostile people have been found to have less desirable plasma lipid profiles (Dujovne & Houston, 1991; Siegler et al., 1991). Plasma cholesterol could serve as a proxy variable for health behaviors, creating the potential problem previously described. However, given the possible effects of stress and sympathetic activation on lipids, elevated plasma total cholesterol or low-density lipoprotein cholesterol could also reflect the psychophysiological correlates of hostility. Thus, statistical control of cholesterol in multivariate tests of the association between hostility and health could again eliminate a substantive contribution of hostility to disease, producing an underestimate of its importance as a risk factor.

Recent evidence suggests that this issue is also relevant to the treatment of demographic variables in statistical tests of the health effects of hostility. Two large studies have demonstrated that hostility is inversely associated with socioeconomic status, education, female sex, and white race (Barefoot et al., 1991; Scherwitz, Perkins, Chesney, & Hughes, 1991). In the traditional approach to statistical analysis, these variables would be controlled in an effort to evaluate the unique effects of hostility in predicting health outcomes. Matthews (1989), however, suggested that psychosocial factors such as hostility could actually mediate the association between demographic variables and health. That is, less educated, lower income, male, or nonwhite individuals may be at greater risk because they tend to be more hostile.

Of course, these concerns do not indicate that multivariate analyses controlling traditional risk factors and demographic variables are inappropriate. Rather, they indicate that decisions about statistical control in epidemiological research might be more effective if guided by theory. The models outlined here provide a useful framework in this regard.

Conclusions

In the past decade, considerable support has accumulated for the centuries-old hypothesis that hostility is a threat to health. Although several negative prospective studies have been reported, the bulk of the evidence is consistent with the basic psychosomatic view. The discrepant results provide fuel for skeptics but also contain the outlines of a research agenda for continuing investigation.

Challenges for Future Research

Replications of the basic association between hostility and health are obviously needed. However, they are likely to be more valuable if they include refined assessments of hostility. The measures used currently have produced important results, but they were pressed into service due to their availability in prospective data sets typically predating current interest in the topic. The necessity of lengthy follow-up periods has created a literature in which measures of the central construct are often extracted after the fact rather than developed, validated, and refined in advance. As a result, basic psychometric qualities, most notably construct validity, are often unknown or lacking. Thus, the need to evaluate and refine existing assessment devices underscores the critical role of personality measurement in the continuing evolution of this area.

It is important to note that most of the research on hostility and health has been done with all-male or largely male samples. In the few studies directly comparing men and women, several interesting sex differences have emerged. In the future, research on the assessment of hostility, its association with health, and factors underlying this association should include men and women.

Virtually all the aspects of research on hostility and health could profit from further consideration of interpersonal processes. For example, evaluation of the validity of assessment procedures should include additional tests of their association with behavior and cognition in social contexts, and tests of the models concerning mechanisms underlying the association between hostility and health should incorporate social factors. Perhaps most important, consideration of potential moderating effects of the social environment could enhance the predictive utility of hostility in epidemiological studies. Hostility may be more dangerous in some interpersonal contexts than in others. The inherently interpersonal nature of hostility would seem to make the importance of social factors obvious. Yet, much of the research on this area has focused on the hostile figure and has neglected the surrounding interpersonal ground.

Application of Personality Theory and Research

Recent developments in the study of personality can provide useful tools for future research on hostility and health. For example, many personality theorists and researchers have advocated a specific trait taxonomy for describing personality (e.g., Digman, 1990). The five-factor model posits the traits of neuroticism, agreeableness, conscientiousness, extraversion, and openness to experience as a comprehensive list of personality dimensions. Several authors have recommended this conceptual scheme and the associated measurement procedures in personality and health research (e.g., T. W. Smith & P. G. Williams, 1992). As noted earlier, Costa et al. (1989) argued that the trait of agreeableness versus antagonism and the facet of neuroticism reflecting angry feelings

may provide a valuable framework for future research. Rather than continuing to pursue the development, validation, and refinement of assessment devices in the narrow confines of research on hostility and health, progress in this area might be more rapid if future efforts borrow the well-developed conceptual and measurement systems emerging from decades of research in personality assessment.

The most obvious value of the evolving trait taxonomies lies in the area of personality description and measurement. This approach is less likely to provide major conceptual advances regarding psychological and social mechanisms underlying hostility and its association with illness. However, a second recent development in personality research and theory may explicate these processes. Current cognitive–social perspectives in personality psychology examine the ways in which people construe their social worlds, regulate and evaluate their own actions, and influence and respond to the actions of others (e.g., Cantor, 1990). The focus is on people, social contexts, and the reciprocal relations between them. Given the inherently cognitive and interpersonal nature of hostility, this approach is quite likely to provide important insights into the psychosomatic consequences of ongoing hostile lives.

Advances in research on the biological underpinnings and correlates of hostility are vital to continued progress in this area, as is the thoughtful evaluation of conceptual models of hostility and the association between hostility and health in epidemiological studies. However, the most immediate threats to continued and cumulative progress may be limitations in the current conceptualization and assessment of hostile persons and the dynamic social contexts they inhabit. The resources for overcoming these difficulties are available. As noted at the outset of this review, current research on the topic of hostility and health has come to a crossroads. Additional conflicting findings and lingering interpretive ambiguities may lead to the slow abandonment of this area of research without satisfactory or lasting resolution of the basic issues. Alternatively, thoughtful application of the concepts and methods provided by current personality and health psychology may answer centuries-old questions regarding the impact of hostility on health.

REFERENCES

Allred, K. D., & Smith, T. W. (1991). Social cognition in cynical hostility. *Cognitive Therapy and Research, 15,* 399–412.

Almada, S. J., Zonderman, A. B., Shekelle, R. B., Dyer, A. R., Daviglus, M. L., Costa, P. T., Jr., & Stamler, J. (1991). Neuroticism and cynicism and risk of death in middle aged men: The Western Electric Study. *Psychosomatic Medicine, 53,* 165–175.

Anderson, N. B., Williams, R. B., Jr., Lane, J. D., Haney, T., Simpson, S., & Houseworth, S. J. (1986). Type A behavior, family history of hypertension, and cardiovascular responsivity among Black women. *Health Psychology, 5,* 393–406.

Barefoot, J. C. (1992). Developments in the measurement of hostility. In H. S. Friedman (Ed.), *Hostility, coping, and health* (pp. 13–31). Washington, DC: American Psychological Association.

Barefoot, J. C., Dahlstrom, W. G., & Williams, R. B., Jr. (1983). Hostility, CHD incidence, and total mortality: A 25-year follow-up study of 255 physicians. *Psychosomatic Medicine, 45,* 59–63.

Barefoot, J. C., Dodge, K. A., Peterson, B. L., Dahlstrom, W. G., & Williams, R. B., Jr. (1989). The Cook–Medley Hostility Scale: Item content and ability to predict survival. *Psychosomatic Medicine, 51,* 46–57.

Barefoot, J. C., Peterson, B. L., Dahlstrom, W. G., Siegler, I. C., Anderson, N. B., & Williams, R. B., Jr. (1991). Hostility patterns and health implications: Correlates of Cook–Medley Hostility Scale scores in a national survey. *Health Psychology, 10,* 18–24.

Barefoot, J. C., Siegler, I. C., Nowlin, J. B., Peterson, B. L., Haney, T. L., & Williams, R. B., Jr. (1987). Suspiciousness, health, and mortality: A follow-up study of 500 older adults. *Psychosomatic Medicine, 49,* 450–457.

Biaggio, M. K., Supplee, K., & Curtis, N. (1981). Reliability and validity of four anger scales. *Journal of Personality Assessment, 45,* 639–648.

Bushman, B. J., Cooper, H. M., & Lemke, K. M. (1991). Meta-analysis of factor analyses: An illustration using the Buss–Durkee Hostility Inventory. *Personality and Social Psychology Bulletin, 17,* 344–349.

Buss, A. H. (1961). *The psychology of aggression.* New York: Wiley.

Buss, A. H., & Durkee, A. (1957). An inventory for assessing different kinds of hostility. *Journal of Consulting Psychology, 21,* 343–349.

Cantor, N. (1990). From thought to behavior: "Having" and "doing" in the study of personality and cognition. *American Psychologist, 45,* 735–750.

Carmelli, D., Swan, G. E., & Rosenman, R. H. (1990). The heritability of the Cook and Medley Hostility Scale revisited. *Journal of Social Behavior and Personality, 5,* 107–116.

Chaplin, J. P. (1982). *Dictionary of psychology* (Rev. ed.). New York: Dell.

Christensen, A. J., & Smith, T. W. (1990). *Cynical hostility, self-disclosure, and cardiovascular reactivity.* Manuscript submitted for publication.

Cook, W. W., & Medley, D. M. (1954). Proposed Hostility and Pharisaic-Virtue scales for the MMPI. *Journal of Applied Psychology, 38,* 414–418.

Costa, P. T., Jr., McCrae, R. R., & Dembroski, T. M. (1989). Agreeableness vs. antagonism: Explication of a potential risk factor for CHD. In A. W. Siegman & T. M. Dembroski (Eds.), *In search of coronary-prone behavior* (pp. 41–64). Hillsdale, NJ: Lawrence Erlbaum.

Costa, P. T., Jr., Zonderman, A. B., McCrae, R. R., & Williams, R. B., Jr. (1986). Cynicism and paranoid alienation in the Cook and Medley Ho scale. *Psychosomatic Medicine, 48,* 283–285.

Dembroski, T. M., & Costa, P. T., Jr. (1987). Coronary-prone behavior: Components of the Type A pattern and hostility. *Journal of Personality, 55,* 211–235.

Dembroski, T. M., MacDougall, J. M., Costa, P. T., Jr., & Grandits, G. A. (1989). Components of hostility as predictors of sudden death and myocardial infarction in the Multiple Risk Factor Intervention Trial. *Psychosomatic Medicine, 51,* 514–522.

Dembroski, T. M., MacDougall, J. M., Herd, J. A., & Shields, J. L. (1983). Perspectives on coronary-prone behavior. In D. S. Krantz, A. Baum, & J. E. Singer (Eds.), *Handbook of psychology and health: Vol. 3. Cardiovascular disorders and behavior* (pp. 57–83). Hillsdale, NJ: Lawrence Erlbaum.

Dembroski, T. M., MacDougall, J. M., Shields, J. L., Petitto, J., & Lushene, R. (1978). Components of the Type A coronary-prone behavior pattern and cardiovascular responses to performance challenge. *Journal of Behavioral Medicine, 1,* 159–176.

Dembroski, T. M., MacDougall, J. M., Williams, R. B., Jr., Haney, T. L., & Blumenthal, J. A. (1985). Components of Type A, hostility, and anger in: Relationship to angiographic findings. *Psychosomatic Medicine, 47,* 219–233.

Diamond, E. L. (1982). The role of anger and hostility in essential hypertension and coronary heart disease. *Psychological Bulletin, 92,* 410–433.

Diamond, E. L., Schneiderman, N., Schwartz, D., Smith, J. C., Vorp, R., & Pasin, R. D. (1984). Harassment, hostility, and Type A as determinants of cardiovascular reactivity during competition. *Journal of Behavioral Medicine, 7,* 171–189.

Digman, J. M. (1990). Personality structure: Emergence of the five-factor model. *Annual Review of Psychology, 41,* 417–440.

Dujovne, V. F., & Houston, B. K. (1991). Hostility-related variables and plasma lipid levels. *Journal of Behavioral Medicine, 14,* 555–565.

Fontana, A. F., Kerns, R. D., Blatt, S. J., Rosenberg, R. L., Burg, M. M., & Colonese, K. L. (1989). Cynical mistrust and the search for self-worth. *Journal of Psychosomatic Research, 33,* 449–456.

Friedman, H. S., & Booth-Kewley, S. (1987). Personality, Type A behavior, and coronary heart disease: The role of emotional expression. *Journal of Personality and Social Psychology, 53,* 783–792.

Glass, D. C., Lake, C. R., Contrada, R. J., Kehoe, K., & Erlanger, L. R. (1983). Stability of individual differences in physiological responses to stress. *Health Psychology, 2,* 317–341.

Hardy, J. D., & Smith, T. W. (1988). Cynical hostility and vulnerability to disease: Social support, life stress, and physiological response to conflict. *Health Psychology, 7,* 447–459.

Hearn, M. D., Murray, D. M., & Luepker, R. V. (1989). Hostility, coronary heart disease, and total mortality: A 33-year follow-up study of university students. *Journal of Behavioral Medicine, 12*, 105–121.

Hecker, M. H. L., Chesney, M. A., Black, G. W., & Frautschi, N. (1988). Coronary-prone behaviors in the Western Collaborative Group Study. *Psychosomatic Medicine, 50*, 153–164.

Helmer, D. C., Ragland, D. R., & Syme, S. L. (1991). Hostility and coronary artery disease. *American Journal of Epidemiology, 133*, 112–122.

Holroyd, K. A., & Coyne, J. (1987). Personality and health in the 1980s: Psychosomatic medicine revisited? *Journal of Personality, 55*, 359–375.

Houston, B. K. (1986). Psychological variables and cardiovascular and neuroendocrine reactivity. In K. A. Matthews, S. M. Weiss, T. Detre, T. M. Dembroski, B. Falkner, S. B. Manuck, & R. B. Williams, Jr. (Eds.), *Handbook of stress, reactivity, and cardiovascular disease* (pp. 207–229). New York: Wiley.

Houston, B. K., & Kelly, K. E. (1989). Hostility in employed women: Relation to work and marital experiences, social support, stress, and anger expression. *Personality and Social Psychology Bulletin, 15*, 175–182.

Houston, B. K., & Vavak, C. R. (1991). Hostility: Developmental factors, psychosocial correlates, and health behaviors. *Health Psychology, 10*, 9–17.

Jamner, L. D., Shapiro, D., Goldstein, I. B., & Hug, R. (1991). Ambulatory blood pressure and heart rate in paramedics: Effects of cynical hostility and defensiveness. *Psychosomatic Medicine, 53*, 393–406.

Joesoef, M. R., Wetterhall, S. F., DeStefano, F., Stroup, N. E., & Fronek, A. (1989). The association of peripheral arterial disease with hostility in a young, healthy veteran population. *Psychosomatic Medicine, 51*, 285–289.

Kamarck, T. W., Manuck, S. B., & Jennings, J. R. (1990). Social support reduces cardiovascular reactivity to psychological challenge: A laboratory model. *Psychosomatic Medicine, 52*, 42–58.

Koskenvuo, M., Kapiro, J., Rose, R. J., Kesnaiemi, A., Sarnaa, S., Heikkila, K., & Langinvanio, H. (1988). Hostility as a risk factor for mortality and ischemic heart disease in men. *Psychosomatic Medicine, 50*, 330–340.

Krantz, D. S., & Durel, L. A. (1983). Psychobiological substrates of the Type A behavior pattern. *Health Psychology, 2*, 393–411.

Leiker, M., & Hailey, B. J. (1988). A link between hostility and disease: Poor health habits? *Behavioral Medicine, 3*, 129–133.

Leon, G. R., Finn, S. E., Murray, D., & Bailey, J. M. (1988). The inability to predict cardiovascular disease from hostility scores of MMPI items related to Type A behavior. *Journal of Consulting and Clinical Psychology, 56*, 597–600.

Lundberg, U., Hedman, M., Melin, B., & Frankenhaeuser, M. (1989). Type A behavior in healthy males and females as related to physiological reactivity and blood lipids. *Psychosomatic Medicine, 51*, 113–122.

MacDougall, J. M., Dembroski, T. M., Dimsdale, J. E., & Hackett, T. P. (1985). Components of Type A, hostility, and anger-in: Further relationships to angiographic findings. *Health Psychology, 4*, 137–152.

MacDougall, J. M., Dembroski, T. M., & Krantz, D. S. (1981).

Effects of type of challenge on pressor and heart-rate responses in Type A and B women. *Psychophysiology, 18*, 1–9.

Matthews, K. A. (1988). CHD and Type A behaviors: Update on and alternative to the Booth-Kewley and Friedman quantitative review. *Psychological Bulletin, 104*, 373–380.

Matthews, K. A. (1989). Are sociodemographic variables markers for psychological determinants of health? *Health Psychology, 8*, 641–648.

Matthews, K. A., Glass, D. C., Rosenman, R. H., & Bortner, R. W. (1977). Competitive drive, Pattern A, and coronary heart disease: A further analysis of some data from the Western Collaborative Group Study. *Journal of Chronic Diseases, 30*, 489–498.

Matthews, K. A., Rosenman, R. H., Dembroski, T. M., Harris, E. L., & MacDougall, J. M. (1984). Familial resemblance in components of the Type A behavior pattern: A reanalysis of the California Type A Twin Study. *Psychosomatic Medicine, 46*, 512–522.

McCann, B. S., & Matthews, K. A. (1988). Influences of potential for hostility, Type A behavior, and parental history of hypertension on adolescents' cardiovascular responses during stress. *Psychophysiology, 25*, 503–511.

McCraine, E. W., Watkins, L. O., Brandsma, J. M., & Sisson, B. D. (1986). Hostility, coronary heart disease (CHD), incidence, and total mortality: Lack of association in a 25-year follow-up study of 478 physicians. *Journal of Behavioral Medicine, 9*, 119–125.

Musante, L., MacDougall, J. M., Dembroski, T. M., & Costa, P. T., Jr. (1989). Potential for hostility and dimensions of anger. *Health Psychology, 8*, 343–354.

Ostfeld, A. M., Lebouits, B. Z., Shekelle, R. B., & Paul, O. (1964). A prospective study of the relationship between personality and coronary heart disease. *Journal of Chronic Disease, 17*, 265–276.

Pedersen, N. L., Lichtenstein, P., Plomin, R., DeFaire, U., McClearn, G. E., & Matthews, K. A. (1989). Genetic and environmental influences for Type A–like measures and related traits: A study of twins reared apart and twins reared together. *Psychosomatic Medicine, 51*, 428–440.

Plomin, R., McClearn, G. E., Pedersen, N. L., Nesselroade, J. R., & Bergeman, C. S. (1988). Genetic influence on childhood family environment perceived retrospectively from the last half of the life span. *Developmental Psychology, 24*, 738–745.

Pope, M. K., & Smith, T. W. (1991). Cortisol excretion in high and low cynically hostile men. *Psychosomatic Medicine, 53*, 386–392.

Pope, M. K., Smith, T. W., & Rhodewalt, F. (1990). Cognitive, behavioral, and affective correlates of the Cook and Medley Hostility Scale. *Journal of Personality Assessment, 54*, 501–514.

Rose, R. J. (1988). Genetic and environmental variance in content dimensions of the MMPI. *Journal of Personality and Social Psychology, 55*, 302–311.

Sallis, J. F., Johnson, C. C., Trevorrow, T. R., Kaplan, R. M., & Melbourne, F. H. (1987). The relationship between cynical hostility and blood pressure reactivity. *Journal of Psychosomatic Research, 31*, 111–116.

Scarr, S., & McCartney, K. (1983). How people make their own environments: A theory of genotype-environment effects. *Child Development, 54*, 424–435.

Scherwitz, L., Perkins, L., Chesney, M., & Hughes, G. (1991). Cook–Medley Hostility Scale scores and subsets: Relationship to demographic and psychosocial characteristics in young adults in the CARDIA Study. *Psychosomatic Medicine, 53,* 36–49.

Scherwitz, L. W., Perkins, L. L., Chesney, M. A., Hughes, G. H., Sidney, S., & Manolio, T. A. (1991, March). *Cook–Medley hostility and detrimental health behaviors in young adults: The CARDIA Study.* Paper presented at the meeting of the Society of Behavioral Medicine, Washington, DC.

Shekelle, R. B., Gale, M., Ostfeld, A. M., & Paul, O. (1983). Hostility, risk of coronary heart disease, and mortality. *Psychosomatic Medicine, 45,* 109–114.

Siegler, I. C., Peterson, G. L., Barefoot, J. C., & Williams, R. B. (1991). *Hostility during late adolescence predicts coronary risk factors at midlife.* Unpublished manuscript.

Siegler, I. C., Zonderman, A. B., Barefoot, J. C., Williams, R. B., Jr., Costa, P. T., Jr., & McCrae, R. R. (1990). Predicting personality in adulthood from college MMPI scores: Implications for follow-up studies in psychosomatic medicine. *Psychosomatic Medicine, 52,* 644–652.

Siegman, A. W., Dembroski, T. M., & Ringel, N. (1987). Components of hostility and the severity of coronary artery disease. *Psychosomatic Medicine, 48,* 127–135.

Smith, M. A., & Houston, B. K. (1987). Hostility, anger, expression, cardiovascular responsivity, and social support. *Biological Psychology, 24,* 39–48.

Smith, T. W., & Allred, K. D. (1989). Blood pressure responses during social interaction in high and low cynically hostile males. *Journal of Behavioral Medicine, 12,* 135–143.

Smith, T. W., & Brown, P. (1991). Cynical hostility, attempts to exert social control, and cardiovascular reactivity in married couples. *Journal of Behavioral Medicine, 14,* 579–590.

Smith, T. W., & Frohm, K. D. (1985). What's so unhealthy about hostility? Construct validity and psychosocial correlates of the Cook and Medley Ho scale. *Health Psychology, 4,* 503–520.

Smith, T. W., & McGonigle, M. (1991). Cynical hostility and parental behavior in monozygotic male twins. *Psychosomatic Medicine, 53,* 220.

Smith, T. W., McGonigle, M., Turner, C. W., Ford, M. H., & Slattery, M. L. (1991). Cynical hostility in adult male twins. *Psychosomatic Medicine, 53,* 684–692.

Smith, T. W., & Pope, M. K. (1990). Cynical hostility as a health risk: Current status and future directions. *Journal of Social Behavior and Personality, 5,* 77–88.

Smith, T. W., Pope, M. K., Sanders, J. D., Allred, K. D., & O'Keeffe, J. L. (1988). Cynical hostility at home and work: Psychosocial vulnerability across domains. *Journal of Research in Personality, 22,* 525–548.

Smith, T. W., Sanders, J. D., & Alexander, J. F. (1990). What does the Cook and Medley Hostility Scale measure? Affect, behavior and attributions in the marital context. *Journal of Personality and Social Psychology, 58,* 699–708.

Smith, T. W., & Williams, P. G. (1992). Personality and health: Advantages and limitations of the five factor model. *Journal of Personality, 60,* 395–423.

Spielberger, C. D., Johnson, E. H., Russell, S. F., Crane, R. J., Jacobs, G. A., & Worden, T. J. (1985). The experience and expression of anger. Construction and validation of an anger expression scale. In M. A. Chesney & R. H. Rosenman (Eds.), *Anger and hostility in cardiovascular and behavioral disorders* (pp. 5–30). Washington, DC: Hemisphere.

Suarez, E. C., & Williams, R. B., Jr. (1989). Situational determinants of cardiovascular and emotional reactivity in high and low hostile men. *Psychosomatic Medicine, 51,* 404–418.

Suarez, E. C., & Williams, R. B., Jr. (1990). The relationship between dimensions of hostility and cardiovascular reactivity as a function of task characteristics. *Psychosomatic Medicine, 52,* 558–570.

Suls, J., & Sanders, G. S. (1989). Why do some behavioral styles place people at coronary risk? In A. W. Siegman & T. M. Dembroski (Eds.), *In search of coronary-prone behavior: Beyond Type A* (pp. 1–20). Hillsdale, NJ: Lawrence Erlbaum.

Swan, G. E., Carmelli, D., & Rosenman, R. H. (1990). Cook and Medley hostility and the Type A behavior pattern: Psychological correlates of two coronary-prone behaviors. *Journal of Social Behavior and Personality, 5,* 89–106.

Verrier, R. L., Hagestad, E. L., & Lown, B. (1987). Delayed myocardial ischemia induced by anger. *Circulation, 75,* 249–254.

Watson, D., & Pennebaker, J. W. (1989). Health complaints, stress, and distress: Exploring the central role of negative affectivity. *Psychological Review, 96,* 233–253.

Williams, R. B., Jr., Barefoot, J. C., & Shekelle, R. B. (1985). The health consequences of hostility. In M. A. Chesney & R. H. Rosenman (Eds.), *Anger and hostility in cardiovascular and behavioral disorders* (pp. 173–185). Washington, DC: Hemisphere.

Williams, R. B., Jr., Haney, T. L., Lee, K. L., Kong, Y., Blumenthal, J., & Whalen, R. (1980). Type A behavior, hostility, and coronary atherosclerosis. *Psychosomatic Medicine, 42,* 539–549.

Woodall, K. L., & Matthews, K. A. (1989). Familial environment associated with Type A behaviors and psychophysiological responses to stress in children. *Health Psychology, 8,* 403–426.

Woodall, K. L., & Matthews, K. A. (1993). Changes in and stability of hostile characteristics: Results from a four-year-long longitudinal study. *Journal of Personality and Social Psychology, 64,* 491–499.

Dispositional Optimism and Recovery From Coronary Artery Bypass Surgery: The Beneficial Effects on Physical and Psychological Well-Being

Michael F. Scheier • Carnegie Mellon University

Karen A. Matthews and Jane F. Owens • University of Pittsburgh

George J. Magovern, Sr. • Allegheny General Hospital, Pittsburgh, Pennsylvania

R. Craig Lefebvre • Brown University and Memorial Hospital, Pawtucket, Rhode Island

R. Anne Abbott • University of Wisconsin at Stevens Point and Abbott-Jeffers and Associates

Charles S. Carver • University of Miami

The effect of dispositional optimism on recovery from coronary artery bypass surgery was examined in a group of 51 middle-aged men. Patients provided information at three points in time—(a) on the day before surgery, (b) 6–8 days postoperatively, and (c) 6 months postoperatively. Information was obtained relating to the patient's rate of physical recovery, mood, and postsurgical quality of life. Information was also gathered regarding the manner in which the patients attempted to cope with the stress of the surgery and its aftermath. As expected, dispositional optimism proved to be an important predictor of coping efforts and of surgical outcomes. More specifically, dispositional optimism (as assessed prior to surgery) correlated positively with manifestations of problem-focused coping and negatively with the use of denial. Dispositional optimism was also associated with a faster rate of physical recovery during the period of hospitalization and with a faster rate of return to normal life activities subsequent to discharge. Finally, there was a strong positive association between level of optimism and postsurgical quality of life at 6 months.

I t is commonly held that positive thinking can help a person triumph over adversity—recover from illness, endure a personal hardship, overcome whatever obstacle may be confronted (e.g., Cousins, 1977; Peale, 1956). The scientific community has tended to view such claims with a healthy sense of skepticism, if not motivated disbelief (see, e.g., Angell, 1985). Research evidence is beginning to emerge, however, that suggests that this popular folk wisdom may have some basis in fact.

In this regard, Scheier and Carver (1985, 1987) have suggested that dispositional optimism may have important implications for the manner in which people deal with the stresses of life (cf. Lazarus, Kanner, & Folkman, 1980; Reker & Wong, 1985). This possibility was derived from a consideration of their model of behavioral self-regulation, which describes the processes that underlie purposive, goal-directed activities (Carver & Scheier, 1981, 1982; Scheier & Carver, 1988a). Most relevant here is the idea that people's actions are greatly affected by their beliefs about the probable outcomes of those actions. This notion, of course, has had a long history in psychological theories of motivation (see, e.g., Bandura, 1977, 1982, 1986; Kanfer, 1977; Lewin, 1938; Rotter, 1954; Seligman, 1975; Tolman, 1932, 1938; Wortman & Brehm, 1975).

In Carver and Scheier's (1981) and Scheier and Carver's (1988a) model, people who see desired outcomes as attainable continue to exert efforts to attain those outcomes, even when doing so is difficult or painful. When outcomes seem sufficiently unattainable, whether through personal inadequacies or through externally imposed impediments, people reduce their efforts and eventually disengage themselves from the pursuit of goals. Thus, outcome expectancies are viewed as a major determinant of the disjunction between two classes of behavior: continued striving versus giving up and turning away (see also, Klinger, 1975; Kukla, 1972; Roth & Cohen, 1986; Schmale, 1972).

Previous research on the effects of expectancies has been limited largely to an exploration of situation-specific or domain-specific expectancies, such as being able to deal effectively with a specific fear (Carver, Blaney, & Scheier, 1979) or overcoming the pain produced by a cold-pressor test (Bandura, O'Leary, Taylor, Gauthier, & Gossard, 1987). This has been true even though at least some prior theoretical statements have contained explicit provisions for expectancies that are more global in scope (see, e.g., Rotter, 1954). In general, research on these limited-domain expectancies has borne out their importance as determinants of behavior, and has illustrated the disjunction in behavioral responses to which they are thought to lead (for reviews, see Bandura, 1986, or Scheier & Carver, 1988a).

It seems clear, however, that expectancies are not always limited to only one particular context or applicable to only one behavioral arena. As Scheier and Carver (1985, 1987) noted, expectancy judgments in many stressful circumstances can range from the very specific (e.g., "Can I sit up in my bed today?"), to the moderately general (e.g., "Will I ever fully recover from this surgery?"), to the very general (e.g., "Do good things usually happen to me?"). Most expectancy-based theories implicitly assume that prediction of an outcome is best when the expectancy in question matches the level of specificity implied by the outcome, or when some combination of specific, moderately general, and very general outcome expectancies is used (see, e.g., Lefcourt, 1976; Rotter, 1954).

The kinds of problems encountered by people during the course of daily living are often general in scope, or are multiply determined. In addition, new problems always seem to arise, often before specific expectancies can be developed. Finally, many problems unfold slowly, over a long period of time, making it difficult to know precisely how things will work out in the end. In all of these cases, focusing on expectancies that are specific in nature may be impractical as well as unwise, if not impossible. For such situations, it may be more profitable to focus attention on expectancies that are more global in scope (cf. Rotter, 1954). Scheier and Carver (1985) used the term *dispositional optimism* to refer to generalized expectancies of this sort (i.e., expectations on the part of the person that good, as opposed to bad, outcomes will generally occur when confronting problems across important life domains).

Initial research has supported the notion that dispositional optimism confers benefits on the favorability of the outcomes one receives. In one study (Scheier & Carver, 1985, Study 3), for example, college undergraduates were asked to complete a measure of dispositional optimism and a measure of physical symptoms at two points in time, separated by a 4-week interval. The period in question was presumed to be a stressful period for most undergraduates: the final weeks closing a semester of school. A negative correlation emerged between optimism (measured at Time 1) and symptom reporting (measured at Time 2) that remained significant even when the initial correlation between optimism and symptom reporting was statistically controlled. Nor is this the only study to report beneficial effects of optimism on reports of physical well-being (see also Reker & Wong, 1983; Scheier & Carver, 1987).

Conceptually similar result have been reported for behavioral outcomes (Strack, Carver, & Blaney, 1987), as well as psychological well-being (Carver & Gaines, 1987; Humphries, 1986). Carver and Gaines (1987), for example, had a group of pregnant women complete a measure of optimism and a measure of depression in the third trimester of their pregnancies. Depression was then reassessed several weeks postpartum. The results showed that optimism was negatively associated with depression over time, as predicted, and that this association held even when initial levels of depression were partialed out. Effects similar to these have also been obtained by Humphries (1986), who studied the effects of office automation on the development of depression among office personnel.

While these studies have begun to document the beneficial effects of optimism on the *outcomes* that people receive, other research has begun to explore *underlying mechanisms* by which the effects may be mediated. One possibility is that the differences in well-being between optimists and pessimists derive from differences between them in the kinds of strategies they use to deal with stressful encounters. Consistent with this notion, a number of studies have shown that optimists are more likely to rely on problem-focused coping strategies, whereas pessimists seem to have a preference for emotion-based coping strategies, particularly denial (see, e.g., Carver, Scheier, & Weintraub, 1989; Scheier, Weintraub, & Carver, 1986; Weintraub, Carver, & Scheier, 1986). For example, Scheier et al. (1986, Study 1) asked subjects to write a brief description of the most stressful event they had experienced during the past 2 months. They then completed the Ways of Coping Checklist (Folkman & Lazarus, 1980; Lazarus & Folkman, 1984). Optimism proved to be positively associated with the use of problem-focused coping and negatively correlated with the use of distancing and denial (defined by the subject's refusal to acknowledge that the stressful situation existed). This latter association, between optimism and the use of denial, takes on additional significance in light of meta-analytic findings by Suls and Fletcher (1985) that denial tends to be associated with poorer long-term outcomes.

In spite of these encouraging results, prior research on optimism and coping is not without limi-

tations. First, and perhaps most critically, coping success has generally been assessed by self-reports of symptoms and affect. With the exception of a study by Beck, Steer, Kovacs, and Garrison (1985), which examined the prospective effects of hopelessness on suicide, no study has directly examined the effects of optimism on physical well-being. This is problematic because actual physical well-being may be only modestly related to self-reported symptoms and affect (cf. Costa & McCrae, 1985, 1987). Use of self-reports thus makes it difficult to evaluate whether optimists are actually achieving better outcomes or simply reporting that their outcomes are better. Second, work on the use of different coping strategies has been uniformly retrospective in nature. It would be profitable to examine the issue of strategy choice in the context of an ongoing stressful episode. Finally, no control has been brought to bear over the kind and severity of coping episodes examined. It is no doubt true that much of the prior research has involved coping situations that were relatively benign in scope. It thus would be useful to replicate these prior findings in a context in which the degree of stress is more extreme.

The study described here explored the impact of optimism on physical well-being and coping efforts in a situation in which individuals were attempting to deal with a life-threatening disease. In this project, physical and mental health outcomes were monitored along with coping strategies among a group of middle-aged men as they underwent and recovered from coronary artery bypass surgery (CABS). Both self-reports and objective measures of coping outcomes were obtained.

There are a number of reasons why CABS provides an optimal context in which to study the effects of dispositional optimism. First, CABS patients have coronary artery disease, a disease that is determined by multiple factors, including behavioral and emotional characteristics (Matthews & Haynes, 1986). Thus, it is likely that coping responses to CABS should have a role in determining the course of recovery from CABS and in altering subsequent risk for negative health outcomes. Second, CABS is the most common surgical procedure in use today for treating coronary artery disease. Current figures suggest that more than 170,000 CABS procedures are performed annually (American Heart Association, 1985) and that more than 2 million patients have undergone CABS in the United States since 1967 (Loop & Cosgrove, 1986). Put simply, CABS is an event that has an impact on many people. Third, there can be little doubt that it is an extremely stressful experience for most people. Recent estimates suggest, for example, that 20–40% of all CABS patients exhibit slow and difficult adjustment, a worsening of psychological conditions in spite of normal physiologic improvement, or both (see, e.g., Magni et al., 1987; Mayou & Bryant, 1987).

Fourth, because it is a relatively common procedure, many patients (even first-time bypass patients) come into the setting with some knowledge about what the experience will be like. Thus, bypass patients often arrive at the hospital with some specific expectations about what their operation and recovery will be like. As such, the CABS setting provides a rich environment within which to study the impact of specific versus generalized expectations, such as those embodied by dispositional optimism.

Finally, although a great deal of research effort has been expended trying to identify the presurgical *medical* attributes of those patients most likely to benefit from CABS, that is, survive 2–5 years postoperatively (e.g., Loop, 1983a, 1983b), relatively little research has been directed toward understanding the presurgical *psychosocial* predictors of recovery and benefit from CABS. Nor is much known about the effects of psychosocial factors on the patient's postsurgical quality of life.

The absence of studies relating psychosocial variables to life quality becomes even more noteworthy in light of recent findings that the benefits of CABS seem to lie in the procedure's ability to enhance the quality of life rather than prolong it. That is, patients with one- or two-vessel disease who undergo CABS do not show lower mortality or myocardial infarction (MI) rates compared to patients who receive medical treatment for coronary artery disease. Yet, CABS patients do show an advantage on variables relating to quality of life, usually operationalized in terms of severity of angina (see, e.g., Loop 1983a, 1983b; the Coronary Artery Surgery Study Randomized Trial [CASS], 1983, 1984).

Patients in our study were asked to provide information about various aspects of themselves and their experiences at three points in time: on the day before surgery, 6–8 days after surgery, and 6

months after surgery. A measure of dispositional optimism was obtained during the first point of data collection. Specific expectations were assessed at several different points in time as well. Information regarding choice of coping strategy was obtained both prior to surgery and 6–8 days postoperatively. Data relating to the patient's mood were also obtained at several points in time. Among the outcome measures obtained during the second and third assessment periods were the patient's in-hospital recovery rate (indexed by self-reports, other-reports, and overt behavior), rate of normalization of lifestyle, and self-reported quality of life. A variety of medical information was also obtained from the patient's medical records, surgery report, and catheterization report.

In general, we expected dispositional optimism to have broad, pervasive, beneficial effects on the patient's mood, rate of recovery, and quality of life. We also expected dispositional optimism to have an impact on the choice of coping strategy selected to deal with the stresses of the experience. In particular, we expected positive associations between optimism and manifestations of problem-focused coping (e.g., making of plans for recovery and seeking out information about what was going to happen) and negative associations between optimism and the use of emotion-focused coping strategies and denial.

Method

Setting and Subjects

Participants for the study were recruited through the Division of Cardiac Rehabilitation, a subdivision within the Department of Surgery and Department of Medicine, Allegheny General Hospital (Pittsburgh, PA). The Division of Cardiac Rehabilitation provides consulting and educational services during the hospitalization period to all patients undergoing cardiac surgery. From 1980 through 1982, the Division of Cardiac Rehabilitation provided consult services to 2,216 patients.

Subjects for the study were limited to patients who were having bypass surgery performed for the first time. Additional criteria were that the surgery be scheduled on a nonemergency basis, that the patients be men, and that they be under 58 years of age. Finally, the surgical procedure had to be limited to coronary artery bypass surgery. Patients receiving other types of coincidental surgical procedures (such as valvular surgery) were excluded.

All patients meeting eligibility criteria during the period February 7, 1984, through August 2, 1984, were asked to participate in the study. A total of 57 patients were contacted, 51 of whom agreed to participate. The average age of the sample was 48.5 years ($SD = 6.5$). The majority of the sample was employed full time at the time of hospitalization (74.5%), had 12 years of education or less (78.4%), and was married (86.3%).

In general, this group of bypass patients was relatively healthy. Of the 51 participants in the study, 19 patients (37%) had total blockage in one coronary artery, and 4 patients (8%) had total blockage in two coronary arteries (the remaining patients had no coronary arteries totally occluded). Using a criterion of 50% occlusion (rather than 100%), 16 patients (31%) had one diseased vessel, 24 (47%) had two diseased vessels, and only 9 patients (18%) suffered from three-vessel disease. The relative health status of the patients is important to keep in mind in light of previous findings that the main effect of CABS on patients with less than three-vessel disease seems to be on quality of life rather than mortality (CASS, 1983, 1984) and that quality of life is one of the main focuses of the present research.

Assessing Dispositional Optimism

Dispositional optimism was assessed by the Life Orientation Test (LOT; Scheier & Carver, 1985). The LOT provides a self-report measure of individual differences in global optimism, defined in terms of the favorability of the person's generalized outcome expectancies. The scale has an internal reliability (Cronbach's alpha) of .76 and a test–retest reliability (over a 4-week interval) of .79 (Scheier & Carver, 1985). The LOT is intended to reflect a pervasive orientation to the experiences of life. Thus, the items do not focus on any particular content domain. Nor is there a built-in confound between optimism and perceptions of personal efficacy, or locus of causality dimensions more generally. That is, items for the LOT were explicitly constructed to be devoid of any attribution-based or efficacy-based content. Its items were designed only to reflect the favorability of the person's generalized expectations for success.

Correlations between the LOT and measures of internal–external locus of control tend only to be moderate; for example, correlations with Rotter's (1966) I-E Scale typically fall around .35 (Scheier & Carver, 1985), and the correlation between the LOT and the internality dimension of the Attributional Style Questionnaire (Peterson et al., 1982) is .07 (Scheier & Carver, 1988b). Further details concerning the LOT's convergent and discriminant validity, as well as information about other aspects of its psychometric properties, can be found in Scheier and Carver (1985).

Assessing Situation-Specific Expectancies

In addition to measuring dispositional optimism, we assessed a number of context-specific expectancies. On the day before their surgery, the patients were asked to indicate their specific expectations of what the week following surgery would be like, in terms of the amount of pain, fatigue, nervousness, sadness, anger, and relief or happiness they expected to feel. Ratings in each case were made along 4-point Likert scales with appropriately labeled endpoints.

Six to 8 days postoperatively, patients were asked to provide information of a somewhat different sort. Specifically, they were asked to estimate (in weeks) the amount of time that they thought it would take for various aspects of their lives to return to normal—including how long it would take for them to return to work; resume social, recreational, and sexual activities; and begin vigorous physical exercise.

Assessing Reactions to Surgery

A number of intraoperative and perioperative measures were assembled, in order to assess the duration of the surgery and index how favorably the patients responded to it. Included here were measures of intraoperative complications such as treated arrhythmias and MI, as inferred on the basis of changes in the patient's electrocardiogram (EKG) and appearance of high levels of certain enzymes in the blood (e.g., aspartate amino transferase [AST], formerly known as serum glutamic-oxaloacetic transaminase, or SGOT, and creatinine phosphokinase [CPK]). Cross-clamp time and pump time were used to provide measures of the duration of surgery. Finally, a record was kept of the number of grafts performed.

Assessing Recovery

First week after surgery. Several different measures of recovery rate were obtained during the week following surgery. One set of measures involved the patient's self-assessment of his own physical and psychological condition during the immediate postoperative recovery period (e.g., the amount of pain, nervousness, and fatigue being felt). This set of ratings was made approximately 6–8 days postoperatively by using 4-point Likert scales with appropriately labeled endpoints. The patients also answered a set of questions concerning their satisfaction with the level of medical care and information they had been receiving.

In addition to patient ratings, the attending member of the Division of Cardiac Rehabilitation was asked to rate the patient's progress during the immediate postoperative period. Division of Cardiac Rehabilitation members rated the rate of the patient's physical recovery, his morale, and their prognosis for the patient's life to return to normal within 4 months postsurgery. Each of these ratings was made on an appropriately labeled 3-point Likert scale. Given the procedures used to assign staff members to patients, it was not possible to have patients rated by more than one staff member. Consequently, there are no interrater reliability data available for these ratings.

Finally, physical markers of recovery were also measured during the immediate postoperative period. The markers ranged from sitting upright in bed for the first time, to walking around the room for the first time, to walking unassisted for over 10 min straight. In each case, the variable of interest was the length of time needed for the "milestone" of physical recovery to be attained.

Complications at 6 weeks. Approximately 6 weeks following the surgery, patients were asked to return to the attending surgeon for a brief follow-up evaluation. At this time, patients were judged by the surgeon to be making normal progress or to be suffering from some sort of complication (e.g., shortness of breath, lingering pain associated with suturing, congestive heart failure). Data from this 6-week follow-up examination were assembled and treated in a dichotomous manner to divide patients into those who were and were not having complications at the time. The data were dichotomized because only a few of the patients ($n = 6$) had developed complications at 6 weeks. This made subdivision of the data into finer subcategories impractical.

Recovery at 6 months. Several aspects of the patient's recovery were assessed 6 months following surgery. First, patients were queried about the degree of satisfaction they felt over their current health status and about whether they thought that their surgery had generally improved their health. In addition, a measure of angina was obtained by asking patients to complete the seven items relating to angina from the Rose Questionnaire, a measure frequently used to assess the presence of angina in cardiac patients (Rose, 1965). Patients also responded to another item from the Rose Questionnaire that is used to assess the occurrence of a probable MI. The time frame for all items on the Rose Questionnaire was limited to that which had passed since the surgery was performed. Information regarding the psychometric properties of the Rose Questionnaire, including its validity, can be found in Rose (1965).

The final aspect of recovery measured at 6 months was the rapidity with which various areas of the patient's life had returned to normal. Recovery within each area was assessed in two ways: First, patients were asked whether they had yet resumed the activity in question. If they answered yes, they then indicated how long it took them to resume the activity (in weeks). The activities covered were the same ones for which patients had indicated expectations the week following surgery. Thus, the patient indicated if and when he had returned to work, begun vigorous physical exercise (e.g., walking briskly for 50–60 min, running or jogging, doing manual labor for 8–10 hr), resumed socializing with friends, returned to hobby and recreational activities, and reinstituted sexual activity.

Assessing Quality of Life

Perceived quality of life was assessed at the 6-month follow-up with Andrews and Withey's (1976) Perceived Quality of Life Scale. The scale consists of 123 Likert-type items, which cover a broad spectrum of life quality, ranging from satisfaction with home, family, and health to satisfaction with one's sexual relations and recreational activities. Typically, the scale is used to generate one overall quality-of-life measure. Psychometrically, the scale is sound. Complete information about the scale (e.g., its factor structure, reliability, and validity) can be found in Andrews and Withey (1976).

Assessing Coping Strategies

In addition to rate of improvement, we also wanted to assess the relation between optimism and the different ways in which the patients attempted to cope with the difficulties of their surgery and recovery period. Of particular interest were strategies involving attentional mechanisms, such as the attempt to cope by not thinking about ongoing procedures and feelings. Coping strategies were assessed on the day before surgery by asking patients to indicate how much thought they had given to their symptoms, emotions, and stay in the hospital during the preceding 2-day period. In an effort to measure thought suppression and denial, patients were also asked to indicate the extent to which they had tried to ignore or not think about such things during the same period of time. Finally, patients were asked to indicate the degree to which they had sought out information relevant to their operation and recovery period, as well as the degree to which they had made plans and set goals for the immediate period of time postsurgically. A similar set of questions was readministered 6–8 days postsurgery, except that the time frame for the items dealing with seeking out information and formulating plans was extended to cover the months ahead. Because of time constraints surrounding patient access, each separate coping strategy was assessed by a single coping item. In all cases, responses were obtained with appropriately labeled 4-point Likert scales.

Assessing Mood

The patient's mood was assessed presurgically and 6–8 days postoperatively by the Multiple Affect Adjective Check List (MAACL; Zuckerman, 1960; Zuckerman, Lubin, & Robins, 1965). This instrument provides a measure of three separate emotional states: depression, anxiety, and hostility. The factor structure of the MAACL, its internal consistency, and its predictive and construct validity are

well documented (for details, see Zuckerman, 1960; Zuckerman et al., 1965).

Medical Information Obtained

Medical information was obtained about each patient through medical history records as well as laboratory reports. Preoperative medical measures included length of time since coronary heart disease was first diagnosed. Prior history of MI, congestive heart failure, and angina were also recorded. Available from the patient's catheterization report was a listing of the number of coronary artery segments occluded 50% or greater. Data concerning left ventricular ejection fraction, left ventricular end diastolic pressure, and left ventricular function were too incomplete to be of use (because of variations in laboratory reporting). Information about blood cholesterol level, smoking history, and history of hypertension was also gathered on each patient.

Procedures of Data Collection

On the day of admission to Allegheny General Hospital (typically the day prior to CABS), all patients were contacted by a member of the Division of Cardiac Rehabilitation and told about the option to participate in the study. Patients were informed about the general nature of the study (to examine psychosocial predictors of recovery from surgery), as well as what would be required of them during the course of the project. If the patient chose to participate, he signed an informed consent sheet and received a brief self-administered questionnaire to complete (which took approximately 15 min).

Contained on this questionnaire were the LOT and the MAACL. The questionnaire also contained the series of items designed to tap attentional strategies for coping with the surgery and its aftermath, as well as the questions dealing with the specific expectancies the patients held for their short-term recovery.

The second patient contact occurred 6–8 days postsurgically, following the patient's return to the regular cardiac surgery ward after release from intensive care. At this time the patient was administered a second questionnaire. Contained on the questionnaire were the MAACL and the item sets designed to assess the patient's current level of fatigue, pain, and morale. Questions dealing with the nature of the coping strategies being used were also repeated for a second time on this questionnaire. Finally, the questionnaire contained the items dealing with the patient's expectations about the rate of normalization of his lifestyle during the coming months postsurgery.

The final contact occurred 6 months postoperatively by mail and telephone. Patients were mailed a packet of materials containing a cover letter, a self-administered questionnaire, and a self-addressed envelope in which to return the forms. The cover letter reminded the patients of the project in which they had agreed to participate and briefly described the nature of the questionnaire that was enclosed. Patients were told that they could complete the questionnaire on their own (with no help from others) if they wanted, and then return it in the enclosed self-addressed envelope. Alternatively, they could wait until they were contacted by phone by a member of the research team, who would help them complete the forms.

Following a 2–3-day delay (to allow the mail to reach the patient), the patient was contacted by phone and queried about the status of the questionnaire. Patients who needed assistance were given aid. If the patient's questionnaire was not received within a week of the first telephone call, the patient was called again to see what had happened. This procedure of phoning and rephoning was continued until either the questionnaire was received or the patient had been contacted four times. Of the 51 patients who were enrolled in the project, 6-month questionnaire data were obtained from 48 (94%). In each case, the missing data were a product of the patient's refusal to participate further.

Two general sets of items were of interest on the 6-month follow-up questionnaire. One item set designed assessed the rate at which various aspects of the patient's lifestyle had returned to normal (i.e., when he had returned to work, begun recreational activities, etc.). The second item set consisted of Andrews and Withey's (1976) Quality of Life Scale.

Because of limited patient access it was impossible to administer all of the items from some of the longer psychosocial scales of interest. Our response was to administer only a subset of items from each of the longer psychosocial scales. Items were selected on the basis of the magnitude of the item-scale correlations (as determined through pretesting procedures). The specific scales truncated in this fashion were the LOT, the three subscales of the MAACL, and Andrews and Withey's (1976) Quality of Life Scale. The abbreviated LOT contained four items; each shortened subscale of the MAACL contained five items; and the abbreviated Quality of Life Scale contained 31 items. Pretesting procedures revealed that the correlations between the subset of items actually administered and the total items to which the subsets of items belonged were acceptably high, both at one point in time and across a 4-week interval (the rs ranged in value from .78 to .89). Thus, relatively little information was lost by using the abbreviated scale format (see also Burisch, 1984).

Results

Adjusting Analyses for Medical Variables

Our primary interest in conducting this research was to document the beneficial effects of dispositional optimism on recovery from CABS, independent of major medical factors that might also have affected the results. In this regard, three aspects of the patient's medical status seemed particularly important to control. These were the extensiveness of the patient's surgery, the severity of the patient's underlying coronary artery disease, and the patient's standing on the major risk factors for coronary heart disease.

As a measure of extensiveness of surgery, we used the number of grafts that were performed. Values on this variable ranged from 1 to 6 ($M = 2.2$, $SD = 1.0$). The correlation between the number of grafts performed and optimism was nonsignificant, $r(51) = -.12$, $p > .39$. (All tests of statistical significance reported in this article are two-tailed.) As may be expected, number of grafts was highly correlated with several measures reflecting the duration of surgery. For example, number of grafts was highly correlated with both cross-clamp time, $r(43) = .50$, $p < .0001$, and pump time, $r(45) = .65$, $p < .0001$. Dispositional optimism was not a significant correlate of either cross-clamp time, $r(45) = -.03$, $p > .50$, or pump time, $r(47) = -.24$, $p > .10$.

As an index of the extent of the patient's coronary artery disease, we used the number of main coronary arteries (out of four) that were occluded 50% or more. This variable has been used extensively in prior research to assess progression of disease (e.g., Frank, Heller, Kornfeld, Sporn, & Weiss, 1978; Krantz et al., 1981). The correlation between the number of arteries occluded and dispositional optimism was .03 (nonsignificant). The mean number of arteries occluded 50% or more in this sample was 1.78 ($SD = 0.78$).

The final medical covariate was a composite variable, comprised of the patient's standing on the three risk factors for coronary heart disease (each scored dichotomously as being present or absent). Patients were given one point each if they (a) were currently smoking, (b) had been diagnosed as hypertensive, or (c) had cholesterol values greater than 240 mg/dl. Scores on this composite ranged from 0 to 3 ($M = 1.0$, $SD = 0.75$). Dispositional optimism was uncorrelated ($r = .00$) with the composite risk-factor variable.

For all analyses that follow, the data were first adjusted for the (simultaneous) effects of the three medical variables just described (i.e., number of grafts performed, number of main coronary arteries occluded 50% or more, and total score on the composite risk-factor variable). This was done using multiple linear regression analyses, in which the three medical variables were entered together in Step 1 of each analysis, followed by the relevant predictor variable in Step 2. The significance of the predictor was evaluated by determining whether it accounted for a significant increment in variance beyond that accounted for by the three medical factors alone. For simplicity in presentation, only the F values associated with the R^2 change are reported in the text. Also, unless otherwise noted, all variables in the regression analyses were treated in a continuous fashion, rather than dichotomized artificially.

Reactions to Surgery

A variety of measures were taken while the surgery was underway in order to assess how favorably the patient responded. Dispositional optimism proved to be related to several perioperative physiologic reactions. First, optimists were significantly less likely than pessimists to have developed new Q-waves on their EKGs as a result of the surgery,

$F(1, 46) = 7.82$, $p < .01$. The appearance of new Q-waves is generally taken as a sign of MI (see, e.g., CASS, 1984; Loop & Cosgrove, 1986).

Consistent with this finding, optimists were also significantly less likely to have shown a clinically significant release (i.e., greater than 100 mU/ml) of AST, an enzyme indicative of general muscle damage that is also released coincident with MI, $F(1, 46) = 4.70$, $p < .05$. Dispositional optimism was also associated in a similar direction with a clinically significant release (i.e., greater than 1,000 mU/ml) of CPK, another enzyme related to general muscle damage. This latter association was not significant, however.

Taken together, these data suggest that optimists were significantly less likely than pessimists to have shown physiologic evidence indicative of MI during the course of surgery. We should note, however, that these findings need to be interpreted cautiously. This is so because the base rate for MIs in studies of this type is low, averaging around 6% (CASS, 1984). Indeed, perhaps the best single marker of MI available to us was the development of new Q-waves following surgery, and only 1 patient showed evidence of new Q-waves. Still, this person did have the lowest optimism score of any patient in the sample, and the effect for dispositional optimism was significant. Moreover, the association between optimism and the development of new Q-waves remained significant even when cross-clamp time and pump time were entered into the multiple regression equation in Step 1 along with the three regular medical covariates, $F(1, 38) = 6.36$, $p < .02$.

Rate of Recovery

Recovery during the first week. Two different types of measures were used to assess recovery during the week immediately following the patient's surgery. The first concerned markers of physical recovery. In all, five discrete markers were used to assess rate of recovery, ranging from the time it took patients to first sit up in bed to the time it took them to walk around the room for 5–10 min. Optimists achieved each of these markers of recovery more quickly than did pessimists (average part correlation equaled –.16), although the size of the effect attained statistical significance for only one of the events monitored. Specifically, optimists took significantly fewer days to begin walking around their hospital rooms following their surgery than did pessimists, $F(1, 44) = 6.67$, $p < .02$.

The second measure relevant to recovery during the first week involved two ratings made by Division of Cardiac Rehabilitation staff members of the extent of the patient's physical progress. One rating asked staff members to judge the patient's progress taking into account the medical factors contained in the patient's medical file. The second rating was made relative to other CABS patients the staff member had seen. Optimistic patients were rated by the staff members as showing a more favorable physical recovery than were pessimists vis-à-vis the patient's specific medical profile, $F(1, 44) = 6.25$, $p < .02$. Optimists also received a more favorable rating when the judgment was made relative to other CABS patients, although this effect was only marginally significant, $F(1, 44) = 2.90$, $p < .10$.

In addition to rating the patient's physical progress, Cardiac Rehabilitation staff members made two other ratings of interest. First, they were asked to judge the patient's morale. Optimists were rated as having nonsignificantly higher morale than were pessimists, $F(1, 44) = 2.42$, $p < .13$. Second, staff members were asked to make a prognosis concerning the rate at which the patient's lifestyle would return to normal in the months ahead. Optimists received a more favorable prognosis than did pessimists. Again, however, the magnitude of the effect was nonsignificant ($p > .35$).

Six weeks postoperative. Review of medical records revealed that optimists tended to have fewer complications at the 6-week follow-up than did pessimists, but the effect was not significant, $F(1, 43) = 2.50$, $p > .10$.

Six months postoperative. At 6 months, the patients were asked to indicate the extent to which their lives had returned to normal across a number of life domains (e.g., whether they had returned to full-time work, resumed physical exercise, etc.). Patients responded to the questions in two steps. First, they were asked whether they had resumed the activity in question. Analyses revealed that optimists were significantly more likely than pessimists to have resumed vigorous physical exercise, $F(1, 43) = 5.13$, $p < .03$. In addition, there was a marginally significant tendency for optimists to have already returned to work on a full-time basis, $F(1, 42) = 3.66$, $p < .07$.

In order to obtain a more general measure of the extent to which the patient's life had normalized, a composite index was created by summing for each patient the number of life domains that had returned to normal (five domains were assessed). A significant association emerged between dispositional optimism and this composite, such that optimists were more likely to have normalized their lives across a greater number of domains, $F(1, 42) = 6.92$, $p < .02$.

In the second step of the question, patients who had responded yes at the first step were asked to indicate how long (in weeks) it took for their life to return to normal (for each domain in question). For purposes of analyses, if a patient had not yet resumed a particular activity, he was given a score (in weeks) equal to the length of time that had passed since his operation. Two marginally significant effects emerged from these analyses. Optimists tended to resume vigorous physical exercise more quickly than did pessimists, $F(1, 42) = 3.17$, $p < .09$. They also tended to return to their recreational activities more quickly, $F(1, 43) = 3.31$, $p < .08$.

As with the dichotomous data, a composite variable was formed using the temporal data in order to derive a more general index of the rate at which the patient's life returned to normal across domains. Prior to adding scores across the five life domains, the raw data for each domain were transformed to z scores, so that each domain would contribute an equal weight to the composite. The change in R^2 due to dispositional optimism was significant, $F(1, 42) = 6.53$, $p < .02$. Thus, optimists normalized their lives across domains in a fewer number of weeks than did pessimists.

In addition to questions about returning to activities, patients also responded to a set of items that were designed to assess both the presence of angina and the possibility of MI during the time since the surgery was performed. Although optimism was not a significant predictor of angina, it was marginally related to probable MI, $F(1, 43) = 4.00$, $p < .06$. Specifically, optimists were less likely to endorse signs of a probable MI than were pessimists at the time of the 6-month follow-up. We should also note here, as we did when describing reactions to the surgery, that the base rate of probable MI in the sample was small (only 3 patients). Still, as with the surgical data, dispositional optimism did prove to be a significant predictor.

Quality of Life at 6 Months

Dispositional optimism had a strong effect on the patient's quality of life measured 6 months postoperatively, $F(1, 43) = 34.16, p < .0001$. Optimists reported a higher quality of life than did pessimists.

Mood and Satisfaction With Treatment

We measured the patient's mood twice, once on the day prior to surgery and once 6–8 days postoperatively. There was a significant effect of optimism on hostility, $F(1, 46) = 9.80, p < .005$, and a marginally significant effect of optimism on depression, $F(1, 46) = 3.20, p < .09$, such that optimists had lower levels of presurgical hostility and depression. Optimism was unrelated to anxiety prior to surgery. There was no significant relation between optimism and mood 6–8 days postoperatively (as assessed by the MAACL), although a significant positive association did emerge between optimism and self-rated happiness or relief at that time, as assessed by a separate item, $F(1, 45) = 8.34, p < .007$.

In addition to rating mood during the immediate postoperative period, the patient was also asked to indicate his level of satisfaction with the quality of his medical care, the amount of emotional support he was receiving from friends, and other aspects of his experience. Optimists reported significantly more satisfaction with the level of medical care they had been receiving than did pessimists, $F(1, 45) = 10.54, p < .003$. There was also a marginally significant tendency for optimists to report greater satisfaction with the amount of emotional support and backing they had been receiving from friends and relatives, $F(1, 45) = 3.06, p < .09$.

As just mentioned, optimism correlated significantly with both presurgical hostility and depression. This covariation raises the possibility that the effects described thus far for optimism were in fact attributable to the association between optimism and these presurgical affects, not to optimism per se. To evaluate this possibility, we performed three sets of supplementary regression analyses on the data. Each set of analyses focused on a different affect (i.e., either hostility, depression, or anxiety) as determined by scores on the MAACL. In each case, the relevant affect was entered along with the three regular medical covariates in Step 1 of the multiple regression. The independent contribution of dispositional optimism was then evaluated by entering it (by itself) in Step 2. In this way, all of the major findings described thus far for dispositional optimism were reexamined.

The results of these analyses can be summarized succinctly. Entering presurgical affect into the multiple regression analyses had little effect on the findings relating to dispositional optimism. Specifically, one significant effect out of seven (involving return to vigorous exercise) became marginally significant when presurgical depression and hostility were each individually controlled ($ps < .07$ and $.08$, respectively). On the other hand, one effect (involving probable MI), which was marginally significant when presurgical affect was uncontrolled, became significant when presurgical anxiety and hostility were each individually controlled ($ps < .03$ and $.02$, respectively). In all other respects, previously reported findings remained the same. Indeed, findings relating to dispositional optimism tended to remain intact even when all three presurgical affects were entered into the multiple regression equation simultaneously (along with the three regular medical covariates). In brief, effects attributed to dispositional optimism seemed not to be due to the associations between optimism and level of presurgical anxiety, depression, and hostility.

Coping Strategies

Coping strategies were measured twice, once on the day prior to surgery and once 6–8 days postoperatively. Strategy effectiveness was also assessed, but only once (6–8 days postoperatively). Prior to surgery, optimists were more likely than pessimists to be making plans for themselves and setting goals for their recovery, $F(1, 46) = 4.52, p < .04$. At the same time, optimists were less likely to be focusing on the negative aspects of their emotional reaction (e.g., their nervousness), although this latter finding was only marginally significant, $F(1, 46) = 3.56, p < .07$.

Four effects emerged from analyses of the data from Postsurgical Days 6–8, although one of these effects was only marginally significant. First, optimists were more likely than pessimists to report seeking out and requesting information about what the physician would be requiring of them in the months ahead, $F(1, 45) = 10.18, p < .005$. In contrast, optimists were marginally less likely than pessimists to cope by trying to ignore or suppress thoughts about their physical symptoms, $F(1, 45) = 3.31, p < .08$. They were also less likely to report being helped by thinking about the negative aspects of their emotional experience, $F(1, 42) = 4.23, p < .05$. Finally, optimists were less likely than pessimists to report being helped by the attempt to ignore or not think about what their recovery would be like in the months ahead, $F(1, 44) = 4.20, p < .05$.

Specific Expectancies

Expectations regarding experiences during the immediate postoperative period. Two different sets of specific expectancies were assessed. One set had to do with the patients' expectations (measured on the day prior to surgery) about what the week following surgery would be like in terms of the amount of pain, nervousness, relief they expected to feel, and so on. In all, six different specific expectancies were assessed. The effects of these expectancies on the patient's subsequent experience were somewhat mixed. That is, of the six specific expectancies measured, three were largely unrelated to their corresponding outcomes (average $ps > .45$), and two were marginally related to their corresponding outcomes (average $ps < .07$). Only one expectancy (expected happiness) was strongly related to its corresponding outcome (actual happiness), $F(1, 44) = 18.11, p < .001$.

The same mixed pattern of results emerged when the relations between these specific expectancies and other types of outcomes were examined. In fact, only one specific expectancy (anticipated nervousness) produced consistent effects. The effect of anticipated nervousness was always negative (i.e., those who expected to be more nervous during the first postoperative week experienced more negative outcomes than those who expected to be less nervous). More specifically, expectations regarding nervousness predicted (a) the rate at which certain recovery milestones were achieved, such as number of days to walk for 5–10 min, $F(1, 42) = 9.34, p < .005$, and length of hospitalization, $F(1, 43) = 5.79, p < .05$; (b) amount of time spent in intensive care, $F(1, 39) = 3.99, p < .06$; (c) ratings made by Division of Cardiac Rehabilitation

members regarding patient morale, $F(1, 43) = 3.86, p < .06$, and anticipated rate of normalization of lifestyle, $F(1, 43) = 11.15, p < .002$; (d) whether the patient had returned to work, $F(1, 41) = 4.32, p < .05$, as well as how quickly they return to work, $F(1, 41) = 4.32, p < .05$, as well as how quickly the return to work took place, $F(1, 41) = 7.30, p < .01$; (e) how quickly the patient began socializing again with friends, $F(1, 42) = 3.92, p < .06$; (f) overall rate of normalization of life function 6 months postoperatively, $F(1, 41) = 4.82, p < .05$; and (g) life quality 6 months postoperatively, $F(1, 42) = 3.62, p < .07$. Although other specific expectancies correlated with certain outcome measures—for example, expected sadness correlated significantly with both length of hospitalization and time spent in intensive care, $F(1, 43) = 10.06, p < .005$, and $F(1, 39) = 13.21, p < .001$, respectively—only expected nervousness correlated in a broad fashion with a number of the outcomes assessed.

The results just described for expected nervousness controlled for the three major medical factors but did not control for the effects of dispositional optimism, which correlated with expected nervousness, $r(49) = -.26, p < .08$. When the effects of optimism were also controlled, exactly half of the significant effects for expected nervousness diminished to a p value greater than .10. In contrast, when expectations regarding nervousness were controlled and the effects of optimism reanalyzed, only four effects (out of the 19 significant and marginally significant effects previously reported) assumed a p value greater than .10.

Expectations regarding normalization of life functions. The second set of specific expectancies concerned the patient's estimate (in weeks) of the amount of time that would be needed for various aspects of his life to return to normal. These estimates were made during the week following surgery. Table 22.1 shows the results of regression analyses between these expectancy variables and the two types of outcome variables involving normalization of life functions (described earlier in conjunction with the findings for dispositional optimism).

As can be seen, specific expectancy about returning to sexual activities was a significant predictor of each type of relevant outcome measure; that is, specific expectancies about sex predicted both if and how soon sexual activities had resumed,

TABLE 22.1. Multiple Linear Regression of Domain-Specific Outcomes 6 Months Postsurgery on Domain-Specific Expectancies, Controlling for the Three Medical Factors

Criterion	Predictor	R^2 total	R^2 change	β	F
Have resumed:	Expectations for:				
Working	Work	.16	.01	.07	0.18
Exercising	Exercise	.01	.00	.01	0.00
Having sex	Sex	.34	.28	.54	15.11***
Socializing	Socializing	N/Aª	N/Aª	N/Aª	N/Aª
Doing hobbies	Hobbies	.05	.01	.11	0.43
Rate (in weeks) to resume:	Expectations for:				
Working	Work	.29	.16	−.43	7.72**
Exercising	Exercise	.07	.06	−.26	2.10
Having sex	Sex	.37	.34	−.60	19.48***
Socializing	Socializing	.28	.17	−.45	8.56**
Doing hobbies	Hobbies	.07	.02	−.13	0.64

ªN/A = not available. It was not possible to compute a multiple regression in this case because there was no variability on the criterion (i.e., all patients for whom data were available had resumed socializing activities by the time of the 6-month follow-up).
*$p < .05$. **$p < .01$. ***$p < .001$.

Fs(1, 36) = 15.11 and 19.48, ps < .001, respectively. In addition, specific expectancies about work predicted how soon work was resumed, F(1, 34) = 7.72, $p < .01$, and specific expectancies about socializing predicted how soon socializing activities were resumed, F(1, 36) = 8.56, $p < .01$. In each case, the direction of association was such that a more favorable expectancy was associated with a greater likelihood of a faster rate of return.

Table 22.2 shows the results of multiple regression analyses between the domain-specific expect-ancies and the two composite variables that were formed by summing normalization outcomes across behavioral domains. As can be seen in Table 22.2, only one effect (involving expectations about sexual activities and overall rate of return to life activities) reached an acceptable level of statistical significance, F(1, 36) = 11.60, $p < .01$. This drop in the number of significant associations (from four to one) as one moves from specific to general outcomes suggests that domain-specific expectancies may be better predictors of domain-

Table 22.2. Multiple Linear Regression of Composite Outcomes 6 Months Postsurgery on Domain-Specific Expectancies, Controlling for the Three Medical Factors

Criterion	Predictor	R^2 total	R^2 change	β	F
	Expectations for:				
Resumed activities or not, summed across activities	Work	.07	.01	.08	0.22
"	Exercise	.08	.01	−.12	0.47
"	Sex	.07	.01	.09	0.30
"	Socializing	.06	.00	−.02	0.01
"	Hobbies	.13	.06	.25	2.55
	Expectations for:				
Rate (in weeks) to resume activities, summed across activities	Work	.10	.05	−.24	1.92
"	Exercise	.05	.00	−.04	0.05
"	Sex	.28	.23	−.49	11.60**
"	Socializing	.14	.09	−.32	3.63
"	Hobbies	.10	.05	−.23	2.02

*$p < .05$. **$p < .01$.

specific outcomes than they are of outcomes that are more general in nature.

The analyses just described controlled for the effects of the three medical variables, but did not control for the effects of dispositional optimism. In order to determine whether similar effects would emerge if optimism were also controlled, additional regression analyses were performed, controlling for dispositional optimism as well as the three medical variables. These analyses yielded generally the same results as when dispositional optimism was uncontrolled. The only difference was the appearance of one additional significant effect—namely, when optimism was also controlled, specific expectancies regarding return to hobbies was a significant predictor of overall resumption of life activities, $F(1, 35) = 4.75, p < .05$.

In general, effects involving the patient's specific expectancies remained significant when dispositional optimism was controlled along with the three medical factors. Is the reverse also true? Do the effects of dispositional optimism remain significant when the patient's specific expectations are controlled? Findings relevant to this question are presented in Tables 22.3 and 22.4. As can be seen, the answer to this question is generally yes. In terms of domain-specific outcomes, four effects (corresponding to Entries 1, 2, 7, and 10 in Table 22.3) were significant (or marginally significant) when domain-specific expectations were uncontrolled. These same effects remained significant or marginally so after controlling for the effects of the relevant domain-specific expectancy (the first and last entries in Table 22.3 have p values of .09 and .08, respectively). Indeed, one effect (involving the rate at which the patient returned to work) became significant in these analyses, $F(1, 33) = 4.30, p < .05$, when before it was not.

The effects of dispositional optimism fared equally well when composite outcome variables were considered (see Table 22.4). Recall that dispositional optimism was a significant predictor of both composite variables, when specific expectations were uncontrolled. Dispositional optimism continued to predict both composite outcomes, not only when domain-specific expectancies were each controlled in turn, but also when the influence of all five specific expectancies were controlled simultaneously (see Table 22.4 for relevant Fs). The only exception to this characterization involved the effect of optimism on the overall likelihood of having resumed activities, which attained only a marginal level of statistical significance when all domain-specific expectancies were controlled simultaneously, $F(1, 28) = 2.35, p < .07$. These findings, taken in conjunction with those presented earlier, suggest that domain-specific expectancies and dispositional optimism can both predict important outcomes relating to recovery from CABS. The data also suggest that specific expectancies and dispositional optimism can each account for some portion of variance that is unique from the other (at least for some of the outcome variables that were considered).

TABLE 22.3. Multiple Linear Regression of Domain-Specific Outcomes 6 Months Postsurgery on Dispositional Optimism, Controlling for Relevant Domain-Specific Expectancies and the Three Medical Factors

Criterion	Predictor	R^2 total	R^2 change	β	F
Have resumed:					
Working	Dispositional optimism	.23	.07	.28	3.20
Exercising	"	.12	.11	.35	4.46*
Having sex	"	.34	.00	.04	0.08
Socializing	"	.11	.02	.12	0.73
Doing hobbies	"	.05	.01	.08	0.21
Rate (in weeks) to resume:					
Working	Dispositional optimism	.37	.08	−.29	4.30*
Exercising	"	.17	.10	−.33	4.22*
Having sex	"	.37	.00	−.04	0.07
Socializing	"	.32	.04	−.19	1.83
Doing hobbies	"	.15	.08	−.29	3.41

*$p < .05$.

TABLE 22.4. Multiple Linear Regression of Composite Outcomes 6 Months Postsurgery on Dispositional Optimism, Controlling for Different Domain-Specific Expectancies and the Three Medical Factors

Criterion	Predictor	Controlling for domain-specific expectancy about	R^2 total	R^2 change	β	F
Resumed activities or not, summed across activities	Dispositional optimism	Work	.21	.14	.39	6.03*
"	"	Exercise	.20	.12	.36	5.14*
"	"	Sex	.20	.13	.36	5.45*
"	"	Socializing	.20	.14	.37	5.73*
"	"	Hobbies	.29	.17	.42	8.24*
"	"	All	.43	.24	.40	2.35
Rate (in weeks) to resume activities, summed across activities	Dispositional optimism	Work	.25	.16	−.40	6.91*
"	"	Exercise	.19	.14	−.39	5.89*
"	"	Sex	.35	.08	−.28	4.12*
"	"	Socializing	.24	.11	−.34	4.88*
"	"	Hobbies	.26	.16	−.41	7.48**
"	"	All	.50	.33	−.36	3.74*

*$p < .05$. **$p < .01$.

Discussion

Effects of Dispositional Optimism

We began this research with the expectation that dispositional optimism would have a broad effect on the patient's responses to and recovery from CABS. This indeed proved to be the case. Optimists were less likely than pessimists to have shown signs of perioperative MI. They tended to achieve various markers of physical recovery in the week following their surgery more quickly than did pessimists (significantly so in some case, marginally so in others). At the same time, they were judged by members of the cardiac rehabilitation team as evidencing a significantly faster rate of recovery. Finally, optimists were more likely than pessimists to have returned to several different life activities by the time of the 6-month follow-up, as well as more likely to have resumed those activities more quickly.

Taken together, these findings strongly suggest that optimism exerted a pervasive effect on the patient's physical well-being and rate of recovery, both during and following surgery. Moreover, in all analyses conducted, procedures were used that controlled for (a) the number of grafts performed

during surgery, (b) the extent of the patient's coronary artery disease, and (c) the patient's standing on traditional risk factors for coronary heart disease. It thus becomes more difficult to dismiss the findings relevant to physical well-being and recovery with the argument that optimists did better because they were healthier, or had less radical surgery performed.

In addition to these effects involving physical well-being and recovery, optimism was also implicated in a number of other effects. For example, optimists reported being less hostile and (marginally) less depressed than did pessimists just prior to their surgery. They also reported greater satisfaction with the care they were receiving from the medical staff and with the amount of emotional support they were receiving from friends and family.

Two additional findings are particularly interesting because of the relation of those findings to prior research. The first concerns the presence in the data of a strong positive association between dispositional optimism (assessed presurgically) and self-reported quality of life (assessed 6 months postoperatively). This finding is particularly significant because of the importance currently afforded quality-of-life measures in studies of

CABS. That is, recent research suggests that the benefits of CABS (relative to medical treatment for angina) lies in its ability to enhance the quality of life rather than to prolong life's duration (see, e.g., Loop, 1983a, 1983b; CASS, 1983, 1984). Our finding suggests that this consequence is more marked among people who are optimistic than among those who are pessimistic.

The other noteworthy finding concerns differences between optimists and pessimists in how they coped with the stresses surrounding their experience. Prior to surgery, optimists were much less likely to be dwelling on the negative aspects of their emotional experience (e.g., their feelings of nervousness and sadness). In contrast, optimists were more likely than pessimists to be making plans for themselves and setting goals for their recovery. To cast this finding differently, pessimists were more disengaged than optimists from postoperative goals. This relative tendency for pessimists to disengage was even more pronounced postsurgically. By then, pessimists were actively trying to block out thinking about aspects of their experience such as their symptoms. Optimists, on the other hand, were trying to acquire as much information as possible about their recommended regimens.

We find these coping-strategy differences interesting for three reasons. First, they fit well with suggestions made in the past regarding disengagement in the face of stressful occurrences. Specifically, Carver and Scheier (1981, 1983, 1986) have argued that negative expectations give rise to an impetus to physically remove oneself from the context in which the stress is occurring, but that this initial impetus is replaced by a tendency toward mental disengagement if physical withdrawal is not possible. Clearly, patients who have just had major surgery cannot run away from the experience. With no possibility of physical escape, the only recourse available to someone with negative expectations is to withdraw mentally. It is of substantial interest, then, that pessimists actively tried to not think about aspects of their experience.

The second reason we find these differences in coping strategies interesting is the similarity they have to other data on coping strategies collected in a different context (Carver et al., 1989; Scheier et al., 1986). That other research also showed optimists to be more likely to deal with stressful encounters by formulating plans for action and not thinking about the negative emotions with which the stress was associated. The present findings add to those earlier findings by replicating them in a naturalistic setting in which the stress level was high.

The third reason is that optimism appears to exert its influence on quality of life in part through coping strategies. Quality of life is the most substantiated outcome of CABS (e.g., CASS, 1983), and the coping strategies used by optimists in the present study seemed to promote that outcome. These data only establish prospective associations, however, between optimism, coping, and quality of life. They do not determine causality. An experiment-based intervention study with CABS patients would thus seem to be in order. The specific purpose of the study would be to document more directly the utility of adopting optimistic coping strategies by designing intervention programs to enhance the use of those strategies among pessimistic patients. These programs could include specific and advance information about the recovery process, setting of attainable and realistic goals during the months ahead, and not suppressing fears and thoughts about the negative aspects of the experience. The results from such a study, if positive, would offer persuasive evidence for the causal role played by optimistic coping strategies in promoting a more favorable quality of life.

In contrast to quality of life, however, the effects of optimism on intraoperative complications, ratings of physical recovery by medical personnel, and normalization of activities seem not to be mediated by coping strategies, at least not by those that were measured. This fact suggests that optimism may have direct, perhaps physiological, effects. Relevant here are the findings of Van Treuren and Hull (1986) that showed that optimists exhibit smaller blood pressure and heart rate responses during a stressful task than do pessimists. Individual differences in the magnitude of blood pressure and heart rate responses, called *cardiovascular reactivity*, are hypothesized to be a risk factor for coronary heart and artery disease (Krantz & Manuck, 1984; Matthews et al., 1986). Thus, to the extent that optimists are less reactive to the stress of surgery and its aftermath than pessimists, they may be expected to have a better and quicker recovery.

Specific Expectancies Versus Dispositional Optimism

Our interest in conducting this project was not to study the effects of specific expectancies per se, but to examine the interplay between specific and generalized expectations (i.e., dispositional optimism). Still, it is interesting to note that specific expectancies (by themselves) played a significant role in certain aspects of the recovery process. For example, expectations about when sexual activities would be initiated significantly predicted whether such activities had been resumed by the time of the 6-month follow-up, as well as the rate with which they were resumed. Expectations about work and about socializing activities also predicted the rate with which those activities were begun again. More generally, expectations regarding sexual activity predicted the overall rate with which activities were resumed. These various findings suggest that specific expectancies were playing a far from trivial role in the patient's experience. Indeed, the apparent predictive power of expectations about sexual activity takes on additional significance in light of the increased attention being given sexual behavior in recent research on recovery from CABS (see, e.g., Papadopoulos, Shelley, Piccolo, Beaumont, & Barnett, 1986).

Although these findings involving domain-specific expectations are of considerable interest in their own right, the differences that emerged between these domain-specific expectations and dispositional optimism are of even greater interest. Three points seem relevant in this regard. First, although it does not constitute a systematic aspect of data analysis, many of the patients had difficulty in generating specific expectancies when so requested. For example, when asked how long in weeks it would take them to resume a particular activity, a fair number of men simply replied, "I'll go back as soon as I can" or "Whenever I feel well enough." When asked to be more precise about how many weeks would be required, the men often became evasive, saying that they could not be more precise because they just did not know what exactly to expect. These anecdotal accounts provide support for the notion that people who have no prior experience with or information about an event often have problems generating specific expectancies about it.

The second interesting aspect of the findings concerns the relative predictive power of generalized versus specific expectancies in predicting actual normalization of activities across the various domains. Consider first the prediction of domain-specific outcomes. In general, specific expectancies did a better job predicting specific outcomes than did general optimism. For example, a greater number of significant effects were associated with specific expectancies than with dispositional optimism. This finding, of course, is perfectly consistent with the "specificity-matching" analysis described earlier in this article.

On the other hand, the findings involving dispositional optimism were not completely negative, even when domain-specific outcomes are considered. For example, optimism was a significant predictor of the rate at which vigorous physical exercise was renewed, whereas the patient's relevant domain-specific expectancy was not. In other domains, the effects attributable to dispositional optimism were nearly as strong as those due to domain-specific expectancies.

The pattern of findings becomes even more favorable with respect to dispositional optimism when generalized outcomes are considered. Indeed, only one domain-specific expectancy (for the resumption of sexual activities) bore any relation at all to the general index of outcomes. In contrast, dispositional optimism was a strong predictor of both types of composite outcome variables that were examined. Taken together, these findings are also consistent with a specificity-matching analysis.

The final point of interest concerns the relative independence of the patient's domain-specific and generalized expectancies. Although optimism tended to correlate positively with the patient's specific expectations, the correlations were moderate in magnitude, and sometimes they even reversed. Although these reversals may appear puzzling, they really are not. Consider, for example, a person who is generally pessimistic, but who happens to have a good friend who underwent successful bypass surgery in the past. The friend may instill in the patient specific expectations toward recovery that are fairly favorable ("Don't worry, I was back on the job in three weeks!"), all the while leaving the patient's general sense of pessimism reasonably intact. A few patients like this in the sample could have resulted in some weak negative correlations between certain domain-specific expectations and dispositional optimism.

This relative independence between the two types of expectancies was also reflected in the results of the regression analyses that were performed, which examined the effects of one type of expectancy while statistically controlling for the effects of the other. In general, these analyses produced the same results as were produced by the analyses in which the complementary expectation went uncontrolled. In fact, sometimes effects that were not significant became significant when the complementary type of expectancy was controlled. This suggests that one type of expectancy was having a suppressor effect on the other—a finding that is no doubt indicative of the slight negative correlation that sometimes occurred between the two.

The currently prevailing view among many psychologists is that specific expectations account for the majority of variance in most settings (see, e.g., Bandura, 1982, 1986; Barrios, 1985; Kaplan, Atkins, & Reinsch, 1984). Although that may be the case for predicting single outcomes, most stressors of any importance must be conceptualized as having multiple outcomes. Unless one has a highly circumscribed interest, prediction of multiple outcomes is of crucial importance, not the prediction of single outcomes. In addition, the findings presented here suggest that global optimism as a generalized personality quality played an important role in responses to recovery from CABS, which was often independent of any domain-specific expectancies that were also operating. By extrapolation, the effects of dispositional optimism may turn out to be important in other contexts as well.

Implications for the Treatment of CABS Patients

Throughout this article we have focused on the beneficial effects of optimism on physical and psychological well-being following CABS. In closing the article, we shift perspective somewhat and focus on the pessimists in the sample. In particular, we focus on the implications that the findings hold for health care professionals who interact with the CABS patients on a daily basis. On one level, our findings simply suggest that patients who are pessimistic (both in a generalized sense and in a domain-specific sense) may be at considerable risk for a difficult and extended recovery. Given their orientation, patients who exhibit a pessimistic style may need extra care to see them through.

On a somewhat different level, however, providing the extra care that is needed may not be the easiest thing to do. Consider for a moment some of the findings associated with a pessimistic orientation. Compared with optimists, pessimists were more hostile, more depressed, and expressed less satisfaction with the treatment they had been receiving by the medical staff. They also asked fewer questions of the medical team and were generally less involved in the recovery process.

As a group, these are not the kinds of characteristics that would particularly endear a patient to a health care provider. As such, pessimism on the part of the patient may exact a subtle cost from the care provider in terms of the amount if not the quality of care that is given. In this regard, it is interesting to note that Schulz, Tompkins, Wood, and Decker (1987) have recently found that one of the best predictors of the favorability of a caretaker's response to the task of providing care to a spinal-cord-injured patient is the *patient's* sense of generalized optimism. To the extent that pessimism on the part of the CABS patient produces a similar kind of negative effect on the surrounding medical team, pessimists may inadvertently be putting themselves at double jeopardy by driving away the very people whose support they so obviously need.

ACKNOWLEDGMENTS

We would like to thank all of the members of the Division of Cardiac Rehabilitation of Allegheny General Hospital for the assistance they provided in the conduct of this research. We would also like to thank Amy Peterman, Lynn Barrett, and Nanci Lebowitz for the help they provided in the data collection phase of the project and B. Kent Houston for reading and commenting on a prepublication draft of the manuscript. Last, but not least, we thank Ellen Ahwesh for the extraordinary amount of effort and care she put into data analyses. Without the help and dedication of these people, the research could not have been done.

This research was supported in part by National Science Foundation Grants BNS-8414601, BNS-8406235, BNS-8706271, and BNS-8717783. Data collection was also facilitated by National Institute of Mental Health Grant MH30915 and National Heart, Lung, and Blood Institute Grant HL07560.

REFERENCES

American Heart Association. (1985). *Heart facts*. Dallas, TX: American Heart Association Office of Communications.

Andrews, F. M., & Withey, S. B. (1976). *Social indicators of well being: Americans' perceptions of life quality*. New York: Plenum Press.

Angell, M. (1985). Disease as a reflection of the psyche. *New England Journal of Medicine, 312*, 1570–1572.

Bandura, A. (1977). Self-efficacy: Toward a unifying theory of behavior change. *Psychological Review, 84*, 191–215.

Bandura, A. (1982). Self-efficacy mechanism in human agency. *American Psychologist, 37*, 122–147.

Bandura, A. (1986). *Social foundations of thought and action: A social cognitive theory*. Englewood Cliffs, NJ: Prentice-Hall.

Bandura, A., O'Leary, A., Taylor, C. B., Gauthier, J., & Gossard, D. (1987). Perceived self-efficacy and pain control: Opioid and nonopioid mechanisms. *Journal of Personality and Social Psychology, 53*, 563–571.

Barrios, F. X. (1985). A comparison of global and specific estimates of self-control. *Cognitive Therapy and Research, 9*, 455–469.

Beck, A. T., Steer, R. A., Kovacs, M., & Garrison, B. (1985). Hopelessness and eventual suicide: A 10-year prospective study of patients hospitalized with suicidal ideation. *American Journal of Psychiatry, 142*, 559–563.

Burisch, M. (1984). Approaches to personality inventory construction. *American Psychologist, 39*, 214–227.

Carver, C. S., Blaney, P. H., & Scheier, M. F. (1979). Focus of attention, chronic expectancy, and responses to a feared stimulus. *Journal of Personality and Social Psychology, 37*, 1186–1195.

Carver, C. S., & Gaines, J. G. (1987). Optimism, pessimism, and postpartum depression. *Cognitive Therapy and Research, 11*, 449–462.

Carver, C. S., & Scheier, M. F. (1981). *Attention and self-regulation: A control-theory approach to human behavior*. New York: Springer-Verlag.

Carver, C. S., & Scheier, M. F. (1982). Control theory: A useful conceptual framework for personality-social, clinical, and health psychology. *Psychological Bulletin, 92*, 111–135.

Carver, C. S., & Scheier, M. F. (1983). A control-theory approach to human behavior and implications for self-management. In P. C. Kendall (Ed.), *Advances in cognitive behavioral research and therapy* (Vol. 2, pp. 127–194). New York: Academic Press.

Carver, C. S., & Scheier, M. F. (1986). Functional and dysfunctional responses to anxiety: The interaction between expectancies and self-focused attention. In R. Schwarzer (Ed.), *Self-related cognitions in anxiety and motivation* (pp. 111–141). Hillsdale, NJ: Erlbaum.

Carver, C. S., Scheier, M. F., & Weintraub, J. K. (1989). Assessing coping strategies: A theoretically based approach. *Journal of Personality and Social Psychology, 56*, 267–283.

CASS principal investigators and their associates. (1983). Coronary artery surgery study (CASS): A randomized trial of coronary artery by pass surgery. Quality of life in patients randomly assigned to treatment groups. *Pathophysiology and Natural History of Coronary Artery Disease, 68*, 951–960.

CASS principal investigators and their associates. (1984). Myocardial infarction and mortality in the coronary artery surgery study (CASS) randomized trial. *New England Journal of Medicine, 310*, 750–758.

Costa, P. T., Jr. (1988, August). *Personality and health: Is there a link?* Paper presented as part of an invited debate at the 96th annual meeting of the American Psychological Association, Atlanta, GA.

Costa, P. T., Jr., & McCrae, R. R. (1985). Hypochondriasis, neuroticism, and aging: When are somatic complaints unfounded? *American Psychologist, 40*, 19–28.

Costa, P. T., Jr., & McCrae, R. R. (1987). Neuroticism, somatic complaints, and disease: Is the bark worse than the bite? *Journal of Personality, 55*, 299–316.

Cousins, N. (1977, May 28). Anatomy of an illness (as perceived by the patient). *Saturday Review*, pp. 4–6, 48–51.

Folkman, S., & Lazarus, R. S. (1980). An analysis of coping in a middleaged community sample. *Journal of Health and Social Behavior, 21*, 219–239.

Frank, K. A., Heller, S. S., Kornfeld, D. S., Sporn, A. A., & Weiss, M. B. (1978). Type A behavior and coronary angiographic findings. *Journal of the American Medical Association, 240*, 761–763.

Guilford, J. S., Zimmerman, W. S., & Guilford, J. P. (1976). *The Guilford-Zimmerman Temperament Survey Handbook: Twenty-five years of research and application*. San Diego, CA: EDITS Publishers.

Humphries, C. (1986). *An investigation of stress and stress outcomes among mortgage company employees as a function of implementation of a computerized information management system*. Unpublished doctoral dissertation, University of Miami, Coral Gables, FL.

Kanfer, F. H. (1977). The many faces of self-control, or behavior modification changes its focus. In R. B. Stuart (Ed.), *Behavioral self-management: Strategies, techniques, and outcomes* (pp. 1–48). New York: Brunner/Mazel.

Kaplan, R. M., Atkins, C. J., & Reinsch, S. (1984). Specific efficacy expectations mediate exercise compliance in patients with COPD. *Health Psychology, 3*, 223–242.

Klinger, E. (1975). Consequences of commitment to and disengagement from incentives. *Psychological Review, 82*, 1–25.

Krantz, D. S., & Manuck, S. B. (1984). Acute psychophysiologic reactivity and risk of cardiovascular disease: A review and methodologic critique. *Psychological Bulletin, 96*, 435–464.

Krantz, D. S., Schaeffer, M. A., Davia, J. E., Dembroski, T. M., MacDougall, J. M., & Shaffer, R. T. (1981). Extent of coronary atherosclerosis, Type A behavior, and cardiovascular response to social interaction. *Psychophysiology, 18*, 654–664.

Kukla, A. (1972). Foundations of an attributional theory of performance. *Psychological Review, 79*, 454–470.

Lazarus, R. S., & Folkman, S. (1984). *Stress, appraisal, and coping*. New York: Springer.

Lazarus, R. S., Kanner, A. D., & Folkman, S. (1980). Emotions: A cognitive-phenomenological analysis. In R. Plutchik & H. Kellerman (Eds.), *Emotion: Theory, research, and experience* (pp. 189–217). New York: Academic Press.

Lefcourt, H. M. (1976). *Locus of control: Current trends in theory and research*. Hillsdale, NJ: Erlbaum.

Lewin, K. (1938). *The conceptual representation and the*

measurement of psychological forces. Durham, NC: Duke University Press.

Loop, F. D. (1983a). Progress in surgical treatment of coronary atherosclerosis (Pt. 1). *Chest, 84,* 611–623.

Loop, F. D. (1983b) Progress in surgical treatment of coronary atherosclerosis (Pt. 2). *Chest, 84,* 740–755.

Loop, F. D., & Cosgrove, D. M. (1986). Repeat coronary bypass surgery: Selection of cases, surgical risks, and long-term outlook. *Modern Concepts of Cardiovascular Disease, 55,* 31–36.

Magni, G., Unger, H. P., Valfre, C., Polesel, E., Cesari, F., Rizzardo, R., Paruzzolo, P., & Gallucci, V. (1987). Psychosocial outcome one year after heart surgery. *Archives of Internal Medicine, 147,* 473–477.

Matthews, K. A., & Haynes, S. G. (1986). Type A behavior pattern and coronary risk: Update and critical evaluation. *American Journal of Epidemiology, 123,* 923–960.

Matthews, K. A., Weiss, S. M., Detre, T., Dembroski, T. M., Falkner, B., Manuck, S. B., & Williams, R. B., Jr. (Eds.). (1986). *Handbook of stress, reactivity, and cardiovascular disease.* New York: Wiley.

Mayou, R., & Bryant, B. (1987). Quality of life after coronary artery surgery. *Quarterly Journal of Medicine, 62,* 239–248.

Papadopoulos, C., Shelley, S. I., Piccolo, M., Beaumont, R. M., & Barnett, L. (1986). Sexual activity after coronary bypass surgery. *Chest, 90,* 681–685.

Peale, N. V. (1956). *The power of positive thinking.* Englewood Cliffs, NJ: Prentice-Hall.

Peterson, C., Semmel, A., von Baeyer, C., Abramson, L. Y., Metalsky, G. I., & Seligman, M. E. P. (1982). The Attributional Style Questionnaire. *Cognitive Therapy and Research, 6,* 287–300.

Reker, G. T., & Wong, P. T. P. (1983, April). *The salutary effects of personal optimism and meaningfulness on the physical and psychological well-being of the elderly.* Paper presented at the 29th annual meeting of the Western Gerontological Society, Albuquerque, NM.

Reker, G. T., & Wong, P. T. P. (1985). Personal optimism, physical and mental health: The triumph of successful aging. In J. E. Birren and J. Livingston (Eds.), *Cognition, stress and aging* (pp. 134–173). Englewood Cliffs, NJ: Prentice-Hall.

Rose, G. A. (1965). Chest pain questionnaire. *Milbank Memorial Fund Quarterly, 43,* 32–39.

Roth, S., & Cohen, L. J. (1986). Approach, avoidance, and coping with stress. *American Psychologist, 41,* 813–819.

Rotter, J. B. (1954). *Social learning and clinical psychology.* Englewood Cliffs, NJ: Prentice-Hall.

Rotter, J. B. (1966). Generalized expectancies for internal versus external control of reinforcement. *Psychological Monographs, 80*(1, Whole No. 609).

Scheier, M. F., & Carver, C. S. (1985). Optimism, coping, and health: Assessment and implications of generalized outcome expectancies. *Health Psychology, 4,* 219–247.

Scheier, M. F., & Carver, C. S. (1987). Dispositional optimism and physical well-being: The influence of generalized outcome expectancies on health. *Journal of Personality, 55,* 169–210.

Scheier, M. F., & Carver, C. S. (1988a). A model of behavioral self-regulation: Translating intention into action. In L. Berkowitz (Ed.), *Advances in experimental social psy-*

chology (Vol. 21, pp. 303–346). New York: Academic Press.

Scheier, M. F., & Carver, C. S. (1988b). [Relationships between dispositional optimism and attributional style.] Unpublished raw data.

Scheier, M. F., & Carver, C. S. (1989). *On the nature of dispositional optimism: Associations with neuroticism, negative affectivity, and self-mastery.* Unpublished manuscript.

Scheier, M. F., Weintraub, J. K., & Carver, C. S. (1986). Coping with stress: Divergent strategies of optimists and pessimists. *Journal of Personality and Social Psychology, 51,* 1257–1264.

Schmale, A. H. (1972). Giving up as a final common pathway to changes in health. *Advances in Psychosomatic Medicine, 8,* 2–40.

Schulz, R., Tompkins, C. A., Wood, D., & Decker, S. (1987). Social psychology of caregiving: Physical and psychological costs of providing support to the disabled. *Journal of Applied Social Psychology, 17,* 401–428.

Seligman, M. E. P. (1975). *Helplessness: On depression, development, and death.* San Francisco: Freeman.

Smith, T. W., Pope, M. K., Rhodewalt, F., & Poulton, J. L. (1989). Optimism, neuroticism, coping and symptom reports: An alternative interpretation of the Life Orientation Test. *Journal of Personality and Social Psychology, 56,* 640–648.

Spielberger, C. D., Gorsuch, R. L., & Lushene, R. E. (1970). *Manual for the State-Trait Anxiety Inventory.* Palo Alto, CA: Consulting Psychologists Press.

Strack, S., Carver, C. S., & Blaney, P. H. (1987). Predicting successful completion of an aftercare program following treatment for alcoholism: The role of dispositional optimism. *Journal of Personality and Social Psychology, 53,* 579–584.

Suls, J., & Fletcher, B. (1985). The relative efficacy of avoidant and nonavoidant coping strategies: A meta-analysis. *Health Psychology, 4,* 249–288.

Tolman, E. C. (1932). *Purposive behavior in animals and men.* New York: Appleton-Century-Crofts.

Tolman, E. C. (1938). The determiners of behavior at a choice point. *Psychological Review, 45,* 1–41.

Van Treuren, R. R., & Hull, J. G. (1986, October). *Health and stress: Dispositional optimism and psychophysiological responses.* Paper presented at the annual meeting of the Society for Psychophysiological Research, Montreal, Quebec, Canada.

Weintraub, J. K., Carver, C. S., & Scheier, M. F. (1986, April). *A theoretically derived measure of coping responses, and correlations with the personality dimension of optimism-pessimism.* Paper presented at the annual meeting of the Eastern Psychological Association, New York.

Wortman, C. B., & Brehm, J. W. (1975). Responses to uncontrollable outcomes: An integration of reactance theory and the learned helplessness model. In L. Berkowitz (Ed.), *Advances in experimental social psychology* (Vol. 8, pp. 277–336). New York: Academic Press.

Zuckerman, M. (1960). The development of an Affect Adjective Check List for the measurement of anxiety. *Journal of Consulting Psychology, 24,* 457–462.

Zuckerman, M., Lubin, B., & Robins, S. (1965). Validation of the Multiple Affect Adjective Checklist in clinical situations. *Journal of Consulting Psychology, 29,* 594.

READING 23

Writing About Emotional Experiences as a Therapeutic Process

James W. Pennebaker • Southern Methodist University

For the past decade, an increasing number of studies have demonstrated that when individuals write about emotional experiences, significant physical and mental health improvements follow. The basic paradigm and findings are summarized along with some boundary conditions. Although a reduction in inhibition may contribute to the disclosure phenomenon, changes in basic cognitive and linguistic processes during writing predict better health. Implications for theory and treatment are discussed.

Virtually all forms of psychotherapy—from psychoanalysis to behavioral and cognitive therapies—have been shown to reduce distress and to promote physical and mental well-being (Mumford, Schlesinger, & Glass, 1983; Smith, Glass, & Miller, 1980). A process common to most therapies is labeling the problem and discussing its causes and consequences. Further, participating in therapy presupposes that the individual acknowledges the existence of a problem and openly discusses it with another person. As discussed in this article, the mere act of disclosure is a powerful therapeutic agent that may account for a substantial percentage of the variance in the healing process.

Parameters of Writing and Talking Associated with Health Improvements

Over the past decade, several laboratories have been exploring the value of writing or talking about emotional experiences. Confronting deeply personal issues has been found to promote physical health, subjective well-being, and selected adaptive behaviors. In this section, the general findings of the disclosure paradigm are discussed. Whereas individuals have been asked to disclose personal experiences through talking in a few studies, most studies involve writing.

The Basic Writing Paradigm

The standard laboratory writing technique has involved randomly assigning each participant to one of two or more groups. All writing groups are asked to write about assigned topics for 3 to 5 consecutive days, 15 to 30 min each day. Writing is generally done in the laboratory with no feedback given. Participants assigned to the control conditions are typically asked to write about superficial topics, such as how they use their time. The standard instructions for those assigned to the experimental group are a variation on the following:

> For the next 3 days, I would like for you to write about your very deepest thoughts and feelings

about an extremely important emotional issue that has affected you and your life. In your writing, I'd like you to really let go and explore your very deepest emotions and thoughts. You might tie your topic to your relationships with others, including parents, lovers, friends, or relatives; to your past, your present, or your future; or to who you have been, who you would like to be, or who you are now. You may write about the same general issues or experiences on all days of writing or on different topics each day. All of your writing will be completely confidential. Don't worry about spelling, sentence structure, or grammar. The only rule is that once you begin writing, continue to do so until your time is up.

The writing paradigm is exceptionally powerful. Participants—from children to the elderly, from honor students to maximum-security prisoners—disclose a remarkable range and depth of traumatic experiences. Lost loves, deaths, incidents of sexual and physical abuse, and tragic failures are common themes in all of the studies. If nothing else, the paradigm demonstrates that when individuals are given the opportunity to disclose deeply personal aspects of their lives, they readily do so. Even though a large number of participants report crying or being deeply upset by the experience, the overwhelming majority report that the writing experience was valuable and meaningful in their lives.

Effects of Disclosure on Outcome Measures

Researchers have relied on a variety of physical and mental health measures to evaluate the effect of writing. As depicted in Table 23.1, writing or talking about emotional experiences, relative to writing about superficial control topics, has been found to be associated with significant drops in physician visits from before to after writing among relatively healthy samples. Writing or talking about emotional topics has also been found to have beneficial influences on immune function, including t-helper cell growth (using a blastogenesis procedure with the mitogen phytohemagglutinin), antibody response to Epstein-Barr virus, and antibody response to hepatitis B vaccinations. Disclosure also has produced short-term changes in autonomic activity (e.g., lowered heart rate and electroder-

mal activity) and muscular activity (i.e., reduced phasic corrugator activity).

Self-reports also suggest that writing about upsetting experiences, although painful in the days of writing, produces long-term improvements in mood and indicators of well-being compared with writing about control topics. Although a number of studies have failed to find consistent effects on mood or self-reported distress, Smyth's (1996) recent meta-analysis on written-disclosure studies indicates that, in general, writing about emotional topics is associated with significant reductions in distress.

Behavioral changes have also been found. Students who write about emotional topics show improvements in grades in the months following the study. Senior professionals who have been laid off from their jobs get new jobs more quickly after writing. Consistent with the direct health measures, university staff members who write about emotional topics are subsequently absent from their work at lower rates than control participants. Interestingly, relatively few reliable changes emerge using self-reports of health-related behaviors. That is, after writing, experimental participants do not exercise more or smoke less. The one exception is that the study with laid-off professionals found that writing reduced self-reported alcohol intake.

Procedural Differences That Affect the Disclosure Effects

Writing about emotional experiences clearly influences measures of physical and mental health. In recent years, several investigators have attempted to define the boundary conditions of the disclosure effects. Some of the most important findings are as follows:

- *Writing versus talking about traumas.* Most studies comparing writing versus talking either into a tape recorder (Esterling, Antoni, Fletcher, Margulies, & Schneiderman, 1994) or to a therapist (Donnelly & Murray, 1991; Murray, Lamnin, & Carver, 1989) find comparable biological, mood, and cognitive effects. Talking and writing about emotional experiences are both superior to writing about superficial topics.
- *Topic of disclosure.* Whereas two studies have found that health effects occur only among in-

TABLE 23.1. Effects of Disclosure on Various Outcome Parameters

Outcome	Studies
Physician visits (comparison of number before and after writing)	
Reductions lasting 2 months after writing	Cameron & Nicholls (1996); Greenberg & Stone (1992); Greenberg, Wortman, & Stone (1996); Krantz & Pennebaker (1996); Pennebaker & Francis (1996); Pennebaker, Kiecolt-Glaser, & Glaser (1988); Richards, Pennebaker, & Beal (1995)
Reductions lasting 6 months after writing	Francis & Pennebaker (1992); Pennebaker & Beall (1986); Pennebaker, Colder, & Sharp (1990)
Reductions lasting 1.4 years after writing	Pennebaker, Barger, & Tiebout (1989)
Physiological markers	
Long-term immune and other serum measures	Pennebaker et al. (1988)
Blastogenesis (t-helper cell response to phytohemagglutinin)	
Epstein-Barr virus antibody titers	Esterling, Antoni, Fletcher, Margulies, & Schneiderman (1994); Lutgendorf, Antoni, Kumar, & Schneiderman (1994)
Hepatitis B antibody levels	Petrie, Booth, Pennebaker, Davison, & Thomas (1995)
Natural killer cell activity	Christensen et al. (1996)
CD-4 (t-lymphocyte) levels	Booth, Petrie, & Pennebaker (1997)
Liver enzyme levels (SGOT)	Francis & Pennebaker (1992)
Immediate changes in autonomic and muscular activity	
Skin conductance, heart rate	Dominguez et al. (1995); Hughes, Uhlmann, & Pennebaker (1994); Pennebaker, Hughes, & O'Heeron (1987); Petrie et al. (1995)
Corrugator activity	Pennebaker et al. (1987)
Behavioral markers	
Grade point average	Cameron & Nicholls (1996); Krantz & Pennebaker (1996); Pennebaker et al. (1990); Pennebaker & Francis (1996)
Reemployment following job loss	Spera, Buhrfeind, & Pennebaker (1994)
Absenteeism from work	Francis & Pennebaker (1992)
Self-reports	
Physical symptoms	Greenberg & Stone (1992); Pennebaker & Beall (1986); Richards et al. (1995). Failure to find effects: Pennebaker et al. (1988, 1990); Petrie et al. (1995)
Distress, negative affect, or depression	Greenberg & Stone (1992); Greenberg et al. (1996); Murray & Segal (1994); Rimé (1995); Spera et al. (1994). Failure to find effects: Pennebaker & Beall (1986); Pennebaker et al. (1988); Pennebaker & Francis (1996); Petrie et al. (1995)

Note. Only studies published or submitted for publication are included. Several studies found effects that were qualified by a second variable (e.g., stressfulness of topic). See also Smyth (1996) for a detailed account.

dividuals who write about particularly traumatic experiences (Greenberg & Stone, 1992; Lutgendorf, Antoni, Kumar, & Schneiderman, 1994), most studies have found that disclosure is more broadly beneficial. Choice of topic, however, may selectively influence the outcome. For beginning college students, for example, writing about emotional issues related to coming to

college influences grades more than writing about traumatic experiences (Pennebaker & Beall, 1986; Pennebaker, Colder, & Sharp, 1990).

• *Length or days of writing.* Different experiments have variously asked participants to write for 1 to 5 days, ranging from consecutive days to sessions separated by a week; writing sessions have ranged from 15 to 30 min in length. In Smyth's (1996) meta-analysis, he found a promising trend suggesting that the more days over which the experiment lapses, the stronger the effects. Although this was a weak trend, it suggests that writing once each week over a month may be more effective than writing four times within a single week. Self-reports of the value of writing do not distinguish shorter from longer writing sessions.

• *Actual or implied social feedback.* Unlike psychotherapy, the writing paradigm does not employ feedback to the participant. Rather, after individuals write about their own experiences, they are asked to place their essays into an anonymous-looking box with the promise that their writing will not be linked to their names. In one study comparing the effects of having students either write on paper that would be handed in to the experimenter or write on a "magic pad" (on which the writing disappears when the person lifts the plastic writing cover), no autonomic or self-report differences were found (Czajka, 1987).

• *Individual differences.* No consistent personality or individual difference measures have distinguished who does versus who does not benefit from writing. The most commonly examined variables that have not been found to relate to outcomes include sex, age, anxiety (or negative affectivity), and inhibition or constraint. The one study that preselected participants on hostility found that those high in hostility benefited more from writing than those low in hostility (Christensen et al., 1996).

• *Educational, linguistic, or cultural effects.* Within the United States, the disclosure paradigm has benefited senior professionals with advanced degrees at rates comparable to those for maximum-security prisoners with sixth-grade educations (Richards, Pennebaker, & Beal, 1995; Spera, Buhrfeind, & Pennebaker, 1994). Among college students, no differences have been found as a function of the students' ethnicity or native language. The disclosure paradigm has produced consistently positive results among French-speaking Belgians (Rimé, 1995), Spanish-speaking residents of Mexico City (Dominguez et al., 1995), and English-speaking New Zealanders (Petrie, Booth, Pennebaker, Davison, & Thomas, 1995).

Summary

When individuals write or talk about personally upsetting experiences in the laboratory, consistent and significant health improvements are found. The effects are found in both subjective and objective markers of health and well-being. The disclosure phenomenon appears to generalize across settings, most individual differences, and many Western cultures, and is independent of social feedback.

Why Does Writing Work?

Most of the research on disclosure has been devoted to demonstrating its effectiveness rather than on identifying the underlying mechanisms. Two very broad models that have been proposed to explain the value of disclosure invoke inhibitory processes and cognitive processes.

Inhibition and Disclosure

The original theory that motivated the first studies on writing was based on the assumption that not talking about important psychological phenomena is a form of inhibition. Drawing on the animal and psychophysiological literatures, we posited that active inhibition is a form of physiological work. This inhibitory work, which is reflected in autonomic and central nervous system activity, could be viewed as a long-term low-level stressor (cf. Selye, 1976). Such stress, then, could cause or exacerbate psychosomatic processes, thereby increasing the risk of illness and other stress-related disturbances. Just as constraining thoughts, feelings, or behaviors linked to an emotional upheaval is stressful, letting go and talking about these experiences should, in theory, reduce the stress of inhibition (for a full discussion of this theory, see Pennebaker, 1989).

Findings to support the inhibition model of psychosomatics are accumulating. Individuals who conceal their gay status (Cole, Kemeny, Taylor, & Visscher, 1996), conceal traumatic experiences in their past (Pennebaker, 1993a), or are considered inhibited or shy by other people (e.g., Kagan, Reznick, & Snidman, 1988) exhibit more health problems than those who are less inhibited. Whereas inhibition appears to contribute to long-term health problems, the evidence that disclosure reduces inhibition and thereby improves health has not materialized. For example, Greenberg and Stone (1992) found that individuals benefited as much from writing about traumas about which they had told others as from writing about traumas that they had kept secret. Self-reports of inhibition before and after writing have not consistently related to health changes. At this point, then, the precise role of inhibition in promoting health within the writing paradigm is not proven.

Cognitive Changes Associated With Writing

In the past decade, several studies have persuasively demonstrated that writing about a trauma does more than allow for the reduction of inhibitory processes. For example, in a recent study, students were randomly assigned either to express a traumatic experience using bodily movement, to express a traumatic experience first through movement and then in written form, or to exercise in a prescribed manner for 3 days, 10 min per day (Krantz & Pennebaker, 1996). Whereas participants in the two movement-expression groups reported that they felt happier and mentally healthier in the months after the study, only the movement-plus-writing group showed significant improvements in physical health and grade point average. The mere expression of a trauma is not sufficient. Health gains appear to require translating experiences into language.

In recent years, we have begun analyzing the language that individuals use in writing about emotional topics. Our first strategy was to have independent raters evaluate the essays' overall contents to see if it was possible to predict who would benefit most from writing. Interestingly, judges noted that essays of people who benefited from writing appeared to be "smarter," "more thoughtful," and "more emotional" (Pennebaker, 1993b). However, the relatively poor interjudge reliability led us to develop a computerized text-analysis system.

In 1991, we created a computer program called LIWC (Linguistic Inquiry and Word Count) that analyzed essays in text format. LIWC was developed by having groups of judges evaluate the degree to which about 2,000 words or word stems were related to each of several dozen categories

(for a full description, see Pennebaker & Francis, 1996). The categories included negative emotion words (*sad, angry*), positive emotion words (*happy, laugh*), causal words (*because, reason*), and insight words (*understand, realize*). For each essay that a person wrote, we were able to quickly compute the percentage of total words that represented these and other linguistic categories.

Analyzing the experimental subjects' data from six writing studies, we found three linguistic factors reliably predicted improved physical health. First, the more that individuals used positive emotion words, the better their subsequent health. Second, a moderate number of negative emotion words predicted health. Both very high and very low levels of negative emotion words correlated with poorer health. Third, and most important, an increase in both causal and insight words over the course of writing was strongly associated with improved health (Pennebaker, Mayne, & Francis, 1997). Indeed, this increase in cognitive words covaried with judges' evaluations of the construction of the narratives. That is, people who benefited from writing began with poorly organized descriptions and progressed to coherent stories by the last day of writing.

The language analyses are particularly promising in that they suggest that certain features of essays predict long-term physical health. Further, these features are congruent with psychologists' current views on narratives. The next issue, which is currently being addressed, is the degree to which cohesive stories or narratives predict changes in real-world cognitive processes. Further, does a coherent story about a trauma produce improvements in health by reducing ruminations or flashbacks? Does a story ultimately result in the assimilation of an unexplained experience, thereby allowing the person to get on with life? These are the theoretical questions that psychologists must address.

Implications for Treatment

Almost by definition, psychotherapy requires a certain degree of self-disclosure. Over the past 100 years, the nature of the disclosure has changed depending on the prevailing therapeutic winds. Whether the therapy is directive or evocative, insight-oriented or behavioral, the patient and therapist have worked together to derive a coherent story that explains the problem and, directly or indirectly, the cure. As the research summarized here suggests, the mere disclosing of the person's problem may have tremendous therapeutic value in and of itself.

The writing paradigm points to one of several possible active ingredients associated with psychotherapy. Most studies that have been conducted using this technique have not examined individuals with major emotional or physical health problems or substance abuse problems. One obvious question is the degree to which writing can serve as a supplement to—or even a substitute for—some medical and psychological treatments. Translating important psychological events into words is uniquely human. Therapists and religious leaders have known this intuitively for generations. Psychologists specializing in language, cognition, social processes, and psychotherapy can work together in better understanding the basic mechanisms of this phenomenon.

ACKNOWLEDGMENTS

Preparation of this article was aided by grants from the National Science Foundation (SBR-9411674) and the National Institutes of Health (MH52391).

REFERENCES

Booth, R. J., Petrie, K. J., & Pennebaker, J. W. (1997). Changes in circulating lymphocyte numbers following emotional disclosure: Evidence of buffering? *Stress Medicine, 13*, 23–29.

Cameron, L. D., & Nicholls, G. (1996). *Expression of stressful experiences through writing: A self-regulation approach.* Manuscript submitted for publication.

Christensen, A. J., Edwards, D. L., Wiebe, J. S., Benotsch, E. G., McKelvey, L., Andrews, M., & Lubaroff, D. M. (1996). Effect of verbal self-disclosure on natural killer cell activity: Moderation influence on cynical hostility. *Psychosomatic Medicine, 58*, 150–155.

Cole, S. W., Kemeny, M. W., Taylor, S. E., & Visscher, B. R. (1996). Elevated health risk among gay men who conceal their homosexual identity. *Health Psychology, 15*, 243–251.

Czajka, J. A. (1987). *Behavioral inhibition and short term physiological responses.* Unpublished master's thesis, Southern Methodist University, Dallas, TX.

Dominguez, B., Valderrama, P., Meza, M. A., Perez, S. L., Silva, A., Martinez, G., Mendez, V. M., & Olvera, Y. (1995). The roles of emotional reversal and disclosure in clinical practice. In J. W. Pennebaker (Ed.), *Emotion, disclosure, and health* (pp. 255–270). Washington, DC: American Psychological Association.

Donnelly, D. A., & Murray, E. J. (1991). Cognitive and emotional changes in written essays and therapy interviews. *Journal of Social and Clinical Psychology, 10*, 334–350.

Esterling, B. A., Antoni, M. H., Fletcher, M. A., Margulies, S., & Schneiderman, N. (1994). Emotional disclosure through writing or speaking modulates latent Epstein-Barr virus antibody titers. *Journal of Consulting and Clinical Psychology, 62*, 130–140.

Francis, M. E., & Pennebaker, J. W. (1992). Putting stress into words: Writing about personal upheavals and health. *American Journal of Health Promotion, 6*, 280–287.

Greenberg, M. A., & Stone, A. A. (1992). Writing about disclosed versus undisclosed traumas: Immediate and long-term effects on mood and health. *Journal of Personality and Social Psychology, 63*, 75–84.

Greenberg, M. A., Wortman, C. B., & Stone, A. A. (1996). Emotional expression and physical health: Revising traumatic memories or fostering self-regulation. *Journal of Personality and Social Psychology, 71*, 588–602.

Hughes, C. F., Uhlmann, C., & Pennebaker, J. W. (1994). The body's response to psychological defense. *Journal of Personality, 62*, 565–585.

Kagan, J., Reznick, J. S., & Snidman, N. (1988). Biological bases of childhood shyness. *Science, 240*, 167–171.

Krantz, A., & Pennebaker, J. W. (1996). *Bodily versus written expression of traumatic experience.* Manuscript submitted for publication.

Lutgendorf, S. K., Antoni, M. H., Kumar, M., & Schneiderman, N. (1994). Changes in cognitive coping strategies predict EBV-antibody titre change following a stressor disclosure induction. *Journal of Psychosomatic Research, 38*, 63–78.

Mumford, E., Schlesinger, H. J., & Glass, G. V. (1983). Reducing medical costs through mental health treatment: Research problems and recommendations. In A. Broskowski, E. Marks, & S. H. Budman (Eds.), *Linking health and mental health* (pp. 257–273). Beverly Hills, CA: Sage.

Murray, E. J., Lamnin, A. D., & Carver, C. S. (1989). Emotional expression in written essays and psychotherapy. *Journal of Social and Clinical Psychology, 8*, 414–429.

Murray, E. J., & Segal, D. L. (1994). Emotional processing in vocal and written expression of feelings about traumatic experiences. *Journal of Traumatic Stress, 7*, 391–405.

Pennebaker, J. W. (1989). Confession, inhibition, and disease. In L. Berkowitz (Ed.), *Advances in experimental social psychology* (Vol. 22, pp. 211–244). New York: Academic Press.

Pennebaker, J. W. (1993a). Mechanisms of social constraint. In D. M. Wegner & J. W. Pennebaker (Eds.), *Handbook of mental control* (pp. 200–219). Englewood Cliffs, NJ: Prentice-Hall.

Pennebaker, J. W. (1993b). Putting stress into words: Health, linguistic, and therapeutic implications. *Behaviour Research and Therapy, 31*, 539–548.

Pennebaker, J. W., Barger, S. D., & Tiebout, J. (1989). Disclosure of traumas and health among Holocaust survivors. *Psychosomatic Medicine, 51*, 577–589.

Pennebaker, J. W., & Beall, S. K. (1986). Confronting a traumatic event: Toward an understanding of inhibition and disease. *Journal of Abnormal Psychology, 95*, 274–281.

Pennebaker, J. W., Colder, M., & Sharp, L. K. (1990). Accelerating the coping process. *Journal of Personality and Social Psychology, 58*, 528–537.

Pennebaker, J. W., & Francis, M. E. (1996). Cognitive, emotional, and language processes in disclosure. *Cognition and Emotion, 10*, 601–626.

Pennebaker, J. W., Hughes, C. F., & O'Heeron, R. C. (1987). The psychophysiology of confession: Linking inhibitory and psychosomatic processes. *Journal of Personality and Social Psychology, 52*, 781–793.

Pennebaker, J. W., Kiecolt-Glaser, J., & Glaser, R. (1988). Disclosure of traumas and immune function: Health implications for psychotherapy. *Journal of Consulting and Clinical Psychology, 56*, 239–245.

Pennebaker, J. W., Mayne, T. J., & Francis, M. E. (1997). Linguistic predictors of adaptive bereavement. *Journal of Personality and Social Psychology, 72*, 863–871.

Petrie, K. J., Booth, R. J., Pennebaker, J. W., Davison, K. P., & Thomas, M. G. (1995). Disclosure of trauma and immune response to a hepatitis B vaccination program. *Journal of Consulting and Clinical Psychology, 63*, 787–792.

Richards, J. M., Pennebaker, J. W., & Beal, W. E. (1995, May). *The effects of criminal offense and disclosure of trauma on anxiety and illness in prison inmates.* Paper presented at the annual meeting of the Midwest Psychological Association, Chicago.

Rimé, B. (1995). Mental rumination, social sharing, and the recovery from emotional exposure. In J. W. Pennebaker (Ed.), *Emotion, disclosure, and health* (pp. 271–292). Washington, DC: American Psychological Association.

Selye, H. (1976). *The stress of life.* New York: McGraw-Hill.

Smith, M. L., Glass, G. V., & Miller, R. L. (1980). *The benefits of psychotherapy.* Baltimore: Johns Hopkins University Press.

Smyth, J. M. (1996). *Written emotional expression: Effect sizes, outcome types, and moderating variables.* Manuscript submitted for publication.

Spera, S. P., Buhrfeind, E. D., & Pennebaker, J. W. (1994). Expressive writing and coping with job loss. *Academy of Management Journal, 37*, 722–733.

Appendix: How to Read a Journal Article in Social Psychology

Christian H. Jordan and Mark P. Zanna • University of Waterloo

When approaching a journal article for the first time, and often on subsequent occasions, most people try to digest it as they would any piece of prose. They start at the beginning and read word for word, until eventually they arrive at the end, perhaps a little bewildered, but with a vague sense of relief. This is not an altogether terrible strategy; journal articles do have a logical structure that lends itself to this sort of reading. There are, however, more efficient approaches–approaches that enable you, a student of social psychology, to cut through peripheral details, avoid sophisticated statistics with which you may not be familiar, and focus on the central ideas in an article. Arming yourself with a little foreknowledge of what is contained in journal articles, as well as some practical advice on how to read them, should help you read journal articles more effectively. If this sounds tempting, read on.

Journal articles offer a window into the inner workings of social psychology. They document how social psychologists formulate hypotheses, design empirical studies, analyze the observations they collect, and interpret their results. Journal articles also serve an invaluable archival function: They contain the full store of common and cumulative knowledge of social psychology. Having documentation of past research allows researchers to build on past findings and advance our understanding of social behavior, without pursuing avenues of investigation that have already been explored. Perhaps most importantly, a research study is never complete until its results have been shared with others, colleagues and students alike. Journal articles are a primary means of communicating research findings. As such, they can be genuinely exciting and interesting to read.

That last claim may have caught you off guard. For beginning readers, journal articles may seem anything but interesting and exciting. They may, on the contrary, appear daunting and esoteric, laden with jargon and obscured by menacing statistics. Recognizing this fact, we hope to arm you, through this paper, with the basic information you will need to read journal articles with a greater sense of comfort and perspective.

Social psychologists study many fascinating topics, ranging from prejudice and discrimination, to culture, persuasion, liking and love, conformity and obedience, aggression, and the self. In our daily lives, these are issues we often struggle to understand. Social psychologists present systematic observations of, as well as a wealth of ideas about,

369

such issues in journal articles. It would be a shame if the fascination and intrigue these topics have were lost in their translation into journal publications. We don't think they are, and by the end of this paper, hopefully you won't either.

Journal articles come in a variety of forms, including research reports, review articles, and theoretical articles. Put briefly, a *research report* is a formal presentation of an original research study, or series of studies. A *review article* is an evaluative survey of previously published work, usually organized by a guiding theory or point of view. The author of a review article summarizes previous investigations of a circumscribed problem, comments on what progress has been made toward its resolution, and suggests areas of the problem that require further study. A *theoretical article* also evaluates past research, but focuses on the development of theories used to explain empirical findings. Here, the author may present a new theory to explain a set of findings, or may compare and contrast a set of competing theories, suggesting why one theory might be the superior one.

This paper focuses primarily on how to read research reports, for several reasons. First, the bulk of published literature in social psychology consists of research reports. Second, the summaries presented in review articles, and the ideas set forth in theoretical articles, are built on findings presented in research reports. To get a deep understanding of how research is done in social psychology, fluency in reading original research reports is essential. Moreover, theoretical articles frequently report new studies that pit one theory against another, or test a novel prediction derived from a new theory. In order to appraise the validity of such theoretical contentions, a grounded understanding of basic findings is invaluable. Finally, most research reports are written in a standard format that is likely unfamiliar to new readers. The format of review and theoretical articles is less standardized, and more like that of textbooks and other scholarly writings, with which most readers are familiar. This is not to suggest that such articles are easier to read and comprehend than research reports; they can be quite challenging indeed. It is simply the case that, because more rules apply to the writing of research reports, more guidelines can be offered on how to read them.

The Anatomy of Research Reports

Most research reports in social psychology, and in psychology in general, are written in a standard format prescribed by the American Psychological Association (1994). This is a great boon to both readers and writers. It allows writers to present their ideas and findings in a clear, systematic manner. Consequently, as a reader, once you understand this format, you will not be on completely foreign ground when you approach a new research report— regardless of its specific content. You will know where in the paper particular information is found, making it easier to locate. No matter what your reasons for reading a research report, a firm understanding of the format in which they are written will ease your task. We discuss the format of research reports next, with some practical suggestions on how to read them. Later, we discuss how this format reflects the process of scientific investigation, illustrating how research reports have a coherent narrative structure.

Title and Abstract

Though you can't judge a book by its cover, you can learn a lot about a research report simply by reading its title. The title presents a concise statement of the theoretical issues investigated, and/or the variables that were studied. For example, the following title was taken almost at random from a prestigious journal in social psychology: "Sad and guilty? Affective influences on the explanation of conflict in close relationships" (Forgas, 1994, p. 56). Just by reading the title, it can be inferred that the study investigated how emotional states change the way people explain conflict in close relationships. It also suggests that when feeling sad, people accept more personal blame for such conflicts (i.e., feel more guilty).

The abstract is also an invaluable source of information. It is a brief synopsis of the study, and packs a lot of information into 150 words or less. The abstract contains information about the problem that was investigated, how it was investigated, the major findings of the study, and hints at the theoretical and practical implications of the findings. Thus, the abstract is a useful summary of the research that provides the gist of the investigation. Reading this outline first can be very helpful, because it tells you where the report is going, and gives you a useful framework for organizing information contained in the article.

The title and abstract of a research report are like a movie preview. A movie preview highlights the important aspects of a movie's plot, and provides just enough information for one to decide whether to watch the whole movie. Just so with titles and abstracts; they highlight the key features of a research report to allow you to decide if you want to read the whole paper. And just as with movie previews, they do not give the whole story. Reading just the title and abstract is never enough to fully understand a research report.

Introduction

A research report has four main sections: introduction, method, results, and discussion. Though it is not explicitly labeled, the introduction begins the main body of a research report. Here, the researchers set the stage for the study. They present the problem under investigation, and state why it was important to study. By providing a brief review of past research and theory relevant to the central issue of investigation, the researchers place the study in an historical context and suggest how the study advances knowledge of the problem. Beginning with broad theoretical and practical considerations, the researchers delineate the rationale that led them to the specific set of hypotheses tested in the study. They also describe how they decided on their research strategy (e.g., why they chose an experiment or a correlational study).

The introduction generally begins with a broad consideration of the problem investigated. Here, the researchers want to illustrate that the problem they studied is a real problem about which people should care. If the researchers are studying prejudice, they may cite statistics that suggest discrimination is prevalent, or describe specific cases of discrimination. Such information helps illustrate why the research is both practically and theoretically meaningful, and why you should bother reading about it. Such discussions are often quite interesting and useful. They can help you decide for yourself if the research has merit. But they may not be essential for understanding the study at hand. Read the introduction carefully, but choose judiciously what to focus on and remember. To understand a study, what you really need to understand is what the researchers' hypotheses were, and how they were derived from theory, informal observation, or intuition. Other background information may be intriguing, but may not be critical to understand what the researchers did and why they did it.

While reading the introduction, try answering these questions: What problem was studied, and why? How does this study relate to, and go beyond, past investigations of the problem? How did the researchers derive their hypotheses? What questions do the researchers hope to answer with this study?

Method

In the method section, the researchers translate their hypotheses into a set of specific, testable questions. Here, the researchers introduce the main characters of the study—the subjects or participants—describing their characteristics (gender, age, etc.) and how many of them were involved. Then, they describe the materials (or apparatus), such as any questionnaires or special equipment, used in the study. Finally, they describe chronologically the procedures of the study; that is, how the study was conducted. Often, an overview of the research design will begin the method section. This overview provides a broad outline of the design, alerting you to what you should attend.

The method is presented in great detail so that other researchers can recreate the study to confirm (or question) its results. This degree of detail is normally not necessary to understand a study, so don't get bogged down trying to memorize the particulars of the procedures. Focus on how the independent variables were manipulated (or measured) and how the dependent variables were measured.

Measuring variables adequately is not always an easy matter. Many of the variables psychologists are interested in cannot be directly observed, so they must be inferred from participants' behavior. Happiness, for example, cannot be directly observed. Thus, researchers interested in how being happy influences people's judgments must infer happiness (or its absence) from their behavior—perhaps by asking people how happy they are, and judging their degree of happiness from their responses; perhaps by studying people's facial expressions for signs of happiness, such as smiling. Think about the measures researchers use while reading the method section. Do they adequately reflect or capture the concepts they are meant to measure? If a measure seems odd, consider carefully how the researchers justify its use.

Oftentimes in social psychology, getting there is half the fun. In other words, how a result is obtained can be just as interesting as the result itself. Social psychologists often strive to have participants behave in a natural, spontaneous manner, while controlling enough of their environment to pinpoint the causes of their behavior. Sometimes, the major contribution of a research report is its presentation of a novel method of investigation. When this is the case, the method will be discussed in some detail in the introduction.

Participants in social psychology studies are intelligent and inquisitive people who are responsive to what happens around them. Because of this, they are not always initially told the true purpose of a study. If they were told, they might not act naturally. Thus, researchers frequently need to be creative, presenting a credible rationale for complying with procedures, without revealing the study's purpose. This rationale is known as a *cover story*, and is often an elaborate scenario. While reading the method section, try putting yourself in the shoes of a participant in the study, and ask yourself if the instructions given to participants seem sensible, realistic, and engaging. Imagining what it was like to be in the study will also help you remember the study's procedure, and aid you in interpreting the study's results.

While reading the method section, try answering these questions: How were the hypotheses translated into testable questions? How were the variables of interest manipulated and/or measured? Did the measures used adequately reflect the variables of interest? For example, is self-reported income an adequate measure of social class? Why or why not?

Results

The results section describes how the observations collected were analyzed to determine whether the original hypotheses were supported. Here, the data (observations of behavior) are described, and statistical tests are presented. Because of this, the results section is often intimidating to readers who have little or no training in statistics. Wading through complex and unfamiliar statistical analyses is understandably confusing and frustrating. As a result, many students are tempted to skip over reading this section. We advise you not to do so. Empirical findings are the foundation of any science and results sections are where such findings are presented.

Take heart. Even the most prestigious researchers were once in your shoes and sympathize with you. Though space in psychology journals is limited, researchers try to strike a balance between the need to be clear and the need to be brief in describing their results. In an influential paper on how to write good research reports, Bem (1987) offered this advice to researchers:

> No matter how technical or abstruse your article is in its particulars, intelligent nonpsychologists with no expertise in statistics or experimental design should be able to comprehend the broad outlines of what you did and why. They should understand in general terms what was learned. (p. 74)

Generally speaking, social psychologists try to practice this advice.

Most statistical analyses presented in research reports test specific hypotheses. Often, each analysis presented is preceded by a reminder of the hypothesis it is meant to test. After an analysis is presented, researchers usually provide a narrative description of the result in plain English. When the hypothesis tested by a statistical analysis is not explicitly stated, you can usually determine the hypothesis that was tested by reading this narrative description of the result, and referring back to the introduction to locate an hypothesis that corresponds to that result. After even the most complex statistical analysis, there will be a written description of what the result means conceptually. Turn your attention to these descriptions. Focus on the conceptual meaning of research findings, not on the mechanics of how they were obtained (unless you're comfortable with statistics).

Aside from statistical tests and narrative descriptions of results, results sections also frequently contain tables and graphs. These are efficient summaries of data. Even if you are not familiar with statistics, look closely at tables and graphs, and pay attention to the means or correlations presented in them. Researchers always include written descriptions of the pertinent aspects of tables and graphs. While reading these descriptions, check the tables and graphs to make sure what the researchers say accurately reflects their data. If they say there was a difference between two groups on a particular dependent measure, look at the means in the table that correspond to those two groups, and see if the means do differ as described. Occasionally, results seem to become stronger in their narrative description than an examination of the data would warrant.

Statistics *can* be misused. When they are, results are difficult to interpret. Having said this, a lack of statistical knowledge should not make you overly cautious while reading results sections. Though not a perfect antidote, journal articles undergo extensive review by professional researchers before publication. Thus, most misapplications of statistics are caught and corrected before an article is published. So, if you are unfamiliar with statistics, you can be reasonably confident that findings are accurately reported.

While reading the results section, try answering these questions: Did the researchers provide evidence that any independent variable manipulations were effective? For example, if testing for behavioral differences between happy and sad participants, did the researchers demonstrate that one group was in fact happier than the other? What were the major findings of the study? Were the researchers' original hypotheses supported by their observations? If not, look in the discussion section for how the researchers explain the findings that were obtained.

Discussion

The discussion section frequently opens with a summary of what the study found, and an evaluation of whether the findings supported the original hypotheses. Here, the researchers evaluate the theoretical and practical implications of their results. This can be particularly interesting when the results did not work out exactly as the researchers anticipated. When such is the case, consider the researchers' explanations carefully, and see if they seem plausible to you. Often, researchers will also report any aspects of their study that limit their interpretation of its results, and suggest further research that could overcome these limitations to provide a better understanding of the problem under investigation.

Some readers find it useful to read the first few paragraphs of the discussion section before reading any other part of a research report. Like the abstract, these few paragraphs usually contain all of the main ideas of a research report: what the hypotheses were, the major findings and whether they supported the original hypotheses, and how the findings relate to past research and theory. Having this information before reading a research report can guide your reading, allowing you to focus on the specific details you need to complete your understanding of a study. The description of the results, for example, will alert you to the major variables that were studied. If they are unfamiliar to you, you can pay special attention to how they are defined in the introduction, and how they are operationalized in the method section.

After you have finished reading an article, it can also be helpful to reread the first few paragraphs of the discussion and the abstract. As noted, these two passages present highly distilled summaries of the major ideas in a research report. Just as they can help guide your reading of a report, they can also help you consolidate your understanding of a report once you have finished reading it. They provide a check on whether you have understood the main points of a report, and offer a succinct digest of the research in the authors' own words.

While reading the discussion section, try answering these questions: What conclusions can be drawn from the study? What new information does the study provide about the problem under investigation? Does the study help resolve the problem? What are the practical and theoretical implications of the study's findings? Did the results contradict past research findings? If so, how do the researchers explain this discrepancy?

Some Notes on Reports of Multiple Studies

Up to this point, we have implicitly assumed that a research report describes just one study. It is also quite common, however, for a research report to describe a series of studies of the same problem in a single article. When such is the case, each study reported will have the same basic structure (introduction, method, results, and discussion sections) that we have outlined, with the notable exception that sometimes the results and discussion section for each study are combined. Combined "results and discussion" sections contain the same information that separate results and discussion sections normally contain. Sometimes, the authors present all their results first, and only then discuss the implications of these results, just as they would in separate results and discussion sections. Other times, however, the authors alternate between describing results and discussing their implications, as each result is presented. In either case, you should be on the lookout for the same information, as outlined above in our consideration of separate results and discussion sections.

Reports including multiple studies also differ from single study reports in that they include more general introduction and discussion sections. The general introduction, which begins the main body of a research report, is similar in essence to the introduction of a single study report. In both cases, the researchers describe the problem investigated and its practical and theoretical significance. They also demonstrate how they derived their hypotheses, and explain how their research relates to past investigations of the problem. In contrast, the separate introductions to each individual study in reports of multiple studies are usually quite brief, and focus more specifically on the logic and rationale of each particular study presented. Such introductions generally describe the methods used in the particular study, outlining how they answer questions that have not been adequately addressed by past research, including studies reported earlier in the same article.

General discussion sections parallel discussions of single studies, except on a somewhat grander scale. They present all of the information contained in discussions of single studies, but consider the implications of all the studies presented together. A general discussion section brings the main ideas of a research program into bold relief. It typically begins with a concise summary of a research program's main findings, their relation to the original hypotheses, and their practical and theoretical implications. Thus, the summaries that begin general discussion sections are counterparts of the summaries that begin discussion sections of single study reports. Each presents a digest of the research presented in an article that can serve as both an organizing framework (when read first), and as a check on how well you have understood the main points of an article (when read last).

Research Reporting as Story Telling

A research report tells the story of how a researcher or group of researchers investigated a specific problem. Thus, a research report has a linear, narrative structure with a beginning, middle, and end. In his paper on writing research reports, Bem noted that a research report

> is shaped like an hourglass. It begins with broad general statements, progressively narrows down to the specifics of [the] study, and then broadens out again to more general considerations. (1987, p. 175)

This format roughly mirrors the process of scientific investigation, wherein researchers do the following: (1) start with a broad idea from which they formulate a narrower set of hypotheses, informed by past empirical findings (introduction); (2) design a specific set of concrete operations to test these hypotheses (method); (3) analyze the observations collected in this way, and decide if they support the original hypotheses (results); and (4) explore the broader theoretical and practical implications of the findings, and consider how they contribute to an understanding of the problem under investigation (discussion). Though these stages are somewhat arbitrary distinctions—research actually proceeds in a number of different ways—they help elucidate the inner logic of research reports.

While reading a research report, keep this linear structure in mind. Though it is difficult to remember a series of seemingly disjointed facts, when these facts are joined together in a logical, narrative structure, they become easier to comprehend and recall. Thus, always remember that a research report tells a story. It will help you to organize the information you read, and remember it later.

Describing research reports as stories is not just a convenient metaphor. Research reports *are* stories. Stories can be said to consist of two components: a telling of what happened, and an explanation of why it happened. It is tempting to view science as an endeavor that simply catalogues facts, but nothing is further from the truth. The goal of science, social psychology included, is to *explain* facts, to explain *why* what happened happened. Social psychology is built on the dynamic interplay of discovery and justification, the dialogue between systematic observation of relations and their theoretical explanation. Though research reports do present novel facts based on systematic observation, these facts are presented in the service of ideas. Facts in isolation are trivia. Facts tied together by an explanatory theory are science. Therein lies the story. To really understand what researchers have to say, you need consider how their explanations relate to their findings.

The Rest of the Story

> There is really no such thing as research. There is only search, more search,
> keep on searching. (Bowering, 1988, p. 95)

Once you have read through a research report, and understand the researchers' findings and their explanations of them, the story does not end there. There is more than one interpretation for any set of findings. Different researchers often explain the same set of facts in different ways.

Let's take a moment to dispel a nasty rumor. The rumor is this: Researchers present their studies in a dispassionate manner, intending only to inform readers of their findings and their interpretation of those findings. In truth, researchers aim not only to inform readers, but also to *persuade* them (Sternberg, 1995). Researchers want to convince you their ideas are right. There is never only one explanation for a set of findings. Certainly, some explanations are better than others; some fit the available data better, are more parsimonious, or require fewer questionable assumptions. The point here is that researchers are very passionate about their ideas, and want you to believe them. It's up to you to decide if you want to buy their ideas or not.

Let's compare social psychologists to salesclerks. Both social psychologists and salesclerks want to sell you something; either their ideas: or their wares. You need to decide if you want to buy what they're selling or not—and there are potentially negative consequences for either decision. If you let a sales clerk dazzle you with a sales pitch, without thinking about it carefully, you might end up buying a substandard product that you don't really need. After having done this a few times, people tend to become cynical, steeling themselves against any and all sales pitches. This too is dangerous. If you are overly critical of sales pitches, you could end up foregoing genuinely useful products. Thus, by analogy, when you are too critical in your reading of research reports, you might dismiss, out of hand, some genuinely useful ideas—ideas that can help shed light on why people behave the way they do.

This discussion raises the important question of how critical one should be while reading a research report. In part, this will depend on why one is reading the report. If you are reading it simply to learn what the researchers have to say about a particular issue, for example, then there is usually no need to be overly critical. If you want to use the research as a basis for planning a new study, then you should be more critical. As you develop an understanding of psychological theory and research methods, you will also develop an ability to criticize research on many different levels. And *any* piece of research can be criticized at some level. As Jacob Cohen put it, "A successful piece of research doesn't conclusively settle an issue, it just makes some theoretical proposition to some degree more likely" (1990, p. 1311). Thus, as a consumer of research reports, you have to strike a delicate balance between being overly critical and overly accepting.

While reading a research report, at least initially, try to suspend your disbelief. Try to understand the researchers' story; that is, try to understand the facts—the findings and how they were obtained—and the suggested explanation of those facts—the researchers' interpretation of the findings and what they mean. Take the research to task only after you feel you understand what the authors are trying to say.

Research reports serve not only an important archival function, documenting research and its findings, but also an invaluable stimulus function. They can excite other researchers to join the investigation of a particular issue, or to apply new methods or theory to a different, perhaps novel, issue. It is this stimulus function that Elliot Aronson, an eminent social psychologist, referred to when he admitted that, in publishing a study, he hopes his colleagues will "look at it, be stimulated by it, be provoked by it, annoyed by it, and then go ahead and do it better. . . . That's the exciting thing about science; it progresses by people taking off on one another's work" (1995, p. 5). Science is indeed a cumulative enterprise, and each new study builds on what has (or, sometimes, has not) gone before it. In this way, research articles keep social psychology vibrant.

A study can inspire new research in a number of different ways, such as: (1) it can lead one to conduct a better test of the hypotheses, trying to rule out alternative explanations of the findings; (2) it can lead one to explore the limits of the findings, to see how widely applicable they are, perhaps exploring situations to which they do not apply; (3) it can lead one to test the implications of the findings, furthering scientific investigation of the phenomenon; (4) it can inspire one to apply the findings, or a novel methodology, to a different area of investigation; and (5) it can provoke one to test the findings in the context of a specific real world problem, to see if they can shed light on it. All of these are excellent extensions of the original research, and there are, undoubtedly, other ways that research findings can spur new investigations.

The problem with being too critical, too soon, while reading research reports is that the only further research one may be willing to attempt is research of the first type: redoing a study better. Sometimes this is desirable, particularly in the early stages of investigating a particular issue, when the findings are novel and perhaps unexpected. But redoing a reasonably compelling study, without extending it in any way, does little to advance our understanding of human behavior. Although the new study might be "better," it will not be "perfect," so *it* would have to be run again, and again, likely never reaching a stage where it is beyond criticism. At some point, researchers have to decide that the evidence is compelling enough to warrant investigation of the last four types. It is these types of studies that most advance our knowledge of social behavior. As you read more research reports, you will become more comfortable deciding when a study is "good enough" to move beyond it. This is a somewhat subjective judgment, and should be made carefully.

When social psychologists write up a research report for publication, it is because they believe they have something new and exciting to communicate about social behavior. Most research reports that are submitted for publication are rejected. Thus, the reports that are eventually published are deemed pertinent not only by the researchers who wrote them, but also by the reviewers and editors of the journals in which they are published. These people, at least, believe the research reports they write and publish have something important and interesting to say. Sometimes, you'll disagree; not all journal articles are created equal, after all. But we recommend that you, at least initially, give these well-meaning social psychologists the benefit of the doubt. Look for what they're excited about. Try to understand the authors' story, and see where it leads you.

ACKNOWLEDGMENTS

Preparation of this paper was facilitated by a Natural Sciences and Engineering Research Council of Canada doctoral fellowship to Christian H. Jordan. Thanks to Roy Baumeister, Arie Kruglanski, Ziva Kunda, John Levine, Geoff MacDonald, Richard Moreland, Ian Newby-Clark, Steve Spencer, and Adam Zanna for their insightful comments on, and appraisals of, various drafts of this paper. Thanks also to Arie Kruglanski and four anonymous editors of volumes in the series *Key Readings in Social Psychology* for their helpful critiques of an initial outline of this paper. Correspondence concerning this article should be addressed to Christian H. Jordan, Department of Psychology, University of Waterloo, Waterloo, Ontario, Canada N2L 3G1. Electronic mail can be sent to chjordan@watarts.uwaterloo.ca

REFERENCES

American Psychological Association. (1994). *Publication manual* (4th ed.). Washington, D.C.

Aronson, E. (1995). Research in social psychology as a leap of faith. In E. Aronson (Ed.), *Readings about the social animal* (7th ed., pp. 3–9). New York: W. H. Freeman and Company.

Bem, D. J. (1987). Writing the empirical journal article. In M. P. Zanna & J. M. Darley (Eds.), *The compleat academic: A practical guide for the beginning social scientist* (pp. 171–201). New York: Random House.

Bowering, G. (1988). *Errata*. Red Deer, Alta.: Red Deer College Press.

Cohen, J. (1990). Things I have learned (so far). *American Psychologist, 45,* 1304–1312.

Forgas, J. P. (1994). Sad and guilty? Affective influences on the explanation of conflict in close relationships. *Journal of Personality and Social Psychology, 66,* 56–68.

Sternberg, R. J. (1995). *The psychologist's companion: A guide to scientific writing for students and researchers* (3rd ed.). Cambridge: Cambridge University Press.

Author Index

Abbott, R. A., xii, 302, 342–361
Abelson, R. P., 269
Abraham, C., 61, 143
Abrams, D. B., 49– 50, 56, 63, 67, 69, 71, 236–237
Adams, D., 288
Adams, H. E., 310
Adams, M., 268
Adams, M. L., 270
Adams, R. D., 108
Addy, M., 288
Ader, R., 232, 308
Adler, N. E., 80, 272
Ahwesh, E., 359
Aiken, L. S., 263
Aitken-Swan, J., 105
Ajzen, I., 18, 33, 37–38, 39n, 51, 60, 78–79, 81, 83, 85, 90, 92, 113, 148, 166, 201, 250, 258
Alagna, S. W., 227, 231
Albarracin, D., 49
Alberta Heritage Foundation for Medical Research, 144
Alexander, F., 306, 310
Alexander, J. F., 328
Alford, B. A., 71
Allen, M. G., 80
Allison, S. T., 27
Allport, F. H., 184
Allport, G. W., 305
Allred, K. D., 328, 333–334
Almada, S. J., 331
American Cancer Society, 263–264, 298
American Heart Association, 344
American Lung Association, 253
American Medical Association, 263
American Psychological Association, 273, 370
Ammerman, A. S., 59, 250
Ander, S., 16
Ander-Pecivas, S., 220
Andersen, B. L., 54

Anderson, J. B., 50, 55–56, 250
Anderson, K. O., 310
Anderson, N. B., 332, 337
Andres, L. W., 10
Andrews, F. M., 347–349
Andrews, M., 364–365
Angell, M., 309, 320, 342
Anson, C., 319
Antone, C., 269, 287, 296, 298
Antoni, M. H., 308, 363–364
Antonovsky, A., 224
Aronson, E., xii, 99, 245, 272–285, 376–377
Arrowood, A. J., 164, 200
Asch, S. E., 184
Ashe, J., 320
Aspinwall, L. G., 97, 199
Atkins, C. J., 359
Atkins, E., 37
Axsom, D., 118, 126, 273

Back, K. W., 184, 222
Backbier, E., 53, 56
Bacon, J. M., 185
Baer, J. S., 63, 237
Bagozzi, R. P., 80
Bahnson, C. B., 301
Bailey, J. M., 331–332
Bakal, D. A., 310
Baker, L. H., 263
Bales, C. B., 303
Banaji, M. R., 269
Bandura, A., 11, 18, 38, 49, 51, 343, 359
Banks, M. H., 180
Banks, S. M., 287, 296–298
Baranowski, T., 43, 249–250
Barbee, A. P., 217
Barefoot, J. C., 229, 326–328, 330–332, 334–335, 337
Barger, S. D., 364
Barnett, L., 358
Baron, M., 269

Baron, R. M., 207, 295
Barrett, L., 359
Barringer, F., 185
Barrios, F. X., 359
Barton, J., 167
Bastani, R., 269
Baum, A., 237, 272–273, 308, 311
Baum, J. K., 263
Baumann, L. J., 16, 110–111, 279
Baumeister, R., 377
Baxter, J. S., 79
Beal, W. E., 364–365
Beall, S. K., 364
Beaumont, R. M., 358
Beauvais, J., 287, 296–298
Beck, A. T., 344
Beck, K. H., 36, 38
Beck, L., 81, 90
Becker, M. H., 11, 21, 33–34, 49, 51, 273
Bedell, B. T., xii, 246, 286–287, 298
Beitman, B. D., 64
Bekiaris, J., 80
Bem, D. J., 373, 375
Bendham, L., 63
Benjamin, A., 65
Benner, L. A., 153
Bennett, P., 304
Benotsch, E. G., 364–365
Benthin, A. C., xi, 6, 21–32, 80, 82, 84
Bentler, P. M., 79–81, 83, 87, 185
Bergin, A. E., 63
Berglund, G., 16
Berkman, L. F., 215, 220, 222–223, 227–229, 233, 236, 238, 240
Berkowitz, A. D., 185, 189
Berkowitz, L., 118–120
Berndt, T. J., 180
Beutler, L. E., 74
Bewley, B. R., 180
Beyer, J. M., 196
Biaggio, M. K., 333
Biener, L., 63, 67

Billings, J. H., 311
Black, G. W., 326–327, 330–332, 337
Blair, L. W., 262
Blalock, S. J., 50, 55–56, 250
Bland, J. M., 180
Blaney, N., 284
Blaney, P. H., 308, 343–344
Blanton, H., xi, 30, 48, 78–94, 149, 178
Blatt, S. F., 329
Blazer, D. G., 222, 227, 229, 236
Block, L. G., 287, 289, 297
Bloomquist, J. N., 212
Blumenthal, J. A., 229, 327–332, 335, 337
Bluming, A., 164
Bodmer, J., 144
Bogdonoff, M. D., 222
Bois, J. L., 212
Boldero, J., 79
Boney-McCoy, S., 24, 79, 81–82, 84–85, 171, 177–178, 180
Bongaarts, J., 225
Booth, R. J., 364–365
Booth-Kewley, S., xii, 301–302, 305–308, 329
Borgida, E., 43, 127
Borhani, N. O., 311
Bortner, R. W., 327, 331
Bossenberry, J., 144
Boster, F. J., 125
Bovard, E. W., 222–223, 234
Bowering, G., 376
Bowlby, J., 222, 224
Boyce, W. T., 230
Boyd, G. M., 71
Bradley, L. A., 310
Bragg, B. W., 22
Brandenburg, N., 65
Brandsma, J. M., 331
Braunwald, E., 108, 203
Breed, W., 184–185
Brehm, J. W., 127, 343
Breslow, L., 229, 236
Brickman, P., 152–153, 162, 200, 262, 269
Broadhead, W. E., 223, 227
Brock, B. M., 37
Bronfenbrenner, U., 180
Brooks-Gunn, J., 79, 89, 168
Brown, B. B., 24, 167, 170, 179–180
Brown, J., 22
Brown, L. K., 79
Brown, P., 333
Brown, R., 236
Brown, S., 79, 89
Brownell, A., 228
Brownell, K. D., 64, 66
Brubaker, R. G., 34, 39
Brunhart, S. M., 97
Bryant, B., 345
Buck, R., 307
Buhrfeind, E. D., 364–365
Bulman, R. J., 152–153, 162, 200

Bulpitt, C. J., 16
Burciaga, A. R., 167, 169
Burg, M. M., 229, 329
Burgess, A. W., 163
Burisch, M., 349
Burke, P. J., 167
Burton, D., 167, 169, 179
Burzette, B., 79
Busemeyer, J. R., 42
Bush, R. R., 142. , 314
Bushman, B. J., 22, 329
Buss, A. H., 326, 328
Buunk, B. P., 91, 150, 199, 201
Bynner, J. M., 167
Byrne, D. H., 237

Cacioppo, J. T., 54, 118, 126–128, 215, 217, 283
Cahaland, D., 63
Caldwell, J., 10
Cameron, J. M., 110–111
Cameron, L. D., 364
Campbell, M. K., 59, 250
Cantor, N., 167, 338
Caplan, G., 219
Caplan, R. D., 10
Carbonari, J. P., 250
Carey, M. P., 132
Carlsmith, J. M., 99
Carlston, D. E., 168
Carmelli, D., 327–328
Carne, S., 16
Carr, C. R., 63, 67
Carter, H., 218
Carver, C. S., xii, 302, 342–361, 363
Cashdan, S., 64
Casperson, C., 205
Cassel, J. C., 219, 222–224, 227, 230, 232, 234, 239
Cassem, N. H., 101
Catania, J. A., 54, 279, 282
Cates, W., 170
Cather, C., 303
Centers for Disease Control, 22, 263, 272
Cerkovnik, M., 237
Cesari, F., 345
Chaiken, S., xi, 95, 118–129, 287–289, 296–297
Chaplin, J. P., 326
Charlin, V., 167, 169
Chassin, L. A., 23, 80, 167, 179–180, 195, 273
Chatterson, M., 144
Chaudhary, B. S., 222, 229
Cherlin, 225
Chesney, M. A., 308, 311, 326–327, 330–332, 334–335, 337
Chesterton, G. K., 65
Chilman, C. S., 79
Chitwood, D. D., 279, 282
Christenfeld, N., 212, 215
Christensen, A. J., 333, 364–365
Christensen, D. B., 35, 37

Christman, N. J., 202
Christophersen, E. R., 287
Chu, G. C., 11
Chu, L., 128
Chung, N. K., 30
Chwalow, J., 10
Cialdini, R. B., 184
Cioffi, D., 112
Clark, M. S., 224
Clarkin, J. F., 74
Clasen, D. N., 24, 170, 179–180
Clausen, J. A., 218
Cleary, P. D., 80, 167, 178
Clitherow, R., 185
Coates, D., 262, 269
Coates, T. J., 54, 272–273, 279, 282
Cobb, S., 219, 223–224
Coh, E., 262, 269
Cohen, F., 103, 115, 151–152, 306–307
Cohen, J., 283, 285, 376
Cohen, L. J., 343
Cohen, N., 232, 308
Cohen, P., 237, 283
Cohen, R., 222
Cohen, S., xii, 63, 67, 216–217, 220, 223–224, 227–244
Cohen-Silver, R. C., 262, 269
Cohn, L. D., 22
Colder, M., 364
Cole, S. W., 365
Coley, B., 287, 296
College Health Association, 185
Colletti, G., 262
Collins, B., 164
Collins, L. M., 23, 30
Colonese, K. L., 329
Conger, K. J., 80–81, 85, 88
Connecticut Department of Health Services, 264, 268
Conner, M., 61, 79, 88, 249, 260
Constantian, C. A., 212
Constantinou, C., 80
Contrada, R. J., 303, 332
Conway, T. L., 231
Conway, V. J., 79–80
Cook, D. A., 273
Cook, W. W., 326
Cooper, C., 260
Cooper, H. M., 329
Cooper, J., 273, 283–284
Cooper, W. H., 167
Cornhill, J. F., 222
Coronary Artery Surgery Study Randomized Trial, 345, 350, 357
Corty, E., 23, 80, 167, 195
Cosgrove, D. M., 345, 350
Costa, A., 68
Costa, F. M., 167, 173
Costa, P. T., Jr., 317, 325–329, 331, 338, 344
Costanzo, M., 273
Cottingham, D. R., 118–120
Cottler, L., 63

Cottrell, N. B., 151, 210
Cousins, N., 342
Coyne, J. C., 237, 325
Craig, S., 167, 169
Crain, A. L., xii, 245, 272–285
Cramer, P., 192
Crandall, C., 150, 184
Crane, R. J., 326
Creer, T., 310
Critchlow, B., 130–131, 143
Cross, S., 30
Croyle, R. T., xi, 22, 95–96, 98–117
Cuite, C. L., xii, 59, 246, 249–260
Cummings, K. M., 34, 37, 63, 67
Cunningham, M. R., 217
Curry, S., 63, 67
Curtis, N., 333
Cutler, P., 108
Czajka, J. A., 365

D'Avernas, J. R., 79
Dabbs, J. M., 11
Dahlstrom, W. G., 328, 331–332, 334, 337
Dakin, S., 164
Darley, J. M., 22, 101–104, 110, 113–114, 153, 162, 185, 195, 211
Darwin, C., 218
Davia, J. E., 350
Davidson, A. R., 92
Daviglus, M. L., 331
Davison, G. C., 262
Davison, K. P., 364–365
de Haan, W., 35
de la Hoz, V., 128
De Vries, H., 53, 56
Dean, A., 237
deAraujo, G., 230
Decker, S., 163, 224, 359
DeCourville, N. H., 79
Deeds, S. G., 10
Deich, J. D., 215
Dembroski, T. M., 325–332, 335, 337–338, 350, 357
DeMichele, J. T., 71
Den-Boer, D.-J., 61
Dent, C. W., 23, 167, 169
Derogatis, L. R., 154
Des Jarlais, D. C., 272
Desharnais, R., 79
DeStefano, F., 329
Detre, T., 357
Detweiler, J. B., xii, 246, 286–287, 298
DeVellis, B. M., 50, 55–56, 59, 227, 231, 250
DeVellis, R. F., 50, 55–56, 59, 227, 231, 250
Devine, E. C., 202, 209
Diamond, E. L., 325, 332, 334
DiClemente, C. C., xi, 43, 48, 50, 54, 57–59, 61, 63–77, 79, 250
Diefenbach, M. A., 43, 303
Digman, J. M., 338

DiMatteo, M. R., 24, 231, 307
Dimsdale, J. E., 330
Ditto, P. H., xi, 22, 95–117
Divlahan, D. R., 63
Dodd, G. D., 263
Dodge, K. A., 328, 331–332
Dohrenwend, B. P., 306
Dollery, C. T., 16
Dominguez, B., 364–365
Donald, C. A., 237
Donnelly, D. A., 363
Donovan, D. M., 63, 66
Donovan, J. E., 167, 173
Dooley, M. A., 50, 55–56, 250
Dosik, G., 164
Douvan, B., 225
Douvan, E., 63
Downey, G., 262, 269
Doyle, J. K., 251
Drake, C., 269
Dryden, W., 64
Dube, C. E., 50, 56
Dudley, D. L., 230
Dujovne, V. F., 337
Dunbar, F. H., 306
Duncan-Jones, P., 237
Dunkel-Schetter, C., 151–152, 162, 164, 269, 306
Dunlap, W. P., 42
Durel, L. A., 307, 336
Durkee, A., 326, 328
Durkheim, E., 217–218, 224
Dusenbury, L., 227
Dyer, A. R., 331

Eagly, A. H., 119, 126–128, 192, 289
Earnest, A., 208, 211–212
Easson, E. C., 105
Ebel, A., 144
Eckenrode, J., 237
Eddy, D. M., 263
Edgarton, R. B., 130
Edwards, D. L., 364–365
Edwards, J. R., 230
Edwards, W., 33
Egan, G., 64
Eicher, S. A., 24, 170, 179–180
Eisenberg, L., 79, 89, 107
Eiser, C., 22
Eiser, J. R., 22, 36, 39, 167, 236
Ellice, J., 144
Ellickson, P. L., 88
Ellsworth, P. C., 99
Elstein, A. S., 108
Emerson, S., 284
Emmons, K. M., 49
Emont, S. L., 63, 67
Engel, G. L., 306
Engstrom, P. F., 263, 269
Ensel, W. M., 237
Epley, S. W., 151, 210
Eppel, E., 287, 296–298
Epstein, J. A., 262

Erdelyi, M. H., 101
Erikson, E. H., 80
Erlanger, L. R., 332
Ershoff, D. H., 68
Esterling, B. A., 363–364
Evans, M. G., 42
Eysenck, H. J., 307

Fairhurst, S. K., 50, 54, 57, 65, 67, 71–72
Falkner, B., 357
Fang, C. Y., 303
Faris, R. E. L., 218
Farmer, J., 37
Fava, J. S., 54, 67, 69–70
Fazio, R. H., 90, 283, 285
Feinleib, M., 219, 222, 229–230
Feshbach, S., 118–119, 126
Festinger, L. A., 22, 106, 126, 147, 151, 153, 162, 184, 199–200, 273
Feuerstein, M., 310
Fiedler, J., 67, 170
Fields, J. M., 185, 193
Fink, D. J., 263
Finlay, J., 10
Finn, P., 22
Finn, S. E., 331–332
Finnerty, F., 10
Fiore, C., 54, 250
Fischer, G. W., 287
Fischhoff, B., 41, 43, 287
Fishbein, M., 18, 33, 37, 49, 51, 78, 85, 90, 113, 148, 166, 201, 250
Fisher, E. B., 262
Fisher, J. D., 79, 166, 273
Fisher, W. A., 79, 273
Fishkin, S. A., xii, 246, 261–271
Fiske, S. T., 29, 169
Flay, B. R., 23, 79, 81, 167, 169, 179
Fleck-Kandath, C., 273
Fleming, R., 22–23, 237
Fletcher, B., 112, 344
Fletcher, M. A., 363–364
Folkman, S., 112, 114, 224, 232, 343–344
Follick, M. J., 67, 69, 71
Fong, G. T., xi, 96, 130–145
Fontana, A. F., 329
Ford, B., 80
Forgas, J. P., 370
Formica, R., 200
Forsterling, F., 262
Foster, F. G., 205
Foster, R. S. J., 37
Fowler, J. L., 67, 69, 71, 310
Fox, S. A., 263, 269
Francis, M. E., 364, 366
Francis, V., 107
Frank, K. A., 307, 350
Frankenhaeuser, M., 333
Frankowski, B., 37
Frautschi, N., 326–327, 330–332, 337
Fredman, L., 220, 227–228, 240

French, J., 10
Freud, S., 306
Frey, D., 127
Frey, K. S., 180
Fried, C. B., xii, 245, 272–285
Friedman, H. S., xii, 301, 305–368
Friedman, J., 301–302
Friedman, M., 311, 319
Friedman, S. R., 272
Friedson, E., 107
Frieze, I. H., 167, 180
Frohm, K. D., 327–328, 334
Fronek, A., 329
Furstenberg, F. F., Jr., 79, 89, 168
Futterman, B., 164

Gaines, J. G., 344
Galavotti, C., 67
Gale, M., 328, 331, 334–335, 337
Galen, 305
Galligan, R. F., 79–80
Gallucci, V., 345
Galton, L., 9
Gardner, G., 92, 288
Garner, W., 238
Garrison, B., 344
Gatchel, R. J., 237
Gauthier, J., 343
Gehlbach, S. R., 227, 223
Gehred-Schultz, A., 64
Genevie, L. E., 237
Gerace, T. A., 311
Gerin, W., 215
German, P., 63
Gerrard, M., xi–xii, 6, 21–32, 29, 48, 78–94, 148–149, 166–182, 260
Getzlaf, S., 167
Gibbons, F. X., xi–xii, 6, 21–32, 29, 48, 78–94, 148–150, 166–182
Gibson, D. R., 279, 282
Gilbertini, M., 64
Gilbertson, V. A. 105
Gill, J., 319
Ginpil, S., 54, 58, 71
Gioia, D., 80, 167, 179
Giorgino, K. B., 50, 55–56, 250
Giovino, G., 63, 67
Gisriel, M. M., 237
Giunta, L. C., 70
Glanz, K., 34
Glaser, R., 238, 364
Glasgow, R. E., 43, 92, 236–237, 248
Glass, D. C., 231–232, 239, 327, 331–332
Glass, G. V., 63, 202, 209, 311, 362
Glassman, B., 247
Glick, P. C., 218
Glynn, K., 22–23
Glynn, T. J., 71
Godin, G., 79
Goethals, G. R., 27, 108, 153, 162, 211
Goffman, E., 194
Goitein, B., 41

Gold, D., 50, 55–56, 250
Gold, R. H., 263
Goldberg, J. D., 222, 229
Goldbourt, U., 230
Goldfried, M. R., 70–71
Goldman, A. E., 22
Goldman, R., 126
Goldmeier, J., 222
Goldstein, I. B., 333
Goldstein, J., 169
Goldstein, M. G., 54, 250
Gonzales, M. H., 99, 273
Good, B., 107
Goodkins, K., 308
Goodstadt, M. S., 29
Gordon, C. M., 132
Gordon, E. I., 97
Gordon, J. R., 64
Gordon, R. A., 84
Gore, S., 227, 232
Gorsuch, R. L., 203
Goss, M. E., 101
Gossard, D., 343
Gottlieb, B. H., 217
Gottlieb, N. H., 67
Gove, W. R., 221
Grafton, H. E., 252, 260
Graham, J. W., 23, 30, 185, 195
Grandits, G. A., 326
Grant, M., 80
Green, L. W., 10, 21, 262
Greenberg, J., 63, 126–127
Greenberg, M. A., 364, 366
Greene, D., 23, 27, 108, 195
Greener, S., 269, 287, 296–298
Grencavage, L. M., 70
Grimson, R., 223, 227
Gritz, E. R., 63, 67
Grube, J. W., 83, 167
Gruder, C. L., 152–153
Gruman, J. C., 71
Grusky, O., 164
Guadagnoli, E., 57, 73
Guest, F., 170
Guralnik, J., 222
Gurung, R. A. R., 215
Gutmann, M., xi, 6, 9–20, 43, 110–111
Gyulay, J. E., 287

Haan, N., 114
Haberman, S., 268
Habgood, R., 80
Hackett, T. P., 101, 330
Haefner, D. P., 37
Hagestad, E. L., 334
Hailey, B. J., 335
Hakmiller, K. L., 152–153, 163, 200
Hallett, R., 39
Hamburg, D. A., 101
Hammen, C., 164
Hammer, G. P., 55
Hammer, M., 234
Hampton, M., 269

Haney, T. L., 229, 327–332, 335, 337
Hansen, D. N., 203–204
Hansen, W. B., 23, 30, 167, 169, 179, 185, 195
Harackiewicz, J. M., 262
Hardy, J. D., 333–334
Harel, Y., 36, 39
Harlow, L. L., 54, 250
Harrison, J. A., 21
Harrison, R. H., 230
Hart, J., 203
Hartman, K. A., 7, 16
Hartwick, J., 79, 81, 166
Harvey, A., 232
Harvey, J. H., 262
Harvey, O. J., 120
Hasselbald, V., 263
Hastie, R., 127
Hatcher, R. A., 170
Hauser, P. H., 218
Hayes-Bautista, D., 17
Haynes, R. B., 10, 17
Haynes, S. G., 230, 344
Haynie, D. L., 80
Hays, R. D., 24, 34, 88, 231
Hazlewood, D., 127–128
Health Today Newsletter, 121
Healthy People 2010, 2
Hearn, M. D., 331–332
Heather, N., 61
Hecker, M. H. L., 326–327, 330–332, 337
Hedman, M., 333
Heikkila, K., 330–331, 335, 337
Helgeson, V. S., 200
Heller, K., 219, 227
Heller, S. S., 307, 350
Hellerstedt, W. L., 67
Helmer, D. C., 320–330
Helsing, K. J., 221
Helweg-Larsen, M., 23–24, 27, 80–81, 171, 178
Hendee, W., 263
Henderson, S., 237
Henning, P., 35, 37
Herd, J. A., 325
Herink, R., 70
Hersey, J. C., 34
Hershey, M., 80, 167, 180
Herzog, T. A., 49
Hessling, R. M., xi, 6, 21–32, 80, 82, 84
Hester, R. R., 63, 71
Heyden, S., 223, 227
Hill, D., 92, 288
Hill, J. F., 153
Hill, M., 212
Himmelsback, F., 10
Hinsz, V. B., 79
Hippocrates, 305
Hoar, P. F., 307
Hobbs, G. E., 218
Hoberman, H., 237
Hochbaum, G. M., 37

Hoff, C. C., 272
Hollatz-Brown, A., 269
Holliday, J. E., 238
Holmes, D. S., 232
Holmes, J. G., 144
Holmes, T. H., 230, 306
Holmstrom, L., 163
Holroyd, K. A., 325
Holt, K., 126
Hoogstraten, J., 35
Horn, D., 64, 250
Hospers, H. J., 59, 61, 250
House, J. S., xii, 216, 218–229, 232–233, 239, 241
House, P., 23, 27, 108, 195
Houseworth, S. J., 332
Houston, B. K., 333–335, 337, 359
Hovland, C. I., 120, 126
Howard, J., 263, 267
Howard-Pitney, B., 127
Huba, C. J., 83, 87, 185
Hug, R., 333
Hughes, C. F., 364
Hughes, C. F., 364
Hughes, G., 334–335, 337
Hughes, S. L., 64
Hull, J. G., 357
Hulley, S. B., 311
Humphries, C., 344
Hungerford, L. R., 220
Hunt, J. R., 107–109, 113–114
Hunter, T., 61

Imai, W. K., 22
Ingham, R., 79
Institute of Medicine, 71
Irwin, C. E., 80, 272
Isenberg, J. I., 310
Isselbacher, K. J., 108
Iverson, D. C., 34

Jaccard, J. J., 92
Jackson, T., 18, 43, 54
Jacobs, D. R., 311
Jacobs, G. A., 326
Jacobus, S., 236
James, S. A., 223, 227
Jamner, L. D., 333
Janis, I. L., 22, 101, 103, 118–120, 126, 139, 250, 297
Janoff-Bulman, R., 262
Janus, C., 22, 166
Janus, S., 22, 166
Janz, N. K., 21, 33, 49, 51
Jeffery, R. W., 61, 67, 295
Jemmott, J. B., III, 22, 101–104, 106–110, 113–114, 232, 308
Jennings, J. R., 333
Jessor, R., 167, 173
Jette, A. M., 37
Joesoef, M. R., 329
Joffres, M., 230
Johansson, E., 301

John, O. P., 105
Johnson, B. T., 49, 127–128
Johnson, C. A., 23, 167, 179
Johnson, C. C., 333
Johnson, E. H., 326
Johnson, J. V., 202, 220–221, 228, 230
Johnson, M. P., 113
Johnson, S., 260
Johnson, V., 79
Jonas, B. S., 301
Jones, E. E., 10
Jones, L. E., 42
Jones, S., 11
Jordan, C. H., 369–378
Jöreskog, K. G., 86
Joseph, J. G., 229, 273
Josephs, R. A., 130–131
Journal of Behavioral Medicine, 312
Journal of Chronic Disease, 312
Journal of Psychosomatic Research, 312

Kagan, J., 365
Kahn, J. P., 307
Kahn, R. L., 228, 239, 241
Kahneman, D., 107, 113, 246, 287
Kalichman, S. C., 61, 287, 296
Kallgren, C. A., 184
Kamarck, T. W., 237, 333
Kandel, D. B., 23, 185, 195
Kanfer, F. H., 18, 64, 343
Kanfer, P., 18
Kanner, A. D., 343
Kapiro, J., 330–331, 335, 337
Kaplan, B. A., 67
Kaplan, B. H., 220, 223, 227–228, 230, 240
Kaplan, G. A., 220, 222
Kaplan, J. R., 232
Kaplan, R. M., 320, 333, 359
Kaplan, S. R., 237
Karasu, T. B., 70
Karoly, F., 18
Karuza, J., 262, 269
Kashani, J. H., 37
Kasl, S. V., 222
Katz, I. R., 306
Kauffman, K., 193
Kean, K., 273
Kegeles, S. M., 54, 80, 272, 279
Kegeles, S. S., 10, 262
Kehoe, K., 332
Keintz, M. K., 263, 269
Keller, P. A., 287, 289, 297
Kelley, H. H., 126, 246, 262
Kelly, J., 61
Kelly, K. E., 334
Kelman, H., 185
Kemeny, M. W., 365
Kemery, E. R., 42
Kenny, D. A., 207, 295
Keough, K., 270, 287, 296, 298
Kerns, R. D., 329
Kesnaiemi, A., 330–331, 335, 337

Kessler, H. B., 263, 269
Kessler, L., 63
Kessler, R. C., 227, 233, 236–237
Kidder, L., 262, 269
Kiecolt-Glaser, J. K., 215, 217, 238, 364
Kihlstrom, J. F., 167
Killian, L., 195
Kilty, K. M., 79
King, J. B., 262
Kingslover, K., 237
Kirkpatrick, L. A., 200
Kirscht, J. P., 11, 33
Kitigawa, E. M., 218
Klein, W. M., 22
Kleinbaum, D. G., 220, 227–228, 240
Kleinman, A., 17, 107
Klinger, E., 343
Klinger, M. R., 170
Klinnert, M., 210
Klos, D. S., 263
Knowles, A., 35, 37
Kobasa, S., 307
Kobrin, S., 61
Kohn, M. L., 218
Kohn, P. M., 167
Kong, Y., 329
Koopman, C., 22, 166
Kopel, S. A., 262
Kornfeld, D. S., 307, 350
Korsch, B. M., 107
Korte, C., 193
Koskenvuo, M., 330–331, 335, 337
Kovacs, M., 344
Kowal, D., 170
Krantz, A., 364, 366
Krantz, D. S., 232, 307–308, 311, 332, 336, 350, 357
Kraus, A. S., 218
Krause, N., 87
Kraxberger, B. E., 97
Kreuter, M. W., 61, 247
Kristellar, J., 68
Krosnick, Judd, 180
Kruger, G., 237
Kruger, T. L., 22, 166
Kruglanski, A., 377
Ktsanes, T., 184–185
Kubler-Ross, E., 101
Kukla, A., 343
Kulik, J. A., xii, 148–149, 199–214, 320
Kulka, R. A., 63, 225
Kuller, L. H., 205
Kumar, M., 364
Kunda, Z., 120, 122, 126–128, 195, 377
Kundson, L., 222
Kupfer, D. J., 205
Kushner, M., 212

Lacey, J. I., 203
Lake, C. R., 332
Lakey, B., 240
Lam, C. S., 64
Lambert, M. J., 63

Lamnin, A. D., 363
Landis, K. R., xii, 216, 218–226
Lando, H. A., 29, 167–168, 173, 177
Lando, J. F., 301
Lane, J. D., 22, 332
Lang, P. J., 203
Langinvanio, H., 330–331, 335, 337
LaPorte, R. E., 205
Lasser, N. L., 311
Latané, B., 185, 195
Lau, R. R., 7, 16, 272
Lawton, M. P., 22
Lazarus, R. S., 23, 101, 103, 112, 114–115, 151–152, 224, 232, 237, 306–307, 343, 344
Leary, M. R., 97
Leavy, R. L., 227
Lebouits, B. Z., 331
Lebovitz, B. A., 101
Lebowitz, N.,359
Lechleiter, S., 232
Lee, K. L., 329
Lefcourt, H. M., 240, 343
Lefebvre, R. C., xii, 302, 342–361
Lehman, D. R., 112
Lehrer, P., 260
Leibowitz, R., 164
Leigh, B. C., 144
Leiker, M., 335
Lemke, K. M., 329
Leon, G. R., 331–332
Leon, P., 63
Lepage, L., 79
Lepper, M. R., 120, 126
Levenkron, J. C., 262
Leventhal, E. A., 43
Leventhal, H., xi, 6, 9–20, 22–23, 37, 43–44, 54, 80, 103, 107, 110–111, 114, 139, 141, 167, 202, 240, 247, 287
Leventhal, J. A., 167, 178
Levesque, J. M., 222
Levi, A., 101
Levin, S., 152, 162
Levine, D. M., 10
Levine, J., 377
Levit, D. B., 192
Levy, S., 306, 308, 311
Lewin, K., 343
Lewis, F. M., 34
Lewis, J., 230
Lewis, M. A., 216
Liang, J., 87
Liberman, A., xi, 95, 118–129
Lichtenstein, E., 63–64, 66–67, 236–237
Lichtenstein, S., 43
Lichtman, R. R., xii, 147, 149, 151–165, 262
Lieberman, M. A., 237
Light, R. J., 311
Lightdale, J., 196
Lilienfeld, A. M., 223
Lilienfeld, A. N., 218
Lilienfeld, D. E., 223

Lilly, C., 284
Lindberg, P., 301
Linden, W., 215
Lindstrom, B., 16
Linnan, L. A., 49
Linville, P. W., 287
Lipowski, Z. J., 101
Liska, A. E., 39, 90
Liu, T. J., 131
Lobel, M., 148, 150, 200
Locke, H. J., 154, 161
Locke, S. E., 232, 308
Loftus, E. F., 170
Loftus, P., 164
Lohr, M. J., 167
Loop, F. D., 345, 350, 357
Lopez, D. F., 97, 104–105, 108, 115
Lord, C. G., 120, 126
Lorenz, F., 180
Loro, A. D., 262
Lotzkar, S., 10
Louie, D. H., 109, 113–114
Lounsbury, P., 97
Lowe, M. R., 262
Lown, B., 334
Lubaroff, D. M., 364–365
Lubin, B., 348
Luepker, R. V., 331–332
Lukasqewski, M., 164
Lund, A. K., 36, 38, 262
Lundberg, U., 333
Lushene, R. E., 203, 332
Lutgendorf, S. K., 364
Luus, C. E., 22, 79
Lynch, J. J., 222, 224
Lyon, J. E., xii, 55, 59, 246, 249–260

Maack, M., 80
MacAndrew, G., 130
MacDonald, G., 144, 377
MacDonald, T. K., xi, 96, 130–145
MacDougall, J. M., 325–332, 335, 337, 350
Macfarlane, S., 22
Macgovern, G. J., Sr., 342–361
MacMillan, J., 144
MacPherson, B., 144
Madden, T. J., 38, 39n, 51, 60, 250, 258
Maddox, G. L., 185
Maddux, J. E., 33, 51, 53
Magni, G., 345
Magovern, G. F., Sr., xii, 302
Maheswaran, D., 118, 287, 289, 297
Mahler, H. I. M., xii, 148–149, 199–214
Mahoney. M. J., 74
Maides, S., 262
Maile, M. C., 34
Maiman, L. A., 11
Manderlink, G., 262
Mann, L., 250
Manning, M. L., 80
Manolio, T. A., 335, 337
Manske, S. R., 79

Manstead, A. S., 79
Manuck, S. B., 232, 333, 357
Marcus, A. C., 269
Marcus, B. H., 50, 54, 56, 250
Margulies, S., 363–364
Marks, G. A., 23, 30, 63–64, 66–67, 185, 195
Markus, H. R., 105, 167
Marteau, T. M., 287
Martin, B., 203
Martin, C. D., 287, 296, 298
Martin, J. B., 108
Martin, R. A., 97, 240
Martineau, A. M., xi, 96, 130–145
Martinez, G., 364–365
Martino, S. C., xii, 246, 286, 295
Marx, J., 308
Matarazzo, J. D., 2
Mathur, J., 215
Mattei, L., 270
Matthews, G., 205
Matthews, K. A., xii, 229, 232, 239, 302, 325, 327–328, 330–333, 337, 342–361
Matza, D., 194
Mayer, J. A., 288
Mayne, T. J., 366
Mayou, R., 345
Mazen, R., 18
McAdams, D. P., 212
McAlister, A. L., 67
McCann, B. S., 333
McCaul, K. D., 43, 79, 92, 97, 110–112, 114, 232, 248
McClelland, G. H., 251
McConnaughy, E. A., 54, 64–65
McCoughlin, L., 80
McCrady, B., 260
McCrae, R. R., 317, 327–329, 338, 344
McCraine, E. W., 331
McCuan, R. S., 67
McCurdy, L., 260
McDaniel, L. K., 310
McDougall, K., 273
McFarland, C., 184–185, 194
McGaw, B., 311
McGee, D., 219, 222, 229–230
McGivney, W., 263
McGovern, P. G., 29, 167–168, 173, 177
McGuire, C. V., 296n
McGuire, W. J., 2, 53, 248, 296n
McKay, G., 232, 235
McKelvey, L., 364–365
McKennel, A. C., 167
McKinlay, J. B., 234
McLeod, J. D., 227, 233, 237
McLoughlin, L., 167, 179
McMahan, B. T., 64
McPartland, R. J., 205
Mechanic. D., 152, 307
Medalie, J. H., 230
Medieros, M., 71
Medley, D. M., 326

Melamed, B. G., 203
Melbourne, F. H., 333
Melin, B., 333
Menaghan, E. G., 237
Mendez, V. M., 364–365
Mendoza, S. P., 223–224
Menken, J. A., 225
Mermelstein, R., 237
Messick, D. M., 27
Mestel-Rauch, J., 23
Metzner, H. L., 227–229
Metzner, H. M., 220
Mewborn, C. R., 36
Meyer, D. L., xi, 6, 9–20, 43, 103, 110–111, 240
Meyerowitz, B. E., 287–288, 296–297
Meyers-Levy, J., 287, 289, 297
Meza, M. A., 364–365
Michela, J. L., 164, 246, 262, 269
Mickelson, K. D., 200
Miller, A., 263
Miller, D. T., xii, 30, 101, 148–149, 183–198
Miller, N., 195, 212
Miller, R. L., 362
Miller, S. M., 303
Miller, T. I., 63
Miller, W. R., 63, 71
Mirsky, I. A., 310
Misovich, S. J., 166, 273
Mittlemark, M. B., 311
Moffitt, P. B., 34
Molleman, E., 200
Mongeau, P., 125
Monti, P. M., 236
Moore, P. J., xii, 148–149, 199–214
Moore, S., 79
Moos, R. H., 310
Mordkoff, J. T., 167
Moreland, R., 377
Morgan, M., 83
Morojele, N. K., 79, 81
Morris, M. J., 107
Morris, W. N., 212
Morrison, D. M., 144
Mosbach, P., 167
Moscovici, S., 183, 189
Moss, A. K., 167, 180
Mosteller, F. M., 142, 314
Moyer, A., 287, 296–298
Muellerleile, P. A., 49
Muhlin, G. L., 237
Mullan, J. T., 237
Mullen, B., 142, 180
Mullen, P. D., 21, 34, 68
Mumford, E., 202, 209, 362
Murata, P. J., 269
Murdock, G. P., 309
Murphy, D., 61
Murphy, S., 304
Murray, D., 331–332
Murray, E. J., 363–364
Musante, L., 327–328

Nadler, A., 79
Nadler, S., 128
National Academy of Sciences, 251
National Cancer Institute, 61, 71, 75, 259, 263, 270, 298
National Center for Health Statistics, 270
National Heart, Lung, and Blood Institute, 223, 359
National High Blood Pressure Education Program, 10
National Institute of Allergies and Infectious Diseases, 242
National Institute of Health, 270
National Institute of Mental Health, 30, 92, 115, 128, 165, 180, 196, 242, 298, 359
    Multisite HIV Prevention Trial Group, 248
National Institute on Alcohol Abuse and Alcoholism, 30, 92
National Institute on Drug Abuse, 30, 180
National Institutes of Health, 367
    Biomedical Research Support Group, 165
National Safety Council, 253
National Science Foundation, 270, 359, 367
Natural Sciences and Engineering Research Council of Canada, 377
Neal, K., 232
Neaton, J. D., 311
Nelson, G. D., 34
Nerem, R. M., 222
Nerenz, D. R., 16, 103, 107, 114, 240
Nesselhof-Kendall, S., 273
New England Journal of Medicine, 122, 309
New Jersey Experiment Station, 259
Newby-Clark, I., 377
Newcomb, M. D., 81, 185
Newcomb, T. M., 184
Newell, G. R., 263
Nezlek, J., 222
Nicholls, G., 364
Nickle, V., 212
Nicolich, M. M., 22–23, 40
Niedenthal, P. M., 167
Nisbett, R. E., 10, 43, 195, 262
Noll, R. B., 185
Nomura, A. M. Y., 230
Norbeck, J. S., 230
Norcross, J. C., xi, 48, 54, 58, 63–77
Norman, P., 61, 249, 304
Nowlin, J. B., 331–332
Nuckolls, K. B., 230
Nurius, P., 167

O'Connell, D., 70
O'Gorman, H. J., 184
O'Hara, M. W., 87
O'Heeron, R. C., 364
O'Keeffe, J. L., 328, 334

O'Keeffe, M. K., 273
O'Leary, A., 260, 303, 343
O'Neill, H. K., 43, 79, 92, 203–204, 248
Oates, C., 196
Obrist, P. A., 232
Ockene, I., 68
Ockene, J., 68
Ogé, M., 259
Olshansky, R. W., 23, 80, 167, 195
Olvera, Y., 364–365
Omoto, A. M., 127
Orbell, S., 143
Orford, J., 63
Orleans, C. T., 63, 67
Orth-Gomer, K., 220–222, 228
Ossip-Klein, D., , 63, 67
Ostfeld, A. M., 222, 328, 331, 334–335, 337
Ouelette, J., 79, 89
Owens, J. F., xii, 302, 342–361

Packard, J. S., 184, 193
Page, J. A., 260
Palermo, N. B., 260
Pallack, M. S., 273
Pallonen, U. E., 67
Papadopoulos, C., 358
Parker, D., 79
Paruzzolo, P., 345
Pasin, R. D., 332, 334
Paul, O., 328, 331, 334–335, 337
Pavlov, I. P., 307
Payne, D., 67
Peale, N. V., 342
Pearlin, L. I., 152–153, 237
Pearson, D. C., 67
Pearson, J. A., 212
Peck, H. B., 237
Penn, G. M., 238
Pennebaker, J. W., xii, 16, 240, 302, 328, 362–368
Perez, S. L., 364–365
Perkins, H. W., 185, 189
Perkins, K., 334–335, 337
Pervin, L. A., 22
Peterman, A., 359
Petersdorf, R. G., 108
Peterson, B. L., 328, 331–332, 337
Peterson, G. L., 335, 337
Peterson, L., 37
Petitto, J., 332
Petravich, C., 212
Petrie, K. J.. 7, 364–365
Petty, R. E., 118. 126–128, 283, 289, 297–298
Piccolo, M., 358
Pickering, T. G., 215
Pierce, G. R., 241
Pillemer, D. B.. 311
Pinto. R. P., 236
Poettcker, K., 144
Polesel, E., 345
Pollard, V., 180

Polyzoidis, H., 80
Pomerantz, E. M., 127
Pompili, M., 260
Pope, M. K., 328, 333–335
Porter, C. Q., 67
Powell, L., 319
Pratkanis, A. R., 284
Pratto, F., 105
Prentice, D. A., xii, 30, 148–149, 183–198
Prentice-Dunn, S., 33, 37, 40
President's Commission on Mental Health, 219
Presson, C. C., 23, 80, 167, 179, 195, 273
Priddy, D. A., 64
Prochaska, J. O., xi, 43, 48, 50, 54, 56–59, 61, 63–77, 250
Pronin, E., 287, 297–298
Pruyn, J., 200
Psychological Abstracts, 312
Psychosomatic Medicine, 312
Puskin, J. S., 251
Pyszczynski, T. A., 126–127

Quade, D., 67
Quadrel, M. J., 262
Quattrone, G. A., 113
Quinn, V., 68

Rabinowitz, V. C., 262, 269
Ragland, D. R., 329–330
Rahe, R. H., 306
Rakowski, W., 50, 54, 56, 250
Ramirez, M. S., 284
Rassaby, J., 92, 288
Ratzin, A. C., 67
Rauch, J. M., 23
Reason, J. T., 79
Redding, C. A., 50, 54, 250
Reed, D. M., 219, 222, 229–230
Regier, D., 63
Rehbein, F., 260
Reinsch, S., 359
Reis, H., 226
Reiser, M. F., 310
Reitzes, D. C., 167
Reker, G. T., 343–344
Reno, R. R., 184
Report of the Joint National Committee on Detection, Evaluation, and Treatment of High Blood Pressure, 12
Revenson, T., 320
Reynolds, K. D., 263
Reynolds, L. A., 79
Reznick, J. S., 365
Rhodewalt, F., 328
Rice, L. N., 63
Richards, J. M., 364–365
Ried, L. D., 35, 37
Right, A. L., 230
Rimé, B., 364–365
Rimer, B. K., 34, 263, 269
Ringel, N., 16, 330

Rizzardo, R., 345
Robbins, C., 220, 227–229
Roberts, D. C., 54
Roberts, N. E., 41, 251, 257
Robins, S., 348
Robinson, E., 10
Rodin, J., 4, 8, 245, 261, 286
Roeser, R., 263
Rofe, Y., 210
Rogers, R. W., 33, 36–38, 40, 51, 53, 78
Roizen, R., 63
Rokeach, M., 167
Ronis, D. L., 33, 35–36, 39, 51, 78, 250
Rook, K. S., 216, 224, 238
Rosan, J. R., 263, 269
Roscoe, B., 22, 166
Rose, G. A., 347
Rose, R. J., 330–331, 335, 337
Rosen, 11
Rosenberg, R. L., 329
Rosenbloom, D., 54, 250
Rosenman, R. H., 301, 308, 311, 327–328, 331
Rosenstock, I., 11, 37
Rosenthal, D., 79
Rosenthal, R., 142, 311, 314–315, 319
Ross, L., 23, 27, 108, 120, 126, 195
Ross, M., 101
Rossi, J. S., 50, 54, 57, 59, 61, 63, 65, 67, 71–73, 250
Rossi, S. R., 54, 250
Roth, S., 343
Rotheram-Borres, M. L., 22, 166
Rothman, A. J., ix, xi–xii, 1–4, 8, 22, 48, 50–62, 245–246, 248, 260–271, 286–289, 294–298
Rothman, A. M., 250
Rotter, J. B., 343, 346
Rountree, C. A., 212
Rowson, D., 259
Ruberman, W. E., 222, 229
Rubin, D. B., 142, 315
Ruble, D. N., 180
Russell, D. W., xi, 48, 78–94, 178, 180
Russell, P., 10
Russell, S. F., 326
Rye, B. J., 79

Sackett, 10
Saetermoe, C., 320
Safer, M. A., 43, 54
Saleh, W. E., 240
Sallis, J. F., 333
Salmon, M. A., 67
Salonen, J. T., 67
Salovey, P., ix, xii, 1–4, 8, 61, 245–246, 261–271, 286–289, 294, 296–298
Saltzman, N., 70
Samaha, G. M., 212
Sande, G. N., 22, 102–103, 108, 110–112, 114
Sanders, G. S., 27, 234, 335–336
Sanders, J. D., 328, 334

Sanders, M., 215
Sandgren, A. K., 79
Sandler, I., 240
Sandler, R. S., 59, 250
Sandman, P. M., xii, 41, 50, 54–57, 59, 246, 249–260
Sansone, C., 262
Sanstad, K. H., 273
Sarason, B. R., 215, 241
Sarason, I. G., 215, 241
Sarnaa, S., 330–331, 335, 337
Sayer, N., 269
Sayles, M., 234, 237, 240
Schachter, S., 16, 63, 66–67, 151, 184, 200–201, 210
Schaefer, C. H., 230, 237
Schaeffer, M. A., 350
Schanck, R. L., 184, 194
Schechter, D., 128
Scheier, M. F., xii, 302, 342–361
Scher, S. J., 284
Scherwitz, L., 334–335, 337
Schifter, D. E., 79
Schlegel, R. P., 79
Schlesinger, H. J., 202, 209, 362
Schmale, A. H., 306, 343
Schmid, T. L., 67
Schneiderman, N., 332, 334, 363–364
Schoemaker, P. J. H., 41
Schoenbach, V. J., 63, 67, 220, 223, 227–228, 240
Schoenberger, 10
Schooler, C., 152–153
Schulman, M., 260
Schultz, R., 163, 224, 359
Schulze, W. D., 251
Schuman, H., 113, 185, 193
Schumann, D., 118
Schustack, M., 320
Schuster, M. M., 320
Schwartz, D., 332, 334
Schwartzenberger, P., 144
Schwarz, N., 105
Schwarzer, R., 54
Seeman, M., 234, 237, 240
Seeman, T. E., 222, 229, 234, 237, 240
Segal, D. L., 364
Seligman, M. E. P., 343
Selye, H., 239, 306–307, 320, 365
Seydel, E., 39
Shadel, W. G., 49
Shaffer, R. T., 350
Shanks, R., 63
Shapira, Z., 41
Shapiro, D. A., 63, 333
Shapiro, S., 63, 263
Sharp, L. K., 364
Shaver, K., 262
Shaver, P., 200, 210
Shawl, L., 10
Shearin, E. N., 241
Sheeran, P., 61, 143
Shekelle, 10

Shekelle, 10
Shekelle, R. B., 311, 328, 331–332, 334–335, 337
Shelley, S. I., 358
Shepherd, R., 79
Sheppard, B. H., 79, 81, 166
Sheppard, M. A., 29
Sheppard, S. L., 37
Sherif, M., 120, 183–184
Sherman, S. J., 23, 80, 167, 179, 195, 273
Sherrod, D. R., 224
Shields, J. L., 325, 332
Shinn, M., 10
Shulman, L. S., 108
Shumaker, S. A., 228, 242
Sidney, S., 335, 337
Siegel, K., 279
Siegel, L. J., 203
Siegler, I. C., 328, 331–332, 335, 337
Siegman, A. W., 330
Sikes, J., 284
Silva, A., 364–365
Silver Platter, Inc., 33
Silver, R. L., 152
Silverman, I., 99
Simpson, S., 332
Singer, J. E., 152–153, 308, 311
Singer, R. P., 11, 16
Sisson, B. D., 331
Skelton, J. A., 110
Skinner, C. S., 59, 61, 250
Skinner, E., 63
Skowronski, J. J., 168
Slovic, P., 43, 113
Smith, C., 304
Smith, G. E., 23, 29, 80–81, 85, 88–89
Smith, J. C., 332, 334
Smith, K. D., 170
Smith, M. A., 333
Smith, M. L., 63, 311, 362
Smith, S. L., 50, 55–56, 250
Smith, S. M., 289, 297–298
Smith, T. W., xii, 302, 325–341
Smyth, J. M., 363, 365
Snapp, M., 284
Snidman, N., 365
Snyder, C. R., 273
Snyder, M. L., 23, 108
Sobel, M. E., 88
Social Sciences and Humanities Research Council of Canada, 144
Soll, A. H., 310
Solomon, G. F., 308
Solomon, L. J., 37, 288
Solomon, S., 232
Sontag, S., 309
Sörbom, D., 86
Southwick, L., 131
Sparks, P., 79, 88
Speckart, G., 80
Speicher, C. E., 238
Spencer, D., 144

Spencer, S., 377
Spera, S. P., 364–365
Spielberger, C. D., 203–204, 326
Sporn, A. A., 350
Sprafka, S. A., 108
Stacy, A. W., 24, 79, 81, 167, 169
Stall, R. D., 144, 272
Stamler, J., 10, 311, 331
Stangor, C., 126
Stanwyck, D., 319
Steele, 17
Steele, C. M., 130–131
Steele, D. J., 103, 107, 114
Steer, R. A., 344
Steffen, V., 35–36
Stein, J. A., 185, 269
Stenner, K., 79
Stephan, C., 284
Stephenson, G. M., 79, 81
Sternberg, R. J., 376
Stewart, F., 170
Stewart, G. K., 170
Stimson, 10
Stitt, C., 202
Stone, A. A., 364, 366
Stone, J., xii, 245, 272–285
Storms, M. D., 262
Strack, S., 344
Stradling, S. G., 79
Strasser, T., 284
Straus, R., 185
Strawbridge, W. J., 220
Strax, P., 263
Strecher, V. J., 59, 61, 247, 250
Stroebe, M., 221
Stroebe, W., 221
Stroufe, L. A., 203
Stroup, N. E., 329
Struening, E. L., 237
Stuart, A. E., 149
Suarez, E. C., 333–334
Sullivan, J. J., 273
Suls, J., 27, 112, 180, 195, 202, 209, 335–336, 344
Sun, Y., 109, 113–114
Supplee, K., 333
Surtees, P. G., 237
Sussman, D., 167, 169
Sussman, S., 23, 167, 179
Sutton, S. R., xi, 33–36, 38–39, 48, 50–62, 120, 125, 250, 259–260, 297
Svardgudd, K., 220
Svarstad, 10
Swan, G. E., 327–328
Swindle, R. W., Jr., 227
Syme, S. L., 215, 220, 222–223, 227–229, 233–234, 236, 240–241, 329–330
Szklo, M., 221

Taal, E., 39
Tanaka, J. S., 87
Tarazi, R. Y., 212

Taylor, C. B., 343
Taylor, S. E., xii, 2, 29, 115, 147–165, 169, 199–200, 238, 262, 304, 365
Taylor, V., 144
Tchividjian, L. R., 97
Temoshok, L., 272, 301
ter Horst, G., 35
Terpstra, J., 144
Terry, D. J., 11, 79–80
Terwilliger, R., 119–120
Tetlock, P. E., 101
Tetzloff, C., 80, 167, 180
Thaler, M., 310
Tharps, Q., 43, 54
Thibodeau, R., 273, 279, 284
Thiesse-Duffy, E., 97, 110–112, 114
Thoits, P. A., 219, 234, 236
Thomas, M. G., 364–365
Thompson, L., 319
Thoreson, C. E., 74, 319
Thornton, D. A., 200
Tibblin, G., 16, 220, 223, 227
Tiebout, J., 364
Tilden, V. P., 230
Tillman, W. A., 218
Tischler, G., 63
Tolman, E. C., 343
Tompkins, C. A., 359
Torrence, D., 212
Trevorrow, T. R., 333
Trice, H. M., 196
Trussel, J., 170
Tsou, C. V., 263
Tuchfeld, B., 63
Turner, G. E., 167, 169
Turner, J., 183
Turner, K. L., 200
Turner, R. J., 195, 228
Turtle, A. M., 80
Turvey, C., xii, 246, 261–271
Tversky, A., 107, 113, 246, 287
Tyler, R., 61

U.S. Department of Health and Human Services, 25, 286
U.S. Environmental Protection Agency, 251–252, 259
U.S. Public Health Service, 22, 166, 172, 212
Agency for Health Care Policy and Research, 115, 212
U.S. Surgeon General, 252
Advisory Committee, 219, 223
Uchino, B. N., 215, 217
Uhlmann, C., 364
Ulmer, D., 319
Ulrich-Jakubowski, D., 87
Umberson, D., xii, 216., 218–226
Underwood, L. G., 217
Unger, H. P., 345
University of California
  at Los Angeles, 164–165
  at Riverside, 320

University of Michigan Survey Research Center, 79
University of Minnesota, 298

Vaccaro, D., 179
Valderrama, P., 364–365
Valfre, C., 345
Valins, S., 262
Valois, P., 79
van Arsdel, P. P., 230
van den Putte, B., 79, 88
van Knippenberg, A., 200
Van Korff, M., 63
Van Treuren, R. R., 357
vandenEijnden, R. J. J. M., 149
Vanet, L., 263
Vanet, W., 263
Vangarelli, D. J., 66–67
Vavak, C. R., 335
Velasquez, M. M., 50, 54, 57, 65, 67, 71–72, 250
Velicer, W. F., 50, 54, 56–59, 61, 64–65, 67, 69–73, 250
Verkaaik, C., 212
Vernberg, E., 228
Veroff, J., 63, 225
Verrier, R. L., 334
Visotsky, H. M., 101
Visscher, B. R., 365
Viviano, A., 260
Vorp, R., 332, 334

Wachtel, P. L., 69
Wachtler, J., 212
Wagner, D., 259–260
Wagner, E. A., 67
Wagner, E. H., 223, 227
Waingrow, S., 64
Wallace, K. M., 154, 161
Wallston, B. S., 34, 227, 231, 262
Wallston, K. A., 34, 262
Wan, C. K., 27, 202, 209
Wangersteen, O. H., 105
Ware, J. E., Jr., 237
Warner, T. D., 22–23, 170
Warshaw, P. R., 79, 81, 166
Watkins, L. O., 331
Watkins, S. C., 225

Watson, D., 328
Weary, G., 262
Wegener, D., 298
Weinblatt, E., 222, 229
Weiner, H., 307, 310
Weinman, J. A., 7
Weinstein, N. D., xi–xii, 6, 22–23, 30, 33–46, 48–62, 246, 249–260
Weintraub, J. K., 344, 357
Weir, I. L., 167
Weisman, A. D., 22
Weiss, J. M., 306, 310
Weiss, M. B., 350
Weiss, S. M., 357
Weisse, C. S., 273
Weitzman, L. J., 225
Welin, L., 220
Wellisch, D., 164
West, D., 260
West, S. G., 263
Wethington, E., 236
Wetterhall, S. F., 329
Whalen, R., 329
Wheeler, L., 153, 222
Wicker, A. W., 18, 113
Wickersham, D., 34, 39
Wicklund, R. A., 23
Widaman, K. F., 24
Wiebe, J. S., 364–365
Wiegman, O., 39
Wilcox, B. L., 228, 237
Wilcox, N., 71
Williams, A. F., 112
Williams, A. W., 237
Williams, K. D., 111
Williams, P. G., 330, 338
Williams, R. B., Jr., 229, 301, 327–335, 337, 357
Willower, D. J., 184, 193
Wills, T. A., 153, 161, 163, 179, 200, 215, 227–228, 233–235, 237, 242
Wilson, D. K., 287, 297
Wilson, G. T., 64, 66
Wilson, J. D., 108
Wilson, P., 97, 110–112, 114
Wilson, S. R., 153
Winer, B. J., 142
Wingard, J. A., 83

Winslow, M. P., xii, 245, 272–285
Winter, L., 79
Wise, C. M., 310
Withey, S. B., 347–349
Wixom, C., 164
Wong, P. T. P., 343–344
Wood, D., 359
Wood, J. V., xii, 147, 149, 151–165, 200, 262, 269
Woodall, K. L., 327–328
Woodcock, A., 79
Worchel, S., 212
Worden, T. J., 326
Wortman, C. B., 112, 151–152, 162, 231, 262, 269, 306, 343, 364
Wright, D., 29
Wright, G., 144
Wright, S. L., 212
Wrightsman, L. S., Jr., 222
Wugalter, S. E., 30
Wurf, E., 105
Wurtele, S. K., 38–39
Wyer, R. S., 127

Yale Cancer Prevention Unit, 264
Yanez, C., 22
Yano, K., 219, 222, 229–230
Yates, S. M., 118, 126
Yatko, R. J., 22
Yatomi, N., 87
Ybema, J.-F., 180
Young, L. D., 310
Youniss, J., 80

Zabin, L. S., 80
Zajonc, R. B., 224, 307
Zanna, A., 377
Zanna, M. P., xi, 79, 96, 130–145, 153, 283, 369–378
Zimbardo, P. G., 200, 212
Zimet, G., 229
Zimmerman, R. S., 10, 110–111
Zola, I. K., 101
Zonderman, A. B., 328, 331
Zucker, R. A., 185
Zuckerman, D. M., 222
Zuckerman, M., 153, 348

Subject Index

Action stage, 54, 63
  change processes, 71–72
  defined, 66
Addictive behaviors
  cross-sectional perspective, 71–72
  how people change, 63–77
  integrating processes and stages, 71–74
  integrative conclusions, 74–75
  longitudinal perspective, 72–74
  mismatching stage and treatment, 68
  processes as change predictors, 71
  processes of change, 69–71
  spiral pattern of change, 66–67
  stage movements during treatment, 68–69
  stages of change, 64–69
  transtheoretical model, 54, 63–77, 250
  treatment implications, 67–68
Adherence, 12
  patient beliefs and, 14–16
Adjustment
  self-enhancement and, 152
  self-evaluation and, 151–152
  social comparison theory, 151–164
Adolescents
  affect of cognitions, 21
  behavior changes, 25, 28
  cognitive shifts, 25–28
  health risk, 79–80
  motivated shifts in cognition, 29–30
  peer pressure, 79–81
  perceived vulnerability, 21, 24–25, 28–30
  prototype/willingness model, 80–81
  risk behavior predictors, 78–94
  risk behaviors and beliefs, 6, 21–32
  risk/cognition reciprocity, 21–22, 29
  treatment, 30
Advocating, 70–71
Affect
  social support and, 237

Aggression, 312–313, 315–320
Alcohol myopia, 130–145
  discussion, 141–144
  field study, 135–141
  intentions, 134–135, 137, 140–141
  justifications, 134, 136–138
  laboratory experiment, 133–135
  manipulation check, 134, 140
  study discussion, 135
  study measures, 134, 136–137, 140
  study methods, 133–134, 136–137, 139–140
  study results, 134–135, 137–138, 140–141
  study subjects, 133, 136, 139
  treatment implications, 144
  vs. disinhibition, 143–144
Alcohol use
  assessing, 24–25
  beliefs and, 6, 21–32
  cognition changes, 27
  on campus, 185–186
  prototype model, 166–182
  risk and beliefs, 6
  social norms, 183–198
Allegheny General Hospital (Pittsburgh), 345
Anger, 312–313, 315–320
Anxiety, 312–313, 315–320
Assertion, 70–71
Attitudes, 5–46
  about breast cancer, 265–267
  about treatment efficacy, 10–11
  based on symptoms and concepts, 13–14, 16
  commonsense models, 9–20
  discussion questions, 7
  effects on health behavior, 3
  expected utility theory, 33–46
  health-belief model, 33–46
  linking attributes, 14
  measuring, 84

  protection motivation theory, 33–46
  reasoned action theory, 33–46
  risk behaviors and cognitions, 21–32
  social norms, 190–191
  suggested readings, 7–8
  testing competing theories, 33–46
  toward hypertension, 12–13
  toward treatment efficacy, 9–20, 35, 39
Attributional Style Questionnaire, 346
Attributions of responsibility, 261–271
  breast cancer and, 266–267
  discussion, 268–269
  health behaviors, 261–263
  obtaining mammograms, 267–268
  persuasive message presentation, 264
  screening mammography use, 263
  study measures, 264–265
  study method, 263–265
  study results, 265–268
  study subjects, 264
Avoiding stimuli, 70–71

Bayh, Marvella, 152
Behavioral intention
  health risk predictor, 78–94
Behaviors
  addictive, 63–77
  affected by beliefs, 5–8
  affected by commonsense models, 17–18
  affected by social support, 231–232
  alcohol myopia, 130–145
  attributions of responsibility, 261–271
  changing, 25, 28, 63–77, 245–299
  combinatorial rules, 35–37
  commonsense models, 9–20
  competing theories, 33–46
  concept differentiation, 42–43
  costs, 37–38
  discussion questions, 48–49
  effectiveness, 39

Behaviors (*continued*)
generalizing from appraisal to, 113–114
health beliefs and, 14–16, 47–94
health-belief model, 33–46
health-protective, 33–46
healthy process, 39–40
illness, 307, 317–318
inducing hypocrisy, 272–285
integrating stages and processes, 71–74
integrative conclusions, 74–75
measuring, 85
mental content, 34–35
message framing, 286–299
model content, 40–41
model testing implications, 40–43
motivation, 34–35
nonhealth considerations, 38
nonrisk variables, 35
perceived vulnerability, 21, 24–2528–30
precaution adoption process model, 55, 249–261
predicting, 78–94, 256–257
preventive vs. detection, 296–297
problems in model testing, 41–42
processes of change, 69–71
protection motivation theory, 33–46
prototype/willingness model, 78–94
pseudostage models, 53–54
risk and cognitions, 6, 21–32, 78–94, 130–145
self-efficacy, 38
stage theories of, 50–62, 64–69
static vs. dynamic models, 43
study conclusion, 43–44
subjective expected utility theory, 33–46
suggested readings, 49
testing competing theories, 33–46
theory of reasoned action, 33–46
transtheoretical model of change, 54, 63–77, 250
Beliefs, 5–46, 122–124
about hypertension, 12–13
about treatment efficacy, 9–20
addictive behaviors, 63–77
based on symptoms, 13–14, 16
commonsense models, 9–20
discussion questions, 7, 48–49
expected utility theory, 33–46
health behaviors and, 47–94
health-belief model, 33–46
how people change, 63–77
integrating stages and processes, 71–74
integrative conclusions, 74–75
linking attributes, 14
processes of change, 69–71
protection motivation theory, 33–46
prototype/willingness model, 78–94
reasoned action theory, 33–46

risk behaviors and cognitions, 21–32
stage theories of, 50–62, 64–69
suggested readings, 7–8, 49
testing competing theories, 33–46
Bibliotherapy, 70–71
Black, Shirley Temple, 152
Breast Cancer Demonstration Project, 263
Breast cancer
attributions of responsibility, 261–271
early detection, 1–2
increasing mammography use, 261–271
social comparison and adjustment, 151–165
Bronchial asthma
personality affecting, 310, 313, 315–320
Buss-Durkee Hostility Inventory, 326

Cancer. *See also* Breast Cancer
personality affecting, 311, 315–320
Causes
mental models, 6, 9–20
patient representations, 13
treatment adherence and, 14–16
Cellular car telephones, 1
Change processes, 69–71
as predictors of changes, 71
cross-sectional perspective, 71–72
integrating with stages, 71–74
longitudinal perspective, 72–74
progressive patterns, 73
recycling patterns, 73
regressive patterns, 73
spiral pattern, 66–67
stable patterns, 73
static patterns, 73
Changing behavior, 245–299
attributions of responsibility, 261–271
discussion questions, 247
inducing hypocrisy, 272–285
message framing, 286–299
precaution adoption process model, 55, 249–261
stages of changes, 249–250
suggested readings, 247–248
Changing behaviors, 3
Chemotherapy, 1
Cigarette smoking, 1, 47–48
adolescents, 82–83
assessing, 24–25
beliefs and, 6, 21–32
cognition changes, 27–28
effects of quitting, 2
prototype model, 166–182
Cognitions
affecting behavior, 25–26, 28
altering, 22, 26–28
motivated shifts, 29–30
perceived vulnerability, 24–25, 28–30
reciprocity with risk behaviors, 21–22, 29

risk behaviors and, 6, 21–32
study discussion, 28–30
study measures, 23–24
study method, 23–24
study parameters, 22–24
study results, 25–28
study subjects, 23
treatment implications, 30
Combinatorial rules, 35–37
Commitment enhancing techniques, 70–71
Commitment manipulation, 275
Commonsense models, 9–20
affecting behaviors, 17–18
information representation, 12–13
study discussion, 16–18
study interview, 12–13
study method, 11–13
study results, 13–16
study subjects, 11–12
themes of, 6
Compliance failures, 9–10
patient beliefs and, 15–16
Condom use
alcohol myopia and, 130–145
encouraging by inducing hypocrisy, 272–285
Confrontations, 70–71
Consciousness raising, 69–71
stage of change, 71–72
Consequences
disregarding, 23
mental models, 6, 9–20
Contemplation stage, 54, 63
defined, 65
change processes, 71–72
Contingency contracts, 70–71
Continuum-based approach, 47–48
vs. stage theories, 53
Coping, 12
downward comparison perspective, 153–154, 156–158, 160–163
similarity perspective, 153, 155–156, 159–160, 162–163
supercoper perspective, 152, 155, 158–159, 162
upward comparison perspective, 153, 156–158, 160–163
Coronary heart disease
hostility and, 325–341
optimism and recovery, 342–361
personality and, 310–311, 313, 315–320
Corrective emotional experience, 70–71
Costs of acting, 35, 37–38
Counterconditioning, 69–71
change patterns, 73–74
stage of change, 71–72
Covert reinforcement, 70–71

Decision-making stage, 55
Decision-making therapy, 70–71
Defensive processing, 118–129

beliefs, 122–124
checks on design, 122
correlations, 125–126
defense mechanisms, 126–127
dependent measures, 122–125
effort, 123–124
heuristic-systematic model, 119
intentions, 122–124
message threat, 121–125
objective processing, 127–128
premeasures, 121
study methods, 121–123
study results, 123–126
study subjects, 121
Denial, 114–115
    and expectations, 103–104
    confirmatory symptom reporting,
        102–103
    nature of, 104–105
    perceived treatability, 102–103
    risk factor information, 101–102
Depression, 312–313, 315–320
Desensitization, 70–71
Diagnostic context, 111–112
Disclosure, 362–368
    effects of, 363
    procedural differences, 363–365
    vs. inhibition, 362
Discussion questions
    health beliefs and behaviors, 48–49
    information processing, 96
    mental models, 7
    personality and health, 303
    social norms/comparisons, 149
    social support, 217
Disease-prone personality, 302, 305–324
    biological variables, 307
    construct validity, 309
    direct influence, 306–307
    discussion, 318–320
    disease outcomes, 313
    disease-caused changes, 306
    future research, 320
    hostility, 325–341
    illness behaviors, 307, 317–318
    literature search, 312
    meta-analysis, 311–312
    multiple influences, 307–308
    overall findings, 316–317
    personality variables, 312–313
    physiological mechanisms, 308–309
    psychosomatic diseases, 309–311
    specific findings, 315–316
    study inclusion criteria, 312
    study method, 312–314
    study results, 314–318
    study techniques, 313–314
    unhealthy habits, 306
Disinhibition
    theory, 130–145
    vs. alcohol myopia, 143–144
Dispositional optimism. See Optimism
Documentaries, 70–71

Downward comparison perspective,
        153–154, 162–163
    predictors of, 161–163
    relevant comparisons, 156–158
    vs. upward comparison, 160–161
Dramatic relief, 69–71
    stage of change, 71–72
Duration of illness
    mental models, 6, 9–20

Educational programs, 10–11
    risk behaviors and, 22–23
Effort, 123–124
Empathy training, 70–71
Empowering, 70–71
Environmental reevaluation, 69–71
    stage of change, 71–72
Etiology of disease
    differentiating, 228
    generic models, 231–232
    main-effect models, 233–234
    psychosocial models, 227–244
    research priorities, 238–241
    role for psychologists, 238
    role of social support, 227–244
    separate links, 236–238
    social links to illness onset, 231
    stress-buffering models, 235–236
    stress-centered models, 232–233
Expectancies, 34–35
    denial and, 103–104
    measuring, 86
    optimism, 342–361
    situation-specific, 346, 353–356
    specific vs. optimism, 358–359
    vs. intentions, 81
Expected utility theory. See Subjective
    expected utility theory
Extraversion, 312–313, 315–320

Fading techniques, 70–71
False consensus bias, 108–109
Fear-inducing messages, 119–122

Gain/loss messages, 286–299
    actions, 294
    attitudes, 293
    behavioral intentions, 293–294
    dental health, 288–298
    discussion, 295–298
    influencing behavior, 297–298
    integrating framing, 287
    manipulation checks, 291–292
    mediational analyses, 294–295
    pamphlet evaluation, 291
    pamphlets, 289–290
    prevention vs. detection behaviors,
        296–297
    risk perception, 292
    study measures, 290–291
    study method, 289–291
    study participants, 289
    study results, 291–295

thought reactions, 292–293
Generalizability
    diagnostic context, 111–112
    from appraisal to behavior, 113–114
    immediate vs. delayed reactions, 112–
        113
    reactions to risk factors, 109–111
    reactions to serious conditions, 113
Generic models, 231–232
Global Adjustment to Illness Scale, 154
Goals, 1–2
Grieving losses, 70–71

Headaches
    personality affecting, 310, 313, 315–
        320
Health belief model
    tested, 33–46
Health information
    affected by beliefs, 9–20
    alcohol myopia, 96, 130145
    beliefs, 122–124
    checks on design, 122
    confirmatory symptom reporting,
        102–103
    correlations, 125–126
    defense mechanisms, 126–127
    defensive, 118–129
    denial, 102–106
    dependent measures, 122–125
    diagnostic context, 111–112
    discussion questions, 96
    effort, 123–124
    expectations, 103–104
    factors in understanding, 3
    false consensus bias, 108–109
    favorable vs. unfavorable, 96, 98–117
    framing, 286–299
    from appraisal to behavior, 113–115
    generalizability, 109–115
    heuristic-systematic model, 119
    illness appraisals, 107–109
    immediate vs. delayed reactions, 112–
        113
    inducing hypocrisy, 272–285
    intentions, 122–124
    internally-oriented, 261–271
    intervention messages, 245–246
    message threat, 121–125
    motivational determinants, 101–102
    nature of denial, 104–105
    objective processing, 127–128
    organizing, 3
    perceived treatability, 102–103
    personal relevance of, 118–129
    persuasive presentation, 264
    preconceived biases, 95
    premeasures, 121
    previous research limitations, 99
    processing, 95–145
    reactions to serious conditions, 113
    reactions to risk factors, 109–111
    research reports, 369–378

Health information (*continued*)
 risk factor test results, 98–117
 social determinants, 101–102
 social influences, 106–109
 study methods, 121–123
 study results, 123–126
 study subjects, 121
 suggested readings, 97
 TAA enzyme paradigm, 100–101
 targeting, 95, 45–246
Health-protective behaviors, 33–46
 combinatorial rules, 35–37
 competing theories, 33–46
 concept differentiation, 42–43
 costs, 37–38
 effectiveness, 39
 health-belief model, 33–46
 healthy process, 39–40
 mental content, 34–35
 model content, 40–41
 model testing implications, 40–43
 motivation, 34–35
 nonhealth considerations, 38
 nonrisk variables, 35
 problems in model testing, 41–42
 protection motivation theory, 33–46
 self-efficacy, 38
 static vs. dynamic models, 43
 study conclusion, 43–44
 subjective expected utility theory, 33–46
 theory of reasoned action, 33–46
Helping relationships, 69–71
 stage of change, 71–72
Heuristic-systematic model, 119
High blood pressure. *See* Hypertension
HIV/AIDS, 2
 alcohol myopia and condom use, 130–145
 preventing, 272–285
 stage theories, 50–51
Hostility, 3
 assessing, 326–329
 Buss-Durkee Hostility Inventory, 326, 328–329
 causing disease, 325–341
 common issues, 336–337
 concepts defined, 326
 constitutional vulnerability model, 336
 cross-sectional studies, 329–330
 future research, 337–338
 health behavior model, 335–336
 health effects, 325–341
 Ho Scale, 327–328
 interview methods, 326–327
 potential for, 326–327
 prospective studies, 330–332
 psychophysiological reactivity model, 332–334
 psychosocial vulnerability model, 334–335
 theory application, 338
 transactional model, 335

Hypertension, 6, 9–20
Identity model, 234–236
Illness appraisals
 false consensus bias, 108–109
 social influence, 107–108
Illness behaviors, 307, 317–318
Illness onset, 231
Imagery, 70–71
Immune function
 physiological mechanisms, 308–309
 social support and, 238
Increasing alternatives, 70–71
Inducing hypocrisy, 272–285
 acknowledging risk, 279–281
 behavioral effects, 277–279
 commitment manipulation, 275
 dependent measures, 275–277
 follow-up interviews, 277, 281–283
 mindfulness manipulation, 275
 practical implications, 284
 self-reports of intent, 279
 study method, 274–275
 study results, 277–284
 study subjects, 274
 theoretical implications, 283–284
Information-based model, 233–235
Inhibition vs. disclosure, 365–366
Intentions, 122–124, 170–171
 alcohol myopia studies, 134–135, 137, 140–141
 measuring, 81
 self-reports, 279
 vs. expectations, 81
 vs. willingness, 89–90
Interpersonal control, 73–74
Interviewing
 biases, 12
 recruitment, 254
 social comparison, 155

Journaling, 362–368
 associated with health, 362–
 basic writing paradigm, 362–363
 cognitive changes, 366
 disclosure, 363, 365–366
 inhibition, 365–366
 procedural differences, 363–365
 treatment implications, 366–367
 why it works, 365–366
Justifications, 134, 136–138

Life Orientation Test, 346
Locke-Wallace Scale of Marital Adjustment, 154
Logotherapy, 70–71

Main-effect model, 233–235
Maintenance stage, 54, 63
 change processes, 71–72
 defined, 66
Mammography, 1–2
 increasing use, 261–271

Medications, 73–74
Melanoma, 1
Mental models, 5–46
 commonsense models, 9–20
 discussion questions, 7
 risk behaviors and cognitions, 21–32
 suggested readings, 7–8
 testing competing theories, 33–46
Message framing, 286–299
 actions, 294
 attitudes, 293
 behavioral intentions, 293–294
 dental health, 288–298
 discussion, 295–298
 influencing behavior, 297–298
 integrating, 287–288
 manipulation checks, 291–292
 mediational analyses, 294–295
 pamphlet evaluation, 291
 pamphlets, 289–290
 prevention vs. detection behaviors, 296–297
 risk perception, 292
 study measures, 290–291
 study method, 289–291
 study participants, 289
 study results, 291–295
 thought reactions, 292–293
Message threat, 121–122
Meta-analysis, 311–312
 discussion, 318–320
 disease outcomes, 313
 future research, 320
 illness behaviors, 317–318
 literature search, 312
 overall findings, 316–317
 personality variables, 312–313
 specific findings, 315–316
 study inclusion criteria, 312
 study method, 312–314
 study results, 314–318
 study techniques, 313–314
Milwaukee Blood Pressure Program, 11–12
Mindfulness manipulation, 275
Minimizing threats, 73–74
Model testing, 40–44
 concept differentiation, 42–43
 key questions, 44
 problems in, 41–42
 static vs. dynamic models, 43
 tests matched to content, 40–41
Moderation, 91
Morbidity studies, 229–230
Mortality studies, 220–222, 228–229
 interpretation limits, 229
Motivation
 denial and, 102–103
 protection motivation theory, 33–46
 risk factor appraisal, 101–102
 to take action, 34–35
 treatment compliance, 10

Mount Sinai Medical Center (Milwaukee), 11–12

Negativity, 3
Neuroendocrine response
  social support and, 237–238
New Year's resolutions, 70–71
Nonhealth considerations, 38–39

Optimism, 3, 342–361
  adjusting analyses, 349–350
  assessing, 356
  coping strategies, 348, 352–353
  data collection, 348–349
  discussion, 356–359
  effects of, 356–357
  medical information obtained, 348
  mood, 348, 352
  quality of life, 347–348, 352
  reactions to surgery, 346–347, 350
  recovery rate, 347, 350–352
  specific expectancies, 346, 353–356, 358–359
  study method, 345–349
  study results, 349–356
  study subjects, 345–346
  treatment implications, 359
  treatment satisfaction, 352

PAP testing, 2
Patient affiliations, 208
Patient representations, 13–14
  behaviors and, 14–16
  linking attributes, 14
Peer pressure. *See* Social influence
Peptic ulcers
  personality affecting, 310, 313, 315–320
Perceived risk, 34–35, 254–255
Perceived treatability, 102–103
Perceived vulnerability, 21
  affecting risk behaviors, 28–30
  assessing, 24–25
  impact of risk behaviors, 28–29
  limits of increases, 30
  motivation and, 34–35
Personal control
  social support and, 237
Personality, 3
  biological variables, 307
  construct validity, 309
  direct influence, 306–307
  discussion questions, 303
  discussion of, 318–320
  disease outcomes, 313
  disease-caused changes, 306
  disease-prone, 302, 305–324
  future research, 320
  health and, 301–368
  hostility, 302, 325–341
  illness behaviors, 307, 317–318
  journaling, 302, 362–368
  literature search, 312

meta-analysis, 311–312
multiple influences, 307–308
optimism, 302, 342–361
overall findings, 316–317
personality variables, 312–313
physiological mechanisms, 308–309
psychosomatic diseases, 309–311
specific findings, 315–316
study inclusion criteria, 312
study method, 312–314
study results, 314–318
study techniques, 313–314
suggested readings, 303–304
treatment compliance and, 10
unhealthy habits, 306
Physiological mechanisms, 308–309
  patient representations, 13–14
Pluralistic ignorance, 183–198defined, 184–185
Policy interventions, 70–71
Positive self-statements, 70–71
Precaution adoption process model, 55, 249–261
  combination condition, 253, 259
  defined, 250
  home radon testing context, 251
  manipulation checks, 254–255
  predicting action, 256–257
  predicting progress, 255–256
  predictions of, 258–259
  preintervention differences, 254–255
  study method, 251–254
  study results, 254–258
  two-stage transitions, 257–258
Preconceived biases, 95, 108–109
Precontemplation stage, 54, 63
  change processes, 71–72
  defined, 65
Preparation stage, 54, 63
  change processes, 71–72
  defined, 65–66
Prevalence estimates, 23, 25
Princeton University
  alcohol use, 183–198
Progressive patterns, 73
Protection motivation theory, 78
  tested, 33–46
Prototype model, 166–182
  assimilation, 168
  behavioral prediction, 168
  change, 167–168, 172–175
  current research, 169–171
  developmental differences, 179–180
  distancing, 168
  favorability, 167
  gender, 179
  images, 167
  intention, 170–171
  predicting change, 175–177
  prototype perception, 171, 177–179
  prototypes, 167–168
  social comparison, 171–172, 179
  study discussion, 177–180

study measures, 170–172
study methods, 170–172
study results, 172–175
study subjects, 170
Prototype/willingness model, 78–94
  defined, 80–81
  descriptive statistics, 82–83, 86
  discussion, 89–91
  empirical support, 81
  impact of previous behavior, 90
  intention vs. willingness, 89–90
  measuring intentions, 81
  measuring prototype, 85–86
  measuring willingness, 81
  model parameters, 91
  moderation, 91
  prototypes, 80–81
  regression analyses, 83
  social desirability, 90
  specificity, 90
  structural equation analyses, 86–88
  study discussions, 83–84, 88–89
  study measures, 82, 85–86
  study methods, 82, 84
  study results, 82–83, 86–88
  temporal sequence, 90–91
  willingness, 80
Pseudostage models, 53–54
PsychLit database, 34
Psychodrama, 70–71
Psychosocial process models, 233–234
  identity, 234–236
  information-based, 233–235
  main-effect, 233–234
  self-esteem, 234–236
  separate links, 236–238
  social influence, 234–236
  tangible-resource, 234–236
Psychosomatic diseases, 309–311
Psychotherapy
  cross-sectional perspective, 71–72
  integrating processes and stages, 71–74
  integrative conclusions, 74–75
  longitudinal perspective, 72–74
  mismatching stage and treatment, 68
  processes as change predictors, 71
  processes of change, 69–71
  spiral pattern of change, 66–67
  stage movements during treatment, 68–69
  stages of change, 64–69
  transtheoretical model of behavior change, 54, 63–77, 250
  treatment implications, 67–68

Reactions
  immediate vs. delayed, 112–113
Reasoned action theory, 33–46
  prototype/willingness model, 78–94
Recall, 124
Reciprocity
  altering cognitions, 22
  associations with changes, 28

Reciprocity (*continued*)
behavior changes, 25, 28
changes in cognitions, 26–28
motivated shifts, 29–30
perceived vulnerability, 21, 24–25, 28–30
risk behaviors and beliefs, 6, 21–32, 90
study discussion, 28–30
study measures, 23–24
study method, 23–24
study parameters, 22–24
study results, 25–28
study subjects, 23
treatment implications, 30
Reckless driving
assessing, 24–25
beliefs and, 6, 21
cognition changes, 26–27
prototype model, 166–182
Recycling patterns, 73
Re-entry patients
treatment adherence, 15
Regressive patterns, 73
Reinforcement management, 69–71
change patterns, 73–74
stage of change, 71–72
Relaxation, 70–71
Relevance of information, 118–129
beliefs, 122–124
checks on design, 122
correlations, 125–126
defense mechanisms, 126–127
dependent measures, 122–125
effort, 123–124
intentions, 122–124
message threat, 121–125
objective processing, 127–128
premeasures, 121
study methods, 121–123
study results, 123–126
study subjects, 121
Research reports, 369–378
abstract, 370–371
anatomy of, 370–374
as storytelling, 375–377
discussion, 373–374
introduction, 371
method, 371–372
multiple studies, 374–375
results, 372–373
title, 370–371
Rewarding change, 70–71
Rheumatoid arthritis
personality affecting, 310, 313, 315–320
Risk behaviors
alcohol myopia, 130–145
assessing, 24–25
beliefs and, 6, 21–32
impact of cognitions, 21–22, 25–26, 29
altering cognition, 22

study parameters, 22–24
study method, 23–24, 170–172
study subjects, 23, 170
study measures, 23–24, 170–172
study results, 25–28, 172–
changes in, 25–28
study discussion, 28–30, 177–
perceived vulnerability, 21, 24–25, 28–30
motivated shifts in cognition, 29–30
treatment implications, 30
prevalence estimates, 23
disregarding consequences, 23
reasoned action, 78–94
social reaction, 78–94
predictors of, 78–94
predicting, 166–183
social comparison theory, 166–183
images, 167
prototypes, 167–168, 172–175, 178–179
comparison process, 179
gender, 179
developmental differences, 179–180
current research, 169–
distancing, 168
assimilation, 168
favorability, 167
changes, 167–168, 172–175
predicting changes, 175–177
social support and, 238–241
Risk factor information, 98–117
confirmatory symptom reporting, 102–103
denial, 102–106
diagnostic context, 111–112
expectations and denial, 103–104
false consensus bias, 108–109
from appraisal to behavior, 113–115
generalizability, 109–115
illness appraisals, 107–109
immediate vs. delayed reactions, 112–113
motivational determinants, 101–102
nature of denial, 104–105
perceived treatability, 102–103
previous research limitations, 99
reactions to serious conditions, 113
reactions to well-known, 109–111
social determinants, 101–102
social influences, 106–109
social relationships, 223
TAA enzyme paradigm, 100–101
Role playing, 70–71
Rose Questionnaire, 347

San Diego Veterans Affairs Medical Center, 202
"Scarlett O'Hara strategy," 28
Self-efficacy, 35, 38
Self-enhancement
and adjustment, 152

Self-esteem
model, 234–236
social support and, 237
Self-evaluation
adjustment and, 151–152
similarity perspective, 153, 155–156, 159–160, 162–163
supercoper perspective, 152, 155, 158–159, 162
Self-help groups, 70–71
Self-initiated changes, 63–77
cross-sectional perspective, 71–72
integrating processes and stages, 71–74
integrative conclusions, 74–75
longitudinal perspective, 72–74
mismatching stage and treatment, 68
processes as change predictors, 71
processes of change, 69–71
spiral pattern of change, 66–67
stage movements during treatment, 68–69
stages of change, 64–69
transtheoretical model, 54, 63–77, 250
treatment implications, 67–68
Self-liberation, 69–71
change patterns, 73–74
stage of change, 71–72
Self-reevaluation, 69–71
stage of change, 71–72
Self-reports
of future intent, 279
Self-reward, 70–71
Serious conditions
breast cancer, 151–165
downward comparison perspective, 153–154, 156–158, 160–163
similarity perspective, 153, 155–156, 159–160, 162–163
supercoper perspective, 152, 155, 158–159, 162
upward comparison perspective, 153, 156–158, 160–163
Sexually transmitted diseases, 1–2
alcohol myopia and condom use, 130–145
beliefs about, 6, 21–32diseases
college students, 84–89
predicting risk behavior, 166–182
preventing, 272–285
Similarity perspective, 153, 159–160, 162–163
dimension-specific similarity, 159
patient affiliation, 199–212
related attributes similarity, 160
relevant comparisons, 155–156
Situational approach, 10
Social class, 10
Social comparison theory, 3, 147–182
adjusting to breast cancer, 151–165
affiliation under threat, 199–214
assimilation, 168
behavior change, 172

behavioral prediction, 168, 175–177
change, 167–168
comparison in adjustment, 155–163
current research, 169–170
dependent measures, 203–205
developmental difference, 179–180
discussion questions, 149
discussion, 177–180, 208–212
distancing, 168
downward comparison perspective, 153–154, 156–158, 160–163
favorability, 167
free-response measures, 155
gender, 179
health-related outcomes, 208–209
images, 167
interviewing, 155
mediational analyses, 207–208
patient affiliations, 208
predicting risk behaviors, 166–182
primary analyses, 205–207
process of, 179
prototype perception change, 173–175
prototypes, 167–168, 178–179
research implications, 163–164
self-enhancement, 152
self-evaluation, 151–152
similarity perspective, 153, 155–156, 159–160, 162–163, 199–212
studies, 154–155, 170–180, 202–208
suggested readings, 149–150
supercoper perspective, 152, 155, 158–159, 162
theoretical considerations, 210–212
upward comparison perspective, 153, 156–158, 160–163
Social desirability, 90
Social influence model, 234–236
Social liberation, 69–71
Social norms, 3
    alcohol use, 185–186
    discussion, 192–
    misperceiving, 183–198
    pluralistic ignorance, 184–185
    possible interpretations, 193–195
    psychological consequences, 196
    social consequences, 195–196
    studies, 186–192
Social relationships
    determinants, 224–225
    false consensus bias, 108–109
    health consequences of, 3, 218–226
    illness appraisals, 107–109
    risk factor appraisal, 101–102, 106–109, 223
Social support, 70–71, 215–244
    affect on health, 218–226
    affecting treatment compliance, 10
    and affect, 237
    determinants, 224–225
    differentiating, 228
    discussion questions, 217
    experimental research, 222–223

for risk behaviors, 79–81
generic models, 231–232
helping relationships, 69–71
illness onset, 231
immune function and, 238
main-effect models, 233–234
morbidity studies, 229–230
mortality studies, 220–222, 228–229
neuroendocrine response, 237–238
policy issues, 223
psychosocial models, 227–244
research priorities, 238–241
risk factors, 223
role for psychologists, 238
role in disease etiology, 227–244
science issues, 224–225
separate links, 236–238
stress-buffering models, 235–236
stress-centered models, 232–233
suggested readings, 217
theory and research, 219–220
Spiral change pattern, 66–67
"Spontaneous remission," 63–64
Stable patterns, 73
Stage theories, 47–48
    assessing stages, 55–56
    category system, 50–51
    common barriers to change, 50, 52
    conceptual and methodological issues, 50–62
    cross-sectional comparisons, 56–57, 71–72
    current models, 54–55
    defined, 51–53
    designing interventions, 61
    different barriers to change, 50, 52–53
    evaluating interventions, 61
    examining stage sequences, 57
    how people change, 63–77
    integrating processes and stages, 71–74
    integrative conclusions, 74–75
    longitudinal perspectives, 57–58, 72–74
    matched/mismatched interventions, 58–60, 68
    ordering of categories, 50–52
    precaution adoption process model, 55, 249–261
    processes as change predictors, 71
    processes of change, 69–71
    pseudostage models, 53–54
    spiral pattern of change, 66–67
    stage movements during treatment, 68–69
    stages of change, 64–69
    testing validity of, 55–60
    transtheoretical model, 54, 63–77, 250
    treatment implications, 67–68
    two-stage transitions, 257–258
    vs. continuum-based approach, 53
Static patterns, 73

Stimulus control, 69–71
    change patterns, 73–74
    stage of change, 71–72
Stress-centered models, 232–233
Subjective expected utility theory, 2, 78
    tested, 33–46
Subjective norms, 85
Subjective probability, 34–35
Substituting alternatives, 70–71
Suggested readings
    health beliefs and behaviors, 49
    information processing, 97
    mental models, 7–8
    personality and health, 303–304
    social norms/comparisons, 149–150
    social support, 217
Supercoper perspective, 152, 158–159, 162
    relevant comparisons, 155
Symptoms
    confirmatory reporting, 102–103
    mental models, 6, 9–20
    patient representations, 13
    treatment adherence and, 14–16
    validity in disease prediction, 16

TAA enzyme paradigm, 100–101
Tangible-resource model, 234–236
Temporal sequence, 90–91
Theories
    alcohol myopia, 130–145
    attribution, 261–271
    disinhibition, 130–145
    health belief model, 33–46
    heuristic-systematic model, 119
    mental models tested, 6, 33–46
    personality, 301–368
    planned behavior, 78
    precaution adoption process model, 249–261
    protection motivation theory, 33–46, 78
    prototype/willingness model, 78–94
    reasoned action, 33–46, 78–94
    social comparison, 3, 147–182
    social reaction, 78–94
    social support, 215–244
    subjective expected utility theory, 33–46, 78
    tested, 33–46
    transtheoretical model, 54, 63–77, 250
Therapeutic alliance, 70–71
Time-lines
    patient representations, 13
    treatment compliance and, 14–16
Transtheoretical model of behavior change, 54, 63–77, 250
    cross-sectional perspective, 71–72
    integrating processes and stages, 71–74
    integrative conclusions, 74–75
    longitudinal perspective, 72–74
    mismatching stage and treatment, 68

Transtheoretical model of behavior change (*continued*)
  processes of change, 69–71
  spiral pattern of change, 66–67
  stage movements during treatment, 68–69
  stages of change, 64–69
  treatment implications, 67–68
Treatment adherence
  hypertension, 9–10

Treatment efficacy, 9–20, 35, 39
Two-stage transitions, 257–258

Uncertainty, 111–112
Upward comparison perspective, 153
  relevant comparisons, 156–158
  vs. downward comparison, 160–163

Value clarification, 70–71

Value of acting, 35

Willingness
  defined, 80
  health risk predictor, 78–94
  measuring, 86
  vs. intention, 89–90
Wishful thinking, 73–74
Writing. *See* Journaling